OR... SOCIETY

England was the first country to experience the emergence of a modern
... society. The period of transition which we inadequately call the In-

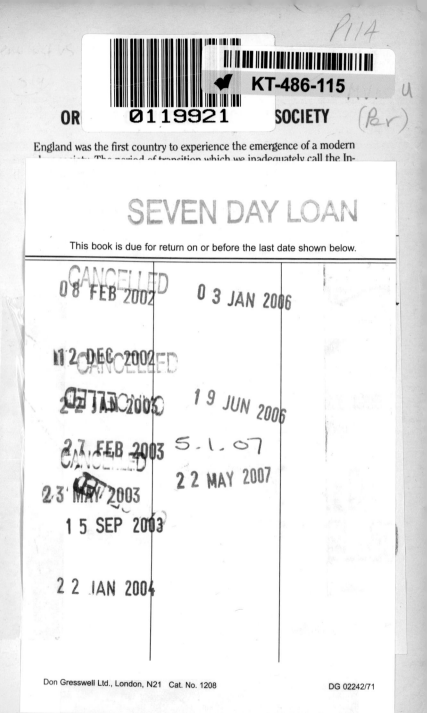

HAROLD PERKIN
ORIGINS OF MODERN ENGLISH SOCIETY

London and New York

First published in 1969
Reprinted 1969
Reprinted 1971
Published as a Routledge Paperback 1972
Reprinted 1973
Reprinted 1976 (twice)
Reprinted 1977
Reprinted 1981
ARK edition 1985
Reprinted 1986
Reprinted in 1991 by Routledge
11 New Fetter Lane, London EC4P 4EE
29 West 35th Street, New York, NY 10001

Printed and bound in Great Britain by
Cox & Wyman Ltd, Reading

ISBN 0–415–05922–4

To Joan

It is not more than seventy or eighty years since, that a few humble mechanics in Lanarkshire, distinguished by scarcely anything more than mechanical ingenuity and perseverance of character, succeeded in forming a few, but important mechanical combinations, the effect of which has been to revolutionize the whole of British society, and to influence, in a marked degree, the progress of civilization in every quarter of the globe.

'A MEMBER OF THE MANCHESTER ATHENAEUM', 1844

Contents

CONTENTS

Preface

SOME years ago I argued the case for social history as a vertebrate discipline built around a central organizing theme, the history of society *quâ* society, of social structure in all its manifold and constantly changing ramifications. I added that this kind of comprehensive social history should—indeed, could only—deal with one society at a time and over a finite period.[1] By thus nailing my historical colours to the mast I took on the obligation of attempting such a comprehensive social history. This book is the result—the inadequate result, it goes without saying, where both the society and the period are so large and complete comprehension unattainable—of that attempt. It concerns the emergence in England of that modern class society which we in the twentieth century have inherited from our Victorian predecessors, and are engaged in reshaping in ways which fall outside the compass of this volume. The origins of modern English society, as indeed of all modern developed and developing societies, go back to the seminal period both for Britain and for the rest of the world which we inadequately call the Industrial Revolution.

The central organizing theme of the book is the belief that the Industrial Revolution was no mere sequence of changes in industrial techniques and production, but a social revolution with social causes and a social process as well as profound social effects. It was a revolution in human productivity, in the capacity of men to wring a living from nature, and therefore in both the number of human beings who could be supported on a given area of land and the abundance of their means and enjoyment of

[1] 'Social History', in H. P. R. Finberg, ed., *Approaches to History* (1962), pp. 51–82.

life. Since it was the first and only spontaneous industrial revolution of modern times, it required a society of a peculiar, not to say unique, kind to generate it, and the first three chapters lay out the problem of its causation, attempt to delineate the peculiarities and uniqueness of pre-industrial society in England, and explain the specific ways in which, if it did not create, it at least drew together into productive harmony the traditional economic, technological, political, intellectual and cultural causes of industrialism. Chapter IV deals, all too briefly, with the social process of industrialization, through the rise in the number, size and complexity of human institutions, political and administrative, educational and even religious, as well as purely industrial and economic, and the migration of people from old to new communities, jobs and social roles which it entailed. Chapter V summarizes the more obvious social effects of industrialism, upon living standards, family life, and the growth of towns. The most important social effects, however, and the heart of the book, are the growth of a new social structure within and its ultimate replacement of the old, the birth of a new society based on the horizontal solidarities of class in place of the old vertical connections of dependency or patronage (chapter VI), and its growth through the violent conflicts of its early nineteenth-century adolescence into the viable class society of its mid-Victorian maturity (chapters VII–IX). Finally, chapter X explores the tensions between the ideal and the reality of this viable class society, and the underlying instability which brought it, by 1880, to the threatened loss of viability and a further round of social change.

Comprehensive social history of this kind, however limited its success, obviously cannot be the unaided work of one historian. Ideally, perhaps, it should be teamwork, with many specialists, and not only historians, contributing their expertise, though the whole at the end best refined in the reverberating furnace of a single mind. Failing that, the lone historian, as in this case, must gather his raw or semi-finished materials—and, occasionally, highly finished components—wherever he can, and from whoever can supply them. As will be apparent from the footnotes, a vast number of historians have contributed, unwittingly for the most part, to the making of this book, and I should like to thank all of them unreservedly for their invaluable help, while freely absolving them from any responsibility for the author's errors. Amongst so many names it would be invidious to anticipate any here, but I cannot forbear to mention my debt to the other authors in the Series to which this book belongs for what I have learned as editor from them, especially from those who have written on aspects of the same period. I am also indebted to numberless friends and colleagues, some of them far removed from my own field, for patiently discussing and constructively criticizing some of my themes and views, notably W. H. G. Armytage, T. C. Barker, D. E. C. Eversley, H. E. Hallam, J. F. C. Harrison, E. J. Hobsbawm, H. G. Koenigsberger, J. M. Lee, Gordon Leff, J. D. Marshall, G. E. Mingay, A. E. Musson, Henry Parris, Eric Robinson, W. W. Rostow, Brian Simon, Frank Glover Smith, E. P. Thompson, F. M. L. Thompson, Penry Williams, and the late R. H. Tawney. Some went further still, and undertook the onerous burden of reading and commenting on part or all of the manuscript, and these deserve a special thank-you: Asa Briggs, J. D. Chambers, R. J. White, T. S. Willan, and my colleagues A. H. Woolrych, J. A. Tuck and G. A. Phillips. I should also like to record my gratitude to Sir William Mansfield Cooper, Vice-Chancellor, and the Council of the Victoria University of Manchester for granting me two sabbatical terms in 1965, which proved invaluable for collecting material and writing part of the work before the exciting but laborious demands of an appointment in a new university engulfed me.

To my teachers I owe a special debt and would like to express my special gratitude: above all to Mr. J. C. W. Ludlow, formerly senior history master at Hanley High School, Stoke-on-Trent, and now of Worthing, who first showed me that the Industrial Revolution was important and a problem, to Professor Charles Wilson of Jesus College, Cambridge, who showed me the breadth and unity of modern British history, and to Mr. R. J. White of Downing College, Cambridge, who showed me the crucial historical role of social ideas and beliefs, and the centrality of the Regency period in the transition from pre-industrial to industrial society. Finally, I should like to single out for gratitude as large, if that is possible, as his boundless encouragement and support, Professor Asa Briggs, Vice-Chancellor of the University of Sussex and doyen of English social historians, who showed the way and travelled most of it—though not, he would agree, in quite the same manner—before me.

Borwicks,
Caton,
Lancaster.
September 1967.

HAROLD PERKIN

ABBREVIATIONS
USED IN THE FOOTNOTES

Blackwood's	*Blackwood's Edinburgh Magazine*
B.J. Sociology	*British Journal of Sociology*
C.R.O.	County Record Office
D.N.B.	*Dictionary of National Biography*
E.H.R.	*English Historical Review*
Ec.H.R.	*Economic History Review*
Ec.H.(Ec.J.)	*Economic History* (Supplement to *Economic Journal*)
Ec.J.	*Economic Journal*
Edin.Rev.	*Edinburgh Review*
H. of C.	House of Commons
H. of L.	House of Lords
Hist.J.	*Historical Journal*
Int.Rev. of Soc.Hist.	*International Review of Social History*
J.Ec.H.	*Journal of Economic History*
J.Mod.H.	*Journal of Modern History*
P.P.	*Parliamentary Papers*
Q.R.	*Quarterly Review*
R.C.	Royal Commission
S.C.	Select Committee
Stat.J.	*Journal of the London* (later *Royal*) *Statistical Society*

Trans.N.A.P.S.S.	*Transactions of the National Association for the Promotion of Social Science*
Trans.R.H.S.	*Transactions of the Royal Historical Society*
West.Rev.	*Westminster Review*

NOTE: in citing periodicals no reference is made to new, second or subsequent series, the date and volume number being deemed sufficient identification.

I

The More Than Industrial Revolution

MODERN society in Britain, as in all the 'developed' societies of East and West, stems directly from that 'vast increase of natural resources, labour, capital and enterprise'[1] which began in Britain in the late eighteenth century and, spreading outwards from there like the ripples on a pond, is still in process of transforming the whole world. The effects of the Industrial Revolution, as it is inadequately called, are still working themselves out, not only on the global stage, but in Britain itself, the first country affected by it and, with the exception of the United States, the one which it has most completely transformed. Much of what we recognize around us as most contemporary, most characteristic of the mid-twentieth century, not merely in the achievements of science and technology but in the most recently recognized trends in social and political organization, is the direct, logistic development of forces set in motion in the Britain of George III. Modern society, no less than its immediate predecessor, the half-way house of Victorian industrial capitalism, has its roots in the Industrial Revolution, and so it is with the Industrial Revolution that we must begin.

Contemporaries were aware of the remarkable acceleration of economic growth which began in Britain in the last decades of

[1] T. S. Ashton, 'Some Statistics of the Industrial Revolution in Britain', *Manchester School*, 1948, XVI. 215.

the eighteenth century. 'An aera has arrived in the affairs of the British Empire, discovering resources which have excited the wonder, the astonishment, and perhaps the envy of the civilized world,' wrote Patrick Colquhoun in 1814, and went on to describe 'the accumulation of property, extensive beyond all credibility, and (during a war of unexampled expense) rapid in its growth beyond what the most sanguine mind could have conceived. . . . It is scarcely necessary to enter into details for the purpose of proving that the prosperity of the British nation has been rapid beyond all example, particularly within the last sixty years.'[1] Whether or not we accept all the implications of Rostow's 'take-off into self-sustained economic growth' between 1783 and 1802,[2] it is clear that these years spanned the central phase of a transition which was to carry the British economy from a lower to a higher plane of productiveness, and create the framework of the modern industrial system. Between 1780 and 1800 British foreign trade, whether measured in shipping tonnage cleared from the ports or in export and import values, nearly trebled. Between 1750 and 1800 coal production doubled, from under five to ten million tons. Between 1788 and 1806 pig iron production, already four times that of 1740, almost quadrupled again, from 68,000 to 250,000 tons. Most spectacular of all was the growth of the pioneer machine industry, cotton: between 1781 and 1800 raw cotton imports quintupled, from 10·9 to 51·6 million pounds.[3] Though other industries were not advancing so rapidly, and the growth industries are perhaps overweighted in the figures, total industrial production in the last twenty years of the century is estimated to have doubled,[4] and the transition to modern industrialism had begun.

The acceleration of that transition, let us remind ourselves,

[1] P. Colquhoun, *A Treatise on the Wealth, Power and Resources of the British Empire* (1814), p. 49.

[2] W. W. Rostow, *The Stages of Economic Growth* (Cambridge, 1960), p. 38.

[3] T. Chalmers, *An Estimate of the Comparative Strength of Great Britain* (1803), pp. 231f.; P. Deane and W. A. Cole, *British Economic Growth, 1688–1959* (Cambridge, 1962), p. 321; T. S. Ashton, *The Industrial Revolution, 1760–1830* (Oxford, 1948), p. 39; G. R. Porter, *The Progress of the Nation* (ed F. W. Hirst, 1912), pp. 237–8; J. A. Mann, *The Cotton Trade of Great Britain* (1860), p. 93.

[4] W. G. Hoffmann, *British Industry, 1700–1950* (trans. W. H. Chaloner and W. O. Henderson, Oxford, 1955), table 54: indices of total industrial production 1780 and 1800, excluding building, 2·43 and 5·65; including building, 3·67 and 8·87 (1913 = 100).

was astonishing. During the course of the nineteenth century the British economy grew prodigiously. Exports rose sevenfold (allowing for falling prices, tenfold) from about £40 million to over £280 million a year; imports still faster, from about £30 million to over £500 million a year; while the widening gap between them was filled to overflowing by the growth of the 'invisibles'—shipping, banking, insurance, and returns on investments—which rewarded the first competitor in the field, and built up an accumulated balance of overseas credit which grew nearly a hundredfold, from £25 million in 1816 to £2,400 million in 1900. Production in the leading industries advanced in step with trade: coal output rose more than twentyfold, from 10 to 225 million tons a year; pig-iron more than thirty-fold, from 250,000 to 9 million tons; raw cotton consumed more than thirtyfold, from 52 to 1,624 million pounds; paper more than forty-fold, from under 15,000 to over 600,000 tons. Older industries—agriculture, wool and worsted, silk and linen—grew less fast, but newer ones—engineering, steel, chemicals, gas and electricity—still faster. Total industrial production may have grown as much as fourteen-fold during the century—a rough indicator, but one which gives some idea of the unprecedented scale of economic growth which the Industrial Revolution set in motion.[1]

The Industrial Revolution, however, was more than an expansion of commerce, more than a series of changes in the technology of certain industries, more even than an acceleration of general economic growth. It was a revolution in men's access to the means of life, in control over their ecological environment, in their capacity to escape from the tyranny and niggardliness of nature. At the material level it can be described as a rise in human productivity, industrial, agricultural and demographic, *on such a scale* that it raised as it were, the logarithmic index of society: that is, it increased by a multiple (rather than a fraction) both the number of human beings which a given area of land could support, and their standard of life, or consumption per head of goods and services. In the course of six centuries after the Norman Conquest the population of England and

[1] Porter, *op. cit.*, pp. 222, 242, 309, 477, 520; A. H. Imlah, 'British Balance of Payments and Export of Capital, 1816–1913', *Ec.H.R.*, 1952, V. 234–8; Hoffmann, table 54 and sources cited pp. ix–xi.

Wales perhaps quadrupled, while for the majority of the people the standard of life fluctuated between actual starvation and mere poverty, and rose, when at all, with painful slowness. During the nineteenth century population more than trebled, while *per capita* industrial production and real income quadrupled. Such a rise in the scale of life required, involved and implied drastic changes in society itself: in the size and distribution of the population, in its social structure and organization, and in the political and administrative superstructure which they demanded and supported. It was in brief *a social revolution*: a revolution in social organization, with social causes as well as social effects.

This view implies that the Industrial Revolution was—and is—a unique phase of historical development: the one-way road which, if travelled successfully, leads from the undeveloped society's comparative poverty, insecurity, and dependence on the bounty of nature to the comparative wealth, security and freedom of choice of the developed society. It is an irreversible revolution, in that any return to lower levels of productiveness would involve a catastrophe of such magnitude as almost certainly to bring down civilization with it, if not to destroy human life itself, and one compared with which the hydrogen bomb would be but a preliminary disaster.

On this view, the discovery of industrial revolutions wherever there occurred considerable technological changes, however innovatory and dramatic, such as thirteenth-century fulling mills, sixteenth-century blast furnaces, or early eighteenth-century silk-throwing mills, is unjustified. Important as such technical innovations undoubtedly were, they did not have the profound, large-scale implications for the whole of society of *the* Industrial Revolution. For a parallel worthy of the name we have to go back to pre-history, to the Neolithic Revolution which substituted for the hunting and food-gathering economy settled agriculture and stock-rearing, raised the maximum population the land could support from perhaps four to upwards of twenty-five per square mile, and provided surplus resources for the first towns, and so for the advent of civilization itself.[1]

The Neolithic Revolution was a precisely similar revolution

[1] Cf. V. G. Childe, 'The Birth of Civilisation', *Past and Present*, 1952, no. 2, and *Man makes Himself* (1956), esp. chap. v.

in human productivity, with similarly profound implications for social organization and political and military power. The process of change was fundamentally the same: an advance in technology involving a more refined division of labour which released from the production of food much larger numbers of more variegated specialists in the arts and crafts, religion and science, government and warfare. It thus increased the collective power for construction and destruction, good and evil, life and death, for organized human welfare and for the organized exploitation of human beings. And the increased collective power over nature was bought at the cost of a loss of simplicity and 'wholeness' and an added burden of social discipline for the individual. The parallel even extends to the problems of prehistorian and historian: in both cases knowledge of the origins and process of change is limited by the fact that the means of knowledge, in the one case written language, in the other precise social and economic statistics, were only produced in the course and as a consequence of the revolution itself.[1]

But here the parallel ends, for the Neolithic Revolution was but a partial emancipation from the tyranny and niggardliness of nature. Starvation and premature death were held at bay, not within human power to conquer, and the wealth, leisure, knowledge and culture of the few were bought by the poverty, drudgery, and ignorance of the many. Culture and civilization were not possible in the pre-industrial world without exploitation, of slaves, serfs, or the 'labouring poor'. Though industrialism in the short run increased the possibility and perhaps the degree of exploitation, in the long run it abolished the necessity. The uniqueness of the historical Industrial Revolution is that it opened the road for men to complete mastery of their physical environment, without the inescapable need to exploit each other. If life and the ends of life are more than the material means, it was a more than material revolution: in principle at least, it made it possible that *all* men might have life, and might have it more abundantly, in that wider choice of ends hitherto restricted to the few.

Only since the Second World War have economists and economic historians, faced with the politically urgent problem of the

[1] For the origins of modern analytical statistics see *Stat.J.*, 1838, I, Introduction, pp. 1–5, and *Annals of the Royal Statistical Society, 1834–1934* (1934), chap. i.

under-developed majority of countries, turned their attention to the comparative study of industrialization and its causes. What has emerged most clearly from the attempt is the total inadequacy of purely economic explanation of economic growth. The two most brilliant and clear-sighted approaches to the problem, Arthur Lewis's *Theory of Economic Growth* and W. W. Rostow's *Stages of Economic Growth*, rapidly move beyond the economic causes to the social and political factors underlying them. Professor Lewis keeps in the forefront throughout his book the fundamental role, in encouraging or inhibiting growth of the non-economic institutions: the family, religion, property law, social class, government, and so on, and the human attitudes and beliefs which shape them. Professor Rostow defines the 'take-off into self-sustained economic growth' as the period in which 'the economy and *the society of which it is a part* transform themselves in such ways that economic growth is, subsequently, more or less automatic'; and its fundamental characteristic—together with 'a rise in the rate of productive investment from, say, 5 per cent or less to over 10 per cent of national income (or net national product)' and 'the development of one or more substantial manufacturing sectors, with a high rate of growth'—as 'the existence or quick emergence of *a political, social and institutional framework* which exploits the impulses to expansion . . . and gives to growth an on-going character.'[1] Both Lewis and Rostow reject out of hand the naïve assumption that capital investment alone is the sole necessary and sufficient cause of economic growth.

Yet neither of them offers a satisfactory alternative analysis of the *causes* of the pioneer Industrial Revolution in Britain. Professor Lewis does not set out to do so: his suggestive work, though bursting with ideas for such an analysis, seeks only 'to provide an appropriate framework for studying economic development' in the world today. Professor Rostow's model is a descriptive not a causal one, in which the stages of the process are delineated but the causes lie outside, largely in the deliberate choice of societies to industrialize. Aside from his economic contribution of 'sectoral analysis', the nearest approach to

[1] Rostow, 'The Take-off into Self-Sustained Economic Growth', *Ec.J.*, 1956, LXVI. 25, and *Stages*, p. 39 (my italics); cf. W. A. Lewis, *Theory of Economic Growth* (1955), pp. 84–90.

consideration of the antecedent causes is in the first stage, that of the 'preconditions' of take-off. These preconditions are, on the economic side, a rise in productivity in agriculture and the extractive industries, and the building of 'social overhead capital' in the form of railways, ports and roads; on the non-economic side, certain types of 'societal change', notably the lifting of the 'horizon of expectations', the readiness of certain groups to invest and of others to accept industrial training, and the appearance of a new élite of entrepreneurs and their allies, able to divert flows of income into creative investment and exploit the elasticities of consumer demand. Neither kind of precondition has the status of an autonomous cause, even acting in conjunction with the other. For historians concerned less with establishing the concept of take-off than with the origins of industrialization, the changes in agriculture, mining and transport are an integral part of the Industrial Revolution, not some antecedent cause, and are therefore part of the thing to be explained. As for the non-economic preconditions, we may readily accept as axiomatic that industrialization required fundamental changes in the traditional society, but this does not answer the crucial causal question. Why did such changes occur? What brought them about? And why did they occur in one society rather than another?

Rostow's answer to these questions is in terms of the deliberate choice of societies to industrialize, and, leaving aside the small group of nations 'born free' as offshoots of a Britain already in possession of the preconditions, he attributes this choice in practically all cases to a 'reactive nationalism' against intrusion or the threat of intrusion by industrially and militarily more advanced societies.[1] As Rostow is aware, this explanation is more satisfactory for all later examples than it is for the pioneer industrial revolution, that of Britain. It is easy to see, once the pattern and potentialities of industrialism had been exemplified in one tremendously successful case, why undeveloped societies should seek development, and how industrial revolutions in Western Europe, America, Japan and Russia could be motivated by envy and engineered by imitation. But the pioneer country had no such ready-made blueprint and no such patent motivation. The Industrial Revolution in Britain was an unsought,

[1] *Ibid*. pp. 17, 34–5.

unplanned, unprecedented phenomenon. Why did it happen at all? Why when it did? And why in Britain first, and not some other country?

The causes of the Industrial Revolution are so complex and manifold as at first sight to constitute almost the whole antecedent history of Britain. Which causes are to be given primacy depends on the level of explanation demanded and found satisfying.

At the first level, the immediate cause of the increase in productiveness was undoubtedly technological. The factory system and all that went with it was manifestly the product of the great inventions in metallurgy, cotton-manufacture, and powered machinery: Darby's coke-smelting of iron, Huntsman's spring steel, Cort's puddling and rolling process, Hargreave's jenny, Arkwright's water-frame and carding engine, Crompton's mule, Cartwright's power-loom, the Fourdriniers' paper-making machine, Bramah, Maudslay, Nasmyth and Whitworth's machine tools, above all the great development of the steam engine from Savery and Newcomen to Watt and Stephenson.

But the technological factor has only to be stated for it to be seen to be a necessary but not a sufficient cause. Underlying it and making its operation possible was a wealth of factors equally material. First there were the favourable natural circumstances: a healthy, boisterous climate, with abundant supplies of water for power and processing; the proximity of large deposits of coal, iron ore and limestone; an island position with good harbours and ready access to navigable water and the ocean trade routes. Next came the peculiar combination of economic factors enjoyed by Britain at the critical period: a population expanding fast enough to provide both an expanding working force and a vigorous, elastic home demand for cheap consumer goods, yet slowly enough to provide incentives for labour-saving inventions, and to avoid the Malthusian threat of population outrunning resources; cheap and plentiful supplies of capital and extraordinarily low rates of interest; land owned in conveniently large blocks by owners willing to develop it; above all perhaps, a body of active and willing entrepreneurs ready to seize opportunities of profit wherever they occurred.

Together these natural, technological and economic advantages enabled Britain to take the decisive lead among European nations in exploiting the enormous expansion of international trade, the springs of which can ultimately be traced back to the geographical discoveries of the post-medieval period, which transposed Britain from the periphery to the cross-roads of the commercial world. It has been argued that the growth of the international market, slowly ripening up to 1780, was 'the most vital circumstance for the first industrial revolution', presenting a glittering prize for the first country in the European trading area able to seize it by the mass-production of some line of cheap consumer goods, a prize which would within a very short time have been seized, if not by Britain, then by Belgium, France, the Prussian Rhineland, or some other well-placed Continental country with adequate resources and access to maritime trade.[1] The argument has the important merit of re-emphasizing the ecumenical, even the world-wide economic context of the British transition, and the inadequacy of tackling economic growth in terms of close homogeneous societies. Though it has not quite the same logical status, it is of course as incontrovertible as the proximate technological causation of industrialism: without the rapid growth of foreign trade the British economy could not have expanded so fast, and *a fortiori* might not have 'taken off'.

Large exports of manufactures, nevertheless, can be mounted only on the basis of a substantial home market. From the 1770's to the 1840's overseas trade, according to the best available estimates, kept roughly in step with total industrial production, the index of relationship standing much the same in the 1840's as in the 1770's and 1790's. In the crucial decade of the 1780's it was actually lower than in the previous three decades, that is, production was expanding faster than foreign trade.[2] Moreover, Britain from as early as 1796 was on balance an importing country, financing allies and building up trading credits by the profits on the invisible exports of shipping, banking and insurance services.[3] Thus throughout the Industrial Revolution by far the greater part, perhaps four-fifths, of the growing total

[1] K. Berrill, 'International Trade and the Rate of Economic Growth', *Ec.H.R.*, 1960, XII. 351–8.

[2] W. Schlote, *British Overseas Trade from 1700 to the 1930s* (trans. W. H. Chaloner and W. O. Henderson, Oxford, 1952), p. 51, table 11.

[3] A. H. Imlah, *Economic Elements in the Pax Britannica* (Cambridge, Mass., 1958), pp. 40–1.

production, together with the still faster growth of net imports, was absorbed by the home market, and it is the remarkable expansion of home demand which needs to be explained.

Even in cotton, the trade on which this argument heavily leans since an extraordinarily large proportion of total production was exported, the ratio of exports to production was scarcely more than a third at the beginning and about half towards the end of the Industrial Revolution, in spite of a 75-fold increase in the consumption of raw cotton.[1] Colquhoun, voicing the cotton manufacturers' resentment at Indian competition in the crisis of 1787–8, clearly considered the home market to be the vital one: 'From the rapid increase in trade, it is plain to demonstration, that in the common article of apparel there is not room in the British markets both for home manufacturers, and for the same species of goods imported from India.'[2] And the tribulations of the export trade during the great French Wars of 1793–1815, though they slowed up the rate of growth, did not apparently prevent the industry from completing its 'take-off'. Moreover, more recently, those economies, such as the Southern United States, Arabia, Iran and Malaya, which have enormously expanded their foreign earnings without an adequate foundation of home demand have singularly failed to 'take off'.

Thus the question of foreign trade, like that of technological causation, merely pushes the problem a stage further back without completely solving it. Why was Britain so pre-eminently fitted to seize the opportunity offered by expanding foreign trade? What accounts for the extraordinary elasticity of home demand for cheap manufactured goods on which the export trade was built? Why was Britain not merely first in the race, but half a century ahead of the nearest competitor? To these questions foreign trade, open by definition to all comers, offers a helpful but necessarily partial and inadequate answer.

The purely material factors, then, prove to be a necessary but insufficient cause. At a somewhat deeper level of explanation we can point, as patriotic contemporaries did, to Britain's political good fortune. Centuries of freedom from invasion and distracting frontier troubles, save for the interlude of the Civil

[1] E. Baines, *History of the Cotton Manufacture in Great Britain* (1835), pp. 217–18.
[2] P. Colquhoun, *An Important Crisis in the Callico and Muslin Manufactory of Great Britain Explained* (1788), p. 15.

War, gave her the best of both worlds, encouragement for the arts of peace together with the periodical stimulus of safely external war. After 1603 or at latest 1707, internal unity and freedom from artificial barriers to commercial intercourse made her the largest free-trade area in Europe, a wide market in which to practise the enlargement of the division of labour. Entrepreneurs were encouraged by low internal taxes, high external tariffs and navigation laws, and by the almost sacrosanct security of property and profits. There was, moreover, from 1660 onwards an almost complete absence of government interference with innovating enterprise, which amounted to effective *laissez-faire* in internal trade and industry a full century before it was put forward as a conscious object of policy, here or elsewhere. *Laissez-faire* may not be the best policy for mounting a deliberately imitative or reactive industrial revolution, where it may become 'the inescapable responsibility of the state to make sure the stock of social overhead capital required for take-off is built',[1] but there can be no doubt of the importance of its role in the British case of a spontaneous revolution in a dogmatically mercantilist world. Even so, the role of the state was an important if negative one: to look benevolently on economic innovation, and to permit the provision in the shape of private enclosure, canal and turnpike bills and the like of the necessary legislative framework of industrial change. There can be no doubt that political causes played a highly significant part in the genesis of the Industrial Revolution. Yet, as with the technological and economic causes we cannot rest there, but are driven beyond them, to ask why and how the rulers and the political structure of Britain became so favourable to economic growth?

At a still deeper level of causation, there was the profound change in human expectations of life in this world and its potentialities for mankind which stemmed from the Renaissance and the Scientific Revolution. At this subtlest and most discreet, yet not the least effective, of levels there was a causal chain, elusive as gossamer, strong as steel, connecting the Industrial Revolution with the philosophical transformation of Western man's outlook on the universe in the sixteenth and seventeenth centuries. How far the new optimistic rationalism had become

[1] Rostow, *Stages*, p. 30.

11

part of the texture of common thought can be seen from that conservative mirror of the age, the *Annual Register's* review in 1800 of the closing century, which confidently expected social progress from the mere enlargement of 'the sphere of facts':

> On a general recollection or review of the state of society, or human nature, in the eighteenth century, the ideas that recur oftenest, and remain uppermost in the mind, are the three following: the inter-courses of men were more extensive than at any former period with which we are acquainted; the progression of knowledge was more rapid; and the discoveries of philosophy were applied more than they had been before to practical purposes.

It noted the effect of improved communications in science, commerce, colonial expansion, psychology, the revolutionary politics of the day, and the increasing scale of warfare. Even such moral advance as there had been came not from an increase in Christian morality, which was the same as in 'harsher centuries': 'the present age may be called the age of humanity. Whence this happy change? Not from the progressive effects of moral disquisitions and lectures: not even from the progressive effects of preaching, trimmed up by the artifices of composition taught by professors of rhetoric; but from the progressive inter-courses of men with men, minds with minds, of navigation, commerce, arts, and sciences?'[1]

The practical application of the 'discoveries of philosophy' is familiar from the well-known evolution of Watt's steam engine via Newcomen's atmospheric engine and Savery's steam pump from Robert Boyle's air-pump experiments before the Royal Society. Such direct causality was rare, however, and since most inventions were made by practical men with few pretensions to scientific training, we must fall back on the in-direct connection, 'the impulse to contrive',[2] to solve practical problems by rational experiment, which was so large and fashionable a feature of the age which founded the Society of Arts, and which interested the rich and influential like Lords Dundonald, Bridgewater, Townshend and Leicester in the humble techniques of metallurgy, civil engineering and agri-culture. Perhaps most important of all was the mere belief in the

[1] *Annual Register*, 1800, pp. 222, 236.
[2] T. S. Ashton, *An Economic History of England: the 18th Century* (1955), p. 104.

worth and possibility of material progress, which the seventeenth century postulated and the eighteenth century established. As Carl Becker has brilliantly illustrated, 'the heavenly city of the eighteenth-century philosophers' was the future itself.[1] Whether or not the apotheosis of the future was any more rational than the apotheosis of the past which it victoriously displaced in the famous literary battle of the Ancients and Moderns, or than that of some other world than this, which the Renaissance undermined, it was undoubtedly a more potent concept for the purpose of changing the present state of the world. In this wide, general sense the philosophical revolution of the sixteenth and seventeenth centuries prepared men's minds and emotions for profound changes, and so for both the French and Industrial Revolutions.

Yet we are still bound to ask: why a political revolution in France, and an industrial one in Britain? The stream of thought which flowed from the Renaissance and the Scientific Revolution, like the expansion of international trade, fertilized the whole of the western world. As James Keir, the industrial chemist, pointed out in 1789, 'The diffusion of a general knowledge, and of a taste for science, over all classes of men, in every nation of Europe, or of European origin, seems to be the characteristic feature of the present age.'[2] Only in Britain did it stimulate before the middle decades of the nineteenth century the vigorous growth of an industrial civilization; and we are still constrained to ask, why?

At the deepest level of all, that of the individual's relation with his God, lie the religious causes of economic growth. Here we seem to be in the midst of the inmost springs of human character and purpose, where 'the capitalist spirit' and 'the Protestant ethic', 'labouring in one's vocation' and 'the soul naked before God' mingle in psychic turmoil. Max Weber's all-too-famous correlation between capitalism and Protestantism has raised far more problems than it solved. At one extreme stands the problem of medieval commercial and financial capitalism—far more dangerous to the soul than the industrial

---

[1] C. L. Becker, *The Heavenly City of the 18th-Century Philosophers* (New Haven, Conn., 1932).

[2] J. Keir, *Dictionary of Chemistry* (1789), p. iii; A. E. Musson, and E. Robinson, 'Science and Industry in the late 18th Century', *Ec.H.R.*, 1960, XIII. 222.

variety—which reached its highest development in the Catholic cities of Italy, the Rhine and the southern Netherlands and infected the Papacy itself; at the other, the violent denunciations of usury and profiteering in Luther's Germany, Calvin's Geneva and the England of the Puritans. It requires all the subtlety of a Tawney to draw a convincing web of interconnection between the two which does not do violence to either or to history. What remains from the attempt is the original illuminating but irreducible pair of facts: that the kind of mind which was attracted to capitalist dealing was often, though not always, attracted to the sterner sorts of Protestantism; and that the narrowly self-regarding external moral uprightness enjoined, though not always enforced, by Protestant churches was not unconducive to success in business. Whichever came first in their experience and motivation, both capitalism and Protestantism were often found together in the same person.

In the British Industrial Revolution the role of Dissenting iron-masters, factory-masters, bankers and the like, is too well-known to need emphasis. Whether such men chose industrial enterprise because they were shut out by their religious affiliation from the accepted roads to social status or prestige, or whether the exclusion of the social groups whence enterprise could be expected from the higher reaches of social status and prestige did not prejudice the choice of their religion will be discussed later. Meanwhile, since, as Rostow points out, industrial revolutions have occurred in societies with almost every variety of religious belief and, as Arthur Lewis points out, in most countries religion has proved to be a brake on economic development, we may conclude that in the British case the possession of an uninhibiting religion was a significant but strictly ancillary factor.

So much, then, for the fortuitous combination of geographical, technological, economic, political, philosophic and religious causes which Rostow calls 'the classic answer' to the 'interesting historical problem' of why the first industrial revolution took place in Britain and not elsewhere. 'It is, essentially, that in the late eighteenth century, while many parts of Western Europe were caught up in a version of the preconditions process, only in Britain were the necessary and sufficient conditions fulfilled for a take-off. This combination of necessary and sufficient conditions for take-off in Britain was the result of the convergence of a number of quite independent circumstances, a kind of statistical accident of history which, once having occurred, was irreversible, like the loss of innocence.' He too finds the answer not completely satisfying, and refuses to believe that the conjunction of circumstances was altogether accidental. His own answer to the 'deeper questions' of why Britain was specially fitted to enjoy and exploit these advantages 'places Britain back in the general case, to some significant degree,' as 'a society modernizing itself in a nationalist reaction to intrusion or the threat of intrusion from more advanced powers abroad'—the Roman Church and Spain in the sixteenth century, the Dutch in the seventeenth, the French in the eighteenth. Thus 'British nationalism . . . may have been a major force in creating a relatively flexible social matrix within which the process of building the preconditions for take-off was hastened in Britain; and in that limited sense the first take-off takes its place, despite many unique features, with the others.'[1]

While this answer gives a hint of the direction in which a solution might be found, it is no more satisfactory than the rest. What European country in the turbulent post-medieval rise of nation-states was *not* threatened by and forced to react against powerful neighbours? Where in that age of mercantilist competition did nationalism *not* play a part in economic policy? Did government economic policy in fact play any positive part in mounting the first industrial revolution? And if so, why did it not occur in France, where both government policy and government control of industry were consciously directed towards economic growth? Most pertinent of all, how and why did a reactive nationalism lead to a flexible social structure in Britain when elsewhere (except in Holland) it so patently led to the reverse, to the entrenched survival of exclusive, reactionary military aristocracies? Rostow's answer raises more problems than it solves, and no more accounts for the social adaptability and economic opportunism of Britain in the critical period than the fortuitous 'classic answer'.

Fortunately, there is a hint here of the one level of explanation in which all the other levels can be said to meet, and which not only united the foregoing necessary and ancillary causes and

[1] Rostow, *Stages*, pp. 31–5.

brought them into convergent and harmonious operation but made them collectively sufficient. That central, integrating cause was the nature and structure of English society. As W. H. B. Court has said of the Industrial Revolution, 'the first requisite of increased wealth is a society of the kind required to produce it.'[1] The only spontaneous industrial revolution in history, occurred in Britain because Britain alone amongst the nations with the full complement of economic resources and psychological attitudes had the right kind of society to generate a spontaneous industrial revolution. (Holland, the only other country with the right kind of society, had the psychological attitudes but not the natural resources.) As we shall see in Chapter III, whether we consider the general, predisposing political, philosophic and religious factors or the narrowly economic factors of labour, land, capital, enterprise and invention, what brought them to bear in the concrete world of practical realities were the unique institutional features of British society. What those dynamic features were, how they came into being, and how they differed from those of all Continental countries except Holland, is a matter of concrete history. To understand them and their part in the genesis of industrialism we must begin, therefore, by considering the nature and structure of the society which generated the first Industrial Revolution.

[1] W. H. B. Court, *A Concise Economic History of Britain from 1750 to Recent Times* (Cambridge, 1954), p. 16.

II

$\diamond$

The Old Society

$\diamond$

T H E old society which spontaneously generated the Industrial Revolution was *an open aristocracy based on property and patronage*. It was thus differentiated not only from medieval feudal and Victorian class society but, in degree at least, from all contemporary societies except Holland.

1. A CLASSLESS HIERARCHY

Like most pre-industrial, civilized societies, English society on the eve of the Industrial Revolution was first of all an aristocracy, a hierarchical society in which men took their places in an accepted order of precedence, a pyramid stretching down from a tiny minority of the rich and powerful through ever larger and wider layers of lesser wealth and power to the great mass of the poor and powerless.

Something of the shape and character of the old society at the beginning and towards the end of its *aera mirabilis* between the Glorious Revolution and the Great Reform Act can be gauged from Gregory King's and Patrick Colquhoun's famous estimates of income distribution for 1688 and 1803.[1] Though they cannot pretend to the statistical accuracy of a modern social survey, they offer an invaluable sketch of two generations of the same society,

[1] For reference see Table 1.

the one at the point at which it reached maturity, the other at the point of take-off into a new level of existence.

In the accompanying tables their categories have been arranged to throw into relief the major features of the old society: the smallness and yet the extraordinary income range of the landed ruling class; the comparatively huge extent of the 'middle ranks', far wider than what is usually meant by the modern term middle class; the correspondingly smaller, but still large, body of the 'labouring poor', a much narrower group than the Victorian working class, and one which scarcely has a counterpart in mid-twentieth-century Britain; and the importance of the 'great functional interests'—agriculture, and the various branches of trade, industry and the professions—into which, rather than into horizontal classes, the old society for political purposes tended to split.

By contemporary standards it was a prosperous society, as foreigners never failed to comment. According to a Dutch immigrant in the 1720's, 'England, which no other country can with so much justice pretend to, produces of itself all that can really conduce either to the Necessities and Convenience or the Pleasures and Satisfaction of Life'; and, according to a Swiss tourist of the 1790's, this prosperity extended even to the lower orders: 'though the English labourer is better clothed, better fed and better lodged than the French, he does not work so hard.'[1] Yet King's table gives a *per capita* income, at current prices, of only £7 18s. *per annum* while Colquhoun's implies one of £22 15s., at the inflated prices of war-time. After all allowances have been made for inaccuracy and for the many items in modern national incomes not then available or not measured in money, it was, though certainly richer than many underdeveloped countries of today, a poor society in which life for the majority of men and women was a hard struggle for subsistence.

As the tables (pp.20–1) inadequately show, wealth was very unequally divided. At the top of the pyramid the nobility and gentry, amounting to about one family in every 70 or 80—1·2 per cent of families in 1688, 1·4 per cent in 1803—received about a seventh of the national income (14·1 per cent in 1688, 15·7 per cent in 1803). The peak, indeed, was much higher and narrower:

[1] H. Moll, *A New Description of England and Wales* (1724), p. 2; J. H. Meister. *Letters written during a Residence in England* (1799), p. 9.

a small group of peers and rich commoners within the landed order had incomes from land alone far in excess of these averages. The Duke of Bedford's gross rental in 1732 was £31,000, the Duke of Devonshire's in 1764 £35,000, the Earl of Derby's 'neat profit' from thirty-two estates in 1797 £47,366. The second Lord Foley in 1766 left an estate worth £21,000 a year, plus mines worth £7,000 a year and £500,000 in the Funds. So minor and profligate an earl as Sefton had a rental of £11,124 in 1797, though over £5,000 of it was committed to interest on his debts. That great commoner Thomas William Coke inherited in 1776 estates worth £12,332 a year, and increased them by 1816 to £34,679. To some of these enormous incomes should be added the profits of office. The second Earl of Nottingham, with a gross rental in 1695 of about £8,400 a year, gained over £50,000 gross (less office expenses) from his two spells, totalling six years, as Secretary of State. The Duke of Chandos, Paymaster of the Forces in 1705–13, is said to have made £600,000 out of office. As Secretary of State in the 1740's and 1750's, the first Duke of Newcastle, with £30,000 a year from estates in thirteen countries, was receiving an average of £5,780 a year clear from the profits of office.[1] Out of such princely incomes the rural palaces of the English aristocracy— Chatsworth, Holkham, Burley-on-the-Hill, Wentworth Woodhouse and the rest—were built, and furnished with the treasures of France, Italy, Greece, and the Orient.

At the base of the pyramid stood the 'labouring Poor', the labourers, cottagers, seamen and soldiers, paupers and vagrants, with no property or special skill to shield them from the pressures of the daily struggle for existence. These amounted in 1688 to over half, in 1803 to over a third of the population, and received (apart from poor relief, charity, dishonest gains and other transfer payments) about one-fifth (20·7 per cent) and

[1] H. J. Habakkuk, 'England', in A. Goodwin, ed., *The European Nobility in the 18th Century* (1953) p. 7, and 'Daniel Finch, 2nd Earl of Nottingham, his House and Estate', in J. H. Plumb, ed., *Studies in Social History* (1955), pp. 161–2, 165–6; G. Scott Thomson, *The Russells in Bloomsbury* (1940), p. 301; 'G.E.C.', *The Complete Peerage* (1910–59), IV. 346n.; Lancs. C.R.O., Derby Muniments, Ledger 1981 (1795–99), and Molyneux Muniments, DDM 1/177–8, Receipts 1796–97, and 'Observations to Ld. and Ly. Sefton . . . March 1797'; R. A. C. Parker, 'Coke of Norfolk and the Agrarian Revolution', *Ec.H.R.*, 1955, VIII. 157; C.H.C. and M. I. Baker, *Life and Circumstances of James Brydges, 1st Duke of Chandos* (Oxford, 1949), pp. 265f.; J. H. Plumb, *Life of Sir Robert Walpole* (1956), I. 6.

TABLE 1

DISTRIBUTION OF THE NATIONAL INCOME, ENGLAND AND WALES, 1688 AND 1803

	King, 1688			Colquhoun, 1803		
	Families	Income per Family	Aggregate Income	Families	Income per Family	Aggregate Income
		£	£000		£	£000
I.						
Aristocracy						
Sovereign	—	—	—	1	200,000	200
Peers	160	2,800	448	287	8,000	2,296
Bishops	26	1,300	33·8	26	4,000	104
Baronets	800	880	704	540	3,000	1,620
Knights	600	650	390	350	1,500	525
Esquires	3,000	450	1,350*	6,000	1,500	9,000
Gentlemen	12,000	280	3,360*	20,000	700	14,000
Fundholders (included above)	—	—	—	—	—	5,056
	16,586	—	6,285·8	27,204	—	32,801
II.						
Middle Ranks						
(1) Agriculture						
Freeholders (1)	40,000	84	3,360	40,000	200	8,000
Freeholders (2)	140,000	50	7,000	120,000	90	10,800
Farmers	150,000	44	6,600	160,000	120	19,200
(2) Industry and Commerce						
Merchants (1)	2,000	400	800	2,000	2,600	5,200
Merchants (2)	8,000	200	1,600	13,000	800	10,400
Manufacturers	—	—	—	25,000	800	20,000
Warehousemen	—	—	—	500	800	400
Shipbuilders	—	—	—	300	700	210
Shipowners	—	—	—	5,000	500	2,500
Surveyors, engineers	—	—	—	5,000	200	1,000
Tailors, etc.	—	—	—	25,000	150	3,750
Shopkeepers, etc.	40,000	45	1,800	74,500	150	11,175
Innkeepers	—	—	—	50,000	100	5,000
Clerks, shopmen	—	—	—	30,000	75	6,750
(3) Professions						
Civil offices (1)	5,000	240	1,200	2,000	800	1,600
Civil offices (2)	5,000	120	600	10,500	200	2,100
Law	10,000	140	1,400	11,000	350	3,850
Clergy (1)	2,000	60	120	1,000	500	500
Clergy (2)	8,000	45	360	10,000	120	1,200
Dissenting clergy	—	—	—	2,500	120	300

Arts, sciences	16,000	60	960	16,300	260	4,238
Education (1)	—	—	—	500	600	300
Education (2)	—	—	—	20,000	150	3,000
Naval officers	5,000	80	400	3,000	149	1,043
Army officers	4,000	60	240	5,000	139	1,816
Half-pay officers	—	—	—	2,000	45	181
Theatrical	—	—	—	500	200	100
Lunatic keepers	—	—	—	40	500	20
	435,000	—	26,340	634,640	—	124,633

III.

Lower Orders

Artisans	60,000	40	2,400	445,726	55	24,515
Hawkers, pedlars	—	—	—	800	40	32
Mines, canals	—	—	—	40,000	40	1,600
Seamen common ⎫	50,000	20	1,000	⎧ 67,099	40	2,684*
naval ⎭				⎩ 38,175	38	1,451*
Soldiers	35,000	14	490	50,000	29	1,450*
Labourers	364,000	15	5,460	340,000	31	10,540
Lunatics	—	—	—	(2,500)*	30	75
Debtors	—	—	—	2,000	25	50
Pensioners (forces)	—	—	—	30,500	20	610
Paupers, cottagers	400,000	6·5	2,600	260,179	(16·4)	6,869
Vagrants	10,000†	2	60	74,000†	10	2,220
	919,000	—	12,010	1,346,479	—	52,096
	1,370,586	—	44,635·8	2,008,323	—	209,530

Summary: Percentage Distribution

	King, 1688		Colquhoun, 1803	
	Families	Income	Families	Income
I. Aristocracy	1·2	14·1	1·4	15·7
II. Middle Ranks	31·7	59·0	31·6	59·4
III. Lower Orders	67·1	26·9	67·0	24·9
	100·0	100·0	100·0	100·0

NOTES

SOURCES: Gregory King, *Natural and Political Observations and Conclusions upon the State and Condition of England, 1696* (ed. George Chalmers, 1804); and Patrick Colquhoun, *A Treatise on Indigence* (1806).

* Original figures corrected by recalculating from average income of group (and corresponding adjustments made to totals).

† Lunatics assumed to be individuals from other families and excluded from family total.

‡ 30,000 and 222,000 vagrants also treated as individuals and excluded from family totals by King and Colquhoun, but here allowed one family to three vagrants and included in totals.

about one-sixth (16·5 per cent) of the national income respectively. Gregory King estimated their incomes at only £3 3s. per head and their outgoings at £3 7s. 6d., and he described them collectively as 'decreasing the wealth of the country'. Colquhoun, who by contrast closely followed Adam Smith in his belief in labour as the source of all wealth, was alarmed at the increase in pauperism as the labourer was driven by the famine prices of the war years beyond poverty, 'the state of every one who must labour for subsistence', into indigence, the state of want, misery and distress of those destitute of the means of subsistence. In 1803 over a million people, one in nine of the population, were said to be in receipt of poor relief, casual or permanent, to the tune of £5,348,205.[1] At both dates poverty was an inescapable fact of life, and the distance between the rich and the poor almost oriental.

Inequality was mitigated by a wide diffusion of wealth. As Colquhoun put it,

> It is not . . . an excess of property to the few but the extension of it among the mass of the community which appears most likely to prove beneficial with respect to national wealth and national happiness. Perhaps no country in the world possesses greater advantages in this respect than Great Britain, and hence that spirit of enterprise and that profitable employment of diffused capitals which has created so many resources for productive labour beyond any other country in Europe.[2]

Between the landowners and the labouring poor stretched the long, diverse, but unbroken chains of the 'middle ranks'. To quote a nostalgic early nineteenth-century observer, seeking the historical 'secret of our liberty',

> In most other countries, society presents scarcely anything but a void between an ignorant labouring population, and a needy and profligate nobility; . . . but with us the space between the ploughman and the peer, is crammed with circle after circle, fitted in the most admirable manner for sitting upon each other, for connecting the former with the latter, and for rendering the whole perfect in cohesion, strength and beauty.[3]

[1] P.P., 1803–4 (175), XIII, Return of Number of Paupers, 1802–3.
[2] Colquhoun, Treatise on . . . British Empire, p. 6.
[3] 'Y.Y.Y.' [David Robinson], 'The Church of England and the Dissenters', Blackwood's, 1824, XVI. 397.

The middle ranks were distinguished at the top from the gentry and nobility not so much by lower incomes as by the necessity of earning their living, and at the bottom from the labouring poor not so much by higher incomes as by the property, however small, represented by stock in trade, livestock, tools, or the educational investment of skill or expertise. From the great overseas merchants, officials and judges who vied in wealth with many peers, mingled on easy terms with royal ministers, married their daughters into the aristocracy, and crowned their careers by founding landed families, they ranged down to small farmers and semi-independent craftsmen as hard-pressed as the labourer himself. At the higher end were princely merchants like John Howland of Streatham who in King's day married his heiress to the Duke of Bedford's heir, or Sir William Curtis in Colquhoun's, banker, baker to the Navy, and friend of the Prince of Wales.[1] At the lower were the 'enslaved husbandmen' whose lot Richard Baxter in King's time thought worse than that of their own out-servants, the ale-sellers whom Joseph Massie in 1760 classed with poor cottagers, or even the many eighteenth-century curates on stipends of under £40 a year.[2]

Between these extremes the whole interim was filled by parallel business and professional hierarchies of an infinity of graduated statuses. Even domestic service formed a separate hierarchy which curiously typified the rest. At the lowest level scullery maids and stable boys at £4 to £8 a year, plus keep, were retained by the year and regularly fed; at the highest the Duke of Devonshire's steward might earn £1,000 a year, the Earl of Derby's fraudulent steward, James Waring, at £300 a year, have property of his own worth £2,000 a year, or the Duke of Bedford's steward, John Hoskins, marry his daughter to an earlier Duke of Devonshire; while in between were butlers, chefs, head gardeners and the like varying in salary with their own merit and experience but still more with the standing of their employers, from as high as 100 guineas a year to as little as

[1] G. Scott Thomson, *Life in a Noble Household* (1937), pp. 390–4; *D.N.B.*, XIII. 349f.

[2] R. Baxter, *The Poor Husbandman's Advocate to Rich Racking Landlords*, quoted by M. D. George, *England in Transition* (1931), p. 7; P. Mathias, 'The Social Structure in the 18th Century: a Calculation by Joseph Massie', *Ec.H.R.*, 1957, X. 43; D. B. Horn and Mary Ransome, *English Historical Documents*, X, 1714–83 (1957), p. 17.

ten or twenty.[1] Domestic service like every other occupation was marked by internal differences of status greater than any which separated it from those outside.

The old society, then was a finely graded hierarchy of great subtlety and discrimination, in which men were acutely aware of their exact relation to those immediately above and below them, but only vaguely conscious except at the very top of their connections with those on their own level. Blackstone is said to have distinguished some forty different status levels, each with its own place in the hierarchy.[2] There was one horizontal cleavage of great import, that between the 'gentleman' and the 'common people', but it could scarcely be defined in economic terms. 'All are accounted gentlemen in England who maintain themselves without manual labour,' asserted the most popular eighteenth-century handbook on Britain, echoing its Elizabethan models.[3] Most contemporaries pitched it higher: the gentlemen included, besides the nobility and gentry, the clergyman, physician and barrister, but not always the Dissenting minister, the apothecary, the attorney, or the schoolmaster; the overseas merchant but not the inland trader; the amateur author, painter, musician but rarely the professional. But wherever the shifting line was drawn, above and below it stretched long scales of social discrimination. If 'gentleman' described anyone who might be found dining at a landed gentleman's table, the respect due to a duke was as far removed from that to a curate, as the curate's was from the cottager's. And between duke and curate, as between curate and cottager, there was an unbroken continuum through layer after contiguous layer of status.

Differential status was part of the given, unquestioned environment into which men were born, and they proclaimed it by

[1] J. J. Hecht, *The Domestic Servant Class in 18th-Century England* (1956), pp. 141–53; Cavendish Muniments, Chatsworth, Accounts of Executors of 4th Duke of Devonshire; Lancs. C.R.O., Derby Muniments, DDK 1657, Lord Derby's Letters to Johnson, 1795–96, DDK 1687, Weekly Notes of Steward's Correspondence . . . 1796–1802, and Ledger 1981, 1795–99; *Complete Peerage*, IV. 345.

[2] R. R. Palmer, *The Age of Democratic Revolution, 1760–1800* (Princeton, N.J., 1959), I. 63.

[3] John Chamberlayne, *Magnae Britanniae Notitia, or the Present State of Great Britain* (38th ed., 1755), p. 179; cf. William Harrison, *Description of England* (1577, ed. and abridged by L. Withington, as *Elizabethan England*, [1876]), pp. 7–8, and Sir Thomas Smith, *De Republica Anglorum* (1583, ed. L. Alston, Cambridge, 1906), pp. 39–40.

every outward sign: manner, speech, deportment, dress, liveried equipage, size of house and household, the kind and quantity of the food they ate. Noblemen wore the honours and trappings of their order, the gentry displayed their coats of arms, under-graduates wore gowns appropriate to their social rank, and the 'middle ranks' and 'lower orders' dress appropriate to their station, down to the 'labouring poor'. The charity school-children wore 'clothes of the coarsest kind, and of the plainest form, and thus are sufficiently distinguished from children of the better rank, and they ought to be so distinguished.'[1] Social consciousness was formalized, and issued in stylized behaviour. Lord Chesterfield advised his son to desire his dancing-master (a significant figure in eighteenth-century society, who taught deportment as well as dancing) 'to teach you every genteel attitude that the human body can be put into: let him make you go in and out of his room frequently, and present yourself to him, as if he were by turns different persons; such as a (royal) minister, a lady, a superior, an equal, an inferior, etc.'[2] In Samuel Johnson's phrases, the English were 'a people polished by art, and classed by subordination', by 'the fixed, invariable external rules of distinction of rank, which create no jealousy, since they are held to be accidental.'[3]

This formal sense of hierarchy the old society inherited from the medieval world. Chaucer, who stood between the two, spoke for both: 'There is degree above degree, as reason is.' Yet unlike medieval feudalism, and unlike many contemporary Continental societies where feudalism was still a living reality, it was not a caste society with exclusive status categories determined by birth. The serf could not escape his status except by flight. Feudalism as a social system in England disappeared with the fourteenth- and fifteenth-century commutation of labour services, and the rise of peasant families like the Pastons of Norfolk and the Sneyds of Staffordshire into the landed gentry. The feudal label, so casually applied by political and economic historians of the right and left, is wholly inappropriate to a hierarchy based

[1] Isaac Watts, *An Essay towards the Encouragement of Charity Schools* (1728), p. 43.
[2] *Letters of the Earl of Chesterfield to his Son* (ed. C. Strachey, 1932), II. 145–6 (2 May 1751).
[3] S. Johnson, *Dictionary* (1755), preface; J. Boswell, *London Journal* (1950), p. 320.

neither on military nor on labour services, and tempered by an extraordinary degree of social mobility.

Nor was it, like the Victorian, a class society, divided into mutually hostile layers each united by a common source of income. Class indeed was latent in eighteenth-century society. The word itself began to come into use in the second half of the century, mostly in its purely grouping or classifying sense, as in Charles Abbott's 'agricultural class' of the first Census, but also in an apparently modern form as in Jonas Hanway's 'lower classes of the people', or Thomas Gisborne's 'higher and middle classes of society'.[1] But down to the end of the century and beyond the word was still used interchangeably with the traditional concepts, 'ranks', 'degrees' and 'orders', and without its nineteenth-century overtones of social strife and antagonism. As late as the Regency period Robert Owen, who might be called the godfather of working-class consciousness and was among the first to speak of 'the *working* classes', still used the phrase interchangeably with 'the lower orders' in a traditional, paternalistic manner.[2] The appearance of the word was less important than the evolution of the concept.

The concept itself originated in eighteenth-century social thinking. 'No credit is due to me,' wrote Marx in a famous letter, 'for discovering the existence of classes in modern society nor yet the struggle between them. Long before me bourgeois historians had described the historical development of the class struggle and bourgeois economists the economic anatomy of the classes.'[3] The 'bourgeois historians' were the 'classical sociologists' of the eighteenth-century Scottish historical school, notably Adam Ferguson, David Hume, Sir James Steuart, Adam Smith, and John Millar, who between them established the connection between the structure of government and society and

---

[1] C. Abbot, Speech on the Population Bill, *Parliamentary History of England, 1800–1*, XXXV. 601; J. Hanway, *Observations on the Causes of the Dissoluteness which reigns among the Lower Classes of the People* (1772); T. Gisborne, sr., *An Enquiry into the Duties of Men in the Higher and Middle Classes of Society in Great Britain* (1794); cf. Asa Briggs, 'The Language of "Class" in early 19th-Century England', in A. Briggs and J. Saville, eds., *Essays in Labour History* (1960).

[2] R. Owen, *A New View of Society* (1816, Everyman ed., 1927), p. 14 and *passim.*

[3] *Marx and Engels Correspondence, 1846–95 . . . A Selection* (Moscow, 1934), p. 57.

'the mode of subsistence', and so originated the economic interpretation of history.[1] As John Millar put it,

> The whole property of a [commercial] country, and the subsistence of all its inhabitants may . . . be derived from the rent of land and water; from the profits of stock or capital; and from the wages of labour: and, in conformity to this arrangement, the inhabitants may be divided into landlords, capitalists, and labourers.[2]

Here are the three great classes of Marx and the classical economists, which they inherited via Adam Smith.

Although Smith rarely used the word class, the concept underlies his 'three great, original constituent orders of every civilized society, from whose revenue that of every other order is ultimately derived.'[3] For the notion of class was inherent in the very act of analysing society in its economic aspects. The mere division of society into income groups, as in King or Colquhoun, or productive orders, as in Smith or Millar, leads to broad horizontal layers which approximate to classes. Thus political economy in Adam Smith's sense of an inquiry into the nature and causes of the wealth of nations leads straight to political economy in Ricardo's, 'an enquiry into the laws which determine the division of the produce of industry amongst the classes who concur in its formation,'[4] and so to the invidious comparison between contributions and rewards which is the parent of class conflict. Already in Adam Smith there are famous asides and forthright comments which could form the basis of a class war: 'the landlords love to reap where they never sowed'; merchants and master manufacturers 'have generally an interest to deceive and even oppress the public, and . . . accordingly have, upon many occasions, both deceived and oppressed it'; in all countries except new colonies, 'rent and profit eat up wages, and the two superior orders of the people oppress the inferior one.'[5] In fact, his labour theory of value and its corollary, the famous distinction between the productive and unproductive members

[1] Cf. R. L. Meek, 'The Scottish Contribution to Marxist Sociology', in J. Saville, ed., *Democracy and the Labour Movement* (1954).

[2] J. Millar, *An Historical View of the English Government* (1803), IV. 115.

[3] A. Smith, *The Wealth of Nations* (ed. E. B. Bax, 1905), I. 263.

[4] D. Ricardo, *Principles of Political Economy and Taxation*, in *Works and Correspondence* (ed. P. Sraffa, 1962), I. 6.

[5] *Op. cit.*, I. 50, 265, II. 73.

of society, became the starting point for all anti-landlord and anti-capitalist critics of society down to Marx and beyond.

Neither the appearance of the word, nor the provenance of the concept, however, is the same thing as the existence of a mature fact, especially a fact so portentous as a new structuring of society. In spite of his propagandist purpose in favour of freer trade and production, Adam Smith did not set out to change the existing basis of society, still less to undermine the authority of the landed aristocracy. On the contrary, his main target was the very capitalist whose private freedom he espoused but whose public influence he denounced, who though the chief organizer of national wealth was also the protagonist of the selfish and self-defeating mercantile system, and was least to be trusted with politicial power. The labourer, though 'his interest is strictly connected with that of society', was 'incapable either of comprehending that interest, or of understanding its connexion with his own'. Only the landowner was both competent and disinterested enough to be entrusted with responsibility for the general welfare. The interest of the landed order 'is strictly and inseparably connected with the general interest of society. Whatever either promotes or obstructs the one, necessarily promotes or obstructs the other. When the public deliberates concerning any regulation of commerce or policy, the proprietors of land can never mislead it, with a view to promote the interest of their own particular order; at least, if they have any tolerable knowledge of that interest.'[1]

It was only with the Ricardians and their opponents that the full implications of class came to dominate political economy and social thought, and the concept changed from an analytical tool to an instrument of social and political conflict. As we shall see in Chapter VI, it was in the 1810's and 1820's that class and class antagonism became a fact. Ricardo's well-known hostility to the landed interest and the Ricardian socialists' denunciation of the capitalist reflected the overt class struggles of the early nineteenth century.

Until then, however, class remained latent in the old society, as can be seen from its politics, industrial relations, and religion. As the late Richard Pares remarked, 'the distribution of political power between the classes was hardly an issue in politics before

[1] *Ibid.*, I. 263.

1815.'[1] Up to Waterloo, power was unquestionably in the hands of the great landowners and their friends of one or the other faction, whom the 'great functional interests' lobbied not for a share of power but for patronage of their particular policies. In so far as economic questions entered politics at all, it was via these 'interests', the various trades, industries, and professions, considered as hierarchies within the general hierarchy of society, and representing through their leaders all levels of society from the squire, great merchant or industrialist down to the humblest labourer, seaman or handicraft worker.

The General Chamber of Manufacturers declared in 1784:

> It seems hitherto to have escaped the notice of the manufacturers that whilst the *landed* and *funded interests*, the *East India*, and other commercial bodies, have their respective advocates in the great council of the nation, *they* alone are destitute of that advantage; and it is probable from this source that many of their grievances have arisen—that they have so repeatedly and inadvertently been oppressed by ministers unacquainted with their real interests, and misled by the designs of interested individuals.

This was not an anticipation of the class politics of the Anti-Corn Law League, as the use of the word 'manufacturer' in its contemporary sense to cover both master and worker makes clear: 'The manufacturers of Great Britain constituted a very large, if not a principal part of the community; and their industry, ingenuity and wealth have contributed no small share towards raising this kingdom to the distinguished and envied rank which she bears among European nations.'[2] Samuel Garbett, Mathew Boulton, Josiah Wedgwood and other leading industrialists who called the Chamber into being to oppose Pitt's Irish Treaty thought of themselves as the hierarchical representatives of their 'dependants', and were typical of the interest politics of the old society. As late as 1812 the mercantile opposition to the Orders in Council followed an exactly similar pattern.[3] As for the worker, outside his hierarchical 'interest' he had no place in politics: as Adam Smith said, 'his voice is little

---

[1] R. Pares, *King George III and the Politicians* (Oxford, 1953), p. 3.
[2] *Plan of the General Chamber of Manufacturers of Great Britain*, Birmingham Municipal Library.
[3] Cf. C. W. New, *Life of Henry Brougham to 1830* (1961), chaps. iv, vi.

heard and less regarded, except upon some particular occasions, when his clamour is animated, set on, and supported by his employers, not for his, but for their own particular purposes.'[1]

To what extent the pro-Revolutionary parliamentary reformers of the 1790's represented a premature ebullition of class politics is a debatable question. Until 1789, certainly, parliamentary reform was little more than a Whig cry for reducing the power of the Crown and getting themselves back into office, and so for most aristocratic reformers it remained down to the Reform crisis of 1830. In the 1790's Fox's aristocratic 'Friends of the People' could hardly qualify as class agitators. Major Cartwright's Society for Constitutional Information had a mainly 'middle-class' membership and anti-aristocratic aims, but it was under 'gentlemanly' patronage and failed to carry most 'middle-class' opinion with it. Thomas Hardy's London Corresponding Society has been described as the first purely working-class political society, which 'laid the foundations of the working-class movement in England,' but it was in fact sponsored by the 'middle-class' reformers, and Hardy himself described the membership as 'tradesmen, mechanics and shop-keepers', of the traditional, pre-industrial kind.[2] All three societies, in spite of their fame and widespread connections, failed to rally more than a tiny fraction of their own levels of society behind them, though they played a part in frightening the landed aristocracy towards class consciousness.

At all events, as a demonstration of class politics they were completely abortive. Much more impressive was the massive demonstration they provoked of traditional loyalty at all levels to the established social order. As a panic reaction on the part of the propertied, the 'Loyal Association' movement which swept the country in 1792–94 was a more important step on the way to class politics than the 'alleged nation-wide conspiracy to overthrow property and government' which called it forth. But meanwhile the overwhelming success of 'the gentlemen of property in the country', each 'according to his rank and situation in life', in rallying both 'citizens of opulence' and 'the inferior classes in the community' in defence of King and Consti-

[1] *Op. cit.* I. 264.
[2] Henry Collins, 'The London Corresponding Society', in Saville, ed., *op. cit.* pp. 111, 134; *Memoirs of Thomas Hardy* (1832), p. 15.

tution was a triumph for the hierarchical politics of the old society.[1]

Class feeling was nearer to the surface in industrial relations. Capitalism in the sense of production for the market by wage-earners employed by capitalists was as old as the old society. The very conditions which brought the one into being inevitably produced the other. The decline first of serfdom and then of the small peasant demanded the expansion of industrial employment for the surplus population. Apart from small, isolated groups of fully proletarian wage-earners, in mines, ironworks, foundries, alum-works and the like, mainly from the Tudor period onwards, most of the surplus was employed in domestic handicrafts, especially textiles.[2] Because of the initial restrictionism of the craft guilds, most of these domestic handworkers worked in the villages and small unincorporated towns and depended on a merchant for materials and the disposal of the product. Although England remained predominantly rural throughout the old society, by the mid-eighteenth century Joseph Massie estimated that more workers were engaged in trade and manufactures than in agriculture, and this was confirmed by the first Census in 1801, when only just over a third of all families were allocated to agriculture, as against over two-fifths to trade, manufactures and commerce.[3] Some of these domestic workers were self-employed, independent masters, but most worked for a merchant, on his materials and often with his equipment, under the domestic outwork system. As Adam Smith pointed out, 'in all arts and manufactures the greater part of the workmen stand in need of a master to advance them the materials of their work and their wages and maintenance till it be completed.' Whatever form the advance took, it rapidly approximated to a piece-rate wage, and the worker became a proletarian working for a capitalist. Since men do not have to be taught where their economic interest lies, mutually hostile combinations frequently resulted. Adam Smith remarked, 'Masters are always and everywhere in a sort of tacit, but constant and uniform combination, not to raise the wages of labour

[1] A. Mitchell, 'The Association Movement of 1792–93', *Hist.J.*, 1961, IV. 56f., quoting Duke of Buckingham, Col. de Lancey, and other contemporaries.

[2] Cf. G. Unwin, *Industrial Organization in 16th and 17th Centuries* (Oxford, 1904).

[3] Mathias, *loc. cit.*

above their actual rate.'[1] The workers in their turn combined in the local trade clubs which are the ultimate roots of the modern working-class movement.

The roots, however, are not the thing itself. Eighteenth-century industrial relations were often violent, involving machine-breaking, physical intimidation and even occasional murder. But eighteenth-century workers resorted to violence as often against bakers who sold dear bread in hard times, the Irish who undercut wages, or merchants who imported competing products or exported their raw materials, as against their employers.[2] Sporadic violence, moreover, was the resort of the frustrated and ineffectively organized and a compliment to the strength of paternal social control. Most eighteenth-century workers were too scattered, too isolated, too dependent upon a face-to-face relationship with a paternal employer, for extensive permanent, trade-union organization. Some of the most proletarian wage-earners, the agricultural workers, the miners, the general labourers, could scarcely organize at all. For the rest, their occasional resentment showed itself in local, sporadic, temporary combination, frequently accompanied by violence and rioting, and as vigorously suppressed as other forms of social insubordination. In between such outbreaks the workers' organization, if it survived at all, relapsed into the cross between drinking club and friendly society, often frequented by independent craftsmen and small masters, which was the average trade club.

The exceptions, the comparatively rare examples of more widespread and permanent trade unionism, as amongst the felt hatters, the London tailors, the Spitalfields silk weavers, the West of England cloth-workers, or the East Midland framework knitters, prove the rule. For in practically every case they existed, often with the recognition or connivance of the law, to uphold the paternal system of industrial regulation. The tailors earned themselves the first of the eighteenth-century anti-combination acts in 1720, but obtained the control of their wages by the Middlesex justices, and reinforced it by appeals in 1744, 1750–1 and 1767. West of England weavers petitioned the King against their employers in 1726, and were admonished not to

---

[1] *Wealth of Nations*, I. 66, 67.
[2] Cf. Ashton, *18th Century*, pp. 227–9.

combine unlawfully, but 'to lay their grievances in a regular manner before His Majesty.' They obtained a short-lived Act regulating their wages in 1756, and were, with the Yorkshire weavers, trying to obtain redress by legal proceedings in 1802, when their intervention led to the suspension and ultimate repeal of the laws regulating woollen manufacture. The London framework knitters failed to prevent the abolition of their Company's control over the masters in 1753, but the East Midland knitters by prolonged agitation in 1778–80 came near to carrying a regulating Bill. The Spitalfields Acts of 1765 and 1773 led to a unique combination of masters and men for settling silk-weaving rates. Even the workers in the new cotton industry turned first to similar methods of settling their grievances: parliamentary petitions from Lancashire and Glasgow weavers, culminating in a famous and costly battle in the Scottish courts, were only then followed by the 1812 strike of 40,000 looms, and its suppression by the common law.[1]

Ultimately, all such attempts to keep alive the paternal protection of the old society broke down in face of the abandonment by the ruling aristocracy of its old responsibilities. Not so the paternal discipline of the old society, however. The general Combination Acts of 1799 and 1800 were only the last of some 40 acts for particular industries or localities, and the general prohibition of industrial insubordination dates back through the Tudor legislation to the fourteenth-century Statutes of Labourers, and the beginnings of the old society.[2] Like the landed rulers' panic reaction to the 'Jacobin' reformers of the 1790's, with which it was connected, the consolidation of the anti-combination laws—an afterthought to the master millwright's bill, prompted by the generalizing mind of Wilberforce[3]—was a step in the direction of class industrial relations. But in itself it belonged more to the repressive industrial discipline of the old society than to the free class competition of the new.

Religion provided the nearest approach in the old society to

[1] S. and B. Webb, *History of Trade Unionism* (1920), pp. 32, 49–55, 58–9.

[2] Cf. M. D. George, 'The Combination Acts Reconsidered', *Ec.H.* (*Ec.J.*), 1926–9, I. 214; J. H. Clapham, *An Economic History of Modern Britain* (1964), I. 205.

[3] *Parliamentary Register*, 9 April 1799; J. L. and B. Hammond, *The Town Labourer, 1760–1832* (Guild Books ed., 1949), I. 121.

overt class attitudes. From the Restoration settlement, when the Puritan aristocracy and gentry finally opted for the Church and left the sects to their social inferiors, the social structure of English religion became the familiar 'sandwich', with Anglicans (in some areas, such as rural Lancashire, Roman Catholics) at top and bottom, and Dissenters in the middle. The Quaker bankers and ironmasters, Presbyterian, Congregational and Baptist merchant-clothiers and traders of the eighteenth century have usually been accounted for in Weber's terms by the mutual attractions of capitalism and puritanism.[1] No doubt there were conscious or unconscious advantages in the combination of virtue and frugality, spiritual and economic ascetism, worldly and other-worldly wisdom, and the godly life and financial success as interchangeable marks of Calvinist election. But not all Dissenters were capitalists, and not all capitalists were Dissenters: eighteenth-century Dissent embraced many yeoman farmers and ordinary textile workers on the one hand, and excluded many great, especially London, merchants and bankers, West country clothiers, and Liverpool slave-traders, on the other.

The full explanation is both simpler and more complex than the Calvinist-capitalist equation. In the old society Dissent flourished in precisely those groups which both wished and could afford to be somewhat independent of the paternal hierarchy. Only those groups who were not dependent on the landed élite for employment, tenancies, or patronage in the form of preferment, government contracts, or the purchases of the plupart of their wares or services, could afford the luxury of dissent from the landlords' religion; and only those who did not wish or could not hope for admission to the fringes of county society and its pleasures, political, cultural and frivolous, wished to do so. Hence Old Dissent—the original puritan sects of the Presbyterians, Congregationalists and Baptists, and their more recent offshoots, the Quakers and Unitarians—was confined to the 'middle ranks', the yeoman farmers and more independent craftsmen of the countryside, and the traders and master manu-

[1] Cf. Max Weber, *The Protestant Ethic and the Spirit of Capitalism* (1930); R. H. Tawney, *Religion and the Rise of Capitalism* (1926); E. D. Bebb, *Nonconformity and Social Life, 1600–1800* (1935); Isabel Grubb, *Quakerism and Industry before 1800* (1930).

facturers of the towns. The arm of dependency was long, and even in the towns, especially market as distinct from industrial towns, the tenants of local landowners, the professional men who served them, and those business men who hoped for some advantage, social, political or lucrative, from the association, tended to follow the landlords' religion. Thus the Duke of Devonshire's Knaresborough tenants, Walpole's relatives the Turners, attorneys and wine merchants of King's Lynn, and the bankers, East India merchants, and government contractors of the City of London would be Churchmen almost to a man; while a Quaker ironmaster like Ambrose Crowley found it paid to become an Anglican when he moved his headquarters to London.[1] Hence, too, the 'filling' in the sandwich was much thinner than the middle ranks of society: in the first half of the century Old Dissenters probably numbered only about 250,000 to 300,000, and in the second half rose to about 400,000, mainly in the last two decades.[2]

They were reinforced from the 1740's by New Dissent. By the time of Wesley's final separation from the Church in 1784, there were about 50,000 Methodists, though a much larger number of sympathizers and adherents; by 1800 there were over 100,000.[3] Early Methodism was peculiarly fitted by its ambivalence, of loyalty to and rejection by the Church, its conservatism and dissent from Old Dissent, to find a place in the social structure of religion. Appealing mainly to those working men who were just beginning to emerge from complete subordination to landlord or employer, it provided a short first step in either direction from Church or from Dissent. The sandwich, as it were, acquired a second layer of filling below the first, midway between middle and lowest layers. Thus an extra step was provided for the familiar progress from Anglicanism to Dissent and back to Anglicanism again, which usually accompanied social mobility from the labouring poor through the middle ranks to a landed estate.[4] There was nothing cynical

[1] New, *op. cit.*, pp. 402, 407–8; Plumb, *Walpole*, I. 25–7; M. W. Flinn, 'Sir Ambrose Crowley, Ironmonger, 1658–1713', *Explorations in Entrepreneurial History*, 1953, V. 162–80.

[2] Bebb, *op. cit.* pp. 45, 174–7.

[3] *Ibid.* p. 178.

[4] Cf. E. Halévy, *History of the English People in the 19th Century* (1961), I. 424.

about this: one sect contained as much scope for piety or world-liness as another, they were all equally Protestant, and atheism was equally anathema to them all. More important, the religious matrix was completed for the moulding of the classes of the future.

For, at least in part, religious dissent, new and old, was from the social point of view the sublimated form taken by vertical social antagonism in the old society. Since political expression was denied it—not so much by the Test and Corporation Acts, which were easily evaded, but by the hierarchical system which prevented practically all but the landowners and their friends from attaining political power—such resentment of the higher orders as existed was diverted into religion. Of course, religion had always played a large part in politics, and the Old Dissenters, who had never been content with a bare toleration and civic inferiority, were a powerful 'interest' which constantly lobbied through their Whig patrons. Towards the end of the century, however, one of the first signs of the expansion of the independent 'middle ranks' which accompanied industrial growth was the increased force and self-confidence of the Dissenters. A new campaign for their emancipation in the late 1780's led by the 'Rational Dissenters', Priestley, Price and Robinson,[1] together with the fervour for religious and civic equality released by the French Revolution, came near to producing the spark which fuses dissent into class feeling.

Again, however, the reaction of the paternal hierarchy was more powerful than the threat. The rational Dissenters were overwhelmed by the same anti-revolutionary tide which all but drowned the parliamentary Reformers and the trade clubs. Church-and-King mobs sacked Joseph Priestley's house in Birmingham as they sacked Thomas Walker's in Manchester.[2] Priestley fled to America, Dissenters deserted Reform in droves for the defence of property, and the Presbyterians who had been most affected split up between the untainted Baptist and Congregational flocks and the Unitarians who took over the Presbyterian chapels. Even the loyal Methodists did not escape the storm: accused of being 'a system which tended to overthrow

[1] Cf. U. R. Q. Henriques, *Religious Toleration in England, 1787–1833* (1961), pp. 57–67.
[2] *Ibid.* p. 66.

Church and State', whose real objects were sedition and atheism, they felt impelled year after year from the 1793 Conference to pass an abject loyal address.[1] Though latent class feeling and organization were clearly the underlying factor in religious dissent, the time for its emergence was not yet.

In short, although class was latent in the politics, industrial relations, and religion of the old society, it was overlain by powerful bonds and loyalties which effectively prevented its overt expression. The explanation lies in the total social situation of the individual. Of this, source of income and the vertical antagonism it generates are but a part, and, though important, can operate freely and effectively only in large-scale communities, where the individual can unite with many others of his kind to defeat the ubiquitous pressures of personal dependency. In the small communities, the villages and tiny towns, of the old society in which the average individual worked, lived and had his being, the source of income itself, with the rest of the 'life-chances' of the individual, was controlled by a paternal landlord, employer or patron who regarded class attitudes as the insubordination of a dependent child. In a world of personal dependency any breach of 'the great law of subordination', between master and servant, squire and villager, husband and wife, father and child, was a sort of petty treason, to be ruthlessly suppressed.[2] Resentment had therefore to be swallowed, or sublimated in religious dissent, or, when pressed beyond endurance, it exploded in outbursts of desperate violence.

If, as one modern sociologist has put it, a classless society is one with a unified élite, which unites in itself the political, economic and social power of the community,[3] then eighteenth-century England was a classless society. The landed aristocracy, standing at the head of all the 'interests' of the social pyramid, held in its hands the strings of connection and dependency which held society together in a hierarchical system. How and

[1] R. F. Wearmouth, *Methodism and the Working-Class Movements of England, 1800–50* (1937), pp. 54–60.

[2] Literally so in the case of women who murdered, or were accessory to the murder of, their husbands, who were burned at the stake for 'petty treason'; cf. L. Radzinowicz, *A History of the English Criminal Law and its Administration from 1750* (1948), I. 209–10.

[3] R. Aron, 'Social Structure and the Ruling Class', *B. J. Sociology*, 1950, I. 131; for a similar concept of a classless or one-class society, see Peter Laslett, *The World We Have Lost* (1965), chap. ii.

why it achieved this remarkable degree of social control we can best see by considering the principles upon which the hierarchy was based, property and patronage.

2. PROPERTY AND PATRONAGE

The old society was firmly based on the twin principles of property and patronage. One's place in that society was wholly determined by the amount and kind of one's own property—'the great source', as John Millar observed, 'of distinction among individuals'[1]—or that of one's relations and friends. Whereas in feudal society, property, in theory at least, followed status—the knight invested with his fee in return for military service which only he was qualified to perform, the serf with his holding in return for servile labour which only he was lowly enough to render—in post-feudal England status followed property. The English gentry, unlike their Continental counterpart, the minor aristocracy, possessed no legal privilege except the readily purchased coat of arms. Land alone granted them their status. 'Gentility is nothing but ancient riches,' Sir John Holles could say as early as Elizabeth I's reign: his descendants became dukes of Newcastle.[2] His contemporary Sir Thomas Smith declared: 'Who can live idly and without manual labour, and will beare the port, charge and countenaunce of a gentleman, hee . . . shal be taken for a gentleman.'[3]

Title itself came to follow property. From James I's reign knighthoods, baronetcies and Irish peerages could be freely purchased by anyone with sufficient cash and the land to support the dignity. An English peerage was more difficult to obtain, but in practice a great estate, like the fifty-eight manors assembled by Lord Chief Justice Coke, sooner or later drew to itself a title; and a commoner who inherited that estate, as his eighteenth-century descendant Thomas Coke of Holkham did from his grandfather the Earl of Leicester, could normally expect to get the patent revived. The dukedom of Newcastle was thrice resurrected between 1694 and 1756 for non-noble heirs, while the dukedom of Northumberland was re-created in 1750 for Sir

---

[1] J. Millar, *The Origin of the Distinction of Ranks* (1793), p. 4.
[2] Historical Manuscripts Commission, *Portland Manuscripts* (1923), IX. 5.
[3] Sir T. Smith, *op. cit.* p. 40.

Hugh Smithson who had married the heiress of the Percies.[1]
By the eighteenth century only a handful of English peers could
claim continuity in the male line from a medieval feudal grant:
all the rest owed their status to their property.

Below the landed order status, honour and power over others
were distributed according to wealth, down to the very cottager
on the common: 'In his own house he finds those who respect
him, who obey him; those, to whom he says go, and they go, and
come, and they come.'[2] Only the utterly propertyless and friend-
less, the vagrant, the beggar and the outlaw, were excluded
from the hierarchy of prestige.

Nowhere can this be better seen than in the distribution of
political power. Government in the old society was a function of
property, and reflected its distribution. According to Arthur
Young in 1794,

> The principle of our constitution is the representation of property,
> imperfectly in theory, but efficiently in practice . . . the great mass of
> property, both landed, monied and commercial, finds itself repre-
> sented; and that the evils of such representation are trivial, will
> appear from the ease, happiness, and security of all the lower
> classes, hence possibly virtual representation takes place even
> where the real seems most remote.[3]

Descriptive of Parliament, this was no less true of other political
institutions. Even the Crown could be said to come within its
ambit: in the vestigial belief that 'the King should live of his own'
lingered the notion of the supreme responsibility of the largest
property-holder, the first amongst his landed peers, the greatest
of the borough-mongering gentlemen of England. The House of
Lords consisted almost entirely of great landowners. In the
House of Commons, protected by political realities rather than
by property qualifications ancient or modern, three-quarters of
the Members between 1734 and 1832 were landowners or their
near-relations, and those of the rest who were not their friends
or nominees were rich business and professional men often with
one foot on the land.[4] Though within the charmed circle of

[1] *Complete Peerage*, IX. 529–31, 743.
[2] *Information for Cottagers, collected from the Reports of the Society for Bettering the
Condition and Increasing the Comforts of the Poor* (1800), chap. i.
[3] A. Young, *The Example of France . . . a Warning to Britain* (1794), p. 106.
[4] G. P. Judd, *Members of Parliament, 1734–1832* (New Haven, Conn., 1955),
p. 71.

property political ability played some part in selection for high office, 'the chief qualification required of a Cabinet Minister was not so much ability as aristocratic connections and a large landed property', and in every Cabinet between 1783 and 1835 peers and sons of peers formed a clear majority.[1] Under the patronage system administration at all levels from the Household to the Customs and Excise department was carried out by landowners and their clients. In 1726 a quarter of the active peerage held Court or Government office;[2] while the chief qualification for appointment as a mere tide-waiter or exciseman was a noble or genteel friend with the ear of a Minister. Office itself was defined by Blackstone in proprietorial terms, as 'a *right* to exercise a public or private employment and to take the fees and emoluments thereunto belonging,' and was linked by the need to maintain a government majority in the House of Commons to an electoral system in which 'For the elector the vote, for the borough its representation, for the Member his seat . . . were valuable assets from which advantages were expected.'[3]

Local government most perfectly reflected the proportional influence of graduated property. Here the institutions—Quarter Sessions, borough corporations, parish officers—were merely the forms through which a hierarchy of property-holders governed themselves and their dependants. In the counties the lords lieutentant and their deputy lieutenants, the sheriffs and the justices of the peace, were leading landowners, noblemen or squires, together with an occasional clergyman or business man with one foot on the land. The boroughs were ruled under a hotch-potch of charters and customs which almost everywhere amounted to an oligarchy of substantial traders and professional men, often with a stiffening of local landowners. At parish level the constables, churchwardens, overseers of the poor, surveyors of highways and the rest, were drawn in rotation from the middle ranks of yeomen, tenant farmers, tradesmen and independent craftsmen.

Such formal equations, however, give little idea of the informal role of property: the 'extra-legal county oligarchy' of

[1] A. Aspinall, *The Cabinet Council, 1783–1935* (1952), p. 199.
[2] Plumb, *Walpole*, I. 8.
[3] E. W. Cohen, *Growth of the British Civil Service, 1780–1939* (1941), p. 21n.;
L. B. Namier, *The Structure of Politics at the Accession of George III* (1929), I. 199.

justices who came during the eighteenth century to usurp legislative and executive powers conferred by no statute, and to punish without right of appeal offences they had themselves created; the attendance at Quarter Sessions and Assizes of 'county society' which brought propertied opinion subtly to bear on the judgments; the power over their neighbours of the majority of squires who were not J.P.s; the consultation by the wage-fixing justices of 'discreet persons' not on the bench; the 300-odd bodies of 'improvement commissioners' who appointed themselves under private acts to clean, pave and light their towns; the 'extra-legal democracy' of ratepayers which governed some parishes as the oligarchy governed the county, still more the 'close vestry' of substantial property-owners which came to replace it after Sturges Bourne's Act of 1819; or the informal parish opinion, headed by 'the natural and proper overseer, the principal proprietor . . . the provider of the fund', which effectively decided the direction and the level of poor relief.[1]

For political power was merely the most specific institutional form which property assumed. As Defoe approvingly put it,

'Tis in the power of the Gentry of England to reform the whole Kingdom without either Laws, Proclamations, or Informers; and without their concurrence all the Laws, Proclamations and Declarations in the world will have no Effect; the Rigour of the Laws consists in their Executive Power.[2]

It was the social power of property which underlay the rest. It was not confined to the landowning élite, for every man of any kind of property had his 'legitimate influence' with his 'dependants': master with servants, farmer with labourers, industrialist with workers, and so on. But its head and centre was the influence of the landowner, larger or smaller, over a wider or narrower stretch of countryside. 'Landed property,' wrote William Marshall in 1804, 'is the basis on which every other

[1] S. and B. Webb, *English Local Government: The Parish and the County* (1906), pp. 104–45, 152–63, 550–6, *The Manor and the Borough* (1908), chaps. viii and ix, and *Statutory Authorities for Special Purposes* (1922), pp. 242–3; 'Report of General Meeting of Justices of Berkshire at Pelican Inn, Speenhamland, 11 May 1795', in A. E. Bland *et al.*, *English Economic History: Select Documents* (1914), p. 655; *P.P.*, 1834, XXVII, *Report of Poor Law Commission*, p. 384A.
[2] D. Defoe, *The Poor Man's Plea in relation to . . . a Reformation of Manners* (1703), p. 129.

species of material property rests; on it alone mankind can be said—to live, to move, and have its being.'[1]

The life of a hamlet, a village, a parish, a market town and its hinterland, a whole county, might revolve around the big house in its park. Its reception rooms, gardens, stables and kennels were the centre of local social life; its estate office the exchange for farm tenancies, mining and building leases, and a bank for small savings and investments; its home farm a permanent exhibition of the best available agricultural methods and techniques; its law-room, if the landowner was on the bench, the first bulwark of law and order; its portrait gallery, music-room and library the headquarters of local culture; its dining-room the fulcrum of local politics. Such big houses ranged themselves in a hierarchy, from the squire's manor house to the ducal country palace, according to the size of the territory they dominated. And at each level the landowners and their families met at each other's houses, and at the market or county town, and jostled to get invitations from the level above, culminating in the ring of great families which ruled England as a whole, and met to dominate London society in the Season. 'From some eighteenth-century memoirs,' Professor Habakkuk has remarked, 'one might suppose that England was a federation of country houses.'[2] And so indeed it was: for the English nobility and gentry, unlike their Continental counterparts, had learned the amphibious art of dominating both town and countryside by their physical presence. Through seasonal residence in the localities and frequent re-union in metropolis and county and market town they kept in their own hands and concerted their control over all the strings of dependency and influence.

Whatever the political forms it took, however, their power always came back to the social control of the ordinary squire over his tenants and villagers. It manifested itself in the inevitability with which they followed his religion and politics; in the customary treats and charity for the loyal and deserving, and the harsh treatment of poor strangers, vagrants and poachers; and in the continual oversight of the morals and behaviour of all the inhabitants. It can be found crystallized in a phrase, written by a steward to a substantial farmer: 'For a

[1] W. Marshall, *On the Landed Property of England* (1804), p. 1.
[2] Habakkuk, 'England', *loc. cit.* p. 4.

tenant to purchase on his own account premises within his landlord's Estate without any previous intimation to his Landlord that they were on sale is not a fair and upright proceeding, and one which Mr. Littleton desires me to say he will not submit to. *He will require you to give up the purchase.*'[1]

Still more fundamentally, in the process by which society renewed itself in each generation property was by far the most important factor, and so in a sense was the architect of the social structure. Inheritance was the highroad to estate, which by deliberate policy rather than the law of primogeniture, passed to the eldest son; an estate was a family concern, and the inheritor usually a life-tenant under a strict settlement, whose function was to hold the land together from one generation to the next, and use it as a base from which to launch portioned younger sons and dowried daughters into brilliant careers and marriages, as well as provide for his own and his father's widows.[2] Where inheritance failed, a lucky marriage might provide: Johnson's attorney friend Sir John Hawkins married a 'fortune', as did Lieutenant Henry Sneyd, the sixth son of the Staffordshire squire, because her aunt liked his face, while the 4th Duke of Devonshire's younger son married the Earl of Northumberland's heiress.[3] But such marriages were for the few, and most younger sons had to seek a living, backed by family influence and funds, in government service, the professions or in business. The 4th Duke of Devonshire left each of his two younger sons £1,000 a year to go into politics. Squire Ralph Sneyd gave his six younger sons capital sums of £1,000: two went into the Church, two into the Army, one into the Navy, and one into the East India Company's service. Squire John Egerton's two younger sons were apprenticed to merchants in Venice and Holland.[4]

[1] Staffs. C.R.O., Hatherton Papers, D260/M/E, *Steward's Letter Book*, f.159, H. Davison to Mr. Woodward, n.d. [February 1925]; my italics.

[2] H. J. Habakkuk, 'Marriage Settlements in the 18th Century', *Trans. R.H.S.*, 1950, XXXII. 15–20.

[3] *D.N.B.*, XXV. 220f.; John Rylands Library, Sneyd Papers (now transferred to Keele University), Early Correspondence, Henry Sneyd to Ralph Sneyd, 22 December [1780s]; *Complete Peerage*, II. 433–4.

[4] Cavendish Muniments, Accounts of Trustees for Lords Richard and George Henry Cavendish; Sneyd Papers, Col. Walter Sneyd's Estate Accounts, 1798–1800; *Burke's Landed Gentry* (1937), pp. 2091–2; W. H. Chaloner, 'The Egertons in Italy and the Netherlands, 1729–44', *Bulletin of John Rylands Library*, 1949–50, XXXII. 157–70.

All such launchings cost considerable sums, and younger sons of landowners competed with and raised the rates for all the sons of the middle ranks. The education of a lawyer or a clergyman cost several hundreds of pounds, and might be wasted without further expenditure on articles or an advowson. Army commissions in 1765 cost from £400 for an ensign to £3,500 for a lieutenant-colonel.[1] Apprenticeship varied in cost with the trade, the place, and the standing of the master: in London in 1747 from £5–£10 for a hatter, breeches-maker, millwright or potter to £50–£300 for a merchant or banker.[2] A Sussex gentleman gave £180 with his son in 1713 to a London citizen and grocer; a Cheshire widow £420 with her son in 1785 to a London surgeon; a Durham coalowner £600 with his son in 1755 to a London banker.[3] Besides education or apprenticeship, property or influence was needed for setting up in the professions or trade. in 1747 the 'Sums necessary to set up as Master' ranged from £50–£200 for a breeches-maker, cutler, millwright or pinmaker, to '£20,000 *ad lib.*' for a banker, and 'Unlimited' for an overseas merchant or insurance underwriter.[4] So finely adjusted to each status was the cost of acquiring it.

After property, and emanating from it, the most important factor in determining status was patronage. The late Sir Lewis Namier has made familiar the uses of eighteenth-century political patronage: appointments to Court and government offices, sinecures and pensions, contracts and agencies, bishoprics and prebendary stalls, tidewaiterships and excise posts, all geared to the maintenance of a parliamentary majority.[5] Government patronage was no isolated phenomenon, however, but the visible topgrowth of a plant whose roots and branches ramified throughout society, the political aspect of a personal system of recruitment which operated at every level and served to articulate the rigidities of a structure based on property. If govern-

---

[1] E. Robson, 'Purchase and Promotion in the British Army in the 18th Century', *History*, 1951 XXXVI. 59.

[2] R. Campbell, *The London Tradesman* (1747), pp. 331f.

[3] Dorothy Marshall, *English People in the 18th Century* (1956), p. 119; Cheshire C.R.O., Wilson Papers, MTD/24/1, Indenture between Thomas Wilson and William Long, surgeon, 1 December 1785; E. Hughes, *North Country Life in the 18th Century* (Oxford, 1952, 1965), I. 107.

[4] Campbell, *loc. cit.*

[5] Namier, *op. cit.*, I. 164–82.

ment patronage controlled the more lucrative, private patronage controlled the more numerous appointments: most church-livings, salaried county, borough and parish offices, merchants' and lawyers' clerks, estate agents, chaplains, secretaries, tutors and governesses, and the whole pyramid of domestic service, sometimes extending to the very labourers on the estate or home farm. Since there was no central organ or policy of government appointments, and no distinction between the official and the personal influence of individual ministers and their subordinates, public and private patronage were dovetailed at many points. At all levels, patronage, the system of personal selection from amongst one's kinsmen and connections, was the instrument by which property influenced recruitment to those positions in society which were not determined by property alone.

When a man of rank and property had an appointment to make or influence, whether a Clerk of the Pells or footman, a bishop or governess, a colonial governor or workhouse master, an army contractor or a scullery maid, a Treasury agent or an insurance clerk, he looked first, and was expected and actively solicited to look, amongst his 'friends'. This was neither sur-reptitious nor shame-faced, but a matter of pride and principle. Sir Robert Walpole 'frankly owned that while he was in employ-ment, he had endeavoured to serve his friends and relations; than which, in his opinion, nothing was more reasonable, or more just.'[1] Addison, the only man to rise by literary patronage to be Secretary of State and marry a Countess, was

> persuaded that there are few men of generous principles who would seek after great places, were it not rather to have an opportunity of obliging their particular friends, or those whom they look upon as men of worth, than to procure wealth and honour for themselves. To an honest mind the best perquisites of a place are the advan-tages it gives a man of doing good.[2]

Edward Gibbon assumed the common motive for going into Parliament to be 'to acquire a title the most glorious of any in a free country, and to employ the weight and consideration it gives in the service of one's friends'.[3] As clearly as by his property,

[1] Plumb, *Walpole*, I. 247–8.
[2] P. H. B. O. Smithers, *Life of Joseph Addison* (1954), p. 122.
[3] *Private Letters of Edward Gibbon* (ed. R. E. Prothero, 1896), I. 24; Namier *op. cit.*, I. 23.

a man's position in society was measured by the number of 'friends' he could 'oblige'.

Who were one's friends? They were all those who expected or, reciprocally, from whom one could expect the benefits of patronage. They were first of all one's nearest relations. Richardson's *Pamela*, the daughter significantly of her master's tenant, does not just go home to her parents, but 'to her friends'. Mrs. Malaprop in *The Rivals* exhorts her niece to take 'a husband of your friends' choosing', meaning her own. The father of John Millar, the Glasgow Professor of Law, 'was not inflexible in his determination, so that with little opposition from his friends, Mr. Millar was allowed to transfer his attention from the Pulpit to the Bar.'[1] William Wright in *The Complete Tradesman* argued the apprentice's right to the advantages 'for which he served his time, and, perhaps, for which his friends gave a considerable sum of money with him.'[2] Defoe, proposing a university as 'the way to make London the most flourishing city in the Universe', suggested that the 'pupils' could lie and diet 'at home, under the eye of their friends'.[3]

Walpole procured for his three sons sinecures in the Exchequer totalling £13,400 a year. Rutland influence helped the 3rd Duke's grandson, Charles Manners-Sutton, brother of an Irish Lord Chancellor and favourite of the Royal family, to become in rapid succession between 1791 and 1805 Dean of Peterborough, Bishop of Norwich, Dean of Windsor, and Archbishop of Canterbury. In the Navy, where commissions could not be purchased, Admiral Rodney's son during 1780 advanced between the ages of 15 and 16 through all the ranks from midshipman to captain. The clerical sons of the Sneyd family were preferred to the family livings of Keele and Wolstanton. John Powell, a Bristol merchant, apprenticed all his five sons to himself. Thomas Stubbs, a farmer on the Sneyd estate, employed his kinsman William Stubbs, 'a servant', whom he left £40 in his will.[4]

---

[1] J. Craig, 'An Account of the Life and Writings of the Author', prefixed to Millar, *Distinction of Ranks*, p. vi.

[2] W. Wright, *The Complete Tradesman; or a Guide in the Several Parts and Progressions of Trade* (Dublin, 1787), p. 3.

[3] D. Defoe, *Augusta Triumphans, or the Way to make London the most Flourishing City in the Universe* (1841 ed.), p. 5.

[4] Habakkuk, 'England', *loc. cit.*, p. 7; *D.N.B.*, XXXVI. 57f.; A. S. Turberville, ed., *Johnson's England* (Oxford, 1952), I. 58; *Burke's Landed Gentry*, pp. 2091–2; W. E. Minchinton, 'The Merchants in England in the 18th Century', in *The*

They were, secondly, the members of one's wider family or household, and by extension their relations. Bernard Edward Howard, squire of Glossop and later Duke of Norfolk, gave his agent's sons a beneficial lease to develop one of the early cotton mills.[1] Lord Moira, friend of the Prince Regent, later Governor of India and Marquess of Hastings, presented his chaplain and children's tutor, the Rev. John Dalby, the son of his attorney, to the livings of Belton and Castle Donington, and procured him two more in the Lord Chancellor's gift.[2]

They were, thirdly, one's tenants and villagers. The same Lord Moira discovered and educated a local farmer's son with a gift for languages, the orientalist John Shakespeare, and helped him to professorships at the East India colleges at Marlow and Addiscombe. The squire of Charlton, Wiltshire, started Stephen Duck, the 'thresher-poet', on the career which led him to be Yeoman of the Guard, Keeper of the Queen's Library at Richmond, Royal Preacher at Kew, Rector of Byfleet and, sad to relate, to suicide. The cobbler's son, James Mill, was educated in exchange for tuition of the daughter of the laird, Sir John Stuart, after whom he named his famous son.[3]

They were, fourthly, one's political helpers, associates and supporters. Political patronage, the shameless begging for 'place' for one's relative, supporters and constituents, is too well-known to need much illustration. Amongst an embarrassment of examples we might instance John Calcraft, son of the Duke of Rutland's Grantham election agent, who was procured a post in the Paymaster's office, and under the further patronage of Henry Fox became agent for half the regiments in the army, one of the principal channels for the purchase of commissions, and the founder of a landed and parliamentary family at Wareham, Dorset.[4]

[1] T. W. Ellison, 'Glossop Dale Reminiscences', *Glossop Advertizer*, 28 December 1935 *et seq*.

[2] J. M. Lee, 'The Rise and Fall of a Market Town: Castle Donington in the 19th Century', *Trans. Leicestershire Arch. and Hist. Soc.*, 1956, XXXII. 65–9.

[3] *D.N.B.*, LI. 345f.; R. G. Furnivall, 'Stephen Duck, the Wiltshire Phenomenon, 1705–56', *Cambridge Journal*, 1953, VI. 8f.; A. Bain, *Life of James Mill* (1882), pp. 12–13.

[4] E. Hughes, 'The Professions in the 18th Century', *Durham University Journal*, 1952, XIII. 51; *D.N.B.*, VIII. 235–6, 236f.

Entrepreneur (Economic History Society, Cambridge, Mass., 1957), p. 22; Sneyd Papers, Thomas Stubb's Notebook, 1755–88.

They included, finally, almost anyone amongst one's acquaintances in whom one recognized special merit or services to oneself. Lord Moira obtained the Admiralty registrarship at Bermuda for his friend, the poet Thomas Moore, who sailed there in 1803 before discovering it was a sinecure.[1] Through their influence with the trustees of the Duke of Hamilton, Adam Smith and Lord Kames obtained the Glasgow chair of law for Smith's pupil John Millar. Lord Bagot took James Wyatt to Italy as travelling companion to study Italian architecture. Charles Abbott, later Speaker of the Commons and Lord Colchester, himself a beneficiary of patronage in the shape of the clerkship of the rules in the Court of King's Bench at £2,700 a year, made the statistician, John Rickman, his secretary, out of which partnership the first Census Act emerged, and the clerkship of the Commons from which Rickman supervised the first four Censuses.[2]

Indeed, what later ages considered corruption was, in the absence of impersonal examination and selection procedures, the inevitable method of recruitment, and patronage, in the midst of so much self-seeking, has some notable successes to its credit. Through William Hamilton and Lord Rockingham it launched Edmund Burke into politics, though through him it also promoted his dubious kinsman Will Burke. Through Burke's friend William Windham it gave Cobbett his anti-Jacobin start in journalism.[3] Through the Duke of Buccleuch it provided Adam Smith with the leisure to write *The Wealth of Nations*, and through Thomas Wedgwood enabled Coleridge to become one of the 'two seminal minds' of the nineteenth century.[4] It succoured Hobbes, Locke, Addison, Swift, Matthew Prior and, less effectively, Defoe, and even provided that scourge of patrons, Samuel Johnson, with a government pension. In the old society the only alternative for ambition to inheriting, marrying or making a fortune by extraordinary endeavour in business

---

[1] Lee, *loc. cit.*; *D.N.B.*, XXXVIII. 340f.: in 1817 he found that the sinecure was not without care, when his deputy defalcated in the sum of £6,000, and Moore had to flee to the Continent to avoid the debtors' prison.

[2] Craig, in Millar, *Distinction of Ranks*, p. vi; *D.N.B.*, XLVIII. 264f., LXIII. 178f.

[3] *D.N.B.*, VII. 345f., 369f.; W. B. Pemberton, *William Cobbett* (1949), p. 38.

[4] A. Gray, *Adam Smith* (Historical Association, 1948), p. 6; *D.N.B.*, XI. 302f., LX. 146f.

or at the Bar was to obtain the friendship of those already in possession of property and influence.

Patronage, however, was more than a device for filling jobs, fostering talent, and providing pensions for the deserving and the undeserving. In the mesh of continuing loyalties of which appointments were the outward sign, patronage brings us very close to the inner structure of the old society. Hierarchy inhered not so much in the fortuitous juxtaposition of degree above degree, rank upon rank, status over status, as in the permanent vertical links which, rather than the horizontal solidarities of class, bound society together. 'Vertical friendship', a durable two-way relationship between patrons and clients permeating the whole of society, was a social nexus peculiar to the old society, less formal and inescapable than feudal homage, more personal and comprehensive than the contractual, employment relationships of capitalist 'Cash Payment'. For those who lived within its embrace it was so much an integral part of the texture of life that they had no name for it save 'friendship'.

In the Elizabethan springtime of patronage, Francis Bacon had expressed its essence: 'There is little friendship in the world, and least of all between equals . . . that that is, is between superior and inferior, whose fortunes may comprehend the one the other.'[1] In that age of glittering courtiers and competing favourites, patronage shaped society into a complex solar system, planet around planet, moon around moon, all revolving about the sun and centre of their world, the Queen herself. Bacon just managed to extricate himself in time from the collision of two such satellite systems, those of Essex and the Cecils. By the eighteenth century the Court counted for less and the Cabinet for more, and the distribution of rewards depended more on the horse-trading of an oligarchy than on the arbitrary whim of royal favour, but the system was essentially the same. Indeed, patronage was the middle term between feudal homage and capitalist cash nexus. Though it may seem a far cry from the overmighty subjects and armed retainers of fifteenth-century 'bastard feudalism' (so different in content and meaning from its legitimate parent) and the borough-mongering Whig magnates and their 'friends' of the eighteenth, there is a clear

[1] F .Bacon, 'Of Followers and Friends', in *Works* (ed. B. Montague, 1825), I. 164.

line of descent from the one to the other. In both, the important social bonds were the chains of informal vertical loyalty converging at the top in the struggles for power of great landlords.[1]

In this wider sense the relationship of patronage was the module of which the social structure was built. It was all-pervading, from Court and Cabinet to the parish poor. The political parties which manipulated majorities in the Cabinet and House of Commons were groupings of 'friends' around leading aristocratic patrons, held together by the hope and expectation of 'place'. As a client wrote to the Duke of Newcastle, 'Protection is due to attachment, and . . . sentiments of friendship to be reall and lasting must be reciprocall.'[2] The commercial and industrial 'interests' which lobbied them for support were similar groups clustering round leading figures like Sir Josiah Child, Governor Pitt, Samuel Whitbread, Josiah Wedgwood, or Samuel Garbett.[3] Both 'party' and 'interest' based their strength on the local, personal prestige and influence of their members, the politicians amongst their neighbours and tenants in the counties and boroughs, the merchants and industrialists amongst their suppliers, customers and economic dependants in the ports, market towns, and industrial villages.

At the lowest level even the poor were drawn into the system: the 'respectable', those for whom powerful friends, squire, parson or prominent townsman or parishioner would vouch, had first access to local charities. Even the paupers were those acknowledged by 'the gentlemen of the parish' as their own—an acknowledgement merely formalized by the Settlement Act of 1662. Only the poor stranger, the vagrant, the miscreant, the 'masterless man', without a friend to speak for him, was whipped and turned away. Indeed, criminal justice itself was modified, not to say distorted, by the influence of property and patronage. Though the penal code was savage and enjoined the death penalty for a wide range of offences, propertied opinion could in particular cases reduce the value of property involved and so reduce the penalty; the word of a powerful friend could commute a death sentence to transportation or imprisonment; and gen-

---

[1] Cf. J. H. Hexter, 'A New Framework for Social History', *J.Ec.H.*, 1955, XV.

[2] Hans Stanley to Newcastle, 26 June 1757; Namier, *op. cit.*, I. 199.

[3] Cf. Pares, *loc. cit.*; S. H. Beer, *Modern British Politics* (1965), chap. i.

teel, wealthy or influential prisoners could transform their punishment into a pleasant and profitable escapade: Leigh Hunt received his friends in his private garden, or in the cell he had had papered with a 'trellis of roses', while the poor wretches rotted in the dungeons below.[1]

The personal, face-to-face relationships of patronage, unlike the impersonal solidarities of class, could only exist in a society distributed in small units, a society of villages and small towns in which everyone knew everyone else. As we shall see, it was in the expanding towns that a new class society was to outgrow the personal bonds of the old society. Meanwhile, there was by modern standards only one great city in pre-industrial Britain, and although London was in many respects a forcing-ground of many features of modern society—it was, for example, almost the only place where criminals, prostitutes and other ne'er-do-wells extruded by their own small communities could find anonymity—it was nevertheless the focal centre of the personal system of social relationships. The higher one's place in the mesh of vertical loyalties, the wider were one's range of connections. 'County society' was a real entity, a comparatively small, face-to-face group of personal acquaintances. So too at the top was metropolitan society: London in 'the Season' was the literal meeting place of the only real 'class', the finite group of personal friends, rivals, acquaintances and enemies who made up the comparatively small informal aristocracy of landed gentlemen, peers or commoners, in whom the chains of patronage, 'friendship', or connection converged.

Patronage, then, was the other face of property, and brings us back to that first principle on which the old society was based. For Locke, the philosopher *par excellence* of the old society, it was the *raison d'être* of government and of civil society itself: 'The great and chief end . . . of men uniting into commonwealths, and putting themselves under government, is the preservation of their property.'[2] That a government of landowners should have welcomed such a philosophical defence of their interest is not surprising, but it does not explain how they came to have so extraordinary and sophisticated an interest to defend. As David Hume remarked, 'though men be much governed by interest;

[1] *Blackwood's*, 1830, XXVII. 390.
[2] J. Locke, *Two Treatises of Civil Government* (Everyman, 1955), p. 180.

yet even interest itself, and all human affairs, are entirely governed by *opinion*.'[1] The key to Locke, and therefore to eighteenth-century society, lies in the peculiar concept of absolute property bequeathed to them by history.[2]

Whereas the medieval concept of property, especially in land, was contingent, conditional, circumscribed, and subject to the specific claims of God, the Church, the king, the inferior tenants, and the poor, the eighteenth-century concept was absolute, categorical, unconditional; and, whether based with Locke, Blackstone and Adam Smith on a natural right anterior to society, or with Hume, Paley and Bentham on the principle of utility, it was secure from the envy of the poor and the covetousness of kings. Property gave to the owner the right to dispose of it exactly as he wished, short of actual fraud or physical injury to others. As the Dean of Westminster put it in 1798: 'Riches, you may think, are abused; but have not the rich a right over their own wealth, to use it or abuse it? A man may be vicious, or a prodigal, or a fool; but if he injures himself only, he is accountable to himself only, to his family or to God.'[3] But 'May I not do what I will with mine own?' is not a simple common-sense but a highly sophisticated notion, especially when 'mine own' is private land on which all mankind, in William Marshall's phrase, must 'live, and move, and have its being'.

This notion was not invented by Locke. 'The language thinks for us,' says Coleridge. Locke merely worked out, for a specific political purpose (the justification of the Whig view of government in the Exclusion Crisis of 1680, though it served admirably as an apology for the 1688 Revolution[4]), the philosophical implications of the concept of absolute property as it had evolved over the preceding three centuries. It is fully complete as early as 1644, in an anonymous pamphlet which gives the clue to its origin: let us, it says, 'who are English subjects . . . blesse God for his goodness who hath . . . made us absolute proprietors of

---

[1] D. Hume, *Essays, Moral, Political, and Literary* (ed. T. H. Green and T. H. Grose, 1875), I. 125.

[2] Cf. W. P. Larkin, *Property in the 18th Century, with Special Reference to England and Locke* (Cork, 1930); cf. also C. B. Macpherson, *The Political Theory oj Possessive Individualism: Hobbes to Locke* (Oxford, 1962), which appeared after the original draft of this chapter was written, and has not affected the views or the terminology presented here.

[3] W. Vincent, *Sermons* (ed. R. Nares, 1817), I. 281f.; Larkin, *op. cit.* p. 105.

[4] Cf. M. W. Cranston, *John Locke* (1957), pp. 206–8.

what we enjoy, so that our lives, liberties and estates, doe not depend upon, nor are subject to, the sole breath or arbitrary will of our Soveraigne.'[1] For the concept finally rose to supremacy with the victory of the landowners over the Crown, the last stage of the transformation of medieval lordship into modern ownership of the land. Feudal lordship was both something more and something less than the ownership of the land: it was a mere estate upon the land, a claim upon the fruits of the soil and the allegiance of its occupiers, subject to and limited by the parallel claims of royal overlord, church, and sub-tenants. Not by philosophical argument but by a political, legal and sometimes physical struggle lasting from the high middle ages until the seventeenth century, the English landowners shook off the claims of crown, church and peasants, and transformed lordship into ownership.

The struggle with the peasants began with a defeat for the landlords. The disappearance of serfdom by the commutation of labour services was a compromise forced on the landlords by the accident of late medieval population decline, before and after the Black Death. But the copyholders who succeeded the serfs thereby lost in most cases their hold on the land. When population and prices rose again in the Tudor period their very freedom made them vulnerable, and they, or rather their families when they died and their copyholds fell in, were evicted in large numbers to make room for larger tenants farming for the market. Some peasants gained by the change: the larger and more prosperous became new-style 'farmers' paying a 'farm' or commercial rent for what had been several peasant holdings; while the freeholders and other secure tenants did best of all, as inflation rendered their fixed rents negligible and turned freehold into virtual ownership. But the rest were squeezed out by enclosure and the 'engrossing of farms' to become the more or less landless proletariat of agricultural labourers and rural industrial workers noticed above. On all except freehold land the manorial lords were left as residuary owners.[2]

The defeat of the Church was less complete but no less decisive. Lay patronage of bishoprics and livings had already in

---

[1] *England's Monarch, or a Conviction and Refutation of those False Principles . . . of Albericus* (1644); Larkin, *op. cit.* p. 52.
[2] Cf. R. H. Tawney, *The Agrarian Problem of the 16th Century* (1912).

the middle ages subordinated the clergy to a large measure of lay control. In the sixteenth century the Crown and the landlords, acting together as King-in-Parliament, engulfed the Church and by the real Tudor revolution in government replaced clerical statesmen and administrators by laymen, transformed the hierarchy into an arm of the State, and transferred a large part of the Church's lands, tithes and advowsons from clerical to lay ownership. So thorough was the victory that all that remained was to decide what sort of a Church it should be, and which of the aggressors, King or Parliament, should control it. These questions were to be decided by a further struggle, between the landlords and the Crown. Meanwhile the outcome of that further struggle was prejudiced if not determined by the poverty of the Crown, and the consequent redistribution of the bulk of the monastic and other Church lands to families who, whatever their provenance, formed the backbone of the nobility and gentry of the following centuries.[1]

Most singular of all in contemporary Europe, the landlords out-manoeuvred, defeated and tamed the Crown without either (permanently) abolishing it or weakening the international standing of the kingdom. Almost from the establishment of feudalism their main aim became to escape its burdens. By the opening of the seventeenth century they could grant, sell, let or bequeath the land at will, subject only to the fiscal annoyances of wardship and marriage. These vestiges of feudal tenure, the subject of the abortive Great Contract of 1610, were abolished in 1645, and the abolition was confirmed at the Restoration, when the Crown was compensated by an excise on beer, paid mainly by non-landowners.[2] The crucial phase of this third struggle, however, can be pinned down to the year 1641, when the land-

[1] Cf. J. H. Round, *Family Origins* (1930), p. 22; James Harrington, *The Commonwealth of Oceana* (1656); R. H. Tawney, 'The Rise of the Gentry, 1558–1640', *Ec.H.R.*, 1941, XI; H. R. Trevor-Roper, *The Gentry, 1540–1640* (*Ec.H.R* Supplement I, 1953), and the whole 'gentry' controversy—for sources see Lawrence Stone, *Social Change and Revolution in England, 1540–1640* (1965), pp. 179–83.

[2] Cf. a whole literature of 19th-century land reform, including W. Cobbett, *Legacy to Labourers* (1834), letter ii; *Anti-Corn Law League Tract No. 1: A Plea for the Total and Immediate Repeal of the Corn Laws; with remarks on the Land Tax Fraud* (1841); Anti-Corn Law League, *The Constitutional Right to a Revision of the Land Tax* (1842); J. S. Mill, Speech on Land Tenure Reform, 15 May 1871, *Dissertations and Discussions* (1875), IV. 251f.

lords, by abolishing the prerogative courts, stripped the Crown of all the instruments by which it might govern without their aid, approval and consent. That decision was upheld by a sufficient fraction of them on the battlefield, and survived the Restoration, to be amply confirmed at the Revolution. The timely publication of Locke's *Treatises of Civil Government* in 1690 celebrates the final triumph of that concept of absolute, unfettered ownership of their estates for which the landlords had fought and won.

The implications of the concept were far-reaching. For Locke, as for the pamphleteer of 1644, property embraced life and liberty as well as estate, and if the old society held the first two cheap when they offended against the third, the fact that it entrusted their defence to tangible property was a gain in citizenship rights even for non-landowners against the arbitrary State.[1] Even religion came within its embrace, to the benefit of toleration: *A Dissenter's Plea*, about 1790, claimed religion as 'the unalienated property of every individual, for which he is answerable to God alone'.[2] But the most important implication was the social ideal which the concept supported. Emphasizing as it did the owner's right to the enjoyment of his property rather than his function as, say, an investor or entrepreneur, its whole weight went to support the ideal of the leisured gentleman. The landowner was distinguished from the rest not so much by the size of his income as by its unearned character; and the rest paid him the unstinted tribute of admiration, envy and emulation. For the leisured gentleman was the ideal at which the whole society aimed, and by which it measured its happiness and ambitions.

Leisure, it goes without saying, did not necessarily mean idleness, although the right to be idle if one so wished was an integral part of the concept. It meant strictly the freedom to pursue any interest, taste or pleasure consonant with the honour of a gentleman, without the further need to demean oneself by earning a living. Social emulation had, as we have seen, stretched the notion of a gentleman to cover, if not quite 'all . . . who maintain themselves without manual labour', at least a wide variety of the higher professions and occupations. But

[1] Cf. T. H. Marshall, *Citizenship and Social Class* (1950), pp. 14–20.
[2] G. Walker, *A Dissenter's Plea* [c. 1790]. p. 3; Henriques, *op. cit.*, p. 21.

clergymen, lawyers, physicians, bankers and overseas merchants knew, and showed by their ambitions that they knew, that the only worthwhile thing to be in the old society was a completely leisured—which in effect meant landed—gentleman. For, with few exceptions, only the landowners were, in a phrase of Bishop Sprat's to describe the majority of the Royal Society, 'gentlemen, free and unconfined'.[1] And only those who were so had the time and opportunity to enjoy to the full the pursuits of gentlemen.

What were the pursuits of gentlemen? There was scarcely an unpaid activity pleasurable or useful in which gentlemen were not prominent as patrons or protagonists. The Squire Westerns and Osbaldestons lived for the pleasures of the table and the hunting field, the Horace Walpoles, Lord Herveys and Creeveys for political gossip and the polite social round, the Lord Seftons, Sir Francis Dashwoods and Lord Hertfords for gambling, irreligion or vice unadorned. Others excelled in more admirable spheres: the Earl of Leicester, Thomas Coke and the Duke of Bedford in agricultural improvement, the Duke of Bridgewater, Sir Nigel Gresley or the Ayrshire laird John Loudon Macadam in transport undertakings, the Duke of Chandos in commercial investment, Sir George Cayley in aeronautics, the Earl of Burlington and Cork in architecture, the third Earl of Shaftesbury in philosophy, Lord Dartmouth and Lady Huntingdon in religious enthusiasm, Robert Boyle, Sir Joseph Banks or Henry Cavendish in science, Edward Gibbon in history, Sir John Hawkins in musicology, Byron, Shelley, and Beckford in literature, and so on. But the one overriding pursuit of landed gentlemen was government. From the squire who was the unofficial arbiter of village affairs through the J.P. at Quarter Sessions and the M.P. in the Commons to the House of Lords and the Cabinet, government was the right, privilege and responsibility of the landed gentlemen who, besides being the only nation-wide class in that otherwise classless society, were in the most literal sense the ruling class.

3. A DYNAMIC SOCIETY

The old society was, finally, an open aristocracy. The triumph of the English landowners was gained at a price which few oli-

[1] Thomas Sprat, *History of the Royal Society* (1667), p. 67.

garchies have been willing to pay. Not only were they willing to tax themselves, in land and luxury taxes, to defend themselves from counter-revolution and, in poor rates, to buy internal peace from those whose lives they had made insecure. They paid for their unique conception of property, for the freedom to do what they would with their own, by opening their ranks to all who could acquire the one necessary qualification, the purchase-price of an estate. From the dawning of the old society with the decline of feudalism and serfdom in the fourteenth century (though there are traces of it as far back as the reign of Henry I) there began that familiar rise of new men into the gentry and nobility which became the most distinctive feature of English History.

'Apart from fortunate marriages, the leading English families have mainly owed their rise to three great sources: successful trade; the law; and the spoils of monastic houses,' wrote the doyen of genealogists, J. H. Round.[1] If for the last we substitute royal service, for which monastic spoils were merely one kind of reward, this was true for the whole life of the old society. The upflow of new men began in the two centuries or rather more before the Reformation, with the rise of merchants like Sir William de la Pole of Hull, Sir John de Pulteney and Sir Thomas Boleyn of London, or, on a humbler level, William Sneyd of Chester; of judges like Sir William Howard, Sir John Cavendish, William Paston, Thomas Littleton, or Sir Robert Brudenell; and royal servants like Sir Thomas Tresham, the Yorkist Speaker of the Commons, Sir John Throckmorton, under-treasurer of England in 1440, Edmund Dudley, Henry VII's unpopular tax-gatherer, or John Russell, the obscure Devon squire whose chance encounter as interpreter to the landfallen King and Queen of Spain led to Whitehall and the earldom of Bedford.[2] The process is complicated because many families had more than one rise: first into landholding as such and, later and sometimes through a younger son, into the substantial estate which might then or later qualify for a peerage. The first rise might come through good peasant husbandry and laying field to field, as did the early Pastons, Sneyds, and the Spencers

[1] *Op. cit.* p. 22.
[2] The references for 'new men' are too numerous to be cited in full. The bulk of them can be found in standard reference works, including *D.N.B.*, *Burke's Peerage and Baronetage* and *Landed Gentry*, *The Complete Peerage*, and so on.

of Althorp, and then, perhaps, by launching a son into law or trade. The second was most commonly through royal service, like the Tudor Cavendishes, Cecils, and Throckmortons.

The upflow became spectacular between the Reformation and the Civil War, when profit inflation, the rapid expansion of trade and industry, the enormous growth of government administration and the share of the laity in it, and the brisk market in Crown and monastic lands increased both the opportunities and the rewards. It was in that critical century that the landowners, noble and common, consolidated their defeat of the Church and the peasants, and acquired the political means and economic sinews to defeat the Crown. But whether or not there was a rise of the gentry as a social group, there can be no doubt about the rise of larger numbers of individual families into the gentry, and from the gentry into the nobility, which, in spite of defunct peerages, was almost trebled to accommodate them. To mention only the famous, new families were founded by merchants, financiers and industrialists like Alderman Cokayne, Sir William Craven, Baptist Hicks and Paul Bayning, all of whose sons became peers, Lionel Cranfield, Earl of Middlesex, Sir Edward Osborne, ancestor of the dukes of Leeds, the German paper-maker, Sir John Spilman, and the clothiers Thomas Cony, the grandfather of Baron Lexington, and Alexander Langford, whose descendant Anne Hyde became the mother of Queens Mary II and Anne; by judges like Sir Edward Montagu and his younger son Henry, ancestors respectively of the Earls of Cardigan and the earls and dukes of Manchester, Sir Thomas Egerton, ancestor of the earls and dukes of Bridgewater, or the great Sir Edward Coke, ancestor of the earls of Leicester; but above all by the royal officials and favourites who enjoyed so large a share of the monastic lands: Sir William Cavendish, ancestor of the dukes of Newcastle and of Devonshire, Sir Thomas Heneage, ancestor of the Finches, earls of Nottingham, the two Cecils, Burleigh and his younger son Sir Robert, ancestors of the earls of Exeter and the marquesses of Salisbury, and the notorious George Villiers, Duke of Buckingham, founder of the ubiquitous 'Villiers connection'. And the catalogue could be greatly extended.[1]

---

[1] Cf. Trevor-Roper, *op. cit.*, pp. 8f.; Lawrence Stone, *The Crisis of the Aristocracy, 1558–1641* (Oxford, 1965).

After the Restoration the spectacular prizes were reserved for the few, like Walpole, Marlborough, or 'Diamond' Pitt, governor of Madras, the first two significantly from within the landed order. But if the emphasis at the highest level had switched from the rise to the consolidation of the great families,[1] the road to the gentry was now a beaten one, with any number of new gates of access, and a byword to the very journalists:

> Trade is so far here from being inconsistent with a gentleman, that, in short, trade in England makes gentlemen, and has peopled this nation with gentlemen . . . ; for, after a generation or two, the tradesmen's children, or at least their grandchildren, come to be as good gentlemen, statesmen, parliamentmen, privy counsellors, judges, bishops and noblemen as those of the highest birth and most ancient families.[2]

The familiar paths were still open for merchants and industrialists like Sir Josiah Child, Sir James Bateman and Sir George Wombwell, chairman of the East India Company, Paul Medway the Essex clothier, Sir George Dashwood the London brewer, William Stone the Sheffield cutler, whose 'grandfather was a common hammerman', the paper-making Portals of Hampshire and Whatmans of Kent, or the Birmingham 'Japanner to the Queen', Henry Clay; for lawyers from Lords Macclesfield, Hardwicke and the two Camdens down to the Scott brothers Eldon and Stowell, and Thurlow, Erskine and Ellenborough; and for government officials and client-politicians like the Calcrafts, the army agents mentioned above, Charles Abbott, Lord Chichester, or Henry Addington, Lord Sidmouth.

Now there rose, however, a host of substantial squires and minor peers from a great variety of occupations: bankers like the Hoares, Childs, Smiths, or Thorntons; government contractors and agents like Sir Lawrence Dundas, Earl of Zetland, and John Henniker, who became an Irish peer; nabobs—in addition to 'Diamond' Pitt, ancestor of the earls of Londonderry as well as of Chatham—like Henry Vansittart, father of Lord Bexley (who rose still further as Chancellor of the Exchequer), and Robert, Baron Clive; mere attorneys like Sir Joseph Banks's grandfather and his predecessor Thomas Wright of Sheffield, or

---

[1] Cf. H. J. Habakkuk, 'English Landownership, 1680–1740', *Ec.H.R.*, 1939–40, X. 2f.

[2] D. Defoe, *The Complete English Tradesman* (1726), p. 376.

Walpole's friend Philip Case of King's Lynn, who left large estates in Norfolk and £100,000 in the funds; and mere inland traders like the Wilberforces of Beverley, the London booksellers who established J. H. Round's ancestors at Birch Hall, Essex, or Joseph Hague of Glossop, the travelling packman who came home to buy Park Hall at Hayfield. Even domestic service could boast its new landed gentry, like Mr. Poynter, the Duke of Kingston's master of horse, who purchased an estate of £200 a year and 'seven miles of manor for sporting', Mr. Rogers, the stable-boy who rose to be Lord Monson's steward and 'a very great landholder', or Henry Isherwood, M.P., son of an inn-servant who prospered as a brewer. The list could be indefinitely extended, but it is long enough to show how open by the eighteenth century was the door to the landed oligarchy.

Many of these new men were themselves younger sons striving to outdo their elder brothers. For the English landowners jealously preserved one principle of feudal lordship, that of primogeniture. Neither the land, the title nor the status of the father normally descended to the younger sons, who were sent out into the world to fend for themselves. The consequences for English society were profound. The landed gentry, unlike the Continental minor aristocracies, the French *petite noblesse*, the Spanish *hidalgos*, the German *junkers*, and so on, were not impoverished by a demographic burden of proud penury and elegant unemployment or driven into compulsory service of the State or the Church. On the contrary, they increased their demographic chances of wealth by sending into lucrative occupations sons whose success might raise the whole family, or who might themselves inherit the estate and bring back their wealth to enrich the parent stock. At the same time they increased their contacts with and thus their informal control of the society over which they ruled. Meanwhile, since younger sons were not—*pace* Dr Thomas Wilson—left with 'that which the cat left on the malt heap',[1] but were given at least an education or apprenticeship and an allowance or capital sum to launch them on a career, the middle ranks of society benefited by an additional inflow of new, energetic young men of capital and resource.

[1] T. Wilson, *The State of England, A.D. 1600* (ed. F. J. Fisher, Camden Miscellany, XVI, 1936), p. 24; Habakkuk, *op. cit., Trans. R.H.S.*, 1950, XXXII. 19.

The English aristocracy was therefore open in both directions. The upward flow of new men into the landed élite was matched by a downward flow of younger sons into the middle ranks. To these movements we should add the parallel upflow of heiresses —scarcely a noble family of any consequence in the eighteenth century failed to acquire at least one heiress—and a downflow of dowried daughters, both of which served a precisely similar purpose. There was thus a two-way flow of blood and wealth which goes far towards explaining the economic expansion and the political stability of the old society in England.

It is true that there have been *novi homines* in all ages and in most countries,[1] but nothing quite on the same scale of social mobility existed elsewhere. In Venice, Florence, or Holland merchants might acquire land and even corporate sovereignty, but they remained an urban oligarchy wedded to commerce and finance, until at length in the Italian case they abandoned trade without leaving behind adequate successors.[2] In France lawyers might aspire to the *noblesse de robe* and officials to bureaucratic power, but from Louis XIV's reign their hopes of reaching to the top of the social scale in the *noblesse d'épée* were increasingly frustrated, until the angry explosion of the Revolution.[3] Elsewhere the barriers between bourgeoisie and nobility were to all intents impenetrable, and if a handful of newcomers 'passed', as American negroes sometimes 'pass' for white, that in itself was a proof of the effectiveness of the gulf. Only in England was there an easy, continuous and accepted interchange between the two.

There is no English word for *bourgeoisie* because, until the nineteenth century at least, the thing itself did not exist, in the sense of a permanent, self-conscious urban class in opposition to the landed aristocracy. In every generation the richer citizens and townsmen who, if socially frustrated, might have galvanized their neighbours into a powerful class were themselves transmuted into country gentlemen, thus making room for other townsmen at the top, and setting in train a general upward movement. The buoyant effects of this social mobility

[1] Cf. E. Salin, 'European Entrepreneurship', *J.Ec.H.*, 1952, XII. 366–7.

[2] H. G. Koenigsberger, 'Decadence or Shift? Changes in the Civilization of Italy and Europe in the 16th and 17th Centuries', *Trans. R.H.S.*, 1960, X. 1f.

[3] Cf. R. B. Grassby 'Social Status and Commercial Enterprise under Louis XIV', *Ec.H.R.*, 1960, XII.

could be felt almost to the bottom of urban society, and radiated outwards to the countryside, through the urban demand for new men at all levels. Meanwhile, the landed aristocracy and gentry were constantly replenished with men, heiresses and new wealth from below, thus replacing their own wastage by failure of heirs, bankruptcies, competitive expenditure, and family jointures, portions and dowries. *Plus ça change, plus c'est la même chose.* The result was a self-contained system of social movement which left the shape and structure of society precisely as before, a 'stationary state' based on the restless motion of its constituent atoms.

On this dynamic social equilibrium was founded the political stability of the old society. But it was not economically stationary. The two-way flow of men and wealth acted like the circulation of the blood, enriching every organ of the body politic, and creating the most important feature of the old society: economic growth without fundamental change of structure. For two centuries or more before the onset of the Industrial Revolution, England achieved by the standards of the time a remarkable degree of economic expansion without any fundamental reorganization of the structure of industry, trade and society.

But such a *tour de force* could not continue for ever. What if the pace of expansion should accelerate to the point where the new men could not be absorbed and assimilated fast enough to prevent the formation of a *bourgeoisie* hostile to the landowners? What if a set of men should hit upon new ways of making money which, though aimed as before at social climbing, required, like the steam-powered factory, a change in the structure of economy and society? And what if the ruling aristocracy itself should begin to abandon the paternal responsibilities on which the whole system rested? Then the dynamic equilibrium might be shattered, and the forces of stability become themselves the forces of change.

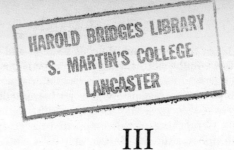
III

The Social Causes of Industrialism

W E can now return to the questions from which we began. Why did the pioneer industrial revolution happen at all? Why when it did? And why in Britain first? Because, alone among nations with the full complement of material resources and adequate access to expanding world trade, Britain had in the fullest degree the right kind of society to produce it. An open, dynamic aristocracy based on absolute property and linked vertically by patronage was the ideal society for generating a spontaneous industrial revolution. The underlying causes were social causes. This is not to say that the social causes were in any sense alternative to the ancillary political, intellectual and religious causes, still less to the necessary economic and techno-logical causes. On the contrary, they worked upon and through these causes, calling them forth, and bringing them to bear in harmonious operation. The nature and structure of the old society were the central, integrating cause, though not of course the sole determinant, of the British Industrial Revolution.

1. SOCIETY AND THE ANCILLARY CAUSES

Britain's political good fortune was not fortuitous. It was the direct consequence of the domination of government and society by a landed aristocracy jealous of the Crown and with a stake in economic growth. If for the encouragement of industrial expansion a combination of internal freedom and external protection—*laissez-faire* in the arms of mercantilism—was the best economic policy, then the seventeenth-century victory of the landowners over the Crown was a decisive step towards industrialism.

The economic significance of this step can be seen by contrasting English policy after the Restoration both with that of contemporary European governments and with that of the Tudors and early Stuarts. Both Continental contemporaries and English predecessors assiduously fostered industry and commerce, and yet neither came near to generating an industrial revolution. Tudor and early Stuart economic paternalism, in-indeed, was deliberately designed to prevent just those changes in the economy and society most necessary to industrialization. The control of industrial processes, the regulation of employment and apprenticeship, the restriction of the internal corn trade, the anti-enclosure acts, the sumptuary laws, the London building restrictions, and the rigorously enforced poor laws, were consciously intended to hinder unwanted economic innovation and maintain the social *status quo*. The 1563 Statute of Artificers set out to keep men in their places in the social hierarchy, and prevent them from rising higher than their fathers.[1] If William Cecil, that second-generation new man, had had his way, there would have been no more new men: he would have prohibited all non-landowners save merchants from buying land worth more than £5 a year, and even merchants land worth more than £50 a year, and so dammed the upward flow of blood and wealth.[2] Because of the administrative inefficiency and financial weakness of the Crown and the frustration of its policies by unsympathetic officials, governments before the Civil War could not prevent the growth of capitalist industry and agriculture, but they did act as a brake on its development, and could conceivably have continued to forestall the essential preconditions of industrialism.

[1] 5 Elizabeth c.4, 1563, by which apprenticeship to the more profitable and prestigious trades was restricted to the sons of existing masters and of holders of certain property qualifications.

[2] 'Considerations delivered to Parliament, 1559', Historical Manuscripts Commission, *Salisbury Manuscripts*, I. 162–3, in Bland *et. al.*, *op. cit.*, pp. 323–4. According to Professor T. S. Willan there is some doubt about whether these notes were in fact by Cecil.

Similarly, in Louis XIV's France and wherever Colbertism was imitated, industry and trade were aggressively encouraged, but only within the framework of accepted techniques and processes. Although Colbert's methods of control might conceivably have been used, given a bureaucracy with the appropriate technical knowledge, to bring about an industrial revolution—and, indeed, French governments from Louis XIV to Napoleon displayed an enlightened interest in industrial invention—in practice the dead hand of State regulation proved inimical to fundamental industrial change. The example of France shows how effectively a victorious English monarchy might have pursued limited economic prosperity while unconsciously preventing the onset of unlimited industrialism.

Instead, the triumphant English landowners from the Restoration, still more from the Revolution, stood the monarchy's traditional policy on its head. They abolished most of the restrictions on internal industry, ignored those on building, forgot the anti-enclosure acts and began to pass private acts in favour of enclosure, and exchanged corn trade controls for bounties on corn exports. During the eighteenth century they allowed the wage-fixing and apprenticeship clauses of the Statute of Artificers to fall gradually into disuse, until only the attenuated poor law remained as the forlorn remnant of the great edifice of Tudor and early Stuart State control. What the Webbs said of the poor law, 'Between the Statute Book and the actual administration of parish officers there was, in the eighteenth century, only a casual connection', could be applied *pari passu* to all branches of social and economic legislation.[1] As Davenant put it in 1699, 'Nowadays Laws are not much observed, which do not in a manner execute themselves.'[2] For the landowners by abolishing the prerogative courts had drawn the teeth of the monarchy, and effectively prevented the Crown from backing up its control over those whom it did not actually pay for their services, by any other means than the weak, haphazard and dilatory processes of the common law. *Laissez-faire* a hundred years and more before the publication of *The Wealth of Nations* was the

[1] S. and B. Webb, *English Poor Law History*, Part I, *The Old Poor Law* (1927), p. 149.
[2] C. Davenant, *Essay upon . . . the Ballance of Trade* (1699), p. 55.

direct consequence of the breakdown at the Civil War of the 'Privy Council system' of central control.

Not that the new landed rulers of England deliberately chose a *laissez-faire* policy. On the contrary, they continued to hold the view, common to all their European contemporaries, that it was the duty of a nation's rulers to take positive action to increase its wealth and power relative to its neighbours. From the Restoration right down to the end of the eighteenth century they reserved the right to regulate internal industry and consumption for mercantilist ends: for example, by the notorious law of 1666 (echoing a proclamation of 1622) requiring burial in woollen, those of 1698 against the use of stuff buttons, of 1700 against Indian calicoes, and of 1726 against home-printed calicoes; or the attempts at regulation of the Kidderminster cloth industry in 1670, of the Yorkshire industry in 1708, 1711 and 1726, and of the treatment of hides outside London as late as 1800.[1] Yet none of these internal controls was more than a capricious remnant of the general regulation of production and consumption by the Tudors and early Stuarts. The very name 'mercantilism', derived from Adam Smith's attack on 'the Mercantile System', is a reminder that, in England as distinct from the Continent, effective State control could only be exercised over foreign trade, and in internal economic affairs was little more than a sporadic nuisance. The reason is to be found in practical administration rather than deliberate policy: the State controlled external trade through professional officials at the ports; when it attempted to control internal trade and industry it was compelled to work through amateur officials who could frustrate it with impunity.[2] And the reason for this in turn was the paradoxical relationship of the landowners to the government which they dominated.

The paradox lies in the unique example of a ruling aristocracy jealous of its own creature, the State. Although the landowners had defeated the old monarchy and replaced it by one more to their liking, they still had no wish to rule in its place. Central

[1] E. F. Hecksher, *Mercantilism* (trans. M. Schapiro, 1935), I. 265–6, 297–301.

[2] *Wealth of Nations*, II. 178, 413. The Excise officers, from 1733, were concerned with very few commodities, and their activities were effectively restricted by the unpopularity of the system. Control at the ports facilitated a considerable increase in tariffs, and therefore in protection to home industry—cf. R. Davis, 'The Rise of Protection in England, 1689–1786', *Ec.H.R.*, 1966, XIX. 306–17.

government in their eyes was still the king's, and all they asked, as the Revolution settlement with its emphasis on impeachment and other *post hoc* controls goes to show, was that the king and his ministers should govern in a way which they could sanction and approve.[1] That in the course of the eighteenth century powerful ministers should transform this simple-minded and impracticable arrangement into a sophisticated working partner-ship between themselves, the Crown and a manipulated Parlia-ment, in no way detracted from the effect: the opposition of the great body of landowners to all effective governmental inter-ference with themselves. So jealous of its power were they that they denied the State any permanent standing army or effective professional police, preferring to rely for the defence of property on their own social power and the loyalty of the lower orders. Least of all would they entrust the State, with the sole exception of the customs officials at the ports and the purely fiscal excise officers inland, with a local bureaucratic civil service through which to outflank their territorial power.

It was, therefore, the peculiar relationship of the English landed aristocracy to society and hence to the State which created the political climate for the germination of industrialism. Out of pure self-interest they created the political conditions —personal liberty, absolute security of property, the minimum of internal intervention, and adequate protection from foreign competition—best suited for generating a spontaneous in-dustrial revolution. More than this, they used their political power to provide the 'preconditions', in agriculture, mining and transport, for the take-off. But this leads us on from the ancillary to the necessary economic causes of the industrial revolution, which will be dealt with in the next section.

The domination of landed patrons played a similar role in the intellectual and scientific causation of industrialism, automati-cally making available to others the advantages they pursued for themselves. If England had the edge on neighbouring countries in giving concrete shape to the 'spirit of improvement', the profound change in human expectations stemming from the Renaissance and the scientific and philosophical revolutions, it was because of the more rapid diffusion and application of practical ideas made possible by the structure of English society.

[1] Cf. Bill of Rights, 1689.

Gentlemen amateurs motivated by curiosity, but not unaware of the value of material progress to the wealth of the nation and themselves, did not disdain to mingle with practical business and professional men and even with skilful artisans with an interest in the new science.

The Royal Society itself symbolized the ease of intercourse between the different levels of English society. Courtiers and landed gentlemen like Lords Brouncker and Brereton, Sir Robert Moray, Sir Gilbert Talbot, John Evelyn and Robert Boyle mingled without restraint or embarrassment with dons like Newton, Wilkins and Wren, physicians like Timothy Clark, George Ent and Jonathan Goddard, lawyers like Dudley Palmer, business men like the clothier and dyer William Petty, and even shopkeepers like John Graunt. The Society 'freely admitted Men of different Religions, Countries, and Professions of Life', and looked for 'Noble Rarities to be every day given in not onely by the Hands of Learned and profess'd Philosophers; but from the Shops of Mechanicks; from the Voyages of Merchants; from the Ploughs of Husbandmen; from the Sports, the Fish-ponds, the Parks, the Gardens of Gentlemen. . . .'[1]

Similarly, the Royal Society of Arts, which by its premiums and bounties did much 'for the encouragement of arts, manufactures and commerce in Great Britain', reads from its early membership lists like a cross-section of mid-eighteenth-century society, from dukes to clockmakers, admirals to actors, bishops to Dissenting ministers, bankers to booksellers, judges to schoolmasters. Its founders in 1754 were a microcosm of English society: Lord Romney and his brother-in-law Lord Folkestone (the latter a 'new man', the son and grandson of Turkey merchants), the botanist and clergyman Stephen Hales, Defoe's son-in-law Henry Baker, journalist and pioneer teacher of the deaf-and-dumb, together with a director of the Bank of England, a surgeon, an optician, a watchmaker, and—the moving spirit, and beneficiary of Lords Romney and Folkestone's patronage— the Northampton drawing-master, William Shipley.[2] The patronage of the brilliant but lowly-born, most notably in the

---

[1] Sprat, *op. cit.*, pp. 53–5, 62–3, 71–2, and Appendix A.

[2] H. T. Wood, *History of the Royal Society of Arts* (1913), pp. 7–17, 28–46.

person of Humphry Davy and Michael Faraday, also characterized the Royal Institution, founded in 1799 by Count Rumford in the house of the celebrated gentleman-amateur (and third-generation 'new man') Sir Joseph Banks, president of the Royal Society.[1] There were, of course, foreign counterparts of such learned societies, but they did not span the whole range of society to anything like the same degree.

The personal interconnections of English society, both between different levels and between the metropolis and the provinces, helped in the second and still more practical wave of the diffusion of scientific ideas. The numerous philosophical societies which sprang into being in Birmingham, Derby, Manchester, Bristol, Bath and many other towns in the last quarter of the eighteenth century were a spontaneous growth, founded, like the Manchester Literary and Philosophical Society in 1781, by 'a few Gentlemen, inhabitants of the town, . . . inspired by a taste for Literature and Philosophy', who 'formed themselves into a kind of weekly club, for the purpose of conversing on subjects of that nature'.[2] The membership was naturally concentrated in the middle ranks of urban society, the professions, especially medicine, being strongly represented, while in industrial towns like Manchester 'the great majority of the members were either engaged or interested in the extension of Science and Art to manufacturing purposes'.[3] Yet they were not without personal encouragement from the aristocracy, as attested for example by Sir Brooke Boothby's membership of the Derby Society, nor without personal contact with fashionable metropolitan science, through the overlapping membership of leading figures with the Royal Society: James Keir and James Watt of the Birmingham Lunar Society, William Strutt, John Whitehurst and Josiah Wedgwood of the Derby Society, John Dalton, Thomas Henry, Charles White and George Walker of the Manchester Society, and so on. Nor, on the other

---

[1] W. H. G. Armytage, *Civic Universities* (1955), pp. 162–4; *D.N.B.*, XIV. 187f., XVIII. 190f.; see also H. Bence Jones, *The Royal Institution* (1871) and T. Martin, *The Royal Institution* (1948).

[2] Manchester Literary and Philosophical Society, *Memoirs*, 1785, I. viii; A. E. Musson and E. Robinson, 'Science and Industry in the 18th Century', *Ec.H.R.*, 1960, XIII. 223.

[3] A. A. Mumford, *The Manchester Grammar School, 1515–1915* (1919), p. 218; Musson and Robinson, *loc. cit.*

side, did they fail to make contact with 'the superior class of artisans', through the extensive provision of scientific lectures, chiefly by itinerant lecturers such as Caleb and John Rotherham, James Ferguson, Gustavus Katterfelto, and the Adam Walkers, father and son, under the auspices of the Societies.[1]

The third and final wave in the diffusion of the new science and technology, through the Mechanics' Institutes and the Society for the Diffusion of Useful Knowledge from the 1820's onwards, though it coincided with the rise of violent social conflict and the division of society into antagonistic classes, benefited nevertheless from what remained of the old vertical personal connections. The Mechanics' Institutes became part of a middle-class mission to the working classes in general, not confined to technical instruction but extending to moral and political education, and their comparative failure at this level will be discussed in Chapter VIII. Meanwhile, their initial success in spreading scientific knowledge amongst the works managers, foremen and skilled workers of the newer industries depended to a large extent on the personal relations between their middle-class founders and patrons and their aspiring working-class membership. In Yorkshire, for example, the Institutes founded and fostered by middle-class leaders like John Marshall and Benjamin Gott, the Leeds industrialists, and the Edward Bainses, father and son, editors of the *Leeds Mercury*, prospered; the few which came under working-class control, like Bradford, collapsed, and had to be refounded on the middle-class model.[2]

More important than the institutional forms taken by personal connection, however, was the direct part taken by patronage in fostering scientific and technical innovation. The lonely inventor, the Crompton or Hargreaves working in isolation, was not a typical figure, and was all too likely to fail or see others reap the harvest of his sowing. The backing of capital, enterprise or influence was essential to success, and it was here that the manifold links of patronage, kinship and connection came into

---

[1] *Ibid.* pp. 222–44; E. Robinson, 'The Derby Philosophical Society', *Annals of Science*, 1953, IX. 359–67; R. E. Schofield, *The Lunar Society of Birmingham* (Oxford, 1963), *passim*; N. A. Hans, *New Trends in 18th Century Education* (1951), pp. 158–60.

[2] J. W. Hudson, *History of Adult Education* (1851); J. F. C. Harrison, *Learning and Living, 1790–1960* (1961), pp. 57–62.

their own. Given the keen amateur interest of a sufficient number of patrons in science and industry, the patronage system might have been designed to encourage scientific and technical genius. The relations at critical stages in their careers of Sir John Denham to Wren, Hooke and Savery to Newcomen, the Duke of Bridgewater to Brindley, Sir William Pulteney to Telford, the Anderson brothers to Watt, Dr. Edwards to Davy, and Davy to Faraday, to mention only a few examples of technological patronage, are a sufficient proof of its importance.[1] The mutual expectations of patronage shaded imperceptibly at the lower margin into those of straightforward partnership, in which kinship, religion, apprenticeship, and other forms of personal connection played a significant part. But here again we encroach on the economic causation of industrialism, to be dealt with later.

Finally, the domination of the landowners played a perverse part in the religious causes of industrialism. Their partial toleration or ineffective intolerance helped to divert the energies of the Dissenters away from politics and towards labouring in their vocations of industry and trade. Nonconformist ironmasters, bankers, brewers, and millowners repaid their exclusion from university, local government, army and navy, parliament and Cabinet by practical education and economic exertion. The iron industry, for example, benefited from every variety of nonconformist endeavour: from the Quaker Darbys, Reynolds, Huntsmans, and Lloyds, through the Independent Roebucks and Dawsons and the Presbyterian Foleys and Hanburys to the Methodist Guests of Dowlais. The Quaker banking and brewing dynasties of Gurney, Fox, Barclay and Perkins are famous, as are the Unitarian cotton millowners, the M'Connells, Gregs and Potters.[2] A single tiny industrial town like Glossop could exhibit in its capitalists the whole gamut of Dissent from Roman Catholic to Methodist.[3] However the Dissenters' challenge to economic exertion operated, whether through superior practical education, labouring in one's vocation, the material rewards of

[1] *D.N.B.*, VI, 345f., XIV. 187f., XVIII. 190f., XL. 326f., LVI. 9f., LX. 51f., LXIII. 80f.

[2] Cf. the list of innovators and religious affiliations in E. E. Hagen, *On the Theory of Social Change* (1964), pp. 303–8.

[3] H. J. Perkin, 'The Development of Modern Glossop', in A. H. Birch, *Small Town Politics* (Oxford, 1959), pp. 18–19.

high moral conduct, or the mere exclusion of unprofitable distractions, the religious structure of English society gave it a helping hand

The argument can, however, be pushed too far. Not every enterprising business man was a Dissenter, nor every Dissenter a successful business man. There were Anglican ironmasters like Crowley, Anglican bankers like the Hoares, Anglican brewers like the Whitbreads, Anglican cotton spinners like Arkwright, Strutt and Peel. And the town of Glossop had in the Woods and Sidebottoms its quota of Anglican millowners. Dissent was of course stronger amongst entrepreneurs than amongst the population in general, but not so much stronger than in the middle ranks alone: a recent sample survey has shown that 49 per cent of the principal inventors and innovators were Dissenters, compared with perhaps a fifth of the population in 1811, and of course a much larger fraction of the middle ranks.[1] And, as we saw in Chapter II, it is at least as arguable that they turned to Dissent because their social status excluded them from the politics and social life of their 'betters' as that they were so excluded by their choice of religion. Certainly, the barriers to their occupation of public offices, after the 1718 Act protecting them after six months from prosecution, or the almost annual indemnity acts after 1727, were frequently surmounted by Dissenters of sufficient wealth and status. They became mayors of towns, high sheriffs of counties, members of the Common Council of London, and even in a few cases Members of Parliament.[2] The alacrity with which many 'new men' changed their religion with their status is a further indication of the connection between social and religious motivations. And, finally, the key part played by religious antagonism in the formation of the mutually hostile social classes which emerged during the Industrial Revolution (a theme which will be taken up in Chapter VI) confirms that Dissent was in the old society the characteristic form assumed by the latent social envy and hostility of the middle ranks for the landed aristocracy. Meanwhile, to beat the morally inferior but socially superior landowners at the game of getting rich was a challenge which rationalized the toil of ambition. Perhaps, after all, the most important economic

[1] Hagen, *loc. cit.*; Halévy, *op. cit.*, I. 428.
[2] Henriques, *op. cit.*, p. 59.

effect of religious dissidence was the added piquancy it gave to material success and social emulation.

One thing at least is certain, that the English system of partial toleration, or intolerance tempered by inefficiency, was more conducive to economic innovation than the almost universal contemporary suppression of heresy, on both sides of the religious iron curtain. What the expulsion of the Huguenots cost France in purely material terms cannot be calculated, but the price cannot have been light; while that of the draconian uniformity of religion further east and south defies all speculation. In England dissenting entrepreneurs were neither expelled nor blighted in the bud, but challenged to prove their moral and economic superiority. In so far as their peculiar situation stemmed from the self-interest of a dominant landed aristocracy in confident *rapprochement* with its society, the religious cause of their industrial exertions becomes a social one.

2. SOCIETY AND THE ECONOMIC FACTORS

Ultimately, however, any interpretation of the Industrial Revolution stands or falls not by the explanation of its ancillary political, scientific and religious causes but by that of its direct, immediate and necessary economic causes, the essential factors of production, to which we should add the most immediate and necessary of all economic factors, the factor of demand. What part did the nature and structure of English society play in the operation of land, capital, labour, and demand?

Of the factors of production, land has been most taken for granted by historians, since in Britain it presented no obstacle to development. Yet in underdeveloped societies the system of land tenure is often one of the most intractable problems. In Britain, by contrast, the land was owned—and by the seventeenth century, owned absolutely—in large viable blocks by a comparatively small number of owners, alert to their interest in every extension of economic activity. By the triumph of their concept of absolute property, the landed aristocracy had determined that land could be freely bought, sold or leased on a wide variety of tenures, for every kind of industrial or ancillary purpose. Even where land was voluntarily tied up in strict family settlements—which from the Civil War became stricter as a result of

Bridgeman and Palmer's invention of 'trustees to preserve contingent remainders'—ample provision was usually made for building and other leases beneficial to the estate.[1] There is no example in the British Industrial Revolution of an industrial project being ultimately frustrated for lack of the necessary land.

Moreover, whatever else they were interested in, landed gentlemen were interested in increasing the returns from their estates. Some of them turned industrialists themselves: the Earl of Derby operated a cotton mill in Preston, the Earl of Dundonald a famous chemical plant, the Sneyds of Staffordshire their own coal-mines, ironworks and brickworks, and a large number, like Lords Dudley, Fitzwilliam, Gower and Middleton, directly exploited their own coal.[2] Few of them, of course, had the temperament or incentive for industrial management and, in that age of the individualist entrepreneur when honest and efficient managers were hard to come by, were nearly always forced to sell or turn such enterprises, other than coal-mines, over to lessees.[3] Their role, however, was not direct industrial enterprise. It was rather to provide both the land, including on occasion the buildings and other fixed capital such as mining gear, and the 'preconditions' for the enterprise of others.

Their most positive economic contribution was in the sphere of the 'preconditions' of industrialism, in agriculture, mining, transport, and town-building, which in later industrial revolutions had so often to be provided by the State or not at all. Out of pure self-interest they spontaneously provided the foundations upon which the new manufacturing industries could rise. The revolution in agricultural techniques without which the expanding industrial population could not have been fed was

[1] W. S. Holdsworth, *History of English Law* (1925), VII. 112–13; Habakkuk, *op. cit., Trans. R.H.S.*, 1950, XXXII. 17.

[2] Derby Muniments, Ledgers 1981–3 (1795–99), entries re 'Preston factory'; A. and N. L. Clow, *The Chemical Revolution* (1952), pp. 100–3; Sneyd Papers, Col. Walter Sneyd's Estate Accounts, 1798–1800, 1882–29, entries re collieries, furnace, and tile-works; G. E. Mingay, *English Landed Society in the 18th Century* (1963), pp. 191–6; T. S. Ashton and J. Sykes, *The Coal Industry of the 18th Century* (Manchester, 1929), pp. 45, 154.

[3] e.g. Derby was forced by the inefficiency or dishonesty of the manager, Leeming, to let the Preston factory—Derby Muniments, DDK 1687, Weekly Notes of Steward's Correspondence, 1796–1802, 20 November 1796; for 'the persistent tendency for mineral landowners to withdraw from their enterprises into the more secure position of rentiers' cf. F. M. L. Thompson, *English Landed Society in the 19th Century* (1963), p. 264.

their responsibility. They were not themselves the chief innovators: this was the work of entrepreneurs, small landowners and large farmers like Jethro Tull, Robert Bakewell and the Colling brothers, from much the same social levels and with much the same ambitions and motivations as their industrial counterparts. But without the inspired advertising of the new methods by great landlords like the Earl of Leicester, the Duke of Bedford and Coke of Holkham, and without the example, encouragement, and persistent pressure upon their tenants of the great majority of ordinary landlords, it is doubtful whether market opportunities alone would have transformed the traditional methods of the average farmer and revolutionized agricultural yields.[1] Further, in so far as the new methods presupposed the enclosure of the open fields—and in that individualist age it would have required an unlikely degree of tenant co-operation to avoid it—the self-interested action of the landowners was indispensable. The moving spirit in every enclosure was the local landowner; and the ultimate sanction for it, whether by private act, Chancery suit, or unregistered agreement, was a Parliament of landowners. The social and political power of the landowners, inside and outside Parliament, determined the pace and process of agriculture change. Pursuing higher rents via expanding agricultural profits they incidentally, as it were, provided the means of life for increased millions. In mining, absolute property still more clearly differentiated the English landowners' role from that of their Continental counterparts. In Britain alone in Western Europe all minerals, save gold and silver, belonged by a judgment of 1568—a significant step in the development of the English concept of property—to the owner of the soil.[2] The landowners, therefore, had a personal stake in their exploitation. Large-scale ownership made State intervention, to grant access to large deposits or to foster joint-stock enterprise, unnecessary. Opportunity and incentive went hand in hand wherever minerals were found in Britain to make landowner and mining exploiter practically synonymous. Along the Tyne, Tees and Wear, for example, landowner in practice

---

[1] Mingay, *op. cit.*, pp. 163–71, 186–8; J. D. Chambers and G. E. Mingay, *The Agricultural Revolution, 1750–1880* (1966), chap. iii.

[2] Ashton and Sykes, *op. cit.*, p. 1, citing Royal Commission on Mining Royalties, *Final Report* (1893), p. 3.

meant colliery proprietor, and *vice versa*. Not every coal-owner directly exploited his own coal, for even in this least complex of industrial operations, direct enterprise through bailiffs or managers was not always compatible with a leisured social life, and a lease was often found to be more profitable. In Derbyshire and Nottinghamshire in 1811, for example, the Duke of Devonshire, Lords Middleton and Manvers, and Messrs. Maundy, Lowe, Morewood, and D'Ewes Coke were the only considerable landowners who commercially worked their own coal, and the majority of pits were on lease.[1] Either way, it was the self-interested initiative and drive of landowners like the Dukes of Argyll and Hamilton in Scotland, the Curwens and Lowthers in Westmorland, the Delavals, Lambtons, Liddells and Ellisons in the North East, the Duke of Norfolk and the Marquess of Rockingham in Yorkshire, Lords Dudley and Granville and the Sneyds and Gresleys in Staffordshire, or Lords Uxbridge and Bute and the Mansels, Bayleys, Symmonds and Protheros in Wales, which touched off the great expansion of the mining and metallurgical industries.[2]

Mining, with its concentration of heavy loads over well-defined routes, gave many landowners an additional interest in improved transport. Most of the early canals and 'navigations', from the famous Bridgewater to carry the Duke's coal from his Worsley mines to Manchester to the little Apedale to carry Sir Nigel Gresley's four miles to Newcastle-under-Lyme, were backed if not initiated by local landowners. Improved transport was a precondition beyond the resources of most individuals, and demanded the co-operation of many others besides the landowners, in turnpike trusts, and canal, dock and railway companies, notably entrepreneurs like Wedgwood, Oldknow, Boulton and Watt, the Crawshays and Guests, and many more. Yet without the active participation of the local landowners no improvement scheme could be set on foot, and the larger landlords with their immense prestige, political influence, local contacts, and material stake in every extension of economic

[1] J. Farey, *General View of the Agriculture and Minerals of Derbyshire* (1811), I. 182.

[2] Cf. Ashton and Sykes, *op. cit.*, pp. 2–6; A. H. Dodd, *The Industrial Revolution in North Wales* (1933), pp. 154–5; A. H. John, *The Industrial Development of South Wales, 1750–1850* (Cardiff, 1950), 7–10, 30, 37; E. Hughes, *op. cit.*, I, chap. v, II, chap. v.

activity on and around their estates were admirably placed to act as impresarios in the early, crucial stages of the transport revolution. The role of Bridgewater was paralleled by the Marquess of Stafford, who built a canal from his ironworks in Shropshire, by the Earl of Thanet who built one to connect his limestone quarries with the Leeds and Liverpool canal, and by the Dukes of Marlborough and Buccleuch and Lords Guilford, North and Spencer, who invested in the Coventry and Oxford canal project of 1768.[1]

Occasionally a landowner might oppose a particular scheme, as the Earl of Kent opposed the Wye navigation to protect the local monopoly of his ironworks,[2] but opposition could be bought off, or overridden by more powerful combinations of landowners, locally or in Parliament. Even the railway companies, which belonged to a phase when the scale of investment and the balance of landed to other fixed capital had greatly altered, still had to win over or buy off the bigger landlords, who formed a considerable proportion of their shareholders and directors—like the Marquess of Stafford who surrendered his opposition to the Liverpool and Manchester Railway in exchange for three seats on the board.[3] Without the active support and, in many cases, the initiative of the landowners individually and in Parliament the transport revolution could scarcely have occurred.

Finally, the landowners played an important part in the process of urbanization. Apart from keeping alive the organizational and technical skills of large-scale building—between the age of cathedral-building and that of the factories, the great country houses were almost the only large buildings raised in Britain—they were in effect the only available planning authorities to direct and control the building of towns. It is commonly assumed that the new or greatly expanded towns of the Industrial Revolution mushroomed haphazardly, without plan or purpose. In some cases this was true, but it was so mainly in those towns without an overriding ground landlord, or manageably small group of them, where the pattern of ownership was a

[1] Mingay, *op. cit.*, p. 196
[2] T. S. Willan, *River Navigation in England, 1600–1750* (1936), p. 36.
[3] C. F. Dendy Marshall, *Centenary History of the Liverpool and Manchester Railway* (1930), p. 13.

patchwork of competing building plots. Elsewhere it was the ground landlord who controlled development, laid out the streets and squares, set aside land for market, town hall, jail and other communal purposes, and leased the building plots for specified and approved development. The plans were not always well-considered, or sufficiently far-seeing to anticipate the needs of future expansion on an unprecedented scale, and they put rentable value high amongst their priorities; but in the contemporary nature of things they were the only ones available, and served at least to prevent chaos. Occasionally, where the economic pressures were not against it, as in the West End estates of the Grosvenors, the Cavendish-Bentincks and the Russells, those of the Duke of Devonshire in Eastbourne or Buxton or those of such lesser landlords as Sir George Tapps-Gervis at Bournemouth, the planning could be elegantly effective. In the industrial towns themselves landlords such as the Dukes of Devonshire and Buccleuch in Barrow-in-Furness, the Lowthers at Whitehaven, the Curwens at Workington and Harrington, or the Dukes of Norfolk in Sheffield and Glossop, performed an indispensable utilitarian service. In Glossop, one of the few entirely new towns of the Industrial Revolution, the 12th Duke of Norfolk and his sons leased out the mills and fostered the turnpike which put the site on the map, laid out the streets, built many of the houses, the town hall, the gasworks, the waterworks, several schools and churches, Anglican and Roman Catholic, helped found the Manchester, Sheffield and Lincolnshire Railway, and finally, when the latter proved dilatory, built the Glossop branch line and sold it back to the Company.[1]

All this is not to say that the landowners made the Industrial Revolution: that was not their function. Their function was, in seeking their own profit by all the means which their special position in English society had made available to them, to create the climate and conditions in which a spontaneous industrial revolution could take place, and to give it effective legislative encouragement when and where it required it. While Continental aristocracies were still preoccupied with preserving

[1] W. Ashworth, *The Genesis of Modern British Town Planning* (1954), pp. 39, 42; J. D. Marshall, *The Industrial Revolution in Furness* (Barrow, 1958), chaps. ix, xiv; E. Hughes, *op. cit.*, II, chaps. ii, v; Perkin, *op. cit.*, 16–18.

their political privileges, military honour, social exclusiveness and feudal rights, sometimes as in France and Poland to the point of self-destruction, English and Scottish landowners were using their unique position as a base for the economic advance of themselves and of the whole nation.

Capital, the second factor of production, is so much of the essence of industrialism that, paradoxically, it is easy to over-estimate its importance in the process. Investment is not a magic wand which can create economic growth unaided. It is at least as much an index, a measure, an effect of growth as a cause. Men are more important than money, capitalists than capital; and as more than one under-developed country has discovered, it is more likely that resourceful entrepreneurs will make shift to raise missing capital than that capital will call forth absent entrepreneurs. Eighteenth-century Britain had the advantage of low interest rates and a fairly advanced banking system, capital was cheap and credit forthcoming, and this in itself was an important cause of the Industrial Revolution. But it was not an autonomous cause. Low interest rates were the effect of complex economic forces which at bottom related to the *rapprochement* between the saving and the enterprising groups in the population. They did not *cause* people to invest in risky innovations—high rates would have done that more effectively—but were the measure of their readiness to invest in production, instead of hoarding their surplus wealth as peasants do, or disbursing it in conspicuous consumption like most aristocracies. Neither the State nor the banking system, as such, could create this readiness. The low legal rate of interest, 5 per cent from 1714, which followed rather than preceded the fall in the 'natural' rate, did not make people invest: on the contrary, it practically prevented them from doing so whenever government stock rose to 5 per cent or more, and they could get a better return from gilt-edged.[1]

Though it helped the flow of credit, the banking system was the beneficiary rather than the cause of low interest rates, which had become low while banking organization was still rudimentary compared with that of several European countries. Indeed, in the English provinces, as opposed to Scotland, it was hardly a system at all: in 1750 there was only a handful of banks outside

[1] Cf. Ashton, *Industrial Revolution*, chap. iv, and *18th Century*, p. 29.

London. It was the Industrial Revolution which created an organized national system of banking, not the reverse.[1] Moreover, the banks as they came into existence did not in general supply fixed capital for industrial enterprise. The country banks were not investment houses but primarily commercial institutions, concerned with the flow of payments and short-term credit required by trade. They thus performed an essential role in the expansion of industry, both in lubricating the wheels of commerce and in releasing entrepreneurs' own funds from circulating for investment in fixed capital; but they did not usually invest in mills, factories and mines, unless the banker, like Arkwright's helper Wright of Nottingham, was personally connected with the enterprise, and then normally he invested only in his personal capacity. The great bulk of the capital for new industrial enterprise did not come from institutional sources,[2] and institutional interest rates were important only in the negative sense that they were not high enough to draw capital away from the informal channels of industrial investment. The low interest rates were a reflection of the readiness and ability to invest via these informal channels, and this in turn was a largely social phenomenon.

English society was specially fitted to provide both the capital and the capitalists for the new industrialism. Here lies the answer to the two crucial questions of industrial investment: where did the initial capital for the new enterprises come from, and what motivated the entrepreneurs to 'scorn delights and live laborious days' long enough to build them up?

To the first the answer lies partly in the wide diffusion of modest wealth which put the means of enterprise within the reach of much larger numbers than elsewhere, partly in the system of kinship and connection which could reinforce the individual's capital from the resources of a wide range of friends and relations. Amongst the numerous and prosperous middle ranks of English society there was no lack of potential entrepreneurs with sufficient capital and self-confidence to back themselves, but not so much as to disdain hard work and appli-

---

[1] L. S. Pressnell, *Country Banking in the Industrial Revolution* (1956), p. 4 and *passim*; Ashton, *Industrial Revolution*, pp. 102–3, 108–9.

[2] Cf. H. Heaton, 'Financing the Industrial Revolution', *Bulletin of Business Historical Society*, 1937, XI.

cation. The burden was lightened by the fact that in the early stages of new or rapidly expanding industries large masses of pre-accumulated capital were not called for. Comparatively small initial capitals were rapidly built on by ploughing back a high proportion of the firstcomers' relatively enormous profits. The Walker brothers' great ironworks at Rotherham was built up from a tiny foundry worth only £600 in 1746, five years after they began. The huge Dowlais concern was founded in 1759 on a capital of £4,000 shared between eight partners. In cotton the humble beginnings of the Arkwrights, Peels, Strutts, and so on, are well known; Samuel Oldknow had assets in 1783 of £2,636, minus debts of £1,548, leaving a net capital of £1,088, plus £148 in buildings and fixtures, on which within a decade he built up a turnover of over £80,000 a year and founded one of the largest contemporary factories. Before the rise of the great porter brewers the equipment for a rented brewhouse could be bought for as little as £200, though a larger circulating capital was required for materials and the like: Henry Isherwood of Eton, an inn servant who married well, built up from a single public house a business worth £8,000 or £9,000 a year. The average paper mill in 1800 was worth only £4,000, some much less, and could be rented. A considerable newspaper like the *Manchester Guardian* could be founded as late as 1821 on a capital of £1,000.[1]

At the end of the process of transformation in each industry, when great cotton mills, ironworks and porter breweries were worth hundreds of thousands of pounds, new entrants to large-scale enterprise required much larger capitals, which only come from banking or mercantile wealth. In heavy industries, especially in areas short of capital, landed or mercantile capitalists might be drawn in from the beginning, as Lords Mansel and Uxbridge, the Bacons and Crawshays of London, or the Harfords of Bristol were into the Welsh coal-mining, iron and copper industries.[2] There was some transfer of mercantile capital into the factory system from domestic industry, as in the case of Arkwright's

---

[1] Ashton, *Iron and Steel*, p. 46; John, *op. cit.*, p. 43; P. Mathias, *The Brewing Industry in England, 1700–1830* (Cambridge, 1959), pp. 253–5; D. C. Coleman, *The British Paper Industry, 1495–1860* (Oxford, 1958), p. 233; A. E. Musson, 'Newspaper Printing in the Industrial Revolution', *Ec.H.R.*, 1958, X. 413.

[2] Dodd, *op. cit.*, p. 155; John, *op. cit.*, pp. 26, 30, 35; J. P. Addis, *The Crawshay Dynasty: a Study in Industrial Development, 1765–1867* (Cardiff, 1957), chap. i.

partner Need, Radcliffe's partner Ross, Benjamin Gott's partners, Wormald and Fountaine, or even Thomas Fox of Wellington in the 'backward' West of England cloth industry.[1] But the great majority of the new entrepreneurs in the early stages of the Industrial Revolution set out from small, though rarely negligible, beginnings: neither too humble to strike out independently, nor too prosperous to work hard and long in new and risky ventures. The Peels, Fieldens, Strutts, Wedgwoods, Darbys, Dobsons, Stubbs, Radcliffes and many more came from yeoman or small farming stock, often uniting domestic industry with husbandry. In the metal industries Aaron Walker, William Hawks, John Parker, George Newton, Benjamin Huntsman, Isaac Wilkinson, Samuel Garbett and others were small, prosperous, independent craftsmen. Arkwright, David Dale, Robert Owen and Oldknow began as apprentices to shopkeepers.[2] The greatest source of new industrialists was the lower levels of the middle ranks, the very levels in short whose prosperity and independence most surpassed those of other countries.

When, as often happened, their own small capital fell short of what was needed, they had to recruit funds wherever they could. Here they fell back, naturally and inevitably, on the old society's system of kinship and connection. Banks were unlikely to help them, unless like the brewers, Truman, Hanbury and Buxton or Barclay and Perkins, they were personally connected with the bankers. Samuel Oldknow set up in the muslin trade with the help of his uncle, a Nottingham draper. Richard Crawshay's ironworks began from the ironmonger's shop bequeathed to a favoured apprentice. Matthew Boulton added to the inheritance of his father, a prosperous silverstamper, by marrying a fortune of £28,000, and borrowing on the security. Matthew Ellison, the Duke of Norfolk's agent in Glossop, leased a cotton mill from the Duke for his sons; it was developed into a very large

---

[1] R. S. Fitton and A. P. Wadsworth, *The Strutts and the Arkwrights, 1758–1830* (Manchester, 1958), chap. iv; W. Radcliffe, *Origin of the New System of Manufacture* (Stockport, 1828), pp. 14–15; H. Heaton, 'Benjamin Gott and the Industrial Revolution in Yorkshire', *Ec.H.R.*, 1931–2, III. 45f.; H. Fox, *Quaker Homespun: Life of Thomas Fox of Wellington, . . . 1747–1821* (1958), p. 15.

[2] Cf. P. Mantoux, *The Industrial Revolution in the 18th Century* (1928), pp. 376–382; M. Dobb, *Studies in the Development of Capitalism* (1947), pp. 278–81; Ashton, *Iron and Steel*, pp. 209–10.

concern by his daughter's stepson, Francis Sumner, a young man with a small capital and great ability. Jedediah Strutt's 'Derby rib' machine was backed by his brother-in-law, a carpenter, and he sought further capital from the clergyman with whom his wife had been in service. The last example illustrates both the tenuous links which might be made to serve, and the indirect connection with institutional finance: the Rev. Dr. Benson, though willing enough to lend at 4 per cent, could not raise the money without selling his government stock at a loss. Even straightforward partnerships often contained elements of personal, beneficial 'connection': Benjamin Gott went into partnership with the Leeds cloth merchants to whom he had been apprenticed, he supplying less than 10 per cent of the capital.[1] The Quaker cousinships in brewing, banking and ironfounding—the Bevans, Barclays, Gurneys, Lloyds and Perkins, and the Darbys, Reynolds, Parkers, Hawkins and Harveys—were perhaps no more than a special case of the general use of kinship. Non-Quaker brewers, for example, pressed their connections into service: when 'Mr. Thrale overbrewed himself last winter' (1772) he 'made an artificial scarcity of money in the family which has extremely lowered his Spirits'; while Samuel Whitbread junior in 1797 and 1807 saved his brewery by extensive borrowing in the aristocratic circles into which he had married.[2] In the absence of institutional methods of financing industrial enterprise through the banking system or the joint-stock company, kinship and connection performed an indispensable service.

To the second question, why entrepreneurs invested their capital and themselves in new and risky industrial enterprises, the answer might seem obvious: to enrich themselves. Yet the limitless pursuit of wealth for its own sake is a rare phenomenon, and historians with a taste for psychology have understandably looked for additional motivations and drives to explain the extraordinary energy and ambition of eighteenth-century industrialists. Weber and Tawney found the answer

[1] Mathias, *Brewing Industry*, pp. 293–4; Unwin *et al.*, *op. cit.*, p. 2; Addis, *op. cit.*, p. 6; S. Smiles, *Lives of the Engineers* (1861–65), IV. 166–7; Perkin, *op. cit.*, p. 11; Fitton and Wadsworth, *op. cit.*, pp. 24–39; Ashton, *18th Century*, p. 29; Heaton, *op. cit.*, *Ec.H.R.*, 1931, III. 48.

[2] Pressnell, *op. cit.*, pp. 114, 283; Ashton, *Iron and Steel*, pp. 214–17; Mathias, pp. 269, 286, 287–99.

in a peculiarly capitalist spirit compounded of unlimited acquisitiveness and the urge to succeed in the face of God and man, deriving ultimately from the Protestant Reformation.[1] More recent variants of this approach seek it in a dramatic change in the psychological outlook of Old and New Dissenters in the eighteenth century itself. Hagen argues that the 'withdrawal of status respect' from such 'subordinate minorities' as the Old Dissenters produced 'retreatism' in the earlier generations, presumably before the mid-eighteenth century, but then, by reaction from this, a driving ambition and 'innovational creativity' in their sons, presumably in the Industrial Revolution itself.[2] McClelland relates the change in outlook to the increased 'need for Achievement' produced by the advent of Methodism and its emphasis in child-rearing on conscious training in self-reliance and mastery: the Methodists' 'uncompromising stress on excellence . . . seems almost certain to have acted to promote the development of achievement motivation in Methodist children. . . . And the picture was similar in other Nonconformist bodies in England in the eighteenth century.'[3]

Such explanations are interesting and important in emphasizing the inadequacy of purely economic motivations, but unfortunately they put the cart before the horse. Against the first it can be argued that the 'capitalist spirit' has been found wherever capitalism has thrived, in the ancient, medieval and modern worlds, both before and after the Reformation. Against the second it can be argued that middle-rank Dissenters enjoyed the same respect, no less and no more, than others of their status, and that no withdrawal of respect, no retreatism, and therefore no innovational reaction can be traced in the historical evidence. Against the third it can be argued that Methodism came too late to affect in childhood more than a handful of the new industrialists—only two of the sample of 92 mentioned above were known to be Methodists[4]—and if the argument from child-rearing is transferred to Old Dissent, the same problem arises as with the second, of explaining the timing of the innovational surge. Above all, against all three it can be argued that they explain the

[1] Weber, *loc. cit.*; R. H. Tawney, *Religion and the Rise of Capitalism.*

[2] Hagen, *op. cit.*, esp. pp. 290–303.

[3] D. C. McClelland, *The Achieving Society* (Princeton, N.J., 1961), esp. pp. 145–9.

[4] Hagen, *op. cit.*, 306, 307.

general case by means of the particular instead, of *vice versa*. Driving ambition and innovational creativity seem to have been common to the English middle ranks, whatever their brand of religion, and, as was argued with their religion, seems more likely to have derived from their position in an open aristocracy offering special opportunities and rewards to ambition and creativity than from a religion which affected only a part of the middle ranks, and was itself arguably derived from that position.

For the old society offered sufficient motivations for ambition and innovation to all equipped to respond to them, whatever their religion. To the perennial desire for wealth the old society added other motivations which gave point and purpose to the pursuit of riches. Compared with neighbouring and more traditional societies it offered both a greater challenge and a greater reward to successful enterprise. On the one hand the greater insecurity of a society in which status followed property rather than property status increased the penalty for lack of effort. On the other, the social prestige and power over one's neighbours which were annexed to property, however acquired, added prizes of a psychologically more satisfying kind to those of mere acquisition. As Malthus put it in his optimistic defence of the 'strikingly beneficial' effect of social inequality, 'If no man could hope to rise or fear to fall in society; if industry did not bring its own reward, and indolence its punishment; we could not hope to see that animated activity in bettering our own condition which now forms the master-spring of public prosperity.'[1] And Adam Smith, who knew the world of the early industrialists still better, asked: 'To what purpose is all the toil and bustle of the world? . . . It is our vanity which urges us on. . . . It is not wealth that men desire, but the consideration and good opinion that wait upon riches.'[2] In the old society 'the consideration and good opinion that wait upon riches' were a synonym for social status. The pursuit of wealth *was* the pursuit of social status, not merely for oneself but for one's family. In the last resort the ultimate motivation of the industrialists, as for most rising men before them, was a dynastic one: to found a family, to endow them splendidly enough to last for ever, and to enjoy a vicarious eternal life in the seed of one's loins.

[1] T. R. Malthus, *Essay on Population* (Everyman, 1951), II. 254.
[2] *The Theory of Moral Sentiments* (1759), quoted by Gray, *op. cit.*, p. 17.

All these motivations can be found in so typical an industrialist as Jedediah Strutt. 'Getting of Money' he wrote to his wife in 1765,

> . . . is the main business of the life of Man & thou knowest not how solicitous I am while life, & youth, & opportunity lasts to acquire something that you & I, should we live so long, may not have the two great calamities of Human Life, poverty and Old Age, come upon us together. Should we succeed in this . . . what think you, in that decline of our days, will afford us a pleasure equal to that of being able to leave a fair patrimony to our children, & to reflect, that they are placed in circumstances that renders them superior to many of these difficulties we were forced to struggle with . . .(?)

To his eldest son he wrote a decade later: 'I need not tell you that you are not to be a Nobleman nor prime minister, but you may possibly be a Tradesman of some emminence. . . .' Finally, near the close of his life—he died in 1797—he wrote in his intended epitaph, 'Here lies JS—who, without Fortune, Family or friends rais'd to himself a fortune, family & Name in the World. . . .' Besides a flourishing business he left a mansion and an estate in Derbyshire, and his grandson, fittingly, became a peer.[1]

'Vanity' took many forms, and not every industrialist, at least at the height of his career, wished to change places with a lord or squire. 'I have but one pride,' wrote William Crawshay senior, 'to be head of the iron trade and land won't do that.' But his father at the end of his career, in a time of fierce competition and price-cutting, thought 'nothing but land can be considered as safe'; his son built Cyfarthfa Castle; and later he himself almost disrupted the firm in his efforts to withdraw his capital and retire.[2] Raising one's status did not necessarily and immediately mean retiring from business to lead the life of a leisured gentleman. In the first generation and often in the second the position of 'eminent tradesman' was a novelty to be enjoyed, and if the business spared mind and leisure enough English society was sufficiently flexible to admit rich entrepreneurs to many of the pleasures and honours of the ruling élite before retirement to the land. Thus active bankers and brewers, merchants and domestic industrialists had long formed a substantial minority in Parliament and on the justices' bench,

[1] Fitton and Wadsworth, *op. cit.*, pp. 108–10, 145, 163; *D.N.B.*, LV. 63f.
[2] John, *op. cit.*, p. 39; Addis, *op. cit.*, pp. 19, 46–9, 54.

and the more successful factory industrialists automatically joined them there.

Landed property, however, in the shape of a large country house and a sufficient estate to support the traditional country sports and pleasures of the gentry was a necessary qualification for full acceptance into genteel society and, once attained, provided a constant counter-attraction to the allurements of business. Moreover, as the Peels found to their satisfaction and Samuel Whitbread junior to his cost,[1] the highest honours were reserved for those not only with wealth and ability but with the complete leisure to exploit them. In the early stages of industrialism at least, before the spectacular rise in the scale of fixed capital investment had made itself fully felt in 'Society' and politics, land was still the most secure and permanent form in which to hold the property which alone conferred high status. Of this the industrialists themselves were keenly aware, instance the arguments of the Birmingham Commercial Society in opposing an excise on manufactures in 1785:

> That manufactures and commerce should only be considered as a means of acquiring that real property which is the proper object of taxation. That property, while exposed to the extreme uncertainty which it is necessarily subject to, while engaged in manufacture and commerce, cannot be justly deemed substantial until it is withdrawn from those dangers.[2]

In 1830, Coleridge, rejoicing in the 'permanence' which landed property conferred upon society, observed: 'To found a family, and to convert his wealth into land, are twin thoughts, births of the same moment, in the mind of the opulent merchant, when he thinks of reposing from his labours;'[3] while Cobden, bemoaning the lack of interest of the industrialists in land reform, could still exclaim in 1851: 'See how every successful trader buys an estate, and tries to perpetuate his name in connexion with "that ilk" by creating an eldest son.'[4]

[1] Whitbread committed suicide in 1815—Roger Fulford, *Samuel Whitbread, 1764–1815* (1967), p. 306.

[2] G. H. Wright, *Chronicles of the Birmingham Chamber of Commerce* ([Birmingham], 1913), p. 15.

[3] S. T. Coleridge, *On the Constitution of Church and State* (1839), p. 25.

[4] J. Morley, *Life of Richard Cobden* (1903), p. 561.

Whether to crown their success as 'eminent tradesmen' or to launch themselves or their families into the landed gentry, then, the entrepreneurs of the Industrial Revolution hastened to acquire land and build or buy a great house. In factory textiles Arkwright built Willersley Castle and became in 1787 the most flamboyant High Sheriff of Derbyshire, the Strutts built Milford House and bought estates in Derbyshire and Nottinghamshire, while the Peels bought the Drayton Manor and Tamworth estates on which they raised their political careers. In the metal industries, the Foleys became barons, the Wortleys Earls of Wharncliffe, the Hardys of Low Moor Earls of Cranbrook, the Guests Lords Wimborne, Isaac Wilkinson leased a country house at Plas Grono near Wrexham, his son John was buried at his seat at Castle Head, Ulverston, Matthew Boulton's son bought Great Tew from the Dashwoods, themselves descendants of a Restoration London brewer, Thomas Williams 'the copper king' bought Plas Llanidan, Anglesey, from Lord Boston, and Michael Hughes, also of the Parys Copper Mining Company, rebuilt Sherdly Hall, near St. Helens. Wedgwood the great potter built Etruria Hall near his works and Barlaston Hall in the country. In brewing, a trade which had produced many new men before them, the 'power-loom brewers' of the late eighteenth century built up large country estates: the Barclays in Norfolk, the Hanburys in Hertfordshire and Essex, the Whitbreads over £420,000's worth of land in Bedfordshire and Hertfordshire. In the paper industry the greatest paper-maker of the eighteenth century, James Whatman junior became High Sheriff of Kent at the age of twenty-six, and retired at fifty-three to his estate at Vinters, near Maidstone.[1]

The list might be indefinitely extended, with lesser men attaining lower social heights, for the rise of new men was a process long familiar and fascinating to contemporaries. As a Manchester 'Cobbler' put it in 1756,

> See, as the Owners of old Family Estates in your Neighbourhood are selling off their patrimonies, how your Townsmen are constantly purchasing; and thereby laying the Foundation of a new

[1] See *D.N.B.* and standard biographies; Fitton and Wadsworth, *op. cit.*, p. 163; Ashton, *Iron and Steel*, p. 218; T. C. Barker and J. R. Harris, *A Merseyside Town in the Industrial Revolution: St. Helens, 1750–1900* (Liverpool, 1954), pp. 89, 152–4; Mathias, *Brewing Industry*, pp. 286–7; Coleman, *op. cit.*, p. 154.

Race of Gentry! Not adorn'd, it's true with Coats of Arms and a long Parchment Pedigree of useless Members of Society, but deck'd with Virtue and Frugality; and who, knowing both how, and when to be content, retire, decently to enjoy their well-got Wealth, leaving the Coast open, for new Adventurers, to follow their worthy Example.[1]

The new industrialists were treading a beaten road, well-trodden by generations of new men before them. In 1820 Malthus accurately summed up the motivations of contemporary capitalists as follows:

It is not the most pleasant employment to spend eight hours a day in a counting-house. Nor will it be submitted to after the common necessaries and conveniences of life are attained, unless adequate motives are presented to the man of business. Among these motives is undoubtedly the desire of advancing his rank, and contending with the landlords in the enjoyment of leisure, as well as of foreign and domestic luxuries. But the desire to realize a fortune as a permanent provision for a family is perhaps the most general motive for the continued exertions of those whose incomes depend upon their own personal skill and efforts.[2]

Industrialism, with its enormous expansion of fixed and visible capital, of the significance of industry in the life of the nation, and thus of the power and prestige of industrialists, was to increase the permanent attractions of business over against land, and change the motivations of business men. In the early stages, however, social emulation, ultimately of the leisured amateurs who ran the old society and enjoyed its highest honours and rewards, was the powerful motivation which English society offered its entrepreneurs in greater measure than elsewhere.

Social emulation also played a significant part in the mobilization of the third factor of production, labour. A regular, disciplined, reliable labour force was—and is—the most hazardous requirement of an industrial revolution, and it was not achieved without trouble, pain and difficulty. A factory proletariat, wholly dependent on industrial wages and innured to regular hours of work at the rhythm of the machines, is a highly sophisticated

---

[1] J. Stot, *A Sequel to the Friendly Advice to the Poor* (Manchester, 1756), p. 19; A. P. Wadsworth and J. de L. Mann, *The Cotton Trade and Industrial Lancashire* (Manchester, 1931), p. 242.

[2] T. R. Malthus, *Principles of Political Economy* (1820), p. 470.

social group, utterly remote from the life of the peasant, with its irregular hours and slow rhythms dependent on season and weather, its alternations between excessive activity and under-employment, and its chronic lack of spendable income. English society, however, had, as we have seen, long got rid of most of its peasants, and though wage-earners of a modern type were to be found only in isolated groups in some of the mines, ironworks, glass-houses and the like, a large proportion, perhaps a majority, of workers had reached what may be considered a half-way stage between peasant and proletarian. Many of them still had one foot on the soil, a few roods of pasture, a cottage garden or a cow on the common to eke out their money-earnings but, in addition to finding the rent for these, most of their needs, of food, clothing, fuel, utensils and so on, were bought in the market and paid for in cash. The habits of earning and spending thus long ingrained were a favourable basis on which the blandishments of the new system could work.

The early factory workers—apart from the parish appren-tices, who probably never numbered more than 20,000—were not driven into the mills, but drawn there by the promise of higher wages than they could earn outside.[1] Except for highly-paid male spinners, skilled craftsmen were not required in the early textile mills, and average factory wages have to be com-pared with those of the unskilled outside, especially women and children. In the early stages of the Industrial Revolution, when weavers and other domestic workers were still earning com-paratively large wages, there can be little doubt that adult factory workers were recruited by attraction rather than com-pulsion. The factory owners, especially in the more remote factories, had to take pains both to stimulate the workers' desire for money and to arrange for the supply of new com-modities on which to spend it. Arkwright, for example, was impelled to build a market place at Cromford and offer prizes for the tradesmen who best supplied it.[2] It was here that social emulation, the desire 'to keep up with the Joneses', which operated at these no less than at higher levels of English society,

---

[1] Cf. F. Engels, *Condition of the Working Class in England* (trans. W. H. Chaloner and W. O. Henderson, Oxford, 1958), pp. 24, 88; and see below, chap. iv, § 2.

[2] Ashton, *18th Century*, p. 214.

came into operation. For the sake of the better food, the whiter bread, the flesh meat, and the new cottons, the pottery, utensils and household goods which industrialism was producing in larger and cheaper quantities, a sufficient body of men and women were prepared to work long hours, which were not new, under unwonted discipline, which was. For this readiness to earn and spend the credit must go once again to the nature and structure of English society. But this brings us to the most important economic factor in the genesis of industrialism, consumer demand.

Consumer demand was the ultimate economic key to the Industrial Revolution, calling into action the factors of land, capital and labour and sustaining them through the vicissitudes of economic change. So powerful was the pressure of contemporary demand that the classical economists took it for granted, and concentrated on the factors of production. Only Malthus glimpsed its significance: without 'a considerable class of persons who have both the will and power to consume more material wealth than they produce . . . the mercantile classes could not continue profitably to produce so much more than they consume.'[1] But Malthus was thinking of the demand of the leisured rich for luxury goods, while industrialism required a rapid expansion of the demand for mass consumer goods. Foreign trade could aid this expansion, but it was most unlikely to operate except on the foundation of an expanding home market. That France led the field in luxury production throughout the British Industrial Revolution and beyond was no accident, but the result of the pattern of demand generated by the French social structure, a structure characterized by a small class of luxury consumers and a large mass of consumption-resisting peasants. Peasants when they have a surplus rarely spend it, but hoard it for an emergency, to replace an ox, dower a daughter, purchase an extra half-acre, or buy out the birthright of the younger son. Not only had Britain practically no peasants, but its social structure might have been designed for the spontaneous and rapid generation of demand for cheap consumer goods.

It was in the elasticity of consumer demand that English society came into its own, and acquired the decisive economic advantage over Continental countries. The graduated hierarchy

[1] Malthus, *Principles*, p. 466.

with its social mobility, together with the diffusion of spendable incomes down to levels scarcely touched by the money economy elsewhere, generated the social emulation, the 'keeping up with the Joneses', the competitive spending which infected all levels of society from the aristocracy down to the very labourers. In the 1720's Defoe commented on 'the alteration which the Humour of the People, and their luxury' had given to the shopping streets of London:

> the same flourishing pride has dictated new methods of living to the people; and while the poorest citizens live like the rich, the rich like the gentry, the gentry like the nobility, and the nobility striving to outshine one another, no wonder all the sumptuary trades increase.[1]

Sixty years later, Henry Meister, a Swiss journalist from Paris on a visit to this country, observed:

> There is as great an inequality of ranks and fortune in England as in France; but in the former the consequence and importance of a man as a member of society is far more respectable. Individuals of the lower classes are better cloathed, better fed, and better lodged than elsewhere; and often, as far as I could learn, with no better means than the same classes enjoy with us. Pride and a desire to preserve the public esteem seem to force upon them that attention to their conduct and outward appearance.[2]

Emulative spending was the real target of the familiar attack on 'luxury' from Defoe to Cobbett. According to Trusler in 1796,

> the great degree of luxury to which this country has arrived within a few years, is not only astonishing, but almost dreadful to think of. Time was, when those articles of indulgence, which now every mechanic aims at possession of, were enjoyed only by the Baron or Lord of a district.[3]

William Green declared in 1800:

> The rapid increase of vanity and extravagance, in this island is a subject pregnant with mischief and alarm. Commercial monopoly and Eastern opulence . . . have already fostered dissipation and immorality into monsters of colossal magnitude, that every moment threatens (sic) the humbler classes of independence, with ruin. That

[1] Defoe, *Complete English Tradesman* (1841 ed.), II. 239.
[2] Meister, *op. cit.*, p. 8.
[3] J. Trusler, *The Way to be Rich and Respectable* (1796), p. 3.

frugality which once characterized the middling and lower classes of society amongst us is no more: the little tradesman and mechanic of the present day, fatally though impotently, ape the luxuries and fashionable vices of their superiors.[1]

The 'luxuries' and 'Eastern opulence' were of course white bread, tea, china cups, cotton prints and muslins, and the like. Cobbett thundered at 'the Italian-like effeminacy' of the modern farmer, who preferred music meetings to hunting, as well as at the tea and sugar of the labourer (because they replaced, he optimistically thought, the beef and beer of an older England).[2] On such 'luxuries' industrial revolutions are based.

English snobbery, long notorious in the old society, bore witness to the emulative social structure. Snobbery is more than pride in rank: it is an active device for preventing upstart inferiors from treading too closely upon one's heels. The *British Magazine* declared in 1763:

> The present rage of imitating the manners of high-life hath spread itself so far among the gentlefolks of lower-life, that in a few years we shall probably have no common people at all.

Henry Fielding blamed emulation *inter alia* for 'the late increase in robbers':

> while the Nobleman will emulate the Grandeur of a Prince: and the Gentleman will aspire to the proper state of a Nobleman; the Tradesman steps from behind his Counter into the vacant place of the Gentleman, Nor doth the Confusion end here: It reaches the very Dregs of the People ...

Another observer, in the *London Chronicle*, 1773, supported them:

> each of the different ranks of men are perpetually pressing upon that above them ... even the lower class both in town and country are so much infected with this preposterous ambition, that all ranks and degrees of men seem to be on the point of being confounded ...

---

[1] W. Green, *Plans of Economy; or the Road to Ease and Independence* (1801); a MS. begging letter attached to the copy in the Manchester Central Reference Library shows the author to be 'a melancholy inhabitant of the King's Bench Prison'.

[2] Cf., *inter alia*, *Political Register*, VI. 617–19, XXIX. 164, LXIV. 712, LXVI. 181; *Cottage Economy* (1821), *Advice to Young Men* (1829) and *Legacy to Labourers* (1835). I owe these references to Mr. J. F. Goodridge of Lancaster University.

Fashions in dress were an obvious vehicle for snobbery and emulation:

> The vanity of the great will ever be affecting new modes, in order to increase that notice to which it thinks itself exclusively entitled. The lower ranks will imitate them as soon as they have discovered the innovation. . . . The pattern is set by a superior; and authority will at any time countenance absurdity. A hat, a coat, a shoe, deemed fit to be worn only by a great grandsire, is no sooner put on by a dictator of fashions, than it becomes graceful in the extreme, and is generally adopted from the first lord of the Treasury to the apprentice in Houndsditch.[1]

Indeed, the fashion cycle aptly illustrates the exact degree of difference between England and the rest of Europe. Since it can only flourish in a society with sufficient openness and emulation between its upper ranks, it was peculiar to European civilization. Beginning in the fifteenth century at the break-up of strict feudalism, with cycles of perhaps half a century, it gradually speeded up until in the eighteenth century it went round about once every decade. Within this European context the peculiarity of English society was that the fashion cycle by the eighteenth century reached so much further down the scale. Foreigners like P. J. Grosley and Per Kalm noticed that the very servants and labourers wore the paniers and sacks, the knee-breeches and occasionally even the peruques, of their betters,[2] and their observations are amply confirmed by the paintings and prints of Hogarth, Stubbs, Rowlandson, Cruikshank and Gillray. Alone amongst European nations, including the Celtic fringe, England was without a 'national costume', that euphemism for peasant dress. With the significant exception of the smock-frock, the working overall worn by the agricultural labourers in the more backward parts of southern England, where the gap between the 'labouring poor' and their 'betters' survived down to the late Victorian age, the common people, at work and especially at leisure, wore a conscious imitation of the dress of their immediate superiors.

[1] *British Magazine*, 1763, IV. 417; H. Fielding, *Enquiry into the Causes of the late Increase of Robbers* (1750), p. 6; *London Chronicle*, 1773, XXXIV. 213a; Vicesimus Knox, *Works* (1824), I. 374; Hecht. *op. cit.* pp. 204–5.

[2] P. J. Grosley, *A Tour to London* (trans. T. Nugent, 1772), I. 75; P. Kalm, *An Account of his Visit to England . . . in 1748* (trans. J. Lucas, 1892), p. 52; Dorothy Marshall, *English People in the 18th Century* (1956), p. 178.

Cotton was the leading industry of the Industrial Revolution because it admirably suited the demands of the emulative fashion cycle. So versatile and yet, potentially, so cheap a fabric, variable in colour, pattern and texture, yet washable and hard-wearing, could make endless reappearances in the salons of high fashion, and just as repeatedly spread down the social scale. Wool was less versatile, yet mass consumer demand played a significant part in the rise of the West Riding and the decline of the older areas: the decline of the West Country cloth industry has been attributed less to the competition of machine-production—which a number of West Country manufacturers adopted—than to the shift in taste from their solid, expensive cloths to the cheaper and lighter woollens and worsteds of the Yorkshire mills.[1] In the pottery trade Josiah Wedgwood consciously used the 'lines, channels and connections' of his noble and royal clientèle to spread the fashion for his wares to the rest of society: 'Few Ladies, you know, dare venture at anything out of the common style till authorized by their betters—by Ladies of superior spirit who set the *ton*'; and he sought out Queen Charlotte's patronage not so much for his artistic productions as for his Queensware, the plain cream earthenware with which to woo the mass market.[2] And even in agriculture and the brewing industry the technical revolutions were due not merely to the increase in population, but to the increasing preference of the 'lower orders' for the fresh meat and wheaten bread of their superiors, and the shift in taste from the lighter ales to the strong, dark, highly-brewed, mass-produced porter.[3] Indeed, social emulation could even operate in bad times, in the refusal to lower standards under the harshest pressure: in the near-famines of the war years the agricultural labourers of the south refused to accept oats or potatoes in place of wheaten bread, and the poor law authorities had to concur.[4]

Mass consumer demand was obviously less directly important in the heavy industries. War was the great stimulator of innovation in metallurgy. But if war had been a sufficient cause of industrialism, the great Continental powers with their much

[1] K. G. Ponting, *The West of England Cloth Industry* (1957), pp, 147–50.

[2] N. McKendrick, 'Josiah Wedgwood: an 18th-Century Entrepreneur in Salesmanship and Marketing Techniques', *Ec.H.R.*, 1960, XII. 415, 418.

[3] Ashton, *18th Century*, p. 216; Mathias, *Brewing Industry*, pp. xxi–xxii, 12–13

[4] Cf. Hammond, *Village Labourer*, I. 119–29.

heavier military commitments and their urgent search for improvements in munitions—France in the late eighteenth century sent missions to try and discover the secret of Britain's superiority in iron and cannon production[1]—would have succeeded long before Britain. War, like foreign trade, was an economic stimulus available to everyone who could respond to it. The peace-time market for heavy industry was clearly the foundation of success even in war. If Henry Cort's puddling and rolling process, developed in the production of iron for the Navy, was called forth by the demands of war, the invention which made it possible, Darby's coke-smelting process, was evoked by the demand for cast-iron pots, pans, firebacks, and similar mass consumer goods.[2] If the production of capital goods could only be indirectly affected by consumer demand, the effect was no less real for that. Even the steam engine owed something to one brand of social emulation, the gradual spread of cleanliness down the social scale from the Restoration period to the Victorian age: 'People now have such a rage for washing their b—ms,' wrote Watt to Robert Milne, engineer of the New River Water Company in the 1790's, that more water and therefore more pumping engines were bound to be needed.[3] To quote Malthus again,

> Inventions to save manual labour are generally called forth by the wants of mankind in the progress of improvement; and therefore seldom exceed those wants. But the same laws apply to machinery as to fertile land: a full use cannot be made of either without an adequate market;

and again:

> In general it may be said that demand is quite as necessary to the increase of capital as the increase of capital is to demand. They mutually act upon and encourage each other, and neither can proceed with vigour if the other be left far behind.[4]

If consumer demand, then, was the key to the Industrial Revolution, social emulation was the key to consumer demand. By the eighteenth century nearly everyone in England and the

---

[1] Cf. the activities of Antoine-Gabriel Jars, 1732–69, Pierre Grimal et al., *Dictionnaire des Biographies* (Paris, 1958), I. 765.

[2] A. Raistrick, *Dynasty of Ironfounders: the Darbys and Coalbrookdale* (1953), pp. 2, 37.

[3] I owe this reference to the Boulton and Watt Papers to Dr. W. H. Chaloner.

[4] Malthus, *Principles*, in *Works and Correspondence of Ricardo* (ed. Sraffa), II. 349, 350.

Scottish Lowlands received a money income, and nearly everyone was prepared to spend a large part of it in 'keeping up with the Joneses'. Even the entrepreneurs, whose emulative spending mainly took the long-term form of capital investment in the hope of raising themselves in the social scale and of ultimately becoming 'new men', were not immune to competitive consumption. The Strutts, for example, filled their home with pictures, books and musical instruments, and they were by no means unusual amongst the entrepreneurs who supported the Lunar and other literary and philosophical societies.[1] As for the workers, although there was in the actual take-off period no spectacular rise in average wages, they were, as we shall see, sufficiently maintained to enable the wage-earners to purchase more of the cheaper consumer goods such as cottons, and in a rising population to expand their aggregate demand significantly. The self-accelerating velocity of circulation resulting from social emulation was the engine which drove the expansion of demand, and so set in motion the take-off into self-sustained economic growth.

From whatever angle we look at the causation of the Industrial Revolution, then, whether from the broader political, scientific or religious, or from the narrowly economic point of view, it was the nature and structure of English society which gave the various causes their opportunity, and set them to work in spontaneous harmony.

By way of postscript, the experience of the 'Celtic fringe' provides a contrast and a test. It was not alone the lack of material resources which frustrated an industrial revolution in Ireland (apart from Belfast and the Lagan Valley) and the Scottish Highlands. Switzerland with no more came to mount one of the earliest and most successful. What thwarted it was the nature of their societies: peasant societies still half immersed in tribalism, dominated by near-feudal or alien landlords, remote and often absentee, and almost completely without the varied prosperous, energetic 'middle ranks' which characterized Anglo-Saxon society in England, the Scottish Lowlands and the Ulster plantation. As long as land was plentiful such peasant societies expanded not by industrialism but by the proliferation of holdings. When, however, by the pressure of population and the

[1] Fitton and Wadsworth, *op. cit.*, pp. 178–9.

imposition of an alien land-law—the Anglo-Saxon concept of absolute property vested in the landlord—land became scarce, the hard-pressed and embittered peasants were driven out in large numbers, to seek new holdings in the colonies or to join the industrial proletariat in the Anglo-Saxon South and East.[1]

Wales, with mineral resources and a similar but slightly more advanced society, is a still more interesting test case. There, handicapped in the early stages by lack of capital, lack of entrepreneurs and lack of a potential proletariat, industrialism had to be induced from outside. The result was a semi-colonial economy in which capital was provided in large blocks by English capitalists, encouraged by favourable concessions from local mineral owners, and recruiting over long distances a heterogeneous and at first partially migratory labour force. Hence the importance of London and Bristol merchants, the long, beneficial mineral leases, and the excessive friction of Welsh industrial relations. Hence too the sense of exploitation by an Anglophile gentry and an alien capitalism. As a contemporary English observer ingenuously put it, 'it was rather curious to observe how few of the inhabitants of South Wales have benefited from the extraordinary wealth their country contains and that the Saxon race of men should have been almost the sole adventurers which have in later times brought this wealth into action, and by their ingenuity, perseverance and adventurous spirit have raised many a noble fortune and laid the foundation of many more.'[2] If South Wales was gradually brought into the mainstream of industrialism, its economy still bears today the scars of its semi-colonial past.

3. THE PROBLEM OF TIMING

There still remains the problem of timing. The old society, the open aristocracy based on property and patronage, lasted a long time, from the decline of feudalism in the fourteenth century to the rise of a class society in the nineteenth. If it was the ideal

[1] K. H. Connell, *The Population of Ireland, 1750–1845* (Oxford, 1950), esp. chaps. v and vi; J. Prebble, *The Highland Clearances* (1963); Ian Grimble, *The Trial of Patrick Sellar: the Tragedy of the Highland Evictions* (1962).

[2] C. Hassall, *General View of Agriculture in the County of Monmouth* (1812), quoted by John, *op. cit.*, p. 24; for rest of this paragraph, cf. *ibid.* chap. vi.

society for generating a spontaneous industrial revolution, why did it not generate it earlier?

The short answer is that the life-cycle of a society takes time. Before one society can give birth to another it must first come to maturity itself. This the old society only achieved with the final triumph of the landowners in the constitutional struggles of the seventeenth century. Even then, there is no inherent reason why a mature society as dynamically stable as the English should not have gone on expanding without fundamental changes of structure indefinitely, at least until the rate of expansion became too great to be contained within the old structure. This, indeed, is precisely what happened, with only temporary setbacks now and then of perhaps a generation long, from the Reformation until the reign of George III. As Adam Smith remarked in 1776:

> Since the time of Henry VIII the wealth and revenue of the country have been continually advancing and, in the course of their progress, their pace seems rather to have been gradually accelerated than retarded. They seem, not only to have been going on, but to have been going on faster and faster.

Yet Adam Smith no more expected the fundamental change in the traditional structure of the economy and society which had actually begun before his death in 1790 than he did the sudden onset of the millennium. On the contrary, he thought that the natural goal towards which this and other advancing countries were moving was 'the stationary state', in which the existing methods of production had been carried as far as they could be made to go, and economic growth ceased.[1] And in the world of 1776, in spite of a handful of water-driven factories and 'fire engines' used exclusively for pumping purposes, this was a thoroughly reasonable expectation.

For economic growth is at first a long, slow, cumulative process, which takes time to reach the critical point at which further advance required a change of structure:

> It is with nations as it is with individuals who are in train of acquiring property. At first progress is slow until a certain amount is obtained, after which, as wealth has a creative power under skilful and judicious management, the accumulation becomes more and more rapid, increasing often beyond a geometrical ratio, expanding

[1] *Op. cit.*, I. 70–4, 91.

in all directions, diffusing its influence wherever talents and industry prevail, and thereby extending the resources by which riches are obtained by communicating the power of acquiring it to thousands, who must have remained without wealth in countries less opulent.[1]

Thus Colquhoun in 1814 expressed what had happened to the British economy during his lifetime: within the last three decades the long, slow acceleration which had been going on since the limit of human memory had suddenly, like a steam-engine coming to the boil, an atomic reactor becoming critical, or an aeroplane taking off, reached the point at which self-intensifying forces began to come into operation, and a completely new level of activity achieved. In contemporary, non-metaphorical language Colquhoun was anticipating Rostow's notion of the take-off into self-sustained economic growth.

Yet, it may still be asked, why after the old society had reached maturity at the Revolution did it take nearly a century to reach the critical point? There were, indeed, signs of a significant surge of economic growth in the late seventeenth century which seemed to contain the promise of an industrial revolution.[2] And there was an upturn in all the curves of growth around 1745 which, although it produced no immediate change in the fundamental structure of economy and society, may be regarded as the initial acceleration of the run-up for take-off.[3] Nevertheless, why so long between taxi-ing and take-off, promise and fulfilment, ripeness and harvest?

If demand was the critical factor, then we must look not only for the causes of the exceptional increase in demand in the last twenty years of the eighteenth century, but also for those which before that date held it within the bounds of buoyant but unrevolutionary growth. In the last two decades of the century there were additional reasons for an acceleration of demand, over and above the normal buoyancy of the old society. Foreign trade, itself stimulated by home demand for foreign goods, took a great leap forward in the recovery from the American War, the only war of the century in which Britain temporarily

---

[1] *Treatise on . . . British Empire*, p. 51.
[2] D. C. Coleman *et al.*, 'The Origins of the Industrial Revolution', *Past and Present*, 1960, No. 17, pp. 71–2.
[3] Deane and Cole, *op. cit.*, pp. 46–7.

lost control of the seas, and was then carried further by the Revolutionary Wars, which benefited the only remaining great sea power at the expense of its Continental competitors. Both home and foreign trade were stimulated by profit inflation, which disproportionately benefited merchants, industrialists, farmers and landowners, the very ranks in which emulative demand began and responded most readily to the new manufactures which, against the general trend, were falling in price. At the same time, although average wages were not rising as fast as profits and rents,[1] aggregate wages were expanding steeply with the rapid growth of the labour force, which was now reaching a critical stage, as we shall see in a moment. Thus there were seemingly fortuitous reasons for the crucial increase in demand between 1783 and 1802.

Yet that they were not so fortuitous as they seem becomes clear when we turn to the main factor holding back demand before the take-off. For the answer to the problem of timing is most likely to be found in the one factor so far left out of account, except as the most important effect of industrialism: population growth. Population growth is the most fundamental of social factors, and its ultimate drives are psychological and historically inaccessible. Between population and economic growth the relationship is never a simple, one-way, causal link but a sensitive, two-way servo-mechanism, which transmits from one to the other the shock of every change of momentum. Varying rates of population growth due to external factors were sufficient to retard or to accelerate the operation of all the causes converging to produce the critical change in the British economy. Certainly, the comparative stagnation of population in the first half, and especially the second quarter, of the eighteenth century, whether it was due to gin, bad weather, a resurgence of endemic disease, notably smallpox, or to the chain reaction throughout the economy of the depression in agriculture, was enough to cancel out all the favourable factors making for a further acceleration of economic growth.

For the Industrial Revolution required, in addition to all the ancillary and economic factors brought into operation by the peculiar structure of English society, a very delicate adjustment

[1] Cf. P. Deane, *The First Industrial Revolution* (Cambridge, 1955), p. 31; and see below, chap. iv, § 2.

of population growth: not too fast, for that would cheapen labour to the point of deadening demand and suppressing the need for labour-saving machinery; nor too slow, for that too would discourage demand while making labour expensive and fractious.

That just such a buoyant rate of growth obtained in the second half of the eighteenth century is beyond doubt. What caused it is a matter for controversy amongst demographers and historians. Indeed, the whole question of the mechanics of population growth during the Industrial Revolution is in dispute. Was the dynamic factor a declining death rate, whether due to medical improvements or to more general environmental causes; or was it an expanding birth rate, due to a lowering of the age of marriage and increased employment opportunities? This larger question must be left to the specialist demographers.[1] Meanwhile, the ultimate significance of the Industrial Revolution for population growth is not in doubt: whatever caused the mid-eighteenth-century surge it could not, but for the extra food and jobs created by industrialism, have led to a revolutionary increase in population. Without them it must soon have received the Malthusian check which had blocked or reversed most population surges in the history of the human race, and which was still to operate in the case of Ireland. Until the famine of 1845, however, the case of Ireland, like that of contemporary Sweden and most of Western Europe, goes to show that a considerable population surge was possible without touching off an industrial revolution. To this extent industrialism in Britain was undoubtedly the long-term cause of the permanent increase in population, and not *vice versa*.

In the short run, however, the initial spurt of population growth in the third quarter of the eighteenth century was the trigger which, given the favourable complex of ancillary and economic causes, set the process in motion. Its causes are still obscure. Such statistics as exist are so open to question that we cannot say with certainty whether the decline in the death rate

---

[1] For this whole discussion see D. V. Glass and D. E. C. Eversley, *Population in History* (1965), Part II, 'Great Britain', esp. the essays by H. J. Habakkuk, D. V. Glass, T. McKeown and R. G. Brown, J. T. Krause and J. D. Chambers; and E. A. Wrigley, ed., *An Introduction to English Historical Demography* (1966).

was greater or less than the acknowledged rise in the birth rate.[1] Even if we could, birth and death rates are not themselves causes but merely the effect and the measure of complex, multiple causes operating through them. Some of the improvement in the death rate may be the merely statistical effect in a younger, healthier population of the high mortality of the second quarter of the century. Equally, some of the rise in the birth rate may be due to the greater numbers in such a population in the child-bearing age groups. In either case, the more stable rate—a comparatively stagnant death rate in the face of a briskly rising birth rate, or a comparatively stationary, but high, birth rate maintained in spite of a declining death rate, especially among infants—may well be the more dynamic factor needing to be explained. And whatever the mechanism of growth, the answer may lie elsewhere: given the philoprogenitive tendency of humanity, growth may as Malthus believed be the norm, and the question turn not on what made the population grow more rapidly after 1750 but on what prevented it from doing so until then.[2]

The field at any rate may be narrowed. Immigration can be ruled out as a major cause. Medical improvements cannot have contributed much until the nineteenth century, but better health and survival may have resulted from improvements in the environment: cleaner, more easily washable clothes; dryer, solider, more vermin-proof housing; and the disappearance of the plague-carrying black rat and other pests. More births may have resulted from a lowering of the age of marriage consequent upon the decline in the custom of apprenticeship and the earlier attainment of full wages; and even from the very losses of the high mortality period which, by making cottages and jobs more available, may have encouraged marriages and births beyond

[1] Cf. Habakkuk, *loc. cit.* 147–58; and J. T. Krause, 'Changes in English Fertility and Mortality, 1781–1850', *Ec.H.R.*, 1958, XI. 52–70, where, however, the effects of the expansion of Dissent on the under-registration of baptisms and burials are exaggerated by assuming the numbers of chapels licensed for worship in each decade from 1771–80 to 1841–50 to be cumulative, and therefore to show the rise of Dissent to 'a peak in the 1810's or 1820's', followed by a decline to the 1840's, when the comparative link with the civil registers comes to be made.

[2] Cf. Habakkuk, *loc. cit.*, p. 158; G. S. L. Tucker, 'English Pre-Industrial Population Trends', *Ec.H.R.*, 1963, XVI. 212–14; P. E. Razzell, 'Population Change in 18th-Century England: a Reinterpretation', *Ec.H.R.*, 1965, XVIII. 312–31.

the strict needs of population replacement. Finally, food was of crucial importance: whether or not the amount per head increased, greater aggregate quantities would certainly be necessary. Here the agricultural revolution, which began, in Norfolk, half a century or more before the industrial, having contributed to the overproduction and low prices of the agricultural depression of the second quarter of the century, may just in the third quarter have begun to have effect. Even more important than the quantity of food, perhaps, was the greater regularity of supply resulting from the winter feeding of cattle; and the increased nutritional value of fresh meat, milk and vegetables available to more, if not to most people, which may have had an effect not only on health but, through improved conception and pregnancy, on fertility also, and on the survival of infants to baptism and beyond.[1]

Whatever the causes, there can be little doubt that the nature and structure of English society contributed to them. Socially the key to a permanent expansion in the number and size of families is the placing of surplus sons in a position to raise a family. Without access to income opportunities the more abundant food, cleaner clothing, better accommodation, and the rest, are of no avail. In practically all Western European countries, at least from the end of the middle ages, marriage was late, since the younger sons, whether of aristocrats, bourgeois or peasants, were restricted by social as well as by economic barriers in their opportunities of employment and therefore of marriage.[2] In England, by contrast, the only barriers to marriage and a family apart from the declining custom of apprenticeships, were the purely economic ones of income opportunity. As we have seen, the provision of income opportunities was very elastic: the early disappearance of a peasant society had necessitated an alternative outlet, notably in domestic outwork industry, for the surplus population, while the upflow of new men into the landed gentry opened up opportunities all the way down the scale for new-comers. There already existed, therefore, a flow of younger sons into new positions which, by earlier marriage, could

---

[1] Cf. McKeown and Brown, *loc. cit.*, pp. 304–7; cf. Habakkuk, *loc. cit.*, pp. 269–84; Chambers and Mingay *op. cit.*, chap. iii.

[2] J. Hajnal, 'European Marriage Patterns in Perspective', in Glass and Eversley, ed., *op. cit.*, pp. 101–43.

respond to every slight improvement in economic prosperity or opportunity.

England was therefore better placed than any European country for exploiting the smallest population surge when it appeared and turning it into a large and permanent one. Whatever the immediate cause of the initial upturn of the third quarter of the eighteenth century, it was seized upon by the dynamic forces operating in English society and sustained long enough to set going the self-reinforcing process of industrialization. For a generation the delicate adjustment of population growth to resources, buoyant enough to expand demand and labour supply, stable enough to intensify the search for labour-saving devices and bring them into practical operation, was maintained. Its role was to concentrate, to compress, to bring to a critical conjunction the built-in forces of economic growth generated by English society. At the end of a generation all that was needed for the final break-through was a suitable cyclical trade boom of a not much more than average kind. That boom came in the 1780's, with the end of the American War and the re-opening of the ocean trade, swept to greater heights by the Revolutionary Wars.

The crucial factor, however, was not the boom itself but the acceleration of population growth, which by then was just sufficient to turn one of the most difficult of economic tricks: to expand aggregate consumer demand without raising labour costs too high for rapid economic growth. This it did by hitting the critical rate of growth squarely in the middle: slow enough to maintain, and even slightly improve, average real wages and encourage labour-saving innovation, fast enough to keep down labour costs and to expand aggregate demand for food and the new cheap manufactured goods. Thus the contemporary profit inflation, which was redistributing income, relatively and on average, away from wages and towards profits and rents,[1] was prevented from having a self-defeating effect on aggregate demand, and for once an expansion of investment and conspicuous consumption on the part of the upper and middle ranks could take place without a corresponding shrinkage of aggregate demand on the part of the lower orders. The effect was to remove the built-in brake from the economic

[1] Cf. Deane, *op. cit.*, p. 31.

system and allow its built-in dynamism full play. In other words, after a long period of acceleration, the lift at last overcame the drag, and the machine was airborne.

Only a machine of the right shape and power, however, could have succeeded in taking off. The economic boom and the population surge were European if not world-wide, and presented an opportunity for any Western European country to seize. In the event only Britain was equipped to seize it. That she was so was due to the unique nature and structure of her society.

IV

The Revolution in Social Organization

THE Industrial Revolution was a social revolution with social causes and social effects. So far we have been concerned with the social causes, in the form of the impact upon industry and economic growth of the unique nature and structure of the old society in England. The rest of the book is concerned with the impact of industrialism upon the nature and structure of English society. In this chapter we attempt to sketch, all too briefly, the central features of the social revolution itself, which consisted in a rise in the scale of human organization, not only in industry, transport and commerce, but in almost every other social activity, from religion to government. This revolution in organization inevitably entailed the migration of large numbers of people between occupations, between industries and sectors of the economy, and between communities, above all between the country villages and the towns.

1. THE RISE IN THE SCALE OF ORGANIZATION

In industry itself the rise in scale consisted chiefly in the gradual replacement of the domestic system by the factory system. The emphasis must fall on the word *system*. All the features of the factory were known long before Arkwright opened his first mill at Cromford in 1771: concentration of labour under one roof or in one place, the use of 'ingenious machines', the application of mechanical power which, in the form of the water wheel, goes back to Domesday Book and beyond, and even large-scale capitalist production, in the sense of large numbers of domestic craftsmen employed by a single merchant-employer. By the eighteenth century it was common for domestic capitalists to employ hundreds and even thousands of outworkers:

> In 1736 two brothers employed 600 looms and 3,000 persons in the Blackburn district; a little before 1750 a Warrington sailcloth manufacturer employed 5,000 persons; in 1758 a small group of Manchester check weavers employed a great many of the weavers of Ashton, Oldham and Royton, and one spoke of employing 500 himself.[1]

But features do not make a system. Thirteenth-century fulling mills were scarcely factories, but a mere adjunct to domestic industry. Sixteenth-century weaving sheds with hundreds of looms, if they existed, were large workshops, examples of unnecessary gigantism doomed to extinction. As Max Weber pointed out,

> The real distinguishing characteristic of the modern factory is in general . . . not the implements of work applied, but the concentration of ownership of workplace, means of work, source of power and raw material in one and the same hand. This combination was only exceptionally met with before the eighteenth century.[2]

Indeed, the first real factory in Britain was almost certainly the Lombe brothers' silk-throwing mill at Derby in 1719, and, though it was imitated, factories remained rare until Arkwright's time.

When they came they represented a rise in scale not because they employed on average more workers than the domestic capitalist—on the contrary, they usually employed fewer—but because they increased the size, complexity and degree of organization of the real unit of production, the working team under the control and leadership of one man. Under the domestic system the merchant merely 'gave employment', often through

---

[1] A. P. Wadsworth and J. de L. Mann, *The Cotton Trade and Industrial Lancashire, 1600–1780* (Manchester, 1931), p. 211; S. Pollard, *The Genesis of Modern Management* (1956), p. 7, to which book some of the industrial detail, though not the general conception, of this section is indebted.

[2] M. Weber, *General Economic History* (1928), p. 302; Pollard, *op. cit.*, p. 7.

agents and intermediaries who themselves were not necessarily in his employ, to domestic craftsmen who were independent of his direct control and discipline, and with whom he was in a purely commercial relationship. The real unit of production was the craftsman's domestic workshop, and the working team the members of his household, including any apprentice or journeyman he might employ. The parallel is with peasant agriculture, in which the unit of production is the family holding, whether or not a merchant supplies the seed and buys the produce, or a landlord shares the cost and the harvest with the *métayer*.

The true comparison, therefore, is between the domestic workshop, with its handful of comparatively unspecialized workers and its £2–£3 worth of equipment, and the factory, with its scores or even hundreds of highly specialized operatives and its £40–£50 of fixed capital per worker. By contrast with the half dozen or so workers in the average domestic weaver's household the average labour force of 41 Glasgow cotton spinning mills in 1816 was 244, of 43 in and around Manchester nearly 300. The average for all cotton mills inspected in 1838 was 137, and in the more comprehensive returns of 1871 177.[1] In 1784 the loom, two spinning wheels and two pairs of hand cards of a Rossendale flannel weaver were valued at £1 16s.[2] Arkwright claimed in 1783 that the investment in factory spinning amounted to £40 per operative, while another estimate in 1833 amounted to £53 per operative.[3] Even the central warehouse of the merchant-employer was modest by comparison. Samuel Oldknow as a muslin merchant in 1784 possessed equipment worth £57 10s. in a warehouse which he doubled in size at a cost of £90. As a factory spinner in 1805 his Mellor mill and estate were valued at £160,584, though this was a giant, and the average mill as late as 1833 was estimated at only £21,000.[4]

Other textile industries followed belatedly behind cotton. In

[1] J. H. Clapham, 'Some Factory Statistics of 1815–16', *Ec.J.*, 1915, XXV 475–9, and *Economic History of Modern Britain* (1964), II. 117; H. D. Fong, *The Triumph of the Factory System in England* (Tientsin, 1930), p. 18.

[2] G. H. Tupling, *Economic History of Rossendale* (Manchester, 1927), p. 190n.

[3] E. Baines, *History of the Cotton Manufacture in Great Britain* (1835), pp. 191, 342–3.

[4] G. Unwin *et al.*, *op. cit.*, pp. 13–15, 202.

1871 woollen mills averaged only 70 workers, but by 1833 Yorkshire mills averaged over 200, at least five of them over 500, and so did another seven in the West Country. Worsted mills came to vie with cotton: only 80 in the West Riding in the 1830's, they reached a national average of 175 in 1871. In silk the typical throwing mill in 1833 had 200–300 operatives; the average establishment in 1871 had 68, but nearly half of these were ribbon shops with an average of only 10. John Heathcote's bobbin lace factory at Tiverton employed 800 in 1833, when his agent, William Felkin estimated the average factory at 200 workers and £10,200 in fixed capital. The average in 1871 was only 37, but this included many workshops. The first hosiery factory, Hine and Mundella's, was built only in 1851, but the average, including workshops, in 1871 was 71 workers. Flax and jute were on a still larger scale, with 202 and 291 workers respectively in 1871.[1]

Most other industries followed the revolution in textiles. Pottery even preceded it: 'near 150 separate potteries' in and around Burslem in 1762 employed 'near 7,000 people', an average of about 47, and by the 1830's 130. North Staffordshire works averaged 165, seven of them employing 500–1,000 each, though the national average in 1871 was only 84. Brewing, at least in London, was contemporary with cotton: in 1785 half a dozen London porter brewers with capitals of over £100,000 and staffs of over 100 each produced more than 100,000 barrels. In 1871 the 44 'factory breweries' had an average of 219, but there were still 929 workshop breweries, and several thousand brewing victuallers and beer-sellers. Engineering closely followed. The prototype heavy engineering works, Boulton and Watt's Soho Foundry, was worth £30,000 in 1797 and twice that in 1830, and grew from about 100 men in 1821 to 251 in 1831. One hundred and fifteen Lancashire engineering firms in 1841 averaged 91 workers, but this included Hibbert and Platt's with 900 and Nasmyth's with 500. By 1871 machine making averaged only 85, but it included many small workshops, as well as vast concerns like Armstrong's and Whitworth's. The largest-scale industry of all, iron shipbuilding, was a sort of

[1] Pollard, *op. cit.*, pp. 94–6; Baines, *op. cit.*, pp. 342–3; Clapham, *Economic History*, II. 117; Charlotte Erickson, *British Industrialists: Steel and Hosiery, 1850–1950* (1959), p. 94.

engineering, with an average in 1871 of 571 workers, in Scotland alone of 800 workers.[1]

Even those industries which had passed beyond the domestic scale before the Industrial Revolution experienced a rise in scale just as profound. A large ironworks in the early eighteenth century, Coalbrookdale or Dowlais, was worth £2,000–£4,000 and employed perhaps a score of workers. By the early nineteenth century, the average was over £50,000 and over 100 men, and giants like Cyfarthfa or John Foster's at Stourbridge would employ up to 5,000 men and be worth half a million pounds or more. The Quaker London Lead Company between 1815 and 1865 employed several hundred smelters besides an average of 865 miners. Thomas Williams, the 'copper king', who in 1800 controlled half the British copper industry, employed 1,200–1,500 in his Anglesey mines, besides smelters at half a dozen refineries, on a capital approaching one million pounds. The four Swansea companies which dominated the industry in 1840 had capitals over £200,000.[2]

Even the little metal fabricating shops of the Birmingham and Sheffield nail, toy and cutlery trades, with averages in 1871 of only 8, 9·5 and 21·5 workers began to go into the factory. In 1841, for example, four steel screw factories employed an average of 200 workers.[3] Many other industries, new and old, followed suit; glass, chemicals, rubber, boots and shoes, 'slop' clothing, and so on. By 1871, the average for all the 23,346 factories in the United Kingdom was 86 workers, that for the 106,988 workshops in the returns only 5.[4] At that point the transition from workshop to factory represented a roughly seventeen-fold rise in the size of the unit of production.

By means of the rise in scale, with its twin principles, of specialization within a large working team and the application of fixed capital in the form of labour-saving machinery—which, indeed, was merely specialized labour in frozen or concrete

---

Clapham, *Economic History*, II. 117–19; Mathias, *Brewing Industry*, pp. 25–6, 36; Pollard, *op. cit.*, p. 79.

[2] Ashton, *Iron and Steel*, p. 100; Fong, *op. cit.*, p. 141; Pollard, *op. cit.*, p. 73; Barker and Harris, *op. cit.*, pp. 77–81; John, *op. cit.*, p. 31.

[3] Fong, *op. cit.*, p. 149.

[4] *P.P.*, 1872, [c. 602], XVI. 37, *Reports of Inspectors of Factories and Workshops*, pp. 82–4.

form—what Marx called the massive and colossal productive forces slumbering in the lap of social labour were awakened,[1] and with them the vast increase in productivity which was the Industrial Revolution in its narrower, technological aspect. According to an estimate of 1827 750 specialized operatives in a cotton mill could produce as much yarn as 200,000 hand spinners. Thomas Bell's calico-printing machine, operated by one man and a boy, replaced a hundred hand-block printers. Heathcote's bobbin-net machine reproduced 2,000-fold, later 10,000-fold, the skilled movements of the pillow-lace maker.[2] Yet however productive the machine, it could not install, supply, and operate itself or dispose of its own products. What mattered was the social unit of production, the divided and re-integrated labour of the working team, under the direction and control of the organizer himself, the entrepreneur.

The entrepreneur, the active, working capitalist who b oth owned and managed his own enterprise, was the key figure in the revolution in organization. He it was who had to see and seize the market opportunity presented by the new technology within the context of existing or potential demand, who had to procure the capital or persuade partners to invest, find a site with, in the early stages, a suitable fall of water and adequate communications, superintend the building of the factory and the making and installation of the machinery, recruit, train, direct and discipline the workers, and purchase the raw materials and dispose of the finished article at remunerative prices. The trials and tribulations of Arkwright, Wedgwood, Boulton, Owen, Oldknow, Heathcote and a great many other early entrepreneurs are well known. On top of all the usual cares and responsibilities of the merchant-employer, notably the mercantile functions of buying and selling, they had the continuous control and direction of what amounted to a whole new community of human beings. They might well have to build houses for them, supply them with water and means of sewage and refuse disposal, provide shops or a market, a church or chapel and a school, procure legislation and build a turnpike road or a canal, maintain law

---

[1] *Communist Manifesto* (1848), in Bottomore and Rubel, *op. cit.*, p. 138.
[2] J. Farey, *A Treatise on the Steam Engine* (1827); Mantoux, *op. cit.*, p. 250; W. Felkin, 'Lace and Hosiery Trades of Nottingham', *Stat.J.*, 1866, XXIX. 540; Fong, *op. cit.*, pp. 41, 204.

and order, or even, as in the case of the parish apprentices, feed, clothe and lodge the workers.[1]

But whether or not they assumed these extraneous, communal responsibilities—and time, usage, steampower and the factory town all tended to reduce them—they could not escape their managerial functions within the factory itself. So onerous were these functions, and so unlike anything that the merchant-capitalist had met with before, that many preferred to continue with the old, less productive system rather than, as the 1806 Committee on the Woollen Manufactures put it, 'submit to the constant trouble and solicitude of watching over a numerous body of Workmen.'[2] Enforcing punctuality and regularity of attendance and steady application to the work, upholding standards of quality and quantity of output, preventing drunkenness, quarrelling, promiscuity, unnecessary conversation, over-lengthy meal breaks or even too frequent visits to the lavatory, awarding praise and very occasionally prizes to the diligent and skilful, and fines or other punishment to the idle and clumsy, these were the functions of the entrepreneur which the merchant-capitalist did not have to think about.[3]

In theory they could have been left to a salaried manager, as Adam Smith suggested when distinguishing the 'profits of stock' from the 'wages of inspection and direction':

> In many great works almost the whole labour of this kind is committed to some principal clerk. His wages properly express the value of this labour of inspection and direction.[4]

In practice honest, efficient, loyal managers without themselves a stake in the firm—which would have made them entrepreneurs themselves—could rarely be found until the later stages of the Industrial Revolution, one of the functions of which was to create the professional manager.[5] In 1796 an ironfounder declared that

> the proprietor of these works by residing on the spot and being brought up to the business in all its subordinate detail may make a

---

[1] Cf. S. Pollard, 'The Factory Village in the Industrial Revolution', *E.H.R.*, 1964, LXXIX. 312f.; Unwin *et al.*, *op. cit.*, chaps. ix, xi, xii, xiv, xvi.

[2] *P.P.*, 1806, III. 268, *S.C. on the Woollen Manufacture of England*, p. 10.

[3] Cf. Pollard, *Management*, chap. v; Baines, *op. cit.*, pp. 184–5; N. McKendrick, 'Josiah Wedgwood and Factory Discipline', *Hist.J.*, 1964, IV.

[4] Smith, *op. cit.*, I. 49–50.

[5] Cf. Pollard, *Management*, esp. chap. iv.

livelihood, but that it would never, I say never, answer conducted by a Manager.[1]

And in 1816 the elder Sir Robert Peel declared:

> It is impossible for a mill at any distance to be managed, unless it is under the direction of a partner or superintendant who has an interest in the success of the business.[2]

The training and supervision of adequate managers and foremen was, as Wedgwood found, just one more of the multitudinous functions of the entrepreneur, and it is the considered opinion of the leading authority on the subject that as a result of the Industrial Revolution

> There were well-defined groups of managers in many industries: there was, by 1830, as yet hardly a managerial profession as such.[3]

By the mid-Victorian age, it is true, the scale of organization had risen in several industries so far as to make delegation to salaried managers inescapable, and to lift the capitalist himself in many cases beyond the plane of the simple owner-manager. But until the rise of the big corporate capitalist in the second half of the nineteenth century—a theme which will be taken up in Chapter X—the entrepreneur was to be the typical business man of the new industrial system.

The new system spread only slowly to many industries, and was by no means complete by the conventional end of the Industrial Revolution, but it had gone far enough to dominate the economy:

> in 1840 the factory system had become the prevalent system ... in textiles such as cotton, woollen, worsted, silk, flax and hemp; in metals such as iron, engine-and-machine, button, screw, steel pen, needle, pin; and in paper, pottery, and glass. In other manufactures, in metals such as nail, anchor and chain, clock and watch, cutlery and gun; in clothing products such as lace, ribbon, glove, hat and wearing apparel, the system was making rapid headway. ... In short, in the English manufactures ... including about one half of the manufacturing population of England in 1840, the factory system had become the predominant system of industrial organization.[4]

[1] A. Birch, 'The Haigh Ironworks 1789–1856', *Bulletin of John Rylands Library*, 1953, XXXV. 330.

[2] *P.P.*, 1816, III, *S.C. on Children employed in the Manufactories of Great Britain*, p. 136; Pollard, *Management*, p. 21.

[3] *Ibid.*, p. 159.   [4] Fong, *op. cit.*, p. 21.

By the time of the comprehensive factory and workshop returns of 1871–72 (which exclude the remaining domestic workers), four out of five of the workers returned worked in factories, representing about half those engaged in manufacturing of all kinds, and a much larger part of the total output.[1]

The revolution in organization could not be confined to manufacturing, and its reverberations were felt throughout the economy. The demand for coal, especially with the general spread of steam power and railways in the second quarter of the nineteenth century, meant deeper mines, larger and more efficient pumping engines, winding gear, ventilation systems, and haulage and handling facilities which, at different times and rates according to the geology and accessibility of the different fields, increased the size, labour force and capital investment of the average colliery. In the north-east, the first field affected, a single pit in 1787 was said to have cost £20,000 to sink, and another by 1833 £70,000. By 1829 41 Tyneside collieries employed 12,000 men, an average of nearly 300. Other fields followed, as the canals and then the railways opened them up. The average British colliery in 1850 employed about 80 workers, above and underground, but there were many in Scotland, Cumberland, Yorkshire and South Wales which employed many times that number.[2]

In transport the revolution in scale went furthest of all, and can best be gauged from the transition from roads through canals to railways. The average turnpike trust at the peak in 1838 had a mortgage debt (loan capital) of £6,300 and employed a score of workers; the average capital of 80 canal companies in 1825 was £165,000, and the labour force averaged several hundred; the average cost of constructing the 27 railways opened between 1830 and 1853 was nearly two million pounds, and the average labour force in 1851, excluding construction workers, was upwards of 2,500.[3] Moreover, the real unit of production, of passenger- or ton-miles, increased from the two-man coach or waggon, to the fleet of boats, and finally,

---

[1] 2,010,637 out of 2,540,789 workers in U.K.—*P.P.*, 1872 [c. 602], XVI. 37, *Reports of Inspectors of Factories for Year ending 30 April 1872*, pp. 82–4.

[2] Clapham, *Economic History*, I. 185–6, 433–4.

[3] S. and B. Webb, *Story of the King's Highway* (1913), p. 224; *Q.R.*, 1825, XXXII. 170–1; H. Pollins, 'A Note on Railway Constructional Costs, 1825–50', *Economica*, 1952, XIX. 407.

since the train could not operate as an independent unit, to the whole railway company, or even, after the rolling-stock clearing house system of 1844, the whole railway network.

The banking system, as a system, was created by the Industrial Revolution. The handful of country banks of 1750 grew to 940 by 1814 (before declining again to 311 in 1842), and the handful of joint-stock banks grew after the 1826 Act to 121, with nearly 1,800 branches, in 1875.[1] More important, they were welded, with the London merchant banks, into an elaborate and highly sophisticated system of national and international payment and credit, and with the Bank of England as the central reserve bank and the arbiter of interest rates and the volume of credit and currency at their head. Insurance, shipping, gas, water, and many other companies experienced a similar growth, and the whole revolution in scale, chiefly outside manufacturing industry, was belatedly and inadequately recognized by the rise of joint-stock companies, which grew from 947 in 1844 to 9,344 (excluding chartered and parliamentary companies) 'believed to be carrying on business' in 1885.[2]

Even agriculture was not untouched by the rise in scale. In spite if the ancient and persistent trend towards larger farms, the average holding remained small—only 111 acres in 1851—and the number of hired hands per farmer grew very slowly, from $1\frac{3}{4}$ in 1688 to $2\frac{1}{2}$ in 1831, although the number of workers per farm, including family members, in 1851 was nearer 6.[3] But the capital investment per farm steadily increased, with improved methods, equipment, livestock, manuring and drainage of the agricultural revolution. The four-course rotation required a 50 per cent increase in seed and other inputs, and facilitated a still larger increase in livestock.[4] Enclosure was estimated in the late eighteenth century by the Board of Agriculture to cost about 28s. per acre in legal expenses, officials' fees, and fencing, while mid-Victorian deep drainage cost as

[1] J. Sykes, *The Amalgamation Movement in English Banking, 1825–1924* (1926), pp. ix–x, 1, 98, 113.

[2] B. C. Hunt, *The Development of the Joint-Stock Company in England, 1800–67* (Cambridge, Mass., 1936), p. 88; Clapham, *Economic History*, III. 201.

[3] J. H. Clapham, 'The Growth of an Agrarian Proletariat, 1688–1832', *Cambridge Hist.J.*, 1923, I. 92–5.

[4] Cf. Chambers and Mingay, *op. cit.*, chaps. iii and iv.

much as £5 per acre.[1] A large part of the steep rise in land values between the mid-eighteenth and mid-nineteenth centuries represented a real rise in capital investment, which enabled a declining number of moderately increasing units of production to feed the bulk of a population which trebled between 1751 and 1851.[2]

The increased efficiency of agriculture not only fed the growing population, but by 1851 had released four out of every five occupied persons for service elsewhere. This meant chiefly in the towns, whose growth was at once the best measure of the revolution in organization and the main transmitter of its reverberations to the non-economic sphere. Four-fifths of the twenty million people added to the population between 1801 and 1891 went to towns with over 5,000 people, two-thirds to towns over 20,000. In 1801 only a third of the population lived in a town of any size, only one in six in a town over 20,000, and most of these, nearly one in ten, in London, the only city over 100,000. By 1851 half the population lived in towns, over a third in towns over 20,000, more than a fifth in towns over 100,000. By 1891 nearly three-quarters lived in towns over 2,000, over half in towns over 20,000, and nearly a third in towns over 100,000.[3] In 1801 London had 865,845, and there were only five other towns with over 50,000. By 1861 London had 2,803,989, Manchester, Liverpool and Birmingham had over 250,000, eight others had over 100,000, and seventeen more—twenty-nine all told—over 50,000. By 1907 London had 4,536,541, eight other towns had over 250,000, twenty-four more over 100,000, and another forty-two—seventy-five in all —over 50,000.[4]

In short, there was a revolutionary rise in the scale of the community in which most people lived. These new or greatly enlarged communities were not just larger versions of the old, simple commercial towns—markets, ports, and organizing

---

[1] *Ibid.*, pp. 85, 163; F. M. L. Thompson, *op. cit.*, p. 248.

[2] *Ibid.*, pp. 122, 218–20; cf. Norton, Trist and Gilbert, 'A Century of Land Values', *Stat J.*, 1891, LIV. 528–32; according to M. B. Mulhall, *Dictionary of Statistics* (1899), p. 15, as corrected by the Rousseaux index of agricultural prices, real agricultural output per worker, at the average of 1865–85 prices, increased from £51 in 1821 to £66 in 1851 and £98 in 1881.

[3] A. F. Weber, *The Growth of Cities in the 19th Century* (New York, 1899), pp. 43, 144.

[4] Census of England and Wales, 1801, 1861, 1901.

centres for domestic industry—of the old society. They were themselves specialized entities with differentiated functions. The 1851 Census distinguished between London, that unique combination of administrative, commercial, residential, tourist resort and every other sort of town, which had grown by 46·4 per cent in the half-century, and the 99 county towns, which had grown by 22·1 per cent, the 26 seaports, by 95·6 per cent, the 28 mining and hardware towns, by 117·3 per cent, the 51 manufacturing towns, by 124·2 per cent, and the 15 watering places, by 154·1 per cent, of which the eleven coastal resorts, the most specialized and fastest growing of all, had grown more than threefold, by 214·1 per cent.[1]

Within each town, too, there was an increasing division of functions between the inhabitants and segregation of areas for different purposes. The larger the town and the more specialized its main activity, the more it required full-time specialists to minister to its needs. Permanent shops and covered markets replaced casual street trading and open-air markets. Slaughterhouses supplemented or replaced the home-killing butcher. Water companies and sewage works eventually replaced wells and cess-pools. Professional police supplemented and eventually took over from elected constables, and local government itself, along with much else, gradually became professionalized. The various functions became localized in different areas, shops and offices in the centre, factories and poorest working-class housing hard by, artisans' and poor clerks' houses somewhat further out, middle-class homes in the inner suburbs, merchants', industrialists' and higher professional men's villas in the outer ring or, when the railways came, in detached satellite suburbs strung along the railway lines.[2]

This segregation by class was the most important social effect of urbanization, and its full significance will be explored in the next and subsequent chapters. Meanwhile, we may just notice that the new class institutions which the very size, anonymity and segregated character of the towns allowed to come into existence experienced an exactly similar rise in scale. The small

[1] Census of England and Wales, 1851, *General Report*, p. xlix.
[2] Cf. H. B. Rodgers, 'The Suburban Growth of Victorian Manchester', *Journal of Manchester Geographical Society*, 1962, LVIII. 1f.; T. C. Barker and M. Robbins, *A History of London Transport*, I, *The 19th Century* (1963), pp. xxv–xxx; Asa Briggs, *Victorian Cities* (1963), pp. 12–15, 24–5.

local, sporadic trade and box clubs of the old society, often frequented by small masters as well as journeymen, evolved into different sets of large-scale institutions, each meant to cope with different aspects of the new scale of social life. The first, and much the larger development, was that of the friendly societies for mutual insurance against sickness and death, which grew from 9,672 in 1803 with 704,350 members and funds of about one million pounds to over 32,000 societies in 1872 with over four million members and funds of nearly twelve million pounds. More significant was the growth from about 1830 of the great affiliated orders, with their headquarters and branch organization, like the Manchester Unity of Oddfellows, which grew from 2,039 lodges with 248,000 members in 1845 to 3,074 lodges with 497,000 in 1875, or the later rise of the national unitary societies like the Hearts of Oak (1841) which grew from 33,000 members in 1872 to 239,000 in 1899.[1]

The second and overlapping development was that of the trade unions, which clearly separated from the first only after the repeal of the Combination Acts in 1824–5. That the emancipating force was urbanization rather than industrialism alone is shown by the fact that traditional crafts were as much affected by it as new factory occupations. The General Union of Carpenters and Joiners, 1827, preceded the more famous Grand General Union of Cotton Spinners of 1829, as did the Operative Builders Union, 1833, and the Miners Association of Great Britain, 1841, the more famous Amalgamated Society of Engineers of 1851. Of the five leading 'New Model' Unions, with their professional officials, high subscriptions, and headquarters and branch organization, three, the carpenters, bricklayers and ladies' shoemakers, belonged to traditional crafts, and only two, the engineers and ironfounders, to new industries. Ignoring the abortive gigantism of the Grand National Consolidated Union of 1834, the movement grew from perhaps 100,000 members in 1842 to 1,200,000 in 1874, and meanwhile managed to grope its way to a measure of unity in the Trade Union Congress of 1868.[2] At the same time it provoked into existence a series of

[1] P. H. J. H. Gosden, *The Friendly Societies in England, 1815–75* (Manchester, 1961), pp. 5, 14, 33–4.
[2] S. and B. Webb, *History of Trade Unionism* (1920), pp. 110, 116–17, 124–31, 181, 211–14, 233, 748–9; H. Pelling, *History of British Trade Unionism* (1963) p. 79.

employers' associations whose nineteenth-century numbers are more fugitive, but amounted in 1900 to forty-three federations and national associations with 810 local associations.[1]

There was also a remarkably similar evolution from the local clubs and guilds of professional men, like the Society of Gentlemen Practisers (in the law courts) or the Company of Surgeons, into the nationwide, monopolistic professional institutions of modern times. The local clubs of solicitors were drawn together in the Law Society in 1825, the medical profession struggled into unity through the Apothecaries Act, 1815, the evolution of the British Medical Association in 1856 from the Provincial Medical and Surgical Association of 1834, and the Medical Registration Act, 1858, and the pharmacists and veterinary surgeons set up their own bodies in 1841 and 1844. Meanwhile, other professions created or greatly enlarged by the Industrial Revolution and the rise in scale sprang into institutional existence: the Civil Engineers (1818), Architects (1848), Ships' Masters and Navigators (1857), Naval Architects (1860), Gas Engineers (1866), Chartered Surveyors (1868), Electrical Engineers (1871), Municipal Engineers (1873), Chemists (1877), Librarians (1877), Teachers (1878) and Chartered Accountants (1880). More important, they began to exercise greater control over the recruitment, competence and conduct of their professions, instituting examinations and seeking parliamentary recognition and registration, like the doctors in 1858, ships' officers under the Acts of 1850 and 1854, and mine managers under those of 1872 and 1877.[2]

At a further remove from industry itself, in education there was a notable rise in scale. The very notion of a school changed from that of a single master with a score or so of pupils to a large multi-class institution with a number of specialist teachers under a non-teaching headmaster. The average eighteenth-century charity school had 18 pupils; the average voluntary school in 1851 had 91, in 1870 125, and by 1900 163, when the

[1] D. C. Marsh, *The Changing Social Structure of England and Wales, 1871–1951* (1958), p. 172.

[2] A. M. Carr-Saunders and P. A. Wilson, *The Professions* (Oxford, 1933), pp. 45–7, 75–83, 127, 133, 146, 151; G. Millerson, *The Qualifying Professions* (1964), pp. 121, 126; cf. also R. Robson, *The Attorney in 18th-Century England* (Cambridge, 1959); C. Newman, *The Evolution of Medical Education in the 19th Century* (1957); W. J. Reader, *Professional Men* (1966).

average Board School would have no less than 430.[1] Ancient grammar schools and public schools were reformed and re-organized on a larger scale, and new ones founded.[2] Even the two ancient universities were reformed, and doubled and re-doubled in size, from 1,128 undergraduates in 1800 to 2,550 in 1850 and to 5,313 in 1900, by which time a further dozen university institutions, beginning with University College, London, in 1826 and Durham University in 1833, had come into existence, and a far wider range of subjects taught and examined.[3]

Hospitals similarly grew in number, size and specialization. The eighteenth century added fifty-seven to the five royal hospitals it inherited, most of them founded since 1750. The nineteenth not only founded between seven and eight hundred more, but developed specialized wards and institutions for maternity, fevers, tuberculosis, mental treatment, convalescence, and so on. In London for example there were only seven hospitals in 1807 with 1,831 beds, an average of 262 per hospital, and in 1843 still only eleven, with 2,884 beds, and the same average. By 1891 there would be seventeen voluntary general hospitals, with 5,272 beds, an average of 310, sixty specialist hospitals with 3,616, an average of 60, and twenty-seven Poor Law infirmaries in what the Webbs called the 'splendid hospital system' run by the Metropolitan Asylums Board and open since 1884 to the general public, with 13,747 beds, an average of 509, plus eight fever and convalescent hospitals with 3,693 beds, an average of 462, and fifteen dispensaries treating over a million outpatients a year.[4] Meanwhile, the range of treatments and the scale of the equipment had also been transformed, so that the idea of a hospital had changed from a last, dangerous refuge for the sick poor to a highly sophisticated fortress in the war against disease.[5]

[1] G. M. Jones, *The Charity School Movement in the 18th Century* (1938), p. 24; E. Baines, *Education best Promoted by Perfect Freedom* (1854), pp. 42–3; Porter, *op. cit.*, (1912), p. 141.

[2] *P.P.*, 1867–8 [3966], XXVIII. Pt. I. 1, *Report of Schools Enquiry [Taunton] Commission*, esp. chap. ii.

[3] A. Mansbridge, *The Older Universities of England* (1923), p. xxn.; Armytage, *Civic Universities*, chaps. viii–x.

[4] J. C. Steele, 'Charitable Aspects of Medical Relief', *Stat.J.*, 1891, LIV. 265–7, 278, 281, 294; S. and B. Webb, *English Poor Law Policy* (1910), p. 123.

[5] Cf. Newman, *op. cit.*, chap. vi; B. Abel-Smith, *The Hospitals, 1800–1948* (1964). esp. chap. viii.

Even religion responded to the rising scale of community organization. Between 1801 and 1873 were built 4,210 new Anglican churches, an increase of about a third, and about 20,000 non-Anglican chapels, a nearly ten-fold increase.[1] As the towns grew, the churches and still more the chapels increased in size. As early as 1811 a Methodist minister wrote to Rev. Jabez Bunting:

> I hear great things of your amphitheatre in Liverpool. A man will need strong lungs to blow his words from one end of it to the other. In Bradford and in Keighley they are building chapels nearly as large as Carver Street Chapel, in Sheffield. To what will Methodism come in a few years?[2]

To cope with the sheer size and paganism of the towns the churches were forced to set up special missionary organizations, like the Nonconformist Home Missionary Society of 1819 or the Anglican London City Mission of 1835, or were overtaken by new mass organizations like the Salvation Army (founded as the 'Christian Mission to the Heathen of our Own Country' in 1865), and had to reorganize themselves by means of new dioceses like Manchester, 1847, or the new Congregational Union of 1832.[3] Charity, religious and secular, expanded likewise. In 1860 Sampson Low junior estimated that there were in London alone 640 charitable bodies, with an annual income of nearly two and a half million pounds. Two hundred and seventy-nine of these had been founded since 1801, 144 of them since 1850.[4] In 1869 the Charity Organization Society was founded to try to weld them into a system, and was imitated in many other cities. Although it failed, it could at least claim to have inaugurated professional casework and the modern theory and practice of social administration.[5]

[1] *P.P.*, 1852–3, LXXVIII. 164, *Returns relating to Dissenters' Places of Worship*, p. 156; Census of England and Wales, 1851, *Religious Worship*, p. xl; H. S. Skeats, 'Statistics relating to Religious Institutions in England and Wales', *Stat.J.*, 1876, XXXIX. 332–3.

[2] T. P. Bunting, *Life of Jabez Bunting* (1887), p. 338; E. P. Thompson, *The Making of the English Working Class* (1963), p. 351.

[3] K. S. Inglis, *Churches and the Working Classes in Victorian England* (1963), pp. 6, 14, 178.

[4] S. Low, jr., *The Charities of London in 1861* (1862), pp. vii–xi; K. Woodroofe, *From Charity to Social Work* (1962), p. 23.

[5] *Ibid.*, chap. ii; C. L. Mowat, *The Charity Organisation Society, 1869–1913* (1961), *passim*.

Finally, if somewhat tardily and reluctantly, the revolution in organization transformed the State itself. To cope with the manifold problems of the growing towns, local government was reorganized and changed from a largely amateur to a professional basis. This was only partly due to the Municipal Corporations Act, 1835, and much more to two other developments of greater significance. One was the series of private Acts beginning in the eighteenth century by which some three hundred towns and cities, such as Liverpool, Manchester and Birmingham, took powers to police, light, pave and drain the streets, and sometimes to provide water, gas, burial grounds, and even to clear slums and rebuild whole areas.[1] The other was the series of public Acts, including the new Poor Law of 1834, the Police Acts of 1839 and 1856, the Public Health Acts of 1848, 1866, 1872 and 1875, the Local Boards Act of 1858, the Food and Drugs Acts of 1860 and 1872, and the Education Act of 1870, which either set up competing local authorities such as the Poor Law Guardians and the School Boards, or loaded the existing ones with additional responsibilities. The resulting rise in scale can be measured by the increase in local government expenditure in England and Wales, from £5·3 million in 1803, to £66·8 million in 1893, and by the increase in the number of officials and other employees, from under 11,000, plus 16,400 police, at the first full occupational Census in 1851 to about 51,000, plus 32,000 police, in 1881.[2]

The revolution in central government was still more striking. The 15,884 'persons in public offices' in Great Britain in 1797, of whom most were Customs and Excise and Post Office officials and only about 1,500 central government clerks, grew to 108,000, in 1869, of whom about 16,700 were central department officers and clerks.[3] Meanwhile, government expenditure, net of debt interest and redemption, grew from £7·7 million in 1792, the last peacetime year of the eighteenth century, to £45·6 million in 1867–8, and to £77·9 million in 1897–8, the last peacetime year of the nineteenth. Altogether, public expenditure, local and national, grew in the course of a century from about £12

---

[1] Cf. S. and B. Webb, *Statutory Authorities*, chap. iv.

[2] Porter, *op. cit.*, (1912), p. 162; Census of England and Wales, 1851 and 1881.

[3] E. W. Cohen, *Growth of the British Civil Service, 1780–1939* (1962), p. 23n.; H. Mann, 'On the Cost and Organization of the Civil Service', *Stat.J.*, 1869, XXXII. 49.

million in 1792 to about £179 million in 1897–8.[1] This fifteen-fold increase in peacetime expenditure—more than fifteen-fold at fixed prices—is the best measure we have of the rise in the scale of government which resulted from the general revolution in organization produced by industrialism.

2. 'PETTY'S LAW'

The revolution in organization naturally required a large-scale redistribution of people between occupations, industries, regions, and communities. The driving force behind this redistribution was the well-known tendency with economic development and the rise in living standards for people to move from lower-paid occupations, notably in agriculture, to higher-paid ones, first in manufacturing and then in services such as commerce, transport, the professions and government. This tendency Colin Clark once christened Petty's law, after Sir William Petty, the pioneer of political arithmetic, who first noticed it as early as the 1670's:

> There is much more to be gained by *Manufacture* than *Husbandry*, and by *Merchandise* than *Manufacture*; . . . . Now here we may take notice that as Trade and Curious Arts increase; so the Trade of Husbandry will decrease, or else the wages of Husbandmen must rise and consequently the Rents of Lands must fall.[2]

The value of this 'wide, simple and far-reaching generalization' is that it both states the trend, which by extension can be held to include the shift of population from the agricultural to the industrial areas and, ultimately, from the countryside to the towns, and offers an explanation of the main, though not the only, mechanism by which it occurs, namely by means of the differential rewards of the different occupations.

In Petty's day about two-thirds of all families in Gregory King's table were primarily engaged in agriculture, although many of them must have spent part of their time in domestic manufacture, general labouring, and the like.[2] By 1760 Joseph

[1] Porter, *op. cit.*, (1912), pp. 617, 641.

[2] W. Petty, *Political Arithmetic* (1690), in *The Economic Writings of Sir William Petty* (ed. C. H. Hull, Cambridge, 1899), pp. 256, 267 (for dating of the *Political Arithmetic* to 1671–76 see p. 235); C. Clark, *Conditions of Economic Progress* (1940), pp. 176–7, and (1951), pp. 395–6; the 1960 ed. drops the term 'Petty's law' and substitutes 'a wide, simple and far-reaching generalization', p. 492.

Massie's figures imply that the proportion had shrunk to about a third, plus a proportion of the time spent in smallholding and harvesting by those in industry and trade—say, about half the population in all.[2] At the first Census in 1801 just over a third of the families in Britain (35·9 per cent) were allocated to agriculture, forestry and fishing. By 1851 the proportion had fallen to just over a fifth (21·7 per cent), and by 1881 to an eighth (12·6 per cent), not very remote from the mid-twentieth-century level of about a twentieth (5 per cent in 1951). Meanwhile, the proportion in manufacturing and mining increased fairly rapidly, from well under a third (29·7 per cent) in 1807 to two-fifths (40·8 per cent) in 1831, and then at a decreasing pace to 43·5 per cent in 1881. The slack was taken up by the increase in services, notably by trade and transport and by domestic and personal, both of which remained at an eighth or less up to 1831 and then began to advance rapidly, the former to more than a fifth (21·3 per cent) in 1881, the latter to nearly a sixth (15·4 per cent).[3] The small residuum was occupied by public and professional services which, because of difficulties of definition, appeared, against the trend, to be shrinking, but when better figures begin with the fuller occupational Censuses were undoubtedly and on any definition expanding faster than population, according to Charles Booth from 3·6 per cent of the occupied population (of England and Wales) in 1841 to 5·6 per cent in 1881.[4]

It used to be held that the main driving force behind the movement from agricultural to industrial occupations was the enclosure movement, which drove small owners and tenants, especially cottagers dependent on the commons, off the land to form the new proletariat. There is no denying, of course, that the enclosure of over six million acres of open field, common pasture and waste between 1760 and 1844, by some 4,000 Acts of Parliament, most of them concentrated in two short bursts from 1760 to 1780 and 1793 to 1815, plus perhaps up to half as much again by agreement,[5] would have a profound effect on the

[1] See above, chap. ii, table 1.
[2] Mathias, *Ec.H.R.*, 1957, X. 44–5.
[3] Deane and Cole, *op. cit.*, p. 142.
[4] C. Booth, *Occupations of the People* (1886), table B(1); figures not comparable with those in previous sentence.
[5] Chambers and Mingay, *op. cit.*, pp. 77–8.

organization of village society, and extremely unpleasant consequences for the majority of countrydwellers who could show no legal or customary rights and lost their access to the commons. The single-minded concern of landlords and farmers with rent and profits which over the main period of enclosures from the 1790's to the 1820's nearly doubled while real wages for the labourer stagnated or declined, the physical segregation of the social strata resulting from the removal of the farmhouses from the village to their consolidated plots and from the decline of the practice of the hired hands living in, and the general sense of betrayal of paternal responsibilities by the naked exercise of the power of property, all contributed to the deterioration in rural social cohesion which culminated in the East Anglian riots of 1815 and the 'last labourers' revolt' of 1830.[1] And the enclosures certainly contributed in one way to the formation of a landless labour force by cutting off—for what it was worth in the new conditions of rapid population growth—the traditional resort of the younger son, squatting on the common.

Nevertheless, it is now clear that the enclosures, allied to the agricultural improvements, were neither necessary nor apt to the creation of the proletariat, save to the extent that they produced the food for it. The sheer growth of population—trebling as it did in the century from 1750 to 1850—was more than ample to the demand for industrial labour. The agricultural population, in spite of its relative fall, continued to grow absolutely, from 565,000 families in England and Wales in 1706 to 660,000 in 1803, according to Massie and Colquhoun, and from 1·7 million persons in Britain in 1801 to a peak of 2·1 million in 1851 according to the Census, and only thereafter began its modern absolute decline, to 1·7 million again in 1881.[2] Except for the, at this period, comparatively rare enclosure of arable for pasture, enclosure and improved agriculture required more, not less, labour, not only for hedging and ditching and the construction of new buildings but for four crops in four years instead of three in two, for labour-intensive crops like turnips and other roots, and for the larger number of animals

[1] A. J. Peacock, *Bread or Blood: The Agrarian Riots in East Anglia, 1816* (1965); J. L. and B. Hammond, *Village Labourer*, II, chap. x.

[2] See above, table 1, pp. 20–1; Mathias, *op. cit.*, *Ec.H.R.*, 1957, X. 45; Deane and Cole, *op. cit.*, p. 143.

which the new fodder crops supported, while machines, apart from the vastly unpopular threshing machines which replaced only traditional winter work, were of little significance before the second half of the nineteenth century. For these reasons the population of almost all agricultural villages continued to rise until mid-century, and that of parliamentary enclosed villages more than any save industrial villages.[1]

Indeed, enclosure, especially that of wasteland, forest, moor and fen, itself illustrates the process of Petty's law. As a result of the enclosure of the Forest of Knaresborough, for example,

> the poor cottager and his family exchanged their indolence for active industry, and obtained extravagant wages; and hundreds were induced to offer their labour from distant quarters; labourers of every denomination, carpenters, joiners, smiths and masons, poured in, and met with constant employment. And though before the allotments were set out, several riots had happened, the scene was now quite changed; for with all the foreign assistance, labour kept extravagantly high. . . . In consequence the product is increased beyond conception, the rents more than trebled and population advanced in a very high degree.[2]

Enclosure did not always raise wages, chiefly because, as Arthur Young, Malthus and many other contemporaries pointed out, the rural labourers preferred to take the benefit of the increased productivity in the form of earlier marriage, more children, and a larger number of survivors to share the gain. In the remoter areas of the south of England, distant from the magnetic pull of the higher wages of the industrial north and of London or the Cornish mines, and especially in areas like the West Country where the alternative employment in domestic industry was shrinking relative to population, the labourers bred faster than the available jobs, and wages stagnated or declined, or after 1795 were only maintained at subsistence level by the Speenhamland system.[3] Their very reluctance to migrate, however, is evidence that they could not be driven to the factories and the towns, but had to be coaxed.

[1] J. D. Chambers, 'Enclosure and Labour Supply in the Industrial Revolution', *Ec.H.R.*, 1953, V. 323–4.

[2] G. B. Rennie, *General View of the Agriculture of the West Riding of Yorkshire* (1794), p. 76, in Chambers, *ibid.*, p. 333.

[3] Cf. M. Blaug, 'The Myth of the Old Poor Law and the Making of the New', *J.Ec.H.*, 1963, XXIII. 151f.

The best evidence for coaxing rather than compulsion is the difference in agricultural wages between the areas adjacent to and remote from the new industries. If we take Caird's well-known division between the high-wage northern and the low-wage southern halves of England in 1850–51 (roughly from mid-Shropshire through Birmingham to the Wash), we find that in Arthur Young's day, about 1770, agricultural wages north of the line averaged ten per cent less than those south of it, 6s. 9d. as against 7s. 6d. a week. By 1850 they were 37 per cent higher, 11s. 6d. as against 8s. 5d. The difference between the remoter agricultural counties and the industrial had widened still further. In Wiltshire, where the decay of the clothing industry exacerbated the glut of labour, wages were the same, 7s. a week, in both 1770 and 1850. In Lancashire they had doubled, from 6s. 6d. to 13s. 6d.[1] The more comprehensive statistics of Bowley show that the advance of northern and north-midland wages had begun with the onset of industrialism, rising by 56 and 35 per cent between 1767/70 and 1795, compared with 10 and 14 per cent in the south-east and the south-west, to become the highest of any region in England. The differential continued to widen until 1850, when northern wages were over 50 per cent higher than south-western, 12s. 2d. as against 8s. 1d. a week, and only narrowed with the coming of the railways and the decline in the agricultural population, to 34 per cent, 16s. 7d. as against 12s. 4d., by 1880.[2] There can be no more graphic illustration of the magnetic pull of industrialism that its effect on the wages of the adjacent farm labourers.

The pull was not so much directly into the new factories, at least in the early stages, as into domestic weaving and ancillary labouring, transport, building, canal and, later, railway construction, and into heavy industry like ironfounding and coal mining. Average weekly wages in cotton factories were lower than in northern agriculture—9s. 10d. and 9s. 2d. in 1824 and 1850 compared with 11s. 7d. and 12s. 2d.—chiefly because the former were weighted by the majority of women and children

[1] J. Caird, *English Agriculture in 1850–51* (1852), p. 474; F. G. Heath, *Peasant Life in the West of England* (1880), pp. 58–61.

[2] A. L. Bowley, 'Statistics of Wages in the United Kingdom during the last Hundred Years, Part I, Agricultural Wages', *Stat.J.*, 1896, LXI. 704–7.

amongst cotton workers while the latter were for men alone.[1] Adult male operatives earned much more—from 15s.–18s. in the blowing and carding room to 33s.–42s. for fine spinning on long mules in the period 1806–46[2]—but they were generally trained up from the children of textile workers and perhaps of farm labourers rather than from the farm labourers themselves. There can be no doubt, however, that it was higher wages which were decisive in recruiting workers, whether men, women or children, for the factories. The fiercest critic of the factory system, Engels, argues that the proletariat was called into existence by machinery and the consequent demand for more labour:

> This caused wages to rise and consequently hordes of workers migrated from the countryside to the towns. There was a very rapid increase in population and nearly the whole of this increase was due to the growth of the working class.[3]

This is confirmed by the very reluctance of the workers to enter the mills. In the early stages especially, when the mills were mostly in the countryside, it was extremely difficult to find satisfactory workers willing to endure the long hours of confinement and harsh discipline in what they clearly regarded as an imitation of the Poor Law workhouse. 'All the scanty evidence available confirms . . . the scarcity of labour for the country mills, the migratory and disreputable character of the early factory population, and the reluctance of the settled population to enter factory life. . . . Factory work in that early period might almost be described as a casual employment for migratory labour. . . .'[4] That is why the early millowners were led to recruit the little parish apprentices from the Poor Law authorities, the only category of workers who were forced into the mills, and who were not cheap labour but often cost more to feed and clothe and lodge than free children.[5] There were, in any

---

[1] T. S. Ashton, 'Some Statistics of the Industrial Revolution in Britain', *Manchester School*, 1948, XVI. 232.

[2] G. H. Wood, *History of Wages in the Cotton Trade during the last Hundred Years* (1910), p. 28.

[3] Engels, *op. cit.*, p. 24; cf. p. 88.

[4] A. Redford, *Labour Migration in England, 1800–50* (Manchester, 1964), pp. 22, 24.

[5] Cf. F. Collier, *The Family Economy of the Working Classes in the Cotton Industry, 1784–1833* (Manchester, 1964), pp. 45–6; Unwin *et al.*, *op. cit.*, pp. 173–5; Pollard, *Management*, pp. 164–5.

case, never more than a few thousand parish apprentices in cotton mills at any one time, and their numbers declined after the first Factory Act in 1802 made their employment more troublesome than that of free labour.[1] By and large it was the prospect of higher wages which was the most effective means of overcoming the natural dislike for the monotony and quasi-imprisonment of the factory.

Even higher wages were not enough in themselves. Traditionally, English workers, according to commentators from Defoe to Arthur Young, preferred to work just long enough to obtain their customary standard of living, and then spend the rest of the week in drinking and pleasure, though, leaving aside the expense of the latter, this does not quite square with the same critics' observations on their love of finery and high living.[2] Nevertheless, the early entrepreneurs, dealing as they did with the lowest stratum of the lower orders, who were the last to be reached by the downward filtration of the fashion for emulation, had to stimulate the consumer appetites of their employees, as Arkwright did by his prizes to the best tradesmen in Cromford market,[3] in order to make them feel higher wages worth working for.

All this is not to deny that there was a large element of compulsion in the worker's situation, however. Given the increased population, however caused, without increased opportunities for settlement on the land, as temporarily in Ireland and more permanently in America, then the choice before the individual worker was either to work or to starve. (In theory he could go on the parish, but in practice the Poor Law authorities would not support a man who refused work, and the actual number of able-bodied unemployed on relief, as distinct from the employed in receipt of allowances, although deliberately obscured by the authorities right down the nineteenth century, was very small.[4]) The fact that 'dismissal and the threat of dismissal were . . . the

[1] Redford, *op. cit.*, pp. 28, 32.

[2] Cf. A. W. Coats, 'Changing Attitudes to Labour in the Mid-18th Century', *Ec.H.R.*, 1958, XI. 35–51, and sources there cited.

[3] Ashton, *18th Century*, p. 214.

[4] Cf. Blaug, *op. cit.*, *J.Ec.H.*, 1963, XXIII. 177n.; M. E. Rose, 'The Allowance System under the New Poor Law', *Ec.H.R.*, 1966, XIX. 608, 614–15; in 1851, for example, the number of adult male outdoor paupers on relief due to 'want of work, or other causes' was only 5,347 out of a total of 137,530—*P.P.*, 1852 [1340] XXVI. 1, *3rd. Annual Report of Poor Law Commissioners, 1851*, p. 96.

main deterrent instruments of enforcing discipline in the factories,' that comparatively huge fines could be levied on workers for being late, for absence, faulty work, swearing, drinking, and so on, and that even physical punishment was applied, especially on children and youths, without them walking out,[1] shows that the fear of unemployment was effective. The fact also that so many handloom weavers and framework knitters in the 1830's and 1840's preferred to starve rather than accept the discipline of the factory shows that many who did accept felt themselves to be driven there as a last resort.

Nevertheless, if compulsion had been the main determinant we should expect to find factory work at the bottom of the list of choices open to the poor, along with scavenging, street trading, sewer hunting, or the sweated workshop trades, with the lowest pay as well as the lowest prestige. This it certainly was not. Although only in a few cases, like the fine spinners, did it rise to the pay and status of the skilled, and especially the apprenticed, crafts which formed the 'aristocracy of labour', it rapidly established for itself a position high in the scale of income and preference of the workers. Aside from the fine spinners, warpers and winders, engineers, iron puddlers and rollers, and a few other factory 'aristocrats', the bulk of the operatives were assigned to the middle category of semi-skilled workers, well above the mass of unskilled labourers and casual workers, not to mention the depressed *lumpen-proletariat* of street-folk, beggars, permanent paupers, criminals and prostitutes who figured in Mayhew's London and other great cities.

This brings us to the wider question of migration from the countryside to the towns. Until the steam engine took the factories into the towns, on a large scale only from the 1820's onwards, this scarcely affected factory operatives at all. Where did the new town-dwellers come from, and why did they go there? The well-attested answer to the first question, when an answer becomes possible from the birthplace enquiry in the Censuses from 1841 onwards, is that they came not by any important transfer of population from the south to the north but mainly from the adjacent countryside.[2] In the cotton and woollen towns of Lancashire and the West Riding and the metal working towns of Warwickshire and Staffordshire, for example, the great

[1] Pollard, *Management*, pp. 187-9. [2] Redford, *op. cit.*, pp. 183-6.

bulk of the newcomers came either from the villages of the same counties or from those of the contiguous counties. There were differences between counties in their attractive power. Staffordshire and the West Riding seemed to be able to provide most of the immigrants to their own towns, while Lancashire and Warwickshire relied more heavily on their neighbours, but this may have been due to accidents of geography, the proportion and positioning of the towns in relation to the area of the county and to the county boundaries.[1] In general, however, the great majority of migrants travelled only a short distance, and the more rapid population growth of the industrial areas was due less to a large-scale transfer of people than to their own greater fecundity. The only important exception to this was the large immigration of the Irish, especially in the 1840's, most of whom went to their nearest English and Scottish towns, in the north-west and the Glasgow area, and accounted for fully thirty per cent of the differential growth of the northern over the south-eastern counties between 1801 and 1851.[2] The bulk of the surplus population of the southern counties was absorbed by southern towns, above all by London. In so far as there was a small drift from south to north it can only have been of the 'wave' variety, short-distance emigrants being replaced by short-distance immigrants in communities across the country, though the evidence for this is extremely scanty.[3]

The general conclusion, that the new industries stimulated the natural increase of the population in the adjacent rural areas, would seem to confirm the view that it was the attractive power of industrial employment at higher wages rather than the compulsive power of enclosure which created the new proletariat. The answer to the second question, why did they go to the towns, even to work outside the factories, would seem to be the same. Even labourers' wages in the towns were higher than those in the countryside. In 1770 when northern farm wages averaged 6s. 6d. a week Lancashire building labourers earned 1s. 6d. a day.[4] In 1824 when northern farm wages averaged 11s. 7d. a

---

[1] Deane and Cole, *op. cit.*. pp. 113–14, 121–2.

[2] Redford, *op. cit.*, p. 187.

[3] *Ibid.*, p. 186; but see Deane and Cole, *op. cit.*, p. 117: 'the statistics suggest little in the way of a drift of population from the predominantly rural South to the industrial North.'

[4] E. W. Gilboy, *Wages in 18th-Century England* (1934), Appendix II.

week those for labourers in Manchester and Bradford were 13s. and 16s. respectively.[1] Perhaps the cost of living was higher in the towns, and rents certainly were, but the difference in wages was still wide enough to attract a steady flow of immigrants from the countryside. To this extent 'Petty's law' adequately explains the change in the distribution of the population which accompanied the revolution in social organization.

[1] Bowley, *op. cit., Stat. J.*, 1898, LXI. 704–7; Porter, *op. cit.*, (1851), p. 415.

V

<hr>

The Social Consequences of Industrialism

<hr>

By far the most important social consequence of the Industrial Revolution was its effect upon the structure of society, and with this effect in its manifold aspects the subsequent chapters are concerned. Meanwhile, the more obvious and immediate social consequences, the controversial effects of industrialism on living standards and the distribution of income, on the role and cohesion of the family, and on life and living conditions in the new and greatly enlarged towns, will be dealt with in this, not so much for their own sake as for the light which they throw on our main theme, the developing structure of society.

1. THE REVOLUTION IN LIVING STANDARDS

A general rise in living standards, by a multiple rather than a fraction, is, we suggested in Chapter I, one of the defining characteristics of an industrial revolution. Of that rise in England in the long term and for the great majority of the population there can be no doubt. Real national income per head quadrupled during the nineteenth century.[1] In the controversy which has raged between 'optimists' and 'pessimists' over the short-term effect upon the living standards of the working class, it is com-

<hr>

[1] From £12·9 in 1801 to £52·5 in 1901, at the average of 1865 and 1885 prices on the Rousseaux index—Deane and Cole, *op. cit.*, p. 282.

mon ground that real incomes were rising throughout for the middle and upper classes and for certain favoured sections of the working class, that they had been rising for most, if not all, of the rest, at least in the north and midlands where industrialism was taking root, for about a generation before 1795, and that, whatever happened to working-class standards between then and about 1842, they began to rise again from the early or middle 1840's, and continued to do so down to the end of the century. Both sides agree that living standards for the mass of the population were higher after 1850 than before 1790. The question can be narrowed down to the distribution of the increase in real national product between the various classes and sub-classes (leaving aside for the moment the definition of those terms) in the period 1790–1850, and the points of time when they, severally and collectively, began to share in the benefits of industrialism.[1] Since the distribution of income is central to the history of social structure, it is on this aspect of the controversy that we shall concentrate in this section.

No one can doubt that the rich and the well-to-do got their full share of the increase in national income. The only question is, did they increase their share and, if so, by how much? Unfortunately, there is only one point in the nineteenth century when we have a return of the actual numbers paying income tax at various levels of income, and that is in 1801. However, we do have two later estimates based on official sources, William Farr's for 1848 and Dudley Baxter's for 1867.[2] Farr's, which was concerned to fix the optimum lower exemption limit, stops short of analysing the taxpayers receiving over £200 a year, but if we compare this group of 236,000 incomes of £200 plus (1·18 per cent of the population), and compare it with the nearest equivalent group in 1801, the 120,873 incomes over £130 a year (1·14 per cent of the population) we find that their share

---

[1] Cf. esp. E. J. Hobsbawm and R. M. Hartwell, 'The Standard of Living in the Industrial Revolution: a Discussion', Ec.H.R., 1963, XVI. 119f., esp. pp. 123–4, 132, 139; for bibliographies of the standard of living controversy see A. J. Taylor, 'Progress and Poverty in Britain, 1780–1850: a Reappraisal', History, 1960, XLV. 16f., J. E. Williams, 'The British Standard of Living, 1750–1850' and R. S. Neale, 'The Standard of Living, 1780–1844: a Regional and Class Study', Ec.H.R., 1966, XIX. 581f. and 590f.

[2] P.P., 1852, IX. 510, 2nd Report of S.C. on the Income and Property Tax, Appendix 10, pp. 462–3, Papers from William Farr, tables i and ii; R. D. Baxter, National Income (1868).

of the national product had risen from 25·4 per cent in 1801 to 34·9 per cent in 1848.[1] Meanwhile, their average income had risen from £489 a year to £741, an increase of 52 per cent in current terms, or in real terms of no less than 98 per cent, compared with an increase in real national product per head of 78 per cent.[2] For a still richer section within this group we can compare Dudley Baxter's 49,500 taxpayers receiving over £1,000 a year in England and Wales in 1867 with exactly the same percentage of the population (0·24 per cent), the 26,366 receiving over £500 a year in Britain in 1801. Their share of the national product increased from 16·8 per cent to 26·3 per cent, while their average income rose from £1,476 to £3,243, an increase of 120 per cent in current terms, or 191 per cent in real terms, compared with an increase in real national product per head of 115 per cent.[3]

This considerable shift in income distribution towards the rich and the well-to-do is confirmed by what we know of the course of average real wages, for what it is worth, in the controversial period. While not necessarily accepting at their full face value the hotly disputed price indices, it is worth applying them to the series of money wages derived by Deane and Cole from Bowley and Wood to discover what the maximum improvement claimed by the meliorists can tell us about the trend in distribution, as well as pinpointing the areas of disagreement between the two sides. In the following table two sequences of general real wages are set out in columns (2) and (3), derived from the money wages in column (1) by means of the Gayer, Rostow and Schwarz and the Rousseaux price indices respectively. Alongside these is placed in column (4), for comparison, a sequence derived from Phelps Brown and Hopkins' series of real wages of builders, based on their own price index of a changing basket of consumables. Since these are given year by year, it enables us to iron out the effects of very high and very

[1] i.e. from £58·99 million to £174·81 million out of a national product which rose from £232 million (at current prices) in 1801 to about £523 million in 1848 —Deane and Cole, *loc. cit.*

[2] Applying the Rousseaux index to both taxpayers' income and to national product per head, and estimating latter in 1848 at £23 at 1865/85 prices—cf. *ibid.*

[3] For another comparison, between Baxter, 1867, and Colquhoun, 1803, see below, chap. X, § 1.

low prices in some of the particular years chosen by Bowley and Wood by averaging real wages over a few years on either side, and in this case five-year averages centred on each date have been taken.[1]

TABLE 2
MONEY AND ESTIMATED REAL WAGES, 1790–1850

| | MONEY WAGES | (1850 = 100) REAL WAGES | | |
	1. Bowley and Wood	2. Gayer, Rostow, Schwarz	3. Rousseaux	4. Phelps Brown and Hopkins (5-year averages)
1790	70	57·8	—	66·1
1800	95	46·2	51·5	54·1
1810	124	59·4	61·0	55·7
1824	105	75·6	81·7	79·8
1840	100	71·7	74·2	77·4
1845	98	86·5	84·6	87·1
1850	100	100·0	100·0	100·0

The most striking point about the table is that it seems to prove both sides to the controversy right. It confirms that there was a long-term rise in the living standards of the working class, but it also confirms that real wages stagnated or declined not only, as is agreed, during the Wars but in the critical period of the 1820's and 1830's. Between 1824 and 1840 there was, according to these estimates, a decline of from three to nine per cent in real wages, a decline which, when allowance is made for those workers who, as we shall see, were making large strides forward in comfort and well-being, the deteriorationists can claim would have been very serious for a large part of the working class. On the other hand, the meliorists can claim that the level of 1824 from which this decline took place was considerably higher—by 20 or 30 per cent—than the pre-war starting point, and that during the 1840's it was rapidly surpassed and left behind.

The extent of the long-term rise, however, depends enormously on the starting and terminal dates chosen. If the very bad year 1800 and the very good one 1850 are taken, then the increase ranges from 85 per cent through 94 per cent to 116 per

[1] Deane and Cole, *op. cit.*, p. 23; E. H. Phelps Brown and Sheila V. Hopkins, 'Seven Centuries of the Prices of Consumables compared with Builders' Wage-Rates', *Economica*, 1956, XXIII. 296f.

cent. If the more normal year 1790 is taken along with the nadir of 1840, the increase is reduced to 17–24 per cent. If for purposes of comparison with the income taxpayers of 1801 and 1848 we take 1800 and 1845, the increase is from 61 per cent through 64 per cent to 87 per cent. Perhaps the fairest comparison would be between the comparatively normal year 1790 and 1845, with an increase of 33–50 per cent.

Whichever years we choose, however, it is significant that (with the exception of the most extreme years exaggerated by the excessive fluctuations of the Gayer, Rostow and Schwarz index) the improvement in real wages did not keep pace with real national income per head. Taking the period as a whole from 1790 to 1850, compared with a doubling of the real national income per head, real wages increased by 51 to 73 per cent, according to the price index used. (The Rousseaux index, which starts in 1800, suggests an increase of 64 per cent from 1810, when real wages were only slightly higher by the other two indices than in 1790.) Thus on the most 'optimistic' view of the question, there occurred a decisive shift in the distribution of income away from wages. The exact size of it depends on many factors, including the changing distribution of the labour force, but assuming that at the end of the process wages accounted for about 40 per cent of the national income, then the order of magnitude of the transfer would be between 6 and 14 per cent of the national income.

An increase in inequality is what we might expect during an industrial revolution, on theoretical grounds. This does not mean that we accept the *a priori* arguments commonly advanced on either side. For the deteriorationists it has been argued that wages *must* fall during the early stages of industrialism, to provide the necessary investment, profit incentive and low labour costs.[1] But the evidence suggests that both the rate of capital investment and the capital-output ratio remained fairly low until the railway age, and that the productivity of the new machines and methods was so great that there was ample means to provide for increased investment, profits and wages.[2] For the

---

[1] S. Pollard, 'Investment, Consumption and the Industrial Revolution', *Ec.H.R.*, 1958, XI. 220–2; Hobsbawm, *op. cit.*, *Ec.H.R.*, 1963, XVI. 126; Taylor, *op. cit.*, *History*, 1960, XLV. 30.

[2] Cf. Deane, *op. cit.*, pp. 156, 270–2.

meliorists it has been argued that the distribution of income between the classes (or the factors of production) remains stable over long periods, and that therefore the working class are likely to have maintained their share of the rising national income.[1] This is not an economic principle, however, but an empirical observation derived from comparatively stable societies and economic systems, such as the periods 1880–1913 and 1906–60 studied by Bowley and Routh.[2] It does not necessarily hold for a period like 1790–1850 when society and its institutions were changing rapidly and when, as we shall see, the classes as we know them were only then emerging into existence and learning their new relationship with each other.

Nevertheless, there were limiting parameters beyond which changes in the distribution of income could not go without frustrating economic growth and bringing the Industrial Revolution to a halt. If, on the one side, wages rose too high, then labour costs, in spite of labour-saving inventions, would become prohibitive, profits and investment would fall, and growth slow down or cease. If, on the other, wages fell too low, demand, especially for the mass consumer goods in which the new industries specialized, would fall with them, and so too would the incentive for labour-saving investment, and once again growth would slow down or cease. The mere fact that production continued to grow so much faster than population is sufficient proof that these limits were not exceeded.

Within those parameters, however, there was room, if not for much absolute decline of average wages, at least for a considerable relative decline, which allowed a large part if not most of the increase in production, over and above what was necessary to induce the workers to co-operate, to accrue to the initiators and organizers of economic growth. In a spontaneous industrial revolution, in which centrally planned development and rewards were out of the question, this was almost inevitable since the engine of the whole process was the profit motive of the individual entrepreneurs (including in this context the enclosing landlords and the improving farmers), and the process

[1] Hartwell, *op. cit.*, *Ec.H.R.*, 1963, XVI. 140–1.
[2] A. L. Bowley, *The Change in the Distribution of the National Income, 1880–1913* (Oxford, 1920); G. Routh, *Occupation and Pay in Great Britain, 1906–60* (Cambridge, 1965).

itself afforded them the means of determining the flow of income to profits and wages, and the return flow back to profitable investment. The opportunities for quasi-monopolistic profits, at least in the early stages, were enormous: Arkwright made half a million pounds in less than two decades; Owen's contemporaries were making with ease twenty per cent or more on their capital.[1] Even where, like Owen, they treated their workers generously, they could scarcely avoid channelling most of the windfall gains of the new technology towards themselves, and they would have been less than human if they had not done so. Again, as long as the wage earners preferred to take a large part of the benefit in early marriage and large families (whether caused by more births or lower infant mortality), then demography was also against them maintaining their relative share, for the supply of labour was the ultimate arbiter of wages, and a glut of labour in the peak decades of population growth and urbanization is the likeliest explanation of the stagnation or decline of real wages in the 1820's and 1830's.

Finally, the structure of the price changes and the pattern of production and demand it reflected favoured the rich rather than the poor. Food prices rose higher and fell more slowly than those of the new manufactured goods, so that consumers, towards the bottom of the social scale, who spent most of their income on food gained much less than those, towards the top, with a considerable surplus for other goods. But this brings us to the larger and more important questions of how not merely the great aggregates of the rent, profit and wage-receiving classes but the different groups within them fared during the Industrial Revolution, and how these different groups came in turn to partake of its benefits. For not only were there great differences in welfare between different sub-classes, especially in the working class, but there were important differences in the timing with which, as it were, they were admitted to the circle of its beneficiaries.

If, as we suggested in the last chapter, social emulation was the key to the expansion of demand which evoked the increased production of the Industrial Revolution, then we should not expect all the different levels of society to enter into full enjoyment of its benefits at one and the same time, but to come to it

[1] Mantoux, *op. cit.*, p. 238; F. Podmore, *Robert Owen* (1923), p. 642.

at varying times and speeds. It is these varying times and speeds which above all account for the wide differences in comfort and well-being at any given point within the Industrial Revolution. Instead of a comparatively static model of a new industrial system showering blessings indiscriminately or in unchanging proportions—more at the top, less at the bottom—on an otherwise stationary social pyramid, we should adopt a dynamic model of a new industrial system growing like a vortex within the old, and gradually pulling into its orbit of production and demand circle after circle of producers and consumers. Higher and more centrally placed circles, like the entrepreneurs and the factory workers themselves, and, perhaps surprisingly, the landowners and larger farmers, were drawn in from the start, to enjoy higher incomes and spend an increasing proportion of them on the new consumer goods. Lower and peripheral circles, like the farm labourers, were the last to be affected, though even here there were gradations: the northern farm labourers felt the effect on their wages as early as the late eighteenth century, while those of the southern counties had to wait until the 1870's or later to begin to feel real benefit. In between, there were not only circles, like the urban labourers or the miners, who were drawn in at varying times and speeds, but other, like the hand-loom weavers and the framework knitters, who early on were drawn into comfort and even, by contemporary standards, luxury, only to be thrust out again by the inexorable whirl of technological change.

It would take too long to catalogue all the aspects, levels, twists and changes of this dynamic process, but enough can be said about each of the major circles to indicate its nature. First of all, there can be no doubt that the upper and middle classes, whose incomes as we have seen more than kept up with economic growth, were the first to enjoy the new consumer goods and other benefits of industrialism. We find the aristocracy from the very beginning enjoying the fashionable new muslins and printed cottons of the 1780's, Wedgwood's 'ornamental ware' which was in fact subsidized by the 'useful', Boulton and Fothergill's Birmingham 'toys', and all the best ironmongery, furniture and gadgets of the new creation.[1] The new factory masters and

[1] N. McKendrick, 'Josiah Wedgwood: an 18th-Century Entrepreneur in Salesmanship and Marketing Techniques', *Ec.H.R.*, 1960, XII. 408f.; E. Robinson,

merchants were only one pace behind, with their fine Georgian houses and furnishings, pianos and pictures, carriages and liveried servants. The lesser business men and shopkeepers came into affluence a generation later, in the early nineteenth century, according to G. R. Porter, 1851:

> In nothing is the improvement here mentioned more apparent than in the condition of the dwellings of the middle classes. As one instance, it is not necessary to go back much beyond half a century to arrive at a time when prosperous shopkeepers in the leading thoroughfares of London were without that now necessary article of furniture, a carpet, in their ordinary sitting-rooms. . . . In the same houses we now see, not carpets merely, but many articles of furniture which were formerly in use only among the nobility and gentry: the walls are now covered with paintings or engravings, and the apartments contain evidence that some among the inmates cultivate one or more of those elegant accomplishments which tend so delightfully to refine the minds of individuals, and to sweeten the intercourse of families.[1]

The falling prices of manufactured goods also left the same circles with more, if they wished, to spend on food. Although they could no doubt already buy as much in quantity as they liked, one gets the impression from the growing obsession with French chefs, gargantuan feasts, and exotic foods, and from the spate of cookery books, that in the early nineteenth century the rich were spending much more on the variety and elaboration of their food than formerly, and that in this they were increasingly emulated by the middle class.[2] And whatever happened to consumption of food per head, they would not go short. They almost alone enjoyed the increase in coffee from one ounce per head in 1801 to one pound seven and a half ounces in 1841, though they also account for the fall in the consumption of wine, from over half a gallon a year to under a third.[3] While general sugar consumption per head undoubtedly fell from thirty pounds ten ounces a head in 1801 to fifteen pounds five ounces in 1840,

[1] Porter, *op. cit.*, (1851), p. 522.
[2] Cf. J. Burnett, *Plenty and Want: a Social History of Diet in England from 1815 to the Present Day* (1966), chap. iv.
[3] Porter, *op. cit.*, (1851), pp. 549, 560.

'18th-Century Commerce and Fashion: Matthew Boulton's Marketing Techniques,' *Ec.H.R.*, 1963, XVI. 39f.

theirs probably rose, and Porter reckoned that, whatever the price and importation, the top fifth of families would take at least forty pounds per head, leaving the rest to fluctuate between nine pounds in 1840 and twenty pounds in 1849.[1] By analogy we can guess that they would take the first pick of all the other foods in the market, in bad years and in good, and that the proportion available for the rest would fluctuate far more markedly than the total figures suggest.

They it was, too, who enjoyed first and most abundantly the other benefits of economic growth: the improved transport, especially the new roads, faster coaches, and the early railways, and the facilities they afforded of living in more salubrious suburbs and taking holidays in the new resorts; the better houses, cleaner drains, piped water, improved medical treatment, and the bonus they offered in longer life and the survival of children; and the spare income for education, entertainment, clubs, societies, books, journals, newspapers, and so on, which all increased in quantity if not always in quality. Finally, they enjoyed a bonus which is now denied to the most advanced industrial societies: cheap and increasingly abundant personal service. The number of servants increased faster than population, from 600,000 in 1801 to 1,300,000 in 1851 (and to two million in 1881)[2]—a clear indication that the rich could afford to buy more of the labour of the poor, and so of the widening gap in income distribution.

Within the working class the first circle to share largely in the benefits of industrialism was not that of the factory workers who, though they improved themselves, did not at the beginning start high enough up the income scale to have a large surplus over and above immediate necessities, but the top ten to fifteen per cent of wage earners who came in the course of the nineteenth century to be called the labour aristocracy. These were chiefly craftsmen—printers, joiners, cabinet makers, cutlers, blacksmiths, wheelwrights, the building crafts, and the like, who we saw in Chapter II were not clearly distinguishable in the old society from the lower echelons of the middle ranks. During the Industrial Revolution many old trades overtaken by machinery, such as the woolcombers and calico-printers, dropped out of

[1] *Ibid.*, pp. 541, 543, 545.
[2] Deane and Cole, *op. cit.*, p. 143.

their circle, and a number of new trades, such as the iron puddlers, the fine spinners and the railway engine drivers, rose into
it. Since they were paid throughout from fifty to one hundred
per cent more than labourers in the same or nearby trades, since
with certain exceptions their skills were in increasing demand,
and since they were far less vulnerable to unemployment than
the rest of the working class, they were a particularly favoured
group who benefited from industrialism as early and nearly as
much as the adjacent middle class.[1] Their real wages at the very
least kept up with the average, as those of the builders in the
above table show, and they were particularly resistant to wage
cuts, so that during slumps and price falls their real wages
did not decline so steeply as the rest, and their margin of
spending power beyond the average worker almost continually
increased. These were the workers who ate meat, vegetables,
fruit and dairy produce, lived in the best and newest cottages
and filled them with furniture and knick-knacks, bought books
and newspapers, supported mechanics' institutes and friendly
societies, and paid the heavy subscriptions to the craft trade
unions.

Below and after them in the scale and speed of improvement
came the factory workers themselves, whose chief claim to
notice in the textbooks is their fight against long hours and bad
working conditions. Since in the chronology of industrial relations grievances about hours and conditions are normally
secondary to those about pay, this in itself is evidence that they
did not consider themselves badly paid, except in periods of
slump and short-time working. It is true that cotton operatives'
average wages were consistently amongst the lowest for any
industry, but this was because only about a quarter of them were
adult men (twenty-seven per cent in 1835) and the rest women,
youths and children.[2] For men wages ranged from about 1·3 to
three times the northern farm labourer's average (14s. 6d.–17s.
for cardroom operatives to 33s. 3d. for fine spinners in 1833 compared with 11s. 1d. for northern farm labourers).[3] Real wages
according to G. D. H. Cole, who was no meliorist, much more
than doubled between the bad year 1800 and 1830 and, after

---

[1] Cf. E. J. Hobsbawm, 'The Labour Aristocracy in 19th-Century Britain',
Labouring Men (1964), chap. xv.   [2] Deane and Cole, *op. cit.*, p. 294.
[3] Wood, *loc. cit.*; Bowley, *op. cit.*, *Stat.J.*, 1898, LXI. 704–7.

falling back somewhat during the 1830's, surged to a new height in 1850 approaching three times the level of 1800.[1] Whatever discount we make for the exaggeration of the price index, it is clear that cotton operatives, and probably most factory workers, enjoyed a markedly rising standard of living from the end of the Wars onwards. By the 1830's 'the majority of the factory operatives were in receipt of wages which brought within their reach a fairly abundant diet of plain food and, if careful and thrifty, tidy clothes and decent household goods.'[2]

Factory workers, however, were a minority of the working class at the end of the Industrial Revolution, and even if we add to them the miners, transport workers, iron shipbuilders and other rapidly expanding occupations who can be presumed to have improved their real wages *pari passu* with them, they would still be outnumbered by those below them. Amongst these were those cruelly tantalized victims of technological progress, the dislocated handicraft workers, above all the handloom weavers and framework knitters. These had been amongst the first and most indulged beneficiaries of industrialism. In the 'golden age of the handloom weavers' from the 1770's to the 1790's, when labour was in brisk demand to weave the new cheap cotton yarn, they could earn twenty-five shillings and more a week, three times the northern farm labourer's average, and clearly lived better than all but the best-paid factory operatives. The trade became overcrowded, however, long before the power loom became general in the 1820's, and their long decline into misery began as early as 1798.[3] Bolton weavers' weekly earnings fell from 25s. in 1800 to 14s. in 1811, 9s. in 1817, 8s. 6d. in the early 1820's, and reached the desperate level of 5s. 6d. in 1829.[4] A private enquiry into 8,362 North Lancashire weavers' families in 1833 revealed average wages of 3s. 8⅝d. a week per worker, or 1s. 9⅝d. per head which, after deducting the cost of rent, fuel and light, left only 1s. 3½d. per head for food and clothing.[5] Mercifully, it became a diminishing occupation, though not decreasing fast enough, since it was learned so

[1] G. D. H. Cole, *Short History of the Working-Class Movement, 1797–1937* (1937), pp. 181–2; based on Wood, *loc. cit.*   [2] Collier, *op. cit.*, p. 49.

[3] N. J. Smelser, *Social Change in the Industrial Revolution: an Application of Theory to the Lancashire Cotton Industry, 1770–1840* (1959), p. 205.

[4] Porter, *op. cit.*, (1851), p. 444.

[5] Collier, *op. cit.*, pp. 47–8.

easily and the Irish in the towns and the children of weavers in the remoter villages often had no other resort. Their numbers fell from 240,000 in 1831 to 110,000 in 1841 and 23,000 in 1856.[1]

In other textiles and in hosiery, in nail and chain making, boots and shoes, tailoring and dressmaking and many other trades, domestic outworkers struggled on much longer, to become in many cases the wretchedly poor and exploited 'sweated trades' of the 1890's and 1900's. Their long agony of poverty, starvation and degradation was part of the social cost of industrialism which must be offset against its benefits.

The displaced domestic workers were driven out from the inner circles of the blessed to the outer circles of the depressed unskilled and casual labourers, the street folk, beggars and criminal underworld of the worst urban slums. Here lay depths of poverty and degradation unimagined by those above them, until accident, sickness or the death of the breadwinner drove them down amongst them.[2] Only the determined investigators, ready to face the filth, stench, disease and the literal risk of death, like Kay, Engels, Chadwick, Southwood Smith, and Mayhew, could have any real notion of life at this level, and even they were incapable of measuring statistically the size and depth of poverty in the worst quarters of the great towns. Not until Booth in the 1880's and Rowntree in 1899 do we have reliable estimates of the numbers in poverty, that is, with too little income to maintain themselves in merely physical health. By that time, at the end of a century and more of steeply rising national income, thirty-one and twenty-eight per cent respectively of the population of London and York, forty and forty-three per cent of the working class, were below the poverty line.[3] Clearly, this huge segment of the working class had not yet benefited from industrialism, except in the crude sense that greater numbers of them had been kept alive to suffer the same

[1] Smelser, *op. cit.*, p. 207.

[2] Cf. E. Chadwick, *Report on the Sanitary Condition of the Labouring Population of Great Britain* (1842, ed. M. W. Flinn, 1965), p. 397: 'The statements of the condition of considerable proportions of the labouring population . . . have been received with surprise by persons of the wealthier classes living in the immediate vicinity, to whom the facts were as strange as if related to foreigners or the natives of an unknown country.'

[3] C. Booth, *Life and Labour of the People: London* (1891), II. 21; B. S. Rowntree, *Poverty: a Study of Town Life* (1901, popular ed., n.d.), pp. 150–1.

life of misery and frustration. Their release from the frozen grip of poverty had to wait for the twentieth century with its disproportionate rise of unskilled wages and of the Welfare State.[1]

The outermost circle of all was that of the farm labourers, especially those of the counties remotest from the industrial towns. Though even their exiguous average wages rose between 1795 and 1850, from 8s. 11d. to 9s. 6d., in real terms by fifteen per cent, this was almost entirely due to the differential rise of northern wages, and in the south and east money wages scarcely rose at all, and real wages almost imperceptibly.[2] Meanwhile, boarding in the farmhouses by unmarried labourers, a system which at least guaranteed them adequate food, declined, encouraging early marriage and more mouths to feed; enclosures, though creating more employment, also whittled away perquisites of fuel and grazing rights and made accommodation more difficult to obtain; and the decline of domestic employment for wives and children reduced incomes and made families more dependent on overcrowded and underpaid agriculture. Small wonder that 'the agricultural labourer was, in fact, the worst fed of all workers in the nineteenth century,' living in the south chiefly on bread with only occasionally a bit of cheese or bacon, potatoes, little or no milk, 'tea' made from used tea-leaves or burnt crusts, and meat only a rare luxury.[3] He was also the worst housed, 'herded together in cottages which, by their imperfect arrangements, violated every sanitary law, generated all kinds of disease, and rendered modesty an unimaginable thing,'[4] and even denied such cottages in 'closed parishes' where landlords forebade them in the interests of keeping down the poor rates. Why such conditions did not produce death rates as high as those of the towns is explained by two factors, the fact that insanitary housing is less dangerous in rural areas, and, a question needing further investigation, the statistical effect of migration on crude death rates, when a large

[1] Cf. Routh, op. cit., pp. 106–8, 144–5; B. S. Rowntree and G. R. Lavers, Poverty and the Welfare State: a Third Social Survey of York (1951).

[2] A. L. Bowley, Wages in the United Kingdom in the 19th Century (1900), table at end.

[3] Burnett, op. cit., p. x and chap. ii.

[4] R. E. Prothero (Lord Ernle), Pioneers and Progress of English Farming (1888), p. 224.

proportion of those born in an area go elsewhere to die. There is no evading the conclusion that 'this was a population existing permanently on the verge of starvation',[1] and it was not until after 1870, when the exodus from the countryside became rapid, money wages rose, and real wages rose sharply with the great price fall, that the southern farm labourers at last joined the outer fringe of those who benefited from industrialism.

There are a great many other aspects of this important question which would have to be investigated before any definitive conclusion could be arrived at about the effect of industrialism on the living standards of the working class: the incidence of unemployment, and whether the cyclical depressions of the early nineteenth century were worse than the chronic under-employment of the eighteenth century; the exact implications for the working class of the available statistics of consumption; the extent and effects of the increase in the adulteration of food as the towns grew and with them the distance between producer and consumer; the incidence and regressive nature of taxation, which increased the burdens on the poorer classes down to Peel's fiscal reforms and income tax in the early 1840's; the chronology of house-building, delayed by the Wars and their aftermath, and the failure of accommodation standards and amenities to keep up with the growth of towns; and the conflicting evidence of demography, setting short-term increases in urban death rates against their overall decline. Some of these will be touched on in the last section of this chapter, on conditions in the towns.

Meanwhile, the direction in which the answer will be found is via a Benthamite calculus of 'the greatest happiness of the greatest number', setting the numbers in the groups which gained against those in the groups which lost by industrialism. This is more difficult than it sounds, since the very process of industrialization was continually changing the proportions, and we do not even have accurate occupational statistics until 1851. It may well be that until the steep decline in handloom weaving and other dying domestic trades after 1840 and the absolute decrease of agricultural labour after 1851, the numbers of those who suffered exceeded those who benefited. Certainly, the Booth and Rowntree figures suggest that fifty or more years

[1] Burnett, *op. cit.*, p. 28.

earlier a majority of the working class might well have been in poverty by the standards of the late Victorian age. Against this, however, it must immediately be said that without the industrial and agricultural revolutions a much larger proportion still of the increased population would not only have been in poverty but would have starved to death. Finally, whatever the proportions at the beginning, there can be no doubt that the long-term trend was, often ruthlessly, in the right direction, towards the diminution and extinction of the losing and the survival and expansion of the gaining groups.[1] In this harsh sense of the survival of the fittest the Industrial Revolution ultimately spread its blessings to what became a majority of the population.

2. INDUSTRIALISM AND THE FAMILY

An exactly parallel controversy raged amongst contemporaries, though less amongst modern historians, about the effects of the factory system on the family. 'When women work in factories,' wrote Engels, 'the most important result is the dissolution of family ties.' Babies and infants were neglected, farmed out to baby-minders who fed them badly and unhygienically or not at all, and quietened them with Godfrey's cordial and other opiates, to their premature destruction. Older children at wages repudiated parental discipline and moral control, demanding to board at minimal charges or leaving home altogether, and the girls were deprived of the domestic education required to make a clean and comfortable home. Working wives had no time to clean and cook for and look after their families, and their husbands were driven out to seek comfort in the public house and gin shop. 'Sometimes, when the husband is unemployed, while his family are at work, the normal structure of the family is reversed', and the man deprived of masculinity and self-respect.[2]

Gaskell, from whom Engels derived most of his notions on the development of the family, declared:

a household thus constituted, in which all the decencies and moral observances of domestic life are constantly violated, reduces its

---

[1] E.g. the number of cotton factory operatives overtook that of the handloom weavers in the 1830's: operatives, 1832, 208,000, 1844–46, 340,000; handloom weavers, 1832, 227,000, 1840, 123,000—Smelser, *op cit.*, pp. 194, 207.

[2] Engels, *op. cit.*, pp. 160–5, 236.

inmates to a condition little elevated above that of the savage. Recklessness, improvidence, and unnecessary poverty, starvation, drunkenness, parental cruelty and carelessness, filial disobedience, neglect of conjugal rights, absence of maternal love, destruction of brotherly and sisterly affection, are too often its constituents, and the results of such a combination are moral degradation, ruin of domestic enjoyments, and social misery.[1]

Lord Ashley concluded similarly:

Domestic life and domestic discipline must soon be at an end; society will consist of individuals no longer grouped into families; so early is the separation of husband and wife, of parents and children.[2]

To these charges Richard Oastler, J. P. Kay (Sir James Kay-Shuttleworth), the Rev. G. S. Bull, Léon Faucher and many others added sexual immorality, both before and after marriage. A witness before the Factory Commission in 1833 declared that 'it would be no strain on his conscience to say that three-quarters of the girls between fourteen and twenty years of age were unchaste,' and another that 'some of the married women were as bad as the girls.'[3] Gaskell, as usual, went further:

The chastity of marriage is but little known among them: husband and wife sin equally, and a habitual indifference to sexual rights is generated which adds one other item to the destruction of domestic habits.[4]

On the other side the factory owners and operatives and their defenders just as vehemently denied the accusations, or claimed that factory workers were unfairly singled out for faults which were universal in the working class, if not indeed in English society as a whole. John Bright denied that factory work broke up the family or degraded the home, since most women left the factory on marriage or when their children arrived. Henry Ashworth, the model cotton employer of Egerton and Turton, declared that he employed no married women, nor did his married workmen wish their wives to work. Dr. Loudon wrote of

[1] P. Gaskell, *Artisans and Machinery: the Moral and Physical Condition of the Manufacturing Population* (1836), p. 89.

[2] E. Hodder, *Life and Work of 7th Earl of Shaftesbury* (1923), p. 234.

[3] *P.P.*, 1833, XX, *Commission on Employment of Children in Factories*, D1, pp. 648, 667.

[4] P. Gaskell, *The Manufacturing Population of England* (1833), p. 147.

Nottingham, 'It is rare to find a mother who has at home a couple of children alive, working in a mill. The duties of domestic life compel her to stay at home.' Dr. Mitchell told the Factory Commission in 1834 that the available evidence showed that 'very few women work in the factories after marriage.' Leonard Horner the Factory Inspector reported in 1844 that of the minority of women who remained at work over twenty-one, only 27·5 per cent were married.[1] Even Engels could not produce more than 10,721 married women out of 61,098 female operatives in 412 Manchester factories, only eighteen per cent of the total, or an average of twenty-six working wives per factory, while the number who supported unemployed husbands was 821, or only two per factory, and there was no evidence that even these few men were permanently unemployed.[2]

The operatives themselves vigorously denied that factory girls made bad wives. One witness before the 1833 Commission replied:

> I have heard it said so, but I know to the contrary, because I married three wives out of the factory, and I take that as proof. I am certain that as good wives may be had from the factories as from any other occupation.

Another claimed that his wife and nineteen-year old daughter, an operative since the age of nine, made all the clothes for the family excepting his coat. A woman witness declared, 'You think we can do nought but work in factories, neither brew, nor bake, nor sew.' Later observers pointed out that factory work was no worse than most occupations, including agricultural labour and domestic industry, in 'unfitting girls to look after a house or for domestic life'. G. W. Hastings told the Social Science Association in 1857 that the 'widespread feeling that the industrial employment of women is prejudicial to the domestic happiness of the working classes' was mistaken:

> The justice of this idea, however, is disproved out and out, by comparing the districts where the industrial employment of women prevails with those districts where it is scarcely known. Take for

[1] John Bright and Sir James Graham in House of Commons, 15 March and 3 May 1844; *Commission on . . . Factories, loc. cit.*, XX. E5, C3, 5, and *Supplementary Report*, Part I, XIX. 38; I. Pinchbeck, *Women Workers and the Industrial Revolution, 1780–1850* (1930), pp. 197–8.

[2] Engels, *op. cit.*, p. 165n.

example, colliery districts, mining districts, towns of metal manufacture, seaport towns without fisheries, and there you find that the squalor, the thriftlessness, the ignorance, and the dissipation are far more universal than in towns and districts devoted to the manufacture of cotton, linen, lace, and suchlike products. In the latter instances, woman has abundant work; in the former she has none. Slatternly habits, therefore, in the lower orders are not a consequence of the industrial employment of women, but constitute an evil to be dealt with on its own grounds.

There were, indeed, plenty of critics to declare that upper and middle-class wives were educated in every accomplishment except how to cook and manage a household, and consequently drove their husbands out to the comfort and gastronomic delights of their clubs.[1]

As for the supposed immorality of factory workers, Cooke Taylor pointed out:

Now, [licentious] conversation in a mill is all but physically impossible; the operatives are separated from each other by frames of working machinery which require their constant attendance, and the overseers would soon dismiss tenters who abandoned the care of their frames to indulge in idle talk.

Though it was difficult to obtain information about the town mills, in the country 'the returns show that seductions are of rare occurrence; that they usually take place in the evenings after work when they do occur; and that, in nine cases out of ten, the seducers do not belong to the same mill as the seduced.'[2] Others claimed for the factory workers what Gaskell and Engels had claimed for the pre-industrial agricultural and domestic workers, that they had their own moral code, and that sexual intercourse took place mainly between couples with a tacit understanding that marriage would precede the birth of a child.[3] Illegitimacy, it was pointed out, was less frequent in Lancashire

---

[1] *Commission on . . . Factories*, 1833, XXI. D1, pp. 707, 877, D2, p. 211; *P.P.*, 1867, XVI, *Children's Employment Commission, 6th Report*, p. 93; G. W. Hastings, 'Remarks on the Industrial Employment of Women', *Trans. N.A.P.S.S.*, 1857, pp. 536–7; 'English Cookery' and 'A Good Plain Cook', *Household Words*, 26 January 1856 and 27 April 1859, in M. Hewitt, *Wives and Mothers in Victorian Industry* (1958), pp. 74–5, 81–2.

[2] W. Cooke Taylor, *Factories and the Factory System* (1844), p. 42.

[3] Allen Clarke, *The Effects of the Factory System* (1913) p. 29; Hewitt, *op. cit.*, p. 55; cf. Gaskell, *Manufacturing Population*, p. 28, and Engels, *op. cit.*, p. 11.

than in Cumberland, Norfolk, and many other counties where factory work for women scarcely existed. An M.P. in the Ten Hours debate in 1844 countered Ashley's charges of profligacy and vice by inquiring:

> When the noble lord . . . asked for interference in the case of factory labourers, had he enquired into the case of the female nailers, employed at Sedgely and Birmingham, of whom his own Commissioners had said that 'morality was nothing among them; in fact, that they had no morals at all'? Look at the lacemaking by hand in Nottinghamshire and Bedfordshire, look at the maids of all work in London and elsewhere.

And the Factory Commission of 1833 reported:

> In regard to morals, we find that though statements and depositions of the different witnesses . . . are to a considerable degree conflicting, yet there is no evidence to show that vice and immorality are more prevalent amongst these people considered as a class than amongst other portions of the community in the same station.[1]

They could, indeed, have added 'or amongst other classes', as the available statistics of prostitutes, recruited chiefly from the working classes, predominantly from amongst domestic servants, but patronized mainly by their 'betters', show.[2]

Modern research has shown that the pictures drawn by the two sides to the controversy were both of them overdrawn and oversimplified.[3] On the one hand, factory workers were no better and no worse as wives and mothers, at least when they gave up work, than the vast majority of working-class women. Domestic workers worked just as long hours and had as little time to cook, bake and clean, and to train their daughters, as their factory sisters, and had the added disadvantage of trying to make a home in the midst of the dirt and disorder of a workshop. Agricultural labourers' wives, as spinning, lace-making, straw-

---

[1] *P.P.*, 1871, VII. 3605, *S.C. on . . . Protecting Infants put out to Nurse*, pp. 1907–8; Ward, M.P., in House of Commons, Hansard, 1844, LXXXIV. 1033; *Commission on . . . Factories*, 1833, XX. p. 36; Hewitt, *op. cit.*, pp. 51–3, 57.

[2] Cf. Mayhew, *op. cit.*, III. 33f.; Faucher, *op. cit.*, pp. 41–2; Steven Marcus, *The Other Victorians* (New York, 1966); Brian Harrison, 'Underneath the Victorians', *Victorian Studies*, 1967, X. 239f.

[3] Cf. Pinchbeck, *op. cit.*, and Hewitt, *op. cit.*, to which a large part of this section is indebted.

plaiting and other by-employments ceased to be available, were increasingly forced to work in the fields to make up the exiguous family income and, in the south of England especially, could not afford the fuel to bake bread or even to cook a hot meal more than once or twice a week. The wives of factory operatives at least had the benefit of larger earnings by their husbands and children, if not of their own, to rent and furnish somewhat better houses and buy the food and fuel for cooking and baking if they so wished. Northern factory workers alive today still remember their mothers, if not themselves, baking bread and brewing beer. 'Shop bread' in many mill towns and villages was looked on with contempt down to the First World War.[1] If, as Kay-Shuttleworth remarked in 1838, 'It is exceedingly lamentable that a very slender acquaintance with domestic economy is generally possessed among the poorer classes, not only in the manufacturing, but also in the agricultural districts,' this was neither new nor the product of industrialism. 'It is indeed difficult,' Ivy Pinchbeck has commented, 'to see how this could have been otherwise, or how the standard could ever have been much higher. . . . Not only factory women, but all women of the working classes were handicapped by ignorance and the lack of any proper system of instruction, and until some measure of education and training was placed within their reach, it was un-reasonable to expect any raising of the general standard of domestic skill or intelligent use of resources.'[2] In the long run better homes and housewifery were the product of higher living standards and education, and so directly and indirectly of industrialism.

On the other hand, the employment in factories or anywhere else outside the home—in workshops, mines, shops and markets, or in the fields—of the mothers of babies and young children undoubtedly had a deleterious effect on their health and survival. Margaret Hewitt has shown that whether the mothers of young children worked in the mills of Lancashire, the Stafford-shire potteries, or the fields of Lincolnshire the infant mortality rate was markedly higher in their families than in those of mothers who did not work. She has also shown that during the

[1] Cf. C. Stella Davies, *North Country Bred* (1963), p. 166; my aunt, Mrs. Ellen Fletcher of Burslem, brewed her own beer down to the Second World War.
[2] Pinchbeck, *op. cit.*, pp. 309–10.

Cotton Famine of the 1860's the infant mortality rate in those areas most affected actually fell, very nearly to the average for England and Wales in 1864, in spite of the poverty and privation of the operatives, thus demonstrating the importance to infant survival of maternal care and, in an epoch ignorant of hygienic and nutritious artificial feeding, of breast feeding. Day nursing by amateur baby-minders, 'infants' preservatives' containing narcotics to keep their charges quiet, and, probably most prejudicial of all to survival, the too early return of mothers to work after confinement, did raise infant mortality rates by as much as fifty per cent or more. A public agitation in the 1860's against this 'sacrifice of infants' and the ineffective Infant Life Protection Act of 1872 did not solve the problem, which had to wait for the child welfare clinics, health visitors and the National Health Insurance of the early twentieth century.[1]

On the still more difficult question of the effect of industrialism on the cohesion of the family Neil Smelser has shown in relation to the cotton industry that the transition was not a simple, once-for-all change from the integration of work, leisure, home-making and child-rearing in the domestic worker's household to the segregation of these activities within the factory operative's family, and between his home and the factory, the school, friendly society, club, and so on. It was a long-drawn-out, syncopated process, proceeding in different ways and at different speeds according to the labour requirements of the new machinery, the social structure of the different types of factory, and the period of their introduction.[2] In spinning, the introduction of the smaller, hand-operated 'cottage' jenny '*increased* the *gains* of the *females* in a family, and of the *family in general*,' and kept the family together.[3] Next, the introduction of the water-frame took some women and children into the mill, but in these early days of country mills and high earnings for domestic weavers these were more often the wives and children of labourers and the like, who usually worked away from home, and so the change was not felt to be revolutionary. Then the factory jenny and the mule took the husband and father into the mill, but it was the normal practice for these highly skilled

---

[1] Hewitt, *op. cit.*, chaps. viii–xi.   [2] Smelser, *op. cit.*, chaps. ix–xi.
[3] D. Ramsbotham, *Thoughts on the Use of Machines in the Cotton Manufacture* (Manchester, 1780), p. 15.

spinners to hire their own piecers and scavengers from amongst their own relatives, thus transferring the family functions of child-rearing and moral education to the factory.[1]

It was only with the longer mules and the self-acting mules of the 1820's, which required more piecers and scavengers than could normally be recruited from the adult spinner's own family—thus leading to the employment of children without their parents, often directly by the factory owner—that the 'break-up of the family' occurred, about half a century after the introduction of the first spinning mills. In factory weaving, on the other hand, it occurred from the beginning, with the general introduction of the power loom in the 1820's and 1830's, since most of the weavers were women and youths, with a few adult men to supervise them. The crisis in the factory worker's family, then, coincided with the factory reform agitation of the 1830's and 1840's, to which it contributed much of the emotional pressure and some of the more paradoxical of its tactical twists and changes. The general aim of the movement from the operatives' point of view was not only to restrict the hours of work for children and, through them, of all other factory workers, but to conserve the technological basis of the existing family structure within the factory system. That is why the spinners especially were incensed by the 1833 Act which restricted the children to eight hours but by allowing them to work in relays broke up the family during working time and required still larger numbers of 'outside' children. It also explains why the operatives, to the chagrin of their aristocratic and middle-class leaders, were willing to extend the hours of the children to twelve in 1835, reduced to ten in 1837, provided that all operatives worked the same hours. Only with the gradual withdrawal of young children from the factories and the development of formal education in the 1850's and 1860's to take over part of the traditional functions of the family did the operatives come to accept the changed role of the family in the new industrial society.[2]

The new role of the family, which was not of course confined to factory workers, was different from the old, but it was not necessarily worse or less important. The migration of work

---

[1] Smelser, *op. cit.*, pp. 184–5, 188–92.
[2] *Ibid.*, pp. 196–201, 239–41, 243–4, 298–303.

outside the home—where, indeed, it had long been for the large part of the population engaged in transport, mining, and agricultural and general labouring—left the family free to concentrate on its more fundamental functions of home-making, child-bearing and rearing, and the emotional satisfaction of affection and companionship. Marx, who was both more perceptive and less romantic than Engels, saw gain as well as loss in the emancipation of the family from the tyranny of the *paterfamilias*:

> However terrible, however repulsive, the break-up of the old family system within the organism of capitalist society may seem; none the less, large-scale industry, by assigning to women and to young persons and children of both sexes, a decisive role in the socially organized process of production, and a role which has to be fulfilled outside the home, is building the new economic foundation for a higher form of the family and of the relations between the sexes.[1]

The emancipation of women was in fact one of the most important and characteristic consequences of industrialism. It began first amongst the factory operatives. A member of the Handloom Weavers' Commission reported in 1840:

> One of the greatest advantages resulting from the progress of manufacturing industry, and from severe manual labour being superseded by machinery, is its tendency to raise the condition of women. Education only is wanting to place the women of Lancashire higher in the social scale than in any other part of the world. The great drawback to female happiness, among the middle and working classes, is, their complete dependence and almost helplessness in securing the means of subsistence. The want of other employment than the needle cheapens their labour, in ordinary cases, until it is almost valueless. In Lancashire profitable employment for females is abundant. . . . A young woman, prudent and careful, and living with her parents, from the age of sixteen to twenty-five, may, in that time, by factory employment, save £100 as a wedding portion. I believe it to be to the interest of the community that every young woman should have this in her power. She is not then driven into an early marriage by the necessity of seeking a home; and a consciousness of independence in being able to earn her own living, is favourable to the development of her best moral energies.[2]

[1] K. Marx, *Capital* (Everyman, 1942), I. 529.
[2] *P.P.*, 1840 (639), XXIV, Commission on . . . Handloom Weavers (W. E. Hickson's Report), p. 44.

The work itself was an agent of emancipation. The factory and workshop, a later observer pointed out,

> take the girl out of 'the home', cribbed, cabined, and confined as to space, light, air, ideas and companions, mould her in habits of punctuality, obedience, promptness, handiness, 'gumption', and sustained attention and effort, spur her on to work well, bring out her capacities for comradeship and social action, and train her in self-respect, self-reliance and courage.[1]

Even in the most fundamental and intimate aspect of emancipation, liberation from the debilitating, health-destroying, life-shortening burden of continuous child-bearing, factory operatives led the way. Margaret Hewitt has shown that textile workers, and not only those whose wives were working, were limiting their families as early as the 1850's, and bore on average fewer children than any social group except the professional and higher administrative.[2]

No doubt the example set by women industrial workers played some part in the emancipation movement amongst middle-class women which, in spite of individual advocates from the anonymous 'Sophia' in 1739 through Mary Wollstonecroft in 1792 and William Thompson in 1825 to Harriet Taylor in 1851, can scarcely be said to have begun until the 1850's.[3] But the connection between industrialism and the emancipation of 'ladies' was more direct than that. While the Industrial Revolution was providing more work for working-class women both inside and outside the home, it was taking it away from their well-to-do sisters. Just as domestic industry was a partnership in which the wife assisted the husband, so too most businesses, professions and trades in the old society were partnerships in which the husband and wife worked as a team. Merchants' and shopkeepers' wives often managed the warehouse or shop, kept accounts, and supervised the apprentices. Doctors' and lawyers' wives not only acted as receptionists and clerks but would turn their hand to dispensing drugs or inditing

---

[1] Caroline Foley, in *Ec.J.*, 1894, IV. 187; Pinchbeck, *op. cit.*, p. 308.

[2] Hewitt, *op. cit.*, p. 87.

[3] 'Sophia', *Woman not Inferior to Man* (1739); Mary Wollstonecraft, *A Vindication of the Rights of Women* (1794); W. Thompson, *The Appeal of One Half of the Human Race, Women, against the Pretensions of the Other Half, Men* (1825); Harriet Taylor, 'Enfranchisement of Women', *West. Rev.*, 1851, LV. 289–311.

documents. Farmers' wives took charge of the dairy and the smaller animals, as well as catering perhaps for a house-full of farm servants. Widows were usually capable of carrying on the business, with or without a new partner selected from amongst the mature apprentices.[1]

Rising living standards and increased specialization, however, undermined these customs. Servants increasingly took over the household chores, and clerks and assistants those of the business, the boarding of apprentices and farm servants declined, social emulation of the gentry and aristocracy increasingly demanded that wives and daughters should not only wear fine clothes and practise 'accomplishments' such as music, drawing and decorative needlework but should patently have the leisure to enjoy them. The result was the rise of the 'perfect lady', the Victorian ideal of the completely leisured, completely ornamental, completely helpless and dependent middle-class wife or daughter, with no function besides inspiring admiration and bearing children. Josephine Butler's aunt, Margaretta Grey, wrote in her diary in 1853:

It appears to me that, with an increase of wealth unequally distributed, and a pressure of population, there has sprung up among us a spurious refinement, that cramps the energy and circumscribes the usefulness of women in the upper classes of society. A lady, to be such, must be a mere lady, and nothing else. She must not work for profit, or engage in any occupation that money can command, lest she invade the rights of the working classes, who live by their labour. Men in want of employment have pressed their way into nearly all the shopping and retail businesses that in my early years were managed, in whole or in part by women. The conventional barrier that pronounces it ungenteel to be behind a counter, or serving the public in any mercantile capacity, is greatly extended. The same in household economy. Servants must be up to their several offices, which is very well; but ladies, dismissed from the dairy, the confectionery, the store-room, the still-room, the poultry-yard, the kitchen-garden, and the orchard, have hardly yet found themselves a sphere equally useful and important in the pursuits of trade and art to which to apply their too abundant leisure.[2]

It was against this life of genteel uselessness that ladies of

---

[1] Cf. Pinchbeck, *op. cit.*, chap. xii.

[2] Josephine Butler, *Memoir of John Grey of Dilston* (1874), p. 228n

character and determination came to rebel. Rebellion did not always or at first take the form of aggressive championship of women's rights. More often it led to charitable works as with Baroness Burdett-Coutts, didactic authorship as with Harriet Martineau, or selfless service to a humane cause as with Florence Nightingale—activities which might well exclude an interest in women's emancipation: ' I am brutally indifferent to the wrongs or the rights of my sex,' Nightingale wrote to Martineau in 1858.[1] But sooner or later the frustrated energies of growing numbers of able and intelligent women with nothing to do but brood on their wrongs were bound to burst out in a concerted movement of protest. That movement, as distinct from individual protests like that of Mrs. Caroline Norton which made the first breach in the monstrous regiment of husbands with the Infants' Custody Act of 1839, began in 1855, when Barbara Bodichon got the support of the Law Amendment Society and collected 26,000 signatures for a Married Women's Property Bill.[2] The Bill was not passed, but by way of countering it Parliament did pass the Matrimonial Causes Act of 1857, which set up the Divorce Court and, though unequal in its treatment of husbands and wives, laid the foundations of modern family law. Though divorce on equal terms did not come until 1923, the essential equality of women within marriage was conferred by a series of Acts culminating in the Married Women's Property Acts of 1870, 1882, and 1893.[3] In this most important respect it was the Industrial Revolution which, if only indirectly, brought about the emancipation of women.

3. URBANIZATION AND SOCIETY

Contemporaries were just as divided about the effects of industrialism on town life as on living standards and the family.[4] The strictures of such anti-urban pessimists as Cobbett and Ruskin apart, even optimistic supporters of industrialism like Cooke

[1] C. Woodham-Smith, *Florence Nightingale* (1952), p. 256.

[2] Josephine Kamm, *Rapiers and Battleaxes: The Women's Movement and its Aftermath* (1966), pp. 23–8, 89–91.

[3] Erna Reiss, *The Rights and Duties of Englishwomen* (Manchester, 1934), chaps. ii, iii, v; P. M. Bromley, *Family Law* (1957), pp. 377–9.

[4] Cf. Asa Briggs, *Victorian Cities* (1963), to which much of this section is indebted.

Taylor and Joseph Fletcher, the school inspector and moral statistician, were disturbed by the social problems of the rapidly growing towns.[1] The latter, for example, thought that the concentration in large towns of 'the masses employed in mining and manufacturing pursuits' was responsible for most of the social problems of the age:

> Here, brought into close neighbourhood, and estranged from the influence of superior example, they are subject to temptations, hazards, and incitements far beyond those which approach the rural cottage; ignorant and largely depraved, they are likewise capable of combination; and combined, they form bodies little prepared to stoop to the exigencies of a reeling alternation of prosperity and adversity; to say nothing of all the evils which improvidence and heathenism pour out upon themselves.

Industrialism, with 'its smoke, its dirt, its bustle, its deformation of the face of nature, and the independent rudeness of its millions,' its 'neglected sanatory police and bad domestic arrangements', 'the greatest amount of ignorance', and 'lost bonds of neighbourhood', had made the towns 'purely places in which to work and make money, not to be at rest and enjoy it,' and demanded a 'higher moral character among the people' which had not been forthcoming.[2] Similar views were expressed by horrified foreign visitors, from de Tocqueville, Faucher and Engels to Hippolyte Taine and, pictorially, Gustave Dore.[3]

On the other side, though admittedly rather later, after the first crushing wave of industrial urban growth had passed, voices were heard extolling town life as the source and centre of civilization and progress. Amongst the first of these was Robert Vaughan, the Unitarian prophet of 'the age of great cities', who looked to them to save the nation from moral and spiritual degeneracy and, one suspects, from aristocracy and

[1] Cf. W. Cobbett, *Rural Rides* (Everyman, 1948), I. 43, 65–6, 226, II. 9, 18, 55–6, 80, 128, 226, amongst many other anti-urban references to 'wens'; J. Ruskin, *The Seven Lamps of Architecture* (1849), p. 359; W. Cooke Taylor, *Notes of a Tour in the Manufacturing Districts of Lancashire* (1842), pp. 12–13; J. Fletcher, 'Moral and Educational Statistics of England and Wales', *Stat. J.*, 1847, X. 193f.

[2] Fletcher, *loc. cit.*, X. 198–200, 214.

[3] A. de Tocqueville, *Journeys to England and Ireland* (ed. J. P. Mayer, 1958), pp. 104–8; Faucher, *op. cit.*, p. 19; Engels, *op. cit.*, chap. iii; H. Taine, *Notes on England* (trans. W. F. Rae, 1874), pp. 273–5, 283–5; G. Doré and W. B. Jerrold, *London* (1872).

what Marx called 'the idiocy of rural life', though even Vaughan compared the crowded capital to a large and intricate forest where criminals and others seeking anonymity could find 'the places of darkness and concealment convenient for them.'[1] His optimism found, especially in the less fearful and conflict-ridden mid-Victorian age, increasing echoes amongst men like himself, born and bred in the cities with the same middle-class, Nonconformist dislike and suspicion of the rural-based, anti-urban aristocracy, men such as Edward Baines, editor of the *Leeds Mercury*, Joseph Chamberlain of Birmingham, and Joseph Cowen, owner of the *Newcastle Chronicle*, who wrote in 1877:

> The gathering of men into crowds has some drawbacks, yet the concentration of citizens, like the concentration of soldiers, is a source of strength. The ancient boroughs were the arks and shrines of freedom. Today, behind the dull roar of our machinery, the bellowing of our blast furnaces, the panting of the locomotives and the gentle ticking of the electric telegraph . . . we can hear the songs of children who are fed and clad, and the acclaim of a world made free by these agencies. When people declaim in doleful numbers against the noise and dirt of the busy centres of population, they should remember the liberty we enjoy as a consequence of the mental activity and enterprise which have been generated by the contact of mind with mind brought together in great towns.[2]

Both sides were right of course, in their different ways. The enormously rapid growth not only of the new industrial but of most towns and cities during the Industrial Revolution did create new social problems and aggravate and expand the scale of old ones. Amongst the more important of these was the new problem of insecurity created by fluctuations in employment amongst concentrated masses of wage-earners without natural protectors to turn to in distress, to add to the old problem of the chronically depressed and abandoned urban poor. Closely connected with both was the vast increase in crime and prostitution which occurred in the towns in the first half of the nineteenth century, and swelled to a new peak in every economic slump. The home of these was in the slums, with their squalid living conditions, overflowing privies, cess-pools and drains, foul water supplies, and excessive disease and death rates for the

[1] R. Vaughan, *The Age of Great Cities* (1843), in Briggs, *Victorian Cities*, p. 61.
[2] *Ibid.*, pp. 64–5.

people forced to inhabit them. Finally, and connected with all these, there was the increasing segregation of urban society into different streets, districts or suburbs according to income and status, which broke it down into isolated and mutually hostile classes.

On the other side it can be said that only the new or greatly enlarged and, ultimately, far more efficiently organized communities of industrial society were capable of solving the moral and physical problems of the towns and of providing the conditions of a civilized social life for a majority of the population. It is no accident that the critics of urbanization were in the ascendant in the first half of the nineteenth century and its protagonists in the second. The problems naturally came first, the solutions only in response to them. In this very brief and inadequate sketch of them as they affected the structure of society we must try to keep a balance between the undoubted enormity of the first and the equally impressive achievement of the second.

We must also remember that neither the problems nor the need for reform were confined to the new industrial towns. Some of the affected towns were old communities of traditional social structure and few or no factories, such as Bristol, Exeter or Edinburgh, while some industrial ones were thought by contemporaries to be superior to them both socially and morally. Birmingham, for example, was a by-word amongst politicians from Attwood through Cobden to Chamberlain for harmony between its classes, while it was also the first town to get a favourable mention in Chadwick's *Sanitary Report* of 1842:

> This town, it will be seen, is distinguished apparently by an immunity from fever, and the general health of the population is high, although the occupations are such as are elsewhere deemed prejudicial to health.[1]

As for Manchester, the 'shock city of the age' as Asa Briggs has so rightly called it,[2] Faucher, who was as uncompromising a critic of it as Engels, wrote in 1844:

> The centres of industrialism are seats of corruption, in which the population enjoy an atmosphere neither more salubrious nor moral,

[1] Chadwick, *op. cit.*, p. 89.
[2] Briggs, *Victorian Cities*, p. 92.

than in those large towns, which are formed by political institutions, or by the demands of commerce. Considered from this point of view, *Manchester appears almost on a level with London or Liverpool.*[1]

Indeed, as Faucher's translator pointed out, Manchester at that very time was giving a lead to the rest of the country, not only towards 'the attainment of entire FREEDOM OF TRADE', but towards 'a comprehensive system of SANATORY REGULATION to secure healthfulness, cleanliness, and order in our vast urban population', and 'a comprehensive and liberal system of SECULAR EDUCATION, combining moral training with intellectual instruction, and open to all classes, without distinction of sect or party.'[2] If the new industrial cities differed in anything from the old commercial ones it was in the means, and still more in the will, to reform.

The first problem of the new and greatly enlarged towns to attract attention was the periodical problem of distress, Fletcher's 'reeling alternation of prosperity and adversity', the increasingly familiar problem of economic depression and cyclical unemployment. Slumps were no new phenomenon, and whether the more acutely observed and keenly analysed depressions of the early nineteenth century were in fact worse in their effects on employment and earnings than those of the eighteenth century we cannot tell. But in the much larger towns of the new age distress was more concentrated, more visible, more vociferous, and, since it affected much larger numbers of the potentially disaffected, more feared as the detonator of revolutionary explosions than in the old society, where the bread riot was less likely to trigger off political discontent. In the first half of the nineteenth century every major slump produced its wave of political protest, every major political crisis coincided with a period of marked distress. The post-war depression of 1815–20 triggered off the first mass movement for Parliamentary Reform. The Reform crisis of 1830–32 coincided with the downswing of a major depression. The birth, climax and dying throes of Chartism in 1837, 1842 and 1848 all occurred in the troughs of slumps, the climax in the worst depression of the nineteenth century. The 'slump explosion', as it has

[1] Faucher, *op. cit.*, pp. 90–1 (my italics).
[2] 'A Member of the Manchester Athenaeum', translator's preface to *ibid.*, pp. xiii–xiv.

been called, was aggravated by a hangover from the old society, the tendency of economic depression to coincide with bad harvests and therefore with high food prices, which doubled the provocation of the distressed workers—a tendency which the repeal of the Corn Laws and the access by railway and steamship to world-wide supplies was to diminish if not to cure.[1]

Distress therefore naturally commanded the attention of politicians and others, though in the climate of thought increasingly dominated by the classical economists and their denial of the possibility of overproduction or underconsumption there was little that could be done about it beyond the humanitarian charity frowned on by Malthus. Among the first to study the problem objectively were those pioneers of empirical sociology, the Statistical Societies, the first of which was set up in Manchester in 1833 'to assist in promoting the progress of social improvements in the manufacturing population by which they are surrounded.'[2] In May and June, 1834, in the aftermath of the 1832 depression, the Society made the first house-to-house social survey on record, under the supervision of Dr. J. P. Kay, in two of the central districts of the town, covering 4,102 familes. The method was taken up by other newly-founded Societies, as for example by the Glasgow and Bristol Societies in the slump of 1837.[3] The general burden of these and other investigations was the desperate plight of thousands of families whenever trade was afflicted by depression. One investigation by a Committee of Relief in Manchester in 1840 found 2,000 families living on an average of 5s. 3¼d. a week, or 1s. 2¼d. per head; another in 1842 discovered a further 2,000 families earning 6s. 3¼d. a week, or 1s. 6½d. per head, and living, as their 22,417 pawn tickets worth £2,781 revealed, chiefly on credit.[4]

[1] E. J. Hobsbawm, 'Economic Fluctuations and Some Social Movements since 1800', *Ec.H.R.*, 1952, V.5; W. W. Rostow, *British Economy of the 19th Century* (Oxford, 1961), chap. v.

[2] T. S. Ashton, *Economic and Social Investigations in Manchester, 1833–1933* (1933), p. 13.

[3] J. P. Kay [-Shuttleworth], *The Moral and Physical Condition of the Working Classes employed in the Cotton Manufacture in Manchester* (1832); 'An Account of an Enquiry into the State of 275 Poor Families in the City of Bristol' by the Statistical Society of Bristol, and C. R. Baird, Secretary of the Glasgow Statistical Society, 'Observations upon the Poorest Class of Operatives in Glasgow in 1837', *Stat. J.*, 1838, I. 86–8, 167–72.

[4] Faucher, *op. cit.*, p. 147n.

In the latter year no less than 60 per cent of the cotton mill operatives in Bolton were unemployed, 36 per cent of the iron-workers, and from 66 to 87 per cent of the building craftsmen—figures which make those of the worst slump of the twentieth century, 1929–33, look moderate.[1]

What such slumps meant in terms of privation and suffering in a population which in prosperity could save little against bad times can only be guessed. Distress committees, soup kitchens and doles scarcely touched the surface of the problem. As an Assistant Commissioner on the Handloom Weavers reported in 1840,

> Few people take the trouble to think of the small proportion which the largest sums raised by the benevolent for such purposes bear to a few weeks' wages. To say that the 10,000 weavers of the district around Leeds were out of employment three months in 1837 is, I am convinced, within the truth; as an average, calling wages only 10s. per week, we have a sum of £65,000, of which the weaving population were deprived. Now, I venture to assert, that from all extraneous sources not a tithe of that sum was distributed among the weavers. We often felicitate ourselves on the large sums raised to relieve the distresses of particular classes during periods of depression; but we are too apt to overlook the extent of the evil to be remedied. No relief, in fact, can make up for a short period of stagnation.[2]

Thus, in spite of the benevolence of the employing classes, it was not surprising that slumps of this magnitude brought to a head the explosive social tensions which, as we shall see in the next chapter, were building up from other causes. In the Plug riots of July and August, 1842, according to Faucher,

> 1,000 men armed with sticks and bludgeons entered Manchester, stopped the engines, compelled the workmen to turn out and join their body, and declared a general suspension of labour until their grievances were redressed. The rioters remained masters of the town for several days, and it was found necessary to recall some troops from Ireland to dislodge them from their position.

But, Faucher went on,

> Happily for England, Industry soon recovers from the convulsions

---

[1] Hobsbawm, 'British Standard of Living, 1790–1850', *Ec.H.R.*, 1957, X. 53.

[2] *P.P.*, 1840, III, *Commission on . . . Handloom Weavers, Reports from Assistant Commissioners*, p. 537.

which from time to time afflict her. That which would be for other nations a revolution, is to her only a shock.[1]

Cyclical unemployment was only one, and not the most important, of the factors making for class conflict in new and growing towns.

What the better-paid industrial workers suffered only temporarily and periodically, large and absolutely if not relatively increasing numbers of towndwellers suffered permanently and without respite. At the base of society in all great cities, especially London, there had always been a substratum of casual labourers, street folk, beggars, petty criminals and prostitutes, familiar enough in the eighteenth century from such diverse sources as *Moll Flanders*, *The Beggars' Opera*, Hogarth's prints, the *Newgate Calendar*, and the exploits of Jonathan Wild and other master criminals. In the nineteenth century the disproportionate growth of the larger towns created many new cities on a par with eighteenth-century London, where poverty, degradation and immorality could breed out of sight and the criminal, wastrel, absconder and 'fallen woman' lose themselves in the anonymity of the urban jungle. In London itself the problem of this underworld of crime and desperate poverty attracted the attention of such sharp-eyed observers as Henry Mayhew, whose aim was not just to describe and moralize, but to 'cause those who are in "high places" and those of whom much is expected, to bestir themselves to improve the condition of a class of people whose misery, ignorance and vice, amidst all the immense wealth and great knowledge of "the first city of the world" is, to say the very least, a national disgrace to us.'[2]

Given the common belief of those in high places that poverty was a moral and individual rather than a social and economic problem, however, what most alarmed contemporaries about the condition of the great towns was the vast increase in crime and prostitution. Between 1805 when comprehensive records first began and 1848 the numbers committed for trial for indictable offences in England and Wales increased more than six-fold, from 4,605 to 30,349, and the numbers convicted more than eight-fold, from 2,783 to 22,900.[3] That this increase was

---

[1] Faucher, *op. cit.*, pp. 150–1.   [2] Mayhew, *op. cit.*, I. iv.
[3] Porter, *op. cit.*, (1851), p. 635.

real and not the statistical effect of the activity of the new police
has been shown recently by Dr. K. K. Macnab, who has demonstrated that most of the increase came before the new police
were appointed, in London in 1829 and in the municipal
boroughs from 1839, that most of the arrests and committals
were at the instance of the public and not of the police, and that
the unpopularity and inefficiency of the police plus the fact that
their orders were to prevent crime by their vigilance rather than
to apprehend criminals and that when they prosecuted they had
to do so at their own, individual risk and expense, all tended to
depress rather than inflate the statistics. Moreover, these figures
are only the tip of the iceberg, since committals were only a
small minority, under ten per cent in London, of those taken into
custody, the rest either being dealt with by the magistrates or
released without being charged. He has also shown that, within
this huge secular increase, the amount of crime varied inversely
with economic prosperity, rising steeply during slumps, with
major peaks in 1817–19, 1842 and 1848, and falling back less
rapidly and not so far in the ensuing recovery, and that in these
waves upon the tide the committals for industrial and political
offences played a statistically insignificant part.[1] The vast bulk,
74–82 per cent, were offences against property without violence,
that is, crimes with a purely economic motive.[2]

Prostitution rather than crime is the traditional resort of
women in desperate straits, and it is significant that the number
of women committed for trial increased much less than that of
men.[3] Contemporaries were convinced that prostitution was a
vast and widespread evil—'*the* social problem', as many of them
called it—and that it was rapidly increasing, but the statistics
are naturally fugitive and unreliable. One estimate in 1844 put
the known prostitutes in Manchester at 750, compared with
15,000 in London, 2,000 in Liverpool, 300 in Hull, and 250 in
Paisley, and expected the total, including 'a large number
of female workers who eke out a living' by part-time prostitution, to be double those numbers.[4] Estimates for London in the
1840's varied from 7,000 to 80,000, with the consensus of

[1] K. K. Macnab, 'Aspects of the History of Crime in England and Wales between
1805 and 1860', D. Phil. dissertation, University of Sussex, 1965.

[2] Porter, *op. cit.*, (1851), p. 646.   [3] *Ibid.*, p. 635.

[4] Faucher, *op. cit.*, p. 42n.

opinion nearer to the latter according to Mayhew, who also gave the only reliable figure, of 41,954 'disorderly prostitutes' arrested in the eleven years from 1850 to 1860.[1] Informed observers like Faucher's translator thought that prostitution increased with commercial distress in exactly the same way as crime, and owing to similar economic causes. Others, like Joseph Fletcher, put it down to the decay of morality and paternal social control in the urban slums.[2]

Whatever the causes of the increase in crime and prostitution, public order and outward moral conduct were, paradoxically, improving. Bryan Donkin and other London engineers all bore witness before the Select Committee on Artizans and Machinery in 1824 on the improved behaviour of the working men.[3] Faucher in 1844 reported that 'public order in Manchester has advanced. Since the establishment of the new police the streets have been more tranquil, if not more safe.'[4] Porter in 1850 noted that 'however prevalent offences may now be against property, we enjoy a far greater degree of protection from personal violence than our forefathers,' and recalled the highway robberies and unsafe streets of half a century earlier. The criminal statistics confirm the decline in offences against the person, at least from 1834 when classification begins.[5] In so far as this paradox forms part of the 'moral revolution' which was transforming the conduct of Englishmen towards everything and everyone from animals and cruel sports to women, children lunatics, and convicts, and, indeed, towards each other, we shall be exploring its significance for society in Chapter VII. Meanwhile, the divergence in behaviour between the comparatively few criminals and prostitutes and the bulk of the respectable working class was part of a larger divergence between the ways of life of different sections of the urban population which presented itself to contemporaries in the shape of the problem of the slums.

As well as a political, moral and criminal problem, the urban slums were felt as a physical threat to the health not only of

---

[1] R. Vaughan, *The Age of Great Cities* (1843), p. 227; Mayhew, *op. cit.*, (1862 ed.). IV. 215, 262-3.

[2] Faucher, *op. cit.*, p. 43n.; Fletcher, *loc. cit.*, pp. 212–14.

[3] *P.P.*, 1824, V, *S.C. on Artizans and Machinery*, pp. 37-8.

[4] Faucher, *op. cit.*, pp. 33–4.

[5] Porter, *op. cit.*, (1851), pp. 634, 646.

their inhabitants but of their well-to-do fellow-townsmen and of the nation as a whole. This was most obviously so at times when epidemics struck, particularly of diseases which were no respecters of persons, like cholera, which galvanized the local and central authorities into frantic action whenever it appeared, as in 1831–32, 1848–49, 1854 and 1866–67. In between such epidemics, however, the threat was apt to be overlooked, except by those valiant Poor Law doctors who spent their lives fighting the more lethal endemic diseases like the ubiquitous 'fever'— typhus, the flea-borne 'poor man's disease'—and tuberculosis, which probably accounted in the early nineteenth century for a third of all deaths.[1] Through the doctors, notably Southwood Smith, Kay and Arnott, the extent of disease became known to the Poor Law authorities, whose concern was to save as much as possible of the vast expense attributable to sickness and to the death of breadwinners in an age when widows and orphans were the largest single category in receipt of poor relief.[2]

The role of Edwin Chadwick, Secretary to the Poor Law Commission, in thrusting the problem of the slums upon the attention of Parliament and the public is the classic example of that process of reform through the pressure of unpleasant facts revealed by government officials which we shall have occasion to pursue further in Chapter VIII. His great *Report on the Sanitary Condition of the Labouring Population of Great Britain* of 1842, although based on the false 'miasmatic' theory of the causation of disease, for that very reason focused public attention on the foul privies, cess pools, drains, sewers and polluted water supplies of the slums from whence the poisonous miasma arose. From the point of view of social structure the most striking thing in the Report was its lengthy demonstration of the differential chances of life as between the different classes and as between town and country. This was most graphically displayed in the following table, quoted from a report of the Manchester Statistical Society for 1837:[3]

---

[1] Flinn, Introduction to Chadwick, *op. cit.*, p. 11.

[2] *Ibid.*, p. 71; cf. Rose, *op. cit.*, *Ec.H.R.*, 1966, XIX. 616.

[3] Chadwick, *op. cit.*, p. 223; Chadwick's correspondent notes that the figures may be affected, though not materially, by migration from Rutland and by the larger proportion of children in Manchester.

	Average Age of Death	
	In Manchester Years	In Rutland Years
Professional persons and gentry, and their families	38	52
Tradesmen and their families (in Rutland, including farmers and graziers)	20	41
Mechanics, labourers and their families	17	38

The astounding fact that the comparatively well-paid workers of Manchester had an expectation of life less than half that of their well-to-do neighbours, who in turn had one no greater than the low-paid agricultural labourers of Rutland, was sufficient proof that conditions in the towns were dangerous to the health of all, and conditions in the urban slums lethal.

Chadwick's *Report* galvanized some of the municipal authorities, such as Leicester, St. Helens and Glasgow, into initiating sanitary reforms and Peel's government into appointing the Health of Towns Commission of 1843, which Chadwick attended, largely wrote its first Report and influenced the second. These, along with the public meetings and publications of the Health of Towns Association, 1844, and the visitation of the cholera in 1848, led to the first Public Health Act, 1848, the 'tentative and uncertain start' to all subsequent government action in cleaning up the slums.[1] It was not in fact the start of urban public health measures, which began with the local improvement commissioners of the eighteenth century, those bodies of 'trustees appointed under sundry Acts of Parliament for paving, lighting, cleaning, watching, regulating, supplying with water, and improving' the towns, 108 of whom were enumerated amongst the 178 boroughs of the Municipal Corporation Act of 1835, though they rarely carried their improvements beyond the central thoroughfares.[2] Nor was it the beginning of the modern wave of sanitary reform, which began with the local boards of health of 1831–34, while local acts such as the Manchester Improvement Act of 1845 went far beyond the 1848 Act in their provisions.[3] Nevertheless, it took two further Royal Commissions,

[1] Flinn, *ibid.*, pp. 66n., 73.
[2] Cf. J. Fletcher, 'Statistics of the Municipal Institutions of the English Towns', *Stat.J.*, 1842, V. 104.
[3] Cf. Fraser Brockington, 'Public Health at the Privy Council, 1831–34',

and three more major Acts, in 1866, 1872 and 1875, before there was any substantial reduction of urban death rates, and still longer before the problem of the slums began to recede.[1]

What the slums represented above all was the segregation of the various strata of urban society into different areas, with different rents and therefore different standards of accommodation and amenity. It was not in fact a new phenomenon, the product of industrialism, smoky factory chimneys, or suburban transport. In the larger eighteenth-century towns the merchants, shopkeepers and professional men had tended to live in the principal streets and thoroughfares, the artisans and labourers in the meaner streets behind them. But with the increasing size of towns and the increasing use of coal for domestic fires those who could afford to moved to the green margins of the towns. As early as 1795 Aikin noticed the middle-class flight to the suburbs of Manchester, while Aston in 1804 observed that 'many persons whose business is carried on in the town reside some little way from it that the pure breath of heaven may blow freely upon them.'[2] Nor were the classes necessarily any less segregated for living cheek by jowl, as they continued to do in many towns down to the mid-nineteenth century and beyond. Chadwick reported in 1842:

> When Dr. Arnott with myself and others were examining the abodes of the poorest classes in Glasgow and Edinburgh, we were regarded with astonishment; and it was frequently declared by the inmates, that they had never for many years witnessed the approach or the presence of persons of that condition near them. We have found that the inhabitants of the front houses in many of the main streets of those towns and of the metropolis, have never entered the adjoining courts, or seen the interior of any of the tenements, situate at the backs of their own houses, in which their own workpeople or dependents reside.[3]

[1] Cf. W. Ashworth, *The Genesis of Modern British Town Planning* (1954), esp. chap. iii.

[2] J. Aikin, *A Description of the Country from Thirty to Forty Miles around Manchester* (1795), pp. 205–6; J. Aston, quoted in H. B. Rodgers, 'The Suburban Growth of Victorian Manchester', *Journal of Manchester Geographical Society*, 1962, LVIII. 2.   [3] Chadwick, *op. cit.*, p. 397.

Journal of Medical History, 1961, XVI. 61–85; Faucher, *op. cit.*, translator's preface, pp. xii–xiii; N. J. Frangopulo, *Rich Inheritance: a Guide to the History of Manchester* (1962), pp. 56–7; A. Redford, *History of Local Government in Manchester* (1939–40), II, chap. xix.

The social gulf between the classes, already so deep when they lived side by side, was inevitably widened by the explosive urban growth which accompanied the migration of the factories to the towns with the general spread of steam power in the 1820's and 1830's. By 1844 Faucher noted in central Manchester

> the absence of the higher classes, who, like the aristocracy, do not live in the town. The town, strictly speaking (as Dr. Kay Shuttleworth has remarked before me), is only inhabited by shopkeepers and operatives; the merchants and manufacturers have detached villas situated in the midst of gardens and parks in the country. This mode of existence . . . excludes social intercourse, and leads to a local absenteeism. And thus at the very moment when the engines are stopped, and the counting-houses closed, everything which was the thought—the authority—the impulsive force—the moral order of this immense industrial combination, flies from the town, and disappears in an instant. The rich man spreads his couch amidst the beauties of the surrounding country and abandons the town to the operatives, publicans, mendicants, thieves, and prostitutes, merely taking the precaution to leave behind him a police force, whose duty it is to preserve some little of material order in this pellmell of society.[1]

Manchester was the extreme case—'There is no town in the world,' a contemporary remarked in 1842, 'where the distance between the rich and the poor is so great, or the barrier between them so difficult to be crossed'[2]—but what was true of Manchester became true in time of all the great cities. In Leeds a Unitarian Domestic Missionary remarked in 1856 the social frontier marked by the river:

> The large and densely populated district south of the river is in many respects unfavourably situated. It is the district in which a large proportion of the wealth of the town is created, and where the hands which create it live; but where none of the employers, the more educated and refined reside, who can avoid it; hence it is deprived of all those civilizing influences and mutually respectful feelings which are exercised when rich and poor—employer and employed—know more of each other than they possibly can under present arrangements.[3]

[1] Faucher, *op. cit.*, pp. 26–7.
[2] Rev. R. Parkinson, quoted by Briggs, *Victorian Cities*, p. 110.
[3] Harrison, *Learning and Living*, pp. 8–9.

In the same year the Rev. John Richardson wrote of the East and West Ends of London:

> There was little communication or sympathy between the respective classes by which the two ends of London were occupied. They differed in external appearance; in the fashion of their clothes, in their pursuits, in their pleasures, and in their toils; and on the occasions when they came into contact, which were but seldom, surveyed each other with much the same curiosity and astonishment as would nowadays be exhibited by a native of this town at the appearance of an Esquimaux in Hyde-park or Regent-Street.[1]

Even Birmingham, renowned for the 'harmonious co-operation' of the middle and working classes, was not immune from the trend, particularly after the factories arrived in the late 1840's, and it was the Rev. R. W. Dale himself, the leader of Birmingham middle-class opinion in the 1860's and 1870's, who, concerned like other Nonconformists at the gulf between the churches and the working men, spoke of 'the wider separation of classes in great towns—a separation produced by the increase of commercial wealth.'[2]

The geographical segregation of the classes, and the mutual ignorance, suspicion and misunderstanding which went with it, were a powerful factor in the rise of class conflicts in the early nineteenth century. 'Class stands opposed to class,' wrote James Hole, the Leeds disciple of Robert Owen, 'and so accustomed have men become to pursue their own isolated interests apart from and regardless of that of others, that it has become an acknowledged maxim, that when a man pursues his own interest alone he is most benefiting society—a maxim . . . which would justify every crime and folly.' But the causes of class conflict went far deeper than the mere growth of towns and the physical separation of the classes, as Hole pointed out:

> the progress of population, the increased power of multiplying wealth, the clearer perception of the rights and duties of human beings, have introduced new *problems* into the art of governing society. The result of these causes, to the mass of the people, has been, gradually to isolate them from that intimate relationship with their employers which prevailed in former times. The principle of

[1] Rev. J. Richardson, *Recollections, Political, Literary, Dramatic, and Miscellaneous of the Last Half-Century* (1856), I. 3.
[2] Briggs, *Victorian Cities*, p. 202; cf. Inglis, *op. cit.*, chap. ii.

supply and demand has been extended from *commodities* to *men*. These have obtained thereby more liberty, but less bread. They find, that in parting with the thraldom of Feudalism, they have taken on that of Capital; that slavery has ceased in name but survived in fact. . . .[1]

The alienation between employers and employed, and between both and the landed aristocracy, was inherent in industrialism. The growth of towns and their segregation of the classes explain where but not why it happened. For that more fundamental explanation we must turn back to the origins of class, in the old society which gave it birth.

[1] J. Hole, *Lectures on Social Science and the Organization of Labour* (1851), quoted in Briggs, *Victorian Cities*, p. 140.

VI

<><><><><><><><><><><><><><><><><><><><><><><><>

The Birth of Class

<><><><><><><><><><><><><><><><><><><><><><><><>

T H E most profound and far-reaching consequence of the Industrial Revolution was the birth of a new class society. A class
society is characterized by class feeling, that is, by the existence
of vertical antagonism between a small number of horizontal
groups, each based on a common source of income.[1] Such vertical
antagonism and the horizontal solidarity of each class transcend
the common source of income which supports them. 'The
essence of social class,' T. H. Marshall has pointed out, 'is the
way a man is treated by his fellows (and, reciprocally, the way he
treats them), not the qualities or the possessions which cause
that treatment.'[2] This is precisely because the qualities and the
possessions which cause the treatment may equally support, as
in the old society which was to give birth to class, a totally different social structure, characterized by horizontal antagonism
between vertical interest pyramids, each embracing practically
the whole range of status levels from top to bottom of society.
In the old society, as we saw in Chapter II, class feeling was
often latent, but when it emerged in the form of industrial or
political 'insubordination' it was ruthlessly suppressed. The

[1] Cf. K. Marx, *Capital* (Chicago, 1909), III, chap. lii, pp. 1031–2, where he
considers the idea that class is based on 'the identity of their revenues and their
sources of revenue', but then rejects it, presumably as undermining his theory of
class struggle—see below, chap. vii, § 4.

[2] *Citizenship and Social Class* (1950), p. 92.

birth of class was the process by which the old society itself generated new vertical economic conflicts powerful enough not only to burst through the old bonds of patronage and dependency but to replace the old structure of relationships with a new.

Such a process of social reproduction was necessarily lengthy, preceded by a long gestation with faint but unmistakeable symptoms even in the earliest stages of industrialism, and followed by a long infancy in which the child only gradually escaped from the domination of its mother. If, therefore, we found anticipations of class conflict in the old society, we shall equally find relics of 'connection' and 'interest' in the new. The Anti-Corn Law League itself, 'that uniquely powerful instrument in the forging of middle-class consciousness' as Asa Briggs has called it,[1] we shall find at times behaving very like an eighteenth-century interest group.

It was also a complex, syncopated process, operating at different speeds in different areas. Not only did the old society survive much longer in the countryside, but the new came to birth much more slowly in some towns than in others, 'In 1830,' its modern historian has written, 'Coventry still epitomized the old order, in which there were many ranks and conditions of men within a single, homogeneous society. But Coventry could not stand still while England moved, and in the end Coventry succumbed to the standards of the nineteenth century all the more painfully for her long resistance to them.'[2] Nevertheless, one of the distinguishing features of the new society, by contrast with the localism of the old, was the nationwide character of the classes, in appeal if not always in strength. At some point between the French Revolution and the Great Reform Act, the vertical antagonism and horizontal solidarities of class emerged on a national scale from and overlay the vertical bonds and horizontal rivalries of connection and interest. That moment, which it is one purpose of this chapter to isolate, saw the birth of class.

[1] Asa Briggs, 'The Language of "Class" in early 19th-Century England', A. Briggs and J. Saville, eds., *Essays in Labour History* (1960), p. 59.
[2] John Prest, *The Industrial Revolution in Coventry* (Oxford, 1960), pp. x-xi.

1. INDUSTRIALISM AND CLASS CONFLICT

Where the birth took place is not in doubt. It happened first in the industrial towns. As Engels observed in 1844,

> The cities first saw the rise of the workers and the middle classes into opposing social groups. It was in the towns that the trade union movement, Chartism and Socialism all had their origin.[1]

It might be thought that the factory itself was the link between industrialism and class antagonism. As John Thelwall the Radical lecturer put it in 1794,

> Whatever presses men together . . . , though it may generate some vices, is favourable to the diffusion of knowledge, and ultimately promotive of human liberty. Hence every large workshop and manufactory is a sort of political society which no Act of Parliament can silence and no magistrate disperse.[2]

Yet this was not the case, for two reasons. First, the rural mills of the water-power phase of the Industrial Revolution saw no such development of class feeling. On the contrary, the little communities built by Arkwright at Cromford, Strutt at Belper, Samuel Greg at Bollington, Styal and Caton, and David Dale at New Lanark—to quote only the best known of a famous species —were self-conscious models of paternal benevolence and discipline, ideal examples of the old society in miniature. Robert Owen's development of paternalism at New Lanark was only an extreme form of the same thing, which goes far to explain not only the aristocratic character of the father of Socialism but also, as we shall see in the next chapter, the debt of the working-class ideal to the old society. It was the concentration of factories in the towns which heralded the change, and Sir Walter Scott as early as 1820 shrewdly attributed it to steam power:

> The unhappy dislocation which has taken place betwixt the employer and those in his employment has been attended with very fatal consequences. Much of this is owing to the steam engine. When the machinery was driven by water, the manufacturer had to seek out some sequestered spot where he could obtain a suitable fall of water,

[1] *The Condition of the Working Class in England* (trans. and ed. W. O. Henderson and W. H. Chaloner, Oxford, 1958), pp. 137–8.
[2] H. Collins, 'The London Corresponding Society', J. Saville, ed., *Democracy and the Labour Movement* (1954), p. 126.

and then his workmen formed the inhabitants of a village around him, and he necessarily bestowed some attention, less or more, on their morals and on their necessities, had knowledge of their persons and characters, and exercised a salutary influence as over men depending on and intimately connected with him and his prospects. This is now quite changed; the manufacturers are transferred to great towns, where a man may assemble five hundred workmen one week and dismiss them the next, without having any further connection with them than to receive a week's work for a week's wages, nor any further solicitude about their future fate than if they were so many old shuttles. A superintendance of the workers considered as moral and rational beings is thus a matter totally unconnected with the employer's usual thoughts and cares. They have now seen the danger of suffering a great population to be thus entirely separated from the influence of their employers, and given over to the management of their own societies, in which the cleverest and most impudent fellows always get the management of the others, and become bell-wethers in every sort of mischief.[1]

Yet—and this was the second reason why the factory could not be the sole cause of class—factory masters and workers were never numerous enough, even in the later, steam-power phase of the Industrial Revolution, to bear the whole burden of class conflict, while in the earlier, water-power phase they lagged far behind traditional employers and domestic craftsmen in class-consciousness. From the London craftsmen who joined the shoemaker Thomas Hardy in the London Corresponding Society of 1792 to Samuel Bamford and the domestic weavers at Peterloo in 1819 the emergent working-class movement was dominated by workers of the traditional non-factory kind, while even the later, more definitely class-conscious movements of co-operative socialism, Owenite or Syndicalist trade unionism, and Chartism, it now appears, had more than their share of domestic, transport and other workers less subject to discipline and more footloose than factory operatives.[2]

Urbanization itself was in part the link between industrialism and class, though even here we must draw a distinction between the traditional towns of the old society—mainly small though not entirely so: consider the traditionalism in this respect of London, Bristol and Exeter—where paternal benevolence and

[1] W. Scott, *Familiar Letters* (1894), II. 78.
[2] Cf. G. Rudé, *The Crowd in History, 1730–1848* (1964).

discipline were still effective, and the large industrial towns, where they were not. This was the difference which Thomas Chalmers noticed in 1821 between 'the purely commercial town' in which 'the great mass of the population are retained in kindly and immediate dependence on the wealthy residents of the place' and the manufacturing (not yet necessarily factory) town in which 'the poor and wealthy stand more disjoined from each other. It is true, they often meet, but they meet more often on an arena of contest, than on a field where the patronage and custom of one party are met by the gratitude and goodwill of the other.' 'There is a mighty unfilled space,' he went on, 'between the high and the low of every large manufacturing city. . . .'[1]

There were, of course, differences in class relations between the great industrial towns themselves, such as Cobden was to remark between Birmingham with its 'small manufacturers, employing a few men and boys each' and Manchester where 'the great capitalists . . . form an aristocracy, individual members of which wield an influence over sometimes two thousand persons. The former state of society is natural and healthy in a moral and political sense. There is a freer intercourse between all classes than in the Lancashire town, where a great and impassable gulf separates the workman from his employer.'[2] Moreover, more industrial towns in the early nineteenth century followed the Birmingham than the Manchester pattern—'Radical Leicester,' turbulent Nottingham, and riotous Sheffield, to name but a few—yet did not thereby escape the turmoil of class conflict.[3]

Meanwhile, no city could have been more different from Manchester than London. As Francis Place explained to Cobden in 1840,

London differs very widely from Manchester, and, indeed, from every other place on the face of the earth. It has no local or particular interest as a town, not even as to politics. Its several boroughs in this respect are like so many very populous places at a distance from one another, and the inhabitants of any one of them know nothing, or next to nothing, of the proceedings in any other, and not much

[1] T. Chalmers, *The Christian and Civic Economy of Large Towns* (1821), I. 27.
[2] J. Morley, *Life of Cobden*, (1881), II. 199–200.
[3] Cf. A. T. Patterson, *Radical Leicester, 1780–1850* (Leicester, 1954); R. A. Church, *Victorian Nottingham* (1966); S. Pollard, *History of Labour in Sheffield* (1959), esp. p. 41.

indeed of those of their own. . . . With a very remarkable working population also, each trade divided from every other, and some of the most numerous even from themselves, and who, notwithstanding an occasional display of very small comparative numbers, are a quiescent, inactive race as far as public matters are concerned.

Yet even the traditional, quiescent London workers were inevitably drawn into the class conflicts of the age:

The leaders—those among them who pay attention to public matters—are one and all at enmity with every other class of society. . . . They call the middle class 'shopocrats,' 'usurers' (all profit being usury), 'moneymongers,' 'tyrants and oppressors of the working people,' and they link the middle class with the aristocracy under the dignified appellation of 'murderers of society', 'murderers of the people'.[1]

The most significant point, however, is that class antagonism, if it was brought to birth in the towns, was by no means confined to them. Leaving aside the domestic weavers, coal miners and iron workers of hundreds of industrial villages who were to take a full share in the class conflicts of the early nineteenth century, the very agricultural labourers, the most traditional and dependent of occupational groups, were to break out in class protest for the first time since the fourteenth century. It is true that the East Anglian bread riots of 1815 and 'the last Labourers' Revolt' of 1830 were transitional phenomena, with all the marks of the sporadic, unorganized, 'grass-fire' outbursts of latent class feeling characteristic of the old society.[2] Yet so too were many of the industrial protests of this transitional age, notably the exactly parallel Luddite movement of the East Midland framework knitters. Sporadic, unorganized violence of the type found in the old society was the inevitable accompaniment of the first stage of class development, above all in traditional, dependent occupations. The agricultural labourers, like the Luddites, were protesting in the only way they knew, but in 1815 and 1830 they were protesting on a new and would-be class-wide scale. That it came to nothing—until Joseph Arch produced their first class organization in the 1870's—merely

[1] G. Wallas, *Life of Francis Place, 1771–1854* (1898), pp. 393–4.
[2] Cf. A. J. Peacock, *Bread or Blood: the Agrarian Riots in East Anglia, 1816* (1965); J. L. and B. Hammond, *The Village Labourer* (1948 ed.) II, chaps. x and xi.

shows how powerful the old society was where it survived, how ruthlessly it still suppressed 'insubordination', and why the gestation of class was likely to prove abortive anywhere but in the great towns.[1]

It also shows, however, in the increasing reliance on paternal discipline and force rather than the inward sanctions of connection and dependency, that the old society was already breaking down even in its last bastion, the countryside. And that must lead us to reject the purely mechanical connection between industrialism and urbanization and the birth of class, and seek a more comprehensive explanation which embraces them, but not to the exclusion of the social and psychological media through which they operated.

The birth of class—the breakdown of the old vertical relationships of patronage and dependency and their replacement by vertical class antagonisms—was from the point of view of the old society a process of alienation: alienation, that is, of the middle and lower ranks or orders from each other and from the higher. Yet it was not a single, one-way process of emancipation of the former from dependence on and obedience to the latter. Alienation proceeded from both ends of the scale. Emancipation was counterbalanced, and indeed provoked, by a rejection on the part of the higher ranks not of the whole relationship—for they insisted on paternal discipline and filial obedience long after they were willing to pay the price for them—but of that part which alone justified it by the light and reason of the old society: paternal protection and responsibility.

It was this 'abdication on the part of the governors', as Carlyle was to call it,[2] which, contrary to aristocratic opinion, was the more radical and disruptive half of the process of dissolution. And its connection with industrialism, as we should expect of that extraordinary élite which had for four or five centuries held the initiative in English history and used it to create all the preconditions of an Industrial Revolution, was through the landed aristocracy itself, and the conscious stake which, from the time of Adam Smith if not earlier, many of

[1] There was, however, a great deal more sporadic agrarian violence between 1830 and 1870 than is usually supposed; cf. the forthcoming work of Dr. E. J. Hobsbawm on this topic.

[2] T. Carlyle, *Chartism* (1839), chap. vi.

them held in industrialism. As we saw in Chapter III, it was the landed rulers of England who, from the Restoration, adopted the dynamic policy of *laissez-faire* in internal industry which Adam Smith was in 1776 to advocate in foreign trade. And it was that very policy which, in the hands not of the still protectionist merchants and manufacturers but in those of Pitt, Addington, Liverpool, Canning and even Wellington—practically all the Prime Ministers from the French Revolution to the Reform crisis—was to become the justification for the abdication of paternal responsibility and through it one of the two principal factors in the breakdown of the old society.

2. 'THE ABDICATION ON THE PART OF THE GOVERNORS'

Contemporaries were acutely aware of the social alienation of the lower orders, but attributed it to diverse causes. Walter Scott blamed the steam engine; Engels, the sheer scale of urban factory production and the consequent estrangement of masters and men; Thomas Chalmers, the withering effect of the poor laws and the manufacturing town on personal charity; Lord Liverpool, 'the extensive circulation of seditious and blasphemous publications . . . (which) have gradually weakened, among the lower orders, the attachment to our Government and Constitution, and the respect for law, morality and religion.'[1] Only a few in the higher ranks glimpsed their own share in the process, like the anonymous contributor to *Blackwood's Edinburgh Magazine* who in 1820 lamented the change in 'the style and structure of society' since 'the time of our fathers':

> Everywhere, in every walk of life, it is too evident that the upper orders of Society have been tending, more and more, to a separation of themselves from those whom nature, providence, and law have placed beneath them. . . . The rich and the high have been indolently and slothfully allowing the barriers that separate them from their inferiors to increase and accumulate. : . . Men have come to deride and despise a thousand of those means of communication that in former days knit all orders of the people together.

[1] Scott, *loc. cit.*; Engels, *op. cit.*, chap. vi; Chalmers, *op. cit.*; Lord Liverpool, speech in House of Lords, 12 June 1817, *Blackwood's*, 1817, I. 653.

The fault was universal, but was most understandable and excusable in the new manufactories:

> The immense extent of the manufacturing establishments in many parts of England and Scotland, has rendered it . . . a matter of extreme difficulty for those at the head of them to keep up anything like those habits of minute acquaintance and tangible sympathy with their people, which prevailed among the masters and apprentices of the comparatively limited and trifling establishments of former days.

But it was not confined to the factories or the towns:

> In country life, however, not a little of the same general fault has been gaining ground, as well as in the life of cities and manufactories—although, as in that happier life it is infinitely more inexcusable, so it has also happily made far less dangerous and alarming progress.

After this accurate diagnosis it is disappointing to find that the writer's remedies for 'the deeply and seriously alarming condition of many important districts' were so naïve—in the factories, 'extraordinary personal zeal, and kindly habits of their superintendants'; in the countryside, visits to the poor man's cottage and gifts to his children.[1]

'The abdication on the part of the governors', however, went far beyond snobbish aloofness and the withdrawal of sympathetic contacts. It consisted in the deliberate dismantling of the whole system of paternal protection of the lower orders which had been the pride of the old society and the justification of its inequalities. In the early years of the nineteenth century practically the whole of the centuries-old legislation protecting the workers' standard of living and conditions of work was repealed, and a campaign waged, not less resented for being unsuccessful, to abolish the most symbolic of all paternal protections, the poor law.

It is true that the abandonment of the system began long before 1800, and something of a paradox that it began with scarcely a whimper of class protest. Amid the relatively stable prices and wages of the eighteenth century, and with no active

---

[1] 'The Warder, No. VII', *Blackwood's*, 1820, VII. 90–102; A. L. Strout, *A Bibliography of Articles in Blackwood's Magazine, 1817–25* (Lubbock, Texas, 1959), p. 61, cannot identify the author.

government control to keep them on their toes, the J.P.s and borough authorities had met their duties under the medieval assizes of bread and ale and the Tudor labour legislation, if at all, by fixing the same lists of wages and prices year after year, until in most areas they lapsed altogether and dropped out of memory. A writer of 1795 who discovered a seventy-year-old Lancashire wage assessment was 'much surprised to hear that any magistrates in the present century would venture on so bold a measure.'[1]

The casual nature of the abandonment and the absence of protest, however, go to show that down to the Great French Wars the spirit if not the letter of the paternal system survived, though with a dangerous mutation in the social theory upon which it rested. As late as 1765 and 1773 Parliament was still willing to extend legislative protection to labour, in the case of the Spitalfields silk weavers. The decisive change in the outlook occurred before 1795, when the first bread crisis of the Wars forced upon the ruling élite the question whether to revive wage regulation or to abandon the labouring poor to starvation. That question they answered in a way which rejected the means but preserved for the time being the end of the paternal system. With the exception of the magistrates of Devon, who issued a list of minimum wages, those of Hampshire who proposed to do so if wages did not rise, and of Suffolk who approached the county Members for a bill to regulate the price of labour, the J.P.s as a body could no longer countenance the revival of wage regulation.[2] Indeed, such was their inexperience of the system that they seem to have assumed it to mean the regulation of *maximum* wages, in no way binding on the employers. Yet neither could they face the alternative of letting the labourer starve. And so the J.P.s all over the low-wage counties of Southern England adopted a series of expedients ranging from subsidizing breadstuffs by charitable subscription to making up wages out of the poor rates. The most popular expedient, poor relief in aid of wages fixed according to the price of bread, was first adopted at the Oxford Quarter Sessions in January 1795, spread to most

[1] *Annals of Agriculture* (1795), XXV. 305f.
[2] Cf. J. R. Poynter, 'The Debate on the English Poor Law, 1795–1820', unpublished Ph.D. dissertation, Melbourne, 1961, pp. 113–14, and his forthcoming book, to be published in this Series.

of the southern counties, and reached the Berkshire Hundred of Speenhamland, which for some unknown reason gave it its name, only in May.[1]

The extent and limits of the abandonment of paternalism at this stage can be measured by the debate in the Commons on Whitbread's bill to regulate wages. Whitbread himself accepted the axiom that 'the price of labour, like every other commodity, should be left to find its own level', merely arguing that the present crisis deserved special treatment. He thus made it easy for Pitt to sum up the overwhelming consensus of legislative opinion:

> It was unnecessary to argue the general inexpediency of any legislative interference as the principles had been recognized by the honourable gentleman himself. The most celebrated writers upon political economy and the experience of those states where arts had flourished most, leave ample testimony of their truth.

The question was only whether the present case was exceptional enough, and whether the means proposed would achieve the object. He concluded that regulation would only produce either 'severe oppression' or 'the most profligate idleness and extravagance.'

> It was indeed the most absurd bigotry, in asserting the general principle to exclude the exception; but trade, industry and barter would always find their own level, and be impeded by regulations which violated their natural operation, and deranged their proper effect.[2]

In 1795 the factory system was in its infancy and the large factory town practically unknown. Yet here was the full-blown Manchester doctrine of extreme *laissez-faire* accepted by Government and Parliament half a century ahead of its time. The reason lies in the complete acceptance by the ruling élite of the logic of industrialism before industrialism itself could be said to be a fact. It would be too facile to attribute this, as Pitt himself did, to the influence of 'the most celebrated writers on political economy.' As we have seen, the ruling aristocracy long anticipated Adam Smith in the practice of *laissez-faire*, though he undoubtedly helped them to formulate the theory. More to the

[1] J. L. and B. Hammond, *Village Labourer*, I. 158–62.
[2] *Parliamentary History of England, 1792–1801*, XXXII. 703–12.

point is their acceptance of just those parts of *The Wealth of Nations* which suited their outlook, such as the pernicious effects of wage regulation, and their rejection of those which did not, such as the pernicious effects of corn laws.[1] In the social philosophy of large groups of men the function of theorists is to rationalize practice, reinforce prejudice, clarify or, more commonly, rigidify opinion, but rarely to originate or greatly modify them. The landed rulers who swallowed (selected) Adam Smith were indulging an addiction which would have retched at any other diet.

The truth is that the English landowners, or many of them, had sold their souls to economic development long before the Industrial Revolution, and as the most important precondition of it. When it came they were more than ready to accept its logic, the freedom of industrial employment from state regulation, and so they seized on Adam Smith, as in an earlier age they had seized on Locke, to justify their instincts by the borrowed light of reason.

Indeed, even before *The Wealth of Nations* appeared, an earlier, now forgotten, economist recognized their addiction and warned them of the consequences. Sir James Steuart, the Jacobite mercantilist, wrote in 1767:

> In countries where the government is vested in the hands of the great lords, as is the case in all aristocracies, as was the case under feudal government, and as is still the case in many countries in Europe, where trade, however, and industry are daily gaining ground; the statesman who sets the new system of political economy on foot, may depend upon it, either his attempt will fail, or the constitution of the government will change. If he destroys all arbitrary dependence between individuals, the wealth of the industrious will share, if not totally root out the power of the grandees.[2]

And so, in the long run, it was to prove. But even in the short run the undermining of 'arbitrary dependence between individuals' was destructive of the very principle on which the old society rested, and in the form pursued by the ruling aristocracy in the early nineteenth century exactly calculated to evoke class

---

[1] *Wealth of Nations*, I. 147–8, II. 27–49.
[2] J. Steuart, *Inquiry into the Principles of Political Economy* (1767), in *Works, Political, Metaphysical, and Chronological* (1855), I 327

antagonism. As late as 1795 they were still willing, in the form of Speenhamland, to pay the price of paternal protection in return for filial obedience. But from then onwards they began to exact the fruits of paternalism but refuse to pay the price. As Baldwin was to say of twentieth-century press lords, they claimed the privilege of the whore, power without responsibility.

The first symptom of this provocative change was the Combination Acts of 1799 and 1800. As we have seen, these were a mere generalization of old society attitudes towards industrial 'insubordination' and contained no new principle. What was new, however, was the context in which they were passed. Having within the same five years refused to regulate wages, Parliament now reiterated its traditional denial of the right of the workers to negotiate them for themselves. It was this outrageous demand to have their cake and eat it, to exact paternal discipline while denying paternal protection, which, repeated over the next two decades in the increasingly concrete form of repeal of the whole machinery of paternalism, was to exasperate the lower orders and awaken in them the spirit of class conflict.

How reluctant the lower orders were to be provoked can be seen in the immense efforts which they made to maintain the fabric of the paternal system. For a dozen years, from 1802 to 1814, workers in the traditional crafts petitioned and went to law for the enforcement of the legislation regulating wages and apprenticeship. In 1802 the Yorkshire and West of England weavers combined to employ an attorney and prosecute infringements of the special laws regulating the woollen industry. The response of Parliament was to suspend the laws in 1803, and repeal them six years later. The Edinburgh compositors appealed to the Court of Session instead of to Parliament, and obtained in 1805 an 'Interlocuter' fixing piece-work rates in the printing trade. The cotton weavers were told by a Select Committee in 1809 that their proposal for a minimum wage was 'wholly inadmissable in principle, incapable of being reduced to practice by any means which could possibly be devised, and, if practicable, would be productive of the most fatal consequences'; and by another in 1811 that their 'proposition relative to the number of apprentices is also entirely inadmissable, and would, if adopted by the House, be attended with the greatest injustice to the manufacturer as well as to the labourer.'[1]

The Glasgow cotton weavers obtained a standard piece-rate from the Edinburgh Court of Sessions in 1812, only to have it rejected by the employers, which led to a strike throughout the industry from Aberdeen to Carlisle, and the arrest and imprisonment of the leaders. A number of London trades engaged a solicitor between 1810 and 1812 and at great cost obtained a few convictions for infringement of the apprenticeship clauses of the 1563 Act, only to have Lord Chancellor Ellenborough rule in 1811 that crafts established since 1563 were not covered by the Act. He also ruled, in the case of the journeymen millers of Kent, that the J.P.s must hear a petition to regulate wages, but they need not fix any rate. Finally, massive petitions to put the 1563 Statute in operation were met by the repeal of the wages clauses in 1813 and of the apprenticeship clauses in 1814, and the destruction of the machinery of industrial paternalism was complete.[2]

This was not the end of the aristocratic onslaught on the paternal system, however. It achieved its zenith only with the attack on the poor laws in the years immediately following the Wars. The campaign to abolish the poor laws was the most flagrant breach of the principle of dependency on which the old society rested, and, though unsuccessful, did more to alienate the lower orders and provoke working-class antagonism than any other action of the aristocracy. The case for abolition will always be associated with the name of Malthus, and certainly 'Parson Malthus' was to be the chief devil on whom Cobbett and the leaders of the emerging working class were to fasten their hatred. But, on the one hand, Malthus was only one amongst a host of abolitionists, from Joseph Townsend of *A Dissertation on the Poor Laws* (1786) onwards; while, on the other, abolition, in spite of Malthus's support from 1798 onwards, does not seem to have been taken very seriously as long as the Wars lasted, and with them the need to placate the potentially Jacobin poor. It was only with the mounting distress

---

[1] S. and B. Webb, *History of Trade Unionism* (1950), pp. 56–8.
[2] *Ibid.* pp. 58–61; the Acts regulating the Spitalfields silk industry were not repealed until 1824—J. H. Clapham, 'The Spitalfields Acts, 1773–1824', *Ec.J.*, 1916, XXVI. 471.

and poor rates of the post-war slump that abolition became an aggressive campaign and a real political issue, by which time Malthus was but a general in the army of abolitionists, and, since he never advocated immediate abolition for the existing poor, by no means the most extreme.[1]

Between 1815 and 1820 condemnation of the poor laws as they then existed was all but universal in England, except for the partisans of the emerging working-class movement. The only question was whether their abolition should be immediate or gradual, partial or total. The opposition of the political economists and the 'progressive' Whigs could be taken for granted: the humane Ricardo declared that 'every friend to the poor must ardently wish for their abolition,' while the *Edinburgh Review* asserted in 1820:

> There are two points which we consider are now admitted by *all men of sense*; first, that the Poor Laws must be abolished;—second, that they must be very gradually abolished. We hardly think it worth while to throw away ink and paper upon any one who is inclined to dispute these propositions.[2]

What is much more significant is the apostasy of the traditional friends of the poor laws and the paternal system, the radical conservatives and the High Tories. Even Coleridge and Southey, with nothing but contempt and abuse for the abolitionists, nevertheless condemned the existing poor laws with a zeal which rivalled that of Malthus himself. Coleridge held it 'impossible to exaggerate the pernicious tendency and consequences' of the laws, while Southey talked of the 'crying necessity' for reform, and suggested a special militia to suppress 'jacquerie and insurrection' when it came.[3] Even the Tory *Quarterly Review* turned abolitionist in 1821, while the High Tory *Blackwood's*, the champion of the poor laws when paternalism was a lost cause in the late 1820's and the 1830's, for a time in 1818 swallowed the whole Malthusian doctrine.[4]

---

[1] Cf. Poynter, *op. cit.*, Part III, chap. iii (for Malthus), and Part V, 'Post-War Distress and the Climax of Abolition'.

[2] *Works and Correspondence* (ed. Sraffa), I. 106; *Edin. Rev.*, 1820, XXXIII. 95.

[3] S. T. Coleridge, *Lay Sermon, addressed to the Higher and Middle Classes on the Existing Distresses and Discontents* (1817), p. 112; R. Southey in *Q.R.*, 1816, XVI. 278 and 1818, XVII. 306; Poynter, *op. cit.*, pp. 416–19.

[4] *Q.R.*, 1821, XXVI. 148–68; *Blackwood's*, 1818, III. 9–11 and IV. 207–11—

The abolitionist campaign reached high water mark in 1817 when its case was completely accepted by a Select Committee of the Commons. With unconscious irony it condemned any compulsory system of poor relief on the grounds that it undermined dependency:

> as it proceeds from no impulse of charity, it creates no feeling of gratitude, and not infrequently engenders dispositions and habits calculated to separate rather than unite the interests of the higher and lower orders of the community,

and it declared that abolition of both relief and parish employment would be of inestimable benefit to the poor.[1] The Report surprisingly recommended not abolition but only palliative reforms, but its arguments so alarmed the Government, obsessed with maintaining order in the distress and discontent of 1817, that it hastily convened a Select Committee of the Lords to undo the damage. Its Report, while joining in the general condemnation of existing practice, was the salvation of the poor laws and the remaining shreds of paternalism:

> From the lapse of time, and a departure from the true spirit of the above (1601) act, abuses have undoubtedly been introduced into the general administration of the Poor Laws of England; but the Committee are nevertheless decidedly of opinion, that the general system of those laws, interwoven as it is with the habits of the people, ought, in consideration of any measures to be adopted for their melioration and improvement, to be essentially maintained.[2]

This was in fact the attitude which triumphed in 1834. Yet the later reception by the working class of the New Poor Law gives some idea of the reaction which abolition would have provoked. As one of the Radical opponents of Malthus put it,

> The truth is, the proposal may irritate; but the execution of the project would be found impossible. The mad brained attempt would serve no other purpose than to raise the standard of insurrection.[3]

[1] P.P., 1817, VI, S.C. of H. of C. on the Poor Laws, pp. 4–5 and 17–18.

[2] P.P., 1818, V, 400, S.C. of H. of L. on the Poor Laws, 1817, p. 91.

[3] David Booth, A Letter to Rev. T. R. Malthus ... being an Answer to the Criticism of Mr. Godwin's Work on Population (1823), pp. 109–10; Poynter, op. cit., p. 432n.

but see 1819, V. 173–5, where the evils of the poor laws are said to be much exaggerated.

As it was, the mere threat to abolish the poor laws alienated the working class at the very moment when, as we shall see, it was coming to birth.

The demand of landed rulers for power without responsibility offended not only the lower orders. The middle ranks, too, on whom throughout the Wars the Government had relied for support against its enemies at home and abroad, were alienated by the unseemly haste with which at the first sign of peace the landowners brought in the Corn Laws to protect their rents at the expense of the rest of the community. As late as 1812 the mercantile interest had, over the question of the Orders in Council prohibiting exports to Napoleon's Europe, played the old society game of petitioning the aristocratic Government for redress, and the Government, in marked contrast to its treatment of the workers' petition, had responded according to the old society rules, and repealed them.[1] But now more was at stake than economic warfare. Protest was of only propaganda value. As Francis Place put it to James Mill in 1814,

> It is only for the purpose of diffusing information that it can be at all desirable to interfere with the Corn Laws; for the legislature will certainly do all in its power to keep up the rent of land, and will pass an Act for that purpose next session in spite of everything which can be done to prevent it. The rich landholders will see nothing but the decrease of rents, and having the power they will certainly prevent it, be the consequences whatever they may.[2]

The consequence was that a large number of influential men in the middle ranks, including James Mill, became as disillusioned with the aristocracy's claim to be the 'virtual representatives' of the whole community, the master interest at the head of all the other interests, the unified élite in whom society placed its implicit faith, as the outraged workers. From that moment the alienation of the middle ranks paralleled that of the lower orders. It was only a matter of time before they would unite to bury the old society which had destroyed itself from within.

We have seen, however, the reluctance of the lower orders, and to a less extent of the middle ranks, to abandon paternalism and be provoked into class antagonism. It is true that from the

[1] Cf. C. W. New, *Life of Henry Brougham to 1830* (1961), chaps. iv, vi.
[2] Wallas, *Place*, p. 159.

French Revolution onwards there were those who were not at all reluctant to apply the axe to the old society, Britain's *ancien régime*, root and branch. Tom Paine and his Radical followers— the English Jacobins as the aristocratic Government and its supporters preferred to call them—were at first sight as emancipated from the system of dependency as any class could be. But were they a class, and were they so emancipated as they appeared to be?

Working men like Thomas Hardy, Thomas Evans and (at the time) Francis Place, it is true, joined the Corresponding Societies in their hundreds, indeed, in some places like Sheffield in their thousands, only to be persecuted and brutally suppressed by the Government. This has given rise to what may be called the conspiratorial theory of the birth of class. 'In the 1790's,' writes the leading left-wing historian of the making of the working class, 'something like an "English Revolution" took place, of profound importance in shaping the consciousness of the post-war working class. It is true that the revolutionary impulse was strangled in its infancy; and the first consequence was that of bitterness and despair.'[1] But the tree of liberty had been planted, and the proletarian seedling was nurtured through the long winter of repression by devoted cells of Painites, whose propagandist labours at length united the hot breaths of the revolutionary working class into an artificial spring and made it burst into bloom.

There is enough truth in this romantic theory to attract any generous mind. We all love the underdog, especially when he is dead and posthumously triumphant. And in this case the Painite underdog undoubtedly performed an important role in the emergence of the working class, that of helping to carry over to the new society the working-class ideal, of labour as the creator of all value, which has its roots deep in the old society. The difficulty with the theory is twofold: it is doubtful to what extent Paine and the Radicals of the 1790's were consciously proletarian, and it is still more doubtful whether the workers as a class supported them.

First, it is ironical that the same school of historians treats Paine and the Radicals of the 1790's in another context, that of the provenance of the socialist movement, as representatives of

[1] E. P. Thompson, *The Making of the English Working Class* (1963), p. 177.

THE BIRTH OF CLASS

the 'bourgeois democratic' reaction against 'feudalism'[1]—a view which, though incompatible with the above theory, offers the same combination of plausible half-truth and tendentious interpretation. In fact, Parliamentary Reform in the eighteenth century was as characteristic of the old society as was the defence of the unreformed Parliament, and the Reformers behaved more like an interest group uniting the various status levels than a congeries of class organizations separating them. The London Corresponding Society of 1792—proletarian according to the theory but in fact composed of 'tradesmen, mechanics and shopkeepers'[2] who in old society terms belonged to the middle ranks rather than the lower orders, or at least cut across both— was connected with Major Cartwright and the Society for Constitutional Information. The latter Society, which has equally been taken as the parent of middle-class political organization, was in its turn linked with Charles James Fox and the aristocratic 'Friends of the People'.[3] All three levels were united, perhaps indeed with different motives, in opposing the aristocractic clique which they considered had cornered the system of representation, and in welcoming the French Revolution which, no more proletarian than Parliamentary Reform itself, seemed the answer to all their hopes.

Secondly, it is not the case that here was a mass-movement of the working class prematurely strangled by a tyrannical despotism. However numerous the working-men Reformers, the working-men supporters of the existing order were still more numerous. The Government had no police and only a volunteer army, and it was not so much the mailed fist of the law which put the Jacobins to flight as the Church-and-King mobs, in which the heat and burden were borne by patriotic working men. No doubt these were organized by the two thousand-odd Loyal Associations set on foot by Government agents like John

[1] Christopher Hill, 'The Norman Yoke', in J. Saville, ed., *Democracy and the Labour Movement* (1954).

[2] R. Birley, *The English Jacobins* (1924), p. 8; cf. Henry Collins, 'The London Corresponding Society', in Saville, ed., *op. cit.*

[3] The difference between the three societies was purely a question of status and the cost of their differing social activities, as evidenced by their varying subscriptions: five guineas p.a. for the Friends of the People, half a guinea p.a. for the Society for Constitutional Information, one penny a week for the London Corresponding Society; cf. J. R. M. Butler, *The Passing of the Great Reform Bill* (1914), p. 14.

Reeves, but this was wholly in accord with the old society principle of the legitimate influence of the higher ranks upon the lower orders as the best answer to disaffection and insubordination.[1] If some of the Reformers were proletarian, how much more so were the mobs which burned and pillaged the houses of Thomas Walker and Joseph Priestley?

Indeed, it can be argued that the loyalist reaction played a far greater part in the development of class feeling than the movement which provoked it. While the Reformers were intent on keeping their wings together by playing down class differences, and hotly denied any threat to property or the economic foundations of society, it was their opponents who raised the spectre of class with wild accusations of levelling principles and the threat of social revolution. An erstwhile Reformer turned Loyalist declared in 1792:

> If Mr. Paine should be able to rouse up the lower classes, their interference will probably be marked by wild work, and all we now possess, whether in private property or public liberty, will be at the mercy of a lawless and furious rabble.[2]

The same fear for the safety of property and the preservation of social inequality pervades the parliamentary debates and treason trials of the 1790's, and helps to account for the near-hysteria of the reaction. That fear, engendered more by the French Revolution than by anything which the English Reformers said or did—only the few and isolated followers of Thomas Spence so much as mooted a division of private property—served to draw the propertied closer together as a class, and to emphasize their segregation from the rest of society. To this extent it reinforced the 'abdication of the governors', and was the real connecting link between the French Revolution and the birth of class. But of this more later.

[1] Cf. Austin Mitchell, 'The Association Movement of 1792–93', *Hist.J.*, 1961, IV. 56f.: the Associations were based on Lord Grenville's principle that 'the hands of the government must be strengthened if the country is to be saved; but, above all, the work must not be left to the hands of government, but every man must put his shoulder to it, according to his rank and situation in life . . . .'—*ibid.*, p. 58.

[2] Rev. Christopher Wyvill to James Martin, M.P., 28 April 1792, G. S. Veitch, *The Genesis of Parliamentary Reform* (1913), p. 202.

3. THE MIDWIFE OF CLASS

The emancipation of the middle ranks and lower orders proceeded almost in spite of themselves, and by means which may
be described as paradoxical. Reluctant to be born, the new class
society needed a midwife to help it into existence. It found one
in the unexpected form of sectarian religion.

In the old society, as we saw in Chapter II, such latent vertical
antagonism as existed in normal times took the form of dissent
from the established Church. The resultant religious 'sandwich', with Anglicans (in some areas Roman Catholics) at top
and bottom and Nonconformists old and new, Old Dissenters
and new Methodists, in the middle, was to become, as industrialism enormously expanded the 'filling' and ate away the bottom
layer, a ready-made pattern for the new society.

This is not to say that the nineteenth-century middle class,
any more than the eighteenth-century middle ranks, were all
Old Dissenters, or that the new working class, any more than
the old lower orders, were all Methodists. On the contrary,
sectarian religion was midwife, not mother or child. Old Dissent
was no more than the core of the middle class, as it had been of
the middle ranks, and if one door led into it from the Church,
another led out of it to sophisticated forms of unbelief; and
Methodism was but one religion of the working class, and as
often as not the gate through which large numbers of working
men passed to secularism or religious indifference, the ultimate
spiritual state of the majority in the great towns of the industrial
age. The role of sectarian religion was threefold: to give expression to emancipation from the dependency system before it
hardened into overt class antagonism; to provide the means, or
at least the model, of class organization; and, not so much by
passive teaching of patience as by active example of the benefits
of non-violent organization, to influence class conflict in the
direction of non-violence, and so to administer an analgesic
against the pains of labour.

For the moment, however, we are concerned only with the
first of these roles, the part played by sectarian religion in the
breakdown of the dependency system.[1] The enormous expansion
of the 'filling' in the religious 'sandwich' and the erosion of the

[1] For the other two roles, see chap. ix, § 1, below.

bottom layer during the Industrial Revolution are the best measure we have of the progress of emancipation from the system of dependency. It is not an exact measure, for the only comprehensive statistics of church attendance are those of the Religious Census of 1851. Before this *terminus ad quem*, however, there are the invaluable returns of new Protestant dissenting chapels licensed under the Toleration Act of 1689. The following table shows that chapel founding rose steeply in the last quarter of the eighteenth century, reached a high peak in the 1820's, and, as far as permanent chapels were concerned, continued on a high plateau through to mid-century and beyond. Even the slight falling off in the 1830's and 1840's may have been counterbalanced, as the urban congregations grew larger,

TABLE 3

PLACES NEWLY LICENSED FOR NON-ANGLICAN WORSHIP PER DECADE 1771–1850 AND NEW ANGLICAN CHURCHES 1801–50.

Decade	Houses, Dwelling Houses, Rooms or otherwise as Temporary Buildings	Chapels, Buildings, Meeting-Houses or otherwise as Permanent Buildings	Total Non-Anglican Places Licensed	New Anglican Churches
1688–1770	6,674	442	7,116	
Before 1801	—	—	—	9,667
Date unknown	—	—	—	2,118
1771–80	1,107	175	1,282	—
1781–90	1,266	332	1,598	—
1791–1800	3,479	915	4,394	—
1801–10	3,975	1,485	5,460	55
1811–20	7,497	2,644	10,141	97
1821–30	7,675	2,910	10,585	276
1831–40	4,550	2,872	7,422	667
1841–50	3,090	2,720	5,810	1,197
Total 1771–1850	32,639	14,053	46,692	—
Total 1801–50	—	—	—	2,292
Total 1688–1850	39,313	14,495	53,808	—
Existing in 1851	3,285	17,105	20,390	14,077

SOURCES: *Parl. Papers*, 1852–3, LXXVIII, p. 156; and *Census of England and Wales 1851: Religious Worship*, p. xl. (The statistics of licensed chapels 1688–1770 are very defective.)

more concentrated, and wealthier, by the building of larger chapels.[1] Meanwhile, in spite of help from public funds, notably by the 'Million Pound Act' of 1818, the Anglican Church failed to keep pace with the sects. According to one authority, even at its peak in the 1830's and 1840's the Church's rate of building was doubled by that of the Independents, trebled by that of the Baptists and Roman Catholics, and quintupled by that of the Methodist Connexions.[2] By 1851 there were nearly twenty thousand Nonconformist, and over twenty thousand Non-Anglican, places of worship, against the Church of England's fourteen thousand. Though the Churches were bigger, and contained slightly more sittings, the Non-Anglicans made rather more attendances.[3]

What these figures mean in terms of alienation from the Church is more difficult to say, but the trend is sufficiently obvious. The three main sects of Old Dissenters rose from about a quarter of a million in the mid-eighteenth century to about a million in the 1820's, and to perhaps a million and half attenders in 1851, which represented a larger number of regular members and adherents.[4] The Methodists grew from about twenty-six thousand communicants in 1770 and about sixty thousand communicants at Wesley's death in 1791, and perhaps three times as many attenders at both dates, to nearly two million attenders, and a larger number of regular chapel-goers, in the ten Methodist Connexions of 1851.[5] The Roman Catholics grew, less by conversion than by immigration of the Irish, alienated from the Church of the English rulers before they arrived, from under seventy thousand according to Returns of 1767 and 1780 to about a quarter of a million attenders, and a larger number of

[1] On very large Wesleyan chapels, cf. T. P. Bunting, *Life of Jabez Bunting* (1887), p. 338, and E. P. Thompson, *op. cit.*, p. 351.

[2] Rev. E. Wyatt-Edgell, 'On the Statistics of Places of Worship in England and Wales', *Stat.J.*, 1851, XIV. 343–4; percentage increases in numbers of buildings, 1831–51: Church of England 18·4; Independents 39·8, Roman Catholics 59·2, Methodists (all Connexions) 102·2. For later figures, 1851–73, see H. S. Skeats, 'Statistics relating to Religious Institutions in England and Wales', *ibid.*, 1876, XXXIX. 332–3.

[3] 5·6 as against 5·3 million.

[4] E. D. Bebb, *Nonconformity and Social and Economic Life, 1660–1800* (1935) p. 45; B. L. Manning, *The Protestant Dissenting Deputies* (Cambridge, 1952), p. 235; Census of England and Wales, 1851, *Religious Worship*, pp. xlvii, lxi, clxxviii.

[5] R. F. Wearmouth, *Methodism and Working-Class Movements in England, 1800–50* (1937), pp. 15–16; Census, 1851, *Religious Worship*, p. lxxviii.

communicants, in 1851.[1] Altogether, the Non-Anglicans grew from a small minority, perhaps half a million out of the seven million people in England and Wales, in 1770 to over half the church-going population in 1851.[2] The 'filling' had become the larger part of the 'sandwich'.

Nor was this the full extent of the alienation from the Church. What alarmed the Census reporter, Horace Mann, and his contemporaries more than the scale of dissent was the 'alarming number of the non-attenders at any place of worship'. According to Mann's estimate, no less than half the population failed to attend a religious service on Census Sunday, and, even on his favourable assumption that only seventy per cent could attend even one service out of three, over a quarter of the population were voluntary absentees.[3] By modern standards, of course, this represents an astonishing scale of religious activity, but to contemporaries it marked a severe decline in adherence and belief.

They were in no doubt about where the decline had occurred. While the middle classes had increased their attendance and the upper classes had maintained theirs as being 'among the recognized proprieties of life', Mann remarked, the urban working classes were characterized not so much by 'infidelity' as by 'negative, inert indifference' to religion. 'More especially in cities and large towns it is observable how absolutely insignificant a portion of the congregations is composed of artisans.'[4] In this he was merely echoing the common opinion of middle-class observers, from Thomas Chalmers in 1821 to Mayhew in 1851. As Engels put it in 1844,

All bourgeois writers are agreed that the workers have no religion and do not go to church. Exceptions to this are the Irish, a few of the older workers and those wage-earners who have one foot in the middle-class camp—overlookers, foremen, and so on. Among the

[1] *Ibid.*, pp. ci-cii.

[2] The Census reporter, Horace Mann, p. clii, used a method of estimating attenders (taking the whole morning attendance plus half the afternoon plus one-third of the evening) designed to favour the Church of England, where the most popular service was in the morning, as against the Non-Anglicans, whose largest services were held in the evening, and he succeeded in giving a slight majority of attenders to the Church. On any other method, such as the two-thirds attendance adopted here, the Non-Anglicans retain the majority of attenders as of attendances.

[3] *Ibid.*, pp. clii, clviii.

[4] *Ibid.*, p. clviii.

mass of the working-class population, however, one nearly always finds an utter indifference to religion.[1]

Engels' verdict is amply confirmed by the bourgeois writers themselves and by modern studies of the churches' relations with the Victorian working class.[2] We do not have to accept the (by then) class-ridden views of contemporaries—there was proportionately as much conscious unbelief, if not indifference, in the Victorian middle class as amongst the workers—to recognize that church-going had declined most in the great towns and amongst the urban working class. This could have been proved from the Census returns, but was not, Mann preferring to rely on subjective impressions. The following table attempts to rectify the omission. It shows two broad trends: first, the larger the town the smaller the proportion of the population attending any place of worship; and, secondly, the larger the town, with the exception of London, the smaller the proportion of Anglican to all attenders. The exception to the second trend is important, for London was not then an industrial town in the new sense of the word, and if space permitted it could be shown that other large towns of more traditional social structure, such as Bristol, Exeter and Norwich, followed the London pattern of Anglican majority attendance. But there were few exceptions to the first trend: the majority in all the great towns, as contemporaries put it, were 'pagan'. And, since the working class made up four-fifths of their population, the majority of non-attenders were working-class, especially adults. As Edward Miall put it in 1849,

> The bulk of our manufacturing population stands aloof from our Christian institutions . . . an immense majority of those who in childhood attend our Sabbath schools, neglect throughout the period of manhood all our ordinary appliances of spiritual instruction and culture.[3]

The reasons for this alienation of a large part of the working class not only from the Church but from all the churches were accurately summarized by Mann, and they were entirely social

---

[1] *Op. cit.*, p. 141.

[2] Cf. K. S. Inglis, *Churches and the Working Classes in Victorian England* (1963); E. R. Wickham, *Church and People in an Industrial City* (1957).

[3] E. Miall, *The British Churches in relation to the British People* (1849); Wickham, *op. cit.*, pp. 118–19.

TABLE 4

ESTIMATED ANGLICAN AND NON-ANGLICAN ATTENDERS, 30 MARCH 1851, IN GROUPS OF TOWNS BY POPULATION SIZE, ENGLAND AND WALES

Size of Towns	Population	Anglican Attenders No.	%	Non-Anglican Attenders No.	%	Total No.	%
London	2,362,236	338,617	14·3	260,472	11·1	599,089	25·4
100,000+ (8 towns)	1,268,507	143,808	11·3	201,757	15·9	345,565	27·2
50,000–100,000 (17 towns)	1,105,421	154,155	13·9	236,513	21·4	390,668	35·3
20,000–50,000 (34 towns)	1,033,964	197,555	19·1	210,897	20·4	408,452	39·5
All towns 20,000 +	5,770,128	834,135	14·5	909,639	15·7	1,743,774	30·2
All places 20,000 –	12,156,681	2,694,232	22·2	2,826,038	23·2	5,520,270	45·4
England and Wales	17,927,609	3,528,367	19·7	3,785,677	20·2	7,264,044	40·5

SOURCE: Abstracted from *Census of England and Wales, 1861: Religious Worship*, Tables, pp. cclii *et seq.*; the number of attenders is taken as two-thirds of the total attendances during the day.

201

ones: the feeling that churches were for the well-to-do and respectable—'the labouring myriads have . . . no desire to mingle with persons of a higher grade'; the supposed indifference of the churches to the social conditions of the poor; distrust of the motives of proselytizing ministers; and the poverty and overcrowding of the slums. 'The masses, therefore, of our large and growing towns—connected by no sympathetic tie with those by fortune placed above them—form a world apart, a nation by themselves; divided almost as effectively from the rest as if they spoke another language or inhabited another land. What Dr. Chalmers calls "the influence of locality" is powerless here: the area is too extensive and the multitude too vast.'[1]

In other words, where dependency was weakened, Anglican Church-going declined; where it was dead, church-going of all kinds decayed. Emancipation from both paternal and religious discipline went hand in hand with urbanization. As a later Bishop of London accurately expressed it, 'It is not that the Church of God has lost the great towns; it has never had them. . . .'[2] The migrating workers moved from the countryside, where the social pressures were in favour of going to Church rather than 'lose everything, work and all',[3] to a small town where the social pressures were in favour of going to chapel, or to a large one where they were against going at all.

This 'religious mobility', if so it can be termed, was not an innovation introduced by industrialism. The natural corollary of the religious 'sandwich' of the old society was the progressive change in denominational allegiance as one moved up—or down—the social hierarchy.[4] What was new in the Industrial Revolution, apart from the acceleration and increased scale of change, was the development for the first time not merely of scepticism or atheism in isolated individuals or groups but of entire social layers in which non-allegiance to any church was the norm and adherence the exception. Nor was this confined to the slums of the great towns, to the depressed bottom layer of paupers, street-folk and semi-criminals who, like Mayhew's costermongers or Dickens' brickmaker, never went to church

---

[1] Census, 1851, *Religious Worship*, pp. clviii, cxxviii.

[2] A. F. Winnington-Ingram, *Work in Great Cities* (1896), p. 22.

[3] Engels, *op. cit.*, p. 304.

[4] Cf. chap. ii, § 1, above.

until they were buried.[1] It spread to large areas of the urban working class up to the craftsman level, and even affected a considerable section of the middle class. Indeed, it helps to explain one of the sharpest paradoxes of the nineteenth century, the emergence, in the midst of the greatest revival of religious faith since the middle ages, of the agnosticism or indifference which was to be the dominant spiritual position in modern Britain.

Both can be explained in terms of emancipation from the integrated pattern of socio-religious behaviour of the old society. The first effect of emancipation was a sharpening of belief and discipline by reaction from the easy-going habits of the latitudinarian Church of the old society, and, as it in turn revived, in competition with it and with other sects. But the second effect, reached almost immediately in some of the emancipated, only by stages in others, and not at all in the rest, was alienation from all organized forms of religious belief and worship. And the existence of numerous competing sects, which was more characteristic of Britain than of any other European country, provided a sequence of stepping stones by which the emancipated individual could make his way from the Church to any position of Christian belief, or at last out into the great desert of unbelief on the other side of the Jordan. This was well recognized by a contemporary, who shrewdly connected it with industrialism: 'the same spirit which has produced "free trade" in articles of commerce advocates likewise a free trade in religion.' The resultant division of the Church into competing parties, High and Low, has unsettled the faith of its adherents who

> wander forth . . . never to return. In this manner thousands, and tens of thousands, have been lost to the Church of England; for, so numerous are now the various sects of dissenters, and so nicely are the shades of distinction drawn, that if a man once begin to doubt any article of belief, fastidious indeed must he be if he cannot find some one congregation whose notions accord with his own.[2]

There were in fact two sequences of stepping stones from the Church (three, if we include the lovers' leap from High Church

---

[1] Mayhew, *op. cit.*, (1851, I. 21-2; C. Dickins, *Bleak House* (1853), the brickmaker to Mrs. Pardiggle.

[2] [J. F. Dalton], 'The Influence of the Church of England in Society', *Blackwood's*, 1830, XXVII. 700-1.

to Rome, but this was more an internal upper-class phenomenon than a species of social alienation). Upstream, as it were, there was for the middle ranges of society the ancient sequence of Old Dissent. Downstream, for the emancipated workers there was the new sequence of proliferating Methodist connexions.

Old Dissent had long formed a sequence of steps, but for most of the era of the old society they had been steps arranged in a social hierarchy. A member of the lower orders who raised himself by diligence and frugality to the level of an independent craftsman or shopkeeper of the lower middle ranks would probably mark his partial emancipation by joining one of the Independent congregations or the Baptists. If he prospered and rose still higher in the social scale, he would be likely to become a Presbyterian or Quaker. Finally, if he became so successful as to be able to buy an estate and retire from business he or his family would return to the Anglican fold. During and after the Industrial Revolution this rising sequence continued—as late as the 1850's, for example, the last of the famous Quaker dynasty of ironfounders, the Darbys of Coalbrookdale, retired from business and built an Anglican church.[1] At the same time, a more horizontal sequence developed, though after an almost false start. In the late eighteenth century the strain of 'rational religion' which produced the scepticism of Hume, Bentham and most of the Utilitarians profoundly affected the leading Presbyterians, above all Priestley, Price and Robinson, the apostles of 'Rational Dissent', who led a large part of their followers into the Socinian wilderness of Unitarianism. In the 1790's they were persecuted both for their heresy and for their political sympathy with the Godless Revolution in France, which the Government and its supporters saw as connected. Price and Robinson died, Priestley fled to America, and the bulk of their followers deserted Rational Dissent for politically safe Baptist and Congregationalist havens. Unitarianism, however, survived, to become in the nineteenth century the main link between 'enlightened' Dissent and those 'secular Dissenters' outside the pale of Christianity, the sceptical Utilitarians and, later, the agnostic Positivists. The link with the first is symbolized by the political alliance between the Mills and the Rev. W. J. Fox,

[1] A. Raistrick, *Dynasty of Ironfounders: The Darbys and Coalbrookdale* (1953), pp. 263, 270, 273.

editor of the *Monthly Repository*; with the second, by George Eliot and her circle, including the phrenologists Charles Bray and George Combe, and the Positivists Frederic Harrison and E. S. Beesly. In the 1820's it was a short step from Unitarianism to sceptical Utilitarianism. By mid-century it was an even shorter one, often via phrenology, from Unitarianism to the deeply moral, religiose agnosticism of the Positivists.[1]

Methodism formed a longer and more evenly spaced sequence of stepping stones from the Church to agnosticism. At the hither end the Wesleyanism of the original Connexion, as Tory, loyalist, politically quietist and theologically Anglican as Wesley himself, was the shortest possible step for the timidest emancipated worker to take. Then, as alienation increased both with time and social distance, Methodism threw up a resting place at every stride, each, for a time at least, more radical than the parent stock: the Kilhamites or New Methodist Connexion of 1797, the 'Ranters' or Primitive Methodists of 1810, the Bryanites or Bible Christians of 1815, the Wesleyan Methodist Association of 1834, and a host of 'Tent Methodists', 'Magic Methodists' of Delamere Forest, 'Quaker Methodists' of Warrington, 'Independent Methodists' of Macclesfield, Barkerites of Bradford, and followers of the fiery Rev. J. R. Stephens of Ashton-under-Lyne.[2] It thus became possible for working men to desert the Church without plunging into theological or political radicalism, and then, as disenchantment and political involvement increased, to leave or be expelled from the more conservative for the more radical connexions, until perhaps they passed finally into secularism or indifference. In this way, for example, Joseph Barker, the Bradford Chartist leader imprisoned in 1848, began as a Wesleyan lay preacher, left to become a travelling preacher and minister for the New Connexion, which expelled him for his Chartist activities in 1841,

---

[1] Phrenology had peculiar philosophical and theological attractions for intellectuals who found Christianity no longer credible but still required the emotional support of a 'religion of humanity'. It played an important part in the ritual of Comte's Positivist Church, where adherents were expected to touch the three (phrenological) organs of love, order and progress. George Eliot took it seriously enough to have her head shaved for her friend Charles Bray to read her 'bumps'. Cf. Royden Harrison, *Before the Socialists: Studies in Labour and Politics, 1861 to 1881* (1965), p. 314; J. F. C. Harrison, *Learning and Living, 1790–1960* (1961), pp. 114–17.

[2] Cf. E. P. Thompson, *op. cit.*, p. 388; Census, 1851, *Religious Worship*, pp. lxxf.

when twenty-nine chapels and four thousand, three hundred and forty-eight 'Barkerites' followed him, and, finally, after many spiritual vicissitudes in England and America, found a congenial home in Primitive Methodism.[1] William Lovett traversed the whole distance, beginning as a Wesleyan, joining the Bryanites, and ending as an Owenite who agreed with the sceptic Francis Place that 'this is the best world of which I have any hope.'[2]

Owenism was the final step for many working men. It was not a religion, in spite of the messianic character of Owen himself, but with its millenarian zeal for co-operative heavens on the (by then) capitalist earth it represented for many the ultimate emancipation from both organized religion and the existing social system. Curiously enough, there was in Owenism a half-step for the nostalgic Christian. Though many members of the working-class movement were aggressive secularists in the tradition of Paine, through the publications of Carlile and the working-class press of the 1820's and 1830's, many were not prepared to abandon religion altogether. For these there was the spiritualism which attracted and finally converted Owen, his son, and many of their followers, including William and Mary Howitt, Gerald Massey the Chartist poet, John Culpan the Halifax Chartist, and so on.[3] And spiritualism was the ideal religion for the emancipated working class: a religion with practically no theology, clergy or organization, completely free from any taint of dependency. It was to the working class what Unitarianism was to the middle class, the final stepping stone between Christianity and unbelief.

It was not necessary for very large numbers, either of the middle or the working class, to remain long on any one stone. Indeed, many were influenced by them who never touched them. As a working man who had lived through the intellectual and spiritual upheavals of the transition remarked,

it was not the number of converts made by the Owenites, Barkerites, or Unitarians, but the influence each and all had on the various religious bodies, the thousands of pamphlets scattered about, lent,

[1] Joseph Barker, *History and Confessions of a Man* . . . (Wortley, 1845), *Teachings of Experience* . . . (1869) and *Life of Joseph Barker, Written by Himself* (ed. J. T. Barker, 1880); Joseph Lawson, *Progress in Pudsey during the Last Sixty Years* (Stanningly, 1887), pp. 76–82; J. F. C. Harrison, *op. cit.*, pp. 45–6, 164–5.

[2] W. Lovett, *Life and Struggles* . . . (1876), pp. 7, 22; Wallas, *Place*, p. 364, Lovett to Place, 16 January 1837.　　[3] Cf. J. F. C. Harrison, *op. cit.*, p. 171.

given and sold, and the every-day discussions carried on in the village [of Pudsey, near Leeds], that made people's minds more liberal and rational without their being aware of it.[1]

Emancipation, in fact, was a negative process: it left men free to choose their belief, or non-belief, as best they could. Some—and the Religious Census shows that their numbers were much larger than alarmist contemporaries believed—chose to remain within the bosom of the Church, and these 'unemancipated' or 'loyalist' middle and working-class Anglicans were to become an important factor in the politics of the viable class society of mid-Victorian England. Others expressed their emancipation by fervent adherence to a range of sects from the quietist Quakers or Wesleyans to the hysterical followers of Richard Brothers and Joanna Southcott. Still others—often the same people in a later phase—expressed it via religious indifference or assertive atheism. Whatever form it took, it represented a rupture of the bonds of patronage and dependency which held the old society together, and prepared the way for the birth of class.

By an apt if irrational instinct the old ruling élite recognized this, at least from the French Revolution onwards, and hit out indiscriminately at the sects, however loyalist they might be. All Dissenters were tarred with the same anti-patriotic brush. Price, Priestley and the Rational Dissenters, and by extension all the old denominations, were bracketed with Paine and the Jacobins; while even the, at that time Tory, Methodists, who never tired of declaring their 'dutiful attachment to their King and Country' were accused of upholding 'a system which tended to overthrow Church and State.'[2] The reason is significant: defence of the Church, which in the eighteenth century had been in greater danger from aristocratic Deists and Sceptics than from the Dissenters, became in the age of alienation defence of the alienating class. As usual, Pitt spoke for the whole class when he declared 'the Church of England, as by law established, to be so essential a part of the constitution that whatever endangered it would necessarily affect the security of the whole.'[3] The counter-attack on the sects served the double purpose of

[1] J. Lawson, op. cit., pp. 80–1; ibid., p. 171.
[2] Cf. U. R. Q. Henriques, Religious Toleration in England, 1787–1833 (1961), chap. iii; Wearmouth, op. cit., pp. 54–60.
[3] Parliamentary History of England, 1796–7, III. 557; Wearmouth, op. cit., p. 56.

provoking the middle ranks and lower orders still further along the path of emancipation and, by awakening the defensive class-consciousness of the aristocracy, of helping to transform the integrated élite of the old society into the segregated upper class of the new. Thus religion played its part even in the creation of the upper class, and well deserves to be called the midwife of all three major classes.

4. THE DELAYED BIRTH

As long as the Great French Wars lasted, patriotism reinforced paternalism to hold overt class conflict in check. There were of course increasing social strains, which came near to bursting point towards the end. War enriched the few and put almost intolerable burdens of taxation and high prices on the many, in a way which seemed to some contemporaries to be not inevitable but the artificial result of the Government's policy of paying for it by means of inflationary loans rather than by taxing the rich. This inequitable policy, and the still more inequitable deflation-ary resumption of cash payments in 1819, which increased both the real value of the funds held by the few and the real burden of taxation of the many, were to play an important part in exacer-bating class conflict after the Wars.

Meanwhile, however, after the very effective suppression of the 'Jacobins' between 1793 and 1797, opposition to the war was largely confined to a dwindling group of aristocratic Whigs, led until his death by Fox and thereafter by Earl Grey, who paid the price for their unpopular attitude in almost permanent exclusion from office. Protests from the middle ranks and lower orders were limited to specific economic grievances and had little or no general political import. The most typical of such protests were the agitation of 1810–12 by the merchants and industrialists against the Orders in Council forbidding exports to Napoleon's Europe, and, leaving aside the running campaign from 1802 to 1814 noticed above for the revival of Tudor wage and labour regulation, the Luddite riots of the framework knitters against starvation wages and other industrial mal-practices of 1812–14.[1] The only general political protest was Cartwright and Wyvill's revival from 1812 onwards of the old

[1] i.e. not against new machinery as such; cf. E. J. Hobsbawm, *Labouring Men* (1964), chap. ii, 'The Machine Breakers'.

campaign for Parliamentary Reform, in the shape of the Union and Hampden Clubs. But these were 'highly respectable'[1]—that is, they did not assume the character of a class attack upon the aristocracy, at least until the War was over.

It was the peace which brought the old society to bed of the new. The gestation had been long and the delay unnatural. The pressures of industrialism and urbanization, of aristocratic provocation and reaction from below, had long been building up for a birth, but were held in check not only by the womb of dependency but also by the artificial pressure of the patriotic war effort. The post-war distress, with its acute competition for income and unrequited demand for positive remedies, brought the natal pressures of industrialism and resentment of aristo-cratic abdication to bursting point. One opposing pressure, patriotism, being removed, the other, dependency, failed to hold, and the bawling child came tumbling forth.

In other words, it was in the first five years of peace, between Waterloo and the Queen's Trial, that the vertical antagonisms and horizontal solidarities of class came for the first time, clearly, unmistakably, and irrevocably, to supplant the vertical connec-tions and horizontal rivalries of dependency and interest.

The essence of class is not merely antagonism towards an-other class or classes but organized antagonism with a nation-wide appeal to all members of one broad social level. By this definition the working class almost sprang into existence with the Parliamentary Reform movement of 1816–19. 'In 1816 began a popular agitation for Radical Reform which in three years almost rose to revolution point, and then subsided as suddenly as it had sprung up.'[2] It took its leaders completely by surprise. Cobbett, who had been hammering at Reform for a dozen years without effect but who now characteristically took credit for the first appeal to the working class, avowed: 'The labouring classes seemed as if they had never heard a word on politics before. The effect on their minds was like what might be expected to be produced on the eyes of one bred up in the dark and brought out all of a sudden into broad daylight.'[3]

---

[1] Butler, *op. cit.*, p. 27. [2] *Ibid.*

[3] *Political Register*, 2 August 1817, referring to the *Weekly Register*, 2 Novem-ber 1816, 'An Address to the Journeymen and Labourers of England, Wales and Scotland', which, published separately at 2d., sold 200,000 copies.

It was not the leadership which gave the movement its working-class character: Cobbett was the nearest to a working man amongst them, while Orator Hunt was an independent occupier farming his own land who prided himself on being a gentleman, Sir Charles Wolseley was an officer and a seventh baronet, and Sir Francis Burdett was an aristocrat as snobbish as his wife, one of the banking Coutts, was rich. It was, first of all, the platform of the movement, household and then universal suffrage, and, secondly, the means, vast mass meetings with democratic resolutions carried by acclamation, both of which alienated practically everybody but the emancipated working class. On behalf of the aristocratic Reformers Grey dissociated himself completely, shuddering at 'the principle universal suffrage which is the only one which will be tolerated by the leaders of the popular party, or rather of the Mob, or of the the means by which they are endeavouring to effect their object, which certainly is not Reform but Revolution,' and he declared he must 'avoid even the intercourse of private society with *them* whom I consider to have degraded themselves from the character of gentlemen.'[1] On behalf of the middle-class Radicals Brougham made fun in Parliament of the 'antiquarian research' and 'wild and mischievous schemes' of the popular movement.[2] The unprecedented means were even more offensive to Tories bred in the old society, like Canning, who clearly recognized their socially disruptive significance:

> When . . . it is asserted that such meetings were never before suppressed, the simple answer is, they were never before attempted to be holden.

They were in contradiction to the spirit of the law, which prescribed a corporate character, that is, meetings of the freemen or inhabitants of a particular place or community, not open meetings of rootless individuals:

> Just so at the beginning of the French Revolution: the first work of the Reformers was to loosen every established political relation, every legal holding of man to man, to destroy every corporation, to

[1] Earl Grey to Sir Robert Wilson, the Radical general, 1819; Butler, *op. cit.*, pp. 34–5.
[2] Speech in House of Commons, 14 February 1817, *Blackwood's*, 1817, I. 106.

destroy every subsisting class of society, and to reduce the nation into individuals, in order, afterwards to congregate them into mobs.[1]

But that the movement was not one of rootless individuals is sufficiently testified by the evidence both of its working-class members and of the Government which tried to suppress it. Samuel Bamford, the 'weaver-poet', one of the Lancashire delegates to the great national convention of Reformers at the Crown and Anchor Tavern in January 1817 and leader of the Middleton contingent at Peterloo, gives chapter and verse for the awakening of the working-class political awareness by Cobbett and the Radical press, for the consciously working-class Hampden Clubs and district and national meetings of delegates, and for the quasi-military drilling of contingents to the mass meetings which so alarmed the Government.[2] Lord Sidmouth, the Home Secretary, bombarded by reports from J.P.s, military commanders and informers of secret oaths, midnight drillings, purchase of arms, and the date—three times over—of the planned rising, was convinced of the existence of an 'organized system of rebellion.'[3]

And to the higher ranks generally there was no doubt about the revolutionary character of 'this nuisance of mere plebeian insolence and profligacy which has been gaining strength for the last two or three years.' As a Scottish Tory saw it,

> The Unions became general throughout the manufacturing districts of Scotland—They were divided into classes systematically—A regular communication was kept up among them—Committees and Sub-committees were appointed for the purpose of forming plans, and digesting the means of carrying them into effect.

The higher classes tried to relieve the distress, but failed:

> The views of the reformers became desperate. Their conduct and deportment towards their superiors was totally altered. They had become indifferent and even insolent. Equality of rights and of property was the end at which they aimed, and the particular mode of partition and allotment was already aimed at. As these objectives could not be accomplished without force of arms, it was resolved to have recourse to that alternative.[4]

[1] Speech at Liverpool, January 1820, *Blackwood's*, 1820, VII. 13–15.
[2] *Passages in the Life of a Radical* (1893 ed.), chaps. i, iii-vi, xii, xxiii, xxv.
[3] Pellew, *op. cit.*, esp. III. 82.
[4] 'The Warder, No. I', *Blackwood's*, 1819–20, VI. 208.

The result was the abortive Glasgow rising of 5 April 1820 and the first Scottish treason trials since 1794.[1] The only other risings were the 'Pentrich Revolution' of Jeremy Brandreth and the poor Derbyshire framework knitters misled by Oliver the Spy in 1817, and the Cato Street Conspiracy by Arthur Thistlewood and the Spenceans—the only group which really aimed at a division of property—in 1820.[2]

The significance of the working-class Reform movement in these five years was not the threat of revolution, which was confined to a few cranks and extremists. On the contrary, it was, as Cobbett was never tired of explaining, the direct opposite: for the first time working-class protest, instead of exploding into riots and mob-violence—as indeed still happened in these years amongst the less sophisticated framework knitters and agricultural labourers—was organized on a national scale for a non-violent purpose. A resolution passed at the mass meeting at Hunslet Moor near Leeds a month before Peterloo puts both aristocratic abdication and the national non-violent reaction of the working class in a nutshell:

> That as our legislators have, in innumerable instances, manifested a cruel and criminal indifference to our truly distressed situation, and treated our petitions with contempt, we therefore make this solemn appeal to our oppressed fellow countrymen, praying them to join us in a National Union, the object of which is to obtain an overwhelming majority of the male population, to present such a petition as can scarcely fail to have the desired effect, and to adopt such other constitutional measures as may be deemed most expedient to procure for us the redress of our manifold grievances.[3]

There were other attempts at working-class organization, especially in the industrial field, of which the most notable were the 'Philanthropic Society' or 'General Union of Trades' organized by the Manchester Spinners' Union in 1818, and the London shipwright John Gast's 'Philanthropic Hercules' of 1819, both of which quickly disappeared.[4] One abortive attempt, of

---

[1] 'Thoughts on the Proceedings of the Special Commission', *Blackwood's*, 1820, VII. 561–5.

[2] Cf. R. J. White, *Waterloo to Peterloo* (1957), chap. xiv and pp. 189–90.

[3] *P.P.*, 1819–20, IV, *Papers relating to the Internal State of the Country, November 1819*, No. 8, p. 9.

[4] G. D. H. Cole, *Attempts at General Union* (1953), pp. 7–12.

immense significance for the future, was Robert Owen's first tentative appeal to the working classes to adopt his new social system which the higher classes had rejected—a turning point in the career of the father of socialism, mass trade unionism and the co-operative movement which was signalized by the distance between the titles of two of his works, published in 1818 and 1819 respectively: 'Two Memorials *on Behalf of* the Working Classes' and 'An Address *to* the Working Classes'.[1] At that moment, however, the emancipated working class were too obsessed with politics to listen to his messianic message.

After the 'Peterloo Massacre' of 1819 the working-class Reform movement also subsided, or was diverted by the agitation over the Royal Divorce Bill, to the importance of which in uniting Reformers of all classes we shall return. Nevertheless, it had completed its task of creating a separate working-class consciousness. As a perspicacious opponent of the movement put it in 1820,

> Never in any age or country was there so firm an alliance betwixt the higher and lower orders as there existed in Great Britain, until it was fatally disturbed of late years by . . . the spirit of turbulence and faction; . . . the cord has been snapped by the revolt of the labouring classes from their natural protectors and best friends . . . .[2]

It was between 1815 and 1820 that the working class was born.

The birth of the middle class was less traumatic but no less real. During the Wars patriotism had combined with commercial prosperity to keep the middle ranks loyal and quiescent. As the first editor of the *Manchester Guardian* was to write of the northern manufacturers during wartime,

> they did not interest themselves about the internal policy of their country, or if they meddled at all, saved themselves the trouble of inquiry by a general determination to 'support the government'.[3]

Their political activity was confined to petitioning as an old society interest for the redress of specific grievances, such as the income tax of 1799 or the Orders in Council of 1807–12. It was

---

[1] My italics.

[2] 'The Warder, No. IV', *Blackwood's*, 1819–20, VI. 455.

[3] [J. E. Taylor], *Notes and Observations . . . on the Papers relative to the Internal State of the Country recently presented to Parliament* (1820), p. 202; D. Read, *Press and People, 1790–1850* (1961), p. 41.

the post-war depression with its sharpening of the competition for income and, above all, the provocative use of the landlords' political power to defend rent at the expense of profits and wages, which opened the eyes of the middle ranks and turned them into a class. The Corn Law of 1815 was for them what the repeal of paternal industrial legislation and the attack on the poor laws was for the lower orders: practical proof that the ruling aristocracy, in spite of its philosophy, governed only in its own interest. The Prime Minister might declare that 'it has been well said in a foreign country, when it was asked what should be done to make commerce prosper, the answer was *laissez-faire*' and that in adversity 'the great interests of the country, the agricultural, the manufacturing, and the commercial interests . . . must stand or fall together';[1] but when adversity arrived, it seemed, *laissez-faire* meant full support for agriculture while leaving industry and commerce to sink. 'Perish commerce, let the landed interests live,' was how 'A Manchester Manufacturer' saw Government policy in 1819.[2]

Irresponsible use of aristocratic power, then, provoked the middle class into existence. Old society methods failed. Protest meetings and mass petitions—54,000 signatures from Manchester, 24,000 from Leeds—failed to halt the Corn Law.[3] The old society compact by which the landed interest ruled on behalf of all the rest was therefore broken, and the middle class must assert its own power through its own representatives. The landed and commercial interests, demanded 'A Manchester Manufacturer', must be 'put upon an equal footing in Parliament' through 'a better representation of commercial and artisan towns and districts.'[4]

Still more significantly, the middle class became ready for the first time to listen to a group of thoroughly emancipated and disillusioned intellectuals who up to now had been more often laughed at than read: the Benthamites. In their appropriately more dignified way, Ricardo's *Principles of Political Economy* (1817) and James Mill's *Essay on Government* (1820) did for

[1] *Hansard*, 1819, XXIII. 1249, and 1820, I. 1119; W. R. Brock, *Lord Liverpool and Liberal Toryism, 1820–27* (1941), pp. 41, 43.

[2] 'A Manchester Manufacturer', *National Good, or, the Utility of the Landed and Commercial Interests being United* (1819), p. 7; Read, *op. cit.*, p. 43.

[3] *Ibid.*, p. 42.

[4] *Ibid.*, p. 43.

the middle class what Cobbett's *Address* did for the working class: they gave expression to the emergent fact of class antagonism. In the first Ricardo armed the new-found anti-landlordism of the middle class with economic logic. His theory of rent, that 'the whole surplus produce of the soil, after deducting from it only such moderate profits as are sufficient to encourage accumulation, must finally rest with the landlord', made the landlord a parasite exploiting the other two classes, more especially the profit-making class, and the community as a whole: 'The dealings between the landlord and the public are not like dealings in trade, whereby both the seller and buyer may equally be said to gain, but the loss is wholly on one side, and the gain wholly on the other. . . .'[1] Small wonder that Ricardo, on entering Parliament in 1819, was, to his own surprise, immediately seized upon as the spokesman of the middle class.

James Mill, without whose persuasion and encouragement Ricardo would not have written the *Principles*, was still more explicit in his denunciation of the landed ruling class. His *Essay on Government*, written for the *Encyclopaedia Britannica* but reprinted in 1820 for a much wider audience, is nothing less than a diatribe against government by an aristocracy. Not only will an hereditary aristocracy, deprived by its wealth of the strongest motives for intellectual labour, be defective in the mental powers required for government, but they will have an interest in exploiting the rest of the community:

> they will take from the rest of the community as much as they please of the objects of desire. They will thus defeat the very end for which Government was instituted. The unfitness, therefore, of an Aristocracy to be entrusted with the powers of Government, rests on demonstration.

Direct democracy on the Athenian model being impossible, 'in the Representative System alone the securities for good government are to be found.' And the infallible safeguard in such a system, based on universal suffrage, against the tyranny of the many was 'the wisdom of the middle rank. It is enough that the great majority of the people never cease to be guided by that

[1] Ricardo, *op. cit.*, I. 335, 336; cf. *Notes on Malthus, ibid.*, II. 157, n. 88: '. . . profits are the fund from which all rent is derived. There is no rent which at one time did not constitute profits.'

rank; and we may, with some confidence, challenge the adversaries of the people to produce a single instance to the contrary in the history of the world.'[1] This blatant attempt to substitute middle-class for aristocratic political leadership of society was exactly what increasing numbers of the middle class now wanted to hear. Though few went so far with Mill as universal suffrage, from this point onwards the curbing of the political power of the aristocracy by the combined force of the newly emancipated middle and working classes was only a matter of time and opportunity. In this awakening to consciousness not only of their conflict of economic and political interest with the aristocracy but of their potential strength the same five years saw the birth of the middle class.

The union of the middle and working classes against the aristocracy was hastened and anticipated by two events which together marked the end of the period of birth, Peterloo and the Queen's Trial. The 'Manchester Massacre' hastened it by throwing into glaring contrast the provocative use of force by the ruling class and the manifest lack of revolutionary intent on the part of the working class. From that moment, while the separatist working-class Reform movement subsided, a union of middle and working-class Reformers, under the paradoxical patronage of Whig aristocrats still operating in the context of old society interest politics, became an increasing possibility.

The Royal Divorce Bill, although—or perhaps because—it diverted popular attention away from Reform, actually anticipated the successful alliance of the Great Reform crisis. As a critical Tory put it,

> Upon the radical question I conceive the Queen's trial to have been productive of the most important consequences. Had it been possible to devise a plan to bring all the various ranks and classes of the discontented into simultaneous action against the state and monarchy, it was the agitation of that most inexpedient measure.[2]

And a patrician Whig was moved by it to embrace Reform for the first time:

> I have never been satisfied [as to the necessity of Reform] until the

[1] *Essay on Government* (ed. Sir E. Barker, 1937), pp. 12, 33, 73.

[2] Henry Lascelles, 'On the Present State of Public Affairs at Home', *Blackwood's*, 1821, X. 335–6.

conduct of the House of Commons relative to the Queen. On this question one half of the higher ranks were on one side, while on the other side were the other half of the higher ranks and the whole of the middle and lower classes of society, and yet notwithstanding this extraordinary preponderance of public opinion in one scale, the members of parliament threw themselves into the other scale at the request of Ministers with as little hesitation as if they were voting upon the most trivial and uninteresting question. These considerations have persuaded me that public opinion has not its due weight in the House of Commons, and that therefore some measures ought to be taken to give the people a more adequate representation.[1]

Loss of confidence and division of the aristocracy in the face of the united middle and working classes—this was to be the formula for the passing of the Reform Bill. Meanwhile, in 1820–21 it was a sufficient proof that the dependent middle ranks and lower orders had been emancipated, and that the years between Waterloo and the Queen's Trial saw the birth of class.

[1] Lord Milton (later 3rd Earl Fitzwilliam) to Sir G. Cayley, 11 March 1831; F. M. L. Thompson, *English Landed Society in the Nineteenth Century* (1963), pp. 280–1.

VII

The Struggle between the Ideals

T H E new class society did not, like Pallas Athene, spring into existence full-grown and fully armed. It had a great deal of growing up to do before it became the viable class society of mid-Victorian England. In 1820 the classes were still very immature and scarcely knew their own strength and limits. Contemporaries often talked of the higher, middle and lower or working *classes*, each in the plural, and this was more than a hangover from the pluralistic ranks and orders of the old society. It reflected the vagueness of the social facts, the existence of numerous layers and sections within the three major classes which only time and the experience of class conflict would hammer into something like compact entities.

Nevertheless, it was from the beginning one of the functions of class consciousness to draw a sharp line between each class and the next by means of the conflict taking place across it. The hotter the firing, the better the troops knew where the front line was, and the less they cared about internal divisions—though there would always be those who neither knew nor cared which side they were on, and others whose hearts were on the other side. What kept the armies together was the competition for income between rent, profits and wages, and in the secular deflation which lasted from the post-war slump of 1815–1820 down to the late 1840's the competition for income was extremely sharp. Whatever happened to them in real terms—and this, as we saw in Chapter V, is still the subject of much dispute amongst historians—rents, profits and wages between 1815 and 1848 were all under severe pressure, and the general trend of all three in terms of current values was downward.[1] The great conflicts of the age were all at bottom struggles for income: the struggle over the corn laws classically so, and even Parliamentary Reform was, in large part, a struggle for the control of government spending and taxation, which weighed far more heavily on some incomes than on others. Certainly, the industrial conflicts of this seminal period of trade unionism were obviously so, while Chartism was basically, in the words of J. R. Stephens, 'a knife and fork question'.[2]

Yet income alone, though a necessary, was never a sufficient motivation for class antagonism, or class would be as old as rent, profits and wages. What was also required was a conscious image of the class in its relation to rival classes, and of the ideal society in which it would find its rightful place. The troops, or at least a considerable portion of them, had to have some notion of the army as a whole and its position relative to the enemy, and of the objective at which they were aiming. Moreover, since morale was half the battle, the image had to be flattering to one's own side and demoralizing to one's opponents: it had to be an ideal image of the representative member of one's own class as the lynchpin of society, the only role-bearer who fully justified his place, the ideal citizen whom the rest should emulate, and of the ideal society as one in which this ideal citizen would be suitably honoured and rewarded.

The class ideal thus sublimated the crude material self-interest of the competition for income, sanctified the role of class members by the contribution they made to society and its well-being, and so justified the class and its claim to a special place and special treatment within the social framework. It had a twofold function: first, to act as a catalyst in the formation and growth of class, a 'seed' around which the class could crystallize and coagulate, a magnetic pole radiating lines of force throughout the beneficiaries of the common source of income and

[1] Cf. Rostow, *British Economy*, p. 8; Deane and Cole, *op. cit.*, p. 23; F. M. L. Thompson, *op. cit.*, pp. 231–5.

[2] G. D. H. Cole, *Chartist Portraits* (1965), p. 74.

orienting them towards itself; second, to operate as an instrument of propaganda or psychological warfare *vis-à-vis* the other classes, to undermine their confidence in their own ideal, and try to win them over to one's own. In other words, it was a means of educating both the class itself to class-consciousness, and the rest of society to accept it at its own valuation.

The class which was most successful in this educational and moral struggle, in uniting its own members and imposing its ideal upon others, would win the day and have most influence in determining the actual society in which all had to live and in approximating it more or less closely to its own ideal. The primary conflict in the newly born class society of the early nineteenth century was a struggle for the minds and hearts of men. It was a struggle between the ideals.

Perhaps the most significant effect of the sublimation of the competition for income into a struggle between ideals was that it allowed men to embrace ideals other than that which sprang from their own source of income. If this had not been so the old society in which the aristocratic ideals of the leisured gentlemen and of the open aristocracy based on property and patronage were universally accepted, could never have existed, while in the new society victory would automatically have gone to the biggest battalion, the working class, which it manifestly did not. Further, it helps to explain one of the most puzzling phenomena of class conflict, the large proportion of leaders and spokesmen who led or spoke for classes other than their own. These 'social cranks', as they may be called—men like Professor Malthus, the premier apologist of the landed class, Ricardo their landed opponent, James Mill the civil-servant spokesman of the capitalist class, and Robert Owen, William Thompson and Feargus O'Connor, the respectively capitalist, landowning and gentleman-journalist champions of the working class—played a part out of all proportion to their rarity in the class conflict of their day. Indeed, it might almost be said that only the social crank could be sufficiently disinterested to possess the fervour and evoke the passionate response of charismatic leadership. Certainly, no landowner, capitalist or workman could have made the outrageous claims for their class which Malthus, James Mill and Feargus O'Connor did for those which they adopted.

Finally, since as we shall see there was in the professional middle class a whole ready-made class of potential social cranks, it helps to explain the very special role of professional men in the class conflicts of the new society.

Not that the leaders and spokesmen invented the ideals and imposed them on their followers. For one thing, they were at least as much chosen by the class as the class by them: they 'spoke to their condition', and when they did not were rejected. For another, the ideals of all the major classes had their origins deep in the old society, and welled up to the surface when the old ground was broken up. There was in each enough nostalgia for certain aspects of the old social structure to ease the transition to the new. In other words, the new class ideals were a transmutation of older elements in the heat generated by class conflict. As such they were not the novel creation of any one man or small band of leaders, but the spontaneous response of large social groups to the release of deep and long suppressed yearnings which had been latent in the old society.

1. THE ENTREPRENEURIAL IDEAL

The ideal citizen for the bulk of the middle class was, naturally, the capitalist, and the ideal society a class society based on capital and competition. Yet these terms were used in a more specific sense than today, and they were much more disruptive of the old society than at first sight appears. The capitalist of the ideal was the active owner-manager of the Industrial Revolution, not the passive or remotely controlling financier of later corporate capitalism. So much was he the typical business man of the age that neither Adam Smith nor the Ricardians thought it necessary to distinguish him from any other kind of capitalist, and it was left to the Continentals like J. B. Say to differentiate between the *entrepreneur* and the *rentier*. Capital likewise was active property, as remote—at least until the capitalist's retirement—from the passive investment of the fundholder or (in theory) of the landowner as a work-horse from a hunter. Competition was not the bloodless competition between material products and between abstract corporations of the modern 'free enterprise' economy: it was *individual* competition, the competition of flesh-and-blood men for wealth, power and social status. For these reasons it may, with judicious anachronism, be called not just the capitalist but the entrepreneurial ideal.

The entrepreneur, according to the ideal, was the lynchpin of society. Although labour was the source of all wealth, it was capital which called it forth and set it in operation. The entrepreneur was the impressario, the creative force, the initiator of the economic cycle. He it was who conceived the end, found the means, bore the burden of risk, and paid out the other factors of production. All this he did for the meagre return of a profit fixed by competition, unable ever to rise more than momentarily above the common rate, and subject to a long-term natural tendency to fall as, with the increasing cost and difficulty of producing food, wages and rent trenched in upon it.[1] The worker, although indispensable and deserving of the highest wages which society could afford, took no thought for the morrow and had nothing to do but to perform at the entrepreneur's bidding a full day's work for a wage fixed by competition at the level of customary subsistence.[2] The landlord, on the other hand, was a mere parasite, a member of the 'unproductive class', whose rent was an unearned income equivalent to the whole surplus produce after the subsistence wages and the common rate of profit had been paid.[3] If the worker was the horse and the landlord the non-paying passenger, the entrepreneur was driver, conductor, pathfinder, caterer and provider of provender all rolled into one.

Capital, it followed, was the mainspring of the economic machine: 'that fund by whose extent the extent of the productive industry of the country must always be regulated.' The national capital—the total fund for the employment of labour in the hands of the entrepreneurs—was the real wealth and strength of the country. It could never be too large: 'there is no amount of capital which may not be employed in a country, because demand is only limited by production.'[4] Derived entirely from the capitalist's self-denying abstention from consumption, savings were automatically invested in further production,

[1] Ricardo, *Principles of Political Economy and Taxation*, in *Works and Correspondence* (ed. Sraffa), I. 110–27; cf. J. S. Mill, *Principles of Political Economy* (1904 ed.), p. 416.

[2] Ricardo, *op. cit.*, I. 162; and cf. I. 94, 100–1.   [3] *Ibid.*, I. 270, 335.

[4] *Ibid.*, 151–2, 290.

raising wages and, via the demand for food, the landlord's rent. Capital could easily be diminished, by the selfishness or fecklessness of the other two classes: by the landed rulers who imposed heavy taxes on profits or transferred a portion to themselves by means of corn laws, or by the working class who might underbreed, and so raise wages at the expense of profits, or overbreed beyond the capacity of capital to employ them, and so hasten the 'stationary state' of mass poverty.[1] Capital was the chief benefactor of society, the parent of all progress, the only bulwark between prosperity and the poverty of countries such as Ireland, with 'labourers unfed for want of employment, and land unproductive for want of labour. . . . The connecting link is capital, and that link is wanting.'[2]

It was also, or ought to be in an ideal society, undistorted by aristocratic corruption and jobbery, the chief determinant of social status. In this it was the exact equivalent of property in the old society, except that the emphasis was, naturally, on active acquisition rather than passive endowment. In the words of a typical early Victorian capitalist, 'society will ever remain composed of classes. Some are born with fortune; more are born without any, and the struggle for it is very serious. It is the best educated of these, the most talented and industrious, who take the prize; but *all* may possess industry which is, after all, the starting point and by far the most valuable power.'[3]

The change of emphasis is significant, for it introduces the second principle of the entrepreneurial ideal society, competition. Competition did for capital what patronage did for property in the old society: buttressed its selection to positions of power, wealth and prestige, and filled those positions which the first principle alone could not fill. Indeed, it played a larger part in their ideal than patronage had done in the old society: for whereas passive property, in land or the funds, required active exertion to get rid of, active capital by its nature required constant attention to keep it in being. While patronage, therefore, was never more than an adjunct to property, competition was inherent in the very idea of capital and inseparable from it.

[1] *Ibid.*, I. 108–9.
[2] [John Wilson], 'The Real State of Ireland in 1827', *Blackwood's*, 1827, XXII. 25.
[3] Edmund Potter, *A Picture of a Manufacturing District* (Manchester, 1856), pp. 54–5.

Patronage, as we have seen, contained an element of selection by merit, measured by the judgment and importance of the patron. Competition, on the other hand, appealed to a far more impartial judge, 'fortune', 'market forces', or material success. Adam Smith's 'invisible hand' of competition was doubly benevolent. It led the self-interest of the individual to promote the good of the whole community, and, conversely, it guaranteed success to the most meritorious: those who best served the interest of the whole best promoted their own interest. The elegant moral symmetry of 'the competitive system', which ran throughout classical economics down to the first edition of J. S. Mill's *Principles*, appealed most powerfully to both the moral self-righteousness and the material self-interest of the middle class.[1] Competition, in contrast to the 'monopoly', 'privilege' and 'restriction' of the old economic system, was universally beneficial. It kept up supply and kept down prices in the market; it maintained profits at a remunerative level, neither so high as to exploit the consumer nor so low as to discourage saving and future production; and it fixed wages at exactly the level which was best for the worker and society, low enough to provide full employment for all workers and to make it necessary for them to work full-time in order to earn their customary standard of living, high enough to guarantee them subsistence and to produce the next generation of workers. The only member of society to escape its beneficent discipline was the landlord who, since he provided no service save that of permitting access to nature's gifts, merely enjoyed the fruits of others' competition.

It was, above all, socially beneficial. 'The theory of self-dependence', as J. S. Mill (or Harriet Taylor) was to call it in contrast to 'the theory of dependence and protection' of 'the patriarchial or paternal system',[2] evoked not only manly self-respect and responsibility but also the ambition to rise in social status which was the chief source of the energy and drive behind the progress of society. Cobden challenged the maternal charity of the squire's wife and daughters with that of his own class:

---

[1] Smith, *Wealth of Nations*, I. 456; Mill, *Principles* (1848), I. 239; cf. L. Robbins, *The Theory of Economic Policy in English Classical Political Economy* (1952), pp. 11–19, 150.

[2] Mill, *Principles* (1904), pp. 455–6; for Harriet Taylor's influence cf. Mill's *Autobiography* (World's Classics, 1958), p. 208.

Mine is the masculine species of charity which would lead me to inculcate in the minds of the labouring classes the love of independence, the privilege of self-respect, the disdain of being patronized or petted, the desire to accumulate and the ambition to rise.[1]

By individual competition anyone with energy and ability, however humble his birth, could climb the ladder of entrepreneurial society. From this belief logically stemmed one of the most powerful instruments of propaganda ever developed by any class to justify itself and seduce others to its own ideal: the myth of the self-made man. As Samuel Smiles was to put it in *Self-Help*, 'What some men are, all without difficulty might be. Employ the same means, and the same results will follow.' The self-made man was the ideal entrepreneur, the man without any initial property or patronage, any education other than self-education, or any advantage other than native talent, who by self-help and force of character made his way to wealth and status. It was a real myth, in that it had a sufficient basis in fact —as Samuel Smiles' *Lives of Engineers* from James Brindley to George Stephenson bears witness—to make it eminently plausible, while remaining utterly fictitious as a sociological explanation of the entrepreneurs as a class. The number of industrialists even in the Industrial Revolution who began without capital or connections of any kind was a minute fraction of the whole, yet 'what some men are all without difficulty might be' was an argument which overwhelmed statistics and made the self-made man to the nineteenth century what the football pool winner is to the twentieth. The myth was the apotheosis of the entrepreneurial ideal. In it, as we shall see, the notions of active capital and beneficent competition were fused with that of the entrepreneur as the autogenous benefactor of society into the decisive weapon of the class struggle.

The entrepreneurial ideal, like the other class ideals, had its roots in the old society. Capital, admittedly, was from a neutral standpoint but old society property in its active phase, and implicit in Locke's labour theory of property. 'Who sees not,' Hume, the link between Locke and the Utilitarians, asks on the active swing of the pendulum, '. . . that whatever is produced or improved by man's art or industry ought, for ever, to be secured to him, in order to give encouragement to such *useful* habits and

[1] J. Morley, *Life of Cobden* (1903), p. 137.

accomplishments?' and, immediately returning on the passive swing, 'That the property ought also to descend to children and relations, for the same *useful* purpose?'[1] No family-founding capitalist, least of all Ricardo, could disagree with that.

Competition, similarly, was rooted in the dynamism of the old society, and its justification of inequality. As Malthus, the rearguard of the old system, put it, in the passage already quoted, 'If no man could hope to rise or fear to fall in society; if industry did not bring its own reward, and indolence its punishment; we could not hope to see that animated activity in bettering our own condition which now forms the master-spring of public prosperity.'[2] The condemnation of idleness and the commendation of self-help and independence were old themes amongst the puritans and mercantilists of the old society's middle ranks, as, for example, Thomas Starkey in the 1530's on 'idle and unprofitable persons' or Sir Josiah Child in 1698 on high interest rates which suffer 'Idleness to suck the Breasts of Industry'.[3]

And the ideal of the self-made man was potential, at least, in the pride of the middle ranks in the endless stream of 'new men' who rose to landed property in the old society.[4] It became quite explicit in Tory opponents of the entrepreneurial ideal who nevertheless defended Lord Chancellor Eldon as 'a man who began the world with no fortune but his education and his talents—with no connexions whatever—with no pretence to any sort of external aids. . . . Self-raised and self-sustained . . . a splendid example of the power of merit—a living witness that there is at least one country in the world where merit can do everything.'[5]

These close connections with the older ideal, however, only carried the thrusts of the new one nearer the heart. Active capital, open competition and the productive entrepreneur were a standing indictment of passive property, closed patronage and

[1] D. Hume, *Essays, Moral, Political, and Literary* (ed. T. H. Green and T. H. Grose, 1875), II. 189.

[2] T. R. Malthus, *Essay on Population* (Everyman, 1951), II. 254.

[3] T. Starkey, *A Dialogue between Cardinal Pole and Thomas Lupset* (ed. J. M. Cowper, 1871), p. 89; J. Child, *A New Discourse on Trade* (1698), p. 21.

[4] Cf. chap. ii, § 3, above.

[5] 'The Late Whig Attacks on the Lord Chancellor', *Blackwood's*, 1823, XIV. 202; Eldon did not in fact begin without fortune: his father was a prosperous Tyneside coal-fitter and 'new man'—cf. E. Hughes, *North Country Life*, I. 165–6.

the leisured gentleman. By the light of capital, property meant idleness. Adam Smith bequeathed to the classical economists the distinction between the productive and the unproductive members of society, and singled out the landlords as men who 'love to reap where they never sowed'; but he said worse things about business men, who were in a continuous conspiracy against consumers, against their workers and against the public at large, while the interest of the landlords, like that of the labourers, was 'strictly and inseparably connected with the general interest of society.'[1] It was left to Ricardo and his followers to kick out this prop, and leave the landlords not merely unproductive but parasitic, compared with the least active capitalist. As Nassau Senior put it,

> Wages and profits are the creation of man. They are the recompense for the sacrifice made, in the one case, of ease; in the other, of immediate enjoyment. But a considerable part of the produce of every country is the recompense of no sacrifice whatever; is received by those who neither labour nor put by, but merely hold out their hands to accept the offerings of the rest of the community.[2]

And J. S. Mill: 'They grow richer as it were in their sleep, without working, risking or economizing. What claim have they, on the general principle of social justice, to this accession of riches?'[3] Business men were even more outspoken than the economists. A Glasgow merchant and Tory critic of aristocratic 'abdication' condemned 'the enormous free incomes of the modern landlords' who had shed their responsibilities as 'custodians of the soil, for the behoof of the nation at large' and 'have been reduced to the condition of DRONES', thus anticipating a whole literature of anti-landlord metaphor down to Joseph Chamberlain's 'they toil not, neither do they spin.'[4]

Similarly, by the light of competition patronage meant corruption. For James Mill it was the device by which the aristocracy redistributed to itself what it extracted from the people,

---

[1] Cf. Smith, *Wealth of Nations*, I. 67, 101, 134, 148, 263, 265, 432, 459.

[2] N. W. Senior, *Political Economy* (1872 ed.), p. 89.

[3] J. S. Mill *Principles*, p. 492.

[4] 'Bandana' [John Galt], 'Hints to Country Gentlemen', *Blackwood's*, 1822, XII, 483–4; J. L. Garvin, *Life of Chamberlain* (1931–51), I. 392; cf. 'The Tenure of Land', *Westminster Review*, 1864, XXVI. 122; 'The position of our landlords, "who toil not, neither do they spin", ... is fast becoming unique'; and same phrase in W. Lovett, *Life and Struggles*, p. 131.

and its abuse of government appointments was exemplified by its extension to the colonies:

> 'The Few' . . . find in colonies, a thing which is very dear to them; they find, the one part of them, the precious matter with which to influence; the other, the precious matter with which *to be* influenced; —the one, the precious matter with which to make political dependents; the other, the precious matter with which they are made political dependents;—the one, the precious matter with which they augment their power; the other, the precious matter with which they augment their riches.[1]

John Wade's *Black Book of England; or Corruption Unmasked* (1820) was little more than an account of the acknowledged patronage in Church and State in the form of appointments and pensions in the Civil List and other published sources. Francis Place thought in 1830 that it would take a revolution, or the threat of it, to cure it:

> The whole scheme of our Government is essentially corrupt, and no corrupt system ever reformed itself. Our system could not reform itself if it would. Take away corruption and nothing remains.[2]

For Sydney Smith the opponents of Reform 'want to keep the bees from buzzing and stinging, in order that they may rob the hive in peace.'[3]

It followed, then, that by the light of the productive entrepreneur, the leisured gentleman, the ideal citizen of the old society, was a useless parasite who contributed nothing to society and abused his indefensible wealth and power. The world's largest calico printer boasted of his little town: 'We are literally nearly all workers. We have scarcely a resident amongst us living on independent means—leading a strictly idle life.'[4] And a Tory defender of the aristocracy in 1826 ironically summed up the attitude of the new ideal: '. . . ye proud landholders of England! You are not merely useless—you are an evil to your country!'[5]

Thus the entrepreneurial ideal confronted the aristocratic at every point. In politics it demanded the abolition of patronage and corruption by means of 'such a reform of the House of

---

[1] J. Mill, *Colony, loc. cit.*, pp. 31–2.   [2] Wallas, *Place*, p. 256.
[3] S. Smith, *Works*, (1859), p. 671.   [4] E. Potter, *op. cit.*, p. 24.
[5] [Robinson], 'Mr. M. Culloch's Irish Evidence', *Blackwood's*, 1826, XIX. 69.

Commons as may render its votes the express image of the opinion of the middle orders of Britain.'[1] In commerce it demanded the abolition of protection and monopoly as symbolized by the Corn Laws, and the completion of the system of free trade. In industrial relations it demanded 'free trade in Labour', the abolition of all State interference between employer and (adult) worker, including (be it noted) the Combination Acts, and the substitution of the contractual relations of employer and employed for the paternal relations of master and servant. A Tory critic of the repeal of the Combination Acts rightly blamed the political economists: 'it was not an insulated measure. It formed part of what is called the new system of Free Trade'; and he complained of the 'language employed by the Economists':

> Their anxiety to destroy the obedience of the one, and the authority of the other, was most remarkable. In Mr. Brougham's pamphlet on the Education of the People, we think the terms, servants and masters, are never used; it is constantly—the working classes and their employers. . . . Why are the good old English words—servant and master, to be struck out of our language?[2]

It inevitably extended itself to 'free trade in land', the abolition of the devices by which the landowners kept the great estates together in a few hands: 'The political economists occasionally raise an immense outcry because the land of this country belongs to a comparatively few people. They cannot endure the law of primogeniture and entails; a very large estate they regard as an abomination. Oh! they exclaim, that the land were divided, and owned in small lots by the peasantry!'[3] It became the main argument against slavery:

> Every man has an inborn indefeasible right to the free use of his own bodily strength and exertion: it follows that no man can be kept for one moment in a state of bondage, without the guilt of ROBBERY: therefore, the West Indian negroes should be set free

—a view which scandalized traditionalists, who believed in the prescriptive right of the slave-owners to compensation for their

[1] *Edin. Rev.*, 1829, XCIX. 125.

[2] [Robinson], 'The Repeal of the Combination Laws', *Blackwood's*, 1825, XVIII. 22, 24; the phrase 'free trade in labour' occurs on p. 23.

[3] [Robinson], 'English and Irish Land Letting', *ibid.*, 1825, XVII. 689; the phrase 'free trade in land' is used in *ibid.*, 1830, XXVII. 568.

property.[1] It even extended to free trade in religion, demanding that it should be a 'marketable commodity', that each sect should compete in equality with others, and that the privileged monopoly of the Church of England should be abolished.[2]

Now it is obvious that on all these issues, from Parliamentary Reform through free trade to free trade in labour, land and religion, the ruling aristocracy was divided. Indeed, many aristocrats had taken the 'progressive' side on them long before the bulk of the middle class. Yet that was the weakness of the old ideal and the strength of the new, that the one was defending and the other attacking a position which was already crumbling. When the aristocratic counter-attack came, as we shall see, it failed more because of lack of support from its own side than from lack of effective ammunition.[3] By contrast, the scent of victory and the sense of having history on their side raised middle-class morale to astonishing heights:

> Never in any country beneath the sun, [wrote Edward Baines, editor of the Leeds Mercury, in 1821] was an order of men more estimable and valuable, more praised and praiseworthy, than the middle class of society in England.[4]

James Mill wrote in 1826:

> The value of the middle classes of this country, their growing numbers and importance, are acknowledged by all. These classes have long been spoken of, and not grudgingly, by their superiors themselves, as the glory of England; as that which alone has given us our eminence among nations; as that portion of our people to whom every thing that is good among us may with certainty be traced.[5]

For Brougham they *were* the nation:

> By the people, [he told the House of Lords in 1831], . . . I mean the middle classes, the wealth and intelligence of the country, the glory of the British name.[6]

Meanwhile, however, the main attack on the entrepreneurial ideal came from behind, from the new anti-capitalist working-class movement.

[1] Henry Brougham in *Edinburgh Review*, quoted by [J. G. Lockhart], 'The West India Controversy', *Blackwood's*, 1824, XV. 69.

[2] J. E. Taylor at Manchester vestry meeting, *Manchester Observer*, 20 January 1820; Read, *op. cit.*, p. 35.   [3] Cf. § 3, below.

[4] Read, *op. cit.*, p. 119.   [5] *West. Rev.*, 1826, VI. 269.

[6] Lord Brougham and Vaux, *Speeches on Social and Political Subjects* (1857), II. 373.

2. THE WORKING-CLASS IDEAL

The working class was never so united or self-confident as the capitalist middle class, partly because it was by its nature more fragmented, still more because its ideal was ambiguous in itself and led to diverse and conflicting means of pursuing it. The divisions of the working class, between urban and rural, skilled and unskilled, 'aristocracy of labour' and common or garden workers, were proverbial right down the nineteenth century. A defender of the old society with its infinity of ranks wrote in 1825:

> The case is the same with the lower orders. The ploughmen hold the mechanics in contempt as an inferior race of beings, although the latter can earn the best wages: the journeymen cabinet-makers cannot degrade themselves by associating with the journeyman tailors: the journeymen shoemakers cannot so far forget their dignity as to make companions of the labourers: the gentleman's lacquey cannot, on any account, lower himself to the level of the carman.[1]

The working-class ideal had to be stretched to bridge such gulfs, and its ambiguity owed much to the attempt. Its ideal citizen was the productive, independent worker, and its ideal society an equalitarian one based on labour and co-operation. Every one of these terms was ambiguous. The productive, independent worker normally meant the manual wage-earner on whom the capitalist system rested and for whom freedom from dependence on the arbitrary will of the capitalist was demanded; but for the nostalgic like Cobbett and the domestic workers who formed so large a part of his following the ideal was narrowed to the (in theory) self-employed 'little masters' of the old domestic system, while for some of its more forward-looking protagonists like Thomas Hodgskin it was widened to include the master manufacturer: 'The labour and skill of the contriver, or of the man who arranges and adapts a whole, are as necessary as the labour and skill of him who executes only a part, and they must be paid accordingly.'[2] One view might lead to an attempt to return to an idealized past which never existed; another to acceptance of the capitalist present with mere political safeguards for the worker's rights and welfare; a third

[1] [Robinson], 'The Nobility', *Blackwood's*, 1825, XVIII. 337.
[2] [T. Hodgskin], *Labour Defended against the Claims of Capital*, by 'A Labourer' (1825, ed. G. D. H. Cole, 1922), pp. 88–9.

to the pursuit of a millennial future in which capitalist and landlord were no more, and only the productive, independent worker remained.

An equalitarian society, likewise, could mean a merely political democracy or a socialist utopia, the latter either replacing the class society comprehensively and immediately or growing alongside it in the form of co-operative communities. As for labour, both aristocratic society and entrepreneurial society were admittedly based on it, in the sense that both passive property and active capital justified themselves by Locke's labour theory.[1] The rights of labour might mean anything from a fair day's pay for a fair day's work, which was all that the craft unions for example demanded, to the complete abolition of landed property and/or industrial capital demanded by the Spenceans and extreme socialists. Working-class co-operation, too, could mean anything from friendly societies and trade clubs for mitigating the worst effects of competition to the primitive communism of Owen's parallelograms or the socialist commonwealth achieved by the general strike.

The ideal, nevertheless, was the only principle which could hope to unite the working class, and its ambiguity was to some extent a virtue. It united the divergent elements more by what it opposed than by the monolithic nature of what it stood for. The ideal of the productive, independent worker was a more logical criticism of the unproductive landowner and rentier than the ideal of the entrepreneur, who had to keep open the door to retirement and passive investment. The ideal of labour as the sole justification of remuneration, recruitment and promotion in society was a standing criticism of all forms of unearned income and of recruitment by anything but merit defined as hard work, and above all of the unequal advantages and bargaining power of capital. The ideal of co-operation was a moral condemnation of the selfish, mutually destructive principle of competition.

[1] Cf. Arthur Young, *Tour in Ireland* (1780), Appendix, p. 18: the poor 'form the basis of public prosperity; they feed, clothe, enrich, and fight the battle of all the other ranks of the community'; and *P.P.*, 1817 (462), VI. 1, *S.C. on the Poor Laws*, p. 4: '. . . those exertions on the part of the labouring classes on which, according to the nature of things, the happiness and welfare of mankind has [sic] been made to rest.' For the basis of capital in labour, cf. Hime, *loc. cit.*, and §1, above.

Like the entrepreneurial ideal, the working-class ideal was rooted in the old society. Justification by labour was implicit in the Lockeian labour theory of property, and became explicit in Adam Smith, who asserted that 'the produce of labour constitutes the natural recompense or wages of labour,' and contrasted the early and rude state of society, 'in which the whole produce of labour belongs to the labourer,' with the capitalist system in which the labourer 'must share it with the owner of the stock which employs him.'[1] From the publication of *The Wealth of Nations* (if not before) it was open to critics of property and capital to assert the workers' 'right to the whole produce of labour.' It was so asserted by William Ogilvie in 1782, but with the same confusion as Locke and Hume about the inheritance of the right: 'Whoever enjoys any revenue, not proportioned to industry or exertion of his own, *or of his ancestors*, is a freebooter, who has found means to cheat and rob the public'; and more unequivocally by Charles Hall in 1805: 'Wealth consists not in things but in *power* over the labour of others.'[2] Robert Owen, who was then more a paternalist critic of the new manufacturing system than a socialist, spoke in 1815 of the 'industry of the lower orders, from whose labour this wealth is now drawn.'[3]

Yet it was only with the emergence of a separate working-class consciousness after the Wars that the right to the whole produce of labour became a dynamic instrument of class conflict. This it did most notably, of course, with the so-called Ricardian socialists of the 1820's.[4] They were not specifically Ricardian, except in the sense that Ricardo was then the chief representative, though not the most vulnerable, of the economists whose ideas they were standing on their head. If Ricardo perpetuated

---

[1] *Wealth of Nations*, I. 48, 50, 65.

[2] W. Ogilvie, *Essay on the Right of Property in Land* (1781), p. 46 (my italics); C. Hall, *The Effects of Civilisation on the People in European States* (1805, 1849 ed.), p. 39.

[3] R. Owen, *Observations on the Effect of the Manufacturing System* (1815), in *A New View of Society, etc.* (Everyman, 1927), p. 121; Owen derived his labour theory of value, along with his idea of villages of co-operation, from the Quaker philanthropist, John Bellers, *Proposals for Raising a Colledge of Industry of all Useful Trades and Husbandry* (1695)—cf. M. Beer, *A History of British Socialism* (1953 ed.), I. 174–5.

[4] First so called by H. S. Foxwell, Introduction to Adolf Menger, *The Right to the Whole Produce of Labour* (1899), p. lxxxiii.

the labour theory of value, at least he was free from the confusion between productive and unproductive workers, between the producers of goods and the suppliers of services, which was the orthodox niche into which the heretical doctrine of the right to the whole produce of labour grafted itself. If any one man influenced them all, it was Patrick Colquhoun, the Benthamite popularizer of Adam Smith, whose statistical tables of civil society with their invidious distinction between the productive and the unproductive classes were a gift which no critic of contemporary society could ignore.[1]

Still less were they all socialists. On the contrary, they were fairly evenly divided between those who, like the anonymous author of *A Letter to Lord John Russell* (1821), the Tory democrat 'Piercy Ravenstone', and the Radical ex-naval officer, Thomas Hodgskin, would retain the present structure of society, with political safeguards for the labourer, and avoided socialist remedies, and those who, like the clerk turned professional lecturer John Gray and the Irish landowner William Thompson, advocated forms of socialism.[2] Both groups, however, equally used the ideal of labour to denounce capital and competition. Thomas Hodgskin defined capital as labour, past or present:

> If . . . , as I say, circulating capital is only co-existing labour, and fixed capital only skilled labour, it must be plain that all those numerous advantages, those benefits to civilisation, those vast improvements in the condition of the human race, which have been in general attributed to capital, are caused in fact by labour, and by knowledge and skill informing and directing labour.[3]

Profit and the capitalist—though not, apparently, the manager—were unnecessary. William Thompson denounced 'competition with its unequal remuneration—prizes for the few, blanks, want, and misery for the many; prizes for the idle, blanks for the industrious—mutual antipathy for all,' and opposed to it his system of 'Association, or of labour by Mutual Co-operation.'[4]

---

[1] Colquhoun, *Treatise on . . . British Empire*, pp. 29–47; his tables were used by Robert Owen and John Gray, and repeated by John Wade in *The Extraordinary Black Book* (1831), p. 216; cf. Foxwell, in Menger, *op. cit.*, pp. xlii–xliii, and Briggs, 'Language of Class', *loc. cit.*, pp. 49–50, 51n.

[2] Cf. Beer, *op. cit.*, I. 183–4; for a bibliography of their works see Menger, *op. cit.*, Appendix.   [3] Hodgskin, *op. cit.*, pp. 108–9.

[4] W. Thompson, *Labor Rewarded*, by 'One of the Idle Classes' (1827), p. 30; and *Appeal of One Half of the Human Race*, p. 199.

This group of anti-capitalists, individualist and socialist, are of the first importance in the intellectual history of socialism and their influence, especially through John Francis Bray and Bronterre O'Brien, on Marx and all later socialists is beyond question.[1] Yet this is not to say that this motley collection of 'social cranks' invented the ideal and foisted it on the working class. At best they formulated it in striking form and 'spoke to their condition.' But the working class were not only ready to accept the message: some at least were already in possession of it. The first 'Co-operative and Economic Society' and the first propaganda organ of the co-operative movement, *The Economist*—both names are significant—were started as early as 1821, and the London Co-operative Society was set up in 1824, contemporary with Thompson's first book, and before the publication of all the rest of the group, 'to restore the whole produce of labour to the labourer.'[2] It is true that they were influenced by Owen, but if ever there was a case of a leader being chosen by his followers, this was it. Practically the whole working-class co-operative movement began either without his knowledge or against his opposition, and it was only in 1829 after the failure of his American experiment and the manifest success of theirs that he was reluctantly persuaded to lead them.[3]

By then the working-class ideal was well established. It was used to justify universal manhood suffrage: a speaker in Manchester in 1826 declared that 'the purpose of parliamentary reform was to secure to the labourer the fruits of his own labour,' and the argument became a standard one with working-class Radicals.[4] Francis Place, commenting in 1831 on the National Union of the Working Classes (an offshoot of the original Owenite British Association for Promoting Co-operative Knowledge of 1829), remarked:

> The 'Union' had great influence over a considerable portion of the working class, more especially in the great manufacturing counties. During the time the Reform Bills were before the Parliament this was particularly the case. The attention of the whole people was then

[1] Cf. Foxwell, in Menger, *op. cit.*, pp. lxv–lxxi; A. Plummer, 'The Place of Bronterre O'Brien in the Working-Class Movement', *Ec.H.R.*, 1929, II. 61f.

[2] Beer, *op. cit.*, I. 185.

[3] Cf. Wallas, *Place*, pp. 269–72.

[4] *Wheeler's Manchester Chronicle*, 28 October 1826; Briggs, 'Language of Class', *loc. cit.*, p. 66.

drawn to the subject, and the working people were quite as much excited as any class whatever. The consequence of this excitement was a general persuasion that the whole produce of the labourers' and workmen's hands should remain with them.[1]

The ideal captured the working-class press, joining forces with the Painites—the Carliles, Hetheringtons and Cleaves—who had kept alive the old Jacobin tradition of political democracy, and transformed the merely political Rights of Man into the social revolutionary Rights of Labour. Joshua Hobson announced in the first number of his unstamped *Voice of the West Riding* in 1833:

> It is intended to publish a Weekly Penny Paper, to be called the 'Voice of the West Riding', advocating the Rights of Man against the 'exclusives', and the Rights of Labour against the 'Competatives' and the 'Political Economists', and especially to vindicate the Working Classes from the calumnies and misrepresentations of our parasitical scribes who figure in the Provincial Newspapers.[2]

Wherever it succeeded, it transformed the working-class movement from an ameliorative one which accepted the basic structure of the new class society into a revolutionary one which rejected it altogether. As a disillusioned bricklayer put it at a trade union conference in 1839,

> Trade unions are for botching up the old system; Chartists are for a new one. Trade unions are for making the best of a bad bargain; Chartists are for a fresh one; and everyone must admit that trade unions partake of the tampering spirit of monopoly.[3]

There were many ways in which outright rejection of the system could show itself—too many for the unity of the working class. There was the frontal attack, via political agitation for Reform, aimed at proletarian control of government, or, if that failed, violent revolution as advocated by the physical-force Chartists. There was the undermining operation of syndicalist trade unionism, culminating in a revolutionary general strike—William Benbow's 'national holiday' or 'sacred month'—as in Owen's Grand National Consolidated Trade Union of 1834. And there was the attractively non-violent method of simply

[1] Wallas, *Place*, p. 266n.
[2] *Voice of the West Riding*, No. 1, 8 June 1833.
[3] E. R. Wickham, *Church and People in an Industrial City* (1957), p. 102.

opting out of the competitive system, by setting up proletarian cells or islands within it based on the ideal of labour instead of that of capital. Even these, however, could take various forms, the basic choice lying between millennial co-operative communities on the Owenite model and nostalgic individualist colonies of independent peasants on the lines of O'Connor's Chartist Land Plan.

The fragmentation of the ideal, in practice as well as theory, was its fundamental weakness. Moreover, an apparently unequivocal decision for outright rejection had a habit not merely of failing—which rejectionist experiments did with dismaying regularity—but of evolving by imperceptible degrees into acceptance of the system. This happened in different ways, as we shall see in Chapter IX, to syndicalist trade unionism, the co-operative movement, and even to physical-force Chartism. Meanwhile, the working-class ideal, for all its greater plausibility, was extremely vulnerable to seduction by the other two ideals, the more surprisingly by the remarkable revival of the aristocratic ideal which took place in the 1820's.

3. THE REVIVAL OF THE ARISTOCRATIC IDEAL

The aristocratic ideal never quite died. At its weakest, in the agitation for the abolition of the poor laws between Waterloo and the Queen's Trial, an etiolated sense of responsibility for the lower orders managed to survive amongst the aristocracy. The Lords' Committee on the Poor Laws of 1817 was 'decidedly of the opinion, that the general system of these laws, interwoven as it is with the habits of the people, ought . . . to be essentially maintained.'[1] Even at this low ebb, schemes for the state-aided welfare of the poor, like John Christian Curwen's 'National Benefit Society' or Robert Owen's Plan for Villages of Co-operation, could still get a serious hearing in Parliament, though they were seen chiefly as cheap alternatives to poor relief, and even so had little chance of breaking through the prevailing belief of the Government in *laissez-faire*.[2]

[1] *P.P.*, 1818, V, 400, *S.C. of H. of L. on the Poor Laws, 1817*, p. 7.
[2] J. C. Curwen, *Sketch of a Plan for Bettering the Condition of the Labouring Population* (1817), and *Parliamentary Debates*, XXXIV. 871; R. Owen, *Report to the County of Lanark of a Plan for Relieving Public Distress* (1820), and *P.P.*, 1823, VI, *S.C. on Mr. Owen's Plan*.

Paternal discipline, on the other hand, survived in despotic strength in its home territories, the English countryside and London 'Society'. A Tory paternalist in 1824 advocated English landlordism as a cure for Ireland's woes:

> None but those who have been familiarized with English farmers and cottagers can conceive the degree of awe which actuates them in regard to their landlords. . . . The English landlord's influence does not slumber. We have ourselves seen farmers deprived of their farms for frequent drunkenness—for leading immoral lives—for being bad cultivators; and we have seen a farmer compelled to marry a girl whom he had seduced . . . . This operates in the most powerful manner, in preventing vice and crime; and in giving the best tone to what may be called the rustic world.[1]

Francis Place complained in 1831 of the difficulty of working with 'gentlemen' Reformers who feared 'being looked upon as ungenteel' or of 'being discountenanced by Holland House people and Brooks' Club people' and would sacrifice the public cause so as 'not to lose caste with their fashionable friends and acquaintances.'[2]

The countryside and the West End were not the whole of England, however, and in other spheres the ruling class were not merely yielding ground to the new entrepreneurial ideal, but actually making the pace in accepting its principles. During the 1820's Tory Governments brought in increasing doses of free trade (Huskisson and Peel's reduction of the customs duties, 1823 onwards, and especially the sliding—and lower—scale of corn duties, 1828), free trade in labour (repeal of the Combination Acts and of the laws forbidding the emigration of artisans, 1824–5), and free trade in religion (repeal of the laws against Dissenters and Roman Catholics, 1828–9). The protectionist High Tories were alarmed. As early as 1826 *Blackwood's* was complaining that 'Our policy has been greatly changed—some of our most important laws and systems have been changed—some of the leading relations and regulations of society have been changed,' and that the defenders of the old system had had 'to oppose both the Ministry and the Opposition, a united Parliament, a united Press, and to a very great extent,

[1] 'Y.Y.Y.' [Robinson], 'The Instruction of the Irish Peasantry', *Blackwood's*, 1824, XV. 502.
[2] Wallas, *Place*, pp. 260–2.

public opinion.' 'What is the great object of the new system?' it asked in 1827, 'To carry competition to the highest point. . . .' And it hounded Canning, Huskisson, Peel, and even Wellington, for selling out to 'the Faction' of Whigs and Political Economists, in terms of which the following is a fair sample: 'Saying nothing of the others, Mr. Peel's public life has been one continuing course of despicable, grovelling, mercenary faithlessness to principles and party. . . .'[1] The very shrillness of the tone betrays the nostalgic protectionists as defenders of a lost cause.

Yet there was at the same time and in the same group a remarkable revival of the paternal aristocratic ideal. Malthus has usually been considered the main champion of the leisured, unproductive landed class, and this amongst the classical economists he certainly was. He was himself aware of it: 'It is somewhat singular that Mr. Ricardo, a considerable receiver of rents, should have so much underrated their importance; while I, who never received, nor expect to receive any, shall probably be accused of overrating their importance.'[2] For Malthus, the unproductive landlord was not only a useful but the most necessary member of society. Not only was rent 'an exact measure of the *relief* from labour in the production of food granted to [man] by a most kind Providence,' which 'will always afford a fund for the enjoyments and leisure of the society, sufficient to leaven and animate the whole mass,' and 'the reward of present valour and wisdom, as well as of past strength and cunning', 'a boon most important to the happiness of mankind'. It also supplied the demand which made the landlord the lynchpin of society, the initiator of the economic cycle, the unproductive consumer without whom the productive classes could not continue to produce more than they consumed: 'In the ordinary state of society, the master producers and capitalists, though they may have the power, have not the will, to consume to the necessary extent. And with regard to their workmen, it must

[1] 'Christopher North' (John Wilson *et al.*], Preface to *Blackwood's*, 1826, XIX. xviii–xix; [Robinson], 'The Surplus Population of the United Kingdom', 'The Faction', and 'Political Economy, No. IV', *ibid.*, 1827, XXI. 379, XXII. 403–31, and 1830, XXVII. 41.

[2] Malthus, *Principles* (1820), p. 238n.; Ricardo bought estates worth £275,000 in Gloucestershire, Herefordshire, Worcestershire, Warwickshire and Kent— Ricardo, *op. cit.* (ed. Sraffa), X. 95–9.

be allowed that, if they possessed the will, they have not the power.' It followed, therefore, that 'it is absolutely necessary that a country with great powers of production should possess a body of unproductive consumers.'[1]

On this Ricardo drily remarked: 'A body of unproductive labourers are just as necessary and as useful with a view to future production, as a fire, which should consume in the manufacturers warehouse the goods which those unproductive labourers would otherwise consume.'[2] Malthus's *Principles* and Ricardo's *Notes* on it constitute a dialogue between the aristocratic and entrepreneurial ideals unique in candour and sincerity, which nevertheless breaks off time after time in mutual incomprehension—symbolically, it may be said, since this was the normal relationship between the two ideals.

Yet it was not Malthus who fathered the revival of the aristocratic ideal. On the contrary, he was one of the chief objects of the revivalists' wrath. For Malthus was the champion of the ideal at its most irresponsible, the apologist of power without responsibility, who armed it—and the entrepreneurial ideal—with what his opponents considered the most diabolical instrument ever invented for disciplining the lower orders and grinding the faces of the poor. The 'principle of population'—'the constant tendency in all animated life to increase beyond the nourishment prepared for it'[3]—was used to mock every attempt to improve the condition of the working class, from the poor laws to Owen's 'parallelograms'. The fact that the principle formed, along with Ricardo's theory of rent which was based on it through the law of diminishing returns, one of the twin pillars of the classical school of economics has masked the extent to which it was a product of 'the abdication on the part of the governors'. In its original form it was intended to counteract entrepreneurial criticism of 'idleness'. Francis Place, the first neo–Malthusian, pointed out, 'Mr. Malthus denies to the unemployed poor man the right to eat, but he allows the right to the unemployed rich man.'[4] Nassau Senior, who found the principle 'made the stalking horse of negligence and in-

---

[1] Malthus, *Principles*, pp. 229, 237–9, 463, 471.
[2] Ricardo, *op. cit.*, II. 421n.
[3] Malthus, *Essay on Population* (Everyman, 1951), I. 5.
[4] Wallas, *Place*, p. 165.

justice, the favourite objection to every project for rendering the resources of the country more productive,' later wrote in the report of a Royal Commission:

> the general proposition that such is the influence of the principle of population, that no increase in the supply of provisions can permanently benefit the labouring class, we believe to be absolutely false. That proposition owed its origin to some expressions of Mr. Malthus, not sufficiently qualified by him, and repeated in a still more unqualified form by many of his followers. It owed its currency to the relief which it afforded to the indolence and selfishness of the superior classes. But it is contradicted by the evidence of all experience.[1]

The revivalists of the aristocratic ideal were reacting as much against the betrayers of paternalism as against the new entrepreneurial ideal. They not only bracketed for common enmity Malthus and the other economists, but singled him out for special attack. Michael Thomas Sadler, the acknowledged leader of the High Tory paternalists, made his name by his attacks on Malthus. A Leeds linen merchant, and thus a notable 'social crank', he had the leadership of the revivalists thrust upon him the moment he entered Parliament in 1829.[2] To the principle of population he opposed his own 'law of population', that 'the prolificness of human beings . . . varies inversely as their number' [i.e. density], and to Malthus's purely hypothetical ratios he opposed massive empirical statistics drawn from all over the world to show that human fertility fell as population density, urbanization and comfort increased.[3] It was 'disproved' by Macaulay in the *Edinburgh Review* by the dishonest manipulation of his statistics,[4] and laughed at or ignored by the economists. Nevertheless, in spite of being couched in theological terms of God's providence and 'the ample provision Nature has made for all creatures,' Sadler's 'law' was essentially

---

[1] N. W. Senior, *Two Lectures on Population* (1829), Appendix (Correspondence with Malthus), p. 89; *Extracts from the Reports of the Commissioners on . . . Handloom Weavers* (ed. R. Currie, 1841), p. 12.

[2] [Samuel O'Sullivan], 'Review of the last Session of Parliament', *Blackwood's*, 1829, XXVI. 234–7.

[3] M. T. Sadler, *The Law of Population* (1830); for Malthus's ratios, see *Essay on Population* (*ed. cit.*), I. 10–11.

[4] [R. B. Seeley], *Memoirs of M. T. Sadler* (1842), pp. 630–4.

the belief accepted by modern economists that economic growth and higher living standards are the main prerequisite of population control.[1] 'Mr. Sadler alleged that the only efficient checks to population were, ease and comfort, increasing to luxury.' It led to a conclusion diametrically opposed to Malthus's: 'If you really apprehend an overflow of this kind, the best way to check it, is to improve the condition of the people.'[2]

To be fair to the economists, it must be admitted that Malthus favoured high wages—though he clearly doubted the working class's capacity for 'moral restraint' by which alone they could keep their numbers small enough to obtain them—while Ricardo believed that 'the natural price of labour . . . essentially depends on the habits and customs of the people,' and that 'a taste for comforts and enjoyments' should be encouraged as the best 'security against a superabundant population.'[3] But that their position was poles apart from Sadler's can be seen from their attitude to the poor laws: their pernicious tendency, says Ricardo, 'has been fully developed by the able hand of Mr. Malthus; and every friend to the poor must ardently wish for their abolition.'[4] Sadler, by contrast, argued 'the absolute necessity of such a provision, as regards the labouring classes of England,' and of their extension to Ireland: 'The institution of the Poor Law of England encourages the demand for, and increases the value of labour, as well as abates distress; in Ireland, in consequence of the want of such a law, labour is discouraged, and distress increased.'[5]

To Malthus's 'Selfish System', therefore, Sadler opposed his 'Paternal System'. It was not merely that the rich ought to be charitable towards the poor out of prudence and benevolence. Protection and maintenance were the right of the poor and a duty of the rich implicit in the privilege of property: 'a real and indisputable right, that, after the institutions of the country have sanctioned the monopoly of property, the poor shall have

---

[1] Cf. W. A. Lewis, *Theory of Economic Growth* (1955), pp. 313–15, 434–5; and cf. recent studies by animal behaviourists, who have found a psychological reluctance to breed in overcrowded conditions amongst laboratory mice and amongst species of kangaroo on islands off Western Australia.

[2] Seeley, *op. cit.*, p. 182; contrast Malthus, *Principles*, p. 472.

[3] Ricardo, *op. cit.*, I. 96–7, 100.

[4] *Ibid.*, I. 106.

[5] Sadler in H. of C., 3 June 1830; Seeley, *op. cit.*, p. 203.

some reserved claims to the necessaries of life.'[1] This was the revival of the aristocratic ideal in all its pristine purity. *Blackwood's* commented on his first session in Parliament:

> The Economists for the first time heard their fallibility called in question, and felt their ascendancy in danger. . . . These sages of the Satanic school in politics encountered an adversary by whom their favourite measures were opposed, and their most familiar axioms disputed; . . . Sadler has done this. Be he right or wrong, he is the man whose warning voice called the attention of the honourable House . . . to the first principles of the Economists; who bid them turn their eyes from the capitalist to the labourer; and who had the spirit and the feeling to ask them . . . whether that could be a good system . . . under the influence of which capital must increase at the expense of humanity; where what is called wealth only serves to oppress and to paralyse industry; and national prosperity is made to . . proceed upon its course amidst the sweat, and the blood, and the groans of its victims.[2]

Sadler was the key figure in the revival of the aristocratic ideal. His part in its most successful manifestation, the campaign for factory reform, and his post-mortem influence through his disciples, Richard Oastler and John Wood, on the attack on the New Poor Law of 1834, make him the chief link between the ideal of the old society and all later attempts to unite the upper and the working classes in common opposition to the capitalist middle class. As the youngest son of a large yeoman or small country gentleman, apprenticed to a linen merchant in one of the largest of the northern industrial towns, and as an Anglican brought up under the influence of the Tory Wesleyans, he was specially fitted for the role. But he was the channel rather than the originating spring of the revival. He belonged to a widespread current of social thought which was flowing strongly in the 1820's before it carried him to the top, provided him through the patronage of the Duke of Newcastle with a pocket borough seat in Parliament, and chose him as its leader. That current of thought, signally defeated by the Reform Act (which overthrew Sadler himself), by the New Poor Law, and by the triumph of free trade, and then dissipated in the romantic feudalism of

---

[1] *Ibid.*, pp. 167, 208.
[2] [O'Sullivan], 'Review of the last Session of Parliament', *Blackwood's*, 1829, XXVI, 235.

Disraeli, Lord John Manners and 'Young England', has suffered the neglect and misunderstanding of most lost causes. Yet in the 1820's it produced, quite apart from Sadler's contribution, a counter-attack on aristocratic 'abdication' and the entrepreneurial ideal which not only rejected outright the whole canon of classical economics but anticipated in great measure both Keynesian economics and the social outlook of the Welfare State.

This current of thought can best be traced in the High Tory *Blackwood's Edinburgh Review*, the most widely read journal of the day, which claimed a larger circulation than the *Quarterly Review*, and sold more than twice as many copies as the *Edinburgh Review* or any other Opposition journal.[1] It was by no means confined to it, however. The *Quarterly Review*, for example, rallied to the defence of the poor laws as early as 1823, when *Blackwood's* was still describing them as 'indefensible' and 'an irremediable calamity';[2] while the *New Monthly Magazine* in 1821 published a highly intelligent refutation by Simon Gray of Say's law—that demand must always be equal to production and that over-production, under-consumption and general gluts are impossible—which went beyond Malthus in its anticipation of Keynes.[3]

Blackwood's, nevertheless, was the main channel, and has the advantage of affording a fairly continuous view of the course of the current. Not all the contributors can be identified, but the most important, apart from the editor, 'Christopher North', who was John Wilson, Professor of Moral Philosophy at Edinburgh University, were John Galt, ex-customs official, merchant and now a novelist and playwright, William Stevenson, a Treasury official, W. Johnstone, probably an Irish

[1] For comparative circulations see *Blackwood's*, 1820–21, VIII. 80–1, and 1826, XIX, Preface.

[2] *Q.R.*, 1823, XXVIII. 349. 'A considerable reaction has taken place in public opinion on the subject of the poor laws; and . . . hazardous schemes for their abolition have given way to proposals of a more sober kind for their severe and strict administration . . . .'; contrast *Blackwood's*, 1823, XIV. 83, on 'this wiseacre of the *Quarterly Review*'.

[3] S. Gray, 'To M. Say on Some Fundamental Principles in Statistics, and the Causes of the Present Stagnation of Commerce', *New Monthly Magazine*, 1821, I. 90–7, II. 366–76; the *New Monthly* even anticipated Sadler's 'law of population', in an anonymous letter 'On the Theories of Godwin and Malthus', 1821, I. 195–205: experience shows that, where the population is already dense, further increase will be slow, and that 'It is population that advances arithmetically, while produce, in quality and quantity, advances geometrically.'

journalist living in London, and, by far the most brilliant and original, David Robinson, a London political writer whose Toryism was too reactionary even for the *Quarterly Review*.[1] The revival began as a merely defensive reaction against the attacks of the entrepreneurial ideal. *Blackwood's* brief welcome for Ricardo in 1817 soon turned to criticism. In 1818 it upbraided him for asserting that 'the interest of the landlords is always opposed to that of every other class of the community,' though at this stage it was willing to admit that the error was without malice: 'it is the great and leading defect of one of the ablest critical works that has ever appeared in this, or . . . in any other country or age, that it has a strong, not an intentional, tendency to make mankind unhappy and discontented with their situation. . . .'[2] By 1819 it was attacking Ricardo's doctrine that 'whenever wages rise, the rate of profits must fall' as 'a theory which teaches, that by the nature of human society, there is a constant and irremediable contrariety of interest between its members, and that a general amelioration, in which all should participate alike, is impossible.'[3]

By 1824 the doctrine of rent and the consequent opposition of interest were 'revolting to the best feelings of our nature'; 'If this inference can be fairly drawn from the doctrine, we should not hesitate to pronounce that doctrine as false as it is mournful and mischievous.'[4] By 1825 the economists were satirized as 'the Statesmen of Cockaigne' whose 'State-Medicine', 'the divine science of Political Economy and the divine Liberal System', was contrary to the facts of experience, and who were responsible for setting the classes against each other:

> our political economists carefully filled the labourers with the conviction that their employers were their tyrants and natural enemies;

[1] F. W. Fetter, 'The Economic Articles in *Blackwood's Edinburgh Magazine*, and their Authors, 1817–53', *Scottish Journal of Political Economy*, 1960, VII. 85f. and 213f.; A. L. Strout, *A Bibliography of Articles in Blackwood's Magazine, 1817–25* (Lubbock, Texas, 1959), pp. 121, 133; I owe these references to Prof. Walter E. Houghton of Wellesley College, Mass., editor of *The Wellesley Index to Victorian Periodicals, 1824–1900* (1966).   [2] *Blackwood's*, 1817, I. 175–8; 1818, IV, 59.

[3] 'On the Influence of Wages on the Rate of Profits', *ibid.*, 1819, V. 171–2; this anonymous article is remarkable for an early use and definition of the term *national income*, p. 171: 'The Aggregate annual produce of the land and labour of a nation constitutes what may be termed the national income.'

[4] [W. Stevenson], 'The Political Economist, No. II', *Blackwood's*, 1824, XV. 653–4.

and of course no sooner were the [combination] laws repealed than the two classes became bitter enemies—the servants became the despots of the masters.[1]

And before 1830 the Government and its 'omniscient and infallible guides, the Economists and Philosophers' had produced 'a gigantic increase to the permanent distress of the majority of your population.'[2]

More significant, however, than their rejection of Ricardian economics were their own alternative theories of economy and society. The first anticipated Keynesian analysis of the causes and remedies of depression far more than did Malthus, to whom Keynes gave too much credit.[3] Whereas Malthus was merely concerned with the effective demand of the rich, and expressly denied any significance to that of the working class—'no power of consumption on the part of the labouring class can ever . . . alone furnish an encouragement to the employment of capital'[4] —the contributors to *Blackwood's* made the effective demand of both the cornerstone of their theory. Henry Lascelles, one of the few writers named, opposed the reduction of patronage, on the grounds that 'every man discharged from the public service is a new member added to the number of the needy, and that every diminution of salary subtracts so much from the expenditure among the tradesmen where the placeman is located . . .', that 'profits are derived from prodigality, and that labour, to be lucrative, must be in request.'[5] Other contributors equally opposed the abolition of the poor laws, on the grounds that poor rates, like wages, were spent wholly on consumption: 'they are expended in promoting the business of the agriculturist, manufacturer, and trader':

> The poor laws form the great prop of wages; abolish them, and with your redundant population wages will speedily fall by half. What will follow? The body of your British labouring orders will be

---

[1] [Robinson], 'State Counsel, by the Statesmen of Cockaigne', *ibid.*, 1825, XVII, 34–44, and 'Brougham on the Education of the People', XVII. 534.

[2] [Robinson], 'The Condition of the Empire', *Blackwoods'*, 1829, XXVI. 97, 103.

[3] J. M. Keynes, *Essays in Biography* (1933), pp. 144–7, and *General Theory of Employment, Interest and Money* (1960 ed.), pp. 321, 362–4, 369, 371.

[4] Malthus, *Principles*, p. 471.

[5] H. Lascelles, 'On the Present State of Public Affairs at Home', *Blackwood's*, 1821, X. 340.

compelled to abandon the consumption of taxed articles, to feed
on potatoes and butchers' offal, and to wear rags. In their fall they
must pull down with them not only the small tradesmen, but to a
great extent the larger ones . . .[1]

The *Blackwood's* economists took a far more realistic view
than the Ricardians of booms and slumps and the part played in
them by government monetary policy:

> Consumption and demand can become giants or dwarfs in a moment;
> but protection and supply require some time for enlarging or
> diminishing themselves.

The excessive boom of 1825 and the ensuing slump were explained in Keynesian terms:

> When the advance began in 1824, the Government, instead of
> draining money out of the market, as it had long done by borrowing,
> was pouring money into it, by reducing its debts; and this, with
> some other things, caused money to be abundant for both specu-
> lation and regular trade . . . the glut in the money market became
> excessive. Saving a glut in agricultural produce and labour, no glut
> in a trading country can well be more destructive. . . . The excess
> inevitably resolves itself into one of goods, and destroys itself by
> ruining those who deal in them.[2]

Like Attwood and the advocates of paper money, they blamed
'Mr. Peel's darling folly of a metallic currency' for much of this,
and pointed out that the restriction of note issue by country
banks had actually destroyed wealth by withdrawing this
stimulus to production.[3] But unlike Attwood, they did not think
that paper currency alone would prevent economic fluctuations:

> 'Once in every three or four years commerce and industry will have
> a fit of suffering, let the currency be what it may, so long as this
> country shall be reasonably wealthy. Production and consumption
> cannot possibly be kept together; the powers of the former have
> been rendered gigantic by capital, machinery and knowledge, and
> the market must be very frequently overloaded with merchandise
> and manufactures.[4]

---

[1] [Robinson], 'The Poor Laws', *ibid.*, 1828, XXIII. 923–36, and 'The Condition
of the Empire', *ibid.*, 1829, XXVI. 104.
[2] [Robinson], 'Public Distress', *ibid.*, 1826, XIX, 429.
[3] *Ibid.*, 1829, XXVI, 472 [W. Johnstone] and 98–9 [Robinson].
[4] *Ibid.*, 1826, XIX, 444 [Robinson].

The remedy lay in 'the restrictive system' in place of free trade, that is, in a managed economy designed to maintain the aggregate national income available for distribution between the classes in place of an unmanaged one which allowed the aggregate to be diminished by competition both by foreigners and between the classes. In contradiction of the Ricardian laws of diminishing returns and the inverse relationship of profits and wages,

> The circumstances that have a tendency to increase the productive power of labour, and thus to occasion a simultaneous advance of wages and profits, are much more numerous . . . than might, at first glance, be imagined. They comprise . . . almost everything that can contribute to the wealth and prosperity of a country, and will be found wherever that prosperity is increasing.

Thus, in a protected economy,

> the national income will be augmented, and each of the three classes into which society is divided, may, without injuring the others, receive for its share a greater portion of the annual growth of necessaries and comforts than it enjoyed before.[1]

All these arguments, many of them from his own pen, were drawn together by the most brilliant of the *Blackwood's* economists, David Robinson, in a series of articles on 'Political Economy' by 'One of the Old School' in 1829–30. In these he at least glimpsed the Keynesian roles of money—'the uncouth and stupendous fictions' of the Ricardians 'destroy money altogether'; of the constant need for fresh investment—to keep wages and profits at their proper height it was essential not only to keep up manufactures but continually to extend them; and the self-defeating tendency of the propensity to save—'It is . . . utterly impossible for any country to have generally a high rate of profit, because such a rate must cause capital to increase much more rapidly than profitable employment for capital, and thereby soon destroy itself.'[2] He thoroughly grasped the potential disequilibrium between productive capacity and effective demand, and used it to counter Say's law of the impossibility of gluts:

[1] *Ibid.*, 1819, V. 172.
[2] 'One of the Old School' [Robinson], 'Political Economy', *ibid.*, 1829, XXVI, 518, 674; 1830, XXVII. 32.

Capital, with a high rate of profit, increases infinitely more rapidly than population; it enters very largely into production, and it continually operates in various ways to make the same portion of labour produce a greater quantity of commodities. In consequence, it increases the production of manufactured goods much more on the one hand than the consumption of them on the other; and its general tendency is, to cause a glut in all. . . . If production rise above the aggregate sum expended by the labourers and capitalists, in their maintenance, it will be excessive; it must rise or fall with this sum. The population of the world, like the labourers, can only consume goods in proportion to its income, no matter what abundance of them may be in the market. Thus a high rate of profit must inevitably create an excess of capital, and this must create an excess of goods; such competition must follow as will bring down the rate, and probably for a time wholly destroy profits. . . . All this has its natural effect on wages. The capitalist reduces them, as his only means of protecting himself from loss. . . . The reduction diminishes consumption, and makes the glut greater, and more general.

He also used it to counter Malthus:

The means of subsistence to population are to be found in employment. Whenever they are deficient, it arises not from dearness of food caused by the cultivation of inferior land, but from the want of employment to buy food with. . . . It is because the increase of population does not consume as much as it can produce, that it diminishes the general means of subsistence.

And he saw as the central aim of economic policy the maintenance of full employment:

The grand essential . . . is, EMPLOYMENT FOR CAPITAL AND LABOUR. Comparative cheapness is a national scourge, in so far as it diminishes such employment.[1]

None of this means that Robinson was a Keynes a century before his time. He lacked the essential mathematical formulation of the relations between national income, saving and investment, between effective demand, the marginal efficiency of capital, and the rate of interest, and between all these and the volume of employment. But, in marked contrast to the Ricardians, he was at least aware of the problem, and he was groping after the very concepts in which Keynes was to express it. He rather than Malthus deserves the credit for wrestling a hundred

[1] *Ibid.*, XXVI. 673, 678, 684, 804.

years before Keynes with 'the great puzzle of Effective Demand'.[1] And he certainly anticipated Keynes in considering that the maintenance of full employment was within the government's responsibility and capacity, and even in many of the remedies for depression which he, like most of the *Blackwood's* economists, urged: a reflationary monetary policy (through the increased issue of small bank notes), increased public expenditure (on poor relief and the cultivation of waste lands, etc.) and a controlled economy (through protective tariffs and taxation).[2]

The implications of his proto-Keynesian economics for his theory of society are obvious. He believed in the old harmonious relations between the interests, maintained not by the 'invisible hand' of competition, but by the visible hand of paternalism:

> The landowners, farmers and working classes, husbandry, manufactures, and trading, must thus prosper and suffer together; their interests cannot be separated.

This harmony and prosperity had been undermined by the 'abdication on the part of the governors'—the government's acceptance of the *laissez-faire* philosophy—which he ascribed to 'the appalling degeneracy of the Aristocracy'.[3]

This view of a paternal society betrayed by its aristocratic governors was common to *Blackwood's* in the late 1820's. In 1829 in reply to 'new Tory' critics it set out

> 'our exposition of true Tory principles—of principles which, while they maintain the due order and proportion of each separate rank in society, maintain also that protection and support are the right of all, so long as there are the means, within the state, of affording them. In opposition to those cold and heartless politicians, who, with the words liberty and liberality ever in their mouths, look with composure upon a people's sufferings, we would say, govern the people, and govern them strictly, but see that they are fed. . . . As Tories, we maintain that it is the duty of the people to pay obedience to those in authority over them: but it is also the duty of those set in authority to protect those who are placed below them.[4]

In accordance with these principles *Blackwood's* consistently maintained that 'the poor have a right to be cared for' and the

---

[1] Keynes, *General Theory*, p. 32.   [2] *Blackwood's*, 1830, XXVII. 33–6.
[3] *Ibid.*, XXVII. 29, 43.
[4] [Johnstone], 'Our Domestic Policy, No. 1', *ibid.*, 1829, XXVI. 768.

poor laws ought to be retained, not only to prevent revolution but to keep wages high and maintain demand, that education and high living standards were the antidotes to improvident marriage and overpopulation, and that cottages and gardens should be provided for the rural labourer and home colonies on wastelands for the industrial unemployed.[1] In brief, it anticipated the spirit of the Bismarckian, if not the modern British Welfare State:

> Whoever . . . loves the institutions of his country, and sincerely desires that they may survive unhurt the revolutionary contagion that prevails in the political atmosphere of Europe, let him study how the common people may be made comfortable.[2]

Why did the attempt to revive the aristocratic ideal, so deeply rooted in the traditional interests of the ruling class and so brilliantly argued in the most widely read journal of the day, fail? For fail it did, despite the partial success of Sadler and his followers in the factory reform agitation. It failed because the revivalists were fighting for a cause already lost. Paternal discipline without paternal responsibility was too attractive a principle for most of the landed class to resist. The fact that it made them more vulnerable to the criticisms of the entrepreneurial ideal merely weakened its hold on them still more: the attack on paternalism as a whole had already gone too far for the revival of its better side to save it.

Indeed, the revivalists themselves helped to undermine its defences. In their disgust with the Parliament which had betrayed paternalism and embraced free trade in commerce, labour, and religion, they denounced it more fiercely even than the Radicals, and so, since there were more of them in the old Parliament than there were Radicals, more effectively ensured the success of Reform. Because of 'the notorious incompetency of the present House of Commons,' because the close borough members had become mere tools and mercenaries of a tacit coalition of renegade Tories and treacherous Whigs who had betrayed paternalism and the Church, the High Tory opponents of Reform came to 'feel that no change could well give them a

---

[1] [Robinson], 'The Poor Laws', *ibid.*, 1828, XXVI. 923–36; [Edwards], 'The Influence of Free Trade upon the Condition of the Labouring Classes', 1830, XXVII. 553–68.

[2] [Johnstone], 'The Present Crisis', *ibid.*, XXVIII. 692.

worse House of Commons than the present system gives them, and that the elective franchise could not be in more dangerous hands than those which now hold it.'[1] In the event it was the decision of the High Tories, led by Sadler, to oppose Wellington's Government and let in the Whigs which decisively opened the doors to Reform, and to the new Parliament which was to bury the aristocratic ideal.[2] The ideal did live to see a transfigured resurrection, in Victorian Oxford and Cambridge and, surprisingly, in the East End of London.[3] But that is another story, which involves another class ideal.

4. THE FORGOTTEN MIDDLE CLASS

The aristocratic, entrepreneurial and working-class ideals, then, were the three major class ideals contending for supremacy in early nineteenth-century England. Yet there was another class and another ideal, without analysing which it is still not possible to understand the struggle between them. An extraordinary proportion of the spokesmen of the first three ideals were members of none of the three classes: James Mill, Henry Brougham, and Nassau Senior, for example, of the entrepreneurial ideal; Charles Hall, Thomas Hodgskin, John Gray, and Bronterre O'Brien, of the working-class ideal; T. R. Malthus, John Wilson (editor of *Blackwood's*), Coleridge and Southey, of the aristocratic ideal.[4] To what class did this collection of lawyers, doctors, public officials, journalists, professors and lecturers belong? To the middle class, certainly, but not to the capitalist middle class. They belonged to the noncapitalist or professional middle class, a class curiously neglected in the social theories of the age, but one which played a part out of all proportion to its numbers in both the theory and the practice of class conflict.

To treat them as a separate class seems at first sight to be

---

[1] [Robinson], 'A Dissolution of Parliament', *ibid.*, 1829, XXVI. 251–9; cf. [O'Sullivan], 'Review of the last Session of Parliament', XXVI. 224–37, and [Robinson], 'The Reform of the House of Commons', 1830, XXVII. 640–58.

[2] Seeley, *op. cit.*, pp. 221–2.

[3] Cf. chap. x, § 3, below.

[4] Mill was an India Office official, Brougham a K.C., Senior a Master in Chancery, Hall an M.D., Hodgskin a half-pay naval officer turned lecturer, Gray a commercial clerk turned lecturer, O'Brien a lawyer turned journalist, Malthus and Wilson professors, Coleridge and Southey professional authors.

perverse. Most theorists have treated them as middle class, *tout court*. Marx, who was aware of them to his own embarrassment, treated them in his criticism of their unregenerative role in existing societies as a mere adjunct of the ruling class: 'within this class one part appears as the thinkers of the class (its active conceptualizing ideologists, who make it their chief livelihood to develop and perfect the illusions of the class about itself)'; but in his hopes for their aid in establishing the socialist society of the future, as 'workers by brain', or super-proletarians.[1] All three views express an element of the truth about this Protean class, which could assume the guise of any other class at will. Yet underlying each disguise was Proteus himself, a class, sub-class, or socio-economic group whose members had enough in common to support a separate social ideal which had a profound effect upon the rest of society.

Curiously enough, their existence as a separate class follows logically from Marx's own definition of class as determined principally by source of income. Indeed, when Marx came to wrestle systematically with his definition, in the abortive last chapter of *Capital*, he uncovered Proteus, and shied away:

> what constitutes a class? . . . What constitutes wage-labourers, capitalists and landlords as the three great social classes? At first glance it might seem that the identity of revenues and of sources of revenue is responsible. . . . However, from this point of view, doctors and officials would also form two distinct classes, for they belong to two different social groups, and the revenues of the members of each group come from the same source.

And he tailed off in an infinite regression of different sub-classes of workers, capitalists and landowners.[2]

Doctors and officials do indeed belong to a distinct class. They receive incomes which differ less from each other than they do from rent, profits and wages. Though not altogether immune from market forces, their incomes are not the direct result of bargaining in the market, but are in a sense set aside by society according to the value set by it on their services, under their persuasion. The first profession was that of the clergy, whose income, significantly, was called a 'living': an income set aside by the laity, not as a reward for their service—which, once

---

[1] Marx, *German Ideology* (1845–6), in Bottomore and Rubel, *op. cit.*, p. 79.

[2] Marx, *Capital* (Chicago, 1909), III, chap. xlii, pp. 1038–40.

incumbent in the living, they were free except in conscience to supply or omit—but a guaranteed income to enable them to perform their office. The second and third were those of law and medicine, in which fees might seem to bear some relation in detail to piece-rates and in aggregate to profits. Yet fees, too, were not (in theory) fixed by competition, but by the value set by the profession, and accepted by society, on services which the client could not judge and had therefore to take on trust. All 'true' professions stem from these three, and are characterized by expert, esoteric service demanding integrity in the purveyor and trust in the client and the community, and by noncompetitive reward in the form of a fixed salary or standard and unquestioned fee.

This is not, of course, to say that either the professional man or the community always lived up to these high standards. In the old society there were always plenty of 'hedge priests', 'pettifogging attorneys', 'dishonest apothecaries', 'fee-snatching office-holders', and 'writers prostituted to Ministers'; and both clients and society were apt to treat all but the very highest levels of the professions with scant respect and scantier reward, viz. the underpaid curate, the apothecary at the tradesman's entrance, and the threadbare government clerk. The professional man could then be anything from rich, respected *savant* through dependent retainer or licensed jester to despised charlatan. Being by nature hierarchical interests dependent on patronage, stretching from the aristocracy of office on the bishops' and judges' benches down to the level of the petty tradesman, the professions fitted snugly into the old dependency society.

The Industrial Revolution, however, which emancipated the entrepreneur and the wage-earner, also emancipated the professional man. With urbanization and the rise of living standards, doctors, lawyers, writers, and even the clergy (including dissenting ministers) found an enlarged demand for their services, which reduced their dependence on the few rich and increased that on the many comfortable clients of their own social standing. The transition enabled them to acquire a greater measure of self-respect, and to demand corresponding respect from society. 'Respectability' was the conscious aim of the 'gentlemen practisers' who set out to substitute for the eighteenth-century image of the 'pettifogging attorney' the nineteenth-century one of the 'respectable solicitor', through the local societies which culminated in the Law Society of 1825.[1] The surgeons and apothecaries, the general practitioners of the eighteenth century, achieved enhanced status through the Royal College of Surgeons of 1800 and the Apothecaries' Act of 1815.[2] Even the Anglican clergy, the most dependent of professions and the most consistent defenders of the aristocratic system, were not immune. In raising the standards, self-respect and independence of the profession the Evangelical and Oxford movements were for once on the same side, the first by demanding a more sober standard of conduct, morality, speech and dress than the average gentlemanly cleric of the eighteenth century, the second by emphasising the sacerdotal character of the clerical office which segregated them from the laity and freed them from lay control.[3]

At the same time new professions proliferated, and organized themselves to demand the same kind of status and independence as the old: the civil engineers in 1818, the architects in 1837, the pharmacists in 1841, the mechanical engineers in 1847, and so on—though many of these took some time to differentiate themselves from the adjacent entrepreneurial occupations of building and contract, shop-keeping, machine-making, and the like.[4]

More significant than any of these particular developments, however, was the general rise in the status of the professional intellectual in society. This can best be seen in the most intellectual of professions, the profession of letters, at both the mundane and sublime levels. At the mundane level, authorship at last became a profession in the material sense. It was no longer mainly a pastime for gentlemen like Dryden, Addison and Pope and a low-paid occupation for Grubb Street hacks like Defoe or Johnson, but a regular profession at which a Walter Scott, a Southey or a Cobbett could make a comfortable, sometimes a handsome living.[5] Aristocratic clients like Thomas Moore

[1] R. Robson, *The Attorney in 18th-Century England* (Cambridge, 1959), esp. chap. x, 'The Road to Respectability'.

[2] C. Newman, *The Evolution of Medical Education in the 19th Century* (1957), pp. 2, 73.

[3] Cf., *inter alia*, M. M. Hennell, *John Venn and the Clapham Sect* (1958) and Geoffrey Faber, *Oxford Apostles* (Penguin, 1954).

[4] G. Millerson, *The Qualifying Professions* (1964), pp. 121, 126.

[5] Cf. J. W. Saunders, *The Profession of English Letters* (1964), esp. chaps. viii and ix.

might condemn the 'lowering of standards that must necessarily arise from extending the circle of judges; from letting the mob in to vote, particularly at a time when the market is such an object to authors,' but they could not resist the rewards of the mass market for best-sellers.[1]

At the sublime level—whatever one thinks of the rise or fall of literary standards—there is no doubt that inordinately higher claims were made in the early nineteenth century for the importance and influence of authors. They were no longer Adam Smith's 'unprosperous race of men, commonly called men of letters', but Shelley's 'unacknowledged legislators of the world'; Coleridge's 'men of genius' whose imagination was 'an echo in the finite mind of the eternal act of creation in the infinite I am'; Carlyle's 'Man-of-Letters Hero . . . our most important modern person . . . the light of the world; the world's Priest:—guiding it like a sacred Pillar of Fire in its dark pilgrimage through the waste of Time.'[2] The evolution of the romantic conception of genius deserves an unromantic monograph, but meanwhile it can be said that the romantic movement represents a social emancipation of the intellectual and the artist exactly parallel to the birth of class.

What characterized the emancipated professional men as a class was their comparative aloofness from the struggle for income. It was of course only comparative. Individuals found the struggle only too real, while each profession collectively knew that its value in the market could be increased by restricting entry and 'closing the shop' like any skilled trade union. Nevertheless, there was a sense in which professional incomes were only indirectly influenced by the market, or rather, that it was implicit in the professional outlook to pretend that the rewards demanded for their services were not to be questioned. At any rate, once established, the professional man could generally rely on a steady income not subject to the same mutual competition as rent, profits and wages. To a certain extent, then, he was above the economic battle, with the same freedom to

[1] T. Moore, *Memoirs, Journal and Correspondence* (ed. Lord John Russell, 1853–1856), VII. 46; Murray, the publisher, was said to have paid Moore £3,000 for *Lallah Rookh*—Saunders, *op. cit.*, p. 177.

[2] Smith, *Wealth of Nations*, I. 38; P. B. Shelley, *A Defence of Poetry*, in *Essays and Letters* (ed. E. Rhys, 1886), p. 7; S. T. Coleridge, *Table Talk* (1835), II. 87; T. Carlyle, *Heroes and Hero-Worship* (1893 ed.), pp. 144–6.

take sides, to turn his thumbs up or down, as a spectator in the Roman Colosseum. More often than not, no doubt, he went with the crowd, or the most influential part of it, the middle tiers or the patrician boxes. But, not being involved, he had the more freedom to choose on the merits of the contest. He was, in short, a ready-made 'social crank', who could be relied upon to come to the aid of any class but his own.

In any other class, to be a 'social crank' required great strength or at least perversity of character. 'No high-sounding maxims can influence the rich as a body,' that remarkable 'social crank', the Owenite landowner William Thompson, pointed out. However, 'a few individuals may rise above the impulses of their class'; these few should be 'numbered among the heroes and philosophers of society.'[1] Professional men, once emancipated, did not need to be heroes. They were the philosophers of society by inclination and training. It was they who supplied the major part of the social analysis and terminology used by the three major classes. It was Adam Smith and the Scottish historical school of philosophy, academics all, who first systematized the language of class.[2] It was the classical economists, all professional men except Ricardo, who, according to their opponents, set the classes at loggerheads. Their professional opponents thought in exactly the same terms of the tripartite class system: Carlyle of 'Workers, Master Workers, and Master Unworkers', Matthew Arnold of 'Barbarians, Philistines, and Populace', F. D. Maurice of 'the aristocracy, the trading classes, and the working classes'.[3] Indeed, what J. S. Mill said of the political economists could be applied to them all:

> They revolve in their eternal circle of landlords, capitalists, and labourers, until they seem to think of the distinction of society into those three classes, as if it were one of God's ordinances, not man's, and as little under human control as the division of day and night.[4]

They were the forgotten middle class, in short, because they forgot themselves. Except when postulating a place for their

[1] R. K. P. Pankhurst, *William Thompson . . . 1775–1833* (1954), pp. 21–2.
[2] Cf. chap. ii, § 1, above.
[3] Carlyle, *Past and Present* (1893 ed.), pp. 5–6; M. Arnold, *Culture and Anarchy* (1869), chap. iii; F. D. Maurice, *On the Reformation of Society* (Southampton, 1851), pp. 10–13.
[4] 'A' [J. S. Mill], 'On Miss Martineau's Summary of Political Economy', *Monthly Repository*, 1834, VIII. 320; Briggs, 'Language of Class', *loc. cit.*, p. 44.

idealized selves in other classes' ideal societies, they generally left themselves out of their social analysis. Nevertheless, professional men had a separate, if sometimes subconscious, social ideal which underlay their versions of the other class ideals. Their ideal society was a functional one based on expertise and selection by merit. For them trained and qualified expertise rather than property, capital or labour, should be the chief determinant and justification of status and power in society. For James Mill, for example, it was 'intellectual powers', not birth or wealth, which alone fitted men to rule. For Carlyle the natural rulers were 'the unclassed Aristocracy by nature . . . "who derive their patent of nobility direct from Almighty God".'[1]

Similarly, selection by merit, rather than patronage, market competition (as distinct from competitive examination), or co-operative endeavour, ought to be the supporting principle of recruitment. Merit of course entered into all systems of recruitment: merit adjudged by the patron, by the impersonal market, or the acceptance of one's fellow workers. But in the professional ideal merit meant ability and diligence in one's chosen field of expertise, and could be judged only by other professional experts in the same field. The principal technique for such selection was the examination. The cult of the examination amongst the Benthamites is proverbial. Bentham himself regarded it as the perfect device for 'maximizing aptitude' and 'minimizing expense', and it was the cornerstone of his followers' educational endeavours from the Lancastrian schools of 1808 to the Society of Arts Examination Board of 1854.[2] It was no less a cult amongst their rivals: Thomas Arnold laid a new emphasis on examinations at Rugby, where in addition he replaced free entry for local boys by scholarship examinations, while his son Matthew devoted his professional career to examining elementary schoolchildren.[3] Examinations inevitably preoccupied the new professional institutes of the nineteenth century, and were absorbed into the

---

[1] J. Mill, *Government*, p. 7; Carlyle, 'Shooting Niagara, and After?', *Macmillan's Magazine*, 1867, XVI. 319.

[2] Cf. Brian Simon, *Studies in the History of Education, 1780–1870* (1960), pp. 79–84, 149–50; F. E. Foden, 'A History of Technical Examinations in England to 1918', Ph.D. dissertation, Leicester University, 1961, pp. 3–4, 10–14, 19–20.

[3] T. W. Bamford, *Thomas Arnold* (1960), chap. xii; M. Arnold, *Reports on Elementary Schools* (1910).

framework of the State by Macaulay's and Trevelyan Northcote's reforms of the Indian and home civil services.[1]

Examinations were a method of ensuring that the candidate was capable of performing the function for which he was selected. For the ideal society was a functional one in which trained and qualified experts provided efficiently and disinterestedly the services necessary to keep it functioning. The professions were bound to justify the privileges—incorporation, self-government, control of entry, and ultimately a legal monopoly of the occupation—which they increasingly claimed from the State, by the service which they provided for the community. They naturally extended the demand for justification by service to the rest of society. The Ricardians, for example, justified the capitalist by his service of managing industry and initiating the cycle of economic activity, and condemned the landlord for giving nothing in return for his unearned rent. Malthus, on the other hand, justified the landowner by his service of unproductive consumption which initiated the activities of the other classes. John Gray, the professional lecturer, hoped that all men would justify themselves in the society of the future by their labour, manual or mental:

> In the old world, men are respected in proportion as they are enabled by the possession of wealth to command the labour of others. . . . In the new, we hope to secure to all men the value of their services to society in whatever way they may be given; to respect men in proportion to their *utility* in promoting in any shape or way, the happiness of our species; and to attach value, not to pieces of metal, but to *every thing* which tends to improve the condition of the human race, physically, morally, or intellectually.[2]

Gray's definition of service in terms of human happiness and improvement was characteristic of the professional ideal. It followed naturally from the concern with function, which could be defined as the increasingly efficient satisfaction of human needs. The Benthamite 'principle of utility', of 'the greatest happiness of the greatest number', obviously fits the same model:

the only rational foundation of government . . . is, expediency—the

[1] Millerson, *op. cit.*, pp. 120–9; Wyn Griffith, *The British Civil Service, 1854–1954* (1954), pp. 12–16; E. W. Cohen, *The Growth of the British Civil Service, 1780–1939* (1941), pp. 118–23.

[2] J. Gray, *A Lecture on Human Happiness* (1825), p. 3.

general benefit of the community. It is the duty of a government to do whatever is conducive to the welfare of the governed.[1]

More remarkably, the anti-Benthamite professional thinkers used identical language. For Coleridge the 'outward object of virtue' was 'the greatest producible sum of happiness of all men', and his 'positive ends of the State' were:

1. To make the means of subsistence more easy to each individual:
2. To secure to each of its members the hope of bettering his own condition or that of his children:
3. The development of those faculties which are essential to his humanity, that is, to his rational and moral being.[2]

The concern of professional men with happiness, progress and efficiency was not entirely altruistic. It was the function of the nineteenth century, Sir George Young has said, 'to disengage the disinterested intelligence, to release it from the entanglements of party and sect, . . . and to set it operating over the whole range of human life and circumstance.'[3] In so far as it did this institutionally, it was the disinterested intelligence of professional men—doctors, lawyers, civil servants, engineers, scientists, social workers, teachers and professional thinkers— which it brought to bear upon its problems. These men were not necessarily superior, morally and intellectually, to their fellows in other classes, but they had a professional interest in disinterestedness and intelligence. It was their interest to 'deliver the goods' which they purveyed: expert service and the objective solution of society's problems, whether disease, legislation, administration, material construction, the nature of matter, social misery, education, or social, economic and political theory.

They also had an interest in educating society to demand, and pay for, disinterested, intelligent service, and to differentiate themselves from quacks and charlatans. Hence their interest in what Sir George Young again called 'moralizing society'.[4] They moralized society at both the theoretical and practical levels. At the theoretical level, professional men moralized the

---

[1] N. W. Senior, Oxford Lectures, 1847–48, in *Industrial Efficiency and Social Economy* (ed. S. L. Levy, 1929), II, 302; Robbins, *op. cit.*, p. 45.

[2] Coleridge, *Aids to Reflection* (1825), p. 39; *Second Lay Sermon* (1839), p. 414.

[3] G. M. Young, *Victorian England, Portrait of an Age* (1960).

[4] *Ibid.*, p. 4.

ideals of the other classes by transforming them from mere apologetics for self-interest into moral theories of society. Thus the three main streams of social thought in nineteenth-century England may be regarded as the rival attempts by three streams of professional thinkers to sublimate the economic interests of the other three classes into morally and intellectually coherent social philosophies, by infusing into them large doses of the professional ideal, and coaxing, goading or shaming their members into living up to them. In each case they were at first successful, but increasingly the professional ideal became uppermost in the minds of the professional thinkers, and increasingly alienated their adopted class.

The first, the radical or Utilitarian, stream flowed from the Benthamites and Ricardians, via John Stuart Mill and his followers, down to the Fabians. With the exception of Bentham himself, the Lord Chancellor *manqué*, Ricardo, a stockbroker who would now claim professional status, and Beatrice Webb, the rentier, they were nearly all professional men: lawyers, doctors, civil servants, academics, journalists, professional authors, and so on. At first this stream intertwined with the entrepreneurial ideal, since in the early nineteenth century professional expertise and selection by merit linked arms with capital and competition in opposition to the 'idle' property and 'corrupt' patronage of the aristocratic ideal. Yet by the time we reach the second generation the two ideals are beginning to diverge. John Stuart Mill developed doubts about the competitive system:

> I confess I am not charmed with the ideal of life held out by those who think that the normal state of human beings is struggling to get on; that the trampling, crushing, elbowing, and treading on each other's heels, which form the existing type of social life, are the most desirable lot of human kind, are anything but disagreeable symptoms of the phases of industrial progress.

He began to advocate the proletarian alternative of producer co-operation, for

> the moral revolution that would accompany it: the healing of the standing feud between capital and labour; the transformation of human life, from a conflict of classes struggling for opposite interests to a friendly rivalry in pursuit of a good common to all; the elevation of the dignity of labour, a new sense of security and independence

in the labouring class, and the conversion of each human being's daily occupation into a school of the social sympathies and the practical intelligence.[1]

He revived the anti-landlord death duties and unearned increment taxation of his father and Bentham, but found small response in the capitalist middle class for his land reform campaign or for the collectivist social reforms which he called 'a qualified Socialism'.[2] And other Utilitarians, Morley, Thorold Rogers and J. S. Nicholson to the one side, Henry Sedgwick, A. V. Dicey and J. F. Stephen to the other, divided themselves between advanced Liberalism and paternal Toryism, both equally anathema to the capitalist middle class.[3]

When we come to the Fabians, the intellectual grandchildren of the Benthamites,[4] the divergence is complete. In them, 'the greatest happiness of the greatest number' has completely shed all connection with capitalism and individual competition, and has become the slogan of a purely professional socialist society, in which the capitalist will become 'a public official with a gold band round his hat, a secure income, and a pension', and the wage-earning class will be abolished, and replaced by salaried, professionalized workers.[5]

A similar divergence took place in the second stream, between the aristocratic ideal and its professional apologists. This, the organicist or Idealist stream, flowed from Coleridge and Southey, John Wilson and the *Blackwood's* revivalists of the aristocratic ideal, via the Christian Socialists and the Oxford Idealists, T. H. Green, D. G. Ritchie and Arnold Toynbee, down

[1] J. S. Mill, *Principles*, pp. 453, 475.

[2] J. Bentham, *Supply without Burthen, or Escheat vice Taxation*, in *Bentham's Economic Writings* (ed. W. Stark, 1952), I. 279f.; James Mill, *Elements of Political Economy* (1821), pp. 202–3; J. S. Mill, *Explanatory Programme of the Land Tenure Reform Association* (1870), in *Dissertations and Discussions* (1875), IV. 239f., and *Autobiography*, pp. 161, 195–8, 210; cf. Beer, *op. cit.*, II. 237–45.

[3] Cf. A. V. Dicey, *Law and Public Opinion in England* (1952 ed.), pp. 161, 165; J. Roach, 'Liberalism and the Victorian Intelligentsia', *Cambridge Hist.J.*, 1957, XIII. 1f.

[4] Cf. B. Webb, *Our Partnership* (1948), p. 210 (diary, 25 January 1901): 'Reading Leslie Stephen's *Utilitarians*. Always interesting to compare one's own point of view with that of one's parents! For Bentham was certainly Sidney's intellectual godfather. . . .'

[5] G. B. Shaw, 'How the Middle Class is Fleeced', speech in Chelsea Town Hall, *The Times*, 18 October 1907; R. Lewis and A. Maude, *The English Middle Classes* (1949), p. 75.

to the East End 'settlers' and the Charity Organization Society. *Blackwood's* saw its role as one of shaming the back-sliding aristocracy into living up to the professional and aristocratic ideal of service. It condemned the idle uncharitable landlord, the 'lazy, luxurious good-for-nothing man, monopolizing to his own use the profits of twenty thousand acres of land', who did not fulfil the social and political duties which alone justified his property.[1] We have already seen how the revivalists failed to revive the ideal in any but a handful of the aristocracy. The leader of the handful, Lord Ashley, complained to his diary that he was disliked and shunned for his paternalism towards the farm labourers not merely by his class but by his kinsfolk.[2]

In the second generation the Christian Socialists—'a band of friends, chiefly clergymen and barristers'—again sought to revive the 'moral guidance and leadership' of the aristocracy, but although they sought 'to separate . . . that socialism which Mr. Southey and other eminent Conservatives believed to be the best solution of the practical difficulties of England, from Communism, Red Republicanism, or any other anarchical opinion whatever,' it is clear that their very name alienated the propertied classes whom they hoped to woo, and their influence was practically confined to a section of the clergy—and perhaps their families, including Edward Denison, son of the Bishop of Salisbury, and their main link with the East End 'settlers' and the Charity Organization Society—and to some Idealist academics and 'new model' trade unionists.[3]

In the third generation, Octavia Hill, the East End 'settlers' and the Charity Organization Society still aimed to introduce the 'delight' of the rural landlord 'to keep thus fair the part of the earth over which it has been given to rule' into 'some of the lowest districts of London.'[4] But they found precious few landlords to support them—save such as Ruskin the professional art

---

[1] [Johnstone], 'The Present Crisis', *Blackwood's*, 1830, XXVIII. 692.

[2] E. Hodder, *Life of Shaftesbury*, (1886) I. 358 (diary, Christmas Day, 1851).

[3] J. S. Mill, *Principles*, p. 471; F. D. Maurice, *op. cit.*, p. 32; F. Maurice, *Life of F. D. Maurice* (1884), II, 92; J. Saville, 'The Christian Socialists of 1848', in J. Saville, ed., *Democracy and the Labour Movement* (1954); Woodroofe, *op. cit.*, pp. 48–50, 65–6; C. L. Mowat, *The Charity Organisation Society, 1869–1913* (1961), pp. 8, 11; R. Harrison, *Before the Socialists* (1965), pp. 15, 251, 327n.

[4] Octavia Hill, 'Blank Court, or Landlords and Tenants', *Macmillan's Magazine*, 1871, XXIV. 456f.

critic and Peabody the American millionaire—and were forced to invent the 'university settlement' and the C.O.S. to enable unpropertied academics, clergymen and their kind to perform the paternal duties of the missing squire. In the end, not only was the divergence between the aristocratic and professional versions of the ideal complete, but by a twist of historical irony the professional version split precisely as the aristocratic had done in the last days of the old society. One part indeed, through remarkable clergymen like Stewart Headlam, the Fabian, and Canon Barnett, went on to revive paternal welfare through what the latter called 'practicable socialism'.[1] The other, through C. S. Loch, Helen Bosanquet and the C.O.S., set out to revive paternal discipline and the rigours of the 1834 poor law, and, greatest irony of all, to oppose every collectivist social reform with the most uncompromising adherence to the entrepreneurial principle of *laissez-faire*.[2]

The third stream, that of the professional apologists of the working-class ideal, was a more fugitive one, which ran underground for long distances, and flowed out unexpectedly in individuals as diverse as Charles Hall, Thomas Hodgskin, Bronterre O'Brien, John Minter Morgan, E. S. Beesly, Frederic Harrison, and—for what class if not the professional one did he belong to?—Karl Marx himself. Such men were not, it is true, typical professional men, for it required extraordinary independence of mind and strength of character to adopt the working-class ideal—which is why it attracted only the more remarkable 'social cranks' from the non-professional classes, Robert Owen, William Thompson, Frederick Engels, H. M. Hyndman, and so on. Yet, paradoxically, there was a greater consistency in this stream of thought than in the other two. Although the professional thinkers offered as great a variety of means of curing the ills of society as the infinitely various working-class ideal was capable of, they consistently applied to it the same criteria, the professional criteria of justification by service, and demanded what amounted to the same end: a new-minted professional

---

[1] F. G. Bettany, *Stewart Headlam* (1926); S. A. Barnett, *Practicable Socialism* (1916); Henrietta O. W. Barnett, *Canon Barnett, his Life, Work and Friends* (1919).

[2] Mowat, *op. cit.*, pp. 21-4, 114-17; Woodroofe, *op. cit.*, pp. 34-5; and the *Majority Report of the Royal Commission on the Poor Laws and the Relief of Distress*, P.P., 1909, (Cd. 4499), XXVII. 1, *passim*. (Loch, Bosanquet, and four other members of the C.O.S. were members of the Majority).

society based on expertise (skilled labour by hand and brain) and selection by merit (from each according to his ability).

In the first generation the Owenite and other primitive communist thinkers came nearer to success in inspiring the working class with their Utopian visions than any later group, but the visions faded into the realities of the Rochdale Pioneers or the mirage of O'Connor's Land Plan.[1] In the second, Beesly, Harrison and the Positivists, despite their great services to the trade union movement, never remotely interested the British working class in the Religion of Humanity and the new, functional society of Comte, while Marx had even less success in converting them to the communist theory of revolution.[2] In the third, socialist ideas spread rather more widely in the working class, but, by another historical irony, they were not so much the socialist ideas of William Morris, H. M. Hyndman, and the revolutionary tradition, but those of the evolutionary tradition which derived rather from the other two streams of thought. The very 'socialisms', Christian and Millite, which had alienated the landed and capitalist classes respectively from their professional apologists, now came together, through Davidson and Headlam on the one side, and Shaw and the Webbs on the other, in the Fabian Society, and that apotheosis of the professional ideal which we have already noticed.[3] This gave the professional ideal a fresh start in infiltrating and moralizing the working class, though it can hardly claim to have made much headway before the end of the century. Meanwhile, the alienation from the bulk of the working class of the Utopian visionaries, from the Owenites to Marx, was complete.

In each case the alienation was inevitable. Even when they were expressing the other classes' ideals the ideal citizen for professional men was not at bottom the responsible landlord, the active capitalist or the co-operative labourer. It was the professional man himself. *Blackwood's* complained that 'the Philosophers . . . are getting up what they are pleased to call a New Aristocracy—an Aristocracy of Science' which 'is to be the enemy and ruler of the old one.' William Thompson attacked

[1] Cf. chap. viii, § 3, below.

[2] Cf. R. Harrison, *op. cit.*, chap. vi, 'The Positivists: a Study of Labour's Intellectuals'.

[3] Margaret Cole, *The Story of Fabian Socialism* (1961), chap. i; A. M. McBriar, *Fabian Socialism and English Politics, 1884–1918* (Cambridge, 1966), chap. i.

Hodgskin's stress on 'mental labourers, *literati*, men of science' and James Mill's middle rank exempt from the need to labour 'which gives to science, to art and to legislation itself their most distinguished ornaments, the chief source of all that has exalted and refined human nature.' For Coleridge

> The *Clerisy* of the nation, or national Church in its primary accepta-
> tion and original intention, comprehended the learned of all denom-
> inations, the sages and professors of the law and of jurisprudence, of
> medicine and physiology, of music, of military and civil architecture,
> with the mathematical as the common organ of the preceding; in
> short, all the so-called liberal arts and sciences, the possession and
> application of which constitute the civilization of a country, as well
> as the theological.

J. S. Mill thought that the government should provide 'by means of endowments or salaries for the maintenance of what has been called a learned class.' For Carlyle 'the ancient guides of Nations, Prophets, Priests, or whatever their name,' had been succeeded by 'the modern guides of Nations, who also go under a variety of names, Journalists, Political Economists, Politicians, Pamphleteers,' in a new 'Aristocracy of Talent'.[1]

It was not to be expected that the other classes should share their self-admiration. There was in all three major classes a built-in suspicion of intellectuals, of men who were two disinterested to be reliable, who had no hard economic interest to bind them to their adopted class. This was in fact an extension of the suspicion of all 'social cranks', whose whimsicality had led them into the quixotic championship of a different class, and might at any moment lead them out again. Suspicion of intellectuals led the T.U.C. to exclude Frederic Harrison and all other middle-class sympathizers from membership in 1883, and suspicion of the 'advanced Liberals', the middle-class 'cranks', both professional and capitalist, who were leading the Liberal Party into both land and social reform was to help to alienate the Whig landowners and Liberal business men who drifted to the Tories in the last quarter of the century.[2] In the long run the

---

[1] [Robinson], 'The Nobility', *Blackwood's*, 1825, XVIII. 350; Pankhurst, *Thompson*, p. 27; Coleridge, *On the Constitution of Church and State* (1852 ed.), pp. 54–5; Mill, *Principles*, p. 589; Carlyle, *Past and Present* (1893 ed.), pp. 23–4.

[2] S. and B. Webb, *Trade Unionism*, p. 374n.; R. C. K. Ensor, 'Some Political and Economic Interactions in Later Victorian England', *Trans. R.H.S.*, 1949,

attempt by professional thinkers to moralize the other class ideals failed, as moralizing without a material *quid pro quo* is apt to do.

In the short run, however, they were by no means unsuccessful. At least they persuaded the State and the public to accept what may be called the highest common factor of the three rival streams, notably social justification by service, the need for expertise and selection by merit in public administration, and the principles of happiness, progress and efficiency as the aims of government. Much of this was achieved at the practical level, by moralizing society in and through the process of social reform. The question has been much debated whether the great social reforms of the middle decades of the nineteenth century, in poor law, factory inspection, police and prisons, public health, education, control of the emigration traffic, and so on, were mainly the work of the Benthamites or were brought about by 'an independent historical process', impersonal and anonymous, the effect of a pervasive humanitarianism acting under the pressure of 'intolerable' facts. The controversy has become a scholastic dispute about an unverifiable question: whether the men who discovered the facts and found them 'intolerable' and those, often drawn from the same group, who devised and administered the machinery to reform them, were or were not all Benthamites, in the sense that they had 'read Bentham or heard of his name.'[1] The truth is that the first group of reformers, who discovered and protested about intolerable facts, were primarily 'social cranks' for whom the professional ideal had a special appeal, while the second group, the great reforming civil servants, were by definition professional men, on whom it operated directly.

On the first group—men like Hume and Place against the Combination Acts, Senior and Chadwick against the old poor law, Sadler, Oastler and Ashley in factory reform, Chadwick,

---

[1] Cf., *inter alia*, O. MacDonagh, 'The 19th Century Revolution in Government: a Reappraisal', *Hist.J.*, 1958, I. 52f.; H. Parris, 'The 19th-Century Revolution in Government: a Reappraisal Reappraised', *ibid.*, 1960, III. 17f.; Jenifer Hart, '19th-Century Social Reform: a Tory Interpretation of History', *Past and Present*, 1965, No. 31, 39f.; Valerie Cromwell, 'Interpretations of 19th-Century Administration: an Analysis', *Victorian Studies*, 1966, IX, 245f.

XXXI. 17f., which, however, places too much weight on reaction against Irish violence, to the neglect of English land and social reform.

Bishop Blomfield and Ashley again in public health—the professional ideal operated in two ways. It worked on them through the professional social critics amongst them and the leaven of professionalism which they introduced into the other class ideals, as, for example, when the *Blackwood's* contributors stiffened the aristocratic opposition to the total abolition of the poor law, or McCulloch and Senior overrode the entrepreneurial principle of the free market in labour as applied to children in factories and women in mines.[1] And it offered a professional solution to particular problems—expert, disinterested, administrative control and inspection—which more often than not proved to be the only effective alternative. In factory reform, for example, while Sadler and Ashley clung to the amateur principle of inspection by J.P.s in their bills of 1832–33, it was the professionals on the 1833 Commission, Chadwick, Tooke and Southwood Smith, who pushed full-time inspectors, on the professional ground that no one else would have an interest in enforcing the law.[2]

Two of the three professionals belonged to the second group, the great civil servants on whom the professional ideal worked directly. Chadwick and Smith were conscious Benthamites, and so were many more of them: Leonard Horner, Kay-Shuttleworth, Farr, Mann, Farrer, Helps, Porter, Deacon Hume, Tremenheere, Sir Charles Trevelyan, and so on. Equally, some of them were not: Matthew Arnold, Sir John Simon, Tom Taylor, to name only three. Whether they were or not, they all represented the new conception of a civil service independent of ministerial patronage, based on expertise and selection by merit. Their aims and methods were simply professional: objective study of the problem, fearless recommendation of a creative solution, ruthless lobbying through official and unofficial channels, and shameless empire building to carry it out. Their reports were a vehicle for their professionalism: as a Vice-President of the Council said of those of the education inspectors, 'instead of being collections of facts [they] were essays propounding new theories and startling systems of their own.'[3]

[1] Cf. § 3, above; and Robbins, *op. cit.*, pp. 101–2.
[2] Hart, *loc. cit.*, p. 42.
[3] Mary Sturt, *The Education of the People* (1967), p. 239.

Yet this meant that they were, willy-nilly, Benthamites, conscious or unconscious. Bentham stood above all for efficient, responsible government, what J. S. Mill called 'the combination of complete popular control over public affairs, with the greatest attainable perfection of skilled agency.'[1] Bentham's method of dealing with any problem of government or society—Inquiry, Report, Legislation, Administration, Inspection—was exactly that which was applied by both groups of reformers, but especially by the professional administrators.[2] If he did not specifically forecast the process by which the administrators and inspectors were to be educated by the 'intolerable' facts which they reported on, and used them to evoke still further legislation and administration and inspection, it was at least in the logic of his method.

Does this mean that Bentham influenced the process of reform which he foresaw and advocated? Not necessarily in every case. There were no doubt reforming administrators who had not read Bentham, and some perhaps—although it is very hard to believe—who had not heard of his name. Their professionalism and the pressure of intolerable facts eventually carried them, if more slowly, by the same road to the same goal. But those who had read Bentham, or talked to those who had, could travel all the faster for knowing where they were going. For the important question is not so much *who* Bentham influenced as *why* they were influenced by him, and the answer is that Bentham spoke to their professional condition. Despite his rentier's income and his apparent championship of the entrepreneurial ideal,[3] Bentham was, above all in his chosen field of government, the apotheosis of the professional ideal. He stood for expert, efficient administration in the interests of the greatest happiness of the greatest number.[4]

---

[1] Mill, *Autobiography*, p. 225.

[2] Cf. David Roberts, *The Victorian Origins of the British Welfare State* (New Haven, Conn., 1960), *passim*.

[3] There were considerable differences of economic doctrine and emphasis between Bentham and his disciples James Mill and Ricardo—cf. T. W. Hutchison, 'Bentham as an Economist', *Econ.J.*, 1956, LXVI. 288f.

[4] Cf. Sir Henry Maine, *Ancient Law* (1861), pp. 78–9: 'It is impossible to overrate the importance to a nation *or profession* of having a distinct object to aim at in the pursuit of improvement. The secret of Bentham's immense influence in England during the past thirty years is his success in placing such an object before us. He gave us a clear rule of reform.'—Dicey, *op. cit.*, p. 168n. (my italics).

Whether Benthamite or merely professional, the great social and administrative reforms were part of the professionalization of góvernment which was the greatest political achievement of nineteenth-century Britain. They were also, as we shall see in the next chapter, an aspect of the divergence of the professional ideal from the entrepreneurial in social policy which was ultimately to help to undermine entrepreneurial society. But first we have to see the triumph of the entrepreneurial ideal in nearly every other field, which preceded and determined the establishment of that society.

VIII

<><><><><><><><><><><><><><><><><><><><><><><><><><><><>

The Triumph of the Entrepreneurial Ideal

<><><><><><><><><><><><><><><><><><><><><><><><><><><><>

T H E entrepreneurial ideal, it might be thought in that *post hoc* wisdom which is the besetting sin of historians, was bound to win the struggle between the ideals. Marx, who was among the first to recognize—and welcome—the victory of the *bourgeoisie*, also recognized that like any new ruling class it had to impose its own ideology upon the rest of society:

> For each new class which puts itself in the place of the one ruling before it, is compelled, simply in order to achieve its aims, to represent its interest as the common interest of all members of society, i.e. employing an ideal formula, to give its ideas the form of universally valid ones.[1]

But we have seen that not only the ruling class but every other represents its interest as the common interest, and universalizes its own ideal. It is not so much that the ruling class imposes its ideal upon the rest, but that the class which manages to impose its ideal upon the rest becomes the ruling class.

This interpretation is obviously nearer the truth in Victorian England where the entrepreneurial class ruled, as it were, by, remote control, through the power of its ideal over the ostensible ruling class, the landed aristocracy which continued to occupy the main positions of power down to the 1880's and

---

[1] Marx, *German Ideology* (1845–6), Bottomore and Rubel, *op. cit.*, p. 80.

beyond. The landed class possessed a clear majority of the House of Commons until 1885, of the Cabinet until 1893, if not 1905, and of the House of Lords until long after the Parliament Act of 1911 drastically reduced its powers.[1] It effectively controlled recruitment to the Civil Service until at least 1870, to the Army until 1871, and to the Church for as long as it cared to exercise it. It dominated local government until at least 1888, and in some counties for much longer. Yet neither contemporaries nor historians have doubted that the capitalist middle class were the 'real' rulers of mid-Victorian England, in the sense that the laws which were passed and executed by landed Parliaments and Governments were increasingly those demanded by the business men and—which is not necessarily the same people —their intellectual mentors.

Of course, all power is limited in practice, and power by remote control is subject to what engineers call transmission losses. Not only did the landowners have a veto on matters affecting their own interest, which on occasions of head-on collision required the threat of revolution to remove. The working class, too, made demands which could not be ignored altogether, and, especially when allied with capable 'social cranks' from the politically entrenched classes, had to be met by concessions and compromise. Finally, the professional middle class had a profound influence both on the demands made by the other classes and the language in which they expressed them and on the way in which the laws were framed and administered. Between these three influences power could often be attenuated, or diverted into directions not anticipated by the class wielding it. To this extent the victory of the entrepreneurial class was a highly qualified one.

Nevertheless, and for that very reason, the triumph of the entrepreneurial ideal was complete, and both preceded and went further than that of the class itself. It was by persuading the rest of society, or the great majority of it, to accept their ideal of a class society based on capital and competition, not by personally capturing the institutions of government, that the capitalist middle class was able to achieve its aims: free trade in nearly everything, from commerce, through land, labour, and appointments under the State, to education and religion.

[1] Cf. § 2, below.

Victory in the struggle meant winning three crucial battles: the battle for the heart, for control of the prevailing system of morality; the battle for the mind, for the control of education and of public opinion about society; and the battle for the State, for control not merely of the choice of governors but of legislation and the administrative system. Of the three the first two were infinitely more important than the third. Whichever ideal won them could afford a less than overwhelming victory in the third, and still win the whole campaign. For whichever class came, through the acceptance of its ideal, to control the heart and mind of society could, without itself taking over the State, indirectly control government policy, the content of legislation, and the recruitment and methods of the administrators. This, as we shall see, was the achievement of the capitalist middle class, and the triumph of their ideal.

1. THE MORAL REVOLUTION

The battle for the heart came first, both in time and in importance. John Stuart Mill once said that 'wherever there is an ascendant class, a large portion of the morality of the country emanates from its class interests, and its feelings of class superiority.'[1] Yet, as with Marx above, the argument may be nearer the truth the other way round: whichever class manages to impose its own morality upon the rest of the nation will become the ascendant class. For every class had its feeling of moral superiority, and tried to get the other classes to accept it. Indeed, the ideal in each case was as much a moral as a social ideal, and the ideal citizen a paragon of morality as well as the model for social emulation. It is therefore true to say that the morality it hoped to impose on the rest of the nation emanated from its class interests, but like a sort of ethical ectoplasm it emanated at a very etheral level. The moral ideal was a highly sublimated version of its economic interest.

The aristocratic ideal of the gentleman was a moral ideal based on the chivalrous code of honour. It was not a particularly

---

[1] Pankhurst, *Thompson*, p. 131n.; cf. James Mill, in *West.Rev.*, 1826, VI. 255: 'every class or combination of men have a strong propensity to get up a system of morality for themselves, that is conformable to their own interests, and to urge [it] upon other men. . . .'

gentle code. Originally the gentleman meant a man of gentle birth, i.e. 'good' or 'high' birth in the feudal hierarchy, as opposed to the common or villainous birth of the mere villager, and had no more to do with gentleness than serfdom as such had to do with villainy.[1] Gentleness and villainy were secondary attributes fathered on the language by the snobbery of the gentry. The gentlemanly code of honour, on the contrary, was the paramilitary code of an aristocracy by conquest, which prided itself on its valour on the battlefield rather than its dedication to the arts of peace. It had been somewhat softened by the medieval Christian ideal of the chivalrous knight fighting for the Church and the heretical ideal of the knight of courtly love. But it remained down to the early nineteenth century an aggressive code which demanded that a gentleman should indeed be honest and keep his word—to other gentlemen, though not necessarily to servants and inferiors; be courteous and honourable towards ladies—though not necessarily to mere women and servant-girls; pay his debts, especially his 'debts of honour', i.e. gambling debts—but not necessarily his debts to tradesmen and shopkeepers; and above all to defend any insult to his honour by challenging the offender to a duel—provided the offender were a gentleman, and not a man of inferior birth, in which case he was merely obliged to administer a thrashing. In defence of their honour, half the prime ministers of the period had at some time fought a duel: Shelburne, Pitt, Fox, Canning, Wellington and Peel.[2]

The code of honour was above religion, and stronger than Christian morality. Even so Christian a gentleman and opponent of duelling as Wilberforce could appeal to it where Christian morality failed. Supporting the Catholic Relief Bill in the House of Commons in 1813, he asked, 'Even if the consciences of Roman Catholics should not be bound by the oath which they will take, where can *gentlemen* be found, who after swearing not

---

[1] Gentlemen from *gentium*, (well-)begotten; villain from *villanus*, peasant, serf; the chivalrous code of honour was somewhat overlain during the Renaissance by the ideals of the courtier, the 'complete man' of education and mental and physical culture, *uomo universale*, but the paramilitary concept of personal honour to be defended by appeal to arms survived intact—cf. K. Charlton, *Education in Renaissance England* (1965), chap. ii, esp. pp. 81–3, which emphasizes the essential continuity of Castiglione's *Il Cortegiano* with the chivalric ideal.

[2] Cf. O. F. Christie, *The Transition from Aristocracy, 1832–67* (1927), p. 23.

to disturb or endanger the Established Church, would dare to rise and propose any measure to its detriment?'[1] Religious sanctions were necessary, on the other hand, for the lesser breeds without the code: in the ranks below the gentleman, he said elsewhere, 'that system of honour and responsibility are wanting, which, in the superior classes, supply in some poor degree the place of higher principles.'[2] The gentleman was by definition above the mercenary money-grabbing pursuits of the commercial classes. Even his vices were less vicious because indulged in with decorum and good taste, thus, according to some, 'losing half their evil by losing all their grossness.'[3] Divorce on the grounds of adultery could safely be allowed for him and not for 'the middling and inferior ranks of society', according to Sir Charles Wetherell, because 'the undeniably greater immorality and moral courseness of the poorer classes' would increase too much the occasions for divorce.[4]

His typical vices, moreover—gambling, drunkenness, sexual indulgence—were private and confined chiefly to his own class, whereas his influence for good was public, and spread to all his neighbours. According to *Blackwood's*, 'he is to a very great extent the guide of society.' It was only the influence of the resident gentry which made the countryside of Britain morally superior to the degenerate peasant villages of Ireland and to 'the utter recklessness of impure thought and unclean living, that is so lamentably prevalent in some of the mining and manufacturing districts of England.' 'The morals and intelligence, the good regulations and conduct, that emanate from him, spread through the country.' The answer to the immorality as well as the insubordination of the Irish countryside and of the industrial towns of Britain was to extend to them the aristocratic system of moral control, to the first by means of a resident gentry, to the second by means of Thomas Chalmers' Glasgow system of organized charity dispensed by district visitors. By the latter 'improvement in the Christian and civic economy of large towns; by the assimilation of their various districts to the moral and religious condition of country parishes, . . . such a

[1] R. I. and S. Wilberforce, *Life of William Wilberforce* (1838), IV. 99.
[2] W. Wilberforce, *A Practical View of the Prevailing System of Professing Christians* (1829), p. 203.
[3] *Ibid.*, p. 224.
[4] Speech in H. of C., 3 June 1830, *Blackwood's*, 1830, XXVIII. 228.

mighty reform might be accomplished in the habits and feelings of the labouring classes, as would animate them to unremitting and unconquerable industry' and 'restrict the evils of pauperism within the narrowest possible limits.'[1] In this way aristocratic morality was linked both to its own class interests and to the moral well-being and economic prosperity of the whole society.

In the entrepreneurial ideal, by contrast, it was the middle class which, in the words of James Mill, was 'both the most wise and the most virtuous part of the community.'[2] Even to a Tory merchant the manufacturing and commercial interests were 'the only interests which, after religious belief has been settled, promote the moral advancement of man.'[3] For Patrick Colquhoun, Glasgow merchant, London stipendiary magistrate, and one of the earliest disciples of Bentham, the upper middle class comprised 'a part of the community, whose professional labours shelter them in a considerable degree from the prevailing vices of the age' and the lower middle class contained 'many very useful members of society, but by far the greatest proportion possessing religious and moral habits,' whereas the nobility embraced 'not a few' whose 'time is spent either at the gaming table, or in the pursuit of the most frivolous and contemptible amusements,' and the gentry, 'a considerable proportion' disposed 'rather to imitate the vices than the virtues of the highest orders of society.' The working classes contained 'much usefulness, much virtue, with at the same time a great and evident increase of the corruption of morals,' while the lowest class of paupers, vagrants and criminals 'alas! exhibits a lamentable picture of deformity, comprising indigence, vice, idleness, and criminal delinquency in all its various shades and ramifications.' The idle and vicious were concentrated at the extremes of society, and were bracketed together:

> It is only those who pass their lives in vice and idleness, or who dissipate the surplus labour acquired by inheritance or otherwise in gaming and debauchery, and the idle class of paupers, prostitutes,

---

[1] 'Christian and Civic Economy of Large Towns', *Blackwood's*, 1819–20, VI. 18–24, 177–83; [Robinson], 'English and Irish Land-Letting', *ibid.*, 1825, XVII. 684–701; [John Wilson], 'The Real State of Ireland', *ibid.*, 1827, XXII. 18–31.

[2] J. Mill, *Government*, pp. 31–2.

[3] 'Bandana' [John Galt], 'Hints to Country Gentlemen', *Blackwood's*, 1822, XII, 625.

rogues, vagabonds, vagrants, and persons engaged in criminal pursuits, who are real nuisances to society—who live upon the land and labour of the people, without filling any useful station in the body politic, or making the smallest return or compensation to society for what they consume.[1]

The entrepreneurial class society, in fact, was based on the moral conception of work. For the classical economists, land-owners were idle, and did nothing whatever for their rents; workers justified themselves by work, but manual work of a coarse and inferior kind; only the capitalist fully justified himself by work of a morally superior kind.[2] The same conception was taken over by their middle-class opponents. It was implicit in Sadler's demand for an aristocracy of service, and in Carlyle's distinction between 'Workers, Master Workers, and Master Unworkers'.[3] But the aristocracy were not only idle, they were inevitably corrupt. 'If powers are put into the hands of a com-paratively small number, called an Aristocracy, powers which make them stronger than the rest of the community,' wrote James Mill, 'they will take from the rest of the community as much as they please of the objects of desire.'[4] In the more hysterical language of the Anti-Corn Law League they were a 'foot-pad aristocracy, power-proud plunderers, . . . blood-sucking vampires,' and 'gluttons and debauchees,' whose life was 'a routine of oppression, extravagance and luxury.' Aristocracy and working class were united in their drunkenness, profaneness, sexual indulgence, gambling, and love of cruel sports.[5]

The entrepreneur, by contrast, was virtuous by occupation, a puritan pilgrim seeking both earthly success and heavenly bliss through work. Commerce, according to a Manchester Congre-gational minister,

is constantly teaching men that thought and labour, during the years immediately before them, present the only path to repose and enjoyment during the years in the distance. Men are thus taught, that in relation to the affairs of this world, no less than to the affairs of religion, the man who would be successful 'must take up his cross and deny himself'.[6]

[1] Colquhoun, *Treatise on . . . British Empire*, pp. 106–7, 120–1.
[2] Cf. Chap. vii, § 1, above.   [3] Cf. chap. vii, § 3, above.
[4] J. Mill, *Government*, p. 7.   [5] Read, *op. cit.*, p. 53; McCord, *op. cit.*, p. 59.
[6] Vaughan, *op. cit.*, p. 312.

Moreover, the entrepreneur represented the cause of peace and human brotherhood in place of the aristocrat's love of war and violence. 'The cause of industry is the cause of humanity,' 'A Member of the Manchester Athenaeum' told the Young Men's Anti-Monopoly Association in the 1840's, 'Instead of the sub-jugation of mankind and the devastation of the earth, let *peaceful and attractive Industry* propose as its highest aim, *the enrichment of all by the civilization and embellishment of the Globe.*'[1] Hence Cobden and Bright's fervent belief that free trade was the first step towards world peace. Hence, too, the belief that civilization was, as its name implied, the product of town life and the peaceful arts of the urban middle class.[2] Finally, entrepreneurial morality represented a totally different conception of the gentleman. Duelling and the paramilitary code of honour were barbarous and criminal. Duellists were car-tooned in *Punch* as fools and monsters.[3] The gentleman was not born: he made himself by his conduct and moral character, which was peaceful, not violent. 'Gentleness is indeed the true test of gentlemanliness,' wrote Samuel Smiles. 'Riches and rank have no necessary connexion with genuine gentlemanly qualities. The poor man may be a true gentleman—in spirit and in daily life. He may be honest, truthful, upright, polite, temperate, courageous, self-respecting, and self-helping—that is, be a true gentleman.'[4] The true gentleman, in other words, was the entrepreneurial ideal of the self-made man.

In the working-class ideal there was no place for gentlemen of either kind. Only materially creative workers were morally justified. The aristocratic gentlemen were simply the perpetu-ators of 'the Norman yoke', the descendants of the gang of marauders who had seized the land in 1066 and exploited it and the inhabitants ever since.[5] The entrepreneurial gentlemen were merely a new gang of exploiters, perpetrators of what Owen called 'this thoroughly selfish system', under which

Truth, honesty, virtue, will (always) be mere names, as they are

[1] Faucher, *op. cit.*, translator's introduction, pp., viii-ix.

[2] Vaughan, *op. cit.*, *passim*.

[3] *Punch*, 1842, III. 173; 1843, V. 581; 1844, VI. 130; 1845, IX. 1; 1862, XLII. 95; cf. Christie, *op. cit.*, p. 133.

[4] Smiles, *Self-Help*, pp. 340, 334.

[5] C. Hill, 'The Norman Yoke', in J. Saville, ed., *Democracy and the Labour Movement* (1954).

now, and as they have ever been. Under this system there can be no true civilization; for by it all are trained civilly to oppose one another by their created opposition of interests. It is a low, vulgar, ignorant and inferior mode of conducting the affairs of society; and no permanent, general and substantial improvement can arise until it shall be superseded by a superior mode of forming character and creating wealth.[1]

This quotation illustrates both the strength and the weakness of the ideal and the morality which it supported. On the one hand it mounted a masterly critique of existing systems of morality by appealing to higher moral principles than any actually operative in contemporary society. On the other, to bring the new society into being required the immediate adherence of the working class, or a large part of it, to these higher moral principles, and for this adherence the motive was distant, altruistic, and therefore weak. Whereas the aristocratic and entrepreneurial moralities were based on reward and punishment either in this world or in the next (or in both) there was a strong, and philosophically superior, tendency amongst Radicals, Socialists and Owenites, particularly the Deists and unbelievers, to condemn as amoral all systems dependent on bribery and threat, and to argue that 'virtue is its own reward.'[2] This was the pure Kantian categorical imperative, but scarcely practicable within the existing systems of morality. Hence the insistence on moral regeneration as the prerequisite of any society based on the ideal of labour: Owen's 'New Moral World' and his Society for Promoting National Regeneration, or the 'Educational Chartism' and 'Teetotal Chartism' of the moral-force Chartists. In all three class ethics there was naturally a gap between principles and practice, but in none was it so wide as in the working-class ideal.

The struggle between the moralities was as much a part of the class conflict of the period as Parliamentary Reform or the campaign against the Corn Laws. As with them, too, it was somewhat confused by the ambivalent roles of a section of the traditional ruling class and of competing groups of the forgotten

[1] *Life of R. Owen, by Himself* (1920 ed.), pp. 122–3.
[2] R. Carlile, *The Republican*, 1819, I. 272; cf. W. Godwin, *Enquiry Concerning Political Justice* (1796), I. 179; P. B. Shelley, *Plan of a Treatise on Morals*, in *Prose Works* (ed. R. H. Shepherd, 1906), II. 201–4; Henriques, *op. cit.*, p. 238.

middle class, the professional men who championed one or other of the major classes. But the story is still further confused by its entanglement with what may be called the Moral Revolution, that profound change in the national character which accompanied the Industrial Revolution. Between 1780 and 1850 the English ceased to be one of the most aggressive, brutal, rowdy, outspoken, riotous, cruel and bloodthirsty nations in the world and became one of the most inhibited, polite, orderly, tender-minded, prudish and hypocritical. The transformation diminished cruelty to animals, criminals, lunatics, and children (in that order); suppressed many cruel sports and games, such as bull-baiting and cock-fighting, as well as innocent amusements, including many fairs and wakes; rid the penal code of about two hundred capital offences, abolished transportation, and cleaned up the prisons; turned Sunday into a day of prayer for some and mortification for all; 'bowdlerized' Shakespeare, Gibbon and other 'obscene' classics, inhibited every kind of literature save that suitable for family reading, and almost gave the death-blow to the English stage; and generally removed from the language, except in official publications and medical literature, all words calculated to 'bring a blush to the cheek of the young person.'

The rise of Victorianism, as it is usually called, is usually attributed to the influence of Hannah More, Wilberforce, and the Evangelicals.[1] It would be tempting to connect it with the struggle between the class moralities by claiming the Clapham Sect for the middle class, to which indeed most of them belonged: Wilberforce alone excepted, as the son of a Hull merchant reared as a landed gentleman, and a typical 'social crank' like Bentham or Owen, they were practically all business men and clergymen.[2] But this would be misleading, on four counts. In the first place it falls into the common trap of building far too much on the influence of a comparatively small group of individuals, who in any case were as much an effect of the revolution as a cause, and not enough on the motives of the much larger numbers who are supposed to have absorbed their teaching.

[1] Cf. M. J. Quinlan, *Victorian Prelude: a History of English Manners, 1700–1830* (New York, 1941), esp. chap. ii; Muriel Jaeger, *Before Victoria* (1956); F. K. Brown, *Fathers of the Victorians: the Age of Wilberforce* (Cambridge, 1962).

[2] Cf. Hennell, *op. cit.*, chap. iii.

Secondly, it fails to explain why the Evangelicals
where their numberless predecessors had failed. T
societies and movements similar to Wilberforce's Pr
Society of 1787 and the Society for the Suppression o
Immorality of 1802 in 1757, 1698 and, with the backing of the
State, in the 1650's.[1] Indeed, the attempts by English puritans
to impose their morality upon the nation date back continuously
to the Reformation and beyond. Thirdly, it fails to take account
of other middle-class groups who were at least equally important, such as the Dissenters and the Benthamites, who did more
for temperance and penal reform, for example, than did the
Evangelicals. And, fourthly, it fails to notice the crucial change
in the movement at this period, from the traditional attempt to
bolster the old social system by improving the morals of rich and
poor, into a radical effort to impose a new morality designed to
support a new society. In short, the Evangelical explanation
fails to account for the revolutionary aspect of the moral
revolution.

The true explanation is that the moral revolution was the
imposition on the whole society, and particularly on its upper
and lower levels, of the traditional puritanism of the English
middle ranks. But it was traditional puritanism in a variety of
mutated forms, some of them surprisingly secular and, at least
in the philosophical sense, hedonistic. The most important
mutation was the change from exhortation of the various ranks
to support existing society by doing their duty in that state of
life to which it had pleased God to call them, to the demand for a
new and higher morality than that associated with the traditional ruling class. This gradual change helps to explain the
fact that the revolution began before the birth of class, and not
merely as a fortuitous traditional movement which became
tangled with class conflict. It had an integral part in the gestation of class exactly parallel to and connected with the part
played by sectarian religion. Just as Dissent, old and new, helped
to carry over and transform the latent vertical antagonism of
the old society into the overt class hostility of the new, so the
moral revolution offered moral 'dissenters', both religious and

[1] The 1802 Society was a conscious revival of the Society for the Reformation
of Manners of 1698—cf. its *Address to the Public* (1803), p. 37; Quinlan, *op. cit.*, p.
203.

secular, the opportunity of carrying over and transforming the conservative moral criticism of the old society into revolutionary moral condemnation by the new. If we count the Evangelicals and the Benthamites as two of the leading 'sects', acting alongside and in the same direction as the religious Dissenters, we can see the moral revolution as an aspect of the same movement which swelled the sectarian middle ranks and led them from merely formal protest to complete emancipation. But in this case it went still further, and transformed independence into a kind of moral imperialism.

The moral and social conservatism of the Evangelicals is proverbial. Christianity, wrote Wilberforce in 1798,

> renders the inequalities of the social scale less galling to the lower orders, whom she also instructs, in their turn, to be diligent, humble, patient; reminding them that their more lowly path has been allotted to them by the hand of God; that it is their part faithfully to discharge its duties, and contentedly to bear its inconveniences; that the present state of things is very short; that the objects about which worldly men conflict so eagerly are not worth the contest; that the peace of mind, which religion offers indiscriminately to all ranks, affords more true satisfaction than all the expensive pleasures which are beyond the poor man's reach; that in this view the poor have the advantage, and that, if their superiors enjoy more abundant comforts, they are also exposed to many temptations from which the inferior classes are happily exempted; that, 'having food and raiment, they should be therewith content,' for that their situation in life, with all its evils, is better than they deserved at the hand of God; and finally, that all human distinctions will soon be done away, and the true followers of Christ will all, as children of the same Father, be alike admitted to the possession of the same heavenly inheritance. Such are the blessed effects of Christianity on the temporal well-being of political communities.[1]

The Society for the Suppression of Vice seems to have been as much concerned to suppress Jacobinism as immorality, and it was not without cause that Sydney Smith described it in 1809 as 'a society for suppressing the vices of persons whose income does not exceed £500 per annum.'[2]

Yet if many Evangelicals ascribed existing 'licentiousness' to

---

[1] Wilberforce, *Practical View* (1834 ed.), pp. 301–2.
[2] *Edin.Rev.*, 1809, XIII. 342.

'a want of attention to the conduct of the lower degree of people,'[1] this was not true of them all. Wilberforce told himself at the outset that 'God has set before me as my object the reformation of manners,' and it is clear that he meant the manners of both rich and poor.[2] Now, there is good reason for believing that the Evangelicals had far more effect on the rich than they did on the poor. Their books and pamphlets were largely bought by the rich, and the astonishing circulations of their tracts are very largely accounted for by the widespread practice of bulk purchase by the rich for free distribution to the poor—to much the same effect, no doubt, as modern political and religious hand-outs.[3] Their methods were so transparently propagandist, so politically aggressive, and so socially condescending that they served rather to antagonize than to seduce the emergent working class, as the most cursory reading of Cobbett, Carlile and the other Radicals will show.

They often antagonized the rich also—far more than their historian-admirers admit. *Blackwood's* described their views on the sexual immorality of the sons of George III as 'mere hypocritical cant, overstrained prudery, in those who affect to be scandalized,' and saw in the Evangelical campaign against slavery 'intrigue, worldliness, heartlessness, and the spirit of money-getting in all its crooked ways, mingling with a cause that inscribes upon its banners philanthropy, honour, and religion.'[4] In spite of their social conservatism they were recognized by their opponents as representatives of the entrepreneurial ideal. To the Christian Socialists, Evangelicalism was the only form of Christianity compatible with the selfish economic doctrine of competition, and made religion 'a scheme or method for obtaining selfish prizes which men are to compete for, just as they do for the things of the earth.'[5]

This indeed was their strength, and explains why nearly all the credit for the moral revolution has been claimed for them. They were borne along by the tide of middle-class moral

[1] W. Godschall, *A General Plan of Parochial and Provincial Police* (1787), p. 101; Quinlan, *op. cit.*, p. 56.   [2] Jaeger, *op. cit.*, p. 14.

[3] Cf. J. Lackington, *Confessions* (1804), pp. 165–6: 'I sent for about 3,000 of them, and many of them I have already given away to farmers, labourers, soldiers, etc.'—Quinlan, *op. cit.*, pp. 192–3.

[4] *Blackwood's*, 1824, XV. 197; 1830, XXVII. 465.

[5] Maurice, *On the Reformation of Society*, pp. 10–13.

superiority to the aristocracy which, pushed by economic and demographic pressures entirely outside their influence, was flowing so strongly in the early nineteenth century. If they had a special function it was, paradoxically, to help to undermine from within the morality of the aristocracy. Their connections, through Wilberforce and his friends, with the ruling élite were so good and their credentials as gentlemen so impeccable that criticism which from others might have been brushed aside as impertinent had some chance of sticking. When Wilberforce on religious grounds refused a challenge to a duel his reputation as a man of honour survived intact, and made it possible for others to do the same. Yet the Evangelicals could hardly have succeeded even here if the aristocratic code had not already been crumbling. When the Duke of Wellington fought Lord Winchelsea in 1829, *Blackwood's* asked how the High Tories could trust a premier who 'wantonly exposed his life, and proved that his country was less dear to him than the gratification of a splenetic passion!'[1]

The loss of confidence in aristocratic morality which the Evangelicals exploited.went deeper than a growing sense of the shamefulness of duelling. The use of morality to defend the existing social system was a weakness rather than a strength, in that moral bonds were made to hold together what economic pressures were beginning to push apart, and they eventually found the strain insupportable. There had always been a defensiveness about the inequities of property, which found classic expression in Paley's parable of the pigeons, in which ninety-nine busily heaped up every grain of corn for one, 'and this one, too, oftentimes the feeblest and worst of the whole set—a child, a woman, a madman, or a fool.'[2] With the emergence of class antagonism morality became the last defence of property short of repression by force. In an article on the ineffectiveness of the death penalty which was itself a contribution to the moral revolution, *Blackwood's* in 1830 implicitly admitted that propertied society was unjust and was only held together by the most powerful moral causes:

The division of the ranks of society which, with advancing society, is continually proceeding, while it separates one portion of the

[1] *Blackwood's*, 1829, XXVI. 227.
[2] W. Paley, *Principles of Moral and Political Philosophy* (1817 ed.), pp. 68–9.

community to affluence and refinement, separates another portion to indigence and abasement. The first great distinction which so early takes place, into the holders of property and those who are born to labour, must appear from the beginning to establish a natural warfare between the rights of one part of the community and the cravings of another. Yet moral institution is found sufficiently powerful, while it has power, to keep down this hostility, and to maintain the order of society; but take morality away, and there is no human power of avail to guard against the boundless depredation that is let loose upon it.[1]

It was obvious that the code of honour and the lax versions of the Christian ethic associated with it gave no support to the moral defences of property mounted by the Evangelicals. In the dangerous times for property and aristocracy which followed the French Revolution, the obvious recourse of the propertied class was that very morality which they themselves, armed with Evangelical tracts, preached to the poor. How could the poor be expected to accept the discipline of Christian morality unless the rich set them a good example? As Arthur Young put it in 1798,

> The true Christian will never be a leveller, will never listen to French politics or to French philosophy. He who worships God in spirit and in truth will love the Government and laws which protect him without asking by whom they are administered. But let it not be imagined that such characters will abound among the lower classes while the higher by their Sunday parties, excursions and amusements and vanities; by their neglect of public worship and their families show that they feel not themselves what perhaps they talk of, or recommend for the poor.

Hence the crowded churches and queues of carriages to them noted by the *Annual Register* in the same year.[2] The effect would have lasted no longer than the immediate cause but for the post-war birth of class, which made it permanent. In this way the Evangelicals—if not their own common sense—taught the new morality to the aristocracy.

If the Evangelicals worked from the inside, operating through their friends, such as the Duke of Grafton, Lord Darlington and

[1] *Blackwood's*, 1830, XXVII. 876.
[2] A. Young, *An Enquiry into the State of the Public Mind* (1798), p. 25; *Annual Register*, 1798, p. 229.

Lady Huntingdon, a sort of fifth column within the aristocracy, the Dissenters and the Benthamites worked mainly from the outside, bolstering the self-confidence of the middle-class morality and fostering emancipation and antagonism. With the possible exception of Priestley, Price and the 'Rational Dissenters', the Nonconformists, including the Methodists, were at first as loyal to the established order as the Evangelicals, and the morality of all of them was just as quietist. Indeed, many Dissenters worked closely with the latter and accepted the name, as did the group of Baptists and Congregationalists who joined them to found the *Evangelical Magazine* in 1793.[1] From the beginning, however, they had a propensity to condemn even more vigorously than the Clapham Sect the characteristic vices of the aristocracy: excessive drinking, gambling, sexual transgressions, dancing, theatre-going, and duelling. Condemnation of the vice spilled over more easily into condemnation of the class. For the *Eclectic Review* in 1805 it was not enough to condemn Richardson's Sir Charles Grandison as a duellist and a hypocrite; it had to add: 'To reconcile the modern fine gentleman with the disciple of Christ is impossible.'[2] Competition between the Church and the Sects led to competition between the classes. 'The Dissenting ministers act upon the regular clergy much as the Opposition acts upon the Ministry,' admitted *Blackwood's* in 1824. The result of their competition was that 'Public morals are therefore in an excellent state in every class; conscience operates powerfully; in many of our parties turpitude is punished by the party without the aid of law; and men cannot publicly offend against integrity and good principles, without being gibbetted by public opinion.'[3] The moral superiority of the middle ranks to the aristocracy was forged by the Dissenters long before the birth of class. It required only a small impulsion to turn moral superiority into class antagonism. That impulsion was given by the Benthamites and classical economists.

We have already seen the role of the Benthamites and Ricardians in the birth of the middle class. They acted as the

---

[1] Quinlan, *op. cit.*, p. 185.

[2] *Eclectic Review*, 1805, I. 126.

[3] 'Y.Y.Y.' [Robinson], 'The Church of England and the Dissenters', *Blackwood's*, 1824, XVI. 395, 398.

spokesmen and ideologists of the class, formulating its antagonism towards the aristocracy and rationalizing its claim to superior social worth which was also a claim to moral superiority. Yet, apart from the special contribution of such near-Benthamites as Samuel Romilly and Sir James Mackintosh to penal reform, their share in the moral revolution has largely been passed over. This neglect arises from the common misapprehension that morality in general and the moral revolution in particular are exclusively the concern of religion and the religious, and that a group of men led by the sceptic Bentham and the atheist James Mill could have nothing to do with them. Utilitarianism, however, was as much a movement for moral as for political and social reform. The principle of utility, the universal test of the greatest happiness of the greatest number, was a moral imperative more categorical than the Evangelical version of the Christian ethic, in that it was pursued for its own sake, as good in itself, and not motivated by supernatural reward and punishment.

The Benthamites were in fact 'secular Evangelicals', burning with a passion for moral reform which blazed the more fiercely because it was less inhibited in attacking existing norms and institutions, particularly the aristocracy and the Church. That is why the Dissenters, although theologically closer to the Evangelicals and perfectly aware of the irreligious tendencies of the Benthamites, increasingly turned from the former to the latter in proportion as they became alienated from the political and ecclesiastical establishments. The Benthamites were more reliable allies in every field: toleration, education, the tithe and Church rate questions, Church disestablishment, and so on. And, in spite of their un-Dissenter-like permissiveness in matters of opinion and belief, their attitude to life and work was the apotheosis of puritanism. Religion apart, nothing could have been more puritanical than the education of John Stuart Mill, and if labouring in one's vocation, seriousness of mind, the exclusion of all but intellectual pleasures, the consciousness of being of the elect, compulsive preaching to potential converts, and coercion of the stubbornly unenlightened, are marks of the puritan, then the Benthamites were puritans to a man. They appealed to just those tendencies in the more secular minds of the capitalist middle class which the Dissenters appealed to in the religious.

Their converts were, if anything, still more dedicated to the entrepreneurial ethic.

It was the entrepreneurial ethic, however, with a difference, a difference due to the predominantly professional character and outlook of the Benthamites. With their characteristically professional emphasis on justification by service to society and their denunciation of idleness and waste as anti-social as well as immoral, they helped to add a new dimension to the moral revolution, transforming it from an attempt merely to moralize the individual within the existing social framework into an attempt to moralize society itself. Other professional men were no doubt working in the same direction: the Evangelical clergymen, like John Newton and John Venn, who formed the backbone of the Clapham Sect, the High Churchmen, like Coleridge, Southey and John Sterling, who were trying to moralize the aristocracy, and the Dissenting ministers and editors, like Rev. Dr. Dale and the Baineses, who were trying to moralize the industrial middle class. But it was the Benthamites who consciously put the revolution into the moral revolution, and turned the moral superiority of the Dissenting middle class into a deliberate attack on the 'immorality' of the aristocracy.

The Benthamites and Dissenters, then, worked together to reinforce the moral superiority of the middle class and to impose its puritanism upon the rest of society. With the help of the Evangelicals and the moral inferiority complex of the aristocracy they soon succeeded with the upper class. By 1827 the *Morning Chronicle* could say,

> Our men of rank may occasionally assume a virtue which they have not, they may sometimes be greater hypocrites than their forefathers were, but hypocrisy is, at all events, an homage offered to public opinion, and supposes the existence of a fear of the people.[1]

In 1844 the Army's Articles of War were amended to discourage duelling by making apology for an insult permissible within the code of honour, and the last duel in England is said to have been fought in 1852.[2] Long before that, however, duellists had become evolutionary throwbacks, as out of place as a cannibal at a chapel tea party, and the aristocratic version of the gentleman and his code of honour were dead.

[1] *Morning Chronicle*, 1 October 1827; Quinlan, *op. cit.*, p. 119.
[2] Christie, *op. cit.*, pp. 132, 134.

With the working class the process took somewhat longer, although the Benthamites were claiming good progress by the 1820's. Francis Place told the Select Committee on Artisans and Machinery in 1824 that the journeyman tailors, 'like all other journeymen, are greatly improved in morals,' and instanced the disappearance of the gin bottle from their workshops. Five years later he was writing that the working classes in the last thirty years 'have become wiser, better, more frugal, more honest, more respectable, more virtuous than they ever were before.'[1] James Mill wrote of them in similar strain:

> In manners, in all the little moralities of daily intercourse, there is even within the memory of men still living, a prodigious amelioration. There is a gentleness and a civility in their deportment towards one another, not to speak of their superiors, rarely met with a century ago. Riot and drunkenness are greatly diminished.[2]

This optimism clearly suited the Benthamite belief in the improvability of the working class by middle-class leadership and propaganda. It is difficult to reconcile, however, with the enormous increase in crime between 1800 and 1830, which has now been shown to have been real, and not a statistical effect of more efficient police or a greater willingness with penal reform to prosecute;[3] or with the known and possibly increasing drunkenness and immorality of the great towns observed by Gaskell, Porter, Foucher, Engels, Mayhew and others.

There was of course a considerable gap in all classes between the moral code and moral practice. Indeed, as standards rise the distance by which sinners fall short of them becomes greater, and there is not much doubt that there was *more* prostitution, drunkenness, and furtive pornography amongst rich and poor, as well as a greater consciousness of the sinfulness of sin, in Victorian England than before the moral revolution.[4] Nevertheless,

[1] *P.P.*, 1824, V, *S.C. on Artisans and Machinery*, p. 46; Wallas, *Place*, p. 61.

[2] *West.Rev.*, 1826, VI. 264.

[3] K. K. Macnab, 'Aspects of the History of Crime in England and Wales between 1805 and 1860', D.Phil. dissertation, University of Sussex, 1965; for statistics of crime see Porter, *op. cit.*, (1851), pp. 635, 646-64.

[4] Cf. Steven Marcus, *The Other Victorians: a Study of Sexuality and Pornography in Mid-19th-Century England* (New York, 1966); B. Harrison, 'Underneath the Victorians', *Victorian Studies*, 1967, X. 239f.; P.T. Cominos, 'Late Victorian Sexuality and the Social System', *Int.Rev. of Soc.Hist.*, 1963, VIII. 18f. and 216f., esp. pp. 228-30; for the record consumption of beer in the mid-Victorian age, rising to an all-time maximum in 1876, see Burnett, *op. cit.*, p. 91.

in spite of the efforts of the Methodists and Evangelicals, the Dissenters and the Benthamites, it patently took longer for acceptance of the new moral standards to penetrate the mass of the working class than the more sophisticated, and more readily hypocritical, upper class. Moreover, there was a difference between outward conformity to external, patently middle-class standards and inward conviction of the need for a new moral code. It was, paradoxically, not so much the middle class who imposed their morality on the working class, as the working class who imposed it on themselves. The need recognized by their leaders to moralize the working class in preparation for the new moral world based on the ideal of labour exposed their Achilles' heel to the darts of middle-class moralists. To meet the remoter need for a new and higher morality they were forced to accept the immediate expedient of a puritanical, self-improving attitude to themselves. This exposed them to the entre-preneurial ideal of the self-made man, the capitalist version of the puritan pilgrim. But the role of the myth of the self-made man in the struggle between the ideals brings us to the battle for the mind, where it can best be explained.

2. THE BATTLE FOR THE MIND

By all the rules of intellectual warfare the aristocratic ideal should have won the battle for the mind. The aristocracy was the army in possession, defending a prepared position, and in control of the most powerful organs of opinion and most of the institutions of education. It also had the enormous moral advantage of long and successful experience of preaching its ideal. At the outset it controlled nearly all the most widely read 'quality' journals and newspapers. The largest quarterly, monthly and daily circulations belonged to the Tory *Quarterly Review*, *Blackwood's Edinburgh Magazine*, and *The Times*.[1] The Whig publications were more open to Radical influence, but their editors, taunted their enemies, walked in fear of being 'cut by the great aristocractical Whigs'.[2] Of the leading national

---

[1] *Blackwood's*, 1820, VIII. 80–1; A. P. Wadsworth, *Newspaper Circulations, 1800–1954* (Manchester Statistical Society, 1955), pp. 8–9.

[2] 'Timothy Tickler' [J. G. Lockhart], 'Letter to Francis Jeffrey' [ed. of *Edin. Rev.*], *Blackwood's*, 1824, XV. 147.

journals only the *Westminster Review*, founded by Bentham and James Mill in 1824, and the *Morning Chronicle*, edited by Mill and Place's *protégé* John Black were unequivocally anti-aristocratic, and their circulations were comparatively small.[1]

Below the 'quality' level the only popular papers before Cobbett brought out his 'Twopenny Trash' in 1817 were Sundays like *Bell's Weekly Messenger* and the *Observer*, crude scandal sheets with no politics other than a vague inclination to support the Government. The commonest reading matter at this level were the broadsheet ballads and 'vulgar and indecent penny books', and even here the defenders of the old society were not without success. In the 1790's Hannah More and Sarah Trimmer's Cheap Repository Tracts—'sheep in wolves' clothing'—sold more than two million copies in one year, though most of them to the rich for free distribution to the poor.[2]

The aristocracy, moreover, knew how to use its power to influence the press. Government journals were subsidized, and Tory editors like William Gifford of the *Quarterly*, John Bowles of the *Anti-Jacobin Review*, and John Walter I of *The Times* granted pensions.[3] The newspaper stamp duty was progressively raised between 1789 and 1815 from $1\frac{1}{2}d.$ to $4d.$, with the aim of restricting political discussion to the propertied classes, and regular prosecutions for blasphemous and seditious libel from 1816 to 1834 reinforced the repression.[4]

Aristocratic control over the institutions of education was still more complete. The two English universities, small, expensive and practically closed to Dissenters, were the preserve of 'the aristocractical, political, professional and clerical sections of society', while the Scottish ones were still chiefly schools for 'noisy and illiterate urchins' from twelve to sixteen, with lectures on medicine, law and theology 'for those of rather riper years'.[5] The seven great public schools were monopolized by the landed class and its dependants, and the other secondary

[1] Wadsworth, *op. cit.*, p. 9.

[2] Martha More, *Mendip Annals* (ed. A. Roberts, 1859), p. 6.

[3] [John Wade], *The Black Book* (1820), pp. 43–4.

[4] A. Aspinall, *Politics and the Press, c. 1780–1850* (1949), pp. 16–23; J. Hamburger, *James Mill and the Art of Revolution* (1963), pp. 9–10.

[5] M. Pattison, *Suggestions on Academic Organization* (1869), p. 102; *Blackwood's*, 1823, XIII. 94.

schools, with a few Dissenting exceptions like the Quakers' Ashworth (1777) and the Presbyterian Mill Hill (1807), were ancient grammar schools either moribund or recently transformed into expensive and predominantly Anglican boarding schools for the propertied and professional classes.[1]

Elementary education, apart from the utterly inefficient dame-schools, was dominated by the charity schools organized chiefly by the Church through the auspices of the Society for the Promotion of Christian Knowledge until 1811, and thereafter by the National Society for the Education of the Poor in the Principles of the Church of England.

The aristocracy's position, however, was marred by fatal weaknesses. In spite—or perhaps because—of its fear of an uncontrolled press, it was far more susceptible to public opinion than Continental autocracies. 'The grand characteristic of Mr. Pitt's system,' its supporters claimed, was 'deference to public opinion', and Parliamentary Reform was opposed on the grounds that 'a single newspaper is worth, in this point of view, all the members for the Aberdeen and Fife districts of boroughs—with those of Westminster, Southwark and Winchelsea to boot.'[2] We have already seen, however, how susceptible Pitt and his followers were to certain entrepreneurial ideas, and we shall find that it was by infiltration rather than frontal attack that the aristocratic citadel fell.

Similarly in education, the aristocracy and its church possessed the institutions, but the ideas taught there were increasingly those of their middle-class rivals, who possessed a self-confidence in this field entirely lacking in their opponents. Indeed, Anglican enthusiasts for education of the poor had to contend with enemies in their midst, who from Mandeville's time never ceased to oppose it as politically and morally dangerous.[3] As late as 1827 a High Tory could argue:

> As education has increased amidst the people, infidelity, vice, and crime have increased. At this moment the people are far more

[1] *P.P.*, 1867-8 [3966], XXVIII. Pt. I. 1, *Report of the Schools Inquiry [Taunton] Commission*, esp. chap. ii, § 1.

[2] 'Bandana [John Galt] on the Abandonment of the Pitt System', *Blackwood's* 1823, XIII. 515–18.

[3] Cf. M. G. Jones, *The Charity School Movement: a Study of 18th-Century Puritanism in Action* (1938), pp. 43–4 and *passim*.

vicious and criminal, in proportion to their numbers, than they were when comparatively uneducated. The majority of criminals consist of those who have been 'educated'.[1]

And when the enthusiasts had won the main battle for education, they still had to fight over any extension of it, as in the case of the Mechanics' Institutes in 1825:

> We are as friendly to the instruction of the working classes as Mr. Brougham, . . . (but) the educating of the working *adults* of a great nation is a thing without precedent. . . . Whenever the lower orders of any great nation have obtained a smattering of knowledge, they have generally used it to produce national ruin.[2]

The effect of this division in their ranks was not so much to prevent the development of education as to restrict it to self-consciously elementary education, mainly in reading plus religion and morality. The fact was that they feared education of the poor above their station because they lacked confidence in their own inherent superiority and in the ability of their ideal of property to stand up to intellectual examination by hostile critics:

> It is unquestionable that the natural powers of the poor are quite equal to those of the rich; and it is alike unquestionable, that they are not more equal.[3]

Educated workers, whether by school or by the press, were potential revolutionaries.

In marked contrast to the aristocracy, the middle-class protagonists of working-class education had no such inhibitions. Not that the entrepreneurs themselves were automatically enthusiastic for such education. Charles Knight found it difficult in 1828 to interest Manchester millowners in the Society for the Diffusion of Useful Knowledge, and Engels in 1844 declared them 'so recklessly stupid and smug that in their blind egotism they do not even take the trouble to instruct the workers in their own bourgeois moral code.' Yet Kay-Shuttleworth, who knew Manchester better than either, remarked in 1847 that 'on Sunday many thousands of the middle class devote three hours of

---

[1] [Robinson], 'The Faction', *Blackwood's*, 1827, XXII. 427.
[2] [Robinson], 'Brougham on the Education of the People', *ibid.*, 1825, XVII. 534–5.
[3] *Ibid.*, p. 536.

their rest from business life to the pious office of instructing the children of the humblest ranks.'[1]

Any lack of enthusiasm on their part, however, was more than made up for by the zeal of the spokesmen of their ideal, the Benthamites and classical economists. Their unshakeable faith in education derived from their professional belief in the power of intellectual argument and the innate superiority of the middle class. As James Mill put it in the *Westminster Review* in 1826,

> Of the political and moral importance of this class, there can be but one opinion. It is the strength of the community. It contains, beyond all comparison, the greatest portion of the intelligence, industry, and wealth of the state. . . . The people of the class below are the instruments with which they work; and those of the class above, though they may be called their governors, and may really sometimes seem to rule them, are more often, more truly, more completely, under their control.[2]

The High Tories admitted as much when they complained of 'the Holy Mother Church of Political Popery' which 'assumes its dogmas to be perfectly infallible; and this is acquiesced in by its opponents. Of course this renders everything defenceless to which these dogmas are opposed.'[3] And Earl Grey for the Whigs acknowledged that the middle classes 'form the real and efficient mass of public opinion, . . . without whom the power of the gentry is nothing.'[4]

This meant that, in spite of the failure of the Benthamites and their allies to create alternative systems of education for the various classes capable of completely replacing those of the aristocracy and its Church, they were able to stimulate the latter to reform and extend the existing provision and to do so in accordance with the spirit of the entrepreneurial ideal. Thus, although their British and Foreign Schools Society which grew out of the Royal Lancastrian Society of 1808 failed to make more than a dent in the Anglican monopoly of working-class

---

[1] C. Knight, *Passages of a Working Life* (1863), II. 83; Engels, *op. cit.*, p. 129; J. Kay-Shuttleworth, *On the School in its Relation to State, Church, and Community* (1847), p. 3.

[2] *West.Rev.*, 1826, VI. 254.

[3] *Blackwood's*, 1827, XXII. 411f.

[4] Earl Grey, ed., *Correspondence of William IV and Earl Grey* (1927), I. 376n.

education,[1] they decisively tipped the balance within the Church party in favour of education, provoked into existence the rival National Society, and by their competition and constant agitation for State education stimulated the expansion of elementary education which, with State aid invoked by Roebuck's agitation in 1833, grew from 675,000 attenders, one in seventeen of the population, in 1818 to 2,144,000, one in eight, in 1851.[2]

Even more important was their effect on what was taught in the schools and how it was taught. The traditionalists could no longer confine the teaching to religious and moral education, reading the Bible and learning the Catechism and the Ten Commandments. 'Useful knowledge' became the watchword: all 'three R's'—writing and arithmetic as well as reading—plus the rote learning of geographical locations, historical dates, and elementary 'science' for which Victorian elementary schools became famous. The methods were still more Benthamite: the monitorial system with its emphasis on self-help and emulation, the constant tests and examinations and striving for place in the class, the concentration on work and discipline to the exclusion of play and physical exercise, made the school a microcosm of the competitive, authoritarian, class-ridden world outside.

Again, their attempt to wrest control of middle-class education by reforming the grammar schools and creating a new species of proprietary school was not immediately or entirely successful, but it ultimately provoked the creation of what was to all intents and purposes a completely new system of middle-class schools adapted to the needs of the new society. The attack on the existing system grew out of the movement for working-class education, when Brougham's Select Committee on the Education of the Lower Orders in the Metropolis was extended to cover the endowed schools of the whole country. Its findings led to the appointment in 1818 of the Charity Commissioners, who devoted fourteen years and twenty-six volumes to exposing abuses in the grammar and public schools,

---

[1] The National Society for the Education of the Poor in the Principles of the Church of England claimed grant in 1858 for 1,187,086 scholars out of a total of 1,566,335, and for 19,549 out of 22,712 State-aided elementary schools—H. Mann, 'The Resources of Popular Education in England and Wales, Present and Future', *Stat.J.*, 1862, XXV. 53.

[2] E. Baines, *Education best Promoted by Perfect Freedom* (1854), p. 46.

a sustained indictment of aristocratic 'corruption' and jobbery, 'empty walls without scholars, and everything neglected but the receipt of salaries and emoluments.'[1] The Benthamites mounted an equally sustained campaign for their reform, culminating in the *Quarterly Journal of Education* begun in 1831 and the Central Society of Education founded in 1837, which demanded that, instead of 'the dry husks of ancient learning', they should provide 'sound and substantial food from the great treasury of modern discovery', adapted to 'a race of men whose ingenuity and perseverance have, by one victory after another, subjected to our control the stubborn resistance of matter, and increased in a thousand ways the material resources of enjoyment.'[2] But until the Taunton Commission inquired into them in 1864 most of the endowed schools, with a few exceptions like Birmingham Grammar School which set up an adjoining school for science, art and modern languages in 1831, and a larger number like Rugby which had been transformed into boarding schools for the rich, remained moribund.[3]

The middle classes were forced to create alternatives, such as Hazelwood School, Birmingham, run by Bentham's friend Thomas Hill Wright, the nearest thing to the original model of Bentham's 'Chrestomathic' school, with its exact routine and strict discipline, and its quasi-capitalist system of banking marks for good work and behaviour and discounting them for bad.[4] More than 10,000 private schools, mostly of recent origin, were thought to be in existence in 1864. The biggest and most influential were the new proprietary day schools, entrepreneurial in form as well as spirit, mostly owned and run by joint-stock companies of parents and educationists, which, beginning with the Liverpool Royal Institution School in 1819, proliferated in and around all the major cities. By 1864 there were about a hundred of them. Whether or not they offered classics, they all taught mathematics and modern languages, and a few taught science. Above all, they pioneered the competitive

---

[1] Lord Kenyon, quoted in *Edin.Rev.*, 1819, XXXI. 502.

[2] Thomas Wyse, 'Education in the United Kingdom', *First Publication of the Central Society of Education* (1837), pp. 59–60; G. Long, 'On Endowments in England for the Purposes of Education', *Second Publication* (1838), p. 88.

[3] Cf. *Taunton Report*, chap. ii, § 1.

[4] Cf. Brian Simon, *Studies in the History of Education, 1780–1870* (1960), to which much of this section is indebted, pp. 82–4.

academic spirit and prefectorial discipline so dear to the Benthamites and the new middle class.[1]

Their competition stimulated imitation. Their Anglican rivals founded their own proprietary schools, such as King's College School (1829), Brighton School (1836) and Cheltenham College (1840), and infiltrated others, so that they went the way of many ancient grammer schools and, like Clifton College and Sydney College, Bath, closed their doors to local tradesmen's sons and became boarding schools for the wealthy. But their most notable influence was on the reform of the public schools. Samuel Butler, headmaster of Shrewsbury, told the Bishop of Chichester, 'the traffic in joint-stock schools is ruining, and will ultimately ruin, the old foundations.'[2] He and Dr. Wooll, Thomas Arnold's predecessor at Rugby, Arnold himself, and other reforming heads, met the challenge by outdoing the proprietary schools in their own field. The reform movement, though mounted from inside, was not autonomous, but a response to the bludgeonings of the middle-class critics, who attacked the old-fashioned curricula and methods of the aristocratic schools, which gave an 'utterly useless education in Greek and Latin', without even the history, philosophy and politics of Greece and Rome. 'In ten years of this labour, privation, punishment, slavery, and expense, what is gained even of this useless trash? Nothing.' Their shrewdest blows were aimed at the vice and immorality of the unreformed schools. At Eton the boy 'oscillates between tyrant and slave,' and before he is ready for the university may have acquired 'a confirmed taste for gluttony and drunkenness, an aptitude for brutal sports, and a passion for female society of the most degrading kind.'[3]

It has often been suggested that the reformers, especially Arnold and his followers, set out to adapt the public schools to the needs of the new middle class. That this was patently not the case is proved by their refusal to abandon classics as the foundation of their curricula and substitute science and modern studies, by their exclusion of local middle-class boys wherever possible, and by their continued concentration on preparation

---

[1] *Taunton Report*, pp. 6, 152–9, 310–22; cf. Simon, *op. cit.* pp. 115–17.

[2] S. Butler, *Life and Letters of Dr. Samuel Butler* (1896), II. 96.

[3] *West.Rev.*, 1825, IV. 156; 1835, XXIII. 314; *Quarterly Journal of Education*, 1834, VIII. 286; Simon, *op. cit.*, pp. 100-1.

for the traditional faculties of the two universities, and the Church, the Army and the higher professions.[1] What they did was something far more significant for the new society: they embraced the new entrepreneurial ideal and and its morality and instilled them into the sons of the aristocracy and gentry. The fundamental educational principle at Arnold's Rugby was competition: academic competition stimulated by examinations, prizes and scholarships; social competition stimulated by the prefect system, and the debating and other societies, and athletic competition in the shape of organized games in place of uncompetitive field sports. Here if anywhere was the most successful incarnation of Bentham's 'Chrestomathic' school.[2] And the morality and gentlemanly conduct which Arnold placed before intellectual ability were those of the new rather than the old ideal. His concept of the Christian gentleman was not that of the old chevalier, jealous of his paramilitary honour but otherwise indifferent to morality, but that of the new 'gentle' gentleman, competing not in duels but in consideration for others. If this system attracted a small but growing number of business men's sons, that was a bonus unforeseen. Meanwhile, the main function of the reformed public schools was to educate the aristocracy and gentry and their dependants in the old professions in the entrepreneurial ideal.

The same process of competing provision and bludgeoning criticism followed by pre-emptive emulation and reform, in the hands of much the same people, occurred in the case of the universities. The Benthamites and their allies, the Dissenters, appalled by the cost and unsuitability as well as the 'bigotry' of Oxford and Cambridge, founded University College, London, in 1828. They were immediately attacked and imitated by the Church party, who founded King's College, London, and— though it stemmed from larger fears of Church disestablishment and spoliation—Durham University (1834). Oxford was attacked by the same critics as the public schools for 'a hideous laziness, an enormous and insatiable greediness, and a crapulous self-indulgence.'[3] 'Bigotry and prejudice have doubtless had

---

[1] Cf. W. J. Reader, *Professional Men* (1966), Appendix II, pp. 212–15, 'Public Schoolboys' Occupations, 1807–1911'.

[2] J. Bentham, *Chrestomathia*, in *Works* (ed. J. Bowring, 1838–43), VIII. 1f.; cf. Simon, *op. cit.*, pp. 79–84.

[3] *West.Rev.*, 1831, XV. 59.

their share [in rejecting a proposal to teach mathematics] . . . but indolence and incapacity exercise even a wider and more pernicious influence; and an ascendancy of privileged inertness represses all attempts towards amelioration on the part of the enlightened few.'[1]

But the enlightened few, in the shape of Arnold's pupils, and Arnold himself from 1841 when he became Professor of Modern History, were able to defeat the reactionaries and prepare the way for reform. The secession of Newman and his friends to Rome in 1845 discredited the conservatives, and opened the gates to 'a flood of reform . . . which did not spend itself till it had produced two Government commissions, until we had ourselves enlarged and remodelled all our institutions.'[2] A similar movement at Cambridge, led by Professors Baden Powell and Pryme, aimed at modernizing the Tripos and abolishing subscription to the Thirty-Nine Articles, produced, through Pryme, who was an M.P., the original motion for a Parliamentary Commission.[3]

Internal reform was easier to block than in the public schools, however, and required further agitation by the middle-class reformers, led this time by James Heywood, the Manchester Radical, before the Royal Commissions were appointed in 1850. Even then their authority was challenged, on the old society principle that they contravened the rights of property. When reform finally came it followed familiar lines: the universities opened their doors to Dissenters, modern subjects including science were encouraged, and examinations and open scholarships given a new emphasis.[4] Though still intended chiefly for the landed class and the older professions, the universities, like the public schools, were remodelled nearer to the entrepreneurial ideal.

The complete triumph of the entrepreneurial ideal throughout education was registered by the three great schools commissions of the 1850's and 1860's, which in effect set out to create a tripartite education system for the three classes of the new society. The Newcastle Commission of 1858 set out to

[1] *Quarterly Journal of Education*, 1834, VIII. 61–2.
[2] Mark Pattison, *Memoirs* (1885), pp. 236–8.
[3] Cf. Simon, *op. cit.*, pp. 281–90.
[4] *Ibid.*, pp. 290–9.

provide 'sound and cheap elementary instruction' for the working class, on the characteristically entrepreneurial principles that it should be strictly elementary, that in the interests of 'the peremptory demands of the labour market' and keeping families off the poor rates it should cease by the age of 11, and that payment of State grants should be by results, measured by examination.[1] These principles, only slightly modified, were carried out by Robert Lowe's 'revised code' of 1862 and the 1870 Act, which between them provided the ideal entrepreneurial education for a docile and permanent labour force.

The Clarendon Commission of 1861 on the nine great public schools was provoked by the fear that their inefficiency placed 'the upper classes in a state of inferiority to the middle and lower.'[2] It was anxious to maintain them as seminaries of a governing class, and opted for the retention of classical literature as the main object of study, which 'has had a powerful effect in moulding and animating the statesmanship and political life of England.' But their criticisms and recommendations, carried out by the Executive Commission appointed under the Public Schools Act of 1869, leave no doubt about their acceptance of the entrepreneurial ideal:

> We have been unable to resist the conclusion that these schools, in very different degrees, are too indulgent to idleness, or struggle ineffectually with it, and that they consequently send out a large proportion of men of idle habits and empty and uncultivated minds.

They recommended more modern subjects, more academic competition, prizes, examinations and daily marking of work; healthy sports and exercise; the Arnoldian aim of 'moulding the character of an English gentleman'; and the exclusion of poor scholars and free local boys in favour of fee payers and open scholars from the wealthier classes.[3]

The class basis of the education system was most explicit in the Taunton Commission Report of 1864, which dealt with schooling for 'those large classes of English society which are

[1] *P.P.*, 1861 [2794-1], XXI. Pt. I. 1, *Report of [Newcastle] Commission on the State of Popular Education in England*, terms of reference and pp. 188, 243; cf., Simon, *op. cit.*, pp. 246-50.

[2] *P.P.*, 1864 [3288], XX. I, *Report of Public Schools [Clarendon] Commission*; and Earl of Clarendon, quoted in E. C. Mack, *Public Schools and British Opinion since 1860* (1941), p. 27.

[3] *Clarendon Report*, pp. 52-6; cf. Simon, *op. cit.*, pp. 304-12.

comprised between the humblest and the very highest.' It divided all secondary schools into three grades according to the social class for which they catered, the division to be determined by size of fee, by the careers for which they prepared, and by a strictly enforced leaving age: 'the fixing of the age would be the most certain means of defining the work which the school has to do, and keeping it to that work.' The first grade would charge 12 to 25 guineas a year for day boys, £60 to £120 for boarders, would cater for the gentry, large rentiers, successful professional men, and business men 'whose profits put them on the same level,' have a leaving age of 18 or 19, and prepare for the university. The second grade would charge 6 to 12 guineas a year for day boys, £25 to £40 for boarders, would educate the sons of smaller professional and business men, large shop-keepers, and farmers for the professions, commerce and industry and have a leaving age of 16 so as to prevent them from preparing for the university. The third grade would charge only 2 to 4 guineas a year and be subsidized from public funds, would be for 'a class distinctly lower in the scale,' the sons of small farmers, tradesmen and superior artisans, who should be compelled to leave at 14.[1]

The whole aim was to segregate the classes so as not to educate the lower above their station or embarrass the higher with low company: 'class distinctions within any school are exceedingly mischievous both to those whom they raise and to those whom they lower,' and even a few working-class boys 'seem to form an obstacle to the schools becoming attractive to others.' Free places or closed scholarships for poor or local boys should be abolished and replaced by open exhibitions for 'boys of real ability in whatever rank they may be found.' The latter, which of course gave a decisive advantage to the already educated, enabled the Commission to reaffirm its faith in the ideal of the self-made man:

> We cannot but look on it as one of the glories of this country, that so many men should have risen to eminence from humble stations, and should have found so much in our institutions to enable them to rise.[2]

The Commission, and the Endowed Schools Act of 1869 which

---

[1] *Taunton Report*, pp. 577–84.   [2] *Ibid.*, pp. 152, 309, 596.

carried out most of its recommendations, did their best to ensure that the social climber should indeed be self-made, and get no help whatever from the schools.

The attempt by the Newcastle, Clarendon and Taunton Commissions to put education in a straitjacket of social class could not last, and began to break down in the 1880's with the provision of State technical and higher elementary schools which were the ancestors of secondary education for all. But they mark the mid-Victorian high water mark of the entrepreneurial ideal in formal education.

The key to the triumph of the entrepreneurial ideal in formal education was its victory at the informal level of social education through the press. Again, it was not the battle for circulations which was decisive but the infiltration of existing organs of opinion by entrepreneurial notions. The ideal did win the battle for circulation in its home base, the provincial press of the great industrial towns. Provincial newspapers trebled in number between 1780 and 1830, from about fifty to over a hundred and fifty.[1] In Carlyle's words, 'A preaching friar settles in every village, and builds a pulpit which he calls a newspaper.'[2] The most successful preaching friars were Benthamites and Dissenters: the Edward Bainses, father and son, of the *Leeds Mercury*. John Edward Taylor and Jeremiah Garnett of the *Manchester Guardian*, T. A. Ward and Robert Leader, jr., of the *Sheffield Independent*, Joseph Parkes and Joshua Scholefield of the *Birmingham Journal*, and so on, whose circulations were two or three times those of their Tory, Whig and working-class Radical rivals, and collectively rivalled the London newspaper press.[3]

The national press, however, was dominated by traditional Whig and Tory journals, *The Times*, the *Morning Post*, the *Morning Chronicle*, and, at that time more important in framing public opinion, the great reviews, the *Quarterly*, the *Edinburgh*, and *Blackwood's Magazine*, whose influence on ministers and politicians was greater than all the provincial and national middle-class papers put together. As W. R. Greg observed in 1853,

The *North British*, the *British Quarterly*, the *Westminster Reviews*, the *Leeds Mercury*, the *Manchester Guardian*, wide as their circu-

[1] Read, *op. cit.*, p. 59. [2] Cowherd, *op. cit.*, p. 70.
[3] Cf. Read, *op. cit.*, chap. iv; Wadsworth, *op. cit.*, pp. 12–18.

lation and great as their influence is among the miscellaneous and middle classes, they seldom read, and regard little. Sentiments may be fermenting, and doctrines may be spreading for years in the interior of the community, till they have modified the whole bent and character of the nation, and yet these men may have heard nothing of them till some such startling facts as the Birmingham Political Union, the Anti-Corn Law League, or the Secession of the Free Church, break in upon their apathetic slumbers, and enlarge the narrow and artificial boundaries of their knowledge.[1]

It was therefore by infiltration of the aristocratic press by middle-class notions that the entrepreneurial ideal won the day. It would take too long to chronicle all the subtle twists and turns of this lengthy process, and two examples must suffice. *The Times*, which under the editorships of Barnes and Delane (1817–41 and 1841–77) was almost a fourth arm of the Government, was the last great paper to support the revival of the aristocratic ideal by Sadler and his friends, amongst whom its proprietor, John Walter II, was one of the staunchest critics of factory conditions and the New Poor Law. Yet by 1845 *The Times* was supporting repeal of the Corn Laws and all the dogmas of free trade, and by 1854 was rejoicing, in the name of *laissez-faire*, in the downfall of Chadwick and centralized public health.[2] 'The renegade, inconstant Times, . . . ever strong upon the stronger side,' the *Edinburgh Review* described it after one of its numerous defections.[3] Yet even *Blackwood's*, the organ of the Tory anti-capitalists, was not impervious to unconscious infiltration. It defended landed property against the Ricardians by claiming that rent was merely interest on capital invested in it, thus assisting that assimilation of land to capital which was one of the aims of land reformers.[4]

[1] W. R. Greg, *Essays on Political and Social Science* (1853), II. 402–3.
[2] *History of the Times* (1935–52), I. 293–4, II. 6–7, 12; Finer, *Chadwick*, pp. 472–3.
[3] Quoted in *Blackwood's*, 1823, XIV. 229.
[4] E.g. [Edwards], 'The Influence of Free Trade upon the Condition of the Labouring Classes', *ibid.*, 1830, XXVII. 565, 568: 'that class which has vested its property in the purchase of real property'; and 'Let the people of Britain have but a free trade in land and cottages, and we care not one farthing to what other branches this system [free trade] be extended'; cf. also [Edwards], 'The Revenues of the Church of England', *ibid.*, 1830, XXVIII. 286–7, where the cost of training and purchasing a benefice for an incumbent is treated as an investment yielding no more than interest on the capital, so that 'the time, the talents, and exertions of an ecclesiastic, who owns a purchased living, are conferred in most cases, gratuitously upon the public'!

But the acid test of the conversion of the traditional press to the entrepreneurial ideal was its support for, or acquiescence in, the whole programme of reforms advocated by the middle-class press. On the repeal of the Corn Laws in 1846 Jeremiah Garnett of the *Manchester Guardian* was able to claim:

> With the passing of this important measure, the editor of the *Guardian* has witnessed the completion of that category of reforms which, at the commencement of his labours, he considered absolutely essential to the good government and well-being of his fellow-countrymen, and from the pursuit of which he has never deviated. The removal of exclusions and disabilities on account of religious opinion,—the reform of the representation,—the establishment of a sound paper currency,—and, lastly, the repeal of the laws affecting freedom of commerce,—have all been effected, almost precisely in the form in which they have been advocated in the columns of this journal.[1]

The triumph of the entrepreneurial ideal over that of the working class in education and propaganda was not quite so straightforward. The working-class leaders had no such doubts about the value and importance of education as the aristocratic. Passion for education and zeal for propaganda were the distinguishing features of the working-class movement, since it was by these alone that it existed and could survive. The slogan which Robert Owen, the father of the ideal, bequeathed to the socialist, trade union and co-operative movements and, through Lovett, even to the Chartists, 'The character of man is formed FOR—not BY—himself', was a challenge to educate the working class, and finally 'all classes of all nations', to fit them for the 'New Moral World'. The *raison d'être* of most of the institutions of the movement was educational and propagandist, from the penny-a-week classes of the Political Protestants or the Chartists, through the coffee-house reading rooms of Doherty and Lovett, to the grandiose Rotunda in Blackfriars Road or the Owenite 'Halls of Science'.

The working-class press, too, was vigorous, outspoken, and not so easily infiltrated as the aristocratic. It achieved circulations far in excess of *The Times*, the largest traditional newspaper: Hetherington's *Poor Man's Guardian* 16,000, Carlile's

---

[1] *Manchester Guardian*, 27 June 1846; Read, *op. cit.*, p. 150.

Gauntlet 22,000, O'Connor's *Northern Star* at its peak 42,000, Cobbett's cheap *Register* at times 50,000.[1]

Once again the middle-class Radicals set out to provide alternatives, and once again the direct attack failed and infiltration succeeded. On the educational side their chief instrument was the Mechanics' Institute, which indeed they wrested from the protagonists of the working-class ideal. The first 'Mechanical Institution' was founded in London in 1817 by a mechanic, Timothy Claxton, and lasted three years. The idea was revived in 1823 by Thomas Hodgskin and J. C. Robertson, editors of the *Mechanics' Magazine*, supported by a group of 'working mechanics, tradesmen, and the radical reformers of the day'. They made the mistake of approaching Francis Place for help, and he and the Benthamites rapidly took over the project, provided the funds, jerrymandered the committee, and put a stop to Hodgskin's lectures on 'Labour defended against the claims of Capital', one of the classics of the working-class ideal.[2] Other Institutes managed by working men collapsed, as at Glasgow in 1823, Bradford in 1825, and Manchester in 1829, while those controlled and supported by middle-class managers and money went from strength to strength. From 55 in 1831 with 7,000 members they grew to 1,200 in 1860 with 200,000 members.[3]

They were self-conscious disseminators of the entrepreneurial ideal. Lectures on practical science for industrial application, on the 'truths of political economy', such as the Ricardian law of wages, Malthusian population theory, and the benefits of machinery, and on successful inventors and business men, were their staple diet.[4] Brougham in his address at the opening of the London Institute saw them as a vehicle for social climbing:

> Some will tell us that it is dangerous to teach too much to the working classes, for, say they, it will enable them to tread on the heels of their superiors. Now this is just the sort of treading on the heel that I long to see.[5]

---

[1] S. MacCoby, *English Radicalism, 1832–52* (1935), p. 414; Pemberton, *Cobbett*, pp. 97–8: the cheap *Register* of 2 November 1816 containing the *Address to the Journeymen and Labourers* sold over 200,000 copies in less than two months.

[2] J. W. Hudson, *History of Adult Education* (1851), p. 49; E. Halévy, *Thomas Hodgskin, 1787–1869* (trans. A. J. Taylor, 1956), pp. 87–91; Simon, *op. cit.*, pp. 153–6.

[3] J. F. C. Harrison, *op. cit.*, pp. 57–74; Simon, *op. cit.*, pp. 216–17; J. M. Ludlow and Ll. Jones, *The Progress of the Working Classes* (1867), p. 169.

[4] Simon, *op. cit.*, pp. 157–9.   [5] New, *op. cit.*, p. 340.

And the Bradford Institute, refounded in 1832 under middle-class control, could look back in 1859 on 'an unbroken stream of youths, sons of working men, rising to positions of responsibility, which in all probability they never would have filled without its aid, and in many cases entering upon and pursuing a successful middle-class career by the habits, the knowledge, and the connexions acquired in this Institute.'[1]

They were in fact too successful. Their members tended to prosper and join the middle class and were joined by those already in it. Their first historian in 1851 noted 'the universal complaint that Mechanics' Institutes are attended by persons of a higher rank than those for whom they were designed,' and that they had abandoned practical science in favour of literature, recreation and entertainment.[2] Nevertheless, to the extent that they had diverted a considerable number of intelligent and energetic working men into the paths of social ambition who might otherwise have turned to working-class protest, they had admirably served their purpose.

To beat the working-class press the middle-class Radicals had to reach a wider audience than the Mechanics' Institutes, and so in 1826 they founded the Society for the Diffusion of Useful Knowledge. It began with a sixpenny 'Library', publishing elementary treatises twice a month on popular science and technology, political philosophy and economy, history and biography, supplemented in 1829 by a Library of Entertaining Knowledge, to supply 'a want felt not merely by the working classes, but by persons of every rank in society.' But there was no doubt of where the main aim of the movement lay. Brougham told the House of Commons in 1828:

> The schoolmaster was abroad and he trusted to the schoolmaster armed with his primer more than he did to the soldier in full military array for upholding and extending the liberties of the country.[3]

The Society settled down, particularly after the economic crisis of 1830 with its rick burning and threshing-machine breaking, to carry middle-class views of politics and economics to the working class, in pamphlets such as *An Address to the Labourers*

---

[1] J. V. Godwin, 'The Bradford Mechanics' Institute', *Trans. N.A.P.S.S.*, 1859, p. 343.

[2] Hudson, *op. cit.*, p. vii.   [3] New, *op. cit.*, pp. 349, 357.

on the Subject of Destroying Machinery and *Results of Machinery, Namely, Cheap Production and Increased Employment, Exhibited.* The advice in the latter, 'When there is a glut of labour go at once out of the market; become yourselves capitalists,' caused laughter amongst the Rotunda Radicals, but the Society's publications achieved spectacular circulations, much larger than those of the working-class press. Its main periodical, Charles Knight's *Penny Magazine*, reached a circulation of 200,000, easily a record for the period. And they stimulated rivals and imitators, like *Chambers' Edinburgh Journal*, *Eliza Cook's Journal*, and Dickens's *Household Words*, which purveyed to large audiences a similar mixture of useful information, edifying tales, and cautionary advice against strikes, political agitation, immorality and crime.[1] What effect such publications had on working-class opinion and behaviour it is impossible to say, but it cannot have been small.

More important than their direct effect on their immediate readers, however, was their general contribution to the developing myth of the self-made man, the chief form in which the entrepreneurial ideal sought to win the minds of the working class. It began as the idea of the self-educated man. Brougham in the pamphlet, *Practical Observations on the Education of the People* (1825), which became the Bible of the Mechanics' Institute movement and of the Society for the Diffusion of Useful Knowledge, held up the example of Benjamin Franklin. If the working man would only read his *Life*,

> I am almost quite sure he will resolve to spend his spare time and money in gaining those kinds of knowledge which from a printer's boy made that great man the first philosopher and one of the first statesmen of his age. Few are fitted by nature to go as far as he did . . . But all may go a good way after him, both in temperance and industry and knowledge, and no one can tell before he tries how near he may be able to approach him.[2]

It rapidly became an undiscriminating admiration for anyone of humble origin who had risen to fame and wealth, by whatever means. The original plan of the Library of Useful Knowledge included biographies of 'six Self-Exalted Men', which inaugurated a whole literature of success, on the careers of James Watt,

[1] J. F. C. Harrison, *op. cit.*, pp. 28–34.   [2] New, *op. cit.*, p. 339.

George Stephenson, the Peel family, Sir Humphry Davy, William Hutton the Birmingham bookseller-antiquarian, Joseph Brotherton 'the factory boy', and a host of others, down to Smiles' *Lives of the Engineers* (1861–2). It pervaded the middle-class periodicals for the working-class reader. The *Family Friend* in 1850 printed a list of a hundred names from Aesop, 'a slave', to Shakespeare, 'the son of a butcher', with the injunction: 'As an encouragement to begin, to persevere, and to conquer, read the following list of self-made men.' And the moral was always the same: 'What some men are, all without difficulty might be.'[1]

The myth in fact found the Achilles' heel of the ambitious working man, and diverted many a Radical into the paths of self-education and material success, like Samuel Bamford of Peterloo fame who started the long tradition of self-congratulatory autobiographies of working men, or 'Shepherd' Smith the Owenite 'Universalist' who transferred to elevating middle-class journalism with the *Family Herald*. Even the 'Educational Chartism' of Lovett came down to individual self-education in the end, while O'Connor's Land Plan degenerated into a scheme for establishing self-made peasants. An Anti-Corn Law League Lecturer told a crowd of Chartist hecklers in 1840: 'Denounce the middle classes as you may, there is not a man among you worth a halfpenny a week that is not anxious to elevate himself among them. . . .'[2] It is a measure of the success of the myth and the triumph of the entrepreneurial ideal in the battle for the mind that it was almost certainly true.

3. THE BATTLE FOR THE STATE

The battle for control of the State was really two distinct battles, or two phases of the same battle fought at two quite different levels. The first was the running battle for Parliamentary Reform: a three-cornered fight between the three major classes to decide the form of the constitution and the method of choosing who should rule. The second was the battle for administrative reform, to determine the machinery of

---

[1] Cf. J. F. C. Harrison, *op. cit.*, pp. 204–5.
[2] McCord, *op. cit.*, pp. 57–8.

executive government and the method of recruiting the administrators. The first was an open battle, fought in the widest public arena of politics, with sound and fury and the occasional threat of revolution. The second was partly in the open, with public agitations for particular reforms, but that was the less important part. The more important part was the struggle to determine the means of implementing the reforms, fought mainly in what are now called the corridors of power, by the men who built the corridors and channelled the power through them, the new administrators themselves.

In both battles the two middle-class ideals worked so closely together as at first sight to be nearly indistinguishable. Yet there was a difference of emphasis between the two, of little consequence in the first battle, but of great importance in the second, where the two ideals increasingly diverged. In the battle for Parliamentary Reform the entrepreneurial ideal led the way, with the professional ideal as a discreet and almost unconscious ally. In the battle for administrative reform, especially in the in-fighting behind the scenes, much of the struggle was necessarily in the hands of administrators, whose professional minds and interests led them far beyond the simple-minded demand of the entrepreneurial ideal for cheap and efficient government.

Both battles nevertheless were a triumph for the entrepreneurial ideal, since the mid-Victorian State was at the conscious level of social and economic policy controlled and administered on the principles of that ideal, open competition and the free play of market forces. Yet both victories contained the seeds of future decay: the first because the apparently general acquiescence in the entrepreneurial ideal led to the enfranchisement of a large part of the working class, whose demands were to transform the *laissez-faire* State from without; the second because the necessary utilization of professional administrators to solve urgent social problems was already, in the heyday of *laissez-faire*, modifying it from within. This second triumph, with its more insidious modification by the professionalism of its instruments, will be the subject of the next section, after the more straightforward story of the first has been dealt with in this.

The political history of Parliamentary Reform is too familiar to need repeating here. What interests the social historian is

Reform as a struggle between the class ideals, as an attack on property and patronage by capital and competition (supported by expertise and selection by merit) from the one side and by labour and co-operation from the other. In brief, Reform was at first feared by the aristocracy as destructive of both pillars of their ideal, but they later came to distinguish between Reformers who wished to abolish property and those who were as determined as they to preserve it. They were thus able to save the main pillar, property, by sacrificing the secondary one, patronage. And they were able to do this because in the main middle-class ideal capital was compatible with property while competition was inimical to patronage. The resulting compromise successfully split the Reformers, and stalled off further Reform until it was 'safe', that is, until the working-class ideal had exhausted, at least for the time being, its revolutionary opposition to property and capital, and the middle-class ideal had so permeated the bulk of the population that capital and property were no longer in danger from democracy.

When Parliamentary Reform first became a class issue in the period after Waterloo it was regarded by both aristocratic parties as a threat to property. Canning asked a Liverpool audience apropos of Peterloo, 'Do I exaggerate when I say, that there was not a man of property who did not tremble for his possessions?'[1] And Lord Grey, the erstwhile and future Reformer, told Sir Robert Wilson, the Radical general, that the object of 'the popular party, or rather of the Mob . . . certainly is not Reform but Revolution,' and that if Burdett and his friends succeeded, 'I shall not precede you by many months to the scaffold. . . .'[2] This naturally remained the opinion of the Tory opponents of Reform until the great Reform Act. As *Blackwood's* expressed it in 1830,

> Even against British property in various modes, there exists an organized conspiracy—against the property of the West Indians—against the property of the fundholders, and, finally, against the property of the Church. But above all the great and paramount conspiracy lies against the guardian of all our property and rights—the aristocracy of our land. . . .[3]

[1] *Blackwood's*, 1820, VII. 12.
[2] J. R. M. Butler, *The Passing of the Great Reform Bill* (1914), pp. 34–5.
[3] *Blackwood's*, 1830, XXVII. 717.

Yet even *Blackwood's* had long recognized that landed property no longer stood alone, that the progress of arts, manufactures and commerce had bestowed property on other classes, and that the time had gone by, for example, for Lord Lauderdale's 'absurd and erroneous' theory of 'renovated feudalism'.[1] Incensed at Catholic emancipation and the liberal economic policies of Peel and Huskisson, which they put down to 'the gross incompetency of the House of Commons' and the 'impotence and dependence' of the House of Lords, the High Tories even demanded their own brand of Reform, designed to amalgamate the new capital with the old property: men of non-landed wealth should be allowed to purchase the franchise in the counties and open boroughs for ready money.[2]

This, too, was the grand strategy of the reforming Whigs—in Durham's phrase, 'to attach numbers to property and good order'—with the difference that the Whigs had a shrewder political sense of what would satisfy the moderate Reformers and detach them from the extremists. Francis Jeffrey, who drew up the Bill for Scotland, saw that 'this may be done by extending the Elective Franchise to those classes, who possess property and knowledge . . . any plan must be objectionable which, by keeping the Franchise very high and exclusive, fails to give satisfaction to the middle and respectable ranks of society, and drives them to a union founded on dissatisfaction, with the lower orders. It is of the utmost importance to associate the middle with the higher orders in the love and support of the institutions and government of the country.'[3] He saw that the key division was not between Reformers and reactionaries, but between opponents and defenders of property: 'The real battle is not between Whigs and Tories, Liberals and Illiberals and such gentlemen-like denominations, but between property and no-property—Swing and the law.'[4]

The Whig strategy worked because it fell in exactly with that of the middle-class Radicals. The latter were as appalled as the aristocracy at the danger to property implicit in manhood suffrage when allied to the working-class ideal. James Mill, an

[1] *Ibid.*, 1821, VIII. 581–5.
[2] *Ibid.*, 1830, XXVII. 640, 646; 1829, XVII. 641.
[3] H. Cockburn, *Letters on the Affairs of Scotland* (1874), pp. 258f.
[4] Lord Cockburn, *Life of Lord Jeffrey* (1852), II. 223.

extreme democrat as long as he remained confident that the working class would follow their natural leaders, the middle class, complained to Place of a deputation 'from the working classes' which preached communism to Black of the *Morning Chronicle*:

> Their notions about property look ugly; they not only desire that it should have nothing to do with representation, which is true, though not a truth for the present time, as they ought to see, but they seem to think that it should not exist, and that the existence of it is an evil to them.

Place replied that

> The men who called on Black were not a deputation from the working people, but two out of half-a-dozen who manage, or mismanage, the meetings at the Rotunda in Blackfriars Road, and at the Philadelphian Chapel in Finsbury. The doctrine they are now preaching is that promulgated by Hodgskin in a tract in 1825, entitled 'Labour Defended against the Claims of Capital' . . .[1]

Place drew exactly the same distinction as Grey between Reform and revolution, but pinned them more firmly to the rival middle and working-class organizations:

> The great peculiarity causing a difference between the Political Unions and the Unions of the working classes was, that the first desired the Reform Bill to prevent a revolution, the last desired its destruction as the means of producing a revolution.

Place's strategy, therefore, was to unite 'the People' in the 'Political Unions of the Middle and Working Classes' behind the middle-class ideal, and to isolate the protagonists of the working-class ideal, the Rotundanists, as an extremist and unrepresentative faction. With the aid of the Government, which obligingly prosecuted Lovett, Watson and Benbow for doing exactly the same as it freely allowed Place and his friends to do, it was eminently successful, and the unrevolutionary Reform Bill passed with popular acclamation.[2]

If the middle-class Radicals were not against property as an institution, what were they against? They were against its abuse, as idleness, as privilege, as monopoly, as undue political influence and corruption. It was therefore against patronage

[1] Wallas, *Place*, p. 274n.   [2] *Ibid.*, pp. 290–1.

that their main attack was mounted, all the more successfully because this secondary pillar of the aristocratic ideal was already crumbling. Official patronage had been declining in extent ever since the 'economical reforms' of the 1780's. Lord Liverpool complained in 1817 that 'the Pension fund is now so limited, as to be scarcely able to meet the just claims which were made upon it for the distressed nobility, and for the persons and families of those who have long laboured in the public service', and another observer in 1821 noted that where once there had been 150 placemen in the House of Commons, there were now not half that number.[1] Long before the Reform Bill the giving up of sinecures was cheered in the Commons, and old naval officers complained 'that (in common, however, with every other class) the patronage which was wont to be awarded to admirals, and even to captains, is completely swallowed up.'[2] By 1829 even the High Tories were attacking 'the gentlemen pensioners and placemen of the new system' of Peel and Wellington.[3] The successive editions of the *Black Book* were flogging, if not a dead, at least a dying horse. On this side Reform was almost completely successful. The 1847 edition of the *Black Book* produced a catalogue of pensions with explanations (from Hume's Select Committee of 1837), most of which it considered justified, and commented: 'The preceding List winds up a chapter of British history . . . upon the whole we are satisfied, and we dare say the public will be so likewise.'[4]

Before then the middle-class attack had switched from the particular to the general abuse of the political power of property, in the shape of urban misgovernment, Church administration and the corn laws, and had been successful there also. This was all the more surprising since the Reform Act gave so little direct political power to the urban, emancipated middle class. The Act increased the United Kingdom electorate from 435,000 to only 813,000 in an adult male population of about 6 million.

[1] W. R. Brock, *Lord Liverpool and Liberal Toryism, 1820–27* (1941), p. 91; *Blackwood's*, 1821, VIII. 583.

[2] Lord Castlereagh's announcement in H. of C., 11 February 1817, that Marquess Camden had resigned all the emoluments and profits of his Tellership of the Exchequer except the regulated salary ('cheering'), *Blackwood's*, 1817, I. 106; Capt. J. Griffiths, R. N., quoted in *ibid.*, 1826, XX. 754.

[3] *Ibid.*, 1829, XXVI. 774.

[4] *Black Book of England* (1847 ed.), pp. 221–2.

More important, it gave an overwhelming majority of the seats to the counties and small boroughs, where the deference and 'virtual representation' of the old society survived, over the great towns, where the new class society was already in being.[1] Most important of all, middle-class politicians lacked the unearned wealth and so the leisure early enough in life to gain the experience and training required for high office. They reached Parliament later in life—Grote at 38, Cobden at 37, as against Gladstone at 23, Sidney Herbert at 22—and unless, like Disraeli or Macaulay, they levered themselves up by patronage and professional earnings compatible with parliamentary attendance, rarely gained the indispensable apprenticeship in the House and in junior office. This was the chief reason why property, in the sense of unearned wealth, retained the lead over capital, in the sense of wealth which had to be managed. As the *Westminster Review* reluctantly admitted in 1833,

> The landed interest must always exercise great sway in public affairs; for that class alone have much leisure to meddle in them. The intelligence of the other classes is absorbed, if not exclusively, yet in a great degree, in the business of money-making. . . . The men who have the leisure for intrigue, from whose coteries the ministries are formed, and whose leisure finds no other occupation than to tattle on the politics of the day, to clog the steps of officials, and flutter from club to club,—are of the landed interest.[2]

In 1848 John Bright told the House of Commons:

> This House and the other House of Parliament are exclusively aristocratic in character. The administration is therefore necessarily the same, and on the Treasury Board aristocracy reigns supreme.[3]

And Matthew Arnold was still observing in 1879 that 'In England the government is composed of a string of aristocratical personages, with one or two men from the professional class who are engaged with them.'[4]

How then did the middle class manage to dominate the legislative climate of the age? The answer lies partly in the work-

[1] E.g. in England the small boroughs with under 1,000 electors together with the counties had 341 out of the 471 seats—N. Gash, *Politics in the Age of Peel* (1935), pp. 65–85, 88–9.

[2] *West.Rev.*, 1833, XVIII. 109–10.

[3] G. M. Trevelyan, *Life of Bright* (1913), p. 166.

[4] M. Arnold, *Mixed Essays* (1879), p. 164.

ing of the new political system. In spite of its limitations, Reform was not without effect. If the aristocracy were left in possession of the main positions of power, possession was no longer theirs by automatic right, but had to be bargained for. The radical change produced by the Reform Act was from aristocratic rule by prescription to aristocratic rule by consent. It was not so much the actual existence of a large anti-aristocratic block vote which swayed the politicians, as the fear of creating one. Given that the aristocracy were divided between competing parties not based primarily on class—a situation which could hardly have survived the rise of a great middle-class party—the aristocratic politicians were bound to show themselves increasingly sensitive to the most independent and rapidly growing section of the electorate. They were, indeed, sensitive to every section, even the least independent and the non-electors: they listened to the tenant farmers of the Anti-League on the Corn Laws, and to the working class on factory reform and economic distress.[1] How much more sensitive they were to the demands of the urban middle class, and how high a price they were prepared to pay to placate them, can be seen from the achievement of 'free trade in practically everything' —land alone partially excepted—catalogued above.[2]

At no point, however, can it be said that the pressure of middle-class votes alone forced the aristocracy to yield a specifically middle-class reform. Even repeal of the Corn Laws owed next to nothing to fear of retribution from the electorate if it were not passed. Repeal was due to the conversion of both Peel and Russell, and of a large part of their landed followers, to the necessity of free trade in corn, and this in turn was due to their acceptance of, or acquiescence in, the middle-class view that one species of wealth, namely passive property in land, had no right to abuse its political power to exact a toll from another, namely active capital in industry and commerce. The same moral and intellectual persuasion can be traced in the decline of patronage, the reform of municipal government, the reform of the Church, the abolition of Church rates, the

---

[1] Cf. Mary Lawson-Tancred, 'The Anti-League and the Corn-Law Crisis of 1846', *Hist.J.*, 1960, III. 162f.; M. W. Thomas, *The Early Factory Legislation* (Leigh-on-Sea, 1948), *passim.*

[2] Chap. vii, § 1, above.

reform of Oxford and Cambridge, the free trade budgets, the abrogation of the 'taxes on knowledge', the reform of the civil service, the abolition of the landed property qualification for M.P.s, the virtual prohibition of the enclosure of urban commons, and a great many more diminutions of aristocratic power and privilege. Since all of these were achieved before the landowners lost their overall majority in the House of Commons in the 1880's, and long before they lost their control of the Cabinet, they could only be passed by the landowners themselves.

It was because the entrepreneurial ideal had already won the moral and educational battles, therefore, that it was able, in spite of the failure of the middle class to capture direct political power, to win the battle for the State. It was an imperfect victory, in that the aristocracy still possessed a veto on all legislation which they felt justified in opposing, as in the case of the reform of land itself. Yet so much greater was the force of the ideal than the strength of the class from which it emanated that the veto was used only in extreme cases, as for example in 1837 against the expropriation of the Irish Church.[1] Most remarkable of all, it achieved by the 1860's a degree of self-confidence—or bravado—which enabled it to try, and to survive, the dangerous experiment of admitting to the franchise as a majority of the electorate the very class which in 1832 it had combined with the aristocracy to exclude.

Between the fear of revolution which forbade the working class the vote in 1832 and the cautious but unfeared concession of urban household suffrage in 1867 lies the whole process of educating all three major classes to accept and live with each other which we shall call the rise of a viable class society.[2] For the moment we are simply concerned with the failure of the working-class ideal not merely to capture control of the State but even to maintain its hold on the bulk of the working class. Whether in its extreme political form of manhood suffrage for the purpose of establishing a classless society based on co-operative labour it ever did gain a hold on the bulk of the working class we may well doubt. Because of the size of the

[1] Cf. N. Gash, *Reaction and Reconstruction in English Politics, 1832–52* (Oxford, 1955), pp. 40–1, 58–9.
[2] See chap. ix, below.

working class and the fragmentation of the ideal which we discussed above,[1] the numbers who held to any one version of the ideal can only be guessed. Not all the more than three million people who were claimed to have signed the largest Chartist petition[2] were social revolutionaries, and, although for most of them the Charter probably represented the social and economic hopes as well as the political rights of labour, the number who knew how to use the vote to transform society must have been very small. Nevertheless, so long as the least suspicion remained amongst the party leaders that further Reform meant social revolution, it was certain that the working class would not get the vote. It is true that the Whigs were more tolerant of the Chartists than were the Tories, and less fearful of a revolutionary outbreak as a means of obtaining the Charter, but they were just as determined to prevent the Charter from reaching the statute book, and were prepared to use police, troops and even artillery to that end.[3]

The only means by which the Chartists could placate this intransigent opposition was by convincing Parliament that they were not revolutionaries. One method was by allying themselves with men who were manifestly upholders of order and property. This was tried twice without success, first at the beginning in 1838–39 in the alliance with Attwood and his following of Birmingham business men, secondly in 1841–42 in the alliance with Joseph Sturge and his Dissenting friends in the Complete Suffrage movement. Both broke down on the Chartists' refusal to renounce revolution as a means or as an end, the first over the threat of physical force, the second over the by now revolutionary name of the Charter. There remained one further method of reassuring their opponents, and that a paradoxical one. It was to threaten force and have their bluff called. O'Connor's greatest service to the cause of working-class suffrage was his 'cowardice' on Kennington Common on 10th April 1848, when he obeyed Police Commissioner Maine and called off the march to the Houses of Parliament. From that day when Chartism as an attempt to capture control of the State

[1] § 2, above.
[2] *Northern Star*, 7 May 1842.
[3] Cf. F. C. Mather, 'The Government and the Chartists', in A. Briggs, ed., *Chartist Studies* (1962), pp. 372–405.

died, the process of working-class enfranchisement can be said to have begun. For it convinced the other classes that the working class had renounced revolution as a means and might conceivably be educated to renounce it as an end.

This, indeed, is exactly what happened. When at last the vote came to be granted to the urban working class in 1867 it was granted in a totally different climate of opinion from that of the Chartist period. There were still those politicians, like Robert Lowe, who opposed their enfranchisement as a threat to property:

> Once give the working man the vote, and the machinery is ready to launch these votes in one compact mass upon the institutions of property in this country.[1]

But Lowe and a handful of die-hards were isolated in their Cave of Adullam, while the two major parties vied with each other over which was to gain the credit for Reform. Both sides accepted Gladstone's principle that 'every man who is not presumably incapacitated by some consideration of personal unfitness or of political danger is morally entitled to come within the pale of the Constitution.'[2] The only question at issue was where the line of personal fitness and politicial safety was to be drawn—in the boroughs at £7, £5 or complete household suffrage, with or without personal payment of rates, including or excluding lodgers; in the counties at £15, £14 or £12 tenant franchise. In the event Parliament took the Bill out of the hands of Derby and Disraeli's Government and opted for the lowest line consistent with political safety.[3] The famous 'leap in the dark' was uncertain only for the Tory Party. In the *Punch* cartoon the course and the horses were the same on either side of the fence: the only uncertainty was over which party would win the electoral race.[4]

---

[1] R. Lowe, *Speeches and Letters on Reform* (1867); Briggs, *Age of Improvement* (1959), p. 500.

[2] Disraeli had already talked in 1859 of opening avenues to the mechanic, 'whose virtue, prudence, intelligence and frugality entitle him to enter the privileged pale of the constituent body of the country,' and Stanley (Lord Derby) had used a similar phrase as early as 1853—cf. Briggs, *Age of Improvement*, p. 492.

[3] *Viz.* household suffrage, including lodgers, in the boroughs and £12 tenant franchise in the counties, adding 938,000 voters to the electorate of 1,056,000 in England and Wales.

[4] *Punch,* 1867, LIII. 47.

In short, by 1867 Parliamentary Reform was no longer a struggle between the ideals for control of the State, because that struggle had already been won. The working class had become, in Gladstone's words, 'our fellow-subjects, our fellow-Christians, *our own flesh and blood*, who have been lauded to the skies for their good conduct,'[1] that is, were believed to have accepted so much of the entrepreneurial ideal of a class society based on capital and competition as to be trusted not to use their voting power to undermine it. No doubt in the long term Lowe and the die-hard opponents of the Second Reform Act were right as in the long term the High Tory opponents of the First Reform Act were right. The working class were to use their votes to modify the social system in the direction of their ideal. This suggests that their ideal was not dead but moribund, and ready to spring into life again when the climate changed once more. But no such quickening is discernible until the 1880's at the earliest, and it will be necessary to look very closely at working-class institutions in the mid-Victorian age to see the ideal still operative in an etiolated form.[2] Meanwhile, the entrepreneurial ideal was so confident in its indirect control of the State that it saw no threat in the admission to the electorate of a not as yet large but nevertheless decisive working-class majority.

The threat, curiously enough, came not from outside but from within. At the very time when the minimal, decentralized, regulatory, *laissez-faire* State of the entrepreneurial ideal was consolidating itself as the norm of political theory, the expanding, centralized, bureaucratic, interventionist State of modern times was coming into being in administrative practice. The reason for this was the role of its ally and instrument, the professional ideal, in the second phase of the battle for the State, the struggle for administrative reform.

4. THE PROFESSIONALIZATION OF GOVERNMENT

In the struggle between the ideals so far the entrepreneurial ideal had won partly because it had the assistance of the professional ideal in its most powerful and best organized form. Indeed, in the Benthamites and Classical Economists the two

[1] P. Magnus, *Gladstone* (1963 ed.), p. 178.   [2] See below, chap. ix, § 3.

ideals seemed to be indistinguishable. In the battles for morality, for public opinion, and for political control of the State, the professional ideal of a functional society based on expertise and selection by merit was almost interchangeable with the entrepreneurial ideal of a class society based on capital and competition. In the final battle, to decide the structure of the administrative system, they seemed at first sight to be identical. The cheap and efficient government demanded by the entrepreneurial ideal could only be provided by expert professional administrators selected by merit. As allies they conquered, achieving in the creation of the modern bureaucratic administrative machine and the new civil service qualified and finally selected by examination a clearer-cut victory than in Parliamentary Reform. Yet in the process the professional ideal began to diverge from its ally, and the administrative system which resulted was so different from the minimal, non-interventionist State of the entrepreneurial ideal as almost to be its mirror-image.

At first, however, the two ideals worked closely together, often in the same persons. Together—with the help of those aristocratic statesmen like Peel and Gladstone whom they won to their views—they worked a revolution in government which was as much a consequence of industrialism and urbanization as the rise of class itself. Under the pressure of social problems not new but of unprecedented scale, interpreted and found 'intolerable' by the light of the belief in the possibility of 'improvement' common to both, they demanded and obtained the creation of a series of administrative agencies staffed by experts capable of solving them. In these and the existing government departments they demanded, and to a large extent obtained, the abolition of patronage and 'corruption', of amateurism and inefficiency, extravagance and waste, secrecy and lack of accountability, and their replacement by selection and promotion by merit, by professional efficiency, retrenchment and economy, publicity and full financial accountability. And they made some headway towards the transformation of the old multifarious collection of 'persons in public offices', chiefly the personal appointees and dependants of individual ministers, into a modern, integrated civil service, recruited by an impersonal central agency chiefly for their ability or expertise, and owing loyalty not to any individual but to the State as a whole, or at least to the State bureaucracy to which they belonged.

Yet this revolution in government, by its very extent and success, was itself designed to sever the two ideals and set them at loggerheads. The entrepreneurial ideal was the more easily satisfied by the negative aspects of the revolution: by the destruction of patronage, by efficiency and economy interpreted as cheap government, the smallest possible departmental staffs, and low taxation, and by the reduction of central government intervention in the relations between individuals to the roles of umpire and policeman. For the professional ideal, on the other hand, it was the positive aspects which were important: selection of talent and expertise, efficiency and economy interpreted as the effective solution of social problems and the abolition of waste arising from social and administrative neglect, and the extension of government as and where necessary to meet the social demands upon it. The former ideal was satisfied by the minimal, regulatory, decentralized, *laissez-faire* State of Victorian theory. The latter pressed on towards the expanding, bureaucratic, centralized, interventionalist State of Victorian practice.

Theory was not altogether divorced from practice, but as ever it lagged far behind. In the organicist tradition of social theory, of course, *laissez-faire* was consistently belaboured by professional thinkers like Coleridge, Southey, Carlyle, Thomas Arnold, and the Christian Socialists.[1] But they were influential, if at all, only in modifying the dominant theory of *laissez-faire* from the outside, in the direction of such mild incursions as the State regulation of child labour, supported in any case by the Benthamites and Classical Economists. The important theoretical rift between the ideals came within Benthamism itself, which for so long had united them, above all in this very battle for more efficient government.

We have already noticed that those professional spokesmen for the entrepreneurial ideal, the Classical Economists McCulloch, Senior, and the young J. S. Mill, like Bentham himself, were never unequivocal supporters of *laissez-faire*, and indeed repudiated it as a universal principle.[2] In fact the rift goes back to

[1] Cf. Dicey, *op. cit.*, pp. 214–16.
[2] Cf. chap. vii, § 1, above; and Robbins, *op. cit.*, pp. 43–6.

Bentham and beyond, to the very heart of the Utilitarian philosophy. In Bentham's own thought and in Utilitarianism in general, as Halévy has shown, there was a fundamental ambiguity: between the *natural* harmony of individual interests in society, independent of government action, and the *artificial* harmony of interests, produced by government intervention.[1] Was the greatest happiness of the greatest number to be gained by leaving men alone to pursue their own interests with the minimum of government interference; or was government interference necessary to its achievement? Adam Smith inclined to the first view, though insisting on the necessity of some government, to 'hold the ring' and see fair play between the rival interests; Bentham to the second, though anxious in view of the 'natural' tendency of governments to corruption to restrict the actual amount of intervention in practice. By such conditionals the centrifugal tendencies of Utilitarianism were held in check, and the two ideals could live cheek by jowl, even in the same thinker.

But the revolution in government was to pull them apart. The reformers of government were all equally 'Benthamite', consciously or unconsciously, in that they all aimed through efficient, economical, professional government at the greatest happiness of the greatest number, but the 'pressure of facts', the size and intractability of certain social problems and their failure to respond to *laissez-faire* methods of administration, forced the reformers to choose between the ambiguities of Utilitarianism, between efficient government and cheap government, between more government and less.

It would be foolish, not to say illogical, to pretend that all the entrepreneurs chose one way and all the professional men the other. The whole purpose of an ideal was to sublimate the interest of a class and present it in a form acceptable to men of other classes. Nevertheless, there was a strong tendency for business men to opt for the natural identity of interests, the free play of market forces, and as little government interference as possible, and an increasing tendency, when they were forced to choose by the exigencies of urgent problems, for the professional men to opt for the artificial identity of interests, the

[1] Cf. E. Halévy, *The Growth of Philosophical Radicalism* (1952), Part III, chap. i, esp. pp. 370–2.

limiting of market forces on behalf of 'higher' values such as health or education, and as much government intervention as was necessary to meet the case.

Thus Cobden and Bright and their entrepreneurial friends in the Financial and Administrative Reform Associations from 1848 onwards never wavered in their demand for cheap government and low taxes. Meanwhile, in the academic economists and civil servants the seed of doubt in the universal benevolence of *laissez-faire* grew into a sizeable tree of disaffection. John Stuart Mill as early as 1833 thought that the *laissez-faire* 'principle, like other negative ones, has work to do yet, work, namely, of a destroying kind, & I am glad to think it has strength left to finish that, after which it must soon expire: peace be with its ashes when it does expire, for I doubt much whether it will reach the resurrection.'[1] McCulloch in 1848 thought that although the principle of individual self-reliance should be followed as a general rule, 'the economist or the politician who should propose carrying it out to its full extent in all cases and at all hazards, would be fitter for Bedlam than for the closet or the cabinet.'[2] Senior, as we have seen, went even further:

It is the duty of a government to do whatever is conducive to the welfare of the governed. The only limit to this duty is power. . . . It appears to me that the most fatal of all errors would be the general admission of the proposition that a government has no right to interfere for any purpose except that of affording protection, for such an admission would be preventing us from profiting from experience, and even from acquiring it.[3]

This transition, in economists and public servants so orthodox as McCulloch and Senior, was remarkable enough, but it was in Mill that the complete theoretical evolution from *laissez-faire* to State intervention took place. In 1848 he still thought that 'Letting alone . . . should be the general practice: every departure from it, unless required by some great good, is a certain evil,' and he let this stand in later editions of the *Principles*,

[1] F. E. Mineka, ed., *The Earlier Letters of J. S. Mill, 1812–48* (1963), I. 152.
[2] J. R. McCulloch, *Principles of Political Economy* (1825), preface; Robbins, *op. cit.*, p. 44.
[3] N. W. Senior, Oxford Lectures, 1847–48, in *Industrial Efficiency and Social Economy* (ed. S. L. Levy, 1929), II. 302; Robbins, *op. cit.*, p. 45.

but with increasing qualifications in favour of departures from it:

> In the particular circumstances of a given age or nation, there is scarcely anything, really important to the general interest, which it may not be desirable, or even necessary, that the government should take upon itself, not because private individuals cannot effectually perform it, but because they will not.[1]

In public he became increasingly unwilling to support *laissez-faire*, repudiating it when appealed to in the House of Commons in 1865 with the words, 'I do not know a single practical rule [of political economy] that must be applicable in all cases.'[2] In private, however, his views had evolved so far under the influence of his wife, Harriet Taylor, that he considered himself a Socialist:

> our ideal of ultimate government went far beyond Democracy, and would class us decidedly under the general designation of Socialists. While we repudiated with the greatest energy that tyranny of society over the individual which most Socialistic systems are supposed to involve, we yet looked forward to a time when society will no longer be divided into the idle and the industrious; when the rule that they who do not work shall not eat, will be applied not to paupers only, but impartially to all; when the division of the produce of labour, instead of depending, as in so great a degree it now does, on the accident of birth, will be made by concert on an accepted principle of justice, and when it will no longer either be, or be thought to be, impossible for human beings to exert themselves strenuously in procuring benefits which are not to be exclusively their own, but to be shared with the society they belong to. The social problem of the future we considered to be, how to unite the greatest individual liberty of action, with a common ownership of the raw material of the globe, and an equal participation of all in the benefits of combined labour.[3]

If, as Beatrice Webb recognized, Bentham was the spiritual ancestor of the Fabians, Mill, the evolutionary link between Benthamite and Fabian Utilitarianism, was surely their intellectual godfather.[4] Or, rather, he would have been if Harriet

---

[1] Mill, *Principles*, pp. 573, 590.
[2] D. H. McGregor, *Economic Thought and Policy* (1949), pp. 86–7.
[3] Mill, *Autobiography*, p. 196.
[4] B. Webb, *Our Partnership*, p. 210.

Taylor had lived longer and given him the courage to declare himself in public. As it was, he and his numerous disciples, especially his kindergarten of academic economists, Cairnes, Cliffe Leslie, Nicholson, Thorold Rogers, Fawcett, and the rest, never got beyond the sort of mildly collectivist Radicalism which was compatible with unqualified support of Gladstone and the Liberal Party.[1]

As it was, too, Dicey—himself both a bigoted individualist and a disciple of Mill—was unable or unwilling to father on to Mill, as he had fathered the 'Legislative Quiescence' of the period before the first Reform Act on to Blackstone and the 'Individualism' of the period between the first two Reform Acts on to Bentham, responsibility for the legislative 'Collectivism' which he saw as the dominant policy, and the bane, of the last third of the nineteenth century.[2] And for the purpose of understanding the Victorian revolution in government and social policy this is just as well, for Mill, like Blackstone and Bentham, was responding belatedly to changes which were already occurring in the practice of government and legislation. The transition from *laissez-faire* to State intervention was not a moment of time when one theory of legislation took over from another, but the long-drawn-out evolution of a new legislative and administrative practice, by the gradual segregation of the two allied but increasingly rival ideals, and the growing domination in the governors and administrators themselves of the entrepreneurial by the professional ideal. It is at the practical rather than the theoretical level, therefore, that the key to the transition must be sought.

The professional ideal, it was suggested in the last chapter, contributed in two ways to the process of practical social reform.[3] On the humanitarians and Radicals who initiated the process by discovering social problems and finding them 'intolerable', it operated indirectly, by providing professional methods and

[1] Cf. J. E. Cairnes, 'Political Economy and the Land', *Fortnightly Review*, 1870, XIII, 41; T. E. Cliffe Leslie, *The Land Systems and Industrial Economy of Ireland, England and Continental Countries* (1870), and review by Mill in *ibid.*, XIII. 641; J. S. Nicholson, *Tenant's Gain not Landlord's Loss* (Edinburgh, 1883), p. 163; J. E. T. Rogers, 'Economy and Trade: Some aspects of Laissez-faire and State Control', *Stat.J.* 1883, XLVI. 645; H. Fawcett, 'The Nationalization of the Land', *Fortnightly Review*, 1872, XVIII. 627f.

[2] Dicey, *op. cit., passim.*

[3] See above, chap. vii, § 4.

standards of criticism and suggesting professional solutions. On the professional administrators who had to apply those solutions in the shape of government control and inspection, it operated directly, through their professional concern to identify the real causes of the problems and to modify and extend the legislation and administrative machinery to meet them. Now it is time to look in rather more detail at this process, and in particular at the part played by professional men both in the scientific study of society and social problems and in the professionalization of government.

The scientific study of society goes back to the Scientific Revolution of the seventeenth century and 'political arithmetic' —and, significantly, to the academic Sir John Graunt and the civil servant Gregory King—but it only came into its own as a result of the Industrial Revolution . Indeed, its most important tool, statistics, is to industrialism what written language was to early civilization: at once its product and its means of self-expression—hence the inadequacy of contemporary descriptions of both, which are like the autobiographies of infants learning to speak. The first attempts were heroic compilations like Sir John Sinclair's *Statistical Account of Scotland* (1791) and Patrick Colquhoun's *Treatise on the Wealth, Power and Resources of the British Empire* (1814), but the real breakthrough came only in the 1830's, with the establishment of the Statistical Office of the Board of Trade and the Registrar-General's Office in 1837, and the founding of the Statistical Section of the British Association in 1833, and of Statistical Societies in all the major cities, beginning with Manchester and London in 1833 and 1834, designed 'to collect, digest, and publish facts illustrating the condition and prospects of society, in its material, social and moral relations.' The Societies believed in the empirical method:

> in the business of social science principles are valid for application inasmuch as they are legitimate inductions from facts, accurately observed and methodically qualified;

and they applied it to an immense range of social problems from illiteracy and crime to slum housing and industrial strikes.[1]

---

[1] *Stat.J.*, 1838, I, Introduction, pp. 1–5; 4th Annual Report, pp. 5–9; and 'Provincial Societies in U.K.', pp. 48–50, 115–17; cf. also *Annals of Royal Statistical Society, 1834–1934* (1934), chap. i, and T. S. Ashton, *Economic and Social Investigations in Manchester, 1833–1933* (Manchester, 1934), chap. i.

The Statistical Societies were a symptom of what Bulwer Lytton in 1833 called 'an immense intellectual revolution. . . . Today everybody is looking for what needs mending.'[1] They were also laboratories for the discovery and examination of 'intolerable' facts, often long before they were felt to be intolerable by the press and public opinion. Thorold Rogers told the London Society in 1863:

> One of the greatest advantages which the members of this Society possess . . . is that of discussing on purely abstract and scientific grounds the principles on which economic facts are founded, the effect of social practices, and the speculative consequences which might ensue from the removal or modification of rules in action which are so habitual, as not to be out of the prejudice of men obviously capable of actual alteration . . .

In other words, if economic facts and social practices did not square with the theory of *laissez-faire* the Societies were prepared to discuss changing the theory, and discussion had in fact made it possible in particular cases to change the practice:

> The adoption of a limitation on the hours of labour, of the sex employed in some kinds of labour, of the half-time system in the work and education of children, of the principle that able-bodied labour should not be ordinarily relieved except under the regulation of a workhouse, and a variety of other economical reforms, have, I understand, been discussed before this society in a grave and unprejudiced manner, long before they have been approached as practical questions either by legislation or by the popular press.[2]

When the facts and practices were found intolerable and agitation and action were demanded, the problem became the concern of other bodies such as the education pressure groups or the Health of Towns Association. But the contribution of the Statistical Societies in throwing the first light into dark corners should not be underestimated.

The professionalism of these Societies inhered in their aims and methods rather than their membership, which included a cross-section of the politically influential classes. Lord Lansdowne chaired and Henry Goulburn and Spring Rice attended

[1] A. de Tocqueville, *Journeys to England and Ireland* (ed. J. P. Meyer, 1958), p. 56.

[2] J. E. T. Rogers, 'On the Rationale and Working of the Patent Laws', *Stat.J.*, 1863, XXVI. 121.

the inaugural meeting of the London Society. But a particularly significant group of members were the civil servants with access to official statistics and information: G. R. Porter and James Deacon Hume of the Board of Trade, Kay-Shuttleworth of the Poor Law Commission and the Privy Council Committee on Education, William Farr and Horace Mann of the General Register Office, Rev. Richard Jones of the Charity Commission, Leonard Horner the Factory Inspector, Joseph Fletcher of the Education Inspectorate, John Simon of the Privy Council Medical Department, and the ubiquitous Edwin Chadwick, to mention only the most prominent. Civil servants not only contributed many of the most valuable papers: they used the societies as a platform for urging their own policies, and even as pressure groups to bring public opinion to bear upon their own political chiefs. Thus Porter and Deacon Hume continually pressed their own programme of free trade and repeal of the corn laws on successive governments, Joseph Fletcher his ideas on penal reform and industrial schools, Leonard Horner his demands for increased safety in factories and extension of the factory acts, Chadwick his system of arterial water supply and drainage, and Simon his insistence on medical control and inspection of the local sanitary authorities. They were not above stimulating artificial 'pressure from without' to further internal departmental moves, as Simon, for example, more than once stimulated the Social Science Association, the B.M.A., the Medical Officers' Association, not to say *The Times* and the *Pall Mall Gazette*.[1]

It was within doors, however, that the great pioneering civil servants had most effect on the revolution in government, and it on them. While most business men and a great many professional men out of doors found little reason for changing their basic *laissez-faire* assumptions, until driven to it in particular cases by the revelation of intolerable facts, the civil servants, however doctrinaire the assumptions with which they began, had thrust upon them the educative task of revealing the facts and of seeing the accepted remedies for them repeatedly fail. It was not they, of course, who in most cases originally found a social problem so intolerable that it required the attention of the State,

[1] Royston Lambert, *Sir John Simon, 1816–1904, and English Social Administration* (1963), pp. 300, 373, 611, and *passim*.

though it might justly be said that it was Chadwick and his medical assistants at the Poor Law Board, Arnott, Kay and Southwood Smith, who thrust the public health problem before the public. In most cases that was the work of spontaneous pressure groups to which present and future civil servants might belong, like the classical economists in relation to the old Poor Law, Sadler and company in relation to factory conditions, the Benthamites and Dissenters in relation to popular education, and so on. Yet once an inquiry requiring professional research or assistance was mounted or an act passed creating professional machinery for dealing with a problem, a process of 'factual enlightenment' began for the responsible professionals to which the original movers of reform had access only at second hand.

The most famous example of this process of factual enlightenment is that of Edwin Chadwick. Chadwick began as the most doctrinaire of *laissez-faire* Benthamites, firmly uniting both tendencies, the demand for non-interference with the labour market and the demand for efficient government to solve the problem of excessive poverty, in the Report of the 1832 Poor Law Commission which he wrote with Nassau Senior. As Secretary of the Poor Law Board he and his medical Assistant Commissioners, Drs. Arnott, Kay and Southwood Smith, soon discovered that there were vast causes of poverty not touched by the Report or its remedies, the workhouse test and less eligibility, in particular the enormous human misery, loss of work and earnings, and waste of industrial production caused by ill health and unnecessary deaths arising from insanitary and over-crowded housing, foul drainage, dirty and inadequate water supply, overflowing burial grounds, public nuisances from manure heaps, slaughter-houses and the like, and noxious industrial processes. Their work, culminating in Chadwick's great *Report on the Sanitary Condition of the Labouring Population of Great Britain* (1842), was at once the first great national, empirical social survey and the chief stimulus and starting point of the Victorian public health movement. The Report established both statistically and through case histories the correlation between insanitary living and working conditions and disease and high mortality, calculated the economic and social costs of ill health, and demonstrated the inadequacy of existing law and administration to solve the problem. It led directly to the

Health of Towns Commission and its still more systematic and wide-ranging reports, the first (1844) mostly written by Chadwick and the second (1845) influenced by him, and to the public agitation headed by the Health of Towns Association (1844) which produced the first Public Health Act, 1848, and the Public Health Board, with Chadwick and Southwood Smith along with Lord Ashley as Commissioners.[1]

This was perhaps the greatest example of what, in the language of cybernetics, may be called 'feedback', the reaction of the administrative machine upon itself and its controllers to produce new policy and machinery. That in the short term it failed, with the dismissal of Chadwick and the virtual collapse of the Board in 1854, followed by its abolition in 1858, was due to Chadwick's aggressive personality and (in spite of his empirical re-education) doctrinaire attachment to his dogmatic sanitary principles, and to the fierce opposition he provoked from the defenders of threatened property interests and the equally doctrinaire opponents of centralization. Their confrontation was a paradigm of the severance and internecine conflict of the once conjoint ideals, the one demanding non-interference with capital and profits, whatever the social cost, the other the mitigation of social waste and misery, whatever the fiscal and administrative burden. For the moment, the entrepreneurial ideal and the dominant theory of *laissez-faire* and decentralization triumphed, but, as we shall see in a moment, the professional ideal and administrative practice were to have the last word.

Chadwick had already had a hand in other examples of the feedback process, and was to be involved in yet more. He rarely originated the study of a particular social problem, but he often 'fed back' a professional solution (not always, of course, the right one). Before he entered government service he had produced the memorandum on police for Peel's Committee and his famous 'preventive Police' article of 1829, which, as well as earning him the friendship of Bentham, had some influence on the origins of the professional police force. From then onwards, in and out of office, he continually pressed his views on the Home Office, culminating in his 1839 Report of the Constabulary Commissioners and the 1839 Act to extend the new police to

[1] Cf. Flinn, Introduction to Chadwick, *op. cit.*, pp. 66–73.

the provinces. As a member of the 1833 Factory Commission with Thomas Tooke and Southwood Smith, he drew up the Report which led to the first effective Factory Act, 1833, with the all-important provision for central government inspection. He suggested the provisions in the 1836 Registration Act making registration districts co-extensive with the Poor Law Unions and requiring the recording of the cause of death, thus making the statistics not only more useful for public health purposes but an important source of further 'feedback' reform, under Chadwick himself at the Board of Health, and later under Simon at the Privy Council Medical Department.[1]

The same process of factual enlightenment and feedback operated through Chadwick's colleagues, friends and rivals. Kay and Tufnell, Assistant Commissioners at the Poor Law Board, began under Chadwick their inquiries into pauper education which were to lead to the setting up, under an Act of 1848, of the district schools, those gigantic boarding schools for the children of the poor which were the real beginning of State provision in education, and to the same men's contributions to State-aided education for the non-pauper working class, notably the setting up of the Privy Council Education Inspectorate and the Battersea Normal School for the training of teachers.[2]

William Farr and Horace Mann of the General Register Office transformed the decennial Census into an indispensable tool of government in an enormous range of problems, from housing to education, and the Census Reports into masterly social and economic surveys of the nation, laced with gratuitous comments on current social philosophy and the direction of government policy. The 1851 Report, for example, contains an able critique and empirical refutation of Malthus, and a section on 'Defective Education of the People' beginning, 'Every British child should unquestionably be taught reading, writing and the elements of knowledge . . . '; while that for 1871 refers, in terms anticipatory of the Welfare State, to the poor law as 'that national institution, which, with all its defects,

---

[1] Cf. S. E. Finer, *Life and Times of Sir Edwin Chadwick* (1952), pp. 29–31, 50–68, 124–7, 164–80; Jenifer Hart, *op. cit.*, Past and Present, 1965, No. 31, p. 42.

[2] Cf. Finer, *op. cit.*, pp. 151–3; Sturt, *op. cit.*, chaps. iv and v; D. Robert, *op. cit.*, pp. 218–19, 235–6, 239, 245–6, 260–3.

is a recognized system of insurance of the whole population, secured on property, against death by starvation,' and to the 'great courage' of the Government and the territorial proprietors in disregarding Malthus and of 'the workmen of the country who went on marrying and multiplying; and so instead of revolutions, and agrarian outrages, and great suffering, and high mortality, and a dwindling race, England had a high poor rate, a vaster population, an immense development of industry at home, and of commerce and colonies abroad.'[1]

Even when the civil servants violently disagreed with each other, as did Leonard Horner and the other three Factory Inspectors on the necessity for prosecution or the fencing of shafts seven feet above the floor, they nevertheless exercised a common pressure in the direction of more inspection and the extension of the Factory Acts to an ever-increasing range of industries. Moreover, the most active and outspoken Inspector, provided that, unlike Chadwick, he had the tact not to offend his political masters or make himself a scapegoat with the press, was likely to be the most influential. Horner was increasingly consulted by successive Home Secretaries faced with drawing up and operating the Factory Acts from 1844 onwards, and himself drafted the 1853 Act which, by forbidding the relay system, finally established the ten-hour day.[2]

All the above examples of feedback—and others too numerous to detail, such as the role of the railway, mines and steamship inspectors of 1840, 1842 and 1846 in establishing and extending safety on the line, underground and at sea—were the work of civil servants who were more or less consciously Benthamites. Many of the administrative devices they applied to the solution of social problems, such as central inspection and report, were undoubtedly Benthamite in origin, and their spread can in part be explained by direct contact and colonization between departments, as in the migration of the Poor Law Assistant Commissioners to public health, education, and other fields. Yet this explanation, true as far as it goes, does not explain why these men were attracted by Bentham's ideas, nor why, since they were equally as Benthamite at the end as at the beginning of the

---

[1] Census of England and Wales, 1851, *General Report*, pp. lxiii-lxviii, lxxxix; 1871, *General Report*, p. xvii.

[2] Cf. D. Roberts, *op. cit.*, pp. 234, 247-8.

process of factual enlightenment, they increasingly opted for the interventionist rather than the *laissez-faire* variety of Benthamism.

The answer, we suggested above, lies in their professionalism, and their consequent predilection for a legislative theorist whose ideas, especially when segregated from what they came to explain away as the historical accident of *laissez-faire*, embodied the professional ideal of efficient, disinterested and, in the administrative solution of social problems, effective government. The test of this view is to be found in those examples of feedback which were not obviously due to Benthamites, above all in those which occurred during the period of reaction against Chadwickian centralization in the 1850's and 1860's, and involved civil servants who were in theory loyal to the ideal of limited government which then re-asserted its domination.

There is an obvious drawback to such a test: the logical impossibility of proving a negative. The one fully documented example of non-Benthamite feedback is that of the emigration officers appointed under the Passenger Acts, who, with little help or pressure from Parliament or the public, developed a complete system of legislation and administrative machinery to regulate the scandalous conditions on the emigrant ships which few but they and the departed emigrants knew about. But not even their anti-Benthamite historian can prove that the Emigration Commissioners had *not* 'read Bentham or heard of his name', or at least read or talked to those who had—and in that age of vociferous Benthamites it would be very surprising if they had not.[1]

However, let us for the sake of argument allow that the civil servants who replaced Chadwick and his Benthamite henchmen in the field of public health, notably John Simon at the Privy Council Medical Department and Tom Taylor at the Local Government Act Office, were not committed Benthamites in the Chadwickian sense, and prided themselves on their 'open minds' and their loyalty to the principles of decentralization and local autonomy which characterized the so-called 'era of localism' between the abolition of the Board of Health in 1858 and the establishment

---

[1] O. MacDonagh, *op. cit.*, *Hist.J.*, 1958, I. 52f., and *A Pattern of Government Growth, 1800–60: The Passenger Acts and their Enforcement* (1961).

of the Local Government Board in 1871.[1] Simon began as the personification of the open, scientific mind concerned only to solve the problems of public health by systematic inquiry and report aimed at persuading the local sanitary authorities to do their duty. He and his inspectors were soon disillusioned: 'local self-government, they began to find, meant, on a large and dangerous scale, no government at all.' By 1865 he had been converted by experience to central compulsion:

> I venture to submit that the time has now arrived when it ought not any longer to be discretional in a place whether that place shall be kept filthy or not. Powers sufficient for the local protection of the public health having first been universally conferred, it next, I submit, ought to be an obligation on the local authorities that these powers be exercised in good faith and with reasonable vigour and intelligence.

His seventh Report, the Vice-President of the Council told the Cabinet, was 'meant to be the basis of subsequent legislation,' and Simon's influence over his political masters enabled him to obtain, among much other interventionist legislation, the vital Sanitary Act of 1866 under which 'the grammar of common sanitary legislation acquired the novel virtue of an imperative mood', and the central executive came to exercise 'a coercive, interfering and even superseding power the like of which Chadwick had never possessed.' Even this proved inadequate, and Simon worked on towards his goal of a Ministry of Health with comprehensive powers of regulation and control over the nation's health. When achieved in the uncouth shape of the Local Government Board of 1871, it served only to frustrate and disillusion him. Nevertheless, it began once again with a new generation of officials the process of factual enlightenment and feedback experienced in turn by Chadwick and himself. 'State medicine as it existed in 1871,' Simon's biographer comments, 'was not one of those functions which originated in sheer empirical necessity.'[2] But it did originate in the impact on empirical needs of the professional ideal as embodied in Simon and his colleagues.

Whereas in Simon the process of feedback, if not Benthamite,

[1] R. Lambert, 'Central and Local Relations in Mid-Victorian England: the Local Government Act Office, 1858–71', *Victorian Studies*, 1962, VI. 120f.

[2] Lambert, *Simon*, pp. 355, 370, 372, 386, 390, 460.

was certainly conscious and deliberate, in Tom Taylor of the Local Government Act Office, which had the task between 1858 and 1871 of sanctioning the programmes of the supposedly autonomous local sanitary authorities, it was unconscious and reluctant. He began by declaring that 'all that the Government can properly be called upon to do is to place the means of local improvement as cheaply and as simply as possible within the reach of the population. It cannot coerce people into being clean and healthy.' Eight years later he was still opposed to the idea of systematic central inspection, and it took him until the very last year of the Office's separate existence to enforce upon all the local Boards their elementary duty of making statistical returns. Yet the Office 'was compelled by the nature of its work, its expert authority, and, above all, the demands from the localities, to exercise an influence far beyond its desire, right, or capacity.' It was bombarded by demands from the local Boards themselves for central inspection, expert advice, and engineering schemes. In its thirteen years of existence the Office and its overworked inspectors mounted upwards of 1,200 local inquiries, approved over 1,600 schemes and an expenditure of over £7 million, chiefly for drainage and water supply, issued 350 Provisional Orders and promoted 34 Parliamentary Bills, and, under the coercive clauses of Simon's 1866 Act, in nine cases superseded the local Board altogether. At the end Taylor found that far from giving rise to 'irritation on the part of the local authorities,' coercion by the State had been, 'as a rule, eagerly called for and warmly welcomed by the ratepayers.'[1]

Here, then, was feedback operating from a still lower level of the administrative machine, from the local authorities themselves, and forcing the administrators at the centre to live up to their professional responsibilities. This was the other aspect of professionalism, the fuel of the engine which powered the ideal: the demand of society for the expert solution of social problems, which the professionals, eagerly in some cases, reluctantly in others, met and manipulated. Either response could be Benthamite, for what that ambiguous label is worth; both were certainly professional, and furthered the professionalization of government.

The final example of feedback is in the reform of the civil

[1] Lambert, *op. cit.*, *Victorian Studies*, 1962, VI. 128, 131–3, 136n., 143, 148.

service itself. As with the rest of the revolution in government, the initial demand for reform necessarily came from without, as part of the general denunciation of the patronage, corruption and inefficiency of aristocratic government stemming from both the entrepreneurial and professional ideals. Yet it was 'internalized' remarkably early. Leaving aside the major role of James Mill from his base at the India Office, we find Sir Henry Taylor, himself the product of a reorganization of the Colonial Office, advising Mill's chief, Hyde Villiers, Secretary of the Board of Control, in 1832 on the reorganization of his department on lines which anticipate the Trevelyan-Northcote reforms of the whole service a generation later.[1] In a remarkable letter Taylor recognized the pressure of facts in the increasing complexity of public administration and the consequent need for professional expertise:

> The affairs of nations, and of this country in particular, become every year more multifarious and complicated, and in proportion to the advance of general education more knowledge both general and particular is required in order to deal with public affairs.

Under the old system the clerkships went to 'the sons of people of rank and influence, brought up in idleness,' and inured to intellectual sloth by the mechanical drudgery of copying, the gentlemanly lack of discipline, and the system of promotion by seniority. 'Efficiency should be substituted for influence, . . . but in our present state of transition, influence has been left behind and efficiency we have not yet reached.' The remedies were selection by merit; probationary appointments; promotion chiefly by merit; two distinct classes of clerks, senior and junior, for the intellectual and routine divisions of the work; the use of patronage to pension off the inefficient, and substitute four or five really able principal clerks at the head of the department. Such measures should be applied 'to the work of reinvigorating *not* your establishment only, but those of the Treasury and of the three Secretaries of State.'[2]

The India Office was in fact reorganized on something like these lines in 1833, with James and John Stuart Mill playing a

[1] H. Parris, 'Sir Henry Taylor "On the Best Mode of Constituting Public Offices" ', *Political Studies*, 1961, IX. 181f.

[2] In his book, *The Statesman* (1836), Taylor elaborated his proposals and discussed the question of selection by competitive examination.

key part.[1] The ensuing twenty years, *before* the Trevelyan-Northcote inquiry, were the key period for the reform of the home civil service. Most of the great civil servants who helped to create the Victorian bureaucractic State were already at work evolving the principles and procedures which Trevelyan and Northcote were to generalize and apply to the service as a whole. These men—Chadwick, Drs. J. P. Kay and Southwood Smith, Leonard Horner, Deacon Hume, G. R. Porter, Rowland Hill, William Farr, Horace Mann, Tidd Pratt, T. H. Farrer, and Trevelyan himself—were of necessity transitional figures. They were themselves products of the patronage system, and it is doubtful whether any other system could have produced such a constellation of forceful pioneers. Yet they used patronage to dig its own grave. Under Chadwick and Senior's influence the Poor Law Commissioners, with 'perfect purity and sagacity', chose 'a body of assistants such as . . . no board had ever possessed', including such men as Drs. Arnott, Kay and Southwood Smith. Lansdowne and Kay (now Kay-Shuttleworth) set out to find men *omni exceptione major* as School Inspectors, and found them in such men as H. S. Tremenheere, Joseph Fletcher and Matthew Arnold. They did it by process of selection by interview and references as impartial as they could make it: only two out of twelve of the assistant commissioners were previously known to the Poor Law Commissioners.[2] In the process they became converted to the most impartial system of all, selection by examination.

When the time came, therefore, to give evidence to the Trevelyan-Northcote Committee, most of them were already converted to competitive examinations, promotion by merit, and unification of the service. Only the unregenerate heirs of the old patronage system, like Trollope of the G.P.O. and Arbuthnot, Auditor of the Civil List, were against them. The Committee came down strongly in favour of competitive examination, but failed to get it.[3] What they did get, however, initiated a typical example of feedback which finally achieved their object. The Civil Service Commission was set up to administer the new qualifying examinations, and Horace Mann, the Registrar,

[1] Cf. Eric Stokes, *The English Utilitarians and India* (Oxford, 1959).

[2] D. Roberts, *op. cit.*, pp. 164–5.

[3] E. Hughes, 'Sir Charles Trevelyan and Civil Service Reform, 1853–55', *E.H.R.*, 1949, LXIV. 53f. and 206f.; Wyn Griffith, *op. cit.*, pp. 14–15; E. W. Cohen, *op. cit.*, pp. 97–109.

became the most indefatigable critic of the system and advocate of competitive examination, both inside the Service and on such well-trodden platforms outside as that of the London Statistical Society.[1] It was substantially his scheme of recruitment and organization which was finally adopted by Gladstone's famous 1870 Order in Council.[2]

The professionalization of government might well be summed up in the words of a young man who came first out of 207 candidates in the Indian Civil Service examination in 1861:

> It is easy to be a Company man [appointed before the Crown took over in 1858] and yet be superior to the common run in an intellectual aspect but it is impossible to be first-class—I mean the very first, one of a set of men picked from the whole country for their talents, and fritter your evenings away in walking quadrilles and consuming ices. I aspire to a circle far above the circle of fashion. I mean the circle of Power. . . .[3]

The entrepreneurial ideal had in effect won the battle for control of the administrative system only by creating a Frankenstein's monster in the shape of a professional bureaucracy with an ideal and ambitions of its own. If anyone fathered Victorian collectivism it was not Mill the theorist but Chadwick the practical reformer, who began by uniting the entrepreneurial and professional ideals and ended by divorcing them. In 1859, personally defeated but institutionally victorious, he repudiated the entrepreneurial ideal:

> The earlier politico-economical doctrines as to competition must now receive considerable modifications . . . To the questions sometimes put to me—*where I would stop in the application of my principle* [of authoritive intervention]—*I am at present only prepared to answer: 'Where waste stops.'*[4]

In the shape of the interventionist State the first breaches in the foundations of the entrepreneurial society began even before

---

[1] *P.P.*, 1860, IX, *S.C. on Civil Service Appointments*, pp. ix-xii, and Appendix IV, 'Papers put in by Mr. Horace Mann'; H. Mann, 'On the Cost and Organization of the Civil Service', *Stat.J.*, 1869, XXXII. 32f.

[2] Cohen, *op. cit.*, pp. 118-22.

[3] William Hunter, letter to fiancée, 1862, in D. Kincaid, *British Social Life in India, 1608-1937* (1938), p. 202.

[4] E. Chadwick, *On the Different Principles of Legislation and Administration in Europe* (1859); Finer, *op. cit.*, p. 476.

it reached maturity. The undermining of the society by the crumbling of its ideal we shall take up in Chapter X. But first we must see how it came to maturity in the viable class society of mid-Victorian England.

IX

The Rise of a Viable Class Society

THE struggle between the ideals was an integral part of the struggle between the classes, and the outcome of the one predetermined the outcome of the other. The class struggle on the practical political and economic level took place between institutions which embodied the class ideals, and *were* the classes so far as they had corporeal existence. These institutions— political associations and pressure groups, trade unions and employers' associations, and the like—were, in the traditional metaphor, the organized battalions of the class war.

If we are to understand the nature of class conflict in the nineteenth century, however, and in particular the evolution of a viable class society out of the violent class struggles of the generation after Waterloo, we must insist that class warfare was, and is, only a metaphor. If, as we have seen, the class struggle was at bottom a struggle for income, between the partners in a system of production and distribution which, in the short run at least, made them mutually dependent, then the 'war' had to be so limited in its aims and circumscribed in its methods as scarcely to deserve the name. At any given moment of the struggle the conflicting parties were faced with the choice between accepting, *ad interim* only and without prejudice to their ultimate objectives, the need to carry on the partnership which produced their incomes, and rejecting it, to their own immediate and possibly catastrophic loss. In short, they were faced with the choice between accepting the economic system and precipitating social revolution.

The choice was no more and no less than that faced by the participants in any system of competing and mutually dependent powers. Just as in international diplomacy, for example, the negotiating powers have to choose between war and continuing to pursue their demands by all means short of war, so the parties to the class struggle had to choose between revolution and all means short of it. They could protest, demonstrate, practise temporary non-co-operation, indulge in violence of a limited 'border incident' variety, even carry 'brinkmanship' to the point of threatening revolution itself, without in fact turning class conflict into revolution. And just as diplomacy, in Clausewitz's phrase, might be the pursuit of war by other means without being the same thing as war itself, so class conflict, though it might degenerate into revolution, was not necessarily the same thing as civil war. On the contrary, it was at worst the pursuit of civil war *by other means*, at best a process of bargaining from strength between mutually dependent and therefore potentially equal partners. The rise of a viable class society in Britain in the generation after Waterloo was in round terms an evolution of class conflict from the pursuit of civil war by other means to a process of mutual bargaining.

Before we trace in detail this evolution there are two paradoxes which must be resolved. The first is that in this transition to comparatively peaceful class relations violence and the threat of violence had a special, indeed an inevitable, part to play. Given that class institutions of any kind were regarded by the old society in which they came to birth as vehicles of social insubordination to be suppressed rather than bargaining partners to be conciliated, it was inevitable that class demands, whether for a share in political power or for a say in industrial relations, should have been met by the legal violence of repression and backed in response to this by the illegal violence of intimidation and threatened revolution. From James Mill to Cobden, from Henry Hunt to O'Connor, the leaders of the challenging classes recognized in the *ultima ratio* of the appeal to violence the only unanswerable argument for reform. Why else, it was argued, should the class in possession concede anything? Violence, or at least the threat of violence, was therefore an inevitable concomitant of the institutionalization of class.

Yet to the extent that the *ultima ratio* worked, and succeeded in wringing concessions and recognition from the class in possession, even where these fell far short of what was demanded, violence and the threat of violence played an essential part in the acceptance of the class institutions and the system of bargaining between them which took the violence out of class conflict. Violence itself, in other words, was a major factor in its own demise. Instead, therefore, of violence leading to more violence in a Marxian crescendo culminating in bloody revolution, violence was rather the mark of an immature class society in which the classes had not yet learned to live in peaceful co-existence with each other. In a mature class society such as that of mid-Victorian Britain the relations between the classes are not those of civil war by other means, but those of a familiar kind of marriage in which the partners cannot live together without bickering but are perfectly aware that apart they cannot live at all. Divorce is always an abstract possibility, but it belongs to the pathology rather than the physiology of marriage, just as war belongs to the pathology of international relations, and social revolution belongs to the pathology of class. It is one of the ironies of history that Marx and Engels, brilliantly analyzing the immature class conflict of British industrialism, should have published their thesis of the inevitability of social revolution at the very moment when the bluff of the last Chartist threat of violence was called and the viable class society came of age.

The second paradox is that the period of most violent class conflict coincided with the period when real incomes were rising faster than ever before in modern times, and that the transition around mid-century to more harmonious class relations coincided with a deceleration in their rate of growth.[1] This surprising fact, which we explored in the discussion on living standards in Chapter V, calls in question the widely held belief amongst political, as distinct from economic, historians, that the trans-

---

[1] Cf. Rostow, *British Economy*, p. 8: taking the periods 1813/17–1845/9 and 1845/9–1871/5 the key annual percentage rates of growth dropped as follows: total industrial production 3·5–3·2; consumers' goods production 3·2–2·6; producers' goods production 4·4–4·1; real wages (Tucker) 0·7–0·6.

formation in class relations can be explained entirely in terms of a change in the economic climate, from the 'depression' of the second quarter of the nineteenth century to the 'prosperity' of the third. As we saw in the earlier discussions, the 'hungry forties' were not hungrier than earlier decades nor 'mid-Victorian prosperity' significantly more prosperous. Both terms are myths, fostered by the differing socio-political experience of the two periods, and as explanations of that experience therefore strictly tautological.

This is not to deny, however, that there was some connection between the transition in class relations and a change in the economic climate. The question is, what was the difference in the climate, what was its connection with class relations, and was it sufficient by itself to account for the transition from violent class conflict to comparative social peace? In the first place, the essential change in the climate was not in living standards or production but in prices, not from depression to prosperity but from long-term deflation to long-term inflation. In the earlier period prices fell by an average 1·4 per cent per annum; in the later they rose by an average 0·6 per cent per annum.[1] This change in the long-term trend of prices, which was itself the principal factor in the changing pace of the growth of real incomes, had, as such changes always do have, a most remarkable effect on the struggle for income. Whenever prices fall, not temporarily as in the downswing of the short-term trade cycle, but persistently over a longer period up to a generation or so, they intensify the competition for income. Conversely, when they rise—provided that the inflation is mild enough and the economy expanding sufficiently for money incomes to rise faster—they relax the competition for income. In brief, secular deflation aggravates, secular inflation mollifies, the struggle for income.

The reasons for this are obvious enough. Secular inflation may wipe out most of the gains from rising money incomes, but it creates a glowing illusion of 'prosperity': employers with a steady expectation of rising prices and money profits yield wage increases more readily; workers may strike as often but, finding that strikes tend to be shorter and more frequently successful, are more prone to accept the economic system as tolerable;

[1] *Ibid., loc. cit.*

both find that rents press less heavily upon them, and are less inclined to blame the landlords, who in turn become more amenable to reforms involving loss of privilege or protection for their incomes. All classes feel themselves to be swimming with the economic tide and the system to be relatively benevolent. Conversely, secular deflation may bring large accretions of real income but it creates an illusion of persistent 'depression': employers with an expectation of falling prices and money profits try to cut wages, protest against taxation, and blame trade union intransigence and 'class legislation' like the corn laws for causing 'depression'; workers, always more determined to 'hold the line' against attempts to reduce wages, dig in their heels in bitter long-drawn-out strikes, and become disenchanted with an economic system which seems to threaten their customary standard of living; both blame the landlords for their difficulties, who in turn cling to any device which may prop them up, such as the corn laws. All classes feel themselves to be swimming against the economic tide, and life to be a struggle for existence.

It is possible, of course, for subjective feelings to produce objective facts, and it may be argued that, because of the psychological pessimism of business men, the depressions of the deflationary period were deeper than those of the optimistic, inflationary period. Certainly contemporaries thought so, but that is only evidence of their psychological state and their readiness to believe in long-term 'prosperity' and 'depression' belied by the statistics. The evidence from unemployment rates is too slight before the 1880's to prove the case either way, but what there is of it certainly does not uphold the view that in terms of hardship the slumps of 1858, 1862 or 1868 were in any degree milder than those of 1826, 1837 or 1842. When objective measurement becomes possible in the so-called 'Great Depression' of the late Victorian age the gap between the observations of the economists and the subjective feelings of the business men before the 1886 Commission on the Depression in Trade and Industry shows at least how incompatible contemporary opinions could be.[1] On *a priori* grounds it could be argued that the

---

[1] *P.P.*, 1886 [c. 4621, 4715, 4715–1], XXI. 1, 231, XXII. 1, *Reports, Evidence and Appendices, R.C. on Depression of Trade and Industry*; cf. H. L. Beales, 'The Great Depression in Industry and Trade, 1873–86', *Ec.H.R.*, 1934–35, V. 65f.

pessimism of the one period postponed and the optimism of the other hastened recovery from the troughs of the slumps, and this would be worth investigating, but it is very different from a belief in the secular depression and secular prosperity of the two periods. Rather would it confirm the view, supported by all the objective evidence, that the essential difference was in long-term expectations about the course of money incomes, and that these were related to the secular trend of prices.

Yet was this difference in what may be called the psycho-economic climate sufficient by itself to account for the change from the exceptionally violent class conflict of the earlier period to the exceptionally peaceful class relations of the later one? If so, then every subsequent period of secular deflation should have produced class conflict just as violent. It is true that both the 'Great Depression' of 1874–96 and the inter-war deflation of 1920–39 were periods of bitter class conflict, but they were not periods of violence and threatened revolution in the same degree as 1816–48.[1] There were manifestly other factors at work in the early nineteenth century which still further exacerbated class relations. Two of these were economic. One was the peculiarly explosive combination of high unemployment and high bread prices which characterized trade depressions before the repeal of the corn laws, and touched off the bread riots, machine-breaking and other outbreaks which so often coincided with major political crises.[2] The other was the structural change in the economy which inexorably destroyed the occupations and eroded the incomes of those handworkers who formed the backbone of the more violent working-class movements, from Luddism to physical-force Chartism.

Yet even these do not exhaust the factors involved in the evolution from violent to peaceable class conflict, for there were gradations even in violence, and one of its historians notes that ' "explosiveness" was less, where regular institutions existed

[1] The most violent period in politics and industrial relations since the Chartist period was in fact 1910–14, when an opposite and, in recent times, exceptional conjunction of economic trends was in operation, *viz.* sharp inflation accompanied by stagnating production and falling real wages.

[2] Cf. Rostow, *British Economy*, chap. v, 'Trade Cycles, Harvests, and Politics, 1790–1850', esp. the 'Social Tension' chart and table, pp. 124–5; E. J. Hobsbawm, 'Economic Fluctuations and Some Social Movements since 1800', *Ec.H.R.*, 1952, V. 5; K. K. Macnab, *op. cit.*, p. 352.

which were believed capable of safeguarding the general bargaining position of the men and their basic minimum of life.'[1] The crucial factor in the rise of a viable class society was in fact the institutionalization of class, the creation, recognition and acceptance of the political, social and industrial institutions through which the classes could express themselves, safeguard or ameliorate their standards and conditions of life, and channel their conflicts out of the paths of violence into those of negotiation and compromise. The evolution was much more gradual than the superficial contrast between the two periods before and after 1848 suggests. Many of the institutions, like the Owenite general union of 1834 or the engineering employers' association of 1852, were created for the purpose of threatening the destruction of the institutions of a hostile class, but were driven by events to acceptance and negotiation. Others, like the Dissenters' organizations, evolved more slowly, from old society interest groups into new society class institutions, threatening destruction to some aristocratic institution like the Church. Between the two extremes there was every variety of evolutionary type, with only this in common: that they pursued class ends by means which were less violent the more they were organized and institutionalized.

The transition, then, was not a sudden, dramatic leap from the violent hostility of 'depression' into the sedative complacency of 'prosperity'. It was a gradual evolution from a phase of immature class struggle, aggravated by adverse economic factors, into one of mature class conflict, aided by favourable economic trends. The earlier phase became by degrees much less violent than its image. The later, in spite of its pacific legend, was still an age of class conflict, some of it more violent than is commonly believed, for the threat of violence remained a factor, if an increasingly remote one, in Victorian class society until its close.

The rise of a viable class society depended, more than on anything else, on the extent and speed at which the classes were institutionalized and the institutions learned by experience the sophisticated arts of mutual bargaining. Here, if English class society was unlucky in the economic climate in which it passed through the main stage of institutionalization, it was lucky in

[1] Hobsbawm, *loc. cit.*, p. 17.

institutions which it inherited from the old society. Apart from an array of political, legal and administrative institutions capable in the event of being reformed to meet its needs, it inherited one set of institutions which might have been designed to be the models and mentors of the new class organizations, and to instruct them in the art of non-violent conflict. These were the institutions of sectarian religion.

1. THE ROLE OF RELIGION

The role of religion at the birth of class, we said in Chapter VI, was threefold: to give expression to emancipation from the dependency system before it hardened into class antagonism; to provide a means or model for class organization; and to administer an analgesic against the pains of labour by influencing conflict in the direction of non-violence. For this reason we called sectarian religion the midwife of class, but left the second and third roles to be dealt with in this chapter, where the functions of the midwife can merge with those of nursemaid of the infant and teacher of the adolescent.

In the case of Old Dissent and the middle class there was a direct connection between the 'interest' institutions of the old society and the class institutions of the new. The Dissenting churches themselves were institutions which could serve, consecutively or even simultaneously, the purposes of an interest group supporting the aristocratic Whigs, their traditional patrons, on such issues as toleration or education, and of a class organization pursuing their own middle-class ends, such as the campaign against Church rates or against the Establishment itself. In this way Old Dissent was able to act as an agent in the transition from the interest politics of the old society into the class politics of the new. Its agency can be most economically illustrated by tracing it through three key movements: Parliamentary Reform; the Church rates agitation; and the campaign against the corn laws.

The Dissenters helped to transform Parliamentary Reform from an interest movement into a class movement. For their Whig allies it was always the former, a struggle of the Whig 'outs' against the Tory 'ins', for which they hoped to rally behind them a formidable proportion of the middle ranks and lower orders. In this endeavour the Dissenters were an invaluable ally, a natural bridge connecting them with the middle ranks of the growing industrial towns from which the main pressure for Reform increasingly came, and at the same time a defensive buffer of moderate opinion between themselves and the extreme Radicals. The Dissenters on their side originally looked to Reform to give them 'complete toleration', meaning civic equality with the Anglicans in local government and so on.[1] When the Tories gave it to them in 1828 it was the Whig leaders, Lord Holland and Lord John Russell, they thanked with a dinner in their honour, and pressed on with them for Reform which would make toleration meaningful by defeating the Anglican corporations which in most towns controlled both Parliamentary representation and local government. The Political Unions, including the renegade Tory Attwood's own at Birmingham, were led by middle-class Dissenters like Joseph Parkes at Birmingham and the Potter brothers at Manchester. Their traditional pressure groups, the Committee of Dissenting Deputies and the Protestant Society for the Protection of Religious Liberty, threw themselves into the campaign for Reform, and took an active part in the elections for the Parliament which passed the Reform Bill.[2]

The Dissenters and their friends and enemies expected Reform to increase their political power. Brougham for the Whigs acknowledged in 1828 that they already possessed informal power.

> Of this I am quite satisfied, that the representatives of every town will hear from the places they represent the voice of the constituents, in approval of the vote [in favour of the repeal of the Test and Corporation Acts] . . . ; for everywhere there has arisen a body of constituents, wealthy, and if I may use the expression, intelligent to a degree of which those who have not well considered the subject can form no adequate notion—I mean the Dissenters. . . .[3]

And when Reform came, Wellington expected it to sweep them into formal power:

[1] Cf. U. R. Q. Henriques, *Religious Toleration in England, 1787–1833* (1961), pp. 4, 57–8.

[2] R. G. Cowherd, *The Politics of English Dissent from 1815 to 1848* (1959), pp. 33, 73–83.

[3] *Ibid.*, p. 31.

The revolution is made, that is to say, that power is transferred from one class of society, the gentlemen of England, professing the faith of the Church of England, to another class of society, the shopkeepers, being Dissenters from the Church, many of them Socinians, others atheists.[1]

Yet Reform was almost as disappointing to the Dissenters as it was to the working class. Very few Dissenters were elected to the Commons,[2] and those who were soon began to find, as did their allies the Benthamite Radicals, that the aims of the Whig Government increasingly diverged from their own. Certain gains they did achieve: the right of Quakers and Separatists to take their seats in Parliament without swearing an oath; the reform of municipal government and the replacement of the self-perpetuating Anglican corporations in many boroughs by elected and predominantly Dissenting ones; and the secularization of the registration of births and deaths and of the solemnization of marriage. But on what they considered the most vital issues, the abolition of Church rates and the reform and disestablishment of the Church itself, the Whigs were at bottom as reactionary as the Tories. The Dissenters therefore increasingly turned away from their aristocratic patrons and towards the secular representatives of their own class, the still more rigorously anti-Church and anti-aristocratic Benthamites and their provincial allies in the growing anti-corn law movement.

Class politics decisively superseded interest politics when in 1836 the Dissenters joined the Benthamites in the Church Rates Abolition Society, still more when the Whigs dropped the Church Rates Bill in 1837.[3] Abolition was meant as a step on the way to Church disestablishment, but it had the advantage of enabling the middle class to organize effectively and win victories at the local level, by capturing the parish vestries and blocking the levying of the rate. This had been done in Sheffield since 1824 and in Manchester since 1835. Now the campaign was spread systematically to other towns, producing its 'Church

---

[1] Wellington to Croker, 6 March 1833, *The Correspondence and Diaries of J. W. Croker from 1809 to 1830* (ed. L. J. Jennings, 1884), II. 205–6.

[2] Only one trinitarian Dissenter, John Wilks of Boston, was elected in 1832, though he was joined by Edward Baines in 1834, and there was a handful of Unitarians—Gash, *Reaction and Reconstruction*, p. 66.

[3] *Ibid.*, p. 73.

rate martyrs' who went to prison for non-payment, like John Thorogood of Chelmsford and William Baines of Leeds. It even produced anti-Church rate riots at Birmingham in 1837. Here was an example of legal violence—the harsh treatment of G. F. Muntz and other non-payers of rates—provoking illegal violence even in middle-class chapel-goers, which helped to stoke the anti-aristocratic fires of class. By 1842 rate levies were blocked in 53 towns, and payment refused by Dissenters in many others. After a long-drawn-out series of legal cases, the House of Lords determined in 1853 that a rate levied by a minority of a vestry was illegal, and in effect gave the victory to the Dissenters wherever they could gain a majority, though the question was not finally settled until the Compulsory Church Rates Abolition Act of 1868.[1] Meanwhile, the anti-Church rate agitation had merged with others of wider political import. Its significance lay chiefly in alienating the Whigs and bringing to the fore the class connections of Dissent.

In the anti-Corn Law movement the emphasis shifts still further, from middle-class support for a mainly Dissenting cause, to Dissenting support for a wholly middle-class cause. The Anti-Corn Law League, that 'uniquely powerful instrument in the forging of middle-class consciousness', as Asa Briggs has called it,[2] was as much a crusade against the tithe-collecting Church as against the rent-collecting aristocracy. The Anglican Cobden wrote to the Quaker Bright in 1842:

> The Church clergy are almost to a man guilty of causing the present distress by upholding the Corn Law—they having themselves an interest in the high price of bread,[3]

and declared in public that

> We have, I believe, the majority of every religious denomination with us—I mean the Dissenting denominations; we have them almost *en masse*, both ministers and laymen; and I believe the only body against us, as a body, are the members of the Church of England.[4]

Finally, he practically identified the middle class with Dissent,

---

[1] *Ibid.*, p. 66–7, 72–3; Cowherd, *op. cit.*, pp. 94–5, 155–7.
[2] Briggs, 'Language of Class', *loc. cit.*, p. 59.
[3] Cobden to Bright, 12 May 1842; McCord, *op. cit.*, p 26.
[4] Cowherd, *op. cit.*, p. 131.

and acknowledged their common interest in non-violent agitation:

> We have carried it on by those means by which the middle class usually carries on its movements. We have had our meeting of Dissenting ministers; we have obtained the co-operation of the ladies, we have resorted to [tea?] parties, and taken those pacific means for carrying out our views which mark us as a middle-class set of agitators.[1]

The League was not always so peaceable, either in words or in deeds. Cobden's meeting of Dissenting ministers, at Manchester in July 1841, heard some very unclerical language about 'round-bellied bishops', 'sleek, meek, well-fed ecclesiastics', and 'holy men, who luxuriate in the embraces of the national harlot'. Cobden himself organized, through Edwin Watkin, later the railway magnate, a body of strong-arm men to beat the Chartist hecklers at their own game.[2] Yet there is not much doubt that Dissent taught the League a great deal about non-violent agitation, and the concessions which 'pacific means' wrung from a still aristocratic Parliament certainly helped to reconcile the middle class to the political system.

We might also fairly claim that Dissent taught the middle class the need to come to terms with the working class, at least on the political plane. The Complete Suffrage movement of 1841–42, led by the Birmingham Quaker Joseph Sturge and the Congregationalist editor of the *Nonconformist* Edward Miall, was an attempt to unite the middle- and working-class Radicals, the Anti-Corn Law Leaguers and the Chartists, in a campaign for everything in the Charter except the name. If it failed on this single point, it also hammered home the wedge between the protagonists of physical and moral force which finally split the movement and rendered it impotent—a disservice perhaps to the working-class movement, but a step on the way to social peace.

Ultimately, however, Dissent was not the middle class, for just as Dissent was wider than the middle class, so the middle class was wider than Dissent. The political dissidence of Dissent went beyond that of its middle-class allies, and indeed in the

---

[1] *Anti-Bread Tax Circular*, 8 September 1842.
[2] McCord, *op. cit.*, pp. 26–7, 97.

1840's went to such extremes in its attack on the Church that it alienated many of them and helped to prevent the very thing it hoped to create, a separate middle-class political party. For four years, between 1843 and 1847, it looked as if a third force in the House of Commons might coagulate around the Dissenters, united as they had never been before, for now they had the Wesleyans and the Roman Catholics with them too.[1] The occasion was the victory of the non-Anglicans over Sir James Graham's Factory Education Bill of 1843, which marked the high-water mark of the Church's highly successful counter-attack. Having saved itself by internal reforms in the 1830's from the threat of reform from without, it now set out to reassert its rights as the Established Church of the whole nation, and especially its right to control all education provided by the State. The ensuing outcry, in the form of public meetings and massive petitions, not by unenfranchised Chartists but by solid citizens with votes, stopped the Bill in its tracks. Its defeat began the Victorian deadlock in educational policy: in Lord Ashley's words, 'The Dissenters and the Church have each laid down their limits which they will not pass, and there is no power that can either force, persuade or delude them.'[2]

But the Dissenters, swollen with triumph, tried to exploit their victory. Led by Edward Miall and Edward Baines they set out to create a middle-class Dissenting party, uniting the platforms of the League and the Anti-State Church Association:[3] free trade, Church disestablishment, complete suffrage, and 'voluntaryism' (no State aid) in education. In the 1847 general election they rejected both Conservatives and Whigs as belonging to the same aristocratic party—'so far as we are concerned, they are one'[4]—and managed to defeat not only a few aristocrats but some of their own best friends, such as Macaulay and Roebuck. The net result was a slight gain in Dissenting representation, at the cost of alienating not only the Whigs but the secular Radicals as well. As the 1847 edition of the *Black Book* put it, 'Why . . . should the pastors of any sect meddle with

[1] Cf. Gash, *Reaction and Reconstruction*, pp. 86–8, 100–6.
[2] C. S. Parker, *Life of Sir James Graham* (1907), I. 345.
[3] Formed in 1844 out of the Church Rates Abolition Society.
[4] *Eclectic Review*, 1847, XXII. 365: 'We have learned to walk alone and shall not contentedly sink again into bondage. Whig and Tory have hitherto been charmed words, but their spell is dissolved, their power is broken.'

politics, least of all the Dissenters, who are notoriously men of narrow minds and intolerant conclusions.'[1] Far from uniting the middle class, the resulting 'party'—twenty-six Dissenting M.P.s, sixty in all pledged to Church disestablishment[2]— divided it. Dissent, itself fragmented into endless sects, helped to fragment still further the middle-class political effort and foreshadowed the secular failure of Cobden and Bright, which left it no alternative but to exist as the divided left wing of the Liberal Party.

Yet even this was a contribution to the rise of a viable class society. Though there were also material reasons why the middle class should prefer to be represented in Parliament by upper-class politicians—notably the lack of leisure of the owner-managing capitalist at the crucial period of his career—the main legacy of Old Dissent to the Victorian middle class was the habit of voting Liberal. Thus Old Dissent carried over to the new class society an element of the 'interest' politics of the old society. And that element was to be one of the major factors in the political harmony of the viable class society.

The connection between Methodism and the working-class movements of the early nineteenth century could not by its nature be so direct as that between Old Dissent and middle class. Since the main body of Wesleyans, like Wesley himself, were staunch Tories at the opposite political pole from the working-class Radicals, historians have taken opposite views about what the connection was and how it worked. On the one side, Halévy saw in Methodism the 'key to the problem' of 'the extraordinary stability which English Society was destined to enjoy through a period of revolutions and crises', partly through its influence via Evangelicalism on social reform, but mainly by its mollifying influence on the working-class movement.[3] On the other, Eric Hobsbawm and Edward Thompson argue that the Tory Wesleyans were far too few to make a decisive difference, though after that point they diverge. While Hobsbawm believes that the seceding Methodist sects, the Kilhamites, the Primitive Methodists, the Bryanites or Bible Christians, and so on, were more Radical and provided political

---

[1] *Op. cit.*, p. vii.
[2] Cowherd, *op. cit.*, p. 163.
[3] Halévy, *op. cit.*, I. 387.

and industrial leadership, Thompson thinks it 'ridiculous to describe the participation of rebellious Methodist lay preachers and others in extreme Radical agitations as a "Methodist contribution" to the working-class movement.'[1]

In a paradoxical way, both sides are right. The key to the paradox is the dynamic migration made by so many working men in the early nineteenth century which we noticed in Chapter VI, from Wesleyanism (more often than not after leaving the Church of England) through one or more of the more Radical Methodist sects to secular Radicalism and spiritualism, religious indifference or militant atheism. Whether they remained Tory because they were Wesleyans, or Wesleyan because they were Tories, those who did not migrate *were*, as Halévy shows, a stabilizing influence, in that they provided an alternative, highly-charged, emotional pole towards which a much larger part of the working class than were Methodists at any one time might be diverted from political or industrial protest.

Whether those who migrated did so because they were Radicals or became Radicals as a result of migrating, the Methodists of the smaller seceding sects, as Hobsbawm shows, had an influence out of all proportion to their numbers on the leadership and organization of the political and industrial working-class movements, particularly in certain areas of the country. And whether we call it a Methodist contribution or not, the ex-Methodist political and industrial leaders, however militant or rebellious, made a contribution to political and social stability which was even more important than that of the Wesleyans. As Thompson shows, 'the Methodist political rebel carried through into his radical or revolutionary activity a profound moral earnestness, a sense of righteousness and of "calling", a "Methodist" capacity for sustained organizational dedication and (at its best) a high degree of personal responsibility.'[2] Trained in oratory, initiative and organization, lay preachers naturally gravitated to the leadership of any movement they joined. As leaders they saw and taught the value of clear aims, sound discipline and solid organization which, even

[1] E. J. Hobsbawm, 'Methodism and the Threat of Revolution in Britain', in *Labouring Men* (1964), pp. 23–33; E. P. Thompson, *The Making of the English Working Class* (1963), p. 394.

[2] *Ibid.*, p. 394.

when the aims were illegal and potentially violent, avoided the sporadic, unthinking, unorganized, riotous violence of the old society, and created an institutional framework for the non-violent forms of conflict, protest and demonstration characteristic of a viable class society. The institutionalization and non-violent expression of working-class discontent was a far more penetrating contribution to social peace than the pouring of a small amount of Wesleyan oil on the troubled waters of the class struggle.

Of the Toryism of the Wesleyans, from Wesley himself to Jabez Bunting, who dominated the Connexion during the critical years of class conflict, there can be no doubt. The annual Conference and the Committee of Privileges never ceased to denounce the Radical societies and their 'tumultous assemblies . . . calculated, both from the infidel principles, the wild and delusive political theories, and the violent and inflammatory declamations . . . to bring all government into contempt, and to introduce universal discontent, insubordination, and anarchy,' and to extrude brethren such as Thomas Cooper and J. R. Stephens if they took too active a share in Radical politics of the left or the right.[1] The only question is whether it was effective as an anti-revolutionary force. The statistical evidence is necessarily equivocal. On the one hand, the original Connexion always had more members than all the seceding congregations put together.[2] On the other, Methodists of all kinds were never more than a fraction of the working class—under one in four of church attenders in 1851, and on the most generous estimate not more than the same proportion of the working class[3]—and the Wesleyans, with at best one in eight of the working-class population, needed to reach large numbers to make their message of political quietism effective. The best evidence, however, comes from their opponents. It was not for nothing

---

[1] Methodist Committee of Privileges, 1819, T. P. Bunting, *Life of Jabez Bunting* (1887), p. 528; *Life of Thomas Cooper, written by Himself* (1873), pp. 100–1; G. J. Holyoake, *Life of J. R. Stephens* (1881), pp. 50–3.

[2] E.g. in 1851 the Wesleyans made 1,544,528 attendances, the other Methodist sects 1,182,579—Census of England and Wales, 1851, *Religious Worship*, pp. clxxxiif.

[3] In 1851 c. 1·8 million out of c. 7·9 million attenders (two-thirds of attendances); allowing, on Mann's estimate, p. cxxf., that only 58 per cent could attend at any one time, this represented at most c. 3 million Methodists (not all working-class) out of a total working-class population in England and Wales of c. 14 million.

that Cobbett and the Radicals singled out the Wesleyan ministers as the 'bitterest foes of freedom in England'.[1] They recognized in them their deadliest rivals for the hearts and minds not merely of the working class as a whole but for the relatively small élite of intelligent, talented, morally passionate men who were the natural leaders of the class.

Perhaps the most insidious way in which Wesleyanism, and indeed some of the seceding sects as they grew older and the fire went out of their bellies, undermined working-class Radicalism was by their worldly success in demonstrating the entrepreneurial ideal of the self-made man. Wesley himself had warned his followers in a famous passage:

> religion must necessarily produce both industry and frugality, and these cannot but produce riches. But as riches increase, so will pride, and anger, and love of the world . . . the Methodists in every place grow diligent and frugal; consequently they increase in goods. . . . So, although the form of religion remains, the spirit is swiftly vanishing away.[2]

This proved to be prophetic. By the 1850's a Wesleyan historian could claim that Methodism had raised many a rich man from squalid poverty: 'It was she that saved him from rags—put him on his feet—gave him a character, and placed him in the path of industry in which he has found both affluence and position.' He also admitted that 'we have not taken hold of the poorest—we have not reached the outcast and dregs of society.' 'What a host of noble lay members have proved that "godliness is profitable in all things",' a minister wrote in 1866, but added, 'Gold comes in at one door, and Grace is driven out at another.' By the last quarter of the century the *Methodist Times* no longer thought of Wesleyanism as a mainly working-class religion: 'It is evident at once that Methodism has been much too exclusively the sect of the lower middle class'; 'we make the pulpit and the pew too much a middle-class monopoly.' And a Wesleyan baronet could boast:

> The Methodist people are said to be a thrifty, saving, and sober people: we know that many of them are captains of industry in the great commercial life of the land. Some of them are millionaires.[3]

[1] *Political Register*, 3 January 1824.
[2] R. Southey, *Life of Wesley* (1925), II. 306.
[3] J. B. Dyson, *The History of Wesleyan Methodism in the Congleton Circuit* (1856),

How many potential revolutionaries had been diverted mean-while into the path of social ambition it is impossible to calculate.

Nevertheless, a great many potential Wesleyan ministers and captains of industry had been diverted into the paths of working-class agitation, as the Wesleyan leaders admitted by their constant denunciations, 'expostulations', and expulsions. A correspondent of Bunting's wrote from Newcastle in 1816 about two local preachers who had attended a Radical mass meeting at North Shields:

> I hope no considerable portion of our brethren is found among the Radicals; but a small number of our leaders are among the most determined friends to their spirit and design . . . and some of the really pious, misguided sisterhood have helped to make the colours.[1]

His hope was forlorn. Large numbers of Wesleyans—or rather, since few of them waited for 'expostulation' or expulsion, ex-Wesleyans—like Samuel Bamford, William Lovett, and Joseph Barker, threw themselves into the working-class movement, appearing there mainly as members of the seceding sects, or simply as secular Radicals.[2]

The Methodists and ex-Methodists from whatever Connexion brought great powers of charismatic leadership to the working-class political societies and trade unions. Joseph Capper, the Primitive Methodist Chartist leader of the Potteries, had 'a tongue like the sledge-hammer he used in his shop.' Tommy Hepburn, the Primitive Methodist leader of the Durham miners, 'could be heard at one time by forty thousand people, and always carried the multitude with him.' One coal-owner told a Royal Commission that 'the men professing to be Methodists and Ranters (Primitive Methodists) are the spokesmen on these occasions, and the most difficult to deal with. These men may be superior men to the rest in intelligence, and generally show great skill, and cunning, and circumvention.' H. S. Tremenheere, the inspector of mines, wrote of prayer meetings of striking colliers in 1844, where local preachers,

---

[1] Bunting, *op. cit.*, p. 527.

[2] Cf. R. F. Wearmouth, *Methodism and the Working-Class Movements of England, 1800–50* (1937), pp. 114–15, 213–15.

---

p. 178; 'A Wesleyan Minister', *Temporal Prosperity and Spiritual Decline* (1886), pp. 16, 18; *Methodist Times*, 19 August 1886, 4 February 1897; Sir Robert Perks, in *Methodist Recorder*, 3 February 1898; Inglis, *op. cit.*, pp. 9, 86.

'by a certain command of language and energetic tone and manner, had acquired an influence over their fellow workmen and were invariably the chief promoters and abettors of the strikes.'[1]

Undoubtedly their greatest contribution was their experience and 'skill in organization. Lovett, the indefatigable and self-effacing secretary of so many Radical and Owenite bodies, without whom there would have been no Charter and perhaps no Chartism, is a special case, but it is no accident that practically every working-class political body from the Regency Reform societies to the Chartists was organized on the Methodist model. Of course, one did not have to be a Methodist to see the advantages of the Methodist model. Major Cartwright and Horne Tooke deliberately imitated it in their Hampden Clubs, while T. J. Wooler of the *Black Dwarf* declared in 1818:

> It is by union alone great things can be accomplished; and it is want of co-operative union, that renders reformers inefficient. What enabled the Methodists and Dissenters to dictate toleration to the State and the Church united against them? Nothing but that union, which originated in their class meetings, and daily and weekly associations.

Orator Hunt, from prison in 1821, modelled his National Political Union on the same plan.[2]

It is one thing, however, to recommend from on high a model of organization, quite another to make it work at the local level amongst a mass of discontented workers bewildered by the onslaught of early industrialism, slumps and unemployment, and used to protesting only in the blind, brutal, undisciplined form of riot and violence. What was needed was a cadre of local leaders with experience of persuading and dominating their fellows and a stern sense of the need for organization and discipline, and this is exactly what the Methodists provided.

The essentials of Methodist organization were simple enough: the weekly 'class' of up to twenty members meeting for discussion and mutual instruction, and generally paying a subscription of a penny a week, under a leader who also acted as their delegate to a local district meeting, which in turn sent

[1] *Ibid.*, pp. 213, 227–34.

[2] *Black Dwarf*, 26 January 1818, 10 October 1821; Wearmouth, *op. cit.*, pp. 105, 108.

delegates to a larger district, and so on up to the national Conference. This was the plan adopted by the significantly named Political Protestants of Hull in 1818, which rapidly spread to the rest of the working-class Reform movement. At a delegate meeting at Hunslet, Leeds, in June 1819, twenty-seven towns in the North of England were represented. And the National Conventions which met in London in these years were part of the same general plan. One other feature of the Radical movement was almost certainly derived from Methodism: the great open-air mass meetings which so alarmed the Government from 1815 onwards were a conscious imitation of the huge 'camp meetings' inaugurated by Wesley and revived by practically every new seceding sect, most recently by the Primitive Methodists in 1807 and the Bryanites in 1815 itself.[1]

The class system died out with the Radical societies in the early 1820's, but was revived again in the working-class political unions of 1831–35. The Owenite 'National Union of the Working Classes and Others', Lovett, its secretary, wrote, was organized

> on the plan of the Methodist Connexion. Class-leaders were appointed at public meetings in the proportion of one for about every thirty or forty members; the class leaders mostly meeting with their classes weekly at their own houses, [where] political subjects were discussed, and articles from newspapers and portions of standard political works read and commented on.[2]

The same model was naturally followed by the Chartists. At a delegate meeting in Rochdale in June 1839 it was decided that 'the system of classes . . . should be adopted by the Chartists in every district. Several of the delegates stated that this system had already been acted on by the political unions of their own town.' Camp meetings were held every summer from 1839 to 1850. Unfortunately, there was some doubt about the legality of the delegate system, under the Corresponding Societies Act of 1797, and for a time, 1841–43, it was suspended. Finally, in 1848 it was abandoned when the Attorney-General declared it illegal, but by then Chartism was almost spent as a political force, and the model had served its turn.[3]

[1] *Ibid.* pp. 88–94, 138–44.
[2] W. Lovett, *Life and Struggles*, p. 68.
[3] Wearmouth, *op. cit.*, pp. 142–63.

There is less direct evidence of the Methodist model in the trade union field, where the local units were generally small and obvious enough not to require an artificial class organization, though the delegate system for district, regional and national meetings, as in the various levels of the National Union of Cotton Spinners of Great Britain and Ireland culminating in their Isle of Man conference in 1829, and the prominence of Methodist trade union leaders in certain areas, as in the Potteries, the Lancashire and Yorkshire textile unions, the Cornish tin and copper mines, and even in agriculture with the celebrated, and Methodist, Tolpuddle 'martyrs', argues a parallel. The most famous example is that of the north-eastern coalfield. When in 1832 the Marquess of Londonderry turned over 1,000 miners out of their tied cottages for striking, it is said that half the lay preachers of the local Primitive Methodist circuits were homeless, including the miners' leader, Tommy Hepburn. Five out of the seven 'Jarrow lads' transported for their part in the 1831 strike, and nine of the 'Twelve Apostles' sent round the country in 1844 to win converts for the Miners' Association of Great Britain were Primitive Methodist lay preachers.[1]

Methodists were not always non-violent. Jeremiah Brandreth, 'the Nottingham Captain' executed for his part in the 'Pentrich Revolution' of 1817, was a Methodist. And that more typical Methodist leaders were not above threatening violence no one who has read the speeches of J. R. Stephens can doubt.[2] But, wiser in their generation than working men without their experience and training, they knew the difference between calculated threat and the actual use of force. Above all, they knew that neither was effective without disciplined organization, and that disciplined organization was most effective when it stopped short of violence. A mass meeting or a strike was more likely to gain their ends—manhood suffrage or the restoration of a wages cut —than a riot or an insurrection. When it came to push of pike their influence was almost always on the side of negotiation rather than open warfare. Even J. R. Stephens habitually followed his fiery imperatives with capacious escape clauses, which enabled him to deny in court that he fomented revolution

[1] *Ibid.*, pp. 228–31, 243–4, 251–2, 265–8.
[2] R. J. White, *Waterloo to Peterloo* (1957), chap. xiv, 'The Pentrich Revolution'; Holyoake, *Stephens, passim.*

or even that he was a Chartist: 'down with the throne, and down with the altar itself—burn the church—down with all rank, all dignity, all title, all power; *unless that dignity, authority, and power will and do secure to the honest industrious efforts of the upright and poor man a comfortable maintenance in exchange for his labour.*'[1] More typically, Tommy Hepburn the Durham miners' leader, who brought the Marquess of Londonderry to negotiate, and led off with public prayers in which the Marquess joined, still advised patience even when Londonderry broke faith, locked out the strikers, and turned them out of their homes.[2] And William Lovett, Thomas Cooper and Henry Vincent went on preaching moral-force Chartism long after the main movement had fallen into the hands of the physical-force O'Connorites.[3]

The last example is perhaps symbolic both of the influence of Methodism and of its limitations. Having helped to bring the working-class movement to birth and lead it in the direction of non-violent political and industrial action, the point was reached when the child was big enough to stand on its own feet, and the midwife, nursemaid and teacher could be dispensed with. What it left behind was the training and the organization, the instinct and the framework for non-violent conflict through negotiation and discussion, which, paradoxically, the English working class were to teach to their employers and rulers.[4]

One other sect, if we may call it that, played a part in the institutionalization of all three major classes. We have already noticed the role of the Church of England in awakening the defensive class-consciousness of the landed ruling class in the period of birth.[5] The revival of the Church in the twenty years after the Reform Act, its salvation by internal reforms and skilful politics from the threat of disestablishment and spoliation, the new-found self-respect and missionary responsibility evoked by the Oxford Movement and the Evangelicals alike, and the remarkable if unsuccessful attempt to re-establish itself as the Church of the whole nation, at least in the educational field,[6]

---

[1] *London Democrat*, 8 June 1839; Cole, *Chartist Portraits*, p. 73 (my italics).
[2] Wearmouth, *op. cit.*, pp. 228–9.
[3] See above, chap. viii, § 2.
[4] See below, § 3.
[5] See above, chap. vi, § 3.
[6] Cf. Gash, *Reaction and Reconstruction*, pp. 77–9, 86–8, 107–10.

had an effect on the evolution of all three major classes. Its effect in provoking Dissent to overreach itself and split the middle class we have sufficiently seen. Its effect on the aristocracy was foreshadowed as early as 1834 by Pusey, the Tractarian leader: 'a strong expression of love for the Church has been called forth by the violence of her enemies.'[1] Though he was thinking mainly of the clergy, this became by degrees equally true of the whole landed class. The turning point was the defeat of the Church Rates Bill in 1837, killed not by 'Episcopal fury' in the House of Lords but by the Anglican sympathies of the Whig gentry in the House of Commons.[2] The furious onslaught of the disestablishment movement in the next ten years effectively consolidated the tacit alliance of both aristocratic parties in defence of the Church.

Yet no more than Old Dissent with the middle class or Methodism with the working class was the Church to be simply equated with the landed class. Both halves of the equation were too diverse for that. The Church in particular was rent in these years by movements of the clergy which served mainly to exasperate the laity and alienate their sympathies. Most notoriously, the Oxford Movement was, from a social point of view, an attempt to professionalize the clergy, to emphasize its sacerdotal independence from lay interference of any kind, and to emancipate it from dependence on lay patronage and State control. The Evangelical movement in its different way was equally concerned to professionalize the clergy, to emphasize its moral superiority to the lay world of the flesh, and its responsibilities to other classes than that of its patrons. Both movements, in reviving the Church's claims to speak to and for the whole nation, and in carrying their missions into the slums of the great towns, went beyond her traditional role as the conscience of the rich, and made her for the first time since the Reformation, to a limited extent at least, an independent force of moral and social reform.

It was this partial emancipation from dependence on the ruling class which enabled the Church, or some of its members, to have a somewhat surprising effect on the evolution of the working class. Only because they claimed for the Church an

---

[1] Pusey to Jelf, 16 February 1834, H. P. Liddon, *Life of E. B. Pussey*, I. 285–6.
[2] *West.Rev.*, 1837, XXVII. 126; Gash, *Reaction and Reconstruction*, pp. 72–3.

equal mission to 'the rich and poor, one in Christ'[1] could the factory reformers and the Christian Socialists use it to try and cement the alliance between aristocracy and working class against the capitalist middle class. Though they failed to get the whole-hearted support of the aristocracy they succeeded in winning the confidence of some working men, and so helped to reconcile the working class to the political system.

Factory reform was at least as closely, if informally, associated with the Church as the anti-corn law agitation with Dissent. Its leaders, M.T. Sadler, Richard Oastler, Parson Bull and Lord Ashley—only the last an aristocrat—were Evangelicals consciously doing the Lord's work against the hosts of Satan and industrialism. In the later stages many of the Short Time Committees were presided over by the local vicars, and all of them supported by an active minority amongst the clergy.[2] The Ten Hours Act of 1847 was at least as much a riposte by the Church for the Dissenters' part in the repeal of the Corn Laws as one by the landlords to the manufacturers. And the 1847 Act, as amended in 1851, which settled the question for a generation, did more to allay working-class discontent than any other concession by the ruling class.

Although from the other wing of the Church, Christian Socialism, which took up the task in 1848 where factory reform left off, was the spiritual heir to Sadler and the aristocratic ideal. A union of 'the Church, the gentlemen and the workmen, against the shopkeepers and the Manchester School', it looked to those 'who stand rather upon birth and inheritance than upon the goods or the position which they have purchased by their exertions' to provide moral guidance and leadership to 'the masses'.[3] It drew on a continuous stream of sympathy within the Church for Owenite co-operation which had been kept alive since 1817 by J. M. Ludlow's friend John Minter Morgan, whose scheme of 1846 for self-supporting villages under the superintendence of the Church was blessed by the Bishop of Norwich and the Vice-Chancellor of Oxford.[4] No doubt from

---

[1] Inglis, *op. cit.*, p. 21.   [2] Cf. J. F. C. Harrison, *op. cit.*, p. 160.

[3] Charles Kingsley, quoted by T. Hughes, prefatory Memoir to *Alton Locke* (1881 ed.) I. 52, and F. D. Maurice, *On the Reformation of Society* (Southampton, 1851), pp. 52–3; J. Saville, 'The Christian Socialists of 1848', Saville, ed., *Democracy and the Labour Movement*, p. 140.

[4] W. H. G. Armytage, *Heavens Below* (1961), pp. 209–23.

Marx and Engels' point of view 'Christian Socialism is but the holy water with which the priest consecrates the heartburnings of the aristocrat'[1]—a rare admission that aristocrats had a social conscience. No doubt, too, co-operative production was a failure, and part of that transformation of co-operation from a genuine alternative to capitalism into a mere palliative which we shall notice below.[2] Nevertheless, the Christian Socialists, good professional men all, won the confidence of organized labour, and continued to act as mediators between the classes, and especially between the Government and the working-class movement. They helped to transform the State's attitude towards working-class institutions from one of hostility to one of cautious benevolence; they had a hand in the legalization of co-operative enterprise by the Industrial and Provident Societies Acts of 1852–1862, in the protection of friendly society and trade union funds in 1855, in the legalization of peaceful picketing in 1859, and, through Thomas Hughes, in the favourable report on the unions by the Royal Commission of 1867, and their legalization in 1871.[3]

Though the working class were not won back in large numbers to the Church, many of them at least ceased to regard it with hostility. Dean Hook, the link between the Yorkshire factory reformers and the Christian Socialists, wrote to Maurice in 1860:

> The great good done by yourself and Co., is this, that the working classes have learned to consider Christians and Churchmen, what they are, their friends. I lived for thirty-three years among them in Birmingham, Coventry and Leeds. Three and thirty years ago we were regarded with hatred. It is very different now—at least in Yorkshire. The step our generation has made is this. The working classes respect Christianity though they stand aloof and only a few of them come to Church, but they readily hand over to us the next generation for education.[4]

To this extent even the Church contributed to the rise of a viable class society.

[1] *Communist Manifesto* (1848).
[2] See below, § 3.
[3] Cf. P. N. Backstrom, jr., 'The Practical Side of Christian Socialism in Victorian England', *Victorian Studies*, 1963, VI. 305f.
[4] J. F. C. Harrison, *op. cit.*, p. 161.

2. THE INSTITUTIONALIZATION OF
THE MIDDLE CLASS

The key to the rise of a viable class society was the institution-alization of the middle class and, as we anticipated in Chapter VIII, the imposition of its ideal upon the other classes. Yet the evolution of middle-class institutions is full of paradoxes. The first and most striking is the failure of the middle class to create its own separate, permanent, potentially governing, parlia-mentary party, and the consequent concentration on individual, short-term, practicable reforms—Parliamentary Reform, repeal of the Corn Laws, abolition of the 'taxes on knowledge', and the like—which made the typical middle-class political institution an ephemeral pressure group, like the National Political Union or the Anti-Corn Law League, whose success entailed its own demise. Secondly, because it was outside the pale of the consti-tution, even the 'respectable' middle class was at first forced to use violence, or at least the threat of violence, to gain admission. Thirdly, because they were too weak either in voting strength or in sheer weight of numbers to impose their will, middle-class pressure groups were forced to broaden their appeal to embrace the working class and to compromise with the ruling aristocracy. This gave them a spurious appearance of being 'universal' or 'non-class' bodies which does not stand up to analysis of their aims and ideology. Finally, their failure to create their own political party did not prevent them from capturing the policies of the existing parties. In the last analysis the institutionalization of the middle class was the institution-alization within the traditional framework of politics, and especially in the Liberal Party, of their ideal.

The failure to create a new middle-class party was not from lack of trying. The Political Unions of 1830, the Radicals in the Reformed Parliament, the Anti-Corn Law League and its various successor organizations in the Financial and Parliamentary Reform movement of 1849–52, all attempted to form such a party, without success. Although 100 to 120 Radical M.P.s were elected in 1832 and 150 in 1837, they had evolved by 1841 into 50 Radicals and 100 Liberals. The strictly separatist, independent Radicals were always fewer: Mrs. Grote in 1836 put them at 20 or so; the Conservative Party agent, F. R.

Bonham, in 1840 at no more than eight.[1] The Anti-Corn Law League, in spite of pioneering modern electioneering methods and creating thousands of forty-shilling freehold votes, fared no better. When Repeal was going through Parliament in 1846 Cobden admitted:

> I don't think there are 100 men in the House, & certainly not 40 in the Lords, who *in their hearts* desire the total repeal of the Corn laws.[2]

And Cobden and Hume's financial and parliamentary reform party of 1849 numbered no more than 50 or 60.[3]

The constitutional reasons for this failure we have already seen: the survival of influence, the small size of the electorate, the built-in majority for the counties and the small boroughs in the distribution of seats, and, above all, the lack of unearned wealth and leisure, as well as the right kind of education and experience, which brought most middle-class politicians later into Parliament and, when there, effectively kept them out of office.[4] But in spite of all these defects in the 1832 constitution, the middle class could have created their own party if they had been singled-minded enough to vote for it. The fact is that most middle-class electors positively preferred to be represented by their betters. For one thing, deference was an undoubted fact in British political life, as de Tocqueville, Carlyle, Gladstone and many other astute observers noted long before Bagehot. More important, however, was the political skill or pragmatic realism with which aristocratic statesmen like Peel and Gladstone responded not so much to the crude electoral pressures of the middle-class voters as to the moral and rational demands of their ideal. In this way they not only stole the thunder of one middle-class movement after another, but, by an extraordinary *tour de force*, became more representative of the middle-class ideal than the middle-class politicians themselves, and ultimately saved the middle class from the need to create their own political party.

Thwarted in parliamentary politics, middle-class reformers

---

[1] Gash, *Reaction and Reconstruction*, pp. 167–8. 204–5.
[2] McCord, *op. cit.*, p. 203.
[3] Gash, *Reaction and Reconstruction*, p. 195.
[4] See above, chap. viii, § 3.

were driven to create extra-parliamentary pressure groups and to adopt the politics of persuasion. They found at first that argument was not very persuasive unless backed up by threats. Their self-appointed spokesman, James Mill, told them as early as 1820 that 'where the people have not the power legally and peaceably of removing their governors they can only obtain any considerable ameliorations of their governments by resistance, by applying physical force to their rulers, or at least by threats so likely to be followed by performance, as may frighten their rulers into compliance.'[1] The Reform campaign of 1830–32 was the classic exemplification of this text. It was brilliantly stage-managed by Francis Place and Joseph Parkes, who sedulously fed the Whig Government through Hobhouse and Young, Melbourne's private secretary, with reports of the explosive temper of 'the people' and the press with inflated news from the provinces, and intervened at each moment of acute crisis to frighten the vacillating Whigs and intimidate the reactionary Tories with open threats of revolution.[2] Wellington's resignation in 1830 was precipitated by the threat of violence. 'This is the first time, observe,' Place wrote to Hobhouse about the cancellation of the King's visit to the City which occasioned it, 'that the apprehension of violence by the people against an administration has induced them openly to change their plan of proceeding.' The Lords' rejection of the Reform Bill was greeted by placards proclaiming 'PEERS OR REVOLUTION', by riots, mass meetings and processions, and Place's deputation told Lord Grey that any compromise would mean that 'this country will inevitably be plunged into all the horrors of a violent revolution.' Wellington's attempt to form a Government provoked a plan by Place and Parkes for simultaneous risings in all the major cities, which was only averted by the success of Place's prior campaign to 'go for gold'.[3]

There was, of course, a large element of bluff in all this. Roebuck later recalled a speech, probably by Place, in preparation for the deputation to Lord Grey:

We must frighten them. . . . No reality we can create will be sufficient

[1] James Mill, 'Liberty of the Press', *loc. cit.*, p. 18.
[2] Cf. J. Hamburger, *James Mill and the Art of Revolution* (1963), *passim*.
[3] Wallas, *Place*, pp. 249, 276, 278, 298–301, 310–13.

for our purpose. We must work on Lord Grey's imagination. We must pretend to be frightened ourselves.[1]

But there were real riots in scores of places, some of them, like the burning of Nottingham Castle and the sacking of the Bishop's palace at Bristol, serious, and if these were the work of working-class mobs, the middle-class Reformers believed that only the discipline of organized agitation had forestalled general anarchy:

> Nothing but the establishment of *Political Unions* has prevented us from becoming the victims of the dreadful catastrophe to which the state of things was hurrying us. . . . They have acted as safety valves to prevent a dreadful explosion.[2]

Place wrote privately at the end of the crisis:

> We were within a moment of general rebellion, and had it been possible for the Duke of Wellington to have formed an administration, the King and the people would have been at issue.

Parkes boasted to Mrs. Grote:

> I and two friends should have made the revolution, whatever the cost. . . . I *think* we could have prevented anarchy and set all right in two days.[3]

Nevertheless, the role of violence in the Reform crisis was not quite what it seemed. The Government was not intimidated. The aristocracy, whatever else it was deficient in, did not lack courage. Grey told Place and his deputation emphatically that any disturbances would be put down by military force, and if this was also partly bluff from a Government possessing only 11,000 regular troops there is no doubt that the aristocracy would have fought to the death against the manhood suffrage of the working-class Reformers.[4] As it was, they did not hesitate to use force against the rioting farm labourers and striking midlands colliers and ironworkers, and 'scraped together every disposable *Sword and Bayonet* within 50 miles of London' to overawe the National Union of the Working Classes.[5] The threat of violence worked, not because the aristocracy feared a revolution more than Reform, but because they thought the

---

[1] [J. A. Roebuck], 'Some Chapters in the Life of an Old Politician', *Bentley's Miscellany*, 1848, XXIII. 523.
[2] *Political Union Register*, 1832, I. 3; Hamburger, *op. cit.*, p. 66.
[3] Wallas, *Place*, pp. 302, 321.   [4] *Ibid.*, pp. 278, 294.
[5] Hamburger, *op. cit.*, pp. 184–7, 241.

mild concession represented by the Reform Bill a small price to pay to quieten popular discontent, to transfer the middle class from opposition to support of the political system, and, in Durham's phrase, to 'attach numbers to property and good order.'[1] Even Wellington and the Tories were willing in the last analysis to pay it; most Whigs saw political advantage in it, and if some of them did not abet, they at least welcomed, Place's reports as ammunition against timid brethren and recalcitrant opponents.

The threat of violence was thus an inevitable stage in the institutionalization of the middle class, at once the necessary consequence of their exclusion from the political system and the prerequisite of their admission. Once admitted within the pale of the constitution, they could henceforth rely, if not on what Place called their 'moral power to control the Government,'[2] then on the politics of peaceful persuasion. They were never again forced to use the same naked threat. The Anti-Corn Law League toyed with various illegal or extra-legal actions—a tax strike or a factory lock-out to halt the Government or the economy—but even over these the moderation of the 'respectables' on the Council prevailed.[3] Cobden welcomed Sturge's alliance with the Chartists as 'something in our *rear* to frighten the Aristocracy',[4] but violence had no part in the Complete Suffrage movement. Bright was in the 1860's to make much the same ambivalent use of the threat of violence to obtain the Second Reform Act as Place did to obtain the First, but by then the middle class was on the conceding not the compelling side.[5] For them violence had long done its work and brought about its own demise.

Both before and after the Reform Act middle-class movements were led to broaden their appeal to embrace the working class. This was only partly because they lacked the numbers to overawe or the M.P.s to outvote the aristocracy. They did so on principle and out of policy. Attwood and the Parliamentary Reformers set out 'to form a GENERAL POLITICAL UNION between the Lower and Middle Classes of the People.'[6] Chartism began as

[1] Hansard, 1829, III. 1029.   [2] Wallas, *Place*, p. 322.
[3] McCord, *op. cit.*, pp. 111, 122–4, 128–31.
[4] Briggs, *Chartist Studies*, p. 365.   [5] See below, § 3.
[6] A. Briggs, 'Middle-Class Consciousness in English Politics, 1780–1846', *Past and Present*, 1956, IX. 65.

an attempt by Place and the Parliamentary Radicals to strengthen their following out of doors.[1] The Anti-Corn Law League assiduously wooed the working class with Radical speeches and verses, special working-class lectures, and Operative Anti-Corn Law Associations, as well as by the attempt to ally with the Chartists in the Complete Suffrage movement.[2] It might be argued from such evidence that they were therefore not simply middle-class but joint middle- and working-class institutions, but this would be to mistake the nature of class politics. Every class political movement, if it wishes to succeed in a multi-class society, must persuade as large a fraction of the society as possible to accept its views. The middle-class Parliamentary Reformers made no concession whatever to the demands of their working-class allies. Universal manhood suffrage they eschewed, or consigned to a distant future, as a threat to property and capital. Place used all his immense political skill and cunning to isolate the Rotunda Radicals and deprive them of influence in the National Political Union. He had a bad conscience about it, and salved it by refusing to regard the Bill as a final measure:

> The working people would see in the proceeding the old desire to use them for a purpose and then to abandon them.[3]

But he more than anyone else helped the middle-class Radicals to use them to obtain the Reform Bill and then to abandon them.

To Place's credit, he did not abandon them himself. He it was who, after the failure of Owenite alternatives to capitalism—the labour exchange scheme and the general syndicalist strike—brought together the Parliamentary Radicals and the London Working-Men's Association and wrote, or helped Lovett to write, the People's Charter.[4] Attwood too tried to revive the old Birmingham alliance on the basis of the Charter. But class ideals are more powerful than personalities. Attwood and the

[1] Wallas, *Place*, pp. 359–69.

[2] Lucy Brown, 'The Chartists and the Anti-Corn Law League', in Briggs, ed., *Chartist Studies*, esp. pp. 344, 355–6, 363–6.

[3] Wallas, *Place*, pp. 281–5, 288.

[4] *Ibid.*, p. 367; contrast Lovett, *op. cit.*, pp. 164–5; for a modern discussion of the authorship of the Charter, which concludes in favour of Place's claim, see D. J. Rowe, 'The London Working Men's Association and the "People's Charter"', *Past and Present*, 1967, No. 36, pp. 73f.

other middle-class Chartists could not carry the middle class generally behind a programme of manhood suffrage backed by threats of violence, the working-class Radicals refused to be gulled again by a mixed programme of currency and other reforms designed, they feared, to kill manhood suffrage by compromise, and within the first twelve months most of the Attwoodites resigned and Chartism, in spite of its middle-class demagogues, became an overwhelmingly working-class movement. Joseph Sturge's attempt to unite the two classes behind the Complete Suffrage movement in 1841–42 rapidly met the same fate: the middle-class members would not have the name 'Charter', and the working-class would not have them without it.[1] As for the Anti-Corn Law League itself, as Cobden wrote at about the same time,

> I don't deny that the working classes generally have attended our lectures and signed our petitions; but I will admit, that so far as the fervour and efficiency of our agitation has gone, it has eminently been a middle-class agitation. . . .
>
> Now, our business is, first to show the working men that the question of wages is a question depending altogether on principles apart from party politics . . . that if we had the Charter tomorrow the principles which govern the relations between masters and men would be precisely the same as they are now. . . .[2]

In other words, middle-class institutions would accept working-class support only on their own terms, and without abandoning any part of their ideal.

On the other side, the middle-class reformers were equally led by the politics of persuasion to woo the ruling class. The extra-parliamentary pressure group was in itself a mark of the transitional character of class institutions at this period. As we saw under the role of religion, above, there is a continuity of evolution from the interest group of the old society to the class movement of the new. Leaving Dissent aside, a clear line of development runs from the campaign against the Orders in Council in 1812 to the Anti-Corn Law agitation. If the first was an old society interest group lobbying an aristocratic government for relief but concealing an element of class antagonism, the second was a class movement demanding justice from an

[1] M. Hovell, *The Chartist Movement* (Manchester, 1959), pp. 242–50, 264–5.
[2] *Anti-Bread Tax Circular*, 8 September 1842.

aristocratic parliament but forced by the lack of political power to adopt the tactics of an interest group.

The difference lies in which strand was uppermost, the old warp of interest or the new weft of class. The critical test is their ideal of society and how it should be governed. While the first accepted the old hierarchical society and the aristocracy's right to rule it, merely asking that it should rule equitably as between the various interests, the second rejected that right and tried, by means such as the creation of forty-shilling freehold votes, to end it. If the League was forced to pursue interest politics, it did so with a significant inversion. It was the landed class in its view which was the interest—in class terms the 'selfish' or 'sinister' interest—maintaining a privileged monopoly at the expense of the rest of the community, while the League stood for a class, and one which had the same interests as all the producers and consumers, and therefore of the whole community. As Cobden was to put it some years later, the middle class 'have no interest opposed to the general good, whilst, on the contrary, the feudal governing class exists only by a violation of sound principles of political economy.'[1] This was a complete inversion of old society interest politics, in which the aristocracy was the master interest at the head of all the other interests, the representative and custodian of the overriding national interest. The League's strategy was to isolate it and narrow it down to a mere agricultural interest, and one shorn if possible even of the support of the farmers and farm labourers. It is a curious irony that if the premise had been true the strategy would not have worked. The corn laws were repealed only because Peel and the aristocracy rose above their agricultural interest and acted, in traditional style, as custodians of the national interest.

It was clearly more than that, however. To see the national interest as requiring their own loss of privilege and income went far beyond the demands of old society interest politics. It is true that Peel and many other landlords had made their calculations, and discovered that, with improved methods of high farming, free trade need not be disastrous, but no calculation could make it free of risk or costs.[2] It is also true that many

---

[1] J. Morley, *Life of Cobden*, (1903), p. 860.

[2] Cf. D. C. Moore, 'The Corn Laws and High Farming', and S. Fairlie, 'The

of the larger as distinct from the smaller landowners drew a considerable part of their incomes from non-agricultural sources. But in practically no case did the industrial and commercial part outweigh the agricultural.[1] Repeal was thus tantamount to accepting the middle-class view of the national interest, which placed the needs of consumers and the prosperity of producers before the unearned incomes of the landlords, or at any rate saw the last as secondary to and dependent upon the other two. Whether we call this a 'victory of the middle class' or 'a concession by the aristocracy', a 'timely retreat' to insure the continuation of aristocratic rule,[2] scarcely matters. The important question is, aristocratic rule upon whose terms?

This question helps to resolve the final paradox of the political institutionalization of the middle class, the fact that it survived and indeed thrived upon the successive extinction of most of the specifically middle-class institutions. Victory in each ephemeral campaign, for Parliamentary Reform, the abolition of Church rates, the repeal of the corn laws, the abrogation of 'taxes on knowledge', and so on, promptly led to the disbandment of the army, and a new one had to be recruited when the next campaign was launched. Even failure, as in the case of the Complete Suffrage movement, or only partial success, as with the Financial Reform Associations of 1849–52, seems to have had much the same effect, since pressure groups of this kind were designed for *blitzkrieger*, win, lose or draw. Meanwhile, the troops defected in large numbers, since each victory satiated and each failure or stalemate wearied a fraction of the middle-class dissidents, who henceforth found a political home in one of the traditional parties, and refused to be recruited for the next campaign. Cobden and Bright, for example, were never again able to recruit more than a fraction of the League's men and resources for their later campaigns for public education, financial and parliamentary reform, and 'free trade in land'. The reason

[1] Cf. F. M. L. Thompson, *op. cit.*, pp. 266–7; D. Spring, 'Earl Fitzwilliam and the Corn Laws', *J.Mod.H.*, 1954, LIX. 287.

[2] G. Kitson Clark, 'The Repeal of the Corn Laws and the Politics of the Forties', *Ec.H.R.*, 1951, IV. 12.

19th-Century Corn Law Reconsidered', *Ec.H.R.*, 1965, XVIII. 544f., and 562f.; but see below, chap. x, § 1, for the comparative decline of agricultural real rentals in the period of high farming.

for this they found, like Bagehot, in deference: 'We are a servile, aristocracy-loving, lord-ridden people, who regard the land with as much reverence as we still do the peerage and baronet-age.'[1]

It is true that the 1850's and 1860's saw a revival of the language of deference and of the pejorative use of 'class', as in 'class prejudices' and 'class legislation', and the sub-divisions within classes and the many rungs on the social ladder were given a new emphasis. Yet, as Asa Briggs points out, this revival was superficial, and it is important to get below the surface to the reality it concealed.[2] What Bagehot was trying to explain at bottom was why the electorate remained predomin-antly middle-class, and why that electorate continued to choose a predominantly aristocratic Parliament and Cabinet. In 'def-erential nations', Bagehot suggested, the numerical majority 'abdicates in favour of its élite, and consents to obey whoever that élite may confide in,' and this educated minority prefers to choose its legislators from 'the highest classes'. But he was in no doubt about where political power resided: 'The middle classes—the ordinary majority of educated men—are in the present day the despotic power in England.'[3]

Similarly, the pejorative use of class—the historian of the Anti-Corn Law League on 'a cruel subjection to class interests', Carlyle on 'class legislation', Gladstone on 'the narrow and oblique purposes of class . . . pursued by Parliaments in the choice of which the upper orders had it all their own way'[4]— was directed against the *landed* class, not against the class which *now* dominated legislation. And the emphasis on the many-runged social ladder sprang from the concern with social mobility which was nearer the heart of the middle-class than of the aristocratic ideal, and was the salvation and justification of the new class society: for the aristocratic ideal it was a prop and support, for the middle class the main pillar of the house. Social climbing, according to Cobden, was the ultimate reason why the men who had fought aristocratic privilege would not

[1] Morley, *Cobden*, p. 518.

[2] Cf. Briggs, 'Language of Class', *loc. cit.*, pp. 69–73.

[3] W. Bagehot, *The English Constitution* (World's Classics, 1958), p. 235.

[4] A. Prentice, *History of the Anti-Corn Law League* (1853), II. 444; Carlyle, *Past and Present* (1898 ed.), p. 27; W. E. Gladstone, 'Last Words on the Franchise', *The 19th Century*, 1878, quoted by A. Arnold, *Free Land* (1880), pp. 183–4.

attack aristocracy itself, in the shape of the system of land tenure:

> Public opinion is either indifferent or favourable to the system of large properties kept together by entail. If you want a proof, see how every successful trader buys an estate, and tries to perpetuate his name in connexion with 'that ilk' by creating an eldest son.[1]

Nor was this tenderness towards the aristocracy as distinct from their privileges a product of mid-Victorian 'prosperity'. Alexis de Tocqueville discovered it, somewhat to his surprise, as early as 1833:

> So, too, if you speak to a member of the middle classes; you will find that he hates some aristocrats but not the aristocracy. On the contrary, he is himself full of aristocratic prejudices. . . .

> It is not rare to hear an Englishman complain of the extension of aristocratic privileges and to speak with bitterness of those who exploit them; but come to tell him the one way to destroy the aristocracy, which is to change the law of inheritance, and he will draw back at once. . . . Thus it is true that there is hatred of aristocrats, but public opinion is far from envisaging the destruction of the aristocracy.[2]

The main prerequisite of viable class relations, the belief that class conflict is not a war to the death but a limited contest for power and income between opponents who recognize each other's right to exist, was accepted by the English middle class as far as the aristocracy was concerned—though not, as we shall see, by the organized working class—the moment the Reform Bill was passed.

At the same time, too, began that drift of the middle class into support of the existing political parties which frustrated Cobden and Bright and rejoiced Bagehot. J. S. Mill and Roebuck told de Tocqueville in 1835:

> all the upper class and a large part of the middle class, as you said just now, has [sic] already gone over to the Tories: one section of the middle class, which is nearest to the people, is daily going over.[3]

More objective evidence, such as it is for this period, shows, as one would expect, that urban middle-class electors divided their

[1] Morley, *Cobden*, p. 561.   [2] Tocqueville, *op. cit.*, pp. 70–1.
[3] *Ibid.*, p. 86.

votes, not equally but with a surprising lack of discrimination, between Liberals and Conservatives. The Rochdale poll books of 1841 and 1857 show them both drawing votes from every sub-class and almost every separate occupation, the Liberals gaining substantial but not overwhelming majorities of the textile inter-est, the retailers and the (largely self-employed) craftsmen, the Conservatives similar majorities of the commercial and pro-fessional men and 'capitalists'. The only sub-class to show an overwhelming bias in favour of one party was the drink trade, and that only in 1857 when they swung four to one against Edward Miall, the militant Dissenter.[1]

At first sight, this readiness to vote almost indiscriminately for the existing parties would seem to give the lie to class politics and to argue a *rapprochement* between the middle class and the aristocracy which overrode the interests of class. But this only brings us back to the key question, *rapprochement* on whose terms? The middle class, it appears, was reconciled to the existing parties only in proportion as the latter accepted the principal tenets of the middle-class ideal. We have already seen, in a general way, how that ideal won the battle for the State and came to dominate Government policy and legislation.[2] Now we must see, more particularly, how it captured the minds, or at least the public *personae*, of the party leaders, and came to be institutionalized in the parties themselves, ultimately, though by no means inevitably, in the Liberal Party.

By this it is not meant that the two parties became stereo-typed and exclusive class institutions, the Conservatives the party of the landed interest and protection, the Liberals the party of industrialism and free trade. Class politics in Victorian England were more complex than that, and each party stood for more than one economic interest. Both were primarily constitu-tional and religious rather than economic and social institutions, the Conservatives the party of order and stability, of authority and the High Church, the Liberals the party of progress and reform, of the Low Church and Dissent.[3] But in order to gain and hold power, their rival and equally aristocratic leaders were forced to come to terms with and increasingly to satisfy the

[1] J. Vincent, *The Formation of the Liberal Party, 1857–68* (1966), pp. 97–8, 105–8, 116–18.   [2] See chap. viii, § 3, above.
[3] Cf. Gash, *Reaction and Reconstruction*, pp. 128–30.

aspirations of those who voted for them. It mattered little that the leaders did not belong to the middle class, or share by birth, education, occupation or source of income these aspirations. On the contrary, the fact that the most brilliant and intuitive leaders were more concerned with what they believed to be the national interest than with the immediate economic advantage of any single class, including their own, made them all the quicker to respond to the demands of whichever class could successfully present its own aspirations as the manifest common sense of the age.

In the aristocratic competition to express the sublimated middle-class interest disguised as the spirit of the age, the Liberals with their traditional alliance with the urban middle class and identification with reform held all the cards, but mismanaged them so badly that they nearly threw the game away. It was two supremely patrician Tories—with, it is true, personal advantages of their own in their family connections with the industrial and commercial middle class—who, almost in spite of themselves, came most closely to personify the middle-class ideal. Peel, indeed, sacrificed his party—and thereby saved the Liberals—by doing so. Gladstone, having inherited Peel's mantle and carried it with him into the Liberal Party, found it, to his own surprise, to be the aegis of the symbolic representative not so much of the middle class as of the middle-class civilization of mid-Victorian England.

Peel never ceased to be a landed aristocrat, with all the pride in his order and prickly sense of honour of the second-generation new man, but his flirtation with the middle-class ideal began before the Reform Act, with his tacit acceptance of the whole canon of classical political economy and Benthamite administrative theory as revealed in his and Huskisson's tariff policies and his own police and penal reforms. It was not at this early stage, perhaps, a personal affair, but part of the general capitulation of progressive Tories to the charms of Utilitarianism which we explored in Chapter VI. Peel differed from the rest only in administrative ability and quickness of apprehension of the higher expediency of safeguarding aristocratic rule by organic reform. Having broken off the suit by his rejection of the crude surgery of the Reform Bill, he was forced to re-create the relationship during the long years in opposition and the few brilliant reforming years in office. Meanwhile, the vacillating Whigs, who could never make up their minds whether they were a patrician or a popular party, held the middle-class reformers at arms' length and almost forced them into the arms of Peel, whose fiscal policies and other reforms seemed to promise them all that the Whigs had refused.[1] By 1845 Cobden had transferred his hopes from Russell—'*Now* I am convinced past all change that *he* is not the man to do our work'—to his rival—'The thing is going fast, and Peel is the *man to give us free trade.*' At the end Peel represented middle-class feeling on repeal of the corn laws more accurately than the League:

> the fact is the feeling is so strong among the middle class everywhere (excepting the *Council Room*) in favour of the measure, that it would not be good policy to deny its merits. . . .[2]

As Cobden expressed it after Peel's death and before Gladstone emerged as the apotheosis of the *zeitgeist*, Peel represented 'the idea of the age, and it has no other representative among statesmen.'[3]

Peel's gratuitous act—for he was fully aware that repeal of the corn laws was irrelevant to the ostensible cause, the Irish famine, and he was certainly not forced to accept the poisoned chalice from Russell—achieved what the League had failed to do, that is, to reduce the landed interest as represented by the Tory Party to a mere agricultural, protectionist interest. The chief beneficiary was the Liberal Party, which as a result enjoyed twenty-eight years of power, all but a few months of them in office. The first half of that period presents the curious spectacle of a vast reserve of middle-class adulation looking for a leader to fasten on to. Lord John Russell was too timid or too unimaginative to accept it when offered, as at Sheffield in 1857. Palmerston, with the cynical detachment of the cool patrician, called on it to rescue him from a political corner, as in the Don Pacifico debate, but otherwise disdained to traffic out of doors.[4] Finally it fastened, somewhat surprisingly, on the at first sight unpromising figure of Gladstone.

An austere, High Church landowner whose personal ideal

---

[1] Cf. *ibid.*, pp. 184–9.
[2] McCord, *op. cit.*, pp. 195, 202–3 (Cobden to J. B. Smith and to George Wilson).
[3] Vincent, *op. cit.*, p. 201 (Cobden to Baines, 11 April 1857).
[4] Cf. *ibid.*, pp. 148–9.

was the old rural social order of 'kindly and intimate relations between the higher and the lower classes', who to the end of his life believed in 'the conservation of estates, and the permanence of the families in possession of them, as a principal source of our social strength, and as a large part of true conservatism', 'a firm believer in the aristocratic principle—the rule of the best' and 'an out and out inequalitarian', Gladstone was no more cut out to be the idol of the middle class than Peel.[1] Indeed, it was not until after 1859 when as Chancellor of the Exchequer he took up again Peel's unfinished work of giving the middle class what they wanted—complete free trade, the repeal of the taxes on knowledge, cheap, efficient government, and peace with France—that he found popularity thrust upon him. 'I am become for the first time a popular character,' he wrote in 1864. 'As far as I feel justified in appropriating and enjoying any of this popularity, it is on account of what I did, or prevented from being done, in 1859–61. . . .'[2] He was feted in Liverpool, Manchester, Tyneside, Stoke and Middlesbrough, and importuned to stand for South Lancashire, Leeds and other industrial constituencies. What the industrialists and merchants applauded in him was the personification of middle-class aims, free trade, peace and economic progress, pursued by the same *laissez-faire* policies which had covered Bootle with 'the houses of thinking citizens': 'the beneficial legislation which has struck the fetters from the arms of human industry.'[3]

It is true that Gladstone, with his mercurial—or brilliantly opportunist—mind and his intuitive grasp of the slightest shift in the centre of gravity of politics, claimed to stand for other groups besides the middle class: for the aristocracy, the Church, Dissent, and, from the moment their enfranchisement was seriously in question, for the working-class as well. To his admirers he was all things to all classes; to his enemies, 'the prince of the humbugs of the present day'.[4] His concern for the

---

[1] F. E. Hyde, *Mr. Gladstone at the Board of Trade* (1934), p. 11; J. Morley, *Life of Gladstone* (1901), I. 347; L. March-Phillips and B. Christian, *Some Hawarden Letters* (1917), p. 37; Vincent, *op. cit.*, p. 212.

[2] i.e. the Anglo-French trade treaty and prevention of war with France; Gladstone to A. H. Gordon, 1864, Vincent, *op. cit.*, p. 229.

[3] W. E. Williams, *The Rise of Gladstone to the Leadership of the Liberal Party, 1859–68* (1934), p. 169; Vincent, *op. cit.*, p. 220.

[4] *Manchester Courier and Advertiser*, 10 June 1865.

working class, as well as for the Irish, was later to alienate many of his middle-class followers. But meanwhile, until the 1880's certainly, his policies were those which the middle class would have pursued for themselves if they could have found in their midst a leader as appealing and representative as Gladstone.

Thus it was through identification with Gladstone and his policies that a large part of the Victorian middle class came to institutionalize themselves in the Liberal Party—though a smaller, if increasing, party identified with his Conservative opponents. He had not chosen them: they had chosen him, and their faith in him lasted no longer than the policies by which he deserved it. Already in the mid-Victorian age there were the first signs of that drift of business men to the Tory Party which in the last twenty years of the century was to change the social structure of English politics. That drift can be traced in part to a further change in the representative character of the Protean Gladstone and the Liberal Party, as a result of bringing within the pale of the constitution both the British working class and the Irish peasantry. But, as we shall see in the final chapter, it had even more to do with the change in the character of the middle class and the decline of the entrepreneurial ideal. Meanwhile, as long as entrepreneurial society lasted in a form still recognizably true to its ideal, it found its chief political expression in Gladstone and the Liberal Party.

There was another set of institutions which embodied the industrial middle class and its ideal for the purposes of conflict: the employers' associations. But, since these were called into existence only in response to the challenge of the trade unions, they can best be dealt with in connection with the institutionalization of the working class.

3. THE INSTITUTIONALIZATION OF THE WORKING CLASS

If the key to the rise of a viable class society was the imposition on the rest of society of the major middle-class ideal, one of the locks into which it fitted was the rise of working-class institutions willing to acquiesce in that ideal. This development was all the more remarkable since, with some important exceptions, nearly all the institutions generated by the workers themselves, as distinct from those provided for them by the other classes, were founded for the express purpose of opposing that ideal. The transformation of institutions aimed at checking or reducing the power of the capitalist class and modifying or replacing the competitive system, into ones which accepted the new class society and merely sought to improve the worker's place in it, tended to follow one or both of two evolutionary lines. One of these may be called education by failure, that is, the acceptance born of the frustration, deadlock, or diversion into unintended paths, of institutions built for class antagonism and steered on collision courses with the declared intention of forcing a battle. The other may be called education by success, the internal adaptation of institutions formed for opting out of the competitive system to a highly successful *modus vivendi* within it. The first was the path mainly taken by the overtly revolutionary working-class bodies, the abortive general unions and the physical-force Chartists; the second, by the covertly revolutionary co-operative movement and the moral-force Chartists, and, less obviously, by the unrevolutionary craft, factory and mining unions.

There was, of course, one group of working-class institutions, and that the largest of all, which went through neither evolution, since they were founded from the beginning as instruments of working-class amelioration within the existing social system. These were the friendly societies, which came to embrace a larger proportion of the working class than any other institution and can therefore be considered the most typical of all working-class bodies formed to respond to the problems of industrialism. They grew most rapidly in the period and in the areas of fastest industrial growth, their membership increasing from under a million in 1815 to over three million in 1849 and to an estimated four million in 1872, heavily concentrated throughout in Lancashire, Yorkshire, and the other industrial counties of the north and midlands. In 1872 they had four times as many members as the trade unions, and twelve times as many as the co-operative societies.[1] At mid-century 'nearly half the adult male

[1] P. H. J. H. Gosden, *The Friendly Societies in England, 1815–75* (Manchester, 1961), pp. 7, 16, 22–4.

population,' it was claimed, belonged to friendly societies of one kind or another.[1]

Not all of them were strictly working-class institutions. The so-called county societies were paternal, charitable bodies, 'managed by some of the leading gentlemen in any county, or by the clergy' for the express purpose of saving the poor rates. But these were small and few in number—less than 90,000 out of 1,857,896 registered members in 1872—and the great bulk were founded by working men themselves, 'to enable the industrious classes, by means of the surplus of their earnings, to provide themselves a maintenance during sickness, infirmity and old age.'[2] Some, the burial societies, provided only that barest minimum of social security, a decent, non-pauper funeral. Others provided a great deal more: widows' and orphans' pensions, medical treatment or, especially in the small local societies and lodges of the great affiliated orders with their splendid names— the Oddfellows, Foresters, Druids, Ancient Shepherds, Rechabites, and so on—good fellowship, conviviality, and a sense of belonging to a secret and powerful freemasonry. They all had this in common, however, that they were from the beginning non-revolutionary, ameliorative organizations designed to mitigate by mutual insurance the insecurities of the competitive system without in any way seeking to overturn it.

It is true that some of them, especially the 'particular trade societies' during the period of the Combination Acts, were really trade unions in disguise, but most of these after 1825 died out or were transformed into overt trade unions. It is also true that the State and the 'influential classes' for long had ambivalent feelings about them, encouraging them on the one hand with a series of nineteen benevolent Acts from 1793 to 1875 as instruments of working-class thrift and independence of the poor laws, while on the other suspecting them of secretly supporting 'the system' of political and industrial insubordination, as the ruling aristocracy viewed most working-class organization down to mid-century.[3] As late as 1848 a House of Lords Com-

---

[1] [W. R. Greg], 'Investments for the Working Classes', *Edin.Rev.*, 1852, XCV. 407.

[2] *P.P.*, 1872, XXVI, R.C. on Friendly and Benefit Building Societies, *2nd Report and Evidence*, q. 594; Sir F. Eden, *Observations on Friendly Societies* (1801), p. 1; Gosden, *op. cit.*, pp. 15, 53–4.

[3] Cf. *ibid.*, pp. 155–9.

mittee still saw 'certain customs' of the affiliated orders as 'open to very serious objections, viz. the employment of secret signs, the circulation of lectures, and the introduction of orations after the burial service.'[1] Yet there is no doubt that of all working-class institutions the friendly societies came nearest to the middle-class ideal of self-help and self-dependence. As the Vicar of Harrow put it in 1817,

> It is the great benefit of Friendly Societies that they teach a man to avert his eye from the workhouse: to look to the blessing of God on his own endeavours; to get his bread by the sweat of his brow. . . .[2]

For the Society for the Improvement of the Working Population in the County of Glamorgan in 1831 the friendly society enabled the labourer to say,

> Poor as I am, I am obliged to no man for a farthing, and therefore I consider myself as independent as any gentleman or farmer in the parish.[3]

And a contemporary historian of the Victorian working class could claim with truth in 1890 that 'the record of the progress of Friendly Societies is a record of the sturdy self-help, the self-dependence, the independence of Englishmen, of which as a nation we may well be proud.'[4] These, of course, were the views of members of the higher classes, but in so far as they reflect the cautious and 'responsible' behaviour of the societies themselves, they accurately represent the mutual acceptance and respect between the State and the most widespread of working-class institutions, which not only fostered the benevolent friendly society legislation and the paternal administration of the first Registrar, Tidd Pratt, 'minister of self-help to the whole of the industrious classes,'[5] but paved the way for the mutual acceptance and respect between the State and other working-class institutions.

Friendly society membership was not a life-absorbing role, and no doubt many such members, as concerned as the rest with

---

[1] *Ibid.*, p. 159
[2] J. W. Cunningham, *A Few Observations on Friendly Societies* (1817), p. 22; *ibid.*, p. 161.
[3] Cowbridge Tracts, No. 5, *On the Advantages of Friendly Societies* (1831), p. 2; *ibid.*, p. 163.
[4] C. S. Roundell, *The Progress of the Working Classes* (1890), p. 22.
[5] *P.P.*, 1874, XXIII, R.C. on Friendly Societies, *4th Report*, Appendix I.

social security and the legal protection of their funds, were also ardent co-operators, militant trade unionists, or physical-force Chartists. The co-operative societies, in particular, appealed to similar motives of thrift, self-help, and mutual security. But the co-operative movement in its earlier phase, from the 1820's to the 1840's, was far more than the instrument for the cheap and efficient supply of pure and unadulterated consumables which it later became. It was a revolutionary, if non-violent, movement for 'the transformation of the whole of capitalist society into a socialist commonwealth.'[1] As such it was the purest institutional embodiment of the working-class ideal of an equalitarian society based on labour and co-operation.

The aim of every co-operative society down to and including the Rochdale Pioneers of 1844 was to found a self-sufficient, primitive communist community into which the members would escape from the competitive system and establish their own system of co-operative production and equalitarian distribution. From isolated cells in the capitalistic body politic, or islands in the ocean of selfish competition, the co-operative communities would expand until they were large enough to take over by a silent and peaceable revolution the whole activity of the existing economic system, and so replace the 'old immoral world' with the 'New Moral World' of the founder, Robert Owen.

The transition from community building to shopkeeping, from the making of utopias to the making of dividends, from a visionary alternative to capitalism into an alternative form of capitalism itself, was more than the progressive betrayal of a great ideal. It was the most conspicuous example of education by success, of the process by which the only institution with an immediate, practical programme for establishing a new society based on the working-class ideal transformed itself into a pillar of capitalist society. As such it was a paradigm of the penetration of working-class institutions by the entrepreneurial ideal.

The process was a classic instance of the substitution of means for ends. To make themselves independent of the capitalist the co-operators had to find capital with which to build their com-

---

[1] Specifically the aim of the Leeds Redemption Society—J. F. C. Harrison, *Social Reform in Victorian Leeds: the Work of James Hole, 1820–95* (Leeds, 1954), p. 14; cf. S. Pollard, '19th-Century Co-operation: from Community Building to Shopkeeping', in Briggs and Saville, ed., *Essays in Labour History*, pp. 74f.

munities. When the traditional method of raising weekly subscriptions proved too slow and unpromising, recourse was had to the 'Brighton system' of Dr. William King:

> We must form ourselves into a Society for this essential purpose; we must form a fund by weekly deposits; as soon as it is large enough, we must lay it out in various commodities, which we must place in a common store from which all members must purchase their common necessaries, and the profit will form a common capital again to be again laid out in the commodities most wanted. . . .
>
> When the capital has accumulated sufficiently, the Society may produce any manufactures they please, and so provide for all their wants of food, clothing and houses. The Society will then be called a Community.[1]

Co-operative trading seems to have caught on with most of the 500 or so societies, with 20,000 members, which were in existence at the height of the Owenite enthusiasm of the early 1830's,[2] but most of them were swept away in the deluge of failure which met the grandiose schemes—the Labour Exchanges, the Grand National Consolidated Trades Union, and the Association of All Classes of All Nations—by which Owen tried to hasten the millennium.

Nevertheless, co-operative store-keeping persisted, and manifestly succeeded, in great contrast with the persistent failure of Owenite communities at Orbiston, Ralahine, Manea Fen, Ham Common, and elsewhere, culminating in the collapse of Owen's favourite community, Harmony Hall at Queenwood, East Tytherley, in 1846. In the 1840's the co-operative movement split into three streams. The purest Owenite stream flowed into the 'Redemption Societies', beginning in Leeds in 1846, which under the slogan, 'Labouring Capitalists, not Labourers and Capitalists', tried to build utopias on a penny per week subscription. The failure by 1855 of the Leeds Society's experiment at Garnlwyd, near Swansea, symbolized the petering out of this stream. Another flowed via John Minter Morgan and his 'Church of England self-supporting villages' into the co-operative workshops founded by the Christian Socialists between

---

[1] *The Co-operator*, 1828, No. 1, p. 3, printed in G. D. H. Cole and A. W. Filson, *British Working Class Movements: Select Documents, 1789–1875* (1951), pp. 210–11.

[2] Pollard, *loc. cit.*, p. 86.

1848 and 1854.[1] Although these had little influence, in spite of stimulating the interest of the Amalgamated Society of Engineers, on the future of co-operative production, they did achieve some success in educating the higher classes to accept the co-operative movement as a harmless, indeed a beneficial, development, and to provide in the Industrial and Provident Societies Act of 1852 a legislative framework for it.[2]

The third stream was the main river of the future. The Rochdale Pioneers of 1844 were firmly in the original Owenite stream, in that their ultimate object was 'as soon as practicable . . . to arrange the powers of production, distribution, education and government; or, in other words, to establish a home colony of united interests. . . .'[3] But their invention, or re-invention, of the dividend on purchases ensured both the unbounded success of their shopkeeping venture and the postponement of community building to the Greek kalends. As co-operative trading prospered and expanded amongst the Pioneers and their numerous imitators—by 1872 there were 927 societies with over 300,000 members and annual sales approaching £10 million[4]—co-operative community founding withered away. In 1855 the Pioneers' *Almanack* still paid lip-service to 'the emancipation of the working classes from poverty and degradation, by enabling them to reap the fruits of their own industry,' through self-employment, 'agricultural operations', and 'community of property'. By 1860, however, according to *The Co-operator*, 'the present co-operative movement does not seek to level the social inequalities which exist in society as regards wealth,' but only to mitigate the exploitation of the workman. In the words of their president, Abraham Howarth, 'The Co-operative Movement . . . [joins] together the means, the energies, and the talent of all for the benefit of each' by 'a common bond, that of self-interest'.[5]

Soon many co-operators were deliberately repudiating the Owenite ideal and accepting the existing social system:

We have seen enough of Communism, enough of the Utopian

---

[1] Armytage, *Heavens Below*, pp. 96–112, 145–83, 209–23.
[2] See above, § 1.
[3] G. J. Holyoake, *History of the Rochdale Equitable Pioneers* (1857), p. 11.
[4] B. Potter, *The Co-operative Movement in Great Britain* (1891), Appendix V.
[5] Pollard, *loc. cit.*, pp. 97–8.

ridiculous mummery of Socialism. . . . We don't want it; we have seen the new moral world, and don't like it. . . . Let Co-operation be what it is. . . . Let it inculcate no other spirit but gratitude to God, loyalty to our Sovereign, love to our country, and good-will to all mankind . . . in the cause of constitutional competitive co-operation.

And all agreed that the movement was now an instrument of working-class amelioration rather than social revolution: 'Modern Co-operation', in the words of a prize essay of the 1860's, 'means a union of working men for the improvement of the social circumstances of the class to which they belong . . . it is the working man's lever, by which he may rise in the world.'[1] If this was still an ideal, it was much nearer to the self-help of Samuel Smiles than to the primitive communism of Robert Owen. To that extent the most practical exponents of the working-class ideal had come to embrace the ideal of the capitalist middle class.

The grandiose Owenite institutions which tried around 1834 to find the short cut to the millennium were, equally, the most conspicuous examples of the education of the working class by failure. Of these the Grand National Consolidated Trades Union was the most important. It was the culmination and focus of two diverse traditions of working-class organization: that of the general trades union, the general union of all the trades, which should be so powerful *vis-à-vis* the employers that wage reductions and other forms of exploitation, but not the capitalist system, would be abolished for ever; and that of the revolutionary general strike which should sweep away the capitalist system itself and replace it by one of co-operative production by voluntary associations of working men. The first tradition went back to the Philanthropic Society and the 'Philanthropic Hercules' of 1818, and reached the Grand National Union via John Doherty whose Grand General Union of the Operative Spinners of the United Kingdom in 1829 led on to the National Association for the Protection of Labour in 1830. The latter was in no sense a revolutionary organization but an ameliorative one, aimed at 'preventing such [wage] reductions and securing to the industrious workman a just and adequate remuneration

---

[1] *The Co-operator*, 1861-2, II. 68, and 1866-7, VII. 357; *ibid.*, p. 100.

for his labour.'[1] The second was a short cut to Owen's millennium by way of William Benbow's general strike or 'sacred holiday month', which should 'come suddenly upon society like a thief in the night. One year may disorganize the whole fabric of the old world, and transfer, by a sudden spring, the whole political government of the country from the master to the servant.'[2]

The failure of the general strike and the collapse of the Grand National Union submerged both traditions for half a century or more. The National Association of United Trades for the Protection of Labour of 1845 was not a general union in this sense but a precursor of the T.U.C., which it closely resembled in organization and outlook.[3] The idea of the political general strike was revived only in the Edwardian age, when it was re-imported from France, by the Syndicalists. The manner of the failure, however, was as important as the failure itself for the education of the working class in viable class relations, for out of the defeat of revolution was plucked a victory for non-violent politics. The general strike—if so premature, partial and ill-organized a stoppage, precipitated by the attempts of particular unions to get national backing for local strikes and lock-outs, can be called a general strike—was defeated by the disunity of the members and the rapid exhaustion of the funds.[4] In the midst of the battle, however, came a godsend from the Government, the gratuitous prosecution of the six Tolpuddle labourers for swearing an illegal oath to the Union. The Tolpuddle affair enabled Owen to pull together the disintegrating Union and to divert the whole energy of its half-million members from revolutionary industrial action into peaceful petitioning for a free pardon. The vast meeting at Copenhagen Fields and the procession of 40,000 to 50,000 London Unionists to the Home Office temporarily failed in its ostensible purpose, but it succeeded admirably in its underlying one, that of re-uniting the working-class movement in a cause in which it could hope to achieve a

[1] National Association for Protection of Labour: Resolutions and Laws, in *United Trades Co-operative Journal*, 10 July 1830; Cole and Filson, *op. cit.*, p. 252.

[2] *The Crisis*, 12 October 1833; S. and B. Webb, *Trade Unionism*, p. 164; cf. W. Benbow, *The Grand National Holiday and Congress of the Productive Classes* (1831).

[3] Cf. Report of its inaugural committee, *Northern Star*, 29 March 1845; Cole and Filson, *op. cit.*, pp. 469–70.

[4] Cf. G. D. H. Cole, *Attempts at General Union* (1953), pp. 115–26.

visible, and bloodless, victory.[1] The eventual return and pardon
of the transported labourers not only sweetened the legend of
1834 with triumphant martyrdom: it taught the lesson that the
politics of peaceful petitioning might be more effective than the
head-on collision with capital.

The lesson was taken up by the Chartists, the greatest protagonists of the mass petition and of the working-class ideal as a
political institution. Chartism was more than a movement for
Parliamentary Reform: it was an attempt to restore by political
means the workers' right to the whole produce of labour. In the
view of its most powerful thinker, Bronterre O'Brien,

> Every industrious man who produces more (*in value*) of the goods
> of life than he needs for his own or his family's use, ought to own the
> difference as property. You are almost all in that condition, for
> there are few of you who do not yield more value to society every
> day than society gives you back in return. Why are you not masters
> of the difference? Why is it not your property? Because certain laws
> and institutions, which other people make, take it away from you,
> and give it to the law-makers.[2]

But since, as we have seen, there were almost as many versions
of the right to the whole produce and how to restore it as there
were labourers,[3] and since the Charter was only a means and not
an end in itself, Chartism overlapped with every other working-
class aim and movement of the period.

It derived principally, through Lovett and the London Working Men's Association, from the earlier independent working-
class Reform movement, the National Union of the Working
Classes, and ultimately from the Regency Reformers of the
period of the birth of class. Through the L.W.M.A., too, it was
connected with the campaign for a free, unstamped press and the
secularist movement of Carlile, Hetherington, and company,
and through Lovett with Robert Owen and co-operative
socialism.

Through William Benbow it inherited the revolutionary
general strike from Owenite unionism, threatened in 1839, put
into ineffective practice in 1842. Through J. R. Stephens it
acquired the fiery antinomianism of the anti-poor law campaign

---

[1] Cf. *The Martyrs of Tolpuddle, 1834–1934* (T.U.C., 1934).
[2] *National Reformer*, 15 January 1837; Cole and Filson, *op. cit.*, p. 351.
[3] Cf. chap. vii, § 2, above.

and the moral indignation of the factory reform movement. Through Lovett again it linked up with working-class emancipation via self-education, through Henry Vincent with the temperance movement, and through Arthur O'Neill with 'Christian Chartism'. Finally, through O'Connor himself it reverted to the old, nostalgic working-class dream of a return to the land and the peasant life.

These ideological differences help to account, through the personalities and their local connections, for the local and regional diversity of Chartism. Educational Chartism was connected principally with London, temperance Chartism with Bath and the South West, Christian Chartism with Birmingham and Paisley, the industrial general strike and the threat of physical force with the North of England, the actual use of physical force with Newport and the volatile Welsh.[1] Local research is still needed to elucidate all the manifold currents of this richly complex movement, but local research will not alter the fundamental point, that Chartism was the main attempt in the nineteenth century to forge a single working-class party for the purpose of changing society by political means, which failed chiefly because of the geographical and ideological fragmentation of the working class.

Even so, its different forms failed in different ways, or, rather, contributed in different ways to the education of the working class to accept the viable class society. Moral-force Chartism experienced the education of success. Its various institutions, the Chartist churches, schools and temperance clubs, survived long enough to undergo the same sort of transformation which overtook the co-operative movement, the pathetic evolution of their dissidence into conformity with existing society. Lovett's splendid vision of society transformed by education, for example, petered out in the secular day school which he ran from 1848 to 1857, and in the lectures and textbooks on physiology, astronomy, zoology, geology and a neo-Smilesian brand of *Social and Political Morality*, on which he spent the rest of his long life. His work came to chime with the entrepreneurial spirit of the age. As his friend George Combe wrote after visiting his National Hall school in 1849,

[1] Cf. the contemporary Welsh riots against the turnpikes, David Williams, *The Rebecca Riots: a Study in Agrarian Discontent* (Cardiff, 1955).

This is the true method of promoting the extension of the political franchise to the working classes. If a generation taught and trained in schools like these were fairly to come to maturity, they might be safely trusted with political power.[1]

Physical-force Chartism experienced the education of failure, not only at the end as a movement but continuously through the rejection of violence by a succession of its leaders. For violence and punishment for violence were great educators in themselves, but had to be experienced in person. As a Scottish Chartist put it, 'It is very easy to talk of physical force when warming our toes before the fire. . . .'[2] When it came to push of pike one protagonist of violence after another found he had had enough of physical force. The fiery parson J. R. Stephens repudiated it at his trial in 1839.[3] Thomas Cooper, the Leicester Chartist leader, was similarly cured of his loose talk of violence by a spell in prison, and ended by preaching, in verse, the removal of social wrong by 'the growth of the masses in Knowledge, Temperance, and Self-Respect.'[4] Even John Frost, the Newport draper who led the only organized Chartist rising, seems to have wept like a child and talked of heaven and hell at the prospect of it, and only to have gone through with it out of a sense of loyalty to a supposedly national revolutionary movement.[5] O'Connor himself gratefully allowed his bluff to be called by Police Commissioner Maine on Kensington Common in 1848, and spent his last sane years vainly pursuing an alliance with the middle-class Radicals.[6] Finally, the last great Chartist leader and protagonist of 'the social war', Ernest Jones, who broke with O'Connor in 1850 over his defection from physical force, turned six years later to the same solution: 'He now called upon them to unite with the middle classes for Universal Manhood Suffrage.'[7]

[1] Letter to *The Scotsman*, 17 November 1849, W. Jolly, *Education: its Principles and Practices as developed by George Combe* (1879), p. 228; cf. *ibid.*, pp. 224–30, and Lovett, *op. cit.*, pp. 360–6, 374–9, 408–10.

[2] W. G. Burns at Calton Hill meeting, Edinburgh, 5 December 1838, A. Wilson, 'Chartism in Glasgow', Briggs, ed., *Chartist Studies*, p. 279.

[3] Cole, *Chartist Portraits*, p. 75.

[4] Preface to his poem, *The Spirit, or a Dream in the Woodlands* (1849).

[5] David Williams, 'Chartism in Wales', Briggs, ed., *Chartist Studies*, p. 236.

[6] Read and Glasgow, *O'Connor*, pp. 133–6.

[7] 'The Social War', *The People's Paper*, 13 November 1852; speech at Chartist Conference, *ibid.*, 13 February 1858: 'Mr. Jones sat down amid loud and continued applause.'

As for the movement as a whole, it is doubtful whether it ever had a practical programme of revolution either as a means to gain power or as an end if and when power were achieved. As a means the threat of violence was used in much the same way that Place and the middle-class Radicals used it to obtain the Great Reform Act, but with two differences; first, that the Chartists had no-one in *their* rear with which to frighten the aristocracy, and, secondly, that in case mere threats failed they never had even so much of a plan of action as Place had mounted against the Duke in 1832. Wild talk of collecting muskets and manufacturing pikes there certainly was, but, apart from sporadic arming and drilling by small groups on distant moors, no evidence whatever of centrally organized preparation for rebellion outside the imaginations of romantic rebels like Benbow and Russophobe counter-revolutionaries like David Urquhart. Of this, the fiasco at Newport, which was defeated by a garrison of twenty-eight soldiers, is conclusive proof.[1] Physical force, as far as the national leaders were concerned, was mere bluff, and when their bluff was called they could only retreat.

To revolution as an end they had given even less thought. Even O'Brien, a critic of capitalist society who anticipated and rivalled Marx, could only suggest the gradual nationalization of the land at the death of existing owners with full compensation to their heirs, the proscription of further public debt, a currency based on the labour value of wheat instead of on gold or silver, the nationalization of distribution through public marts or bazaars, and 'an honest system of public credit' through District Banks funded from the rents of public land.[2] Ernest Jones, apart from the purchase of land for self-employment by the workers, seems to have thought mainly in terms of co-operative factories, workshops and stores, the further control of factory hours and conditions, and abolition of the truck system.[3] But the chief contribution of Chartism to the transformation of society was the famous Land Plan of O'Connor. This nostalgic attempt to recreate the supposedly idyllic peasantry of Merry England— or pre-Cromwellian Ireland—was designed not to produce a

[1] Hovell, *op. cit.*, pp. 138, 175–6, 178–80.

[2] J. B. O'Brien, 'Programme of the National Reform League', *National Reformer*, 16 January 1847, in Cole and Filson, *op. cit.*, pp. 407–9.

[3] Cf. Report on the 'Labour Parliament' at Manchester, *The People's Paper*, 11 March 1854, in *ibid.*, pp. 419–21.

social revolution but, through the conservatism of small proprietors, to prevent one. As O'Brien's *National Reformer* put it, 'Every man who joins these land societies is practically enlisting himself on the side of the Government against his own order.'[1]

Thus Chartism both in its practice of the politics of petitioning and in its lack of any constructive theoretical alternative to capitalism was, in spite of its revolutionary appearance, a long step on the way to the viable class society.

The collapse by the 1850's of all the overtly revolutionary working-class institutions and the conversion of all the covertly revolutionary ones into pillars of existing society left only the trade unions as residuary legatees of the working-class ideal. The extinction of general unionism had reduced these to three comparatively small groups of solidly organized unions: the traditional craft unions, mainly in building, printing, woodworking, glass and pottery, and the metal and engineering industries; the textile unions, especially in cotton; and the miners' unions, which last maintained only a flickering life outside the north-eastern coalfield.[2] Their total membership was small—probably under 100,000 in 1842, certainly well under a million before the upsurge of growth in the early 1870's.[3] It was practically confined to the most prosperous stratum of the working class, the so-called labour aristocracy, for one or both of two reasons. Only the highly-paid worker could afford the high subscriptions, as much as a shilling a week or more, charged by the skilled unions, and only a well-organized trade, able to restrict entry to the occupation, could in the competitive labour market of the mid-nineteenth century maintain a high rate of wages.

Indeed, as H. A. Turner has shown, whether a trade was described as skilled and as therefore belonging to the labour aristocracy depended less on its intrinsic skill and the length of training necessary to acquire it than on its ability to restrict

[1] Hovell, *op. cit.*, p. 275.

[2] Cf. H. A. Turner, *Trade Union Growth, Structure and Policy: a Comparative Study of the Cotton Unions* (1962), pp. 169–70; there were a few other unions outside these categories, such as the operative boot and shoe makers and the railway footplatemen and guards, but they were either tiny or to all intents and purposes friendly societies.

[3] S. and B. Webb, *Trade Unionism*, pp. 748–9.

recruitment and so to command an 'aristocratic' wage. Thus a 'closed' union of machine-minders like the cotton spinners' was able to maintain its position as a skilled and highly-paid occupation, while an 'open' one like the cotton weavers' was not.[1] As Eric Hobsbawm has pointed out, 'labour aristocrats generally enjoyed the power of making their labour artificially scarce, by restricting entry to the profession, or by other means. If they lost this—for instance by the uncontrollable rise of machines— they ceased, like the woolcombers, to be labour aristocrats.'[2] For this reason labour aristocrat and trade unionist were, between the collapse of mass unionism in the 1830's and its revival in the late 1880's, almost interchangeable terms. As one of them put it negatively, of the unskilled labourer, in 1879, 'As his title of "unskilled" implies, he has no handicraft and he has no union.'[3]

It might be thought that these aristocratic trade unions of the mid-Victorian age would be the most vulnerable of working-class institutions to the infiltration of the middle-class ideal. They represented a small and highly-privileged fraction: the whole labour aristocracy was probably less than 15 per cent of all industrial wage-earners, earning from 30 to 140 per cent more than unskilled men in the same industry, a differential which was widening between the 1840's and 1890.[4] They were often snobbish and exclusive in their attitude towards the rest: 'The artisan creed with regard to the labourers is that the latter are an inferior class and that they should be made to know and kept in their place.'[5] Many of their members were with the capitalists co-employers of fellow-workers, as the spinners were of the piecers, the colliery 'butties' in the midlands of the other miners, many building craftsmen of their labourers, and so on, and were often harder masters than the capitalists themselves— though it is fair to add that the unions consistently opposed subcontract working arrangements of this kind, with some success in the period 1850-73 and a great deal thereafter.[6]

[1] Turner, *op. cit.*, book III, chap. i, 'The Theory of the Labour Aristocracy'.
[2] Hobsbawm, 'The Labour Aristocracy in 19th-Century Britain', *Labouring Men*, pp. 290-1.
[3] 'A Working Man', *Working Men and Women* (1879), in *ibid.*, p. 275.
[4] *Ibid.*, pp. 279, 291-4.
[5] Thomas Wright, *Our New Masters* (1873); *ibid.*, p. 275.
[6] *Ibid.*, pp. 297-300.

Altogether, there were many reasons why the skilled trade unionists might come nearer to the outlook of their employers than to that of the mass of the unskilled operatives and displaced handworkers who made up so much of the following of the Owenite mass unions or the physical-force Chartists.

To some extent this was so, and was borne out by their patent lack of enthusiasm for mass Radical movements. With certain obvious exceptions like the cotton unions' part in the factory hours agitation or the building crafts' involvement through their co-operative Builders' Guild in the downfall of the Grand National Union in 1834, they held aloof from general unionism and mass politics. The Manchester printers, for example, declined to join Doherty's National Association for the Protection of Labour, or Owen's Society for National Regeneration, condemned the violent and revolutionary tendencies of the Grand National Union and the 'futility' of Chartism, and denounced O'Connor, owner of the *Northern Star*, as an 'unfair employer'.[1] They had even, it seems, refused to celebrate the passing of the 1832 Reform Bill.[2] The 'New Model' Unions' lack of interest in 'all projects of Social Revolution', their dislike of strikes, and their supposed acceptance of 'the economic Individualism of their middle-class opponents' led the Webbs to believe that they had to all intents and purposes abandoned the cause of the working class in exchange for a privileged position within it for themselves.[3] More recently H. A. Turner has blamed the exclusiveness of the 'closed' unions of skilled workers for 'the gap in trade union development' between the two eras of mass unionism in the 1830's and the 1880's and even for 'an apparent *decline* in the general degree of collective association among workers.'[4]

Yet such criticisms, by students of trade union development who wished it had followed a different path, are wide of the mark. Whatever their shortcomings from the point of view of later theorists, not merely were the mid-Victorian unions the only working-class institutions to maintain a recognizable version of the working-class ideal, albeit in the etiolated form of

[1] A. E. Musson, *The Typographical Association* (1954), pp. 76–7, 82–3.
[2] Hobsbawm, *Labouring Men*, p. 278.
[3] S. and B. Webb, *Trade Unionism*, pp. 180, 198–9, 239, 369.
[4] Turner, *op. cit.*, book IV, chap. i, 'The Gap in Trade Union Development'.

'a fair day's wage for a fair day's work'. They were the only working-class institutions which, in the deluge of the entrepreneurial ideal which overwhelmed mid-Victorian Britain, could fully accept the viable class society without either collapsing or capitulating to that ideal. They were a sort of Noah's Ark which rode out the flood and carried an admittedly attenuated working-class ideal through to a later epoch of expansion. More than that, such was their navigational skill that they were able to use their privileged position to achieve political and industrial gains for the working class, and in particular to teach both the employers and the Government something of the art of viable class relations.

This remarkable role, it is true, was not of their own choosing. It was thrust upon them by the economic and political situation in which they found themselves. They were forced to organize to defend and consolidate a privileged position in the labour market which meant everything to them but the abandonment of which would have benefited the rest of the working class but little, merely reducing all occupations to the same buyer's market as unskilled labour. Unlike the Chartists or the co-operators, they were tied to working-class organization by economic rather than ideological ties, and could not abandon it without great financial loss. The craft unions could not, if they wished, escape from class antagonism, since in spite of their dislike of strikes their chosen method, controlling recruitment to their trade, necessarily brought them into repeated collision with the employers, who in turn repeatedly tried to smash them by lock-outs and the demand to sign the notorious 'document' forswearing the union. Indeed, their dislike of strikes was not a measure of their absorption of middle-class thrift and economics but the practical result of their method of raising the individual worker's 'supply price' by creating a relative scarcity of labour: collective bargaining was avoided where possible, and hence also its degeneration into strikes, while the fund was husbanded to pay high unemployment benefit to keep the redundant worker temporarily out of the market. Thus the high benefits and husbanded funds were not a bourgeois luxury but a prerequisite of the 'autonomous regulation' of the trade.[1]

Even their peacemaking role as tutor in industrial relations to

[1] Cf. Turner, *op. cit.*, p. 203.

the employers was thrust upon them. The employers could not be expected to sit back while the craft unions rigged the labour market and set what price, hours and conditions they liked on their labour. They were forced to organize themselves, initially for the purpose of destroying the union, by means of the lock-out and the 'document'. Thus the two greatest craft stoppages of the period, the engineers' dispute of 1852 and the London builders' dispute of 1859, were both lock-outs, concerted by newly-formed employers' associations set up to stamp out the unions. Though the first was a defeat for the union and the second a drawn battle, both ultimately led to negotiation between the two sides and so to mutual recognition and acceptance.[1]

What is more, the craft unions' peaceable and skilful conduct began for the first time to earn them public support, not only from other unions but from middle-class allies, notably through the Christian Socialists and the Positivists, and also from aristocratic sympathizers like Lord Goderich and Lord St. Leonards.[2] The builders' dispute, for example, coincided with and influenced the report of the Social Science Association Committee on Trade Societies, 1860, to which three Christian Socialists and a Positivist contributed, which was the first public attempt by a middle-class organization to look at the unions objectively, and marked a turning point in public opinion on industrial relations.[3] The report concluded that 'the principles upon which trade societies regulate their proceedings are more moderate, and that discussions between the workmen belonging to them and their masters have been managed in a fairer spirit' and 'the strikes, though more frequent, are conducted with less violence than in former days,' that, 'disastrous as have been the immediate results of most strikes to masters as well as to men, they have not been without their use to both, by inducing wiser and more gracious concessions on one side, and less unreasonable demands on the other,' and that 'improved education of masters and men is doing more to avert collisions between them than any mere arrangements could accomplish, whether voluntary or enforced. . . .'[4]

[1] *Ibid., loc. cit.*   [2] Cf. S. and B. Webb, *Trade Unionism*, pp. 215, 231, 246.
[3] *Trade Societies and Strikes* (1860); the Christian Socialists were Ludlow, Hughes and Maurice, the Positivist Lushington, and there was also a trade unionist, T. J. Dunning, Secretary of the Bookbinders.
[4] *Ibid.*, pp. xvii–xx.

In the development of viable industrial relations the textile unions and the miners had a special role, partly because these great piece-working trades could not practice the 'autonomous regulation' of the craft unions. For them, control of recruitment, even where it was possible as in the case of the cotton spinners or the coal hewers, was not enough, but had to be supplemented by some form of collective bargaining to fix the rate for the piece, which because of wide differences in product or working conditions might require very complex negotiation. This fact both increased the likelihood and the severity of strikes and hastened the development of collective bargaining. On the one side, these industries experienced the greatest stoppages of the age, the North-Eastern coal strikes of 1844 and 1863, the Preston lock-out of 1853, the South Wales coal strike of 1875, and the North Lancashire cotton strike of 1878. On the other, they also produced the most advanced and sophisticated systems of collective bargaining, the cotton unions having to negotiate the pay for hundreds of different qualities and sizes of yarn and cloth, the miners' a wide range of working arrangements, from hours and pay for underground travel or 'hard places' to safety inspection and check-weighmen. The weavers, the least aristocratic, with their complete lack of control over entry and their consequently 'open' unions, made the largest advances of all. The famous 'Blackburn List' of piece-rates which they negotiated with the employers in 1853 settled the main principles of wage-fixing in the industry for a century. It also required a permanent staff of expert calculators and skilled negotiators who were the real origin of the professional administration of modern trade unionism.[1]

The non-craft unions also contributed as much as the craft unions to the change in public opinion on trade unionism. The Preston cotton stoppage of 1853 was probably a more important turning point than that of the engineers the previous year. It began as a selective or 'rolling' strike for higher pay (ten per cent)—not a promising basis for public sympathy in mid-Victorian England—but the action of the employers in turning it into a lock-out of over 20,000 workers, their stubbornness in refusing to negotiate, the manifest injustice of the magistrates

[1] Turner, *op. cit.*, pp. 128–32, 138; Smelser, *op. cit.*, p. 339; G. D. H. Cole, *Short History of the British Working-Class Movement* (1948), pp. 61–2.

in arresting the workers' leaders for peaceful dissuasion of Irish blacklegs while allowing the employers to organize a provocative triumphal procession of the latter, and the skill and patience of the strike leaders in presenting their case and discouraging violence, all earned the union the sympathy of the national press. The *Daily News* observed, 'There is something almost sublime in the spectacle of so many thousands of human beings, actuated more or less by angry feelings, waiting quietly while their cause was being decided.' Dickens went to report it in person, and though he deplored the strike in principle, praised the conduct of the strikers in *Household Words*. Even the *Economist* so far overcame its prejudice against trade unions as to regret that the law of conspiracy had been invoked against them, 'when the conduct of the two parties appears to the public almost as similar as two peas.' Money was collected for the strikers all over the country, and a benefit performance of a new play by Mark Lemon was put on for them at Drury Lane.[1] It was the first major strike for increased pay which earned the strikers the sympathy and support, if not the approval, of the middle-class public.

The changed atmosphere resulting from successful strikes and enforced negotiation can best be seen in the rapid growth of industrial conciliation and arbitration machinery. Such machinery had long been advocated—indeed, it had its origins in the wage-fixing customs of many pre-factory handicrafts such as silk-weaving and hosiery—and had been encouraged by the State in the Cotton Arbitration Act of 1800, the general Arbitration Act which accompanied the repeal of the Combination Acts in 1824, and its amendments in 1837 and 1845.[2] But advocacy and legislation had small effect until the mid-Victorian unions became powerful enough to make their employers think negotiation a preferable alternative to industrial deadlock. After three unsuccessful experiments in the 1850's, in the Macclesfield silk, the wooden shipbuilding, and London printing

[1] *Daily News*, 3 May 1854; *Household Words*, 11 February 1854; *Economist*, 25 March 1854; *Reynold's Newspaper*, 22 and 29 January 1854; G. Carnall, 'Dickens, Mrs. Gaskell, and the Preston Strike', *Victorian Studies*, 1964, VIII. 31f.

[2] Cf. J. Prest, *The Industrial Revolution in Coventry* (1960), pp. 53–62; R. A. Church, 'The Social and Economic Development of Nottingham', Ph.D., dissertation, Nottingham University, 1960, pp. 48–52; V. L. Allen, 'The Origins of Industrial Conciliation and Arbitration', *Int.Rev. of Soc.Hist.*, 1964, IX. 237f.

trades, the first successful joint committee of employers and workers appeared in the Nottingham hosiery industry in 1860, as the direct result of three important strikes in a period of heavy demand. 'It is further agreed,' their joint statement read, 'that in order to prevent a recurrence of strikes which have been so disastrous to employers and employed, a Board of Arbitration be at once formed. . . .'[1]

Similar bodies appeared during the 1860's in the Wolverhampton, Leeds, Manchester, Coventry and Worcester building trades, Nottingham lace, Leicester hosiery, the Staffordshire potteries, the glass bottle industry, and the North of England iron trade. Meanwhile, informal arbitration was popularized by an accepted group of arbitrators, including A. J. Mundella, who originated the Nottingham hosiery and lace boards, Judge Rupert Kettle, the Christian Socialists Thomas Hughes and Lloyd Jones, and the Positivist Henry Crompton. In the 1870's an 'arbitration craze' was talked of, and by 1875, when the National Conciliation League was formed, there was, according to a modern expert, 'barely a trade where trade unions existed which did not have either a standing joint committee of employers and workmen to settle disputes, with provision for arbitration, or the experience of settling disputes through arbitration on an *ad hoc* basis.'[2] The machinery was often used by the employers to stave off strikes during booms and ignored during slumps when they were no longer feared, but the institutional treatment of industrial disputes was a large advance upon the violent strikes and lock-outs, the intimidation and repressive legislation of immature industrial relations.

Similarly, the skilful propaganda and new-found prestige of the unions made the politics of persuasion work where they had not worked before, Here again the textile and mining unions led the way, forced, by their inability to apply the 'autonomous regulation' of the craft unions to industries with far more complex problems and dominated by the largest capitalists and landowners of the age, to seek control of hours and safety by the State. As Alexander Macdonald, the miners' leader, told the Royal Commission on Trade Unions in 1867, 'even if without combinations of workmen they might have been passed, yet it

---

[1] *Nottingham Review*, 21 September 1860; Allen, *loc. cit.*, p. 244.
[2] *Ibid.*, p. 240.

was on the representations of the workmen that the laws to destroy truck were passed, and that it is on the representations of the workmen that all the inspection Acts were passed, and that it is owing to the representations of the workmen that education is now a portion of the statutes of this country as far as children working in mines are concerned.'[1] The cotton unions were able, with the help of the revivalists of the aristocratic ideal, Sadler, Oastler and Ashley, to make the first major breach in the *laissez-faire* industrial policy in the shape of the Factory Acts.[2] The miners, with the same help, not only made the second, in the shape of the Mines Act of 1842, but in 1863 began the campaign for the amendment of the Master and Servant Acts which was the true starting point of that remarkable decade of successful pressure from 1866 to 1876 which produced more legislative gains for the working class than all the mass agitations of the preceding half century.[3]

The key to that legislative transformation was of course the working-class vote granted in 1867. Here again the unions, as the only remaining political representatives of the working class, were able, through the Reform League, which in one sense was the trade unions in disguise, to obtain what all the threats and blustering of the Chartists and all the persuasive argument of the middle-class Radicals since 1848 had failed to yield.[4] The problem for Bright and the Reformers of 1866 was exactly that of Place and the Radicals of 1832: to persuade Parliament that it was safer to let in a part of those who were banging on the door than to leave them out. This required a delicate balance between the threat of revolution, or at least of public disorder, and the promise that those who threatened it could be trusted not to impose a revolution once they were in. That balance was symbolized by the demolished railings of Hyde Park and its 'handing over' to Beales and the Reform

---

[1] Cole and Filson, *op. cit.*, pp. 494–5.

[2] Cf. [E. C. Tufnell] (an opponent of trade unions), *The Character, Objects and Effects of Trade Unions* (1834), p. 28: 'the spinners were invariably the most strenuous, and in many cases the only, supporters of the Ten-Hour Limitation Movement. . . .'

[3] Daphne Simon, 'Master and Servant', in Saville, ed., *Democracy and the Labour Movement*.

[4] The Reform League grew, in 1865, out of the Trade Unionists' Manhood Suffrage and Vote by Ballot Association of 1862—cf. George Howell's MS. Reform League Letter Book, 24 September 1867, in Cole and Filson, *op. cit.*, pp. 520–3.

League 'for the express purpose of our maintaining that order in it which the police could not maintain';[1] but no one could pretend that this political comedy was more than a symbol of the changed attitude of both political parties towards the working class as represented by the unions. It was still feared for its potential physical power if provoked by abuse or injustice, but it was no longer feared as a threat to property or the social system.

The change was best summed up by Gladstone, that intuitive barometer of the socio-political weather, two years before the Hyde Park railings collapsed: 'Please to remember that we have got to govern millions of hard hands; that it must be done by force, fraud or good will; that the latter has been tried and is answering. . . .'[2] Good will could answer only if it was reciprocated, and the assurance that it would be was given, not by any speeches of Reformers, whether middle- or working-class, but by the actual behaviour of the trade unionists and their leaders in industrial and political action. In industrial affairs they had shown themselves more 'responsible' and conciliatory than their employers. In foreign politics they had, in their attitudes towards the Russian question, Italian unification, and the American Civil War, shown themselves to be more liberal than their 'betters', less warlike than the aristocracy, more 'patriotic' than the middle-class Radicals led by Cobden and Bright. In domestic politics they had rejected revolution and opted for a programme of particular reforms, from labour legislation to land law reform, which held no threats for property. In short, the labour aristocracy had shown themselves more orthodox than the orthodox liberalism of their day, and admirably fitted for admission within the pale of the Constitution. Finally, the conversion by George Howell of the Reform League after Reform into an election agency of the Liberal Party amply confirmed the confidence reposed in them by Gladstone.[3]

It might be supposed from their consistent 'Lib-Lab-ism' that the mid-Victorian unionists had completely accepted both the politics and the social ideal of their 'betters'. No doubt many of

[1] Edmond Beales, letter in *The Times*, 28 July 1866; R. Harrison, *Before the Socialists* (1965), p. 84.

[2] J. Morley, *Life of Gladstone* (1904), II. 133.

[3] Cf. R. Harrison, *op. cit.*, chaps. iii and iv.

them did. George Howell, founding secretary of the London Trades Council, of the Reform League, and of the Parliamentary Committee of the T.U.C., who worked so assiduously for the Liberal Party, had, like many others, swallowed completely the propaganda of the viable, permanent, inevitable class society:

> I have never been, and never shall be, an advocate for merely changing our masters. I neither want aristocratic rule, nor the rule of the middle classes, nor the rule of the working classes. I want a government of the entire people—where wealth and intellect will have its share of power—no more.[1]

And in his book, *Trade Unions and Strikes* (1860), T. J. Dunning, the bookbinders' secretary, and a respected spokesman for the unions at the Social Science Association, explicitly accepted the classical economic theory of wages as being fixed by the law of supply and demand, merely adding, like McCulloch in 1826, that the workmen were justified in combining to ensure equality of bargaining power, and gain the full market rate.[2]

Yet it would be misleading to make too much of such quotations. On the political side the trade unions were as justified, practical and pragmatic as the Anti-Corn Law League and other middle-class pressure groups had been in looking to the existing parties for redress of their grievances. In the circumstances of the age, where else could they look? And if the middle class had been able to use the existing parties, without actually taking them over, to implement their whole programme of political reforms, why should not the working class do the same? It ill became the Webbs, who as Fabians practised the infiltration of the major parties and until the First World War were unhelpfully ambivalent towards the Labour Party, to blame the 'Lib-Labs' for not creating a separate working-class party. By working with, and playing off against each other, the existing parties, the trade unionists were able to gain the urban household suffrage (1867), the amendment and ultimately the repeal of the unequal Master and Servants Acts (1867 and 1875), the complete legal recognition of trade unions (1871), and the legalization of trade disputes and of all peaceful methods of

---

[1] Howell to Morrison, M.P., 30 November 1868, *ibid.*, p. 144.
[2] Dunning, *op. cit.*, pp. 5, 7; cf. J. R. McCulloch, *Essay on the Circumstances which determine the Rate of Wages* (1826), p. 188; though in later editions (1851, 1854, 1868) he admonished workers for persisting with unions.

pursuing them (1875), as well as helping to obtain a number of more general social reforms, such as the Elementary Education Act (1870), the Public Health Acts (1872 and 1875), and the Artisans' Dwellings Act (1876). With Liberal acquiesence, too, they also carried in 1874 the election of the first two working-class M.P.s, the miners' leaders Alexander Macdonald and Thomas Burt.

The real test of whether the trade unions accepted the entre-preneurial ideal, however, is their attitude to contemporary economic theory. It is easy to collect quotations from trade unionists like Dunning, Newton, Allan, and even from the militant Potter, repudiating class war, deprecating strikes, and favouring arbitration and conciliation. But these were the words of men intent on presenting the unions, for tactical reasons, as responsible, non-violent, unrevolutionary organizations, loyal to the State, but not necessarily in agreement with the existing social and economic system at every point. Beneath the bland words they stood for principles which were incompatible with classical economics, and which derived entirely from the dissident working-class ideal: the fair day's wage, the right to work, the right to gain an adequate, guaranteed standard of living by it, the right to society's protection of their health, safety and even hours, and so on. None of these rights was guaranteed by classical economic theory, which rested on the impersonal laws of the market and repudiated the notion of personal rights. (It is true that classical economic theory was beginning to weaken on the wages fund and the laws of distri-bution, but this was a result of trade union pressure and experi-ence rather than an influence upon them.) The potters in 1844 asserted their right to 'profitable employment' and 'a claim on society for bodily protection and mental development'; the flint glass makers in 1851, ' a perfect right to our trade; we all have a right to claim a living by it'; the Blackburn cotton weavers in 1863, a 'right to toil' as their 'inheritance'.[1] The unions denied the theory of the labour market and the wages fund by words and actions. Daniel Guile of the ironfounders told the Royal

---

[1] *Potters Examiner*, 7 September, 30 November 1844; *Magazine of Flint Glass Makers*, 1851, I. 381; *P.P.*, 1863, XXII, *Reports of Factory Inspectors*, pp. 561–2; R. V. Clements, 'British Trade Unions and Popular Political Economy, 1850–75', *Ec.H.R.*, 1961, XIV. 103.

Commission on Trade Unions that he did not believe that a cut in wages would increase the demand for labour, and asserted that excessive profit margins alone kept wages down. The flint glass makers wrote in 1869: 'it is all very well to talk about the law of supply and demand; we happen to know that there is enough for all and to spare.'[1]

Above all, the unions were forced by the exigencies of industrial conflict to repudiate the central principle of classical economics, the assumed natural harmony of interests between buyer and seller of labour, as of other 'commodities'. Even Dunning, who purported to accept it—'all things being equal, their interest is not one of opposition, but of mutual interest'— and thought that strikes were 'only resorted to on extraordinary, and, generally speaking, most unusual occasions,' considered that industrial conflict was nonetheless inevitable: 'there is no proper alternative, in certain cases, than the position of a strike.'[2] Howell, the self-appointed matchmaker between the classes, concluded reluctantly that strikes

> would appear to be an essential part of the economy of capital and labour, and the natural and inevitable outcome of the relationship now subsisting between employers and employed.... The working classes have to fight for every advantage which they have gained, and for every privilege which they have won; and ... the results which have followed the operations of the unions, the benefits they confer, and the net gains they have realized for their members, have justified their existence, and sanctified the means legitimately employed in securing their several objects.[3]

And William Allan of the engineers, for the Webbs the originator of the pacific 'New Model' unionism, explicitly denied to the Royal Commission the economists' identity of interests:

> There I differ. Every day of the week I hear that the interests are identical. I scarcely see how they can be, while we are in a state of society which recognizes the principle of buying in the cheapest and selling in the dearest market. It is their interest to get the labour at as low a rate as they possibly can, and it is ours to get as

[1] *P.P.*, 1869, R.C. on Trade Unions, *Reports and Evidence*, q. 8756; *Magazine of Flint Glass Makers*, 1869, VI. 711; Clements, *loc. cit.*, p. 102.

[2] Dunning, *op. cit.*, pp. 7, 23.

[3] G. Howell, *The Conflicts of Labour and Capital* (1878), pp. 372, 378.

high a rate of wages as possible, and you never can reconcile these two things.[1]

At bottom the mid-Victorian unions' *raison d'être* was the struggle for income, and for that reason they could not escape their role as class institutions engaged in permanent and inevitable class conflict.

Finally, it was the trade unions which provided the institutional framework which enabled the working class to achieve the political and economic gains outlined above. Again, their role was thrust upon them. The industry-wide amalgamations of the 'New Model' craft unions, the textile unions, and, after several failures, of the mining unions, were necessitated by their chosen methods of action. The 'closed' unions' control of entry to their occupations implied country-wide regulation and a geographical mobility of labour which required industry-wide organization. The 'open' unions' collective negotiation of piece rates and working conditions equally required organization as wide as the region of competing employers and labour. For the cotton unions, concentrated in the two diverse, spinning and weaving, regions of northern and south-eastern Lancashire, this effectively meant industry-wide organization. For the miners, it merely meant coalfield-wide organization, which helps to account for their repeated failure until 1889 to set up a successful, permanent national body.[2]

From a class point of view, a more important step was the amalgamation of all, or most of, the unions into a national entity capable of co-operation in industrial conflict and political agitation. Again, this was an aim as old as the National Association for the Protection of Labour of 1830 or even the 'Philanthropic Hercules' of 1818, but it was not until the solidly-based industry-wide amalgamations came into being that it could be achieved. Even then, it was force of circumstances which thrust it upon the unions. The London Trades Council, one of its founding constituents, grew out of the strike committee which organized support for the London builders' dispute of 1859.[3] Many attempts were made in the 1860's to graft on to it a national

[1] R.C. on Trade Unions, *Evidence*, qq. 8646, 8684, 8924; Clements, *loc. cit.*, p. 103.

[2] Cf. Turner, *op. cit.*, pp. 185–92.

[3] Cole and Filson, *op. cit.*, p. 86.

organization, but they were all thwarted by personal rivalries, notably between Potter of the *Beehive* and the Junta, until a political crisis forced the unions to combine in self-defence.[1] The crisis, brought on by the revival of immature, and now mainly outgrown, violent industrial relations in the Sheffield outrages, and the forensic attack on the security of trade-union funds in the case of Hornby v. Close, demanded concerted countermeasures, especially on the public stage provided by the Royal Commission on Trade Unions appointed in 1867.[2] Even then, it required the separate initiative of the provincial unions, notably the mainly cotton unions of the Manchester and Salford Trades Council, to overcome the divisions of the London crafts and bring the Trades Union Congress into being, and the further crisis, created by the Criminal Law Amendment Act o 1871 and its prohibition of peaceful picketing, to keep it in being, in the shape of its permanent Parliamentary Committee, in its early crucial years.[3]

Reluctant yet inescapable national organization, however, was a solider basis for the institutionalization of the working class than the premature and hollow 'gigantism' of the Grand National Union and its ilk. And if at first it was confined to the few, small and exclusive unions of the labour aristocracy, it was to prove an adequately flexible framework for the enormous expansion of the late Victorian age, and ultimately for the political institutionalization of the working class in the trade unions' creation of the Labour Party.

Thus the aristocratic trade unions of the mid-Victorian age were forced by their class character to create the institutional framework by means of which they not only taught their employers, the Government and the public much of the art of viable class relations, but preserved for a later age with a more favourable socio-political climate the remnant of the working-class ideal. Meanwhile, they also helped to modify and even to undermine the self-confidence of the main middle-class ideal, and so with portentous consequences to open up a fissure between the ideal and the reality of the entrepreneurial society of mid-Victorian England.

[1] Cf. A. E. Musson, *The Trades Union Congress of 1868* (1955).
[2] Cf. S. and B. Webb, *Trade Unionism*, pp. 259–64.
[3] B. C. Roberts, *The Trades Union Congress, 1868–1921* (1958), chap. ii.

X

Entrepreneurial Society: Ideal and Reality

B<small>Y</small> mid-century the entrepreneurial class could feel well pleased with the new society which they had created and persuaded the other classes to accept. In May 1853 Absolom Watkin, Manchester cotton merchant and one of the leading lights of the Anti-Corn Law league, wrote in his diary:

> This is the last day of Whitsun week, and the people of Manchester have never enjoyed it more, nor have I seen clearer evidence of general well-being. Our country is, no doubt, in a most happy and prosperous state. Free trade, peace, and freedom. Oh, happy England! Mayest thou know and deserve thy happiness.[1]

The result of nearly a century of revolutionary industrialism and material progress was that Britain was the richest and most powerful country in the world, the world's workshop, carrier and banker, and head of the greatest empire the world had ever known.

Palmerston in 1850 explained Britain's strength and happiness in terms of the viability and openness of its society:

> We have shown the example of a nation, in which every class in society accepts with cheerfulness the lot which Providence has assigned to it; while at the same time every individual of each class

[1] A. Watkin, *Extracts from his Journal, 1814–56* (ed. A. E. Watkin, 1920), p. 275; Read, *op. cit.*, p. 58.

is constantly striving to raise himself in the social scale—not by injustice and wrong, not by violence and illegality, but by preserving good conduct, and by the steady and energetic execution of the moral and intellectual faculties with which his Creator endowed him.[1]

Here was the aristocratic statesman who almost personified mid-Victorian England embracing on behalf of his order the entrepreneurial ideal of a viable class society tempered by social mobility. The entrepreneurial society had indeed arrived.

But what was the reality underlying the ideal of mid-Victorian society? Was it quite so progressive and prosperous as it has been painted? Or were there already signs of a slackening of industrial growth and technological innovation? Was it, as its champions believed, the best possible society not merely for increasing wealth but for sharing it out more equally between the classes? Or were the rich becoming richer and the poor, if not absolutely, then relatively poorer? Was poverty a relatively minor problem to be solved by individual exertion, or was it a massive one involving a substantial fraction of the population? If upward mobility was the chief compensation for poverty and inequality, how much of it was there, and was it expanding or contracting? If the answers to these questions prove unsatisfactory, then the tensions between ideal and reality were undermining the stability of entrepreneurial society and storing up trouble for the future.

There are still more fundamental questions, however. Did the ideal view of the social structure itself correspond to the reality? Or were changes taking place in the middle class, especially the business middle class, which were transforming the outlook and attitudes of some entrepreneurs and, indeed, evolving them into a new and rather different class of big, corporate business men, the harbingers of the new plutocracy of late Victorian and Edwardian England?

Finally, could the entrepreneurial ideal escape unscathed these tensions and changes in society? Or was it coming under attack from without and defection from within which would ultimately discredit it? And if the ideal lost its grip on society, could the society itself survive unchanged?

So far we have traced the rise of the new class society created

[1] Speech in Don Pacifico debate, 1850, A. Briggs, *Victorian People* (1954), p. 106.

by industrialism. In this last chapter we must look, admittedly beneath the surface, for the first signs of its decline.

1. PROGRESS AND POVERTY

The ideal assumed, first of all, that this was the best of all practicable societies for economic growth. In the 1880's, when the economic system came under open attack for the first time in a generation, Sir Robert Giffen, the representative orthodox economist of his age, told the Statistical Society:

> Whatever may be said as to the ideal perfection or imperfection of the present economic *régime*, the fact of so great an advance having been possible for the masses of the people in the last half-century is encouraging. It is something to know that whether a better *régime* is conceivable or not, human nature being what it is now (and I am one of those who think that the *régime* is the best, the general result of a vast community living as the British nation does, with all the means of healthy life and civilisation at command, being little short of a marvel if we only consider for a moment what vices of anarchy and misrule have had to be rooted out to achieve this marvel); still, whether best or not, it is something to know that vast improvement has been possible with this *régime*. Surely the lesson is that the nation ought to go on improving on the same lines, relaxing none of the efforts which have been so successful. Steady progress in the direction maintained for the last fifty years must soon make the English people vastly superior to what they are now.[1]

It is true that Britain was a much wealthier country than fifty years before; in terms of real national income per head, nearly twice as wealthy, and nearly three times as wealthy as at the beginning of the century. As we saw in Chapter I, it was the defining characteristic of an Industrial Revolution to raise by a multiple both the population and their average real income. Yet there were already signs in the mid-Victorian age that the great acceleration of economic growth inaugurated by the Industrial Revolution had passed its peak and, though it had by no means exhausted itself, was beginning to slow down. General economic growth actually reached its lowest rate for the century in the middle decades centred on the 1850's, the worst decade of

[1] R. Giffen, 'The Progress of the Working Classes in the Last Half-Century', Statistical Society, 20 November 1883, reprinted in *Essays in Finance* (2nd series, 1886), p. 406.

all, and although it regained and even topped the old maximum in the late Victorian age, that was due to the increasing shift from slow growing agriculture to faster growing industry and services rather than to greater productivity in any particular sector.[1] More significantly, industrial production itself, on which everything else hinged, achieved its maximum rate of growth, at 3·5 per cent per annum, in the previous generation, from the 1810's to the late 1840's, and though from then until the early 1870's it was only slightly lower, at 3·2 per cent per annum, in the last few years of the period it slumped to 1·7 per cent per annum, only half the peak rate of the Industrial Revolution.[2]

To a large extent this slackening of the rate of growth was disguised by an increase in the proportion of production exported and in 'invisible exports' like shipping, banking, insurance and overseas investments, the returns from which paid for a considerable but somewhat smaller increase in the rate of growth of imports, until foreign trade too slackened off in the later 1870's.[3] Britain's phenomenal success as firstcomer in the new industrialism was reflected in her record 38 per cent share of the world trade in manufactures in 1876–80, and in her overseas capital balances which quadrupled between 1850 and 1873.[4] But none of this could disguise the fact that it was in the mid-Victorian age that Britain ceased to be the world's only workshop, and that other countries, Belgium, France, Germany and the U.S.A., 'took off' into industrialism, and began, in the last two cases, to achieve rates of growth much faster than anything Britain had ever achieved, which would inevitably take them into the lead in industrial production by the end of the century.[5]

The reasons for this absolute and relative slackening of industrial growth are not altogether clear. There was no slackening of investment. On the contrary, it was in the 1850's and

---

[1] Deane and Cole, *op. cit.*, p. 283.

[2] Rostow, *British Economy*, p. 8; cf. Deane and Cole, *op. cit.*, p. 297: peak rate of growth of industrial production 1820/29–1830/39 1·7 × that of 1850/59–1860/69.

[3] Rostow, *British Economy*, p. 8; Deane and Cole, p. 311.

[4] W. A. Lewis, *Economic Survey, 1919–39* (1960), p. 75; A. H. Imlah, 'British Balance of Payments and Export of Capital', *Ec.H.R.*, 1952, V. 235–7.

[5] The average annual increase of manufacturing production, 1875–1913, in Germany and the United States was 3·9 and 4·8 per cent respectively, as against 1·8 for the United Kingdom, and 3·5 per cent at peak for U.K. in 1813/17–1845/9— Lewis, *op. cit.*, p. 74; Rostow, *loc. cit.*

1860's that capital formation reached its zenith, more indeed than the British economy could absorb, even with the vast amounts sunk in the railways, so that between 3 and 4 per cent of the total national product was invested abroad.[1] The production of producers' goods, although slackening off compared with the previous generation, was still growing at a much faster rate than that of consumers' goods.[2] It was in this period that man-made capital in the shape of buildings, machines, railways and so on came decisively to outweigh the non-man-made, in the form of land—a fact of considerable significance for society.

The explanation would seem to be that most of this vast investment was going into now traditional means of production, textile machinery, coal mining, ironworks, and the like, which had exhausted most of their first, once-for-all potentiality for revolutionary growth in productivity, and now grew more by multiplying plants and workers than by labour-saving machinery. In other words, a broadening of investment, in capital-extensive methods, took over from the deepening of investment, in capital-intensive production. British industrialists were content to exploit on a wider scale the means and devices they knew rather than to risk new and untried lines. There was in fact no lack of British inventions, like Elder's compound marine engine (1845), Bessemer's steel converter (1856), Perkin's aniline dyes (1856), Siemens, Wheatstone and Varley's principle of the dynamo (1867), Bell's telephone (1878), Swan's electric lamp (1878), or the Gilchrist-Thomas steel process (1879). But it is significant that many of these were taken up much faster and on a larger scale in America, Germany and elsewhere, and that many of the most fundamental inventions for future industry, like the sewing machine, the internal combustion engine, and electric traction, now originated overseas. Compared with America, Germany and France, technical education was neglected in Britain, as shrewd observers began to point out.[3] Beneath, and perhaps because of, the undoubted industrial supremacy of Britain there was a complacency to-

[1] Deane, *First Industrial Revolution*, pp. 156, 160.

[2] Rostow, *loc. cit.*

[3] Cf. *P.P.*, 1868, *S.C. on Scientific Instruction*; Michael Argles, *South Kensington to Robbins: an Account of English Technical and Scientific Instruction since 1851* (1964), pp. 25–7.

wards innovation which goes far towards explaining the loss of momentum which ultimately cost her the leadership.

It may of course be argued that this policy of expanding known and traditional lines paid off in the short run, in the prosperity of the so-called mid-Victorian boom. People are as prosperous as they feel, and to this extent the age was prosperous, but by objective standards it was much less prosperous than they supposed. National income per head in terms of current prices rose between 1855 and 1873 by 56 per cent. But part of this was due to inflation, and the increase in real income per head was only 46 per cent, most of it coming in the cyclical boom from 1869 to 1873, so that for most of the 1850's and 1860's real incomes stagnated or crept up very slowly.[1] Moreover, the evidence suggests that real national income per head was rising no faster in the 'prosperous' and 'contented' mid-Victorian period than in the 'depressed' and 'discontented' periods before and after it.[2] As was argued in Chapter IX vis-à-vis the depression and discontent of the previous period, the belief in prosperity and the contentment of the mid-Victorian age were at least in part due to the mollifying effect of inflation on class conflict and the struggle for income.

On the question of the distribution of income between the classes the ideal assumed, secondly, that entrepreneurial society had a built-in mechanism for sharing out the benefits of material progress not merely with reasonable fairness but with increasing equality. Sir Robert Giffen in the paper quoted above proved to his own satisfaction that

the rich have become more numerous but not richer individually; the 'poor' are, to some smaller extent, fewer; and those who remain 'poor' are, individually, twice as well off on the average as they were fifty years ago. The 'poor' have thus had almost all the benefit of the great material advance of the last fifty years.

While aggregate wages had increased by 160 per cent and

[1] Deane and Cole, op. cit., p. 329.

[2] Real national income (at 1900 prices) rose 1855/59–1875/79 by 47 per cent, or 2·4 per cent p.a.; 1875/79–1895/99 by 52 per cent, or 2·5 per cent p.a.—calculated from B. R. Mitchell and P. Deane, Abstract of British Historical Statistics (Cambridge, 1962), p. 367. Reliable comparative figures are not available before 1855, but contemporary estimates suggest a doubling between 1812 and 1851, equal to a rate of c. 2·5 per cent p.a.—P. Deane, 'Contemporary Estimates of National Income in 19th Century', Ec.H.R., 1957, IX. 459.

average wages by 100 per cent, income from capital had increased in aggregate by only 30 per cent and on average 'hardly at all'.[1] His friend Leone Levi went even further, and almost proved too much: while over the shorter period, 1851–80, average wages had increased by 59 per cent, the average business man's 'family income' had actually declined by 30 (strictly, 34) per cent.[2]

These gratifying conclusions were in fact based on elementary statistical errors. Both Giffen and Levi compared subjectively selected wage rates, themselves open to question, with the average income of a taxpaying class which was not a fixed but an increasing fraction of the occupied population, and radically changed its composition between the chosen dates. While money incomes rose steeply, the fixed tax-exemption limit cut off an increasing segment of the income pyramid, thus weighting the average with a large influx of small incomes which automatically reduced it. Giffen's wage statistics, moreover, were a very haphazard collection, showing increases ranging from 20 'and in most cases from 50 to 100 per cent', which he then interpreted as an *average* of 100 per cent.[3] Levi was even more cavalier in his treatment of income tax statistics, and by a species of legerdemain turned a supposed 10 per cent fall in average profits under Schedule D into a 34 per cent fall in 'incomes per family'.[4] In short, both eminent statisticians were so eager to tell their hearers what they wanted to hear that they failed to compare like with like, and even doctored the already erroneous results to fit their theories.

The objective facts of profits and wages for the period 1850–1880 are set out in Table 5. They show that, far from declining, average business profits assessed under Schedule D for the same fraction of the occupied population as paid tax in 1850 had risen by 1880 by no less than 60 per cent, while average wages, allowing for unemployment and for the movement to better-paid occupations, had increased by 47 per cent (39 per cent allowing for unemployment) and for the worker of unchanged occupation by only 31 per cent (24 per cent allowing for unemployment).

[1] Giffen, *op. cit.*, p. 405.
[2] L. Levi, *Wages and Earnings of the Working Classes* (1885 ed.), p. 55.
[3] Giffen, *op. cit.*, pp. 372, 405.   [4] Levi, *op. cit.*, pp. 47–50, 54–5.

TABLE 5

PROFITS AND WAGES, 1850–80

A. Profits returned under Schedule D, 1850/51 and 1879/80

1	1850/51			1879/80			
	2	3	4	5	6	7	8
Income 1850/51 (1879/80)	Number	Amount £000	Mean £	Equivalent Number	Amount £000	Mean £	Percentage increase in mean
£3,000+ (£4,887+)	1,889	14,678	7,770	2,626	33,937	12,924	66·3
£500–£3,000 (£793–£4,887)	18,335	17,054	930	25,486	38,055	1,493	60·5
£150–£500 (£235–£793)	90,231	20,282	223	125,421	43,752	349	56·5
All tax-payers 1850/51 £150+ (£235+)	110,455	52,014	471	153,533	115,744	754	60·1
Non-tax-payers 1850/51 Under £150 (£150–£235)	—	—	—	199,510	34,091	171	—
All tax-payers 1879/80 (£150+)	—	—	—	353,043	149,835	424	—

B. Indices of Money Wages, 1850–80

	1850	1880
Unweighted average (not allowing for changes in occupation):	100	131
Ditto, allowing for unemployment:	100	124
Weighted average (allowing for changes in occupation):	100	147
Ditto, allowing for unemployment:	100	139

SOURCES: A. Return giving Number of Persons and Gross Amount of Profits assessed under Schedule D in Great Britain, 1850–51 and 1879–80, specially supplied by the Commissioners of Inland Revenue to Leone Levi, *Wages and Earnings of the Working Classes* (1885 ed.), p. 58. The 1850–51 returns include a small number of public companies (excluding mines, quarries, ironworks, gasworks, railways, waterworks, canals, etc) not included in 1879–80; in so far as they inflate

The table suggests that distribution of income was becoming more unequal not only between the business and working classes but within the business class itself, where the average income of the highest group of taxpayers was increasing significantly faster than those of the middle and lower groups. This is not surprising in an age when, as we shall see in the next section, a new type of big business man was beginning to emerge from the entrepreneurial class.

A similar increase in inequality was taking place in the landed class, where the small agricultural squires were doing less well than the great landlords with supplementary income from mining, transport and urban property. While non-agricultural rents continued to rise much faster than prices, the rent of land alone lagged behind, so that real income from agricultural land may even have begun to decline. The aggregate rent of land (as distinct from buildings, etc.) returned in England and Wales under Schedule A1 by a practically stationary landed class rose between 1850 and 1873 by no more than 16 per cent, while agricultural prices rose by 29 per cent and general prices by 32 per cent.[1] As their historian writes, 'Behind the façade of the "Golden Age of English Agriculture", a distinct weakening in the economic position of the agricultural landowners can be detected.'[2] It is a wry comment on mid-Victorian 'prosperity' that it began the modern decline of the gentry. Meanwhile, aggregate rents of houses, etc., over the same period increased by over 100 per cent,[3] and though this did not all accrue to the great landlords, enough did so to more than compensate them for their agricultural losses, thus further widening the gap between the great and small landowners. The 'New Domesday Book' of 1873–76 showed that some 2,500 landlords in the United Kingdom owned more than 3,000 acres each, worth

[1] J. C. Stamp, *British Incomes and Property* (1916), p. 49, table A4, Schedule A(1), Lands (including Tithes)—'a very stable series for purposes of comparison', pp. 41–2.

[2] F. M. L. Thompson, *op. cit.*, p. 240.

[3] Stamp, *op. cit.*, p. 50.

the mean for 1850–51 their effect is to depress slightly the real increase in the mean. The 'equivalent number' in column 5 is calculated from column $2 \times 1 \cdot 39$ (= increase in occupied population, 1851–81), and column 6 is their aggregate income estimated by graphing (Lorenz curve: percentage assessment/percentage income). B. G. H. Wood, 'Real Wages and the Standard of Comfort since 1850', *Stat.J.*, 1909, LXXII. 102–3.

more than £3,000 a year, exclusive of London property. Of these, 866 had rentals of over £10,000, 76 of over £50,000, and 15 of over £100,000.[1] These were the owners who had gained and continued to gain most from industrialism and the growth of towns, and to leave their country cousins still further behind.

Within the working class, too, there is some evidence that the skilled workers with their natural or artificial monopoly of their trades did better than the unskilled at the mercy of the free labour market.[2] Authentic unskilled wages are hard to come by, but builders' labourers' wage rates in London and Manchester, for example, rose between 1850 and the later 1870's by 25 and 33 per cent respectively, while the craftsmen's wage rates rose by 50 per cent or more. Agricultural wages, which set the floor for unskilled wages generally, lagged behind the average rate of increase until the spurt associated with Arch's agricultural labourers' union in 1872–74. With the exception of printing, wages in all the higher-paid industries, iron and engineering, building, and mining, advanced until 1874 faster than those in the lower-paid, wool, cotton and agriculture.[3]

Thus what objective evidence there is suggests, contrary to contemporary opinion, not only that the rich were getting richer at a faster rate than the poor, but that the whole scale of income distribution was being stretched, so that inequalities were increasing within as well as between classes, from top to bottom of society. This increasing inequality, at all levels, of income distribution is what we should expect in a free-for-all society rapidly increasing in wealth and population, in which the few possessed of valuable resources or special talents, skills or energy enjoyed unprecedented opportunities for increasing their incomes, while the many were forced by their lack of these and by their own increasing numbers to sell their services in a buyers' market. It is confirmed by all the circumstantial evidence. The peak rate of investment was reached between the 1830's and the 1870's, when man-made or reproducible capital increased between 1833 and 1865 from just over three to about

[1] J. Bateman, *The Great Landowners of Great Britain and Ireland* (1879), pp. 490–1.

[2] Cf. Hobsbawm, *Labouring Men*, p. 293.

[3] A. L. Bowley, *Wages in the United Kingdom in the 19th Century* (1900), pp. 62, graph opp. 90, 130–1, 132–3 and graph.

four-and-a-half times the national income,[1] thus arguing a very considerable shift in income distribution towards profits available for re-investment. The ratio of domestic servants to population reached its peak, at nearly one in six of the occupied population between 1871 and 1891,[2] a sure sign that the servant-keeping class could afford to purchase a larger proportion of the labour of the rest. The specific forms of the new wealth—gargantuan meals for the rich, new and larger houses with gas lighting, hot water, flush lavatories, bathrooms, patent kitchen stoves, the hideously comfortable and expensive furniture and decorations, the 'monumental' fashions in women's dress of the crinoline and bustle periods, the top hats and tails of the men's, all more or less confined to the well-to-do classes—argue a shift of income towards the wealthy. So does the new physical framework of community life, with passenger transport on a much larger scale, horse buses and suburban railways, almost confined to the middle and upper classes, and the new segregated suburbs to provide clean air and decent sanitation, and therefore better health and longer life, as well as social exclusiveness.

It is of course true that industrialism was already providing benefits for many, in increased quantities of food, clothing and, rather more belatedly, decent housing, and that in the long run it would do so for most. But the argument is that in the short run the benefits came first and in larger quantities to the well-to-do, and that the initial effect down to and including the mid-Victorian age was to increase the lead of the rich over the poor. It is a phenomenon exactly parallel to that in population growth, in which the rich were the first to benefit from reduced mortality and, later, from smaller families, so that for a transitional period in each case, although longevity and, later, smaller families were increasing amongst all classes, the gap between rich and poor considerably widened. All the evidence suggests that, in spite of the undoubted improvement in real wages, the transitional gap in income distribution between rich and poor was at its widest in the mid-Victorian age, when the free-for-all society was at its zenith and before the efforts of the State to redress the balance by means of welfare benefits for the poor had begun to have much effect.

[1] Deane, *op. cit.*, pp. 155–6.   [2] Deane and Cole, *op. cit.*, p. 142.

Some statistical confirmation of this may be derived fro..
Dudley Baxter's well-known analysis of the distribution of the
national income in 1867, which he compared to the Atlantic
peak of Teneriffe, 'a good emblem of a wealthy state, with its
long low base of labouring population, with its uplands of the
middle classes, and with its towering peaks and summits of those
with princely incomes.'[1] It is a remarkably accurate analysis,
but for comparative purposes it has three defects: it deals with
individual, not family, incomes; it omits those without incomes
other than poor relief or charity; and it overstates the number of
income taxpayers, according to Stamp by as much as two-
thirds.[2] Happily, these defects tend to cancel out each other,
and we might almost use the figures as they stand. However, an
attempt has been made, in Table 6, to translate them into family
incomes, as explained in the adjacent notes, in order to compare
them with those of Colquhoun for 1803 in Chapter II.[3]

The translation is not completely satisfactory, since the
average family, at 3·4 persons, is somewhat too small, but the
error is much the same for each class, and the Table has the
merit of approximating the division of incomes to the distribution of the occupied population derived by Baxter from the 1861
Census.[4] It also yields much the same distribution of family
incomes as Baxter's distribution of individual incomes, for the
reason given above.

The resulting comparison is so striking that it would require
an enormous margin of error to overturn it. Whereas in 1803
more than one family in a hundred (1·4 per cent) shared less
than a sixth (15·7 per cent) of the national income, in 1867 less
than one family in a thousand (0·07 per cent) shared about the
same proportion (16·2 per cent) of the national income. The
top 2 per cent in 1803 shared about a fifth, in 1867 about two-
fifths of the income; and the top 10 per cent in 1803 about two-
fifths, in 1867 over half the income.[5] Because of the distortion
of the income scale produced by Baxter's peculiar residuary
intermediate class, which contained many clerks, shop assistants,

[1] R. D. Baxter, *National Income* (1868), p. 1.

[2] Stamp, *op. cit.*, p. 449: he estimates 420,000 over £150, compared with
Baxter's 700,000 (deducting 196,000 £100–£150).

[3] See Table 1, pp. 20–1, above.

[4] Baxter, *op. cit.*, p. 15.

[5] Estimated by graphing (Lorenz curves).

TABLE 6

RIBUTION OF THE NATIONAL INCOME BETWEEN FAMILIES,
ENGLAND AND WALES, 1867

	Families		Income	
	Number 000	Per-centage	Amount £000	Per-centage
I. Upper Class				
(1) £5,000+	4·5	0·07	111,104	16·2
(2) £1,000—£5,000	25·2	0·41	69,440	10·1
II. Middle Class				
£300–£1,000	90·0	1·46	72,912	10·6
III. Lower Middle				
(1) £100–£300	510·3	8·29	93,744	13·7
(2) Under £100	946·0	15·37	70,958	10·3
Upper and Middle Classes	1,576·0	25·6	418,158	60·9
IV. Higher Skilled	840·8	13·8	72,028	10·5
V. Lower Skilled	1,610·0	26·1	112,042	16·3
VI. Unskilled and Agricultural	1,516·8	24·6	70,659	10·3
VII. Wageless families	610·4	9·9	13,466	2·0
Manual Labour Classes	4,588·0	74·4	268,195	39·1
All Classes	6,154·0	100·0	686,353	100·0

NOTES:
1. Estimated from R. D. Baxter, *National Income* (1868), as explained below.
2. The number of taxpayers in each class I–III (1) has been reduced by 40 per cent to conform with Stamp's estimate, and one family allowed per taxpayer.
3. The non-taxpaying middle class, III (2), has been increased to absorb the above reduction, and then allowed one and a half income earners per family, and an average family income of £75.
4. The manual labour classes, IV–VI, have been allowed one family per adult male wage-earner (on the assumption that the bachelors would very roughly offset families supported by women or child breadwinners). To even out subsidiary earners, one-third of the women's and children's income in class V has been transferred to class IV. The resultant family incomes average for class IV £85·7 and for class V £69·6.
5. Class VII is a new category based on the daily average number of paupers in 1866, 916,000, plus an equivalent number presumed to be living on charity, etc., and allowed one family to three persons (cf. Rowntree's poorest class A in York, 1899, *Poverty: a Study of Town Life*, p. 58). Their income has been estimated from the average amount of poor relief in the 1860's, £7 10s. per head, or £22 10s. per family.

small dealers and 'collectors', who earned much less than the highly skilled manual workers, the working-class majority appears not to be very much worse off than the equivalent group in 1803 (with 39 per cent as compared with 42 per cent), but when allowance is made for the disproportionate share of this going to the small and relatively prosperous aristocracy of skilled labour (in Baxter's original distribution of individual incomes one worker in seven shared nearly a quarter of the available wages), it is clear that the mass of less skilled workers had lost considerable ground. All this confirms the conclusion we reached in the discussion on living standards in Chapter V, that, whether or not real wages improved in the first half of the nineteenth century, they lagged far behind the general increase in national income per head.[1] The main effect of the Industrial Revolution on the distribution of income was to make it very much more unequal.

Perhaps relative inequality, even increasing inequality, does not matter if living standards for the poor are rising absolutely, and poverty is declining. The entrepreneurial ideal assumed, thirdly, that the economic system provided work for all, at least at subsistence wages, and that such poverty as there was, apart from the inevitable cases of misfortune and hardship dealt with by charity and the poor laws, was voluntary, the result of individual vice, improvidence and idleness. If pauperism was an adequate test, poverty was declining, relatively if not absolutely. In 1803 there were just over a million paupers in England and Wales, or about one in nine of the population. In 1850 and again in 1870 there were still almost exactly the same number (though the mid-Victorian average was slightly lower), but in a much larger population they represented less than half the proportion, about one in eighteen and one in twenty-three respectively.[2] But the tightening of poor-law administration by the 1834 Act and the enormous burgeoning of mid-Victorian charity suggest that pauperism is not an adequate test. The New Poor Law was designed to stamp out outdoor relief for the able-bodied, and within the workhouses the able-bodied declined from 38 per cent of the inmates in 1842 to 15 per cent in 1860, and remained around that proportion for the rest of the century.[3] Meanwhile, contemporary estimates show that in the 1860's far larger sums were dispersed in organized charity than in poor

---

[1] Cf. chap. v, § 1, above.
[2] 1803 1,040,000; 1850 1,009,000; 1870 1,033,000—Colquhoun, *Indigence*, p. 36; Porter, *op. cit.*, (1912 ed.), p. 70.
[3] Porter, *op. cit.*, p. 72.

relief, while the extent of casual charity cannot be gauged at all.[1]

The amount and degree of poverty in mid-Victorian England can therefore only be guessed. Informed contemporaries like Henry Mayhew, who chronicled the starvation earnings and conditions of the London street folk, or Dr. Edward Smith who in 1863 found representative groups of domestic workers in London and the provinces spending sums of from 2s. 6¼d. to 2s. 9½d. a week per adult on food, many of them 'insufficiently nourished, and of feeble health', knew it to be enormous.[2] At the very time when Sir Robert Giffen was arguing that 'The general conclusion from all the facts is, that what has happened to the working classes in the last fifty years is not so much what may properly be called an improvement, as a revolution of the most remarkable description,' Charles Booth was beginning the first modern social survey, which was to show that 30·7 per cent of the population of London was living in poverty.[3]

Where all is guesswork an informed guess may be allowed, by working backwards from the first survey to afford a precise definition of poverty, that of Rowntree in York in 1899. Rowntree defined the poverty line as the 'minimum necessary expenditure for the maintenance of merely physical health', and divided the poor into those families whose total income fell below this line and were therefore in 'primary' poverty, and those whose total income came only slightly above but were pulled down below it by other expenditure, either useful or wasteful, and were therefore in 'secondary' poverty. He found that 27·84 per cent of the population of York in 1899, one of the most prosperous years of the nineteenth century, were in poverty (9·91 per cent in primary and 17·93 per cent in secondary poverty). Rowntree's poverty line was calculated separately for each family, but for a typical family of man, wife and two

[1] Sampson Low, jr., *The Charities of London* (1862), pp. xi, 86, estimated London charities at £2,441,967, as against Metropolitan poor relief in 1857 of £1,425,063; Thomas Hawkesley, *The Charities of London* (1889), p. 7, estimated both together at £7 million, the great bulk of it being charity; Woodroofe, *op. cit.*, pp. 26–7.

[2] Mayhew, *op. cit.*, (1851 ed.), p. iii; Report by Dr. Edward Smith on Food of Labouring Classes in England, *6th Report of the Medical Officer of Privy Council*, 1863, pp. 219f.; Burnett, *op. cit.*, pp. 150–3.

[3] Giffen, 'Further Notes on the Progress of the Working Classes'; *loc. cit.*, p. 473; Booth, *op. cit.*, II. 21.

dependent children in 1899 was 18s. 10d. a week.[1] For 1867, when prices were much higher though rents somewhat lower, we can estimate the same line at 22s. 11d., or nearly £60 a year.[2] In Table 2 the averages of the lowest class of paupers, etc., and of the unskilled working class fall so far below this line that comparatively few families can have risen above it. Those who did would certainly have come within the zone where the slightest misspending of income would thrust them down into poverty, and, judging by the record spending in mid-Victorian England on beer, which reached an all-time peak in 1876,[3] secondary poverty would be larger in 1867 than in 1899. And those in the unskilled class who still managed to escape both kinds of poverty would probably be balanced by those in the class immediately above, with an average income only marginally above the line, who succumbed.

We can therefore guess that the equivalent of the whole of classes VI and VII in Table 6 were in either primary or secondary poverty in 1867, or 35·5 per cent in all, a figure clearly compatible with that for Booth's London in 1889. A society in which a third of the population was in poverty by the low standards of 1899, which Rowntree himself considered inadequate as a basis for his later surveys in 1936 and 1949,[4] cannot be called prosperous in any absolute sense.

The ideal assumed, fourthly, that both poverty and inequality were adequately compensated by increased opportunities for improving one's standard of living by social climbing. The myth of the self-made man was enshrined in Samuel Smiles' *Self-Help* only in 1859. Giffen relied on the movement from lower-paid to higher-paid jobs to double the rate of increase in wages.[5] Levi declared that

> In a large number of instances working men of 1857 have become middle-class men of 1884. Many a workman of that day has now a shop or an hotel, has money in the bank or shares in shipping or

[1] Rowntree, *op. cit.* (2nd. ed., n.d.), pp. 119, 144, 150–1.

[2] Calculated with the aid of commodity prices and rents in G. H. Wood, 'Real Wages and the Standard of Comfort since 1850', *Stat.J.*, 1909, LXXII. 91f.

[3] Burnett, *op. cit.*, pp. 81, 155.

[4] B. S. Rowntree, *Poverty and Progress: a Second Social Survey of York* (1941), pp. 28–30, 101–9; Rowntree and G. R. Lavers, *Poverty and the Welfare State: a Third Social Survey of York* (1951), pp. 8–9.

[5] Giffen, *op. cit.*, pp. 422–4.

mills. Cases of rising from the ranks are by no means so rare as we might imagine.[1]

Even Mill, who doubted whether industrialism had benefited the workers as a class, believed that it had increased their individual chances in life. The distinguishing feature of modern society was the fact that

> human beings are no longer born to their place in life . . . but are free to employ their faculties and such favourable chances as offer, to achieve the lot which may appear to them most desirable.[2]

There is of course no doubt that there was a considerable amount of upward mobility in mid-Victorian England, as in all periods of modern English history. 'Petty's law', the movement of labour with economic growth from agriculture to industry and services, continued to operate, with two significant new features. The relative decline of agricultural employment now became an absolute one, shrinking between 1851 and 1881 from a fifth to an eighth of the occupied population and from 2·1 to 1·7 million persons. And for the first time the proportion employed in manufacturing and mining industry ceased to grow, and the emphasis shifted to the growth of trade, transport and other services.[3] Not all of the expansion was in higher-paid occupations, for shop-assistants, clerks, domestic servants and even teachers were often paid less than skilled manual workers, but the upward movement on balance was strong enough to raise the average increase in money wages over the period 1850–80 from 24 to 39 per cent.[4] There was also a significant expansion of middle-class occupations, and not merely of the lowly white-collar employments mentioned above. All the professions, including central and local government, expanded faster than the occupied population, with the doubtful exception of law and medicine, whose advance the Census probably understates.[5] And the trebling of the number of Schedule D assessments in Table 5 above compared with a 39 per cent growth in the occupied population is probably evidence of an upward movement into and within the business middle class. Against these upward

[1] Levi, *op. cit.*, p. 30.

[2] J. S. Mill, *Principles*, p. 455; *The Subjection of Women* (1869), p. 31.

[3] Deane and Cole, *op. cit.*, pp. 142–3.   [4] G. H. Wood, *loc. cit.*, pp. 102–3.

[5] Cf. H. J. Perkin, 'Middle-Class Education and Employment in the 19th Century: a Critical Note', *Ec.H.R.*, 1961, XIV. 128.

movements must be set certain contrary ones, such as the continuing decline of self-employed workers from perhaps 20 per cent in the 1820's to 11 or 12 per cent towards the end of the century, and, with the growing size of units of production, the increasing proportion of workmen to managers.[1] But on balance the general drift was certainly upward.

The important questions, however, are whether the extent of the upward mobility was greater or smaller than before, and whether in the mid-Victorian period itself it was expanding or contracting. To the first the answer is the more elusive, but it is probably negative. Leslie Stephen believed that 'there is probably no period in English history at which a greater number of poor men have risen to distinction' than at the end of the eighteenth and beginning of the nineteenth century—instancing writers, scientists and scholars rather than inventors and industrialists. Since then, however, patronage and free education for the intelligent poor had substantially declined, and it is doubtful whether the mid-Victorians could produce such a galaxy as that cited by Stephen.[2] Samuel Smiles' industrial heroes risen from the ranks were mostly drawn from the eighteenth and the early rather than the mid-nineteenth century, and even that optimist betrays a feeling that the heroic age is past.[3] Finally, such evidence as there is suggests that fewer new men founded landed families in the nineteenth than in the eighteenth century. In three typical counties, Shropshire, Oxfordshire and Essex, in 1873, fewer estates belonged to new families which had arrived in the nineteenth than to those which had survived from eighteenth-century founders.[4]

On the second question there is much better evidence, and it all points to a contraction of opportunities for social climbing during the mid-Victorian age. In the two industries whose leaders have been studied, steel and factory hosiery, both new industries in this period, the chances of rising from humble origins were comparatively small and steadily declined.[5] The

---

[1] Deane and Cole, *op. cit.*, pp. 149–50.

[2] L. Stephen, *The English Utilitarians* (1900), i. 111–12 (Burns, Paine, Cobbett, Gifford, Dalton, Porson, Joseph White, Owen, Lancaster, Watt, Telford, Rennie).

[3] S. Smiles, *Lives of the Engineers* (1861–65), *passim*.

[4] F. M. L. Thompson, *op. cit.*, pp. 124–5.

[5] Charlotte Erickson, *British Industrialists: Steel and Hosiery, 1850–1950* (Cambridge, 1959), pp. 12, 56, 93, 129.

majority of entrepreneurs and company officials, in hosiery in 1871 52 per cent, in steel in 1865 89 per cent, came from the landed, business or professional classes, and most of the rest, 33 and 7 per cent respectively, from the lower middle class of retailers, clerks, foremen and self-employed craftsmen. Only a small minority, in hosiery 16 per cent, in steel 4 per cent, were the sons of manual workers, and even these small percentages were declining, to 9 in hosiery by 1905, to 3 in steel by 1875–95. The proportion of managers and officials who had themselves started as manual workers was smaller still, and between the same dates declined in hosiery from 11 to 2 per cent, in steel from 13 to 4 per cent. Still more significant for the direction of the trend was the difference between the two industries. The more traditional, small-scale hosiery industry, dominated by old-fashioned individual entrepreneurs and partnerships was the more open to outsiders and social climbers, while the more progressive, large-scale steel industry rapidly became the more closed, exclusive and patrician in its recruitment and connections. Limited companies in both, moreover, recruited still fewer of their leaders from the working class, and in so far as they recruited more from outside existing business families, took them from the clerks and professional men in the office.[1] The incipient managerialism of the joint-stock company favoured the already middle-class office worker rather than the manual worker.

This would perhaps have mattered less if educational opportunities for manual worker's sons had been improving, but they were not. If elementary education was expanding, secondary education for the working class, as we saw in Chapter VIII, was disappearing with the conversion of free grammar schools into fee-charging day and boarding schools and of free places into scholarships requiring expensive preparation.[2] As for higher education, 'from 1854 to 1904 was the most difficult time for the poor scholar to make his way to Oxford and Cambridge,' while the new provincial university colleges were exclusively middle-class.[3] Thus with industrial opportunities declining on

---

[1] *Ibid.*, pp. 189–93.

[2] Cf. chap. viii, § 2 above; and Brian Simon, *op. cit.*, pp. 312–18, 325–35.

[3] A. Mansbridge, *The Older Universities of England* (1923), pp. 108–9; Armytage, *Civic Universities*, chaps. viii–x.

the one side and educational opportunities disappearing on the other, upward mobility for the working class was probably at its nadir, and could scarcely provide adequate compensation for the poverty and inequality of entrepreneurial society.

At the other end of the social scale, too, upward mobility in the form of the rise of individual new men into the landed class was certainly more difficult than before. The greatest single source of new men, government patronage and the perquisites of high office, was drying up. The Lord Chancellorship had once been the high road to landed status, but between 1832 and 1885 six of the eleven Lord Chancellors were virtually landless, and the rest acquired much smaller estates than those of the past. Twenty of the twenty-six 'poor' peers with less than 3,000 acres in 1873 were government servants who would in the past have been amply endowed.[1] At the same time, for them as for business men and others, the cost of acquiring a landed estate was at its highest in the mid-Victorian age, with both rents and the number of years' purchase at their zenith. The cost of a typical 1,000-acre estate had risen since the eighteenth century from about £12,000 to over £30,000, and rose still further in the land boom of the 1860's and early 1870's, when £1,000 a year in rent might cost £40,000 to acquire.[2] The competition for land was fierce, and many wealthy new men had to make do with more modest estates than previously, or even with country seats with little or no land attached.

The high price of land, however, argued no lack of large fortunes made in business. Far from declining, the number of business men who could vie with the landlords in wealth was rapidly increasing. But this was part of a far more disturbing movement in mid-Victorian society than the mere rise of new men, whose function had always been to maintain the dynamic stability of English society. Now the rise of individuals was being overtaken by the rise of a whole class, or, rather, of an important section of a class. For it was not the entrepreneurial class as a whole which was beginning to rise above itself, but a class of new and bigger business men, mostly corporate capitalists in the new large-scale joint-stock companies, who differed in outlook and attitudes in important ways from the traditional individual owner-manager. If the tensions and dichotomies

[1] F. M. L. Thompson, *op. cit.*, pp. 56–7, 61–2.   [2] *Ibid.*, p. 122.

between the ideal and reality of entrepreneurial society in the matters of material progress, poverty, increasing inequality and decreasing social mobility were a threat to its stability and permanence, how much more so was the evolution of a new business class which, as we must now see, did not accept either the traditional place or the whole ideal of the entrepreneur.

2. THE EMERGING PLUTOCRACY

The entrepreneurial ideal assumed that the middle class consisted predominantly of business men, large and small, who, whatever their line of business and scale of operation, were distinguished from the other two major classes by the fact that they both owned and actively managed their businesses, and earned profits which varied with both the size of their capital and the skill and intensity of their activity. In short, they were entrepreneurs, in the sense of active owner-managers individually responsible for their firms and partnerships, who considered themselves morally superior to both idle landowners and irresponsible wage-earners in providing the initiative, drive and direction of the economic system.

We have already seen, of course, that this necessarily oversimplified view—necessarily, because all class ideals can exist only by oversimplifying—left out a major section of the middle class, the professional middle class. Until the mid-nineteenth century, however, the professional class could be readily accommodated within the entrepreneurial ideal, partly because it was the forgotten middle class, which left itself out of its own versions of the class structure, but mainly because until then most professional men were still paid by fees, returned their incomes for tax purposes under Schedule D (profits) like any business man, and lived and worked amongst urban business men who differed very little from themselves in basic outlook and way of life. As we saw in Chapter VIII, it was chiefly in the salaried civil servants from the 1830's onwards that the professional ideal began to diverge from the entrepreneurial.

The mid-Victorian age, however, was the key period for the emergence and consolidation of the leading professions, and for the crystallization of the professional ideal as a separate entity, increasingly critical of the entrepreneurial. Between 1841 and

1881 professional occupations trebled in number, compared with a two-thirds increase in general population, and came to constitute a substantial element in the middle class.[1] Although the professions and public services (omitting the police and armed forces) constituted only about $3·8$ per cent of the male occupied population in 1867, they equalled about a sixth of non-manual occupations, and if they had all paid tax (which they did not) would have constituted over half the taxpaying class.[2] More important, the leading professions were rising in public recognition and status, and more clearly distinguishing themselves and their systems of remuneration from business men and the profit motive. Beginning with the British Medical Association in 1856 a new and much larger wave of professional institutions came into existence for doctors, dentists, mechanical, mining and electrical engineers, naval architects, accountants, surveyors, chemists, teachers and others, expressly to exclude quacks and charlatans who put profit before professional service. Beginning with the Medical Registration Act, 1858, State regulation to ensure professional standards by the exclusion of the free market was introduced for doctors, dentists, pharmacists, ships' masters and mine managers, while the civil service was forged into a profession by the reforms of 1855 and 1870. It is also interesting to note that the salaried professions, education, religion, journalism, and central and local government, were expanding faster than the fee-charging, medicine and law.[3]

Professional men, as we have seen, were freer than most to choose sides in the socio-economic struggle, and no doubt many of them took their conscious political outlook from their families, friends and clients, but their increasing professionalism led many of them increasingly to differentiate themselves from the business class and to play an important part in criticizing the entrepreneurial policy of *laissez-faire* and replacing it by collectivism. The divergence of the professional and entrepreneurial ideals foreshadowed in the previous generation actually took place in the mid-Victorian age.

[1] W. J. Reader, *Professional Men* (1966), p. 211.

[2] I.e. c. 375,000 professional compared with 2,053,000 non-manual workers and 700,000 taxpayers with over £150 (or 420,000 on Stamp's estimate)—C. Booth, 'Occupations of the People of the United Kingdom', *Stat.J.*, 1886, XLIX. 363–6; Baxter, *op. cit.*, p. 36; Stamp, *op. cit.*, p. 449.　　　[3] Cf. Perkin, *loc. cit.*, p. 128.

More significant even than this defection of their chief ally, however, was the undermining of the entrepreneurial class from within by the emergence of a new class of big business men who no longer fitted the simple model of the entrepreneur. This was a logical consequence of the continuing rise in the scale of organization, the first effect of which had been to create the industrial owner-manager. Now a further turn of the spiral was creating enterprises which were too large to be owned and managed by a single entrepreneur or partnership, except by elaborate schemes of delegation. Giant family businesses did indeed survive, but their owners could no longer supervise them daily at shop-floor level. They were forced to act through professional managers, and to become themselves remote controllers of finance and general policy. The more normal device was the joint-stock company which, after its phenomenal success with the railways and the legalization of limited liability under the Companies Acts of 1856–62, spread rapidly throughout large-scale industry. The number of registered companies (excluding railways and other chartered or parliamentary companies) carrying on business grew from under 1,000 in 1844 to nearly 3,000 in 1868 and over 10,000 in 1887.[1] Only a minority were in manufacturing industry, but they were nevertheless in process of becoming the normal form for the largest enterprises, and they naturally dominated the large-scale industries and services, notably railways, shipping, telegraphs, banking, insurance, mining, gas and water.

Whether joint-stock company or giant family business, the large-scale enterprise changed the outlook of the controlling business man. For one thing, it became much more difficult to give up business and retire to the land. As early as the 1820's William Crawshay, senior, of Cyfarthfa found it nearly impossible to withdraw his three-fifths share from the £½ million ironworks without ruining the business.[2] When the joint-stock company solved this problem by creating transferable shares, it still kept the giant concern in being to be controlled by someone, who might by degrees come to own only a minority of the shares,

---

[1] B. C. Hunt, *The Development of the Business Corporation in England, 1800–67* (Cambridge, Mass., 1936), pp. 88, 157; Clapham, *Economic History*, III. 201.

[2] J. P. Addis, *The Crawshay Dynasty: a Study in Industrial Organization and Development, 1765–1867* (Cardiff, 1957), pp. 38, 46–9.

but still wielded the whole power of its capital. Such wealth and power were attractive, and more large owners or directors were drawn to stay in business and to become still larger, wealthier and more powerful. Hence the old cycle of business life, by which the successful moved out to the land, to be replaced by newcomers from below, was in an increasing number of cases broken, a development which helps to explain the declining social mobility of the Victorian age. It was not that the big business men could no longer afford to emulate the landlords. On the contrary, they could buy out the average squire many times over, and they often did buy estates, or country seats without estates, without, however, giving up business.

The result was the rise of a whole new class of permanent big business men, as rich and as powerful as many of the great landowners themselves. During the Industrial Revolution there had been a few individuals, such as the Arkwrights and the Peels, who vied in wealth with the aristocracy. But it was in the mid-Victorian period when, as we have seen, man-made capital at length came decisively to outweigh land in value, that big business as a class finally outstripped the landed class in wealth and numbers. Compared with the 2,500 great landowners in 1873 with rentals of over £3,000 (excluding London property and other income) there were in 1850 under 2,000 business men with profits under Schedule D of £3,000. By 1880 there were over 5,000. And if 866 of the landlords had over £10,000 and 76 over £50,000, the corresponding figures for business men had risen from 338 to 987 and from 26 to 77 respectively.[1]

Thus it was in the mid-Victorian age that the business aristocracy of modern times came into existence. Most of them might not acquire their peerages until after 1880, when the first peerages for continuing industrialists were created, but it was in the previous generation that they emerged to great wealth and began to mingle and intermarry with the landed aristocracy. Great Bankers like Samuel Loyd Jones (Lord Overstone, 1860) and George Carr Glyn (Lord Wolverton, 1869), great brewers like Henry Allsopp (Lord Hindlip, 1880), Arthur Guinness (Lord Ardilaun, 1880) and Michael Bass (Lord Burton, 1886), great ironmasters like Ivor Guest (Lord Wimborne, 1880), armaments manufacturers like William Armstrong (Lord

[1] Bateman, *op cit.*, p. 491; Levi, *op cit.*, p. 58.

Armstrong of Cragside, 1887), machinery manufacturers like Samuel Cunliffe-Lister (Lord Masham, 1891), railway contractors like Thomas Brassey (whose son became Lord Brassey, 1886), and even great retailers like W. H. Smith (whose widow became Baroness Hambleden, 1891) were then acquiring the wealth, the political connections and, without giving up business, the country seats and estates, which their titles belatedly recognized. Some, like Sir John Guest, Lord Wimborne's father, who married a daughter of the Earl of Lindsey, or John Marshall, the Leeds flax spinner, who married two sons and a daughter into the Monteagle family, were already intermarrying with the aristocracy. A few, like the banker, G. J. Goschen (Lord Goschen, 1900) and the newsagent W. H. Smith, became Cabinet ministers.[1] Most frequented London in the Season where they were more sought after than most of the gentry and many of the landed aristocrats themselves.

At what point the traditional tendency of business men to buy up estates prior to retiring and founding a family shaded into the new tendency to buy with the intention of remaining in business it is impossible to say. It was the railways of course which made it possible to live on estates distant from the business, and so to postpone the decision to retire. John Marshall, who bought extensively in Cumberland, Lancashire and the North Riding, followed the old entrepreneurial tradition of settling most of his sons on country estates. Lord Overstone invested £1,670,000 in 30,000 acres of land, but left still more, £2,118,804, in stocks, shares, and personal property. Lord Wolverton purchased only 712 acres in Middlesex and Dorset, though they were worth £2,126 a year, but left nearly £2 million at his death.[2] Beatrice Webb's father, Richard Potter the railway magnate, with nine daughters and no sons, merely leased one country house near his Gloucester timberyards, bought another near his Barrow timberyards, plus an old manor house in Monmouthshire for holidays, and rented a furnished house in London for the Season.[3]

The transition can best be seen in the railway men. George Hudson, in his meteoric career from York draper to 'railway king' and then to the exile of bankruptcy, bought a 'grand

[1] *D.N.B.* and standard biographies.
[2] F. M. L. Thompson, *op. cit.*, pp. 39, 61, 120.
[3] B. Webb, *My Apprenticeship* (1950), pp. 34–5.

estate' and the house at Albert Gate to which the whole of London society came to prostrate themselves at his feet, and he was on familiar terms with the Prince Consort. Lord Wolverton, the banker and chairman of the London and North Western Railway, had only 712 acres but he and his son, the Liberal Chief Whip, were thoroughly at home in the highest political circles. Richard Potter, chairman of the Great Western, president of the Canadian Grand Trunk, and a director of the Dutch-Rhenish railways, with next to no land, was on familiar terms with Napoleon III, who let him use his private cabinet to draw up an army contract. Sir Edward Watkin, chairman of the Great Central, the Metropolitan, and the South Eastern railways, and a later President of the Canadian Grand Trunk, with a small estate in Cheshire, negotiated with both French and British governments to build the Channel Tunnel. Such men belonged to a new international world of big business, and negotiated as equals with prime ministers and emperors.[1]

They also perfectly illustrate the rise in scale and status from the individual entrepreneur to the corporate capitalist. The self-made man like Hudson was a rarity at this level. Wolverton's father was a banker, Lord Mayor of London, and a baronet, but scarcely on the plane inhabited by his son. Both Potter's and Watkin's fathers were self-made cotton merchants, M.P.s, pillars of the Anti-Corn Law League, and leaders of Manchester society, but they could scarcely compare with the international standing of their sons.

Men of such wealth, power and prestige might still emulate the aristocracy, but they had no reason to feel jealous, socially inferior, or morally superior. The main principles of the entrepreneurial ideal, active capital and open competition, they viewed with an increasingly ambivalent or critical eye. At their level the distinction between earned income from capital and unearned income from land, still so clear to old-fashioned entrepreneurs like John Bright or Joseph Chamberlain, made little sense, and limitation of competition by price agreements, amalgamations and mergers was their major interest. They had no

[1] R. S. Lambert, *The Railway King, 1800–71* (1934), esp. chap. ix; F. M. L. Thompson, *op. cit.*, p. 61; B. Webb, *My Apprenticeship*, pp. 3–4; C. Hamilton Ellis, *British Railway History, 1830–1947* (1954–59), I. 307–8, II. chap. iii; cf. the careers of Thomas Brassey, Sir John Aird, Lord Cowdray and Sir John Norton-Griffiths in R. K. Middlemas, *The Master Builders* (1963).

sympathy with Cobden and Bright's attempts at land reform, even in the mild form of 'free trade in land', still less for Chamberlain's talk of 'what ransom will property pay for the security it enjoys?'[1] To them an attack on one form of property was an attack on all.

In fact the threat to passive property mounted by the left wing of the Liberal Party, however innocuous it looks at this distance, was enough to frighten some of them into the arms of the Conservatives. Long before the geological shift in the structure of British politics centred around the Liberal split of 1886, which took so many business men as well as landowners into the Tory Party,[2] it is possible, beneath the overwhelming Liberalism of the mid-Victorian business class,[3] to detect anticipatory traces of the drift. One such trace was the defection of Lord Overstone, who was supporting Tory candidates by 1865, another that of Richard Potter, who deserted the Liberalism of his Mancunian forebears, a third the swing of the biggest railway company, the L.N.W.R., from Liberalism under Lord Wolverton to Conservatism under Sir Richard Moon, a fourth the progressive alienation from as early as the 1850's of the drink interest by the vociferous temperance Liberals.[4] The Liberals of course retained a majority of all categories of business M.P.s except the brewers down to 1885, but the Tory share steadily rose, and when the main break came in 1886 it was the typically corporate interests, finance, railways, shipping and transport, which first gave a majority to the Tories, and the more typically entrepreneurial categories, cotton, coal, metals, engineering, and the merchants, which still remained marginally more loyal to the Liberals.[5] The remoter origins of the modern social structure of politics and particularly the equation of big business and Conservatism, can be traced to the mid-Victorian age.

On their side the aristocracy were more willing to meet the big business men halfway than they had been to meet the

---

[1] Cf. Morley, *Cobden*, p. 561; Garvin, *Chamberlain*, I. 548.

[2] Ensor, *op. cit.*, *Trans. R.H.S.*, 1949, XXXI, 17f.

[3] Cf. H. J. Hanham, *Elections and Party Management in the Age of Disraeli and Gladstone* (1959), p. 74; Vincent, *op. cit.*, pp. 10, 39.

[4] Vincent, *op. cit.*, pp. 8, 97–100; B. Webb, *My Apprenticeship*, p. 7; Hanham, *op. cit.*, p. 87.

[5] J. A. Thomas, *The House of Commons, 1832–1901* (Cardiff, 1939), pp. 4–5, 14–15.

smaller and provincial entrepreneurs. The greater landlords drew an increasing proportion of their incomes from mines, docks, canals, railways, and urban property. Although this did not make them industrialists—in practically no case did they draw a majority of their income from such sources, and they preferred to lease their mines and other industrial undertakings rather than exploit them directly[1]—they at least understood industrialism and could see the benefit of meeting and coming to terms with its new large-scale impresarios. The process of absorption occurred in the dining rooms and ballrooms of country houses and London in the Season, on the hunting field and the parade grounds of the Volunteers, in Church, for Nonconformist business men at this level began to join the Church of England, and at the public schools, for they began to send their sons to Eton, Harrow, Winchester and Rugby.[2] The seeds of many of the aristocratic directorships of late Victorian England—in 1896 167 noblemen, a quarter of the peerage, were directors of companies[3]—were no doubt sown on the playing fields of mid-Victorian public schools.

The best index of the process, however, was the distribution of county offices, notably the Commission of the Peace. It can best be illustrated in so aristocratic a county as Cheshire, with its own industries and excellent railway connections with the nearby cities of Liverpool and Manchester supplying a steady inflow of business men with country seats. The noble landlords who dominated county politics knew and understood the benefits of business: the Marquess of Westminster drew a large part of his vast income from London property and had a private railway station built to serve Eaton Hall, Lord Egerton of Tatton had Manchester property, railway interests and was to become chairman of the Ship Canal, Lord Newton of Lyme had coal mines across the Mersey, and Lord Tollemache's model farms and cottages were built on the profits of his brewery. Between the 1840's and the 1880's they presided, as Lords-Lieutenant and county magnates, over 'the most important revolution in county society, the merging of the landed and business interests.'

[1] F. M. L. Thompson, *op. cit.*, pp. 264–5.

[2] Cf. Erickson, *op. cit.*, pp. 11, 33–4; J. M. Lee, *Social Leaders and Public Persons: a Study of County Government in Cheshire since 1888* (Oxford, 1963), pp. 32–3, 35–6.

[3] F. M. L. Thompson, *op. cit.*, p. 307.

At the beginning there were already a few business men amongst the Justices of the Peace on the northern fringe: a Birkenhead shipbuilder, a file manufacturer, a brewer and two bankers from Warrington, and several well-known cotton spinners in the Hyde division. By the end the Bench included all the great resident industrialists: Sir Edwin Watkin the railway magnate, Sir John Brunner the Northwich chemical manufacturer, John Laird and David MacIver the Birkenhead shipbuilders, Thomas Brocklebank the Liverpool shipowner, Colonel Brocklehurst the Macclesfield silk manufacturer, and a host of others. In 1886 the Daresbury division Bench was 'very similar in composition to the boards of directors of the two principal Warrington companies, Greenall's Brewery and Parr's Bank', while in the Wirrall division a third of the magistrates travelled daily to work in Birkenhead and Liverpool.[1] This silent revolution in county government in the forty years before the democratic reform of the 1888 County Councils Act registered the quiet absorption into county society of the new aristocracy of business.

The revolution was at once the apotheosis of entrepreneurial society and the advent of its demise. From one point of view it celebrated the fulfilment of the entrepreneur's ambition, to be accepted at his own valuation as the natural leader of society and the equal of the landed aristocrats. But from another it marked his transformation into something different, the harbinger of the plutocracy of big business men and great landowners in late Victorian and Edwardian England, in which the old virile, ascetic and radical ideal of active capital was submerged in the still older, supine, hedonistic and conservative ideal of passive property. In a word, the entrepreneurial ideal had triumphed only to throw in its lot with the seemingly defeated aristocratic. This belated capitulation, which was from the first in the logic of the entrepreneurial position with its ambivalent emulation of the landed aristocracy, goes far to explain why Britain, the first to experience the Industrial Revolution, should remain the most traditional and aristocratic of industrialized societies. Both the long-term causes and the long-term effects of industrialism found their key in the peculiar nature and structure of English society, in the dynamic stability derived from the resourcefulness and

[1] Lee, *op. cit.*, pp. 22, 29–38.

flexibility of an open aristocracy which, when at last it failed to absorb the rising men as individuals, ended by absorbing them as a class. In so doing it robbed the entrepreneurial ideal, already under attack from outside, of its inner principle of self-justification, the belief in the moral superiority of active capital to passive property. To the incipient decline of the entrepreneurial ideal, therefore, we must finally turn.

3. THE DECLINE OF THE ENTREPRENEURIAL IDEAL

The incipient moral decline of the entrepreneurial ideal was double-sided. Externally, it was a decline in the degree of almost automatic respect hitherto accorded to it by other classes. Internally, and more significantly, it was a decline in the degree of faith and self-confidence in which it was held by the business men themselves.

The most explicit evidence of the external decline is to be found in social and economic legislation. For A. V. Dicey, still the chief guide to legislative opinion in the nineteenth century, the 1860's marked the turning point between individualism and collectivism.[1] But these terms are too crude and over-simplified to express the change fully. As we saw in Chapter VIII, there were two distinct versions of individualism, corresponding to the distinction between the natural and the artificial harmony of interests broadly associated with Adam Smith and Bentham respectively. The second, Benthamite, version could easily spill over into what the Victorians called collectivism. Was a professional police force, for example, which intervened to protect the liberty of the individual, an individualist or collectivist instrument? If the former, what were the factory, mines, sanitary, and food and drugs inspectors who intervened to protect children, young persons, women, adult men in dangerous trades, and finally the whole community from exploitation, negligence, injury and death by maiming and poisoning? At this point individualism overlapped with collectivism.

The ambiguities of collectivism were more complex still, for

[1] Dicey, *op. cit.*, p. 64, where he pinpoints the change to 1865, though elsewhere, pp. 63 and 217, he gives it as 1870.

the word was used by the Victorians, in relation to State intervention, in at least seven senses. It meant, first, the kind of State intervention which overlapped individualism, essentially an extension of the police function, to protect individuals from the illegal acts of others, as in the regulation of factories, mines, public health, common lodging houses, and food and drugs. This readily spilled over into the second, the enforcement of minimum standards of private provision, as in factory education or general housing legislation. Thirdly, it meant State aid to individuals or bodies making private provision, as in the education grants from 1833. Fourthly, it meant State provision, in whole or in part, for particular groups, such as aged paupers, lunatics, orphan children, or the sick poor, for all of whom special arrangements were made by the 1860's. Fifthly, it meant State provision for all willing to accept it, as in the Public Libraries Act, 1851, the Education Act, 1870, or the Act of 1885 admitting non-paupers to poor-law hospitals. Sixthly, it could mean compulsory State provision, whether or not the individual wanted it, as in the National Insurance Act, 1911, discussed though not achieved in the Victorian age.[1] Finally, it could mean the State ownership, in whole or in part, of the means of production, distribution and exchange, mooted for the railways by Gladstone's Act of 1844, and much discussed in relation to land by the early 1880's.

Dicey, indeed, used collectivism in two further senses, derived from contemporary discussion. For him, 'trade unionism, which means collective bargaining, and involves practical restrictions on individual freedom of contract,' was 'a step in the direction of collectivism', while, still odder to our ears, the joint-stock company, as a collectivity engaged in corporate trade, had 'fostered the growth of collectivist ideas.'[2] In a sense he was right. As a committed individualist, he recognized in both a threat to the entrepreneurial ideal.

Amid so much ambiguity, it is not surprising that Dicey traced the beginnings of collectivism back to the education grants of 1833, at the very start of his 'period of Benthamism or Individualism'. Yet he put his finger right on the mark

[1] Cf. Canon W. L. Blackley, 'National Insurance: a Cheap, Practical and Popular Means of Abolishing Poor Rates', *The 19th Century*, 1878, IV. 834f.
[2] Dicey, *op. cit.*, pp. 241, 248.

when he chose the 1860's as the turning point in legislation. For the transition which took place in and around that decade was crucial for entrepreneurial society and its ideal. It was not a transition from crude, wholesale individualism to crude, wholesale collectivism. Indeed, in some respects it might be better regarded as a transition within individualism, from the negative Smithian to the positive Benthamite variety, and, certainly, it coincided with the 'individualist' reaction against Chadwickian centralization and bureaucracy.[1] For it amounted to a major change in the attitude of the State to the free market, from the assumption that the market could be safely left to the hidden hand of self-interest and competition, save in very exceptional cases where the bargainers were particularly vulnerable to exploitation, to the assumption that, although the market should still be free, the strong could not be expected not to exploit the weak unless the State laid down some very firm rules of conduct for all bargainers. This, in turn, implied a major change in the attitude towards the entrepreneur, from the assumption that he could, unless proved otherwise, be trusted to pursue the common good by pursuing his own self-interest, to the assumption that, unless the temptation to exploit the weak and the community at large were removed, he would pursue his own self-interest to the detriment of the common good. In brief, the game was still free and the State was still the referee, but the rules, which had been few and applied only to proven dirty players, were tightened up, increased in number, and applied universally.

Until the 1860's, for example, the textile millowners could and did justifiably complain that they were singled out amongst employers for special mistrust and regulation, and the Factory Law Amendment Association confidently looked forward to repeal of the legislation.[2] In the 1860's, on the contrary, the Factory Acts were extended, first in 1860 and 1861 to bleach and dye works and lace factories, then in 1864, after the revelation by the Children's Employment Commission of the appalling conditions in the metal trades, the potteries, the brickfields,

---

[1] Cf. R. M. Gutchen, 'Local Improvements and Centralization in 19th-Century England', *Hist.J.*, 1961, IV. 85f.; R. Lambert, 'Central and Local Relations in Mid-Victorian England: the Local Government Act Office, 1858–71', *Victorian Studies*, 1962, VI. 121f.

[2] Clapham, *Economic History*, II. 412.

lucifer match making and other industries, to 'any place in which persons work for hire' in six trades, and, finally, in 1867 by the Factory Act to most industrial processes where fifty or more persons were employed, and by the Workshops Act to 'any room or place whatever' controlled by an employer in which women, children or young persons engaged in handicraft, with or without wages. By 1871 when the workshops were transferred from Local Authority to Home Office inspection, the factory inspectors had legal access to 110,000 workplaces, or practically all non-domestic industrial establishments, and even dwelling-houses where children and young persons were employed on handicrafts were to be brought under the law in 1878.[1] In little more than a decade the presumption of the law had shifted from trusting the industrialist to protect his workers unless he proved unworthy of the trust, to suspecting him of exploitation unless he was inspected by the State.

In the case of the chemical manufacturers, the State intervened not merely to protect the public from injury but to teach the entrepreneur his own business, how to make a profit out of a source of loss. The alkali inspectors under the 1863 Act forced the chemical producers to turn waste hydrochloric acid gas, poured out over the surrounding countryside and population at the rate of 13,000 tons a year, into saleable hypochlorite and commercial bleach. Even then, in a classic example of 'feedback' on the part of the Chief Inspector, Robert Angus Smith, and of the survival of central inspection against the vociferous forces of decentralization, it took twenty years, a Royal Commission, and two more Acts to get all the manufacturers to pursue their own self-interest. Powerful property owners like Lord Stanley of Alderley and the Lancashire and Cheshire Association for Controlling the Escape of Noxious Vapours and Fluids were behind the legislation, but it is significant that it was in the 1860's that the protection of the public at large began to take precedence over the freedom of the industrialist.[2]

It was in the 1860's, too, that the public at large was first protected from wholesale fraud and poisoning by the adulteration of food. The campaign against adulteration, started by

[1] *Ibid.*, II. 415–17.
[2] R. M. MacLeod, 'The Alkali Acts Administration, 1863–84', *Victorian Studies*, 1965, IX. 92.

Fredrick Accum and practically laughed out of court in the
1820's,[1] was revived in the 1850's by Thomas Wakley, the
Radical doctor-M.P. and editor of the *Lancet*, with remarkable
effect. Dr. Arthur Hassall's revelations in the *Lancet* of the
poisonous compounds in thirty of the commonest foods daily
sold by supposedly respectable business firms did perhaps more
than anything else to undermine public confidence in the common honesty of the average tradesman.[2] The *Quarterly Review*
commented:

> A gun fired into a rookery could not cause a greater commotion than
> did the publication of the names of dishonest tradesmen.[3]

A Parliamentary Committee in 1855–56 revealed that the fraud
practised on the public was general and systematic. One medical
witness said:

> Adulteration is a widespread evil which has invaded every branch of
> commerce; everything which can be mixed or adulterated or debased
> in any way is debased.

The Committee finally reported:

> We cannot avoid the conclusion that adulteration widely prevails.
> Not only is the public health thus exposed to danger and pecuniary
> fraud committed on the whole community, but the public morality
> is tainted and the high commercial character of the country seriously
> lowered, both at home and in the eyes of foreign countries.[4]

More damaging than the initial revelations was the resistance
of tradesmen to the reform of proved abuses. The first Adulteration of Foods Act of 1860, a permissive measure empowering
Local Authorities to appoint public analysts, was completely
ineffective. In 1861 a lecturer at the Royal Society of Arts

[1] F. Accum, *A Treatise on the Adulteration of Food and Culinary Poisons* (1820);
cf. review, 'Death in the Pot', *Blackwood's*, 1820, VI. 542–54: 'Mr. Accum puts us
something in mind of an officious blockhead, who, instead of comforting his dying
friend, is continually jogging him on the elbow, with such cheering assurances as
the following: "I am sorry there is no hope, my dear fellow, you must kick the
bucket soon. . . . " '

[2] A. H. Hassall, M.D., *Food and its Adulteration*; *comprising the Reports of the
Analytical Sanitary Commission of 'The Lancet' for the years 1851 to 1854 inclusive*
(1855); Burnett, *op. cit.*, pp. 190–1.

[3] [Andrew Wynter], 'Food and its Adulteration', *Q.R.*, 1855, XCVI. 460f.;
Burnett, *op. cit.*, p. 192.

[4] *P.P.*, 1856 (H.C. 379), VIII. 1, S.C. on Adulteration of Food, *Third Report*;
ibid., pp. 192–3.

demonstrated that 87 per cent of the bread and 74 per cent of the milk sold in London were adulterated, and in 1872 Dr. Hassall showed that half the bread he analysed contained quantities of alum. Public disquiet and parliamentary agitation at length obtained the Acts of 1872 and 1875, under which public analysts were appointed everywhere, and adulteration was dramatically reduced.[1] The long-drawn-out campaign and its ultimate success were a classic demonstration of professional criticism of entrepreneurial morality and the failure to enforce even common honesty amongst a large section of business men without the backing of State inspection.

Even the vaunted financial probity of business men took some hard knocks during the mid-Victorian age. The expansion of large-scale enterprise and joint-stock organization increased the opportunities for negligent management, irresponsible accounting and actual fraud. In these early days of company promotion, before Parliament, the Board of Trade, and the Stock Exchange had learned to control the flotation of companies and the issue of shares, public scandals became frequent, involving fraudulent promotion of companies formed only to collect money from the public and then to be wound up, the formation by directors of separate companies to supply land, buildings or materials at exorbitant prices to the main company or to take its products at cost, the granting of free shares by the directors to themselves or their friends, the spreading of false or withholding of true information to affect the price of shares with a view to profitable dealings on the stock market, the paying of dividends out of capital—the crime for which George Hudson was exiled in 1854—and so on.[2] From the 'railway mania' of 1846–47 onwards the investing public was compulsorily educated in a whole new world and vocabulary of ingenious crime, which could only be perpetrated by business men, and by large, prominent, wealthy or at least credit-worthy business men at that. *The Times* in 1860 even noted the appearance of specialist frauds in the sanctum of Victorian respectability, the great corporate charities.[3] Great bankruptcies periodically shook business con-

---

[1] *Ibid.*, pp. 203–13.

[2] Clapham, *Economic History*, II. 136–8, 182–3; R. S. Lambert, *op. cit.*, chaps. xii, xiii.

[3] *The Times*, 2 January 1860.

fidence, like those of Overend and Gurney's Bank, the London Joint-Stock Bank, and the civil engineering contractor Samuel Peto in 1866.[1] And the banking system as a whole was subject to frequent failures of confidence: the thirty years following the 1844 Act, which 'wrote *laissez-faire* principles into orthodox monetary policy,' were 'amongst the most troubled in the history of the banks.'[2] The Bank Act of 1858 and the general limited liability Act of 1862 owed something to the shocking bank failures of 1857.[3]

Indeed, the Company Acts of 1856–62 which finally generalized limited liability were less a mark of confidence in the probity of business men than a recognition that the shareholder as well as the creditor needed to be protected from the negligence, mismanagement and fraud of the company director. The debate which accompanied them was a prolonged discussion of business morality, unflattering on both sides to the business man. Professional opponents of limited liability argued, like McCulloch, that 'trading requires a degree of unremitting vigilance and attention which it would be visionary to expect from directors or servants of a joint-stock association.' Professional supporters like R. C. Fane, Commissioner in Bankruptcy, asked, 'Why should the law be so harsh against contributors, and so tender to creditors?'[4] Mill even made the suspicion of corporate business men an argument for State enterprise:

> The defects . . . of government management do not seem to be necessarily much greater, if necessarily greater at all, than those of management by joint-stock.[5]

Of course, such arguments could be used to support the old-fashioned entrepreneur, and were so used by McCulloch.[6] But as companies increased in number and the typical business man became a company director the old moral superiority of the entrepreneur faded with him.

[1] Clapham, *Economic History*, II. 375–6.
[2] Deane, *op. cit.*, p. 184.
[3] Clapham, *Economic History*, II. 351.
[4] Hunt, *op. cit.*, pp. 130, 132.
[5] Mill, *Principles*, p. 580.
[6] J. R. McCulloch, 'Partnerships, Limited and Unlimited Liability', *Encyclopaedia Britannica* (1859 ed.), XVII. 321; Hunt, *op. cit.*, p. 117.

The moral superiority of the middle class as a whole came under attack in these years at its most sensitive point, sexual continence. The moral revolution on its sexual side, we saw in Chapter VIII, was the attempted imposition on the upper and lower classes of the traditional puritanism of the middle. What middle-class moralists set out to suppress were the characteristically patrician and plebeian vices: kept mistresses on the one side and promiscuity on the other. Though they naturally failed, they succeeded to some extent in driving them underground. But what they manifestly failed even to drive underground was the characteristic vice of the middle-class male and of mid-Victorian England, resort to prostitutes. Whether or not there were more prostitutes than in earlier periods, it was generally believed that there were, and estimates for London around 1860 ranged from 8,000 to 80,000. Plausible explanations were found for the supposed increase, for example by *The Times* and the *Lancet* in 1857, in the lateness of marriage owing to rising expectations of the accustomed middle-class style of life. Whatever the cause, if any, there was a growing obsession in the 1850's and 1860's with 'the social evil', as it was universally called, which attracted the philanthropic concern of such diverse people as Henry Mayhew, Dickens, Lady Burdett-Coutts, and Gladstone and his wife. From 1857 campaigns were organized by West End clergymen, 'to put down the open exhibition of street prostitution . . . carried on with a disregard of public decency and to an extent tolerated in no other capital city of the civilized world.'[1] Sympathy for the prostitutes, the attempt to rescue 'fallen women' by midnight tea-and-prayer meetings, the common belief that they were driven to the streets by seduction, threw into relief the immorality of their middle-class customers.

Even where the customers were not middle-class, but the soldiers and sailors in the eighteen garrison towns named in the Contagious Diseases Act, 1863–71, which prescribed compulsory medical examinations for known and registered prostitutes, the campaign of Josephine Butler for their repeal highlighted the 'double standard' of middle-class sexual morality, which, in striking contrast with the aristocratic morality of the old society, imposed one code for women and another and more

[1] C. Pearl, *The Girl with the Swansdown Seat* (1956), pp. 31, 47–50, 67–71.

elastic one for men.[1] The double standard was in fact institution-alized by the Matrimonial Causes Act, 1857, which established the Divorce Court to grant in effect middle-class divorces—cheaper than by Act of Parliament, but still much too expensive for the working class—on grounds of adultery alone by the wife but of adultery only if aggravated by cruelty or desertion by the husband.[2] The immediate effect of forensic divorce was to expose the sanctity of the middle-class hearth to the public gaze. The *Saturday Review* declared in 1864:

> We want a Moral Sewers Commission. To purify the Thames is something, but to purify *The Times* would be a greater boon to society. . . . The unsavoury reports of the Divorce Courts, the disgusting details of harlotry and vice, the filthy and nauseous annals of the brothel, the prurient letters of adulterers and adulter-esses, the modes in which intrigues may be carried out, the diaries and meditations of married sinners, these are now part of our domestic life.

Though few in number, such cases helped to create a new legend of the unchastity and hypocrisy of the well-to-do middle class.

The moral state of the great towns in a wider and less bigoted sense became a pressing public question in these years, and it too was unflattering to the middle-class image. The sanitary inquiries of the 1840's and 1860's revealed the moral as well as the physical degradation of the urban slums, and contributed to a conscious revival of paternalism which was registered by the resurgence of the language of paternalism which Asa Briggs has noted.[3] It took the form of 'slumming', or philanthropic visiting of the poor in their homes, and was encouraged by most of the churches and by such missionary and charitable bodies as the Metropolitan Visiting and Relief Association (1843) and the Society for the Relief of Distress (1860).[4] The philosophy behind the movement was that of Thomas Chalmers, who in the earlier revival of the aristocratic ideal in the 1820's had at-tempted to introduce the paternalism of the country village to

[1] E. Moberley Bell, *Josephine Butler*, (1962).

[2] O. R. McGregor, *Divorce in England* (1957), pp. 17–29; P. M. Bromley, *Family Law* (1957), p. 81.

[3] Briggs, 'Language of Class', *loc. cit.*, pp. 69–73.

[4] A. F. Young and E. T. Ashton, *British Social Work in the 19th Century* (1956) pp. 88–90.

the slums of Glasgow.[1] As such it was a practical criticism of the moral neglect of the urban poor by the urban middle class. This neglect, it was felt, was becoming deeper and more critical with the development of the horse bus and suburban railways, which further segregated the classes into the ghettos of the central slums and the more salubrious middle-class suburbs. The result was what *Macmillan's Magazine* in 1867 called 'social disintegration':

> The wall of moral separation between rich and poor appears to have become broader, higher, more impassable. . . . Most land-owners of moderate means, or their families, know something of their peasantry; many country manufacturers know something of their workpeople. . . . Setting aside the few persons actually and personally engaged in benevolent labours, . . . men and women of moderate means in our large towns lead a life altogether apart from that of the poor.[2]

The remedy found by increasing numbers of philanthropic individuals in the 1860's and 1870's was to go and live amongst the urban poor and play benevolent squire. The first of the East End 'settlers', in 1867, was Edward Denison, one of the 'almoners', or visitors, of the Society for the Relief of Distress.[3] There he found Octavia Hill already playing the benevolent landlady. In 1865 she had begun with Ruskin's money her management of slums in Marylebone, where she endeavoured 'to use the power given her by her position to bring order into the lives of her tenants.'[4] Together with others of like mind, they founded in 1869 the Charity Organization Society.[5]

The Charity Organization Society was the key to the ambivalence of the movement and to its paradoxical effect on the decline of the entrepreneurial ideal. In spite of its conscious revival of paternalism and the patronage of Lords Shaftesbury, Derby and Lichfield, it was not a movement of the landed class

---

[1] T. Chalmers, *The Christian and Civic Economy of Large Towns* (1821); *On Charity* (ed. N. Marston, 1900); *On Poverty* (1912); Young and Ashton, *op. cit.*, pp. 67–78.

[2] *Macmillan's Magazine*, 1867, XVI. 28.

[3] Sir Baldwyn Leighton, ed., *Work among the London Poor: Letters and Other Writings of the late Edward Denison* (1872).

[4] Octavia Hill, 'Blank Court; or Landlords and Tenants', *Macmillan's Magazine*, 1871, XXIV. 456.

[5] C. L. Mowat, *The Charity Organisation Society, 1869–1913* (1961), pp. 11-18.

against the urban middle class. It is in fact ironical that at this very time the rural labourers were at last beginning to emulate their urban cousins and to emancipate themselves from the discipline as well as the benevolence of the paternal landlord. In the early 1870's the seething resentment of the agricultural labourers at length took institutional form in Joseph Arch's Union, and if their immediate gains in wages were short-lived, they began with the help of the railways to vote against patern-alism with their feet, in that great rural exodus which did more to raise living standards for those who remained behind than all the charity of the squire and his lady. The effective members of the C.O.S. were not rural landlords but urban business and professional men and their children, like W. M. Wilkinson, Charles Bosanquet, Dr. Thomas Hawksley, Rev. Henry Solly, John Ruskin, Edward Denison, son of the Bishop of Salisbury, and Octavia Hill, grand-daughter of Southwood Smith, the Public Health Commissioner. They were, moreover, against the indiscriminate benevolence and pecuniary almsgiving which characterized traditional charity, which they considered 'a frightful evil', 'among the curses of London', 'a silent working pestilence, . . . an endowment to the hypocrite and a laughing stock to the cynic'.[1] If they looked back at all to the paternalism of the old society, it was to its disciplinary aspect, and its dis-crimination between the deserving and the undeserving poor. What they set out to revive was not the soup and blankets of the squire's lady, but 'the principles of 1834', the workhouse test and less eligibility, which indeed they managed to impose on the East End Poor Law Unions in the early 1870's.[2]

In short, the C.O.S. represented a revival not so much of the aristocratic as of the entrepreneurial ideal, in its original purity and vigour, with all its insistence on individual responsibility for poverty and the demand that charity should only be given in order to set the individual on his feet again. As such it con-stituted a rejection of all criticism which laid the blame at the door of entrepreneurial society, and of all remedies involving State aid or provision of welfare. This remained the position of the C.O.S. down to and including the share of six of its members,

[1] Denison, in Leighton, *op. cit.*, p. 103; C. S. Loch, in *Charity Organisation Reporter*, 1882, XI. 196, and *13th Annual Report of C.O.S.*, 1882, p. 20.
[2] Mowat, *op. cit.*, pp. 114–16.

led by C. S. Loch, Octavia Hill and Helen Bosanquet, in the Royal Commission on the Poor Laws, 1905-9.[1]

And yet, paradoxically, the C.O.S. and the East End settlers played a key part in the decline of the entrepreneurial ideal. On the one side, the very professionalism of the C.O.S., through its invention of caseworkers to examine the causes and remedies of poverty, uncovered depths of undeserved misery and want which could not be put down to the sins of the individuals, and could not be cured by private charity, however well organized. The concern with the facts of poverty led others, like Charles Booth and Beatrice Potter, to try and measure the extent of it, and to conclude that to so vast a problem charity was irrelevant. As Beatrice Webb (as she became) shrewdly noted,

> The pioneers of organized charity had made unwittingly an ominous discovery. . . . They had let loose the tragic truth that, wherever society is divided into a minority of 'Haves' and a majority of 'Have Nots', charity is twice cursed, it curseth him that gives and him that takes.[2]

The remedy was not almsgiving or even social service, but social welfare provided or aided by the State. Charles Booth came to pioneer old age pensions, Beatrice Webb a Socialist 'minimum standard of life',[3] but less idealistic politicians were converted to State intervention in precisely those fields where charity had tried and failed. Chamberlain said in 1883:

> I do not often agree with Lord Salisbury, but I did agree with him when he said that social reform was the great problem of our time and that two of the most important branches of that reform are the better provision of dwellings for the working classes . . . and an improvement in the condition of the agricultural labourers.[4]

Thus the attempt by the C.O.S. to push individual responsibility and self-help to its logical extreme merely led to disillusionment with private charity and recourse to the State.

---

[1] *P.P.*, 1909 [Cd. 4499], XXXVII. 1, *R.C. on Poor Laws and the Relief of Distress*, esp. the Majority Report; cf. S. and B. Webb, *English Poor Law Policy* (1910), chap. vi.

[2] B. Webb, *My Apprenticeship*, p. 175.

[3] C. Booth, *Pauperism, a Picture, and the Endowment of Old Age, an Argument* (1892); *Old Age Pensions and the Aged Poor: a Proposal* (1899); S. and B. Webb, *Poor Law History: the Last Hundred Years*, II. 546.

[4] S. H. Jeyes, *Life and Times of 3rd Marquess of Salisbury* (1895), IV. 66.

On the other side, first-hand acquaintance with the facts of poverty intensified the sense of guilt which so often underlay charitable endeavours. Denison set out to expiate the sin of endowed idleness: 'as I have both the means, time and inclination, I should be a thief and a murderer if I withheld what I so evidently owe.' Even Loch, the tough-minded secretary of the C.O.S., was motivated by 'a vague regret that the lives of others, as he judges them from contrast with his own, are sunless and sad.'[1] As a new generation of young social workers came into close contact with the facts of poverty the sense of guilt and the yearning for expiation became oppressive. Beatrice Potter, who herself took up benevolent slum management in 1878, experienced this change, and illustrated it by Arnold Toynbee's pathetic address to London working men in 1883:

> We—the middle classes, I mean, not merely the very rich—we have neglected you; instead of justice we have offered you charity, and instead of sympathy we have offered you hard and unreal advice; but I think we are changing. If you would only believe it and trust us, I think that many of us would spend our lives in your service. You have—I say it clearly and advisedly—you have to forgive us, for we have wronged you; we have sinned against you grievously— not knowingly always, but, still we have sinned, and let us confess it; but if you will forgive us—nay, whether you will forgive us or not—we will serve you, we will devote our lives to your service, and we cannot do more.[2]

This sense of guilt, expressed admittedly more often by the children of the business middle class than by the business men themselves, brings us to the more significant aspect of the decline of the entrepreneurial ideal, its declining hold on the entrepreneurial class itself. Even though every business man did not feel a sense of sin for the wrongs supposedly done by his class, the old conviction of moral righteousness and superiority was undermined. Faith in the wholly unregulated free market declined as year after year the blue books revealed both the benefits and the lack of threat to profits of government

[1] Leighton, *op. cit.*, p. 48; *Charity Organisation Review*, 1892, VIII. 168; Woodroofe, *op. cit.*, p. 22.

[2] A. Toynbee, *'Progress and Poverty': a Criticism of Mr. Henry George, being a lecture . . . delivered in St. Andrew's Hall, London, 18 January 1883* (1883); B. Webb, *My Apprenticeship*, pp. 157-8.

regulation. The world's largest calico printer told the Social Science Association in 1864:

> The Factory Acts were opposed by many of us as economically unsound, and as an unjust interference with the rights of labour and capital. *They have been soundly beneficial.*[1]

Even the *Economist* welcomed the Acts of 1864, and remarked that no one who knew how the earlier Acts had 'worked in Lancashire and Yorkshire had any doubts *now* of the wisdom of those measures.'[2] A factory inspector in 1870 contrasted the co-operation he now received from factory owners with their obstruction of his predecessors, and added:

> The whole country is now of one mind,—labour should be moderate, workrooms and factories should be made healthy, and the young should be educated.[3]

By 1880 academic economics had capitulated. The Cobden prize essay at Oxford for that year declared that

> We have had too much *laissez-faire.* . . . The truth of Free Trade is clouded over by the *laissez-faire* fallacy. . . . We need a great deal more paternal government—that bugbear of the old economists.[4]

Whether or not that was fair to the old economists, the new economists certainly were opposed to an unqualified *laissez-faire*, and had learned from Mill a new empiricism towards State intervention. Cairnes denied that economic doctrine could be summed up in *laissez-faire*. Cliffe Leslie was destroying the abstract certainties of Ricardo. Jevons struck the new keynote of detachment: 'We must learn to judge each case upon its merits.'[5] But the economists no longer claimed to speak for the united middle-class ideal as they had once done. They appeared as

[1] Edmund Potter, quoted by J. M. Ludlow, and Ll. Jones, *The Progress of the Working Classes, 1832–67* (1867), pp. 109–10.

[2] *Economist*, 21 May 1864.

[3] *P.P.*, 1871 [c. 348], XIV. 525, *Reports of Factory Inspectors: Report of Alexander Redgrave*, p. 9.

[4] A. N. Cumming, *On the Value of Political Economy to Mankind* (Oxford Cobden Prize Essay for 1880, Glasgow, 1881), pp. 46–8.

[5] J. E. Cairnes, 'Political Economy and *Laissez Faire*', *Essays in Political Economy* (1873), pp. 250–1; T. E. Cliffe Leslie, *Essays in Political and Moral Philosophy* (1879); S. Jevons, *The State in Relation to Labour* (1882), p. 6; Clapham, *Economic History*, II. 389, 395.

detached professional critics of the business man rather than as defenders. That was the measure of the gap which had widened between the professional and entrepreneurial ideals. The business men were confused and divided. On the one side, Chamberlain, the typical entrepreneurial politician of the age, was sounding 'the death-knell of the *laissez-faire* system. . . . The goal towards which the advance will probably be made at an accelerated pace is that in the direction of which the legislation of the last quarter of a century has been tending—the intervention, in other words, of the State on behalf of the weak against the strong, in the interest of labour against capital, of want and suffering against luxury and ease.'[1] On the other, Goschen, the typical political representative of the new corporate business men, was being successfully urged not to 'slip down the inclined plane on which we are all now standing;— to the letting go of all that has hitherto been understood as sound Liberal Principles.'[2]

The division and confusion extended to the acid test of the entrepreneurial ideal, the distinction between active capital and passive property. The true entrepreneur was an owner-manager who maintained his moral superiority to the landowner by insisting on the latter's irrelevance to the cycle of production, distribution and consumption. In the mid-Victorian age the chief vehicle for entrepreneurial antagonism towards the landed class was the movement for free trade in land, which aimed by removing the artificial barriers to the free sale of land, in primogeniture, strict settlement, and entail, not only to assimilate passive property to active capital but to force land to 'find its own level' in the hands of prosperous, entrepreneurial owner-occupiers, and so painlessly abolish the landlord class.[3] It is true

[1] T. H. S. Escott, ed., *The Radical Programme* (1885), in Garvin, *Chamberlain*, II. 57.

[2] Duke of Argyll to G. J. Goschen, 31 July 1881, A. D. Elliot, *Life of Lord Goschen, 1831–1907* (1911), I. 253; Goschen, ex-merchant banker and director of the Bank of England, had already refused to join Gladstone's 1880 Government because of his opposition to extending the franchise and his suspicion of Chamberlain's 'setting class against class; all against property, which he implies but does not actually say is *landed* property,' and he was to break with the Liberal Party over Home Rule in 1886—*ibid.*, I. 196, 285–9, 290.

[3] The land reform movement bulked much larger in contemporary politics and public opinion than it does in the histories of Victorian England—cf. F. M. L. Thompson, 'Land and Politics in England in the 19th Century', *Trans. R.H.S.*, 1965, XV. 23f.

that this movement died down after the repeal of the corn laws, in the face of the apparent indifference of the satiated free traders which Cobden and Bright so lamented, but it revived again in the 1860's when in the last speech before his death Cobden called for 'a League for free trade in Land just as we had a League for free trade in Corn.'[1] From then onwards the agitation gradually rose to a crescendo, until in 1880 Disraeli could declare that of the two subjects which most occupied the thought of the country, 'one was the government of Ireland, and the other the principles upon which the landed property of this country should continue to be established.'[2]

Yet free trade in land increasingly divided the business class rather than united it. If business men like Chamberlain, Jesse Collings, P. A. Taylor, J. W. Barclay, James Cowan, W. E. Baxter, T. B. Potter and others still supported it with as much fervour as Cobden and Bright had done, many more were becoming apprehensive about the effect which an attack on one form of wealth would have on the other. In the Parliament elected in 1880 business men formed the largest single group amongst acknowledged land reformers, with 26 out of 62 M.P.s, but they were vastly outnumbered by the business men who were not so committed, and by those who by accepting the Conservative whip could be presumed to oppose it.[3]

It was not so much free trade in land in itself which alienated many business men, for much of the programme could be accepted by landowners and by a Tory ex-Lord Chancellor, Lord Cairns, who brought in a partial measure of it in his pre-emptive Settled Land Act of 1882. But, as with State intervention, many of them feared that land reform, once begun, would not know where to stop. Free trade in land might be the first step towards the unearned increment taxation of Mill and the trade unionist George Odger's Land Tenure Reform Association, the Single Tax of Henry George, and the land nationalization of Alfred Russell Wallace, from which the next step was short to the nationalization of railways, mines and other forms

---

[1] Cobden, Speech at Rochdale, 23 November 1864, *Speeches on Questions of Public Policy*, (ed. J. Bright and J. E. T. Rogers, 1870), II. 367.

[2] Hansard, 1880, CCLVI. 618–19.

[3] I.e. 43 per cent of known land-reforming M.P.s, compared with the 25 per cent which business men formed of all M.P.s in 1880—extracted from *Dod's Parliamentary Companion*, 1880.

of capital, and so to full-blooded socialism.[1] Since Gladstone's Irish policy seemed to many of them to belong, as an interference with the rights of Irish property, to the same declension, they began to think that the Liberal Party was already sliding down the same slippery slope that Goschen feared and that Lord Salisbury warned them off in 1884:

> We are on an inclined plane leading from the position of Lord Hartington to that of Mr. Chamberlain and so on to the depths over which Mr. Henry George rules supreme.[2]

Thus land reform, which began as an instrument of entrepreneurial antagonism towards the landed class, ended in the 1880's, along with State intervention and Irish Home Rule, as one of the bogies which helped to frighten a great many business men as well as landowners out of the Liberal and into the Tory Party. There they contributed to that amalgamation of land and capital, passive and active property, which was to dominate the social structure of politics in the succeeding age.

In short, by 1880 the dominant business class of the new class society were in much the same position as the dominant landed class of the old open aristocracy in 1815: outwardly stable and triumphant and in complete moral and ideological control of their society, inwardly divided and confused and crumbling in their conviction of moral superiority and their faith in their class ideal. Some of them, led by Chamberlain, clung to the old belief in active capital in the shape of free trade in land, but had already abandoned the entrepreneurial rejection of State intervention. Others, led by such men as Goschen, were in process of abandoning the entrepreneurial distinction between land and capital, passive and active property, but still clung to the belief in unmitigated *laissez-faire*, thus, like some of the aristocrats before them, demanding the fruits of their ideal without the price of them, privilege without service, power without responsibility.

---

[1] J. S. Mill, 'Explanatory Statement of the Programme of the Land Tenure Reform Association' (July, 1870), *Dissertations and Discussions* (1875), IV. 239f.; Henry George, *Progress and Poverty* (1883), and the publications of the Land Restoration League; A. R. Wallace, *The 'Why' and the 'How' of Land Nationalization* (1883), and the publications of the Land Nationalization Society; cf. M. Beer, *op. cit.*, II. 237–45.
[2] Salisbury, Speech at Dorchester, 16 January 1884, Garvin, *Chamberlain*, I. 462.

The business class, therefore, was already poised for the geological shift of 1886, which began the landslide which was to carry the bulk of them into the defensive alliance with the landowners against the forces of democracy and socialism. The fact that the split came over the apparently extraneous question of Irish Home Rule, and that Chamberlain and his followers took the unexpected side, only added to the confusion. But when the dust and rubble had settled, the old topography of the simple, stable, would-be-permanent, viable class society created by the Industrial Revolution had been radically changed, and the way lay open to the very different society of the twentieth century. What that society was to be, and how it was to evolve after the earthquake of the 1880's, must await another book.

Index